Praise for *Organisational Behaviour: An Introduction*

'This is an excellent introduction to the field of organisational behaviour, not only of the main topic areas but also very novel ones, such as managing healthy workplaces. Definitely a must for those wanting a comprehensive view of the field.'
 – **Professor Sir Cary Cooper,** *The University of Manchester, UK and founding director of Robertson Cooper*

'In a crowded field of OB textbooks, the new edition of *Organisational Behaviour* by Christine Cross and Ronan Carbery stands out for its comprehensive yet accessible coverage of key contemporary topics. Theory is brought to life through "OB in Practice" case studies and links to resources including video clips and other media. There are ample opportunities for students to reflect on their individuals strengths through simulations and exercises. The result is an engaging and interactive resource which will greatly enhance the learning on any OB course.'
 –**Professor David Collings,** *Professor of HRM and Associate Dean for Research, Dublin City University Business School, Ireland*

'The authors draw upon an extensive review of relevant literature to provide an in-depth understanding of Organisational Behaviour. A range of engaging pedagogical features showcasing current topics in the news, the influence of technology in the workplace, and ethical considerations, will help students understand the complexity of the world of work today. This is a brilliant text.'
 –**Dr Geetha Karunanayake,** *Lecturer in HRM & Organisational Behaviour, University of Hull, UK*

'Cross and Carbery's *Organisational Behaviour* provides excellent coverage of all of the important classical and contemporary topics in organisation and management studies. Each chapter is well informed by research and is presented in a clear and engaging style, in which management theories and concepts are clearly linked to practice in real-world organisational settings.'
 –**Dr Frank Worthington,** *Senior Lecturer in Management, The York Management School, UK*

'This is a brilliant book that looks into the salient issues within organisational behaviour. It is exciting to see how the main issues are unpacked, with room for students to apply their own knowledge. The book also considers contemporary issues and makes outstanding contributions to our understanding of organisational behaviour. I am certain that this book will be an excellent resource for students and lecturers alike.'
 –**Dr Hakeem Ajonbadi,** *Lecturer, Birmingham City Business School, UK*

T0291169

ORGANISATIONAL BEHAVIOUR

AN INTRODUCTION

SECOND EDITION

Edited by

CHRISTINE CROSS

RONAN CARBERY

This edition published 2021 by
RED GLOBE PRESS

Previous editions published under the imprint PALGRAVE

Red Globe Press in the UK is an imprint of Macmillan Education Limited,
registered in England, company number 01755588, of 4 Crinan Street,
London, N1 9XW.

Red Globe Press® is a registered trademark in the United States,
the United Kingdom, Europe and other countries.

ISBN 978-1-352-01251-4 hardback

ISBN 978-1-352-01247-7 paperback

This book is printed on paper suitable for recycling and made from fully
managed and sustained forest sources. Logging, pulping and manufacturing
processes are expected to conform to the environmental regulations of the
country of origin.

A catalogue record for this book is available from the British Library.

A catalog record for this book is available from the Library of Congress.

Printed and bound in Great Britain by Bell and Bain Ltd, Glasgow

Publisher: Ursula Gavin

Senior Development Editor: Lauren Zimmerman

Assistant Development Editor: John Heron

Production Editor: Elizabeth Holmes

Senior Marketing Manager: Amanda Woolf

SHORT CONTENTS

CONTENTS

LIST OF FIGURES

LIST OF TABLES

ABOUT THE EDITORS

Professor Christine Cross is Head of Department, Work and Employment Studies at the University of Limerick (UL). Prior to joining UL she worked for a number of multinational organisations in both management and human resource management roles. This experience has led to a wide range of research, consultancy and publication interests covering areas such as investigating the glass ceiling; the gender pay gap; the lack of women on boards and the workforce experiences of immigrants.

Dr Ronan Carbery is Senior Lecturer in Management at Cork University Business School, University College Cork (UCC), Ireland. He is co-director of the HR Research Centre in UCC and editor of the *European Journal of Training and Development*. Christine and Ronan have co-edited a number of leading international texts including *Human Resource Management* (2019) and *Human Resource Development: A Concise Introduction* (2015).

ABOUT THE CONTRIBUTORS

Dr Ashley Bamberg holds a BSc degree in Industrial and Organisational Psychology from Colorado State University and both an MSc degree in Work and Organisational Behaviour and a PhD degree in Work and Employment Studies from the University of Limerick. She has conducted research on a number of topics relevant to organisational behaviour, including employee perceptions of HR practices and generational differences in work values. She is an expert on generations, work values, and age diversity and lectures in the Department of Work and Employment Studies at the University of Limerick.

Dr Clodagh Butler graduated with a BA in Psychology and an MSc in Health Psychology from NUI, Galway. She moved her studies to the University of Limerick and undertook an MSc in Sport Performance. She received the Kemmy Business Schools Dean scholarship to undertake her PhD in Occupational Health Psychology. Her research interests relate to occupational well-being within high-performance/high-stress environments that focuses on stress, resilience, coping, self-regulation and well-being. Currently, she is lecturing in UL and working on applied research projects within sport, business and psychometrics. She is an accredited psychologist with Sport Ireland Institute and a member of PSI.

Dr Vivienne Byers is a Researcher with the Royal College of Surgeons in Ireland and Adjunct Research Fellow in Health Policy at Technological University Dublin. Her research interests and academic publications are in the areas of professional communication and development, distributed healthcare leadership and person-centred practice, as well as health policy implementation. She has been involved in academia for over two decades in research, lecturing as well as management. She has a background in communications development, having practised as a Speech and Language Therapist for many years. She has extensive experience working in both health services and academia in Ireland, Canada and the UK.

Dr Colette Darcy is Dean of the School of Business at the National College of Ireland and a Senior Lecturer in Human Resource Management. She is a former Government of Ireland Scholar and was awarded the European Foundation for Management Development / Emerald Outstanding Doctoral Thesis Award for her research examining employee fairness perceptions and claiming behaviour. Colette is a graduate of Trinity College Dublin and the University of Limerick. Prior to returning to academia Colette worked in management consultancy and is an honorary fellow of the Recruitment Federation of Ireland. Colette has published her work in a number of international peer reviewed journals including *Human Resource Management* and the *International*

Journal of Human Resource Management. Her main research interests include talent management, human resource development, work–life balance and organisational justice.

Dr Michelle Hammond is an Assistant Professor of Management at Oakland University (OU) in Rochester, Michigan. She earned her PhD in Industrial Organizational Psychology from Penn State University. She was the Program Director of the MSc in Work and Organisational Psychology/Behaviour at the University of Limerick, Ireland until joining OU in 2017. Through her research, she seeks to understand the process of leadership development across multiple domains of life. Her work also focuses on understanding the influence of leadership on employee well-being at work, including factors such as meaningful work, work–life balance, and creativity and innovation.

Lindsay Harrison has a professional background in speech and language therapy and a strong interest in communication, at both an interpersonal and systems level. She is currently studying for a PhD within the healthcare business domain with Technological University Dublin. Her research focuses on the education of healthcare professionals to collaborate with the persons in their care, as part of an effort to incorporate the patient perspective into healthcare systems. Lindsay additionally works as a communications consultant with a digital health company that is developing technical solutions in the field of speech and language therapy.

Dr Jennifer Hennessy is a lecturer in Human Resource Management at the School of Business, Waterford Institute of Technology. She also holds a Postgraduate Diploma in Business Studies and Information Technology and an Occupational Psychometric Testing Course Level 1 (BPS accredited). Her areas of interests include person–organisation fit, career management, work-life interaction strategies and employee engagement. Prior to this she was employed as a human resource management generalist in a multinational high technology organisation where part of her role involved managing a redundancy and career development outreach programme.

Dr Gráinne Kelly is a Lecturer at Queen's University Management School with expertise in the areas of management and international management. Gráinne is interested in individual perspectives on work and organisational change, particularly the health and well-being implications of new types of work arrangements in the globalised digital economy. She has been a lead researcher on a project with the Irish Centre for Manufacturing Research on employees' experience of tacit knowledge management practices. She has engaged in research on employees' experience of work within knowledge intensive firms and multinational organisations, particularly in the pharmaceutical, ICT and financial service sectors. Gráinne is a reviewer for the *International Journal of Human Resource Management* and *Personnel Review*. She is an External Examiner with Carlow Institute of Technology.

Dr T.J. McCabe is a Lecturer in Human Resource Management at the National College of Ireland and visiting Lecturer at the University of Hebei, China. TJ leads a number of postgraduate and undergraduate modules, including Strategic and International Human Resource Management, Employee Relations, Human Resource Development and Research Methods. TJ's research interests extend to Nursing professionals, Human Resource Management issues in the health sector, Graduate Employability, International HRM and National Culture. TJ has presented this work at national and international conferences. He co-chaired the HRM track for the 14th Annual Conference of the Irish Academy of Management. He has published papers in numerous academic journals. TJ received the *Best Paper Award*, for the Healthcare and Public Sector Management Track, Irish Academy of Management: McCabe, T.J. and Sambrook, S. (2011), A Discourse Analysis of Managerialism and Trust among NHS Nurses and Nurse Managers, *14th Annual Irish Academy of Management Conference*, National College of Ireland, Dublin.

Dr Jean McCarthy is a Lecturer in Organisational Behaviour at the University of Limerick. She lectures in the areas of Organisational Behaviour, Workplace Learning & Development and Research Methods within the Department of Work & Employment Studies. She has extensive experience in teaching and supervision at undergraduate, postgraduate, executive, and post-experience levels, as well as working with community-based and youth-reach education and training programmes. Beyond her core interests in multi-level teaching, learning and development, Jean's focus of scholarly research centres on understanding organisational attitudes and behaviour which promote a more inclusive and sustainable workplace.

Dr Ciarán McFadden is a Lecturer in Human Resource Management and Organisational Behaviour at Edinburgh Napier University in Scotland. He is the Programme Leader for the Global Online MBA and the BA Human Resource Management with Organisational Psychology (Top-Up). He is a former Government of Ireland Scholar and a former Fulbright Scholar. He has presented his research at many academic conferences and published in books and journals such as the *International Journal of Human Resource Management*, *Human Resource Development Review*, and the *International Journal of Manpower*. His research interests include workplace diversity and inclusion, human resource development, and employment relations.

Dr Caroline Murphy is a Lecturer in Employment Relations and Director of the BA in HRM at the Kemmy Business School, University of Limerick. She lectures in Employment Relations, Human Resource Analytics, and Human Resource Management. She has worked on a variety of research projects including: The Impact of Technology on Workers in the Finance Sector (2019), Pathways to Better Jobs in the Early Years Childhood Care and Education Sector (2020), Gender Equality in Decision-Making (funded by the European Commission), A Study of Zero Hours Work in Ireland (funded by the DJEI) and Reconciling Employment and Elder Care Together (2016, funded by the Irish Research

Council). Her current research interests include precarious employment, female labour market participation, formal and informal care work and employee representation. She has published in *Economic and Industrial Democracy*, *Industrial Relations Journal*, *International Journal of Human Resource Management*, *Journal of Industrial Relations*, *Personnel Review*, and *Irish Journal of Management*.

Dr Deirdre O'Shea is Senior Lecturer in work and organisational psychology at the University of Limerick, Ireland. She is a chartered psychologist and Fellow of the Psychological Society of Ireland. Deirdre received her PhD from Dublin City University in 2011, awarded with no amendments. Her research focuses on self-regulation, work motivation, and well-being with a particular focus on psychological resource-based interventions. She has published her research in top academic journals and received the 2017 *European Journal of Work and Organisational Psychology* best paper award. Her research has been supported by grants from the Irish Research Council, the Health Research Board and the European Association of Work and Organisational Psychology, among others.

Dr Maeve O'Sullivan lecturers in human resource management and leadership at University College Cork. Her research interests include the effective management of older workers, multi-level implications of part-time and precarious employment, gender equality, and diversity and inclusion in organisations. Previously, Maeve held management and consultancy roles in both public and private sector organisations in Ireland, the UK, and at the European Commission in Brussels. Her research has been published in peer-reviewed academic journals including the *Irish Journal of Management*. In addition to providing policy briefings for think-tanks, Maeve is also a member of the Chartered Institute of Personnel and Development, a registered psychometric tester with the British Psychological Society and a French speaker.

Jill Pearson is a Chartered Work & Organisational Psychologist who has been lecturing in the Kemmy Business School at the University of Limerick for over 20 years. She was the inaugural Programme Director of the MSc in Work & Organisational Psychology/Behaviour and has recently returned to that role. Prior to joining UL, Jill taught at the London Business School and the London School of Economics. She has also worked as a Consultant to a number of multinationals and as an HR Practitioner in both the private and public sectors. Her teaching has included topics such as organisational behaviour, employee well-being, careers, and research methods. Jill received her MSc in Industrial Relations & Personnel Management from the London School of Economics and her BA (Honours) in Psychology from the University of Western Ontario, Canada. Her current research focus is in the areas of careers and career success.

Dr Lorraine Ryan is a Lecturer in Employment Relations and Human Resource Management at the Kemmy Business School, University of Limerick. Lorraine holds a BBS, 2002, MBS, 2003, and PhD, 2010, and is a former Government of Ireland Scholar. She has published widely in leading international journals including *Economic and Industrial Democracy, European Journal of Industrial Relations, International Journal of Human Resource Management* and *Industrial Relations Journal* as well as authoring and co-authoring numerous book chapters and research reports. Her research focuses on precarious work, conflict, workers' attitudes to democracy and the impact of technology on the future of work.

Dr Nuala Ryan is a lecturer and researcher in the Department of Management and Marketing at the Kemmy Business School in the University of Limerick. Her areas of focus include Strategic Management, Leadership and Organisational Behaviour. She has been a lecturer at the University College Cork, UCD Michael Smurfit Graduate Business School, University College Dublin, the National College of Ireland, NUI Galway and currently in the University of Limerick. Prior to becoming a full-time lecturer Dr Ryan has worked in industry where her main responsibilities included HR Business Management, Organisational Development, Team Development and Learning Organisation Management. This experience has led to a wide range of teaching, research and publication interests in the broad area of leadership development, strategic management and general organisational behaviour. She is currently carrying out research in the healthcare sector in the area of Leadership and Strategic Management.

Dr Ultan Sherman lectures in Organisational Behaviour and Human Resource Management at Cork University Business School in University College Cork. His research interests lie broadly in the relationship between work and psychology with specific focus on the psychological contract. His research has been published in leading international journals such as *Human Resource Management Journal, Group & Organization Management, International Journal of Human Resource Management* and *European Journal of Work & Organizational Psychology*. Ultan is a Chartered Psychologist with the Psychological Society of Ireland and has worked with leading organisations on a variety of organisational behaviour issues.

Dr Missie Smith earned her B.S. and M.S. from Mississippi State University in 2010 and 2012, respectively. She earned her PhD in Industrial and Systems Engineering from Virginia Tech in 2018. Dr Smith researches the impact of technology on users' perception, performance, and behaviours.

Paolo Yaranon is Dean's PhD Scholar from the Department of Work and Employment Studies, Kemmy Business School, University of Limerick. He received his MSc in Work and Organisational Psychology in 2018. Currently in his third year of PhD studies, his research lies within the field of workplace incivility and its impact on employee well-being and organisational outcomes. He is a member of the British Psychological Society (BPS) Register of Qualifications in Test Use (RQTU) and the Kemmy Business School Equality & Diversity Committee.

FOREWORD

There are numerous organisational behaviour texts from which to choose. As the composition of university level students is becoming increasingly diverse, our methods and platforms for teaching evidence-based theories and practices in organisations are also changing. The new edition of the Cross and Carbery textbook, *Organisational Behaviour* represents an excellent choice for teaching age-, work-experience, and learning style-diverse students.

Organisations operate in a larger, global context with an increasingly volatile set of economic, political, social and environmental challenges. Navigating work successfully in a complex world requires educating newcomers as well as current employees using multiple methods and perspectives. Cross and Carbery introduce the critical topics on organisational behaviour using best practices in learning and teaching techniques. Each chapter begins with learning objectives followed by an engaging introduction to the topic. Important and frequently used terms uniquely relevant to the topic are highlighted and defined for the learner. Each topic introduction is accompanied by key theoretical frameworks that enhance greater and more nuanced understanding of the topic. These frameworks provide an umbrella to incorporate both practical examples and scientific findings on the topic. Exemplars or applications of the topic to real work situations are provided generously throughout the chapters to link specific material to students' experiences. Chapters are written by selected experts on each topic, thereby ensuring in-depth knowledge of both the scientific basis of each area as well as its application.

Throughout the book, there are a number of simulations presented where students can role play and apply organisational behaviour knowledge. New features in the 2nd edition include chapters on organisational socialisation and managing healthy workplaces. In addition, this updated edition provides numerous discussions and examples that help students understand how technology influences work and ethical considerations at work. Each of these new features again incorporates sound teaching and learning principles with: (1) the use of strategically placed questions for students throughout each chapter as well as at the end of each chapter; (2) spotlight boxes on 'OB in Practice'; (3) links to visual material available on the companion website, highlighting the material, such as TED talks or current event news outlets; (4) additional web or research links available on the companion website (Twitter, Facebook, etc.) so students may choose to dig deeper into a given subject; and (5) often the direct application of chapter material to the students' experiences in their student roles.

The book is written in highly accessible language. One particularly attractive feature of this text is that it engages undergraduates in assessments of their leadership, motivation and stress management styles as well as personality, all designed to enhance self-awareness. Such awareness of self and others is critical in the development of leadership for future managers in an increasingly diverse global workplace.

Organisational Behaviour by Christine Cross and Ronan Carbery is one book that will be on my office shelf. It is sure to be often used to help to develop the next generation of leaders and managers navigate the complex world of work and community.

Jeanette N. Cleveland
Professor
Department of Psychology
Colorado State University

PREFACE AND EDITORS' ACKNOWLEDGEMENTS

Our aim with the first edition of this textbook in 2015 was to write a textbook that we could use for our own teaching in Ireland and so we drew on a large number of Irish examples throughout the book. We were delighted with how the book was received not only in Ireland but throughout Europe and the rest of the world. We therefore chose to broaden the focus of this second edition and have adopted a much more international focus throughout the book.

While there are a large number of excellent organisational behaviour [OB] textbooks available, there are very few dealing with OB at such a concise level. This book has been written not only for 1st and 2nd year undergraduate students who are taking HRM modules for the first time, but also for postgraduate students who are interested in understanding OB. While many of these students may not go on to specialise in OB, the concepts discussed in this book are relevant to any business student and, indeed, anyone in employment.

Once again, the book is written in easy-to-understand language and we have presented the material in such a way as to highlight the practicality of the issues involved in work and organisations. There is a strong emphasis on skills and career development throughout each of the 14 chapters, with key features such as up-to-date news pieces (OB in the News), case studies (OB in Practice), understanding how technology impacts work (Impact of Technology), ethical considerations (Ethical Behaviour in the Workplace), the real-life impact of OB (In Reality) and highlighted key terms with on-page definitions, and video interviews with experienced professionals (Spotlight on Skills – videos available on the companion website). The book's companion website provides extra resources, including videos, self-test questions and more skills development guidance.

We would like to acknowledge the help we received with writing this text. Aléta Bezuidenhout, John Heron, Lauren Zimmerman and Ursula Gavin at Red Globe Press (Bloomsbury) provided tremendous assistance and support throughout the writing of the text.

The authors and publishers are very grateful to the reviewers of the draft chapters who provided excellent feedback, including:

Sam Thiara, Beedie School of Business, Simon Fraser University, Canada
Rita Chan, BNU-HKBU United International College, China
Todd Bridgman, School of Management, Victoria University of Wellington, New Zealand
Ruth Brooks, University of Huddersfield, UK
Roger Leenders, Tilburg University, the Netherlands
Selen Kars, Bristol Business School, University of the West of England, UK
Henrik B. Sørensen, Aarhus University, Denmark

In addition to the contributors to the textbook, we would like to thank colleagues at the University of Limerick and University College Cork who provided us with support along the way.

We are grateful for the time the participants in the Spotlight on Skills video features so readily gave us and for their excellent insights into industry practice.

Finally, we would like to thank our families: Dave, Oisín and Luíseach Cross and Michelle and Julie Carbery.

Christine Cross and Ronan Carbery
February 2021

TOUR OF THE BOOK

Learning Outcomes

A set of learning outcomes are identified at the start of each chapter. After you have studied the chapter, completed the activities and answered the review questions, you should be able to achieve each of the objectives.

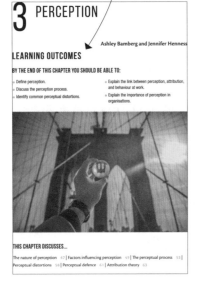

3 PERCEPTION

Ashley Bamberg and Jennifer Henness

LEARNING OUTCOMES

BY THE END OF THIS CHAPTER YOU SHOULD BE ABLE TO:

- Define perception.
- Discuss the perception process.
- Identify common perceptual distortions.
- Explain the link between perception, attribution, and behaviour at work.
- Explain the importance of perception in organisations.

THIS CHAPTER DISCUSSES...

The nature of perception 47 | Factors influencing perception 49 | The perceptual process 53 | Perceptual distortions 58 | Perceptual defence 61 | Attribution theory 63

Key Terms

Each chapter contains an on-page explanation of a number of important words, phrases and concepts that you need to know in order to understand OB, its theoretical basis and its related areas.

Making Links

To allow you to see the interconnected nature of the topics in the field of OB, areas that link to topics and concepts in other chapters are identified.

His statement is no less true today as exploring attitudes allows us to understand how others view the world. The term 'attitude' has entered our everyday vernacular. We have different attitudes towards our families, friends, work, music, and so on which direct how we behave in relation to each one of them. Some of you might *believe* that Taylor Swift is the greatest pop star in the world. As a result, you may have bought all her albums and attended some of her concerts. Others might *feel* she is overrated and *change* the song when they hear her music on a playlist. So, what is an attitude? If we examine the words italicised above it suggests that attitudes are beliefs or feelings or behaviours. Like many concepts within the organisational behaviour field there are competing theories drawn upon to define the term attitude, although Allport is arguably the father of attitude research, and most subsequent research is congruent with his definition. We define attitudes as evaluative judgements relating to people, events or objects.

attitudes are evaluative judgements relating to people, events or objects

There is much debate as to what constitutes an attitude. Some theorists prefer a one-component attitude model, specifically the *affective* component (e.g. Thurstone, 1931). Other theorists propose a two-component attitude model, incorporating a *cognitive* component into the one-component model (e.g. Petty and Cacioppo, 1986). They argue that exploring the cognitive underpinnings of attitudes can tell us something different about how they function in a way that the affective component cannot. A third approach is the three-component model incorporating a *behavioural* component. Therefore, there are potentially three different components of an attitude:

1 ***Cognitive component:*** This refers to the values and beliefs that the individual holds about a particular person or thing. The idea here is that an individual will perceive and make sense of the world in a way that is unique and subjective ▸See Chapter 3◂ For example, a first-year student at the National University of Singapore may hold particular values and beliefs about her new university. One belief may be that she is now studying at one of the world's most prestigious academic institutions. This is likely to be a source of pride for the student – the underlying value supporting the belief.
2 ***Affective component:*** This points to the feelings and emotions arising from an evaluation of the two elements in the cognition component. An individual making sense of an object, event, situation etc. evokes an emotional or affective reaction. For instance, the Singapore student would typically develop feelings about the university related to the inherent beliefs and values she holds about it. For example, she might have a great sense of accomplishment for having been accepted into the university. However, she might also feel greater pressure in terms of her academic performance given the high standards expected of Singapore students. The affective component of attitude structure tends to be learned from our environment (this is discussed below).
3 ***Behavioural component:*** This is about the behavioural outcome of the process. This behaviour stems from the affective component of the model. The affective reaction will

In Reality

These short vignettes demonstrate that OB is not merely 'common sense', but based on rigorous research and evidence which often contradicts our assumptions.

IN REALITY

When faced with difficult problems, when in need of the next product, when trying to improve processes in workplaces, the most common response is to create a working group to come up with creative ideas. Group brainstorming sessions are often the default when trying to come up with a perfect idea. But do they work? No, the research findings do not support this 'idea'. A meta-analysis of over 20 studies (Mullen *et al.*, 1991) has found that group brainstorming leads to the generation of fewer ideas than comparable numbers of solitary brainstormers in both laboratory and organisational settings. Why might this be the case? First, sometimes people slack off in groups, expecting other team members to take the lead. Most often it's the most extroverted person who shares the most ideas, not necessarily the person with the most or best ideas. Quite often people are hesitant to share ideas for fear of saying something stupid – that they'll be judged by others. Other times people get blocked by what someone else said instead of thinking things through on their own, or only come up with ideas that are similar to those already proposed. Research suggests that brainstorming is most effective when individuals take time to process the problem or opportunity individually and bring their ideas to the group. If group brainstorming is to be used, make sure that the leader does not share his or her idea first, be sure to defer judgement on ideas, and focus on trying to come up with as many ideas as possible, regardless of the quality of the idea. Additionally, the use of trained facilitators, diversifying the team members, and creating a 'playground' where members feel a sense of play and positive emotion while engaging in creativity, may reduce some of the threats to group creativity (Thompson, 2003). A further meta-analysis (DeRosa *et al.*, 2007) found evidence that a virtual environment produces more creative ideas with higher group member satisfaction, likely by reducing some of the process loss effects described above.

Impact of Technology on Behaviour

This feature uncovers the persuasive influence of technology in today's workplace.

IMPACT OF TECHNOLOGY ON BEHAVIOUR

Covid-19 forced the entire world to rapidly adjust to new norms, and it was made possible in large part due to virtual communication tools like synchronous document editing and video calls. Although virtual work had long been a part of many people's working lives, Covid-19 forced video communications to be a central feature of work and life for many people. Although this technology has been essential in helping people to connect with each other, it has its drawbacks as the line between work and home life has also become increasingly blurred and some report experiencing what's labelled as 'Zoom Fatigue'. Research in neuropsychology (Lee, 2020) suggests that virtual connections do not offer the brain the same type of neurochemical rewards (in the form of oxytocin and dopamine) that face-to-face communication offers because of increased audio delays and the ability for mutual gaze. At the same time, there is increased cognitive effort to fight the distraction of multitasking, a lack of boundaries with personal life, and the draw to stare at yourself in the screen. So, what to do? In their *Harvard Business Review* article, Liz Fosslien and Mollie West Duffy (2020) propose tips to 'combat zoom fatigue': avoiding multitasking, building in breaks, reducing onscreen stimuli such as by hiding your own face or simplifying background images, making social events opt-in rather than mandatory, and switching to phone calls or e-mails when appropriate.

OB in the News

Each chapter contains an example of coverage of its main topic in the media. The aim here is to highlight how you can apply the constructs and concepts in the chapter to the management of people in the real world of the workplace. A set of questions accompanies each feature to assist with this application to a practical situation.

OB IN THE NEWS

#MeToo

The 'me too' movement was instigated by Tarana Burke to help victims of sexual violence. The website (www.metoomvmt.org) highlights how the 'vision from the beginning was to address both the dearth in resources for survivors of sexual violence and to build a community of advocates, driven by survivors, who will be at the forefront of creating solutions to interrupt sexual violence in their communities'. Although the movement began in 2006, it went 'viral' in 2017 when actor Alyssa Milano brought #MeToo to Twitter denouncing sexual misconduct allegations against film producer Harvey Weinstein. The #MeToo movement quickly gained momentum, cutting across industry and national borders, as a 'beacon of hope that the attention placed on sexual harassment allegations at this time will result in fewer infractions and less tolerance in the workplace for inappropriate sexual behavior in the future' (Atwater *et al.*, 2019, p. 2).

The movement has sparked substantial dialogue and action in individuals and employees. According to a study within the harassment-free workplace series of the Society of Human Resource Management in 2018, one in three executives reported changing their behaviour in the wake of the #MeToo movement, with concerns not only to reduce the occurrence of harassment but also for the morale, engagement, and productivity of the staff. Many organisational responses include expanding training in the areas of sexual harassment and assault, implicit bias, and diversity and inclusion.

Some responses to the #MeToo movement have suggested the movement has highlighted an unequal power distribution, such that those who feel more powerful are more likely to abuse. An article in the *Washington Post*, by Jena McGregor, blames a focus on 'super star' employees that creates a sense of privilege, entitlement, and a view that rules do not apply, which in turn, can foster abuse.

Others have written about a #MeToo backlash, in which men became more reluctant to engage with women in certain circumstances for fear of blame (Atwater *et al.*, 2019). The authors' research suggested that although there have been positive outcomes such as an increase in willingness to report sexual harassment among women and a commitment to reducing inappropriate behaviour of men, some intentional and unintentional backlash also occurs. For example, 41% of men reported that men may be more reluctant to engage in one-to-one meetings with women and 22% of men and 44% of women predicted that women may be more likely to be excluded from social interactions.

1 Identify the main areas of organisational behaviour impacted by the #MeToo movement.
2 Taking a systems thinking approach, how might even one instance of harassment affect the organisation at large?
3 What can you do to reduce the occurrence of sexual harassment in your workplaces and schools?

Sources

Atwater, L.E., Tringale, A.M., Sturm, R.E., Taylor, S.N. and Braddy, P.W. (2019) Looking ahead: How what we know about sexual harassment now informs us of the future. *Organizational Dynamics*, 48(4), 1–9.

https://metoomvmt.org/

https://shrm.org/hr-today/trends-and-forecasting/research-and-surveys/Documents/Harassment-Free%20Workplace%20Series%20Executive%20View%20Topline.pdf

https://www.washingtonpost.com/news/on-leadership/wp/2017/12/19/the-metoo-movement-is-a-warning-sign-about-the-star-system-at-many-companies/

Building Your Employability Skills

This feature asks you to place yourself in the position of a line manager and to think about what you would do in the situation that has been presented to you.

OB in Practice

These short case studies at the end of each chapter provide the opportunity for you to link the material covered in the chapter to a real-life situation. Questions are posed at the end of the case study, which can be answered either in class or as part of an assignment.

Ethical Behaviour in the Workplace

This feature challenges you to consider how you would respond to everyday ethical dilemmas.

Chapter Review Questions

Each chapter ends with questions that can be used as class exercises or for self-testing and evaluating your knowledge about the chapter topic.

Further Reading

The aim of these lists is to highlight a few specific texts and journal articles we believe can assist you in developing your understanding and furthering your knowledge of the many areas introduced in this book.

Useful Websites

An abundance of websites exist on topics related to OB. At the end of each chapter we have identified those we believe you will find most useful in furthering your knowledge and understanding of the discipline.

Spotlight on Skills: text and video feature

This feature encourages you to develop your skills in OB by asking you to consider specific questions and activities. Each one is accompanied by a video interview with a professional that you can view on the book's website. The skills-related questions posed in the text feature are addressed by the practitioner in the video. To maximise this resource, you should first attempt to answer the questions in the book and then watch the video.

DIGITAL RESOURCES

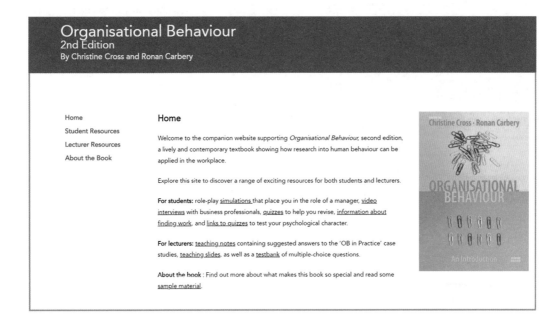

An array of engaging resources for both students and lecturers is available at bloomsbury.pub/organisational-behaviour.

For students

- **Interactive simulations** which put you in the shoes of a manager who must make a difficult decision. Each choice you make will lead to a new scenario
- **Video interviews** with a range of business professionals to accompany the Spotlight on Skills text feature
- **Quizzes and flashcards** to test your understanding of key terms in OB
- **Employability resources**: links to additional information about finding work
- **Psychological character tests**: links to free online quizzes to help you learn more about your unique personality

For instructors

- **A testbank** containing multiple choice questions relating to coverage of each of the book's chapters
- **Teaching notes** containing suggested answers to the 'OB in Practice' case studies found in every chapter
- **Teaching slides** corresponding to every chapter in the book ready for instructors to customise

ABOUT THE SPOTLIGHT ON SKILLS CONTRIBUTORS

There are 14 Spotlight on Skills features in this textbook, each linking to videos on the companion website. Background information about the practitioners and their experience is given below.

Chapter 1: Carla DiBenedetto, Cook Medical

Carla DiBenedetto has been employed by Cook Medical since 2005, working initially as part of the European HR team managing employees based in the UK, Italy, the Netherlands and Scandinavian countries. Carla is currently Senior HR Manager for Cook Ireland. Carla holds a Bachelor of Civil Law degree from University College Cork, and a Graduate Diploma in Business Administration and Master of Science in Human Resource Management from the University of Limerick.

Chapter 2: Fiona Clarke, Aviva

Fiona Clarke worked in HR for 14 years and in programme delivery for four years in a variety of industries – pharmaceuticals, medical devices, Financial Services, global distribution and retail – and in a variety of cultures, including American, Japanese, British and Irish. She is currently Group Transformation Portfolio Lead at Aviva, where she is responsible for collaborating with transformation teams to ensure change and programme management standards are embedded and outcomes are delivered aligned to the strategic ambition. Fiona was previously Project Management Office (PMO) Manager at Eurostar, where she established the PMO function through a partnership approach with the business and managed the quality of a portfolio of company-wide strategic projects.

Fiona holds an Honours Degree in Human Resource Management and Marketing from the University of Stirling, a Diploma in Project Management from Dublin Business School, a professional qualification from the CIPD (Chartered Institute of Personnel and Development) and is a qualified Executive Coach via the ILM (Institute of Leadership & Management).

Chapter 3: Gavin Connell, University of Limerick

Gavin Connell is the Head of Careers, Cooperative Education & Careers Division, University of Limerick. Gavin is Masters-qualified in work and organisational behaviour with a degree in Human Resources. He has 20 years of industrial experience in manufacturing, process engineering, learning and development, recruitment, and has HR experience in Ireland and also across Europe, the Middle East and Africa (EMEA).

Gavin currently supports students in developing employability skills and implementing their career plans, and is also responsible for engaging employers on all matters of graduate recruitment and employability. A significant element of this role is to influence policy formulation and planning within the University on issues relating to career development and employability, as well as graduate employment. He holds a Level A/B Psychological Society qualification in Psychometric testing/Profiling and is also MBTI certified.

Chapter 4: Melissa Challinor, HR and Education Specialist

Melissa Challinor has 18 years' experience in HR across the private, charity and public sectors. She is Vice Chair of Directors at a Multi Academy Trust where she is the HR lead for the performance management and recruitment of senior leadership. Also within Education, Melissa works as a School Business Manager responsible for HR, Finance, Procurement and Premises management. Additionally, Melissa provides guidance to her District Council as a member of their Independent Remuneration Panel, setting annual allowances for elected Councillors.

Previously, Melissa spent 10 years at Which?, initially as Training and Development Manager where she introduced City & Guilds qualifications, which had a positive impact on retention. While there Melissa's role grew to Resourcing and Development Manager. She led on recruiting, onboarding and developing new employees, providing training for existing employees and bespoke development programmes for the Which? legal and financial teams.

Melissa is a Chartered Member of the CIPD and holds an MSc degree from the University of Essex. She is also accredited in the use of the Hogan, SDI and Talent Q psychometric tools.

Chapter 5: Clare Hodder, Freelance Rights Consultant

Clare Hodder is a Rights and Licensing Consultant working with a broad range of publishers and service providers to help develop profitable licensing opportunities and establish compliant rights acquisition practices. Prior to embarking on a consultancy career Clare was the Associate Director of Rights for Palgrave Macmillan, having worked within various rights roles for the company over a 15-year period. In 2018 she launched RightsZone, a cloud-based software app to help rights teams in the publishing industry to manage their workload more effectively. Clare founded the rights networking group rights2gether and is actively involved in various industry fora focusing on copyright and licensing issues in the UK and the US. Clare studied English at Southampton University and holds a Postgraduate Diploma in Publishing.

Chapter 6: Joanna Moriarty, Green Park Interim & Executive Search

Joanna Moriarty is a Partner at Green Park Interim and Executive, and sits in the Civil Society and Government Practice, recruiting senior executive and non-executive leaders, and providing consultancy and governance review. She was Publishing Director for SPCK until 2014, during which time she also developed leadership roles in the third sector. Joanna sits on the boards of several charities, including Feed the Minds, and on the board of a large primary-school Multi-Academy Trust. Joanna's work at Green Park has a strong focus on helping organisations become more diverse, and creating teams which translate different thinking into impact and action.

Chapter 7: Doug Howlett, Munster Rugby

Doug Howlett is a former professional New Zealand rugby union player. He finished his career with Munster Rugby in Ireland. With an outstanding 49 tries in 62 tests, Howlett is currently the seventh-highest try scorer in rugby union history and first on the all-time highest try scorers' list for the All Blacks. Doug is highly experienced in the areas of leadership, motivation and high performance.

Chapter 8: Declan Deegan, Milford Care Centre, Limerick

Declan Deegan has over 20 years' experience in the area of HR. He has worked for Wang, EMC and with Dell Computers in many roles, including Recruitment Manager, Senior Human Resources Manager and EMEA Business Ethics Manager. He was also the HR manager for the overseas facility in Poland. He is currently Head of Human Resources, Education and Learning and Development at Milford Care Centre in Limerick.

Chapter 9: Marcus Kelly, Analog Devices

Marcus Kelly is HR Business Partner for Global Operations & Technology at Analog Devices, a multinational semiconductor company specialising in data conversion, signal processing and power management technology. Upon joining the company in 1997, he worked in Manufacturing, Process Engineering, and Design Engineering before moving to the HR function in 2016. Marcus has also worked as a College Recruitment Specialist and Manager for Analog's sites in EMEA. Marcus holds a BA in Psychology and an MSc in Organisational Psychology from the University of Limerick, and is a Chartered Organisational Psychologist of the Psychological Society of Ireland.

Chapter 10: Lucile Kamar, ITN

Lucile Kamar is Head of Diversity and Inclusion at ITN. She is an award-winning diversity and inclusion expert specialising in driving and implementing change as well as empowering individuals. From a French and North African background, she believes in the power of diverse and inclusive teams to transform the workplace. She's passionate about creating safe and brave spaces to facilitate conversations and connecting with people to create long-lasting relationships.

Lucile has experience driving diversity and inclusion in various industries such as politics, the construction and legal sectors. She has a BA (Hons) in Politics and International Relations and a MA in Human Rights Law from the School of Oriental and African Studies in London.

Chapter 11: Lavinia Duggan, VHI

Lavinia is Corporate Business Manager with VHI Healthcare and recognises that developing a culture of proactive health management in the workplace, in community and at home can result in a positive impact on individuals' physical and mental health. Lavinia holds a Bachelor of Business Studies with the University of Limerick, a Master's in Business Strategy & Marketing Management with Limerick Institute of Technology, and is Chairperson of CIPD Midwest.

Chapter 12: Micheál Clancy, AMCS Group

Micheál Clancy is a Senior Global HR Business Partner with digital software company AMCS Group, based at its corporate headquarters in Limerick. Previously, Micheál worked with Kerry Group plc for over 16 years in various HR roles in Ireland and abroad, having joined the Kerry Group Graduate Development programme directly from the University of Limerick. Throughout his education and career to date he has been immersed in the area of Human Resource Management. He has worked in a variety of HRM roles in both corporate and manufacturing settings. A Masters in HRM graduate of the University of Limerick, Micheál also holds a Bachelor of Business Studies in addition to a number of postgraduate diplomas in areas such as Industrial Relations, Mediation Skills and Executive Coaching.

Chapter 13: Simon Shaw, IBM

Simon Shaw has over 25 years' experience leading international, multi-site customer service operations for organisations such as Expedia, Carnival Cruise Lines, Eurostar, British Airports Authority, Diageo and the BBC. He is currently the Global Lead for Service Transformation at IBM, where he leads clients across all industry sectors and supports customer service, field service and contact centre transformation projects enabled by digital and AI technologies to enhance the customer and agent experience. He has a Diploma in Management Studies from Leicester University.

Chapter 14: Gina London, International Communications Expert

Gina London is a renowned global expert on leadership communications. An Emmy-winning former CNN correspondent and anchor with premier clients in five continents, she guides the top companies and executives in the world to more positively connect and engage with their employees, their board and themselves.

Gina also provides interactive and motivational keynote speeches on the power of communicating with purpose and impact. She brings her network interview skills when she profiles top leaders like Ford Executive Chairman Bill Ford, Jr, and Nobel Peace Prize winners Oscar Arias and Archbishop Desmond Tutu. She has also facilitated or compèred hundreds of events – like the prestigious 2018 International Children's Peace Prize in Cape Town, South Africa.

A published author and regular media analyst, Gina has appeared on the BBC, FOX and CNN. She's been featured in Fast Company and interviewed on radio and TV across the world, from New Zealand to Europe, Africa and the United States. She currently writes a weekly business leadership column, 'The Communicator' in Ireland's largest circulated newspaper, *The Sunday Independent*.

OB IN PRACTICE GRID

Chapter	Title	Industry	Location	Focus
Chapter 1: Organisational Behaviour in the Business Environment	Industry 4.0: Helping or Harming the Human?	Manufacturing	Global	Workplace evolution
Chapter 2: Personality	BrewCo	Food and beverage	USA	Recruitment, selection and organisational culture fit
Chapter 3: Perception	Marwood	Manufacturing	Kenya	Continuous improvement process and employee perceptions
Chapter 4: Attitudes and Job Satisfaction	Pulsate	Home entertainment	China	Employee attitudes to a company takeover
Chapter 5: Motivation and Rewards	HR at Google	Communication services	Global	Effective team performance
Chapter 6: Leadership	Narcissistic Leaders	All	Global	Managing narcissists at work
Chapter 7: Groups and Teams in the Workplace	Teamwork at Madame Chu's: A Case of Too Many Cooks?	Food and beverage	UK	Team conflict
Chapter 8: Management Control, Power and Authority	Power, Control and Ethics at Amazon	Online retail	Online	Control of employees
Chapter 9: Managing Healthy Workplaces	The Vulnerable Heroes of the Pandemic	Health sector	China	Keeping the frontline workers safe
Chapter 10: Managing Diversity	Gender Discrimination	Teaching profession	Ireland	Discrimination in the recruitment and selection process
Chapter 11: Organisational Socialisation	Designing a Graduate Programme	Business consulting	Europe and Asia	Socialising new graduate employees
Chapter 12: Organisational Culture	Encountering a Culture Clash	Manufacturing	USA, Europe and Asia	Implications of cross-cultural differences
Chapter 13: Managing Organisational Change	Change at ChemCo	Pharmaceutical	Asia	Integration of an acquisition
Chapter 14: Communication in the Workplace	Communication in the Health Sector	Health Sector	Ireland	The impact on stakeholders of a communication strategy

BUILDING YOUR SKILLS

In this section we briefly look at four skills that are key to being successful both at college and at work: online learning; managing your phone and social media; presentation skills and persuading and influencing skills.

Online Learning Skills

Covid-19 has resulted in a change to the way we learn. Most of us are forced to learn at home now rather than in our college buildings. This has led to the rise of e-learning, whereby teaching is undertaken remotely and on digital platforms. Research suggests that online learning has been shown to increase retention of information, and take less time, meaning the changes brought about by Covid-19 may be here to stay. Online learning platforms such as Tencent classroom have been used extensively since the arrival of Covid-19. In China, for example, the government instructed a quarter of a billion full-time students to resume their studies through online platforms.

There are a lot of challenges, however, for you as a student. Successful distance learning requires self-discipline, self-motivation, being prepared, being well organised and having good time management skills. It is important to regularly log in to each of your courses, monitor deadlines, and complete your course work regularly.

- **Log in to your learning management system regularly.** The key is to have a dedicated time set aside for your course work and to minimise obstacles that prevent you from studying and participating in online learning.
- **Participate.** Get involved in the online live learning experiences that you are presented with. Proactively turn off or minimise your distractions (including your mobile phone, music, etc.) when it is time for live classes.
- **Use a calendar.** Set up a daily schedule, marking important due dates for learning activities and assessments, and blocking off time for reading course content and participating in course requirements.
- **Read, read and read!** Be sure to read all of your instructor's e-mails, announcements, and communications. Often these will contain important deadlines, 'to do's', assignment instructions, etc.

Managing Mobile Phones

The phone seems to have taken over our lives. We are now no longer able to go anywhere without a mobile phone. Do you check your smartphone compulsively? It is likely the first thing you do when you get up in the morning and the last thing you do at night before going to sleep. The fact is, the more often you check it the more often you feel the need to check it! Research has found that people spend around 3 hours and 15 minutes on their phone every day. Most people check their phones 58 times a day. Thirty of those times are during work hours! Studies have also shown that since Covid-19 people are spending more time on their phones every day.

Therefore:

- Set aside specific time slots for checking your phone, maybe after you have worked for a block of time.
- When your phone beeps you don't always have to check it. In fact, you can avoid temptation by turning off the notifications.
- Set your screen to appear monochrome during work hours: Instagram will not seem so appealing if it is all in black and white. Turn on your phone's greyscale mode when you work.
- Check the Screen Time function on your phone just to see how much you are actually spending on your phone each day. You might be surprised with the results!

WhatsApp, e-mail, Instagram, Snapchat, Facebook, Twitter and other social media platforms have become the standard way of communicating both at university and at work. The biggest problem with this is that they consume large portions of your day, and yet help you achieve relatively little. To deal with these problems and at the same time manage your time better you could try some of the following:

- Check your e-mail/Instagram/Twitter pages just two or three times a day – in the morning, at lunchtime and in the afternoon. If something is really urgent someone will contact you on your phone! Web apps such as Anti-Social for Mac and Cold Turkey for Windows are free productivity programs that you can use to temporarily block yourself off from popular social media sites, addictive websites and games.
- Set up e-mail messages with auto-preview as this will allow you to see if the message needs to be opened and acted on straight away.
- Use a subject message line each time you send an e-mail, even if it's a reply.
- Delete an e-mail once you have read and replied to it or move it to a personal folder.

Presentation Skills

Regardless of the industry sector or size of organisation you work in, you will need to have the ability to present your ideas clearly and succinctly. You will probably also have to make presentations as part of your programme of study. You will use a software programme such as Microsoft PowerPoint to provide an overview of the context and key points. Increasingly, some job vacancies require you to make an oral presentation as part of the selection process. In order to present your ideas and arguments clearly there are a number of stages involved in making an oral presentation. Some of the key issues involved are outlined here in order to assist you in developing this important skill, either through your course work or after college:

Planning your presentation:

- Be clear about what your core message is and repeat this at different stages during the presentation in order to increase its impact. Is it to inform? To sell your idea? To defend a position? To present a new idea? Whatever the answer, keep asking yourself why, in different ways. What is the objective I want to achieve? What will I accept as evidence that my presentation has succeeded? What do I want the audience to think or feel at the end of the presentation?
- Analyse your audience. What are their expectations of your presentation? Do they expect to be informed? Persuaded? Have their existing ideas challenged? What do you think they already know? The key to a successful presentation is to know what your audience expects and that you meet or exceed that expectation.
- How much time do you have for your presentation? Be careful not to run over an allocated time slot. This will detract from your effectiveness.
- What should you wear? This may seem a little strange to include here; however, confidence is an important element in an effective presentation. You need to be comfortable, and appropriately dressed to project the 'right' message.

Handling nerves:

Many people find this the most difficult part of making a presentation.

- Be well prepared and organised. Most people will feel nervous before a presentation. Knowing what you are going to say and being organised will reduce your level of nervousness. The first two minutes of any presentation are the most crucial. If you feel confident and clear about what you are going to say in the early stage of the presentation this will help alleviate your nerves for the remainder of the presentation. Once you have passed the first two minutes and you mentally believe that the presentation is going well, this will allow the remainder of the presentation to run more smoothly.

- Don't read directly from your notes – use visual aids. This means that the words/pictures you use on the screen should act as your 'prompt'. Do not use hand-held notes as they will just act to provide a false sense of security. If you lose your place in the notes or have learned off by heart what to say and then mix up your notes, your level of effectiveness in the eyes of the audience will be diminished.
- Rehearse in advance. Trial runs are an excellent method of preparation and allow you to establish how long your presentation will take. This also develops your self-confidence, which will work to reduce your nervousness.
- Pay attention to your 'mannerisms' and work to overcome them. Ask a friend/family member to highlight any repeated unconscious behaviours you might have, such as running your hands through your hair, shaking the change in your pocket, swaying from side to side or speaking too fast. These are very distracting for the audience.
- Practise deep breathing before you get to the room/place where the presentation is. This will help reduce the overall feeling of nervousness.
- Be in the room in plenty of time and check the equipment and that your presentation is working.
- Thinking positively means you are more likely to feel and behave positively.

Structuring your presentation:

The golden rule is simple:
- Tell them what you are going to tell them (introduction).
- Tell them (main body).
- Tell them what you've told them (conclusion).

The introduction:

- The introduction should comprise approximately 10% of your presentation. It should provide a map for the reader of what is going to come.
- Introduce the topic yourself (if necessary).
- Start with an attention-getting hook – make a bold claim, present a striking fact/statistic, ask a question, use a quotation. If you have a suitable quote, surprising information or a visual aid – use it to grab the audience's attention.

Body language:

- Speak clearly and audibly throughout. Vary the tone of your voice as this creates interest in your message.
- Face the audience, not the screen behind you or your laptop. Speak to the audience and make eye contact with people in the room. This demonstrates that you are paying attention to them and encourages them to pay attention to you.
- Don't speak too fast as your message can get lost in translation.
- Show enthusiasm for the topic/issue/idea, as enthusiasm is contagious.
- Project your voice out towards the audience. Do not speak down to your shoes!
- Regard the presentation as an opportunity to shine.

The conclusion:

- Remind the audience of what you set out to do at the start. That means stressing the key point of your presentation.

- Briefly repeat the main points you made.
- End on an interesting point, as this assists people in remembering your presentation.
- Thank the audience for listening and invite questions.

Persuasion and Influencing Skills

Learning how to influence and persuade people to do something they would otherwise have not done is an important life skill. Influencing is essentially getting your own way, unobtrusively. Managers do it most of the time. People are usually not aware that every human interaction involves a complex process of persuasion and influence. And being unaware, they are usually the ones being persuaded to help others rather than the ones who are doing the persuading!

- Know what you want …! If you are not clear about what you want it will be difficult for you to persuade others around to your way of thinking.
- Look for points of mutual agreement and build on these.
- Build rapport and make a connection with the person you are trying to influence.
- Ask questions. The type of question is important. You need to use a mixture of questions to get the response you are looking for.
  - Find out what the other person is looking for out of the interaction – What do you want to get out of this discussion? What do you want to achieve from this discussion?
  - Probe to find out why they don't agree with you – What is the reason why you can't do that? What is stopping you from agreeing with me?
  - Ask hypothetical questions as this allows you to gather information without the person actually committing to anything – What would happen if you agreed with me? What would happen if we went ahead and did it?
  - Find out what they need you to give them in order for them to agree with you – What do you need to get in order for us to agree? What do I need to give you to get you to agree?
  - Ask challenging questions to test the person's resolve/position. Search for specifics – Why do you not agree with this proposal? What specific reason do you have for not wanting to do this?
- Listen actively. This includes being able to paraphrase what the other person has said.
- Use positive body language and verbal language. This creates the right atmosphere and is more conducive to agreement.
  - Don't use 'flowery language'! Using too many adjectives and adverbs will lose the listener.
  - Use strong words not weak words when trying to persuade people. For example, which of these two sentences would persuade you: *'I think you might like this new product we have'* or *'You're really going to like this new product we are offering.'* 'Think' in this sentence is a weak word. Here is another example: *'I was wondering if you might want to go for a drink with me at the weekend?'* A stronger question would be: *'Would you like to go to for a drink this weekend?'*
  - Focus on using the active voice, not the passive voice. Passive: An account was opened by Mr Smith. Active: Mr Smith opened an account.
- Stress the benefits to them of agreeing with you.
- Work towards a decision. Use all the techniques above to keep building towards their agreement.

PUBLISHER'S ACKNOWLEDGEMENTS

The publishers and the authors would like to thank the organisations and people listed below for permission to reproduce material from their publications.

The Academy of Management, for permission to reproduce:

Figure 11.1 'Feldman model of socialisation'. From Feldman, D. C. (1981). The multiple socialization of organization members. *Academy of Management Review*, 6(2), 309–318. Copyright © The Academy of Management 1981.

American Psychological Association, for permission to reproduce:

Figure 2.1 'Personality dimensions across the life course'. Adapted from B.W. Roberts, K.E. Walton and W. Viechtbauer (2006). Patterns of Mean-Level Change in Personality Traits across the Life Course: A Meta-Analysis of Longitudinal Studies. *Psychological Bulletin*, 132 (2006), 1–25. Copyright © 2006 by the American Psychological Association.

Figure 4.2 'The relationship between job satisfaction and job performance'. From Judge, T.A., Thoresen, C.J., Bono, J.E. and Patton, G.K. (2001). The job satisfaction–job performance relationship: A qualitative and quantitative review. *Psychological bulletin*, 127(3), 376. Copyright © 2001 by the American Psychological Association.

Figure 5.2 'Maslow's hierarchy of needs theory'. From Maslow, A.H, (1943) A theory of human motivation. *Psychological Review*, 50(4), 370–396. This material is now in the public domain.

Figure 13.3 'Three-step model of change'. Adapted from Lewin, Kurt (1997). *Resolving Social Conflicts and Field Theory in Social Science*. Washington, DC: American Psychological Association. Copyright © 1997 by the American Psychological Association.

Table 9.1 'Coping strategies identified by Carver, Scheier and Weintraub'. Adapted from Carver, C.S., Scheier, M.F. and Weintraub, J. K. (1989). Assessing coping strategies: A theoretically based approach. *Journal of Personality and Social Psychology*, 56(2), 267–283. Copyright ©1989 by the American Psychological Association.
All reproduced with permission. The use of APA information does not imply endorsement by the APA.

Deloitte University Press, for Table 10.2 'Diversity and inclusion: Old rules vs new rules'. From 'Diversity and Inclusion: The Reality Gap.' Copyright © 2017 Deloitte University Press.

Elsevier, for permission to reproduce:

Table 2.3 'Measure yourself on the Big Five'. Adapted from Gosling, S.D., Rentfrow, P.J. and Swann Jr., W.B. (2003). A very brief measure of the Big-Five personality domains. *Journal of Research in Personality*, 37, 504–528. Copyright © Elsevier 2003.

Figure 4.1 'Theory of planned behaviour'. Adapted from Ajzen, I. (1991). The theory of planned behavior. *Organizational Behavior and Human Decision Processes*, 50, 179–211. Copyright © Elsevier 1991.

Figure 4.3 'Organisational commitment questionnaire'. In Mowday, R.T., Steers, R.M. and Porter, L.W. (1979). The measurement of organizational commitment. *Journal of Vocational Behaviour*, 14(2), 224–247. Copyright © Elsevier 1979.

Figure 5.3 'Job Characteristics Model'. Adapted from Job Characteristics Model developed by Hackman, J.R. and Oldham, G.R. (1976). Motivation through the design of work: Test of a theory. *Organizational Behavior and Human Performance*, 16, 256. Copyright © Elsevier 1976.

Figure 6.3 'The toxic triangle'. Adapted from Padilla, A., Hogan, R. and Kaiser, R.B. (2007). The toxic triangle: Destructive leaders, susceptible followers, and conducive environments. *The Leadership Quarterly*, 18(3), 176–194. Copyright © Elsevier 2007.

Emerald Publishing, for permission to reproduce Figure 9.2 'Relationships between motivation and strain in the Job Demands–Resources Model'. From Bakker, A.B. and Demerouti, E. (2007). The Job Demands–Resources Model: State of the Art. *Journal of Managerial Psychology*, 22(3), 309–328. Copyright © Emerald Publishing 2007.

Dr Sybil Eysenck (Personality Investigations Publications & Services), for permission to reproduce: Figure 2.3 'Eysenck's personality types and associated traits'. From Eysenck, H. (1965). *Fact and Fiction in Psychology*. Harmondsworth: Penguin. Copyright © Personality Investigations Publications & Services 1965.

Gulf Publishing Company, for permission to reproduce Figure 6.1 'The Managerial Grid'. From Blake, R.R. and Mouton, J.S. (1962). *Managerial Grid: Key Orientations for Achieving Production through People*. Houston, TX: Gulf Publishing Company. Copyright © Gulf Publishing Company 1964.

Institute for Social Research, for permission to reproduce and adapt Table 8.1 'Sources of power'. From French, J.R.P. and Raven, B. (1959). The Bases of Social Power. In D. Cartwright (ed.), *Studies in Social Power*. Ann Arbor, MI: Institute for Social Research. Copyright © Institute for Social Research 1959.

John Wiley & Sons, Incorporated, for permission to reproduce:

Figure 8.1 'The power/interaction model'. From Raven, B.H. (1993). The bases of power: Origins and recent developments. *Journal of Social Issues*, vol. 49, 227–251. Copyright © 1993 John Wiley & Sons, Incorporated.

Figure 12.1 'Schein's model of organisational culture'. Adapted from Schein, E.H. (1985). *Organizational Culture and Leadership*, 1st edition. San Francisco, CA: Jossey-Bass. Copyright © 1985 John Wiley & Sons, Incorporated.

Figure 12.2 'The competing values Framework'. From Cameron, K.S. and Quinn, R.E. (2011). *Diagnosing and Changing Organizational Culture Based on the Competing Values Framework*. Reading, MA: Addison-Wesley. Copyright © 2011 John Wiley & Sons, Incorporated.

Figure 13.1 'Kotter's integrative model of organisational dynamics'. Adapted from Kotter, J.P. (1980). In E.E. Lawler, D.A. Nadler and C.T. Cammann (eds), *Organizational Assessment: Perspectives on the Measurement of Organizational Behaviour and the Quality of Work Life* (p. 282). New York: John Wiley & Sons Incorporated. Copyright © 1980 John Wiley & Sons, Incorporated.

Table 10.1 'Differences between affirmative action programmes and diversity management programmes'. Adapted from 'Exhibit 2-1, Organizational Diversity', from Hitt, M.A., Miller, C.C. and Colella, A. (2009). *Organizational Behavior: A Strategic Approach*, 2nd edition, (p. 40). India: John Wiley & Sons. Copyright © 2009 John Wiley & Sons, Incorporated.

Lidl for permission to reproduce Figure 11.3 'Lidl graduate programme' from their brochure.

Pierce Howard and Jane Howard, for permission to reproduce and adapt Table 2.1 'The Big Five personality dimensions'. From Howard, P.J. and Howard J.M. (2001). *The Owner's Manual for Personality at Work: How the Big Five Personality Traits Affect Performance, Communication, Teamwork, Leadership, and Sales*. Austin, TX: Bard. Copyright © Pierce Howard and Jane Howard 2001.

Profile Books Limited, for permission to reproduce and adapt Figure 13.2 'The McKinsey 7S framework'. From Peters, T. and Waterman, R.H. (2004). *In Search of Excellence: Lessons from America's Best-run Companies*. London: Profile Books Ltd. Copyright © 2004 Profile Books Ltd.

Psychological Assessment Resources, Inc. (PAR), for permission to reproduce Figure 2.5 'RIASEC personality types'. From Holland, J.L. *Making Vocational Choices*, Third Edition. Copyright 1973, 1985, 1992, 1997 by PAR. All rights reserved.

Red Globe Press, for permission to reproduce:

Figure 2.4 'A sample feedback report using Cattell's 16PF'. From Bratton, J. (2021). *Work and Organisational Behaviour: An Introduction*, second edition. London: Red Globe Press. Copyright © Red Globe Press 2021.

Figure 13.4 'Factors affecting employee responses to change'. From Hayes, J. (2021). *The Theory and Practice of Change Management*, sixth edition. London: Red Globe Press. Copyright © Red Globe Press 2021.

Taylor & Francis, for permission to reproduce Figure 9.1 'Four quadrant model of affective well-being'. From Warr, P., Bindl, U.K., Parker, S.K. and Inceoglu, I. (2014). Four-quadrant investigation of job-related affects and behaviours. *European Journal of Work and Organizational Psychology*, 23(3), 342–363. Copyright © Taylor & Francis 2014.

1 ORGANISATIONAL BEHAVIOUR IN THE BUSINESS ENVIRONMENT

Michelle Hammond and Missie Smith

LEARNING OUTCOMES

BY THE END OF THIS CHAPTER, YOU SHOULD BE ABLE TO:

- Define organisational behaviour (OB) and discuss its goals as a field of study.
- Identify the major disciplines that contribute to understanding OB.
- Demonstrate evidence of the value of OB for managers and organisations.
- Identify the main methods used in OB research.
- Identify the major levels of analysis in OB and the interplay among them.
- Summarise contemporary issues facing the field of OB.

CREDIT: PHOTO BY MARVIN MEYER ON UNSPLASH

THIS CHAPTER DISCUSSES...

INTRODUCTION

Take a moment and picture yourself starting your workday 10 years from today. What would make that day great? You might think about doing work that you love, feeling accomplished or recognised by others, working with motivated colleagues, having meaningful conversations and interactions with your co-workers and making a difference in the lives of others. Your ideal workday likely included elements that enhance your well-being and the well-being of others as well as doing great work to benefit your company. If so, your goals are in alignment with the goals of the field of Organisational Behaviour, which highlights both the well-being of employees as well as the performance of the organisation. Within this book, you will study how people think, act and react in the workplace and the influence of many factors on their behaviour. If you have ever wondered about how people act and think the way they do in the workplace, you have been thinking about organisational behaviour (likely without knowing it). By studying concepts and research in OB, you will be able to understand and ultimately affect attitudes and behaviours at your current or future place of work. You will also find personal insight into your preferences and patterns, and ideas for improving your workplaces. You will also be better able to enter into conversations with others about their work, regardless of their industries and positions, by studying the context of work.

This chapter provides an introduction and background in the field of OB. It is broken down into four important questions to consider when studying organisational behaviour: (1) What is organisational behaviour? (2) Why does organisational behaviour matter? (3) What are the sources of OB knowledge? (4) Why is OB more important today than ever? Addressing these questions will give you a solid basis for understanding the field and help you better interact with other people in work regardless of where your career takes you.

WHAT IS ORGANISATIONAL BEHAVIOUR?

organisational behaviour is a field of study that seeks to understand and improve organisational effectiveness by examining factors about individuals, teams, and organisational culture and structure and the way they interact.

What is this business about 'organisational behaviour'? Do organisations really behave? Perhaps not, but people certainly do. The field of OB is really about understanding how people think, act and react in the workplace, and the influence of many factors on their behaviour, including issues around individuals, their relationships with others such as their co-workers and boss, the group or department they are in, and the structure and culture of the organisations they work in. As a field, OB is ultimately concerned with using this information to promote certain desirable attitudes and behaviours of employees as well as the effectiveness of the organisation more broadly.

ORGANISATIONAL BEHAVIOUR IS MULTI-LEVEL

Because factors about people, their relationships and the broader organisational context all affect how people act in the workplace, the field is inherently *multi-level*. By multi-level we mean that individuals operate within groups, and groups operate within organisations, and likewise, organisations operate within a larger environmental context. If we fail to consider the context, we are missing a key piece of the puzzle.

It is unwise to consider one employee or his/her role in isolation. Individual employees both influence and are shaped by their environment. Think about how you act in various settings. If someone saw you give a formal presentation in class, they might draw a conclusion that you are a smart dresser, articulate and formal. However, if they saw you with your friends in a relaxing setting, they might draw a different conclusion. Your behaviour is shaped by the norms around you. However, you also shape those norms. If you were very upset, you might shape the mood of those around you. Likewise, employees' input, personality, knowledge, and so on, have an influence on work teams. Teams are part of departments and departments are part of organisations with their own history, values, culture, policies, and so on. Finally, the whole organisation is all part of a larger environmental context including the market, the economic situation, local, national and global regulations and national culture(s). These influences go from top down, for example from the environment or the organisation to the individual, and in a bottom-up fashion from the individual to the organisation (see Figure 1.1).

While studying OB, it is useful to take a systems thinking approach. This means that if we want to understand a problem, we need to keep in mind how that problem is part of an overall system. In the context of organisational behaviour, systems thinking helps us to realise that an organisation is a system made of different parts that affect and are affected by one another. Similarly, the organisation interacts with its larger environment. Systems thinking has its roots in General Systems Theory, which was originally a theory developed from the physical sciences. Ludwig von Bertalanffy (1968) and Kast and Rosenzweig (1972), who later brought this to the field of OB, suggested that a system is a complex structure of interacting elements and that they are open to, and interact with, their environment. Systems theory suggests that the organisation is a system made of interrelated and interdependent parts. One can study each component in isolation, but when we do so, we fail to capture the essence of the whole. Take, for example, the argument illustrated in the 'Building your Employability Skills' box. How might each individual approach the issue differently and what effect might this interaction have on the rest of the team or department? Likewise, how does the larger workplace context affect this argument?

systems thinking is an approach that considers the organisation as a structure made of different parts that affect and are affected by one another. Similarly, the organisation interacts with its larger environment.

BUILDING YOUR EMPLOYABILITY SKILLS

Managing Conflict

In your role as manager, a dispute between two employees, Mike and John, is brought to your attention. Both employees came to talk to you independently about an issue they cannot seem to work through themselves. Mike and John's desks are next to each other, separated by a small divider. Mike complains that John is loud. Mike is 'constantly distracted and frustrated' by him. John argues that he has been respectful of Mike, but 'has to do his job', which includes taking calls and meeting with others. How do you help Mike and John resolve their issues? What effect might their disagreement have on the rest of the department?

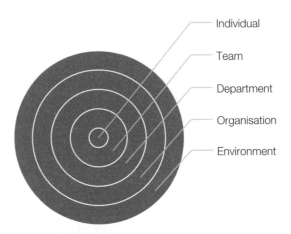

Individual

Team

Department

Organisation

Environment

Figure 1.1 The multi-level nature of the field of OB

As you read the chapter, be sure to keep in mind what level the material is focused on – is it the individual, the team, the organisation? – and remember that they are all influenced by and influencing other levels.

As you are reading each of the chapters in the text, it may feel as if they are independent and unrelated. Try to take a systems perspective and remind yourself that they do influence and are influenced by each other. The chapters of this text are grouped in meaningful sections, or parts, that can be best understood through a systems perspective. Part 1 covers individual differences that reflect the innermost ring of Figure 1.1. In this section, you will read about how people vary in personality ▶**See Chapter 2◀**, the way they perceive information ▶**See Chapter 3◀**, their attitudes and values ▶**See Chapter 4◀** and how they are motivated ▶**See Chapter 5◀**. When reading these chapters, it is easy to think about how employees bring these differences to the workplace. However, we would encourage you to also think about how motivations, attitudes and perceptions are shaped and influenced by the situations, life stages and environments in which they are embedded. Part 2 of the text presents information about bringing diverse individuals together to achieve organisational goals through the management of behaviour at work. This section highlights the relationships between managers and employees and among employees themselves. You might consider this section as the interplay of the first three rings in Figure 1.1. Topics such as leadership ▶**See Chapter 6◀** and power and control ▶**See Chapter 8◀**, groups and teams ▶**See Chapter 7◀** and managing diversity ▶**See Chapter 10◀** highlight the importance of relationships in the workplace, to name a few. Finally, the last section of the text focuses on organisational processes that shape both individuals (Part 1) and relationships (Part 2) in a top-down manner. These processes include formal processes such as policies and programmes and informal processes such as agreed-upon norms in the areas of socialisation ▶**See Chapter 11◀**, culture ▶**See Chapter 12◀** and communication ▶**See Chapter 14◀**. However, we often forget that these formal and informal processes are indeed written, shaped and reinforced by individuals, in a bottom-up fashion. We truly need to take a systems approach when considering the complexities of organisational life.

While reading these chapters, if you have work experience, try to think of how these aspects of the workplace affected your own behaviour. For example, you might think about how your personality and that of others affected the way you worked with others on a team ▶**See Chapters 2 and 7◀** and how that team operated within the larger culture of the organisation ▶**See Chapter 12◀**. If you do not have formal work experience, sports teams, schools and families may operate in a similar way. Additionally, you might think about how you motivate yourself to study ▸See Chapter 5◂ and how you communicate with your lecturers or instructors ▸See Chapter 14◂.

ORGANISATIONAL BEHAVIOUR IS MULTI-DISCIPLINARY

Just as organisational behaviour involves a complex interplay across various levels of analysis, the field itself draws from a variety of fields of research. In order to better understand individual-level phenomena such as personality and job performance, OB draws from **work and organisational psychology**, which is a field dedicated to applying psychological research and principles to the workplace. Research in **cognitive psychology**, a field dedicated to studying the informational processes of the mind, informs our discussion on perception. In order to understand groups and teams, and emotions, OB draws from **social psychology**, which studies the effects of group dynamics on individual well-being. At the organisational level, theories of **sociology and anthropology** help us to understand the structure of the organisation and inform our understanding of culture and values. Whereas psychology generally focuses on individuals, sociology and anthropology have a more macro-level focus on institutions. Sociology teaches about patterns of social relationships whereas anthropology studies the evolution of human characteristics and cultures.

You are probably less familiar with interdisciplinary fields than with more traditional 'vertical' fields such as accounting, marketing or finance. OB cuts across lots of other fields that provide us with some understanding of how people behave in different situations as well as information about work in general, bringing them together with the goal of understanding how and why people act at work. Additionally, there is a concern for both the employee – the person – and the workplace – the bottom line. You may see elements of many different fields, but what makes OB unique is that it brings them all together with the goal of understanding human behaviour at work. While you read about the #MeToo movement, think about how various fields might approach this issue, and how the field of OB might consider both employee well-being and the bottom line of the companies experiencing these injustices.

WHY DOES ORGANISATIONAL BEHAVIOUR MATTER?

First of all, OB matters because the concepts within OB, and in this textbook, do affect the success of a company and the experience of its employees working there. In a 2003 study, Fulmer, Gerhart and Scott suggested that organisations that value the research outcomes within organisational behaviour outperform their counterpart organisations. The study compared the 100 Best Companies to Work for in America with organisations matched for size and industry. The results showed that not only did employees from the 100 best companies have more positive attitudes towards their workplaces, but also these organisations outperformed their counterpart organisations financially. Furthermore, organisations who took a more systematic approach to making changes in their organisation, following good OB practice (called organisational behaviour modification), experienced a 17% increase in performance (Stajkovic and Luthans, 1997). This practice involves identifying, measuring, analysing, intervening in and

#MeToo

The 'me too' movement was instigated by Tarana Burke to help victims of sexual violence. The website (www.metoomvmt.org) highlights how the 'vision from the beginning was to address both the dearth in resources for survivors of sexual violence and to build a community of advocates, driven by survivors, who will be at the forefront of creating solutions to interrupt sexual violence in their communities'. Although the movement began in 2006, it went 'viral' in 2017 when actor Alyssa Milano brought #MeToo to Twitter denouncing sexual misconduct allegations against film producer Harvey Weinstein. The #MeToo movement quickly gained momentum, cutting across industry and national borders, as a 'beacon of hope that the attention placed on sexual harassment allegations at this time will result in fewer infractions and less tolerance in the workplace for inappropriate sexual behavior in the future' (Atwater *et al.*, 2019, p. 2).

OB IN THE NEWS

The movement has sparked substantial dialogue and action in individuals and employees. According to a study within the harassment-free workplace series of the Society of Human Resource Management in 2018, one in three executives reported changing their behaviour in the wake of the #MeToo movement, with concerns not only to reduce the occurrence of harassment but also for the morale, engagement and productivity of the staff. Many organisational responses include expanding training in the areas of sexual harassment and assault, implicit bias, and diversity and inclusion.

Some responses to the #MeToo movement have suggested the movement has highlighted an unequal power distribution, such that those who feel more powerful are more likely to abuse. An article in the *Washington Post*, by Jena McGregor, blames a focus on 'super star' employees that creates a sense of privilege, entitlement and a view that rules do not apply, which in turn, can foster abuse.

Others have written about a #MeToo backlash, in which men became more reluctant to engage with women in certain circumstances for fear of blame (Atwater *et al.*, 2019). The authors' research suggested that although there have been positive outcomes such as an increase in willingness to report sexual harassment among women and a commitment to reducing inappropriate behaviour of men, some intentional and unintentional backlash also occurs. For example, 41% of men reported that men may be more reluctant to engage in one-to-one meetings with women and 22% of men and 44% of women predicted that women may be more likely to be excluded from social interactions.

Questions

1 Identify the main areas of organisational behaviour impacted by the #MeToo movement.
2 Taking a systems thinking approach, how might even one instance of harassment affect the organisation at large?
3 What can you do to reduce the occurrence of sexual harassment in your workplaces and schools?

Sources

Atwater, L.E., Tringale, A.M., Sturm, R.E., Taylor, S.N. and Braddy, P.W. (2019) Looking ahead: How what we know about sexual harassment now informs us of the future. *Organizational Dynamics*, 48(4), 1–9.

https://metoomvmt.org/

https://shrm.org/hr-today/trends-and-forecasting/research-and-surveys/Documents/Harassment-Free%20Workplace%20Series%20Executive%20View%20Topline.pdf

https://www.washingtonpost.com/news/on-leadership/wp/2017/12/19/the-metoo-movement-is-a-warning-sign-about-the-star-system-at-many-companies/

evaluating employees' behaviours in contrast to changes made more haphazardly. These studies highlight the importance of not only the content of OB but also its systematic approach.

While this is all well and good, you might be asking yourself, why does OB matter to *me*, personally? Here are a few reasons why understanding OB may matter to you, regardless of where your career takes you:

1 **It will provide you with a better understanding of the world of work:** Chances are you will have a job at some point in your life, and it will likely make up a significant percentage of your waking hours. Insights coming from OB can help you to work better, to promote more positive relationships with your co-workers and boss, and even to know when quitting your job might be the best move for you. Because OB is the study of why people behave as they do in work settings, it is probably the most applicable material to any job. The content that we will cover has to do with all human behaviour in the workplace and often more generally – it'll give you insights into working with other people, managing stress, and structuring jobs and companies.

   Many people are promoted into management positions based on technical expertise, with little understanding of people – how to manage them, who to hire, how to work through conflict and what motivates people. Even if you don't study OB at degree level or pursue a job in HR or management, the knowledge and skills you learn in this OB module and those after it will be useful regardless of what you do.

2 **It promotes self-insight and personal growth:** In addition to improving your skills working with others, studying OB can be a bit like pointing a microscope at yourself. Because the field is about understanding people in the workplace, it is personally relevant to you. When you study personality ▶**See Chapter 2◀**, you might consider dimensions of your own personality and how they may impact the way you behave and how others respond to you. By studying perception ▶**See Chapter 3◀**, you might consider the way you accurately (or inaccurately) categorise events or the factors that shape how you see yourself and the world. In studying attitudes and values ▶**See Chapter 4◀**, especially in relation to organisational structure and culture ▶**See Chapter 12◀**, you might have a better understanding of the kind of workplace where you might find the most meaning and satisfaction. By studying leadership ▶**See Chapter 6◀** and power and authority ▶**See Chapter 8◀**, you might consider what type of boss inspires you and what type of leader you might like to be. And considering emotions and stress may give you insights into how to maintain and promote your own psychological health. Finally, understanding team dynamics ▶**See Chapter 7◀** and communication ▶**See Chapter 14◀** might help you to make sense of how people speak to you and what they mean, and how to avoid and learn from conflict.

3 **It gives you the ability to speak with others from various disciplines:** One of the things I like about having a background in OB is that I am able to talk to a lot of different people about their jobs. I have friends in diverse fields – engineering, medicine, music, journalism, education – but since I have a background in understanding people at work, I feel I can talk to almost anyone about any job. After studying OB, you might not understand the *content* of their work; you will have a better understanding of the *context* of the workplace. Sure, you won't know the ins and outs of any of it, but you will be able to find common ground.

WHERE DOES OB KNOWLEDGE COME FROM?

People are familiar territory – it is often said that psychology is the science of the obvious. As OB draws heavily on psychology, you may feel this as well. What you read may make sense to you. You might think you know the material already. Granted there will be some new terms and words you've never heard before, but for the most part, you may have some notion from your own life, experience and reading about what you think this is about. One grave mistake students make is opening their book, glancing at it and saying 'I know this stuff.' That is nearly a guaranteed recipe for failure. Just because it may seem at first glance less scary (few formulas, equations, Greek symbols) that does not mean it is purely intuitive either. As OB is a social science, the learning is based on research. Sometimes the research might coincide with your own thoughts on these topics, but other times it might cause you to rethink your own ideas.

It is good to keep in mind that OB may seem like common sense. The thing is, common sense is usually evoked *after* we have all the facts and make sense of them. So you might have read through the answers to the above questions and believed them to be common sense, but according to hindsight bias, you overestimate the accuracy of your intuition, believing that you 'knew it all along'. This tendency comes from a desire to make sense of our lives; to be able to understand – and anticipate – events in our world.

> **hindsight bias** refers to the tendency, after an event has occurred, to overestimate our ability to have foreseen the outcome.

SPOTLIGHT ON SKILLS

There has been a lot of discussion by academics and practitioners about using evidence-based management. Why is it important for organisations? How do you or would you look for information and evidence to make decisions in your organisation?

To help you answer these questions, visit bloomsbury.pub/organisational-behaviour to watch the video of Carla DiBenedetto from Cook Medical talking about evidence-based management.

Managers might fall into the same hindsight bias trap in making sense of the accuracy of their own intuition or personal feeling on a decision. One way to prevent this is to balance the use of intuition in decision-making with evidence-based practices. Through evidence-based practice, managers become more scientific about how they think about organisational problems and changes (Rousseau, 2006). They rely on information from social science and OB research to make decisions. The criminologist Lawrence W. Sherman summed it up well when he said, 'We are all entitled to our own opinions, but not to our own facts' (2002, p. 223). In the 'In Reality …' feature, read about ways in which our intuition might not serve us well, but evidence-based practices could improve our effectiveness and efficiency in brainstorming.

So how and where do we get this evidence?

> **evidence-based practice** means basing decisions on the best presented scientific evidence.

IN REALITY

When faced with difficult problems, when in need of the next product, when trying to improve processes in workplaces, the most common response is to create a working group to come up with creative ideas. Group brainstorming sessions are often the default when trying to come up with a perfect idea. But do they work? No, the research findings do not support this 'idea'. A meta-analysis of over 20 studies (Mullen *et al.*, 1991) has found that group brainstorming leads to the generation of fewer ideas than comparable numbers of solitary brainstormers in both laboratory and organisational settings. Why might this be the case? First, sometimes people slack off in groups, expecting other team members to take the lead. Most often it's the most extroverted person who shares the most ideas, not necessarily the person with the most or best ideas. Quite often people are hesitant to share ideas for fear of saying something stupid – that they'll be judged by others. Other times people get blocked by what someone else said instead of thinking things through on their own, or only come up with ideas that are similar to those already proposed. Research suggests that brainstorming is most effective when individuals take time to process the problem or opportunity individually and bring their ideas to the group. If group brainstorming is to be used, make sure that the leader does not share his or her idea first, be sure to defer judgement on ideas, and focus on trying to come up with as many ideas as possible, regardless of the quality of the idea. Additionally, the use of trained facilitators, diversifying the team members, and creating a 'playground' where members feel a sense of play and positive emotion while engaging in creativity, may reduce some of the threats to group creativity (Thompson, 2003). A further meta-analysis (DeRosa *et al.*, 2007) found evidence that a virtual environment produces more creative ideas with higher group member satisfaction, likely by reducing some of the process loss effects described above.

RESEARCH METHODS IN OB

During this era of huge amounts of information at our disposal, it is hard to know what to trust. One organisational leader might publish a book on '5 steps to becoming a great leader' whereas another produces a podcast on 'the 5 essential aspects to being successful' with contradicting information. How do we know whose advice to follow? One way to ensure the quality of our sourcing is to ensure the conclusions are drawn from rigorous processes, rather than generalised from one person's experience. Within OB, evidence comes from systematic, scientific research. It is important to note the two elements 'systematic' and 'according to scientific principles'. This means that there is a method to what we do and some scientific guidelines governing the quality of the subsequent research. It's not just haphazard observation or testing. It's more than that, as we saw in the 'In Reality ...' box above. The scientific process includes stages of:

> **scientific research** is the systematic study of phenomena according to scientific principles.

1 description – the accurate portrayal or depiction of a phenomenon
2 explanation – understanding why the phenomenon exists and what causes it
3 prediction – anticipating an event prior to its occurrence
4 control – manipulating antecedents to change behaviour

You might consider OB an applied science. As a field, the goal of OB is both to know and to improve. That is, it has a practical focus. OB researchers use scientific methods in order to build this body of knowledge, but seek to do so in order to improve the working world.

In general, research in OB and other social sciences involves developing and testing theories. Theories describe the what, how, when, and why of some phenomena. In short, they describe what the phenomena of interest are like. However interesting or logical the theories are, they are only useful when they have stood up to testing. The verification of theories is necessary to show that they are indeed accurate and applicable. When theories are backed up with evidence, they are incredibly helpful in their practical application. There are different methods of conducting research for the development and verification of theory that are used in OB research, including:

theory is a collection of assertions that specify how and why variables are related, as well as the circumstances in which they should and should not be related.

- **Quantitative survey research** – This methodology involves the use of surveys of a population and attempts to quantify a phenomenon (i.e. to numerically represent something such as performance or attitudes). The data gathered is analysed using statistics to find trends in behaviour across individuals, groups or organisations. Survey research is often very useful for theory testing.
- **Laboratory studies or experiments** – Experiments involve the manipulation of certain variables in controlled environments. In OB research, experiments are often conducted with university students as samples. They provide precision but are often limited in their generalisability to a real-life situation.
- **Qualitative interviews and focus groups** – Interviews provide an in-depth understanding of phenomena through interviewing individuals one at a time or in groups (focus groups). Interviews range from unstructured to highly structured and researchers analyse the data for themes in responses.
- **Case studies** – A case study involves a very in-depth study of one individual, group or organisation. Case studies may include observation over a period of time, analysis of historical records, and interviews. Case studies provide a rich understanding of phenomena and are realistic but they often have limited generalisability to other settings or contexts.
- **Meta-analyses** – A meta-analysis involves the statistical compilation of a previous body of quantitative research on a particular topic. While they often can account for some limitations within any given study, such as small sample size, results of meta-analyses are only as good as the studies that are included.

contingency approach suggests that organisational and individual behaviour is contingent, or depends, on a number of interacting factors.

Scholars and practitioners within OB take a contingency approach. Like a systems thinking approach, the contingency approach highlights the interaction of various factors within organisational life. The contingency approach highlights that there is no 'one best approach' that works for every company in every situation. There are fewer clear cut answers – however, when it comes to your exams, there will clearly be 'correct' answers! But in general, the context is important. So a lot of things we learn will be dependent on different situations. In OB there are not 'laws' that apply to all contexts like the laws of physics. People are less predictable than gravity, but there are basic trends. We might not be able to predict any one person's behaviour at one given point in time, but as humans, we are united in some common experience and have a tendency to act in similar ways. Similar types of people may act similarly in similar situations. There are important lessons to be learned and there is real value in learning about people at work.

BUILDING YOUR EMPLOYABILITY SKILLS

Balancing Empathy and Fairness

Imagine one of your top employees just called a meeting with you. During this meeting, she mentioned that her mother, who lives a two-hour' drive away, is ill. She would like to figure out an arrangement to work from nearer to her mother for an indefinite amount of time. What creative solutions might you work out? How would this arrangement affect the others in the office? How do you consider the fairness of an employee's non-work concerns?

CONTEMPORARY CHALLENGES IN OB

How is the world of work different for you today than for your parents and grandparents? What are the implications of these changes in the field of OB? Several factors affecting what, where and how we work and their implications for OB are described below.

GLOBALISATION

The global economy is continuing to change rapidly due to technological innovations, economic fluctuations, and the rise of service and knowledge work, among other-reasons. Globalisation has meant that goods, services and capital frequently flow across borders and so organisations need to move beyond a local focus. This also means that the context where many people complete work and craft their careers has changed as well. It can be argued that globalisation has changed the job of a manager. Now, managers are more likely to experience the following:

1 **Working with people from different cultural backgrounds.** As a manager, you are likely to be responsible for managing people with very different backgrounds from your own. Your communications, ideas for motivating and recognising others, and even mannerisms may be interpreted very differently from your intentions. Similarly, these miscommunications may be happening among members of your team. How do you ensure everyone is working towards the team's goal and getting on well?

2 **Increased foreign assignments.** As he was leaving General Electric (GE), Jack Welch said this: 'The Jack Welch of the future cannot be like me. I spent my entire career in the United States. The next head of GE will be somebody who spent time in Bombay, in Hong Kong, in Buenos Aires. We have to send our best and brightest overseas and make sure they have the training that will allow them to be the global leaders who will make GE flourish in the future.' What factors might affect the success of a foreign assignment? A manager might be trying to lead a workforce with very different needs, beliefs, expectations and practices from his or her own while facing his or her own need of being away from home.

3 **Managing across time zones and managing virtual teams.** Even if a manager is not on a foreign assignment, some of the same issues may arise at home. Because of globalisation,

many companies are multinational and are spread across many different countries, many have clients or customers in other countries, and others involve collaborations with or outsourcing from other companies across borders. Consider managing a team who are located across the globe. How (and when) do you communicate?

IMPACT OF TECHNOLOGY ON BEHAVIOUR

CREDIT: PHOTO BY GABRIEL BENOIS ON UNSPLASH

Covid-19 forced the entire world to rapidly adjust to new norms, and it was made possible in large part due to virtual communication tools like synchronous document editing and video calls. Although virtual work had long been a part of many people's working lives, Covid-19 forced video communications to be a central feature of work and life for many people. Although this technology has been essential in helping people to connect with each other, it has its drawbacks as the line between work and home life has also become increasingly blurred and some report experiencing what's labelled as 'Zoom Fatigue'. Research in neuropsychology (Lee, 2020) suggests that virtual connections do not offer the brain the same type of neurochemical rewards (in the form of oxytocin and dopamine) that face-to-face communication offers because of increased audio delays and the ability for mutual gaze. At the same time, there is increased cognitive effort to fight the distraction of multitasking, a lack of boundaries with personal life, and the draw to stare at yourself in the screen. So, what to do? In their *Harvard Business Review* article, Liz Fosslien and Mollie West Duffy (2020) propose tips to 'combat zoom fatigue': avoiding multitasking, building in breaks, reducing onscreen stimuli such as by hiding your own face or simplifying background images, making social events opt-in rather than mandatory, and switching to phone calls or e-mails when appropriate.

It is important to take the cultural context into consideration when studying concepts and theories in OB. Did you notice that many of the historical studies mentioned above took place in companies in the USA? What effect might that have on the field? Considering the cultural dimensions is consistent with taking a systems thinking and contingency approach as mentioned before. Let's say you learned all about the importance of rewards and recognition for employees and from this you developed a scheme to motivate your employees that involves giving a weekly bonus to the best worker in each workgroup. It works brilliantly in Ireland. You tell your manager friend in the US. It works brilliantly there. Then you are transferred to Japan and set up the same system and it is a total flop. Why? The cultural differences. Japan is a much more collectivistic culture, which emphasises the needs of the group over the needs of one individual. Within collectivistic cultures, employees may not like to be singled out or given individual attention as this goes against the group norms and values. Therefore, it's important to see how the larger environment affects the individual (systems thinking) as well as how one theory works in one situation but not another (contingency approach). Take the case of an assembly plant described in the film *American Factory* and consider the value of understanding context and learning from others.

BUILDING YOUR EMPLOYABILITY SKILLS

Understanding Cross-Cultural Issues

American Factory, the 2019 Netflix documentary directed by Julia Reichert and Steven Bognar, follows the true story of the opening of Fuyao Glass America in Dayton, Ohio. After a General Motors assembly plant closed in 2008, Chinese billionaire Cho Tak Wong purchased the building and opened his auto glass manufacturing company. The film highlights the ups and downs of cross-cultural relationships as American and Chinese factory workers work together. Watch the trailer, available on YouTube, or the film available on Netflix, and imagine yourself moving to a new country to manage a project like this. What cultural issues are highlighted in the trailer? What factors should be considered when running a multinational company?

INCREASED DIVERSITY IN THE WORKFORCE

There have been a number of changes to the demographic makeup of the workplace, especially in three major ways:

1 There has been an increase of women in the workforce. The increase of women and dual-earner couples has triggered a desire for more family-friendly practices and flexibility in the workplace. Additionally, many men are expressing a desire to reduce time spent at work in favour of increased engagement at home.

2 With the rise of globalisation, emigration and global careers, the workforce is becoming more diverse. It is very common for individuals to work in some capacity with others of a different race or cultural background. For example, within the United States, the Hispanic population is growing much faster than the White population. In fact, minority groups now outnumber the traditional majority group members in California and New Mexico. Interestingly, the region of the world that experienced the most population growth within the last century was the Middle East and North Africa (MENA) region. More recently, regions in Europe, Australia and North America have dropped below replacement levels, whereas populations in regions in Africa and the Middle East have risen.

3 Finally, people are living and continuing to work longer than ever before. In some countries, such as the US, individuals over 85 are the fastest growing segment of the population. In many countries, the mandatory retirement ages are becoming older,

and mandatory retirement limits do not exist in many countries. Stereotypes against older workers are prevalent but meta-analysis suggests no relationship between age and motivation, adaptability, trust or health (Ng and Feldman, 2012) and other research suggests they are actually more engaged in their work (James *et al.*, 2011). Much attention is given to understanding generational differences in work values, style, and preferences. Despite the popularity of this subject of conversation, the research evidence behind generational differences suggests differences are not as dramatic as we might think (Twenge *et al.*, 2010). There may be some impacts from major societal events and some motivations such that younger people are more motivated by growth and career planning, whereas older individuals may be more focused on meaningful relationships. However, people tend to be as different from one another within generations as across them and most employees have similar desires around recognition, quality of life, fairness and training opportunities. In short, what we do know is that seeking to understand one another, learning from one another, extending respect, and meeting individual needs are best practice for all. Good OB principles are important for all workers, across generations.

So why would the changing demographics of the workplace be important in understanding OB? In most countries, legislation exists to prevent discrimination in a wide range of employment and employment-related areas. These include recruitment and promotion, pay, working conditions, training or experience, dismissal and harassment. This legislation often defines discrimination as treating one person in a less favourable way than another person based on any of several grounds, which may include gender, marital or family status, sexual orientation or religion. Employers need to be mindful that their practices are in line with the law.

Additionally, while diversity has the potential to bring about more perspectives, greater innovations and better decision-making, these things do not happen on their own (Stahl *et al.*, 2010). When people are different from one another there are added challenges that need to be overcome and this has implications in the workplace as well. For example, teams comprised of diverse members may pose added challenges ▶See Chapter 10◀; individual stereotypes and perceptual biases ▶See Chapter 3◀ and attitudes and values ▶See Chapter 4◀ may affect the ability of individuals to work together to achieve organisational goals while shaping a positive organisational culture ▶See Chapter 12◀, effectively communicating ▶See Chapter 14◀ and promoting a healthy workplace ▶See Chapter 9◀.

TECHNOLOGICAL GROWTH

It is clear the last few centuries have seen tremendous technological growth. This has changed the nature of work and it has implications for personal privacy and work–life balance. Through technological growth, we have seen a decrease in the manufacturing sector and the huge growth of the services and information industries. Furthermore, this has polarised workforce needs. For example, think about the technology now in place when you go to the airport. In many airports, there are touch screens where you check in for your flight. You can also do it from home and print off your boarding pass or simply show your phone. Highly technical jobs are needed to set up and monitor those systems (therefore there is an increase in highly skilled jobs), but the mid-level jobs which involve the technical aspect of checking you in, confirming seats and dealing with issues, are now handled electronically. But someone is still needed to do the manual job of putting the baggage claim tickets on the baggage and lifting it onto the conveyor belt. Furthermore, there are growing needs for employees to have competence in both technical skills and service skills. Technicians often interact directly with the customers and customers are allowed, even encouraged, to influence the design process.

Currently, being creative and innovative is of utmost importance for organisations to remain competitive. Companies have to continually reinvent themselves, adapting their products or services to adapt to changing customer needs and demands. Furthermore, as an employer, you find that job applicants and employees have access to much more information than before about your company. For example, websites like glassdoor.com provide reviews of companies and CEOs, and even include a place for applicants to post the questions they were asked at the interview. Similarly, employers have more access to information about their employees through social media sources such as LinkedIn and Facebook.

ETHICAL BEHAVIOUR IN THE WORKPLACE

Is it ethical to fire someone for their social media posts? According to www.fileunemployment.org, individuals have been fired for these posts: 'First day at work. Omg!! So dull!!', 'Does anyone know where I can find a very discrete hitman? Yes, it's been that kind of day,' and 'Anyone know how to pass a drug test in 24 hours?' Others  have been fired for political posts, offensive posts or posts that damage the reputation of the company. What do you think? Is it right to discipline or fire employees for certain types of posts? Who decides? Should a company be obligated to retain an employee who expresses distasteful views online?

Additionally, technological advances have opened opportunities for employees to be accessible to their employer just about 24 hours a day, 7 days a week. This brings issues around work–life balance to the forefront. Where is the fine line between open information exchange and privacy?

Industry 4.0: Helping or Harming the Human?

As technology advances, so do we. With steam and water power, we were able to produce using machines rather than our hands. The Industrial Revolution brought us trains and electricity so we could work longer hours, produce more things and transport them more quickly. Computers brought us into the digital age, where we offloaded processing and communication tasks to machines. Now, we have the capability to use computers to do even more advanced work like identify objects (machine vision), build systems that can learn from their environment (machine learning) and more. The application of these advanced technologies to industrial settings is often called Industry 4.0.

OB IN PRACTICE

Industry 4.0 is characterised by four main principles:

1 Interconnection, which means entire systems are connected to each other and to the people involved.
2 Information transparency, which means we can collect more detailed data about the system, which we can use to make decisions.

3 Technical assistance, which means human abilities are supported by the technology we've developed.
4 Decentralised decisions, which means the system can make decisions independent of the human.

With Industry 4.0, the possibilities are seemingly endless. With technology present in Industry 4.0, we may be able to build manufacturing facilities with almost no human workers. This could save companies significant money when they can hire and train fewer workers. Machines never leave work and don't need lunch breaks. Dangerous tasks could be offloaded to machines, resulting in fewer injuries. We could make more, faster, and increase the quality of life for people around the globe.

While automating and integrating systems can be beneficial, it is important to consider how people are affected by these changes. People are good at adapting to new situations and dealing with uncertainty, but machines are not. That means that integrating robots or using machine learning in the workplace will require careful planning. New systems must be incredibly reliable if we rely on them for critical tasks without humans to catch mistakes as they occur.

We have access to massive amounts of data, so we could provide people with detailed reports to help them understand when mistakes are in the process, but so much data is generated every second that it would be impossible to comprehend. Understanding how people process information and how to provide them with useful information requires careful planning and a deep

understanding of the people interacting with the data.

Taking people out of the loop can cause worse performance than having them do the entire task in the first place. Monitoring is a stressful and difficult task for people, so even though the system might be better, people will be less likely to do their part, or they will just be stressed while trying (Warm *et al.*, 2008).

Another concern with interconnected systems is the potential for people to hack into the system. When everything was manually connected, someone would have to physically break into a manufacturing facility to make changes or disrupt the work. When systems are connected online, someone could potentially hack in from anywhere in the world. Even if they do not change the system itself, the data in the system can be hard to protect, leaving valuable trade secrets and productivity measures vulnerable to hackers. As we connect more and more equipment, even more data is vulnerable.

Questions

1 Think about the ways that the workplace has changed in the last 10 years, 100 years and 500 years. How do you think it will change in the next 10 years? Do you really think Industry 4.0 will change the way people work?
2 How do you think Industry 4.0 will change the demographics of people working in manufacturing?
3 What concerns do you have about Industry 4.0? Do you see any ethical concerns not mentioned in the text?
4 How would you feel if you worked next to a robot all day? Do you think human–robot interactions would change the way you feel about work?

MANAGERIAL TAKEAWAYS

The field of OB is really about understanding how people think, act and react in the workplace and the influence of many factors on their behaviour. The field is concerned with both the well-being of employees as well as the performance of the organisation. It is important to remember that OB is multi-level and to consider workplaces through a systems thinking approach. Try to keep this in mind when reading through the following chapters. Remember that each topic cannot be considered in isolation, as each is really affected by the others, so try to see connections across the chapters. When reading the 'In Reality ...' sections, keep in mind the importance of evidence-based practice and consider the methods used in the research. Finally, as you read this text consider the contemporary issues that make OB more important now than ever, such as globalisation, changing workplace demographics, and technology growth. These issues are discussed as we move through the chapters in this textbook.

 CHAPTER REVIEW QUESTIONS

1 In what ways is the field of OB different from other fields of study within business and the social sciences? In which ways is it similar to them?
2 Why does organisational behaviour matter?
3 How might courses on organisational behaviour be useful for someone entering the field of management? Or for someone in a technical field such as engineering or medicine?
4 Describe the roles of evidence-based management and intuition in organisational decision-making. What are the strengths and weaknesses of each approach?
5 Distinguish between qualitative and quantitative methods.
6 How are employment relationships changing in modern times? How might this affect how you prepare yourself for your career?
7 What are the opportunities that come from increased globalisation and diversity?
8 How is technology changing how people are managed in organisations?

 FURTHER READING

Barends, E., Rousseau, D.M. and Briner, R.B. (2015) *Evidence-Based Management: The Basic Principles*. Amsterdam: Center for Evidence-based Management.

Gelfand, M.J., Erez, M. and Aycan, Z. (2007) Cross-cultural Organizational Behavior. *Annual Review of Psychology*, 58, 479–514.

Quick, J.C. and Quick, J.D. (2004) Healthy, happy, productive work: A leadership challenge. *Organizational Dynamics*, 33(4), 329–337. Available at: https://doi.org/10.1016/j.orgdyn.2004.09.001

 USEFUL WEBSITES

http://www.careers.org/

Here is a great site for many career-related issues. There is also a good deal of advice about surviving and prospering in organisations.

http://www.trade.gov

This is the site of the International Trade Administration and is packed with resources with the goal of helping US business succeed globally.

http://www.glassdoor.com

Pick a company. Read a few reviews. What do they reveal about OB constructs?

https://www.siop.org/Research-Publications/SIOP-White-Papers

The Society for Industrial and Organizational Psychology (SIOP) has a series of white papers on important OB topics such as groups/teams, leadership development, attitudes/motivation and well-being. You might find these useful to enhance your understanding.

Online Resources

Visit bloomsbury.pub/organisational-behaviour to access additional materials to support teaching and learning.

PART 1
INDIVIDUAL DIFFERENCES

OVERVIEW

Individuals are unique in terms of their skills, abilities, personalities, perceptions, attitudes, emotions, and motivations. No two people are exactly the same and this is what poses the greatest challenge for managers in trying to understand and predict behaviour at work. This first part of the book provides a foundation for understanding individual differences.

- Chapter 2: Personality
- Chapter 3: Perception
- Chapter 4: Attitudes and job satisfaction
- Chapter 5: Motivation and rewards

 Visit bloomsbury.pub/organisational-behaviour to play an interactive simulation that will allow you to practise what you have learned about individual differences. The simulation puts you in the role of a manager acting out the decision-making process.

2 PERSONALITY

Jill Pearson and Clodagh Butler

LEARNING OUTCOMES

BY THE END OF THIS CHAPTER, YOU SHOULD BE ABLE TO:

- Understand personality and where it comes from.
- Distinguish between nomothetic and idiographic theories of personality.
- Describe each Big Five personality characteristic and map the behaviour of individuals onto these characteristics.
- Discuss how and why organisations measure individual personality characteristics.
- Identify bright and dark personality characteristics that are important in understanding individual-level behaviour at work.

CREDIT: PHOTO BY NONG VANG ON UNSPLASH

THIS CHAPTER DISCUSSES...

INTRODUCTION

Why do you prefer staying in while your friend loves going out all the time? Why are you so messy and your housemate is so neat and tidy? Why are you calm around deadlines when others around you are not? What sets you aside from others? The answer is your personality.

Organisations are interested in the concept of personality because they believe, and research has shown, that personality differences have an impact on behaviour at work. Personality affects motivation, communication, team interaction, and performance in both positive and negative ways. The focus of this chapter is to introduce the concept of personality and to explore personality in the workplace. The chapter is divided into three sections: the past, the present and the future in relation to personality in the workplace. We begin by defining personality and discussing the extent to which our genes versus our environment influence the type of personality we have. We discuss some well-known theories that have influenced our understanding of personality as it is today. We discuss where personality has a role in the workplace by focusing on five specific personality characteristics on which people differ (called the Big Five) and their implications for behaviour in organisations. The issue of assessing personality for organisational-based decisions is also outlined. Finally, we discuss where personality testing is going in the future and discuss the good, the bad and the ugly when it comes to the future of personality in the workplace.

This leads us on to the important issue of if, when and how employers should assess personality when hiring and managing employees, and questions surrounding personality testing. We finish off by discussing alternative lenses on the Big Five.

PERSONALITY, WHAT IS IT?

personality is typically defined as the relatively stable set of psychological characteristics that can distinguish one individual from another and can provide generalised predictions about a person's behaviour.

individual differences are psychological ways in which people differ from each other, and include factors such as intelligence, personality and emotionality.

We have all heard of the term 'personality', and we all have an idea of what we think personality is, but what is it really? A friend tells you that they have a new work colleague and she thinks you'll like her … 'She's got a great personality, so much energy. She tells the best stories and really likes to have a good time. But she works too hard; she stays in late all the time trying to make a good impression on the boss.'

Is your friend describing her new colleague's personality? Or something else? We all have the tendency to describe someone in the same manner. We think we are describing their personality when in fact, we are describing their social reputation, which is the way that we all – friends, family, neighbours, co-workers and supervisors – perceive other people. While social reputation isn't the same thing as personality, someone's social reputation is influenced by their personality.

So, what is personality? While there is no universally accepted definition, we can think about someone's personality as their mental makeup. There are three important points relating to this definition that need to be emphasised.

The first, is that stability implies consistency over time and in different situations. We describe someone as being warm and kind if they are like that most of the time. Secondly, people differ in how they think, feel and act. These individual differences mean we can describe people according to their different personality characteristics. Finally, while someone's behaviour is influenced by their personality, behaviour is also influenced by the social context. Some situations are described as strong situations in that everyone, regardless of their personality, behaves in the same way. For example, personality is likely to have less influence on behaviour in the armed forces where rules are clearly defined and the consequences for not following them are severe, than in an organisation like Google.

There is another interesting point about the personality–behaviour link. As the definition indicates, by knowing someone's personality characteristics, we can make reasonable predictions about their behaviour. Psychologists have studied ways to accurately measure personality and used this information to determine the impact of different personality characteristics on a wide range of behaviours. However, for most of us, the inference goes the other way. Instead of knowing someone's personality and using it to predict their behaviour, we tend to infer what someone's personality is by observing what they do, what they say and by what others say about them (i.e. their social reputations). This is because without specific personality measurement tools (discussed later in this chapter), we as humans cannot measure personality directly. Therefore, our observations and assessments of others may or may not be accurate, but they do influence the impressions and judgements we make about other people.

> strong situations are those in which the rules and expectations of the social context control the behaviour of people regardless of their personality.

SPOTLIGHT ON SKILLS

Personality, Fit and Selection Methods

Organisations want to hire the person who has the best knowledge, skills and abilities for the job they are trying to fill. They also want someone who will fit well into the job, work group and organisational culture ▶See Chapter 12◀. Sometimes the applicant who fits the best is lacking in one or more competencies and sometimes the person with the best skill set doesn't seem quite right in terms of their personality or fit for the job or organisation.

1 Which is more important, skills or fit?

2 Should we rely on psychometric tests and assessments when making selection decisions?

3 How do you integrate a new employee who has the right skills but might not be a clear fit?

To help you answer these questions, visit bloomsbury.pub/organisational-behaviour to watch the video of Fiona Clarke, from Eurostar, talking about personality.

OUR UNDERSTATING OF PERSONALITY OVER TIME

WHERE DOES PERSONALITY COME FROM?

Where does personality come from? Is it from the genes our parents pass on to us or is it influenced by our environment? This question summarises what is known as the nature–nurture debate. Consider the following. Imagine that you are quite imaginative and creative, and your parents are too. It's possible they passed on an 'openness to experience gene' and/or an 'artistic gene' to you. This supports the nature side of the argument. However, it is also likely that you observed and imitated your parents' behaviour growing up. Perhaps they're artists or musicians. Furthermore, your parents not only tolerated your creative pursuits, but they actively encouraged and rewarded them. The presence of these environmental conditions supports the nurture side of the debate. So how do we separate them to understand the role of nature and nurture in the formation of personality?

THE BIOLOGICAL APPROACH

Behavioural scientists have conducted studies of twins who have been adopted by different sets of parents and raised apart, to try to disentangle these two influences. If identical twins (i.e. those who share 100% of their genetic makeup) have the same personality traits, even when they grow up in different environments, then there is strong support for the nature side of the debate. Researchers at the University of Minnesota have been carrying out such studies for several decades and have found that genes do have a significant impact on personality. After reviewing several studies of twins and personality, Loehlin (1992) concluded that genes can explain between a third and a half of the variance in different personality traits.

Another approach is to examine personality traits over time (called life course research). Participants complete personality assessments several times throughout their life. Since people's environments are different at different points in their life, it's thought that personality has a strong genetic component if people's personality profiles are reasonably stable throughout their lives. Roberts *et al.* (2006) reviewed 92 life course studies that included over 50,000 people. As can be seen from Figure 2.1, some traits are reasonably stable while others change quite a bit over time.

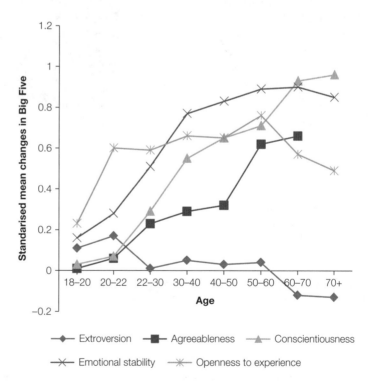

Figure 2.1 Personality dimensions across the life course

Source: Adapted from Roberts et al. *(2006).*

For example, openness to experience is quite stable once people become young adults (it seems teenagers are much less open to new experiences). On the other hand, people become more conscientious as they age. Interestingly, life course studies show that relative positions between people tend not to change on the various traits. In other words, while you and your best friend are both likely to become more conscientious as you get older, if your friend is more conscientious than you are now, chances are she will continue to be into old age.

THE ENVIRONMENTAL APPROACH

While heredity clearly plays a major part in determining one's personality, environmental factors are important too. People's personalities develop in part because they internalise their surroundings. Social, cultural and situation factors all influence personality (see Figure 2.2).

- **Social Factors:** Interactions with parents, siblings, peers and others influence our personality and behaviour throughout our lives through a process of socialisation. Although socialisation takes place throughout our lives, early socialisation (e.g. the result of birth order) is particularly influential in the development of personality.
- **Cultural Factors:** Researchers believe that cultures provide societies with their own unique personalities (e.g. Heine and Buchtel, 2009). A large study of over 50 cultures found variation in the dominance of certain personality traits. For example, people from China, India, Nigeria and Iran tend to be more introverted than people from Iceland, Spain, Australia and Estonia. Of course, this doesn't mean that there are no extroverts in China and no introverts in Iceland; these country differences are merely averages (McCrae *et al.*, 2005).
- **Situational Factors:** Specific situations or experiences also play a role in the development of personality. Traumatic events, such as surviving terrorism attacks or experiencing bullying as a child, teenager or adult, can change a person, often in dramatic ways.

There are several theories of personality that attempt to explain how personalities develop and/or why people differ. These theories can be categorised as either idiographic or nomothetic.

> socialisation is the process of learning how to think, feel and behave by conforming to and imitating influential others within social settings.

> idiographic refers to an approach which describes personality in terms of traits that are unique to the individual.

> nomothetic means an approach which describes personality in terms of specific dimensions that vary across people.

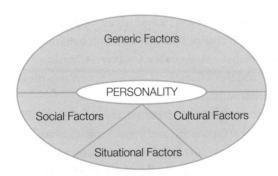

Figure 2.2 Influencing factors on personality

MAJOR THEORIES OF PERSONALITY

IDIOGRAPHIC APPROACHES

The idiographic approach tries to understand the essence of someone's personality and believes that all aspects of personality are unique to that person alone. It also links someone's personality with their perceptions and attitudes ▸See Chapters 3 and 4◂ to understand their behaviour, for example, leadership. Idiographic theories tend to have roots in clinical psychology and are largely concerned with helping people to cope with their everyday demands.

FREUD'S PSYCHODYNAMIC THEORY

No doubt you have heard of Sigmund Freud (1856–1939). His psychodynamic theory is probably the most famous of the idiographic approaches to personality. Freud believed that our personalities are made up of three interacting parts called the id, the ego and the superego. The **id** is something that we are born with, it's an unconscious part of our personality and drives us to seek immediate gratification. The **ego** operates at a conscious level; its function is to think, control and organise. The ego decides when to give in to the impulses of the id and when to succumb to the demands of reality. The **superego** is the moral regulator of personality. It is culturally influenced and tells us what we should and shouldn't do. Furthermore, it punishes us with guilt when we do the wrong thing. It's the ego's job to manage the ongoing tension between the impulses of the id and the moral judgement of the superego. Imagine the anxiety you might feel if you were given a last-minute ticket to the sporting event of the year on a day your boss needed you to chair an important meeting!

HUMANISM

Not happy with the limitations of Freud's psychodynamic approach, particularly its pessimistic lens on personality development, another approach, called humanism, was developed in response. This approach looks at the person as a whole by identifying patterns of behaviour, thoughts and emotions within the individual. Humanism promotes that humans have a need for self-determination and self-realisation, can think consciously and rationally and can control biological urges. In the humanistic view, individuals are responsible for their own actions and have the freedom and will to change their attitudes and behaviour. One popular humanistic approach comes from Abraham Maslow ▸See Chapter 5◂. Maslow (1943) argues that human needs change over time and the fulfilment of needs is essential in the development of personality, which influences behaviour.

Maslow believed that motivation is a central aspect of personality development and is concerned with the subjective experiences and free will that drive an individual toward the highest need of self-actualisation. Maslow found that individuals who experience self-actualisation shared certain personality traits. Self-actualised people indicate a coherent personality syndrome and represent optimal psychological health and functioning; including awareness and acceptance of self, active problem-seeking and solving, and openness and spontaneity. This theory, however, has been known to lack scientific rigour and is culturally biased towards Western countries.

self-actualisation is a state of fulfilment in which a person is achieving at their highest level of capability.

BUILDING YOUR EMPLOYABILITY SKILLS

Making Tough Decisions

As HR manager you would like to utilise personality testing within your organisation. You need to convince the CEO as to why the organisation should invest in personality testing. What advantages will personality testing bring to the organisation? When and why will it be adopted? Who gets access to the reports?

trait theories are theories that describe people in terms of enduring personality characteristics.

type theories are theories that place individuals into predetermined categories, thereby identifying them as a particular personality type.

NOMOTHETIC APPROACHES

Theories that adopt the nomothetic approach focus on identifying dimensions of personality that can be used to measure similarities and differences between people. They assume that personality characteristics are relatively stable within people over time. These theories are typically subdivided into trait theories and type theories. While there are many similarities between trait and type theories, trait theories measure personality dimensions on a continuum from low to high whereas type theories classify people typically using dichotomies of opposites types. Two influential, nomothetic theories were developed by Eysenck (1947, 1965, 1970) and Cattell (1965).

EYSENCK'S TYPE THEORY

Eysenck identified two key dimensions on which he believed that people vary: extroversion and emotional stability, which resulted in four distinct personality types:

- Emotionally Stable Extroverts (Sanguine Types)
- Emotionally Stable Introverts (Phlegmatic Types)
- Emotionally Unstable Extroverts (Choleric Types)
- Emotionally Unstable Introverts (Melancholic Types)

While Eysenck's theory is considered a type theory, he believed that specific traits stem from each of the four types. For example, Emotionally Stable Extroverts (known as Sanguine Types) tend to be sociable, outgoing, lively and carefree. Details of the traits associated with each of the four types are shown in Figure 2.3.

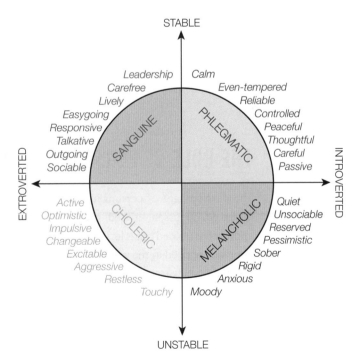

Figure 2.3 Eysenck's personality types and associated traits

Source: Eysenck (1965).

CATTELL'S TRAIT THEORY

Cattell (1965) believed that a distinction should be made between surface traits, which are observable through someone's behaviour, and source traits, which cause behavioural tendencies. He called source traits the fundamental building blocks of personality and through extensive testing with thousands of people he refined his theory and measurement instrument into a scheme of 16 source traits. Cattell's Sixteen Personality Factor Questionnaire (known as the 16PF) is widely used in organisations for selection, career development, team building, leadership assessment and other purposes. A sample feedback report with the continuum of the 16 source traits is shown in Figure 2.4.

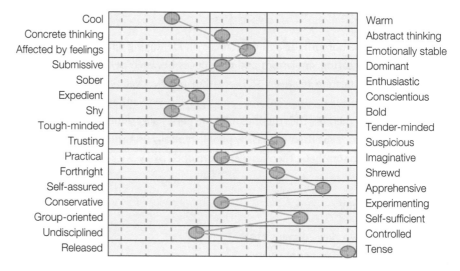

Figure 2.4 A sample feedback report using Cattell's 16PF

Source: Bratton (2020).

THE ROLE OF PERSONALITY IN TODAY'S WORKPLACE

The development of personality theories over the last century has shaped how personality is viewed, discussed, utilised, predicted and measured in today's workplace. The idiographic approach is utilised but is less common (we discuss why later). The most prominent theoretical approach applied in the workplace is the nomothetic approach, with two of the most popular theories coming from McCrae-Costa and Myers-Briggs.

THE NOMOTHETIC VS THE IDIOGRAPHIC APPROACH FOR ORGANISATIONAL USE?

Despite Freud's prominence, there are several reasons why his psychodynamic theory in particular, and idiographic approaches in general as a way of measuring personality, have had limited impact on organisations. First, their origins in clinical psychology mean that the focus has been largely on abnormal rather than normal populations, meaning they are less generalisable to general working populations. Second, their idiosyncratic perspective means that measures of personality dimensions have not been developed or empirically validated, resulting in no measurement tool for comparing the personalities of different employees; which is important in relation to recruitment and selection, employee development, succession planning, etc. Third, the idiographic approaches have limited classification of different personality factors and explanations of behaviour in comparison with other theories, that is, the Big Five. Finally, Freud's theories have come under scrutiny because it's not possible to test them using scientific methods and, as such, they are mostly used to explain employee behaviour but not predict it.

Some companies implement a humanistic approach within their organisation that promotes employees as people, not workers. Identifying and developing the individual needs of employees helps to create a positive productive environment. Common methods for collecting information include case studies, unstructured interviews, self-reports, autobiographies and personal documents. These methods allow for an in-depth insight into individual behaviour. However, questions are raised over the scientific validity of these methods.

IMPACT OF TECHNOLOGY ON BEHAVIOUR

CREDIT: PHOTO BY SVEN ON UNSPLASH

Innovative people like Steve Jobs, Bill Gates, Mark Zuckerberg, and Jeff Bezos have changed the way in which we conduct our day-to-day living. We spend most of our daily or work activities using multiple technological devices, which has both advantages and disadvantages.

Nowadays, even a smartphone can potentially get you a job. Mobile recruiting is using smartphone technology to attract, engage and entice potential candidates. A growing sector of smartphone apps are being developed to connect potential employees with organisations, such as LinkedIn, Glassdoor, ZipRecruiter. However, most of these platforms only describe the organisation or the candidate, they do not measure anything beyond QCA or CVs. One such app, ExitEntry, allows candidates to upload a profile that showcases their full spectrum of skills, including personality. This means that personality and soft skills are already incorporated in the recruitment process before the interview, speedingup the recruitment and selection process before it becomes in-house.

THE FIVE-FACTOR MODEL (KNOWN AS THE BIG FIVE)

How many traits are needed to comprehensively describe an individual's personality? You can see from our discussion in the previous section that Eysenck (4 traits) and Cattell (16 traits) disagreed on the correct number. Over three-quarters of a century ago, Allport and Odbert (1936) identified several thousand words in the dictionary that describe normal everyday personality characteristics. They challenged the psychological research community to figure out how many clusters of personality synonyms are needed to distinguish human behaviour from one individual to another. While researchers will continue to deliberate, most agree a winner was declared over 30 years ago with the emergence of the Five-Factor Model (FFM) known widely as the 'Big Five' (McCrae and Costa, 1987). Most individual differences in personality can be classified into these five broad domains. Importantly, these five domains or dimensions are theoretically independent, that is, someone's level on one of the five dimensions is completely unrelated to their level on the other dimensions.

The five personality dimensions are: **Openness to Experience**, **Conscientiousness**, **Extroversion**, **Agreeableness**, and **Need for emotional stability**. (To note: this last factor is traditionally known as **Neuroticism**; however, many have changed the label to Emotional Stability or Need for Emotional Stability because neuroticism has such negative connotations.) **OCEAN** is a useful acronym to help you remember the five dimensions although you can also use **CANOE**.

Each of the dimensions can be thought of as a continuum so, for example, someone could be high or low on extroversion. Because it is a continuum, the term 'ambivert' has started to gain popularity as a label for those who fall somewhere in the middle. Table 2.1 provides a brief description of the five personality dimensions.

Table 2.1 The Big Five personality dimensions

	Higher score	Trait	Lower score
O	**Explorer** Like to learn about new ideas and experience new things; tend to be inquisitive, creative and easily bored.	Open to Experience	**Preserver** Like operating in familiar territory; tend to be traditional, conventional and conforming.
C	**Focused** Focus their energies on accomplishing goals; tend to be ambitious, hardworking and organised.	Conscientious	**Flexible** Are spontaneous and work to their moods; tend to be good at multiskilling; can be inefficient and disorganised.
E	**Extrovert** Like to be where the action is; tend to be sociable, assertive, gregarious and dominant.	Extroversion	**Introvert** Are happy to let others get stuck into where all the action is; tend to be quiet, reserved and private.
A	**Adapter** Are accommodating when it comes to others' needs or wishes; tend to be kind, sympathetic and courteous.	Open to Agreeableness	**Challenger** Focus on their own priorities over others'; tend to be competitive, quarrelsome and sometimes callous.
N	**Reactive** Can feel crippled by stressful situations; tend to be anxious, emotional and often feel nervous and insecure.	Neuroticism	**Resilient** Can stay quite calm in stressful situations; tend to be secure, relaxed and stable.

Source: Adapted from Howard and Howard (2001).

MYERS-BRIGGS TYPE INDICATOR

Although most psychologists believe that the Five-Factor Model is the best system for examining personality, it is certainly not the only lens available. The Myers-Briggs Type Indicator (MBTI) is the most widely used personality instrument in the business world (see Table 2.2). This may be because of successful commercial marketing or its user-friendliness. The different dimensions are described as being opposite types, but they're not described as being good or bad. Not having negative characteristics is an advantage when introducing personality concepts into the workplace where trainers, managers and consultants are trying to improve morale and effectiveness and do not want to label people as having the 'wrong' personality.

The MBTI, developed by mother–daughter duo Catherine Briggs and Isabel Briggs-Myers, was originally designed to test Carl Jung's theory of personality type. Jung, who once worked with Freud (then split from him), was the first to develop the terms 'extroversion' and 'introversion'. He was drawn to understanding differences in the way people prefer to use their perception and judgement. He strongly believed in the notion of opposites. If you are not an introvert, then you must be an extrovert; there is no middle ground. A major difference between the MBTI's theory and that of the Big Five is this notion of opposite types. Remember, the Big Five dimensions are on a trait continuum. You may be very extroverted, a little bit extroverted, right in the middle of the continuum or somewhere towards the introvert end of it.

In the MBTI classification system, there are four dichotomies, which lead to 16 different personality types.

You can see several similarities between this classification scheme and the Big Five. Intuition is like openness to experience; Feeling is like agreeableness; and Judging is like conscientiousness. The extroversion link is obvious, but neuroticism doesn't have a parallel in the MBTI.

The beauty of the MBTI is its simplicity. Someone's personality type can be captured by four letters. You might be an ENTP or an IFSJ. You can then read a short description of yourself that feels accurate and positive. The MBTI does emphasise individual weak spots, but the tone and language are positive. The MBTI is only available via commercial providers and must be administered, scored and interpreted by qualified practitioners. However, if you would like to complete an online version of Jungian Typology to see what your own type is, you can do so at: http://www.123test.com/jung-personality-test/

Table 2.2 Myers-Briggs type indicator dimensions

E	Extroversion being energised by people and things in the outer world	I	Introversion being energised by thoughts, feelings and impressions in the inner world
S	Sensing gathering information by focusing on facts and details that can be confirmed by experience	N	Intuition gathering information by focusing on possibilities and relationships among ideas
T	Thinking making decisions by using impersonal, objective and logical analysis	F	Feeling making decisions by using subjective analysis and focusing on others' needs
J	Judging approaching tasks by planning, being organised and reaching closure	P	Perceiving approaching tasks by being spontaneous, flexible and open

Source: Adapted from Myers et al. (1993).

Becoming a Billionaire

According to *Forbes Magazine*, https://www.ubs.com/billionaires, there were over 2000 billionaires in the world in 2019. What is the secret to becoming a billionaire? Wouldn't we all like to know! 'The billionaire effect report' conducted by investment bank UBS and PricewaterhouseCoopers (PwC) analysed how entrepreneurs' businesses have excelled over the years. According to the report, 'Over the 15 years to the end of 2018, billionaire-controlled companies listed on the equity markets returned almost twice the average market performance.' You might argue they have more opportunities, resources and money than the average person so they can re-invest in more business opportunities. However, most of the world's billionaires started from nothing at some point, so what makes them excel?

According to the report, billionaires sustain and maintain wealth due to the trifecta of personality characteristics of

IN THE NEWS

'high risk-taking, business-focus, and determination', which together are coined the 'Billionaire effect'. The report's findings align with other research that suggests billionaires think and operate differently from much of the population. Maybe we shouldn't compare traits of billionaires with those of entrepreneurs of start-ups but what is there to learn? The collective impact of entrepreneurs to society is just as important!

A study by Zitelmann (2019) asked 43 high-net-worth entrepreneurs from across the globe to take a personality test based on the Big Five. He found that wealthy entrepreneurs were more open to experience and extroversion than the general population and were lower on neuroticism and less agreeable. In one meta-analytic review (Zhao *et al.*, 2010), **openness to experience**, **conscientiousness**, and **extroversion** appeared to be the personality constructs most strongly and consistently associated with entrepreneurial intentions and performance.

These findings are similar to those of Brandstätter (2011), who also compared entrepreneurs with managers and who also found that entrepreneurs in general have lower levels of neuroticism and agreeableness.

Taken together, research shows that conscientious people are attracted to entrepreneurship and are also more likely to succeed once they become an entrepreneur. Conscientiousness manifests as detail-oriented and very thorough. Openness to experience is closely associated with creativity, performance, and learning in new situations, allowing entrepreneurs to enjoy thinking outside the box. Extreme extroversion is associated with wealth and business success, as those high in extroversion are somewhat likely to establish a social network (Zhao and Seibert, 2006). Overall findings suggest that personality plays a role in the intention to become an entrepreneur and success as an entrepreneur.

Questions

1. List the advantages of personality profiling for entrepreneurs. What are potential drawbacks to using it?
2. Would you recommend personality testing in a creative and innovative environment and for what purpose?
3. Can you think of any entrepreneurs whose personality helps them to be successful? What specific traits do you think they have that are so beneficial? Can you think of any entrepreneurs whose personality gets in the way of their success? What traits are holding them back?

CREDIT: PHOTO BY MUFID MAJNUN ON UNSPLASH

In recent years, psychologists have started coming out strongly against the MBTI, arguing that there are limitations surrounding its measurement and theory. For a non-academic critique, refer to Adam Grant's hard-hitting assessment in the Huffington Post: http://www.huffingtonpost.com/adam-grant/goodbye-to-mbti-the-fad-t_b_3947014.html

PERSONALITY–BEHAVIOUR LINK AT WORK

Classification of different personality factors and how they explain or even predict employee behaviour is an extremely attractive prospect for organisations. Organisations want to hire the right people, see if employees will thrive in a certain role, or even to best understand employees' needs.

There are three questions to consider in relation to how organisations should act based on this information:

1 Are some personality traits better than others for effectiveness at work? Would you insist that your organisation only hire people with these desirable traits?
2 Does effectiveness at work depend more on the situation? Perhaps some work environments suit some personalities better than others. Would you use personality tests to make sure job applicants have the right traits to fit specific jobs?
3 Is it possible to have too much of a good thing? For example, if it's good to have a conscientious employee, is it better to have a very conscientious employee? Or are moderate amounts of desirable traits better?

Using the Big Five we can use each of the five traits to help understand how personality can influence behaviour.

- **Openness to experience** People who are open (i.e. those who are high on the openness to experience dimension) are creative, curious, complex and cultured (Howard and Howard, 2001; Saucier, 1994). Open employees tend to perform well in creative jobs that require them to come up with novel ideas and solutions. Since they have a built-in desire to learn and experience new things, they also tend to thrive in jobs that are dynamic and have rapidly changing job demands. Because they tend to get bored doing things 'the same old way' they are quick to adapt and improve existing procedures that aren't working well. They are less suited to jobs that are repetitive, require precise rules to be followed and have little autonomy, such as accounting, police work, sales and some service occupations.

- **Conscientiousness** Conscientious people are motivated, committed, self-confident, hardworking, organised, ambitious and persevering (McCrae and Costa, 1987; Saucier, 1994). Conscientiousness is thought to be important for all jobs and occupations. While people who are low on conscientiousness are spontaneous, good at multitasking and comfortable dealing with chaos (Howard and Howard, 2001), most research shows that conscientious employees are indeed productive employees (Barrick *et al.*, 2001; Judge *et al.*, 2008). Conscientious workers are more likely to employ citizenship behaviours and less likely to engage in counterproductive work behaviours. This is due to high levels of job satisfaction, which promotes unprompted acts of citizenship and diminishes any feeling that they need to retaliate (Barrick *et al.*, 2001).

- **Extroversion** Extroverts are sociable, talkative, assertive and dominant. Extroversion is important for some but not all jobs (Barrick *et al.*, 2001). Jobs that require long periods of working on one's own (e.g. computer programmers, archivists, chemists, writers) would be unsuitable for people high on the extroversion–introversion continuum. Jobs like project

citizenship behaviour is discretionary behaviour that is often not formally recognised or rewarded by organisations but benefits the organisation and/or its members.

counterproductive work behaviour is any intentional behaviour by an employee that is seen to be contrary to the organisation's interests.

managers, teachers, sales representatives and healthcare professionals are often recommended for high extroverts. Surprisingly, extroverts don't always perform better in jobs that require lots of social interaction, mainly because extroverts tend to make their presence felt by dominating situations when a backseat is sometimes more appropriate (Stewart and Carson, 1995). Research found that extroversion is easier than any of the other Big Five factors to guess correctly (Levesque and Kenny, 1993). In a group of people, it doesn't take long to figure out who the extroverts are. Extroverts are concerned with being influential and successful; they often emerge as leaders in group situations ▶See Chapter 8◀. Extroverts are typically high in positive affectivity across a wide range of situations (Thoresen *et al.*, 2003).

positive affectivity is a dispositional tendency to experience pleasant moods such as enthusiasm and excitement.

- **Agreeableness** Agreeable people are kind, helpful, warm and cooperative. They focus more on getting along with others than they do on getting ahead in organisations. Once again, this trait is not right for all occupations. Agreeableness is very useful in jobs like nursing, teaching and service jobs in business, but may be less useful in jobs where being disagreeable is required, to be effective. For example, managers often make tough decisions that don't please staff or other relevant stakeholders. Worrying about making everyone happy may lead to poor decisions or even complete indecision, which would make no one happy. People high on agreeableness tend to have lower levels of career success when it's measured objectively as one's salary (Seibert and Kraimer, 2001). This is undoubtedly linked to their interest in getting along rather than getting ahead. Agreeable people are less likely to get involved in conflicts ▶See Chapter 6◀. However, if a conflict does arise, they are more likely to take a productive, integrative approach to resolve it, but they are also more likely to feel distressed as a result of the conflict situation (Dijkstra *et al.*, 2004).

negative affectivity is a dispositional tendency to experience negative moods such as nervousness, annoyance and hostility.

objective career success is career success that can be assessed by a third party, and is usually measured by the hierarchical level reached, salary attained and/or number of promotions received.

- **Need for emotional stability** People high on need for emotional stability (sometimes referred to as Neuroticism) are nervous, insecure, moody and emotional. Like conscientiousness, this dimension relates to all jobs and occupations but unlike conscientiousness, jobs benefit from employees who are low rather than high on this domain. Employees who are calm under pressure are much more attractive to employers than those who are anxious and insecure. You recall that extroversion is associated with positive affectivity. Well, emotional stability is associated with negative affectivity, which undoubtedly explains their lower levels of job, career and life satisfaction (Barrick *et al.*, 2001; Judge *et al.*, 2002). Some research has found that emotional stability correlates negatively with objective career success although the results are mixed (Judge *et al.*, 2002). Stress is also an issue for people high on emotional stability ▶See Chapter 9◀. They perceive that they are exposed to greater amounts of stress, regardless of their actual workload; feel more threatened by stressful situations; and use less effective coping strategies when trying to deal with stressful events (Bolger and Zuckerman, 1995).

BUILDING YOUR EMPLOYABILITY SKILLS

Managing Diversity

As project manager, you are tasked with putting together a multi-disciplinary group to work on a high-profile project ▶See Chapter 10◀. The team will be diverse, members will all work in different roles and will all come from different countries. Should you consider personality when designing the team? What are the most desirable traits you would look for in future team members?

MEASURING INDIVIDUAL PERSONALITY CHARACTERISTICS

Personality is often 'assessed' during interviews, or by asking former employers about the person's personality during reference checking. A study carried out by Barrick *et al.* (2000) set out to determine how good interviewers are at assessing personality during interviews. They found that interviewers were pretty good at assessing openness, agreeableness and extroversion, but not at determining levels of conscientiousness or neuroticism. As you now know, conscientiousness and neuroticism are extremely important personality traits for job performance, therefore it seems reliable methods of assessment are needed. How do organisations measure the personality traits they want to assess for hiring decisions? It's much easier said than done.

First, how can you measure what you cannot see or touch? It's not like height and weight and other physical entities that simply require agreed measurement tools. At best we can infer what someone's personality is based on what is observable. For example, we know that some people are more sociable and talkative than others. However, just because measuring personality is difficult and cannot be done directly, it doesn't mean it's a complete guessing game. Psychologists have developed a number of 'yard sticks' to assess personality, called self-report personality inventories. These are often referred to as personality tests (even in this chapter) but that's technically incorrect, as the term 'test' implies there are right and wrong answers and that's not the case when measuring personality. It's an assessment of personality on a scale of high to low. Again, there is nothing wrong with a low score, it's just that some people score higher or lower on certain personality factors than others and these variances help to explain differences in behaviour between people.

SELF-REPORT PERSONALITY INVENTORIES

Some self-report personality inventories are completed using pencil and paper methods while others are administered online. Some are developed by academics and have been critiqued through the blind peer review process while others are available commercially, where the quality can be variable. It's important that these instruments are of a very high standard, especially if they are going to be used for making selection decisions. They need to have both reliability and validity. There are several types of validity, but the most important in this context is predictive validity. If you were to look in academic journals, you'd find that some measures of the Big Five include 240 items. These longer tools typically have very good psychometric properties (i.e. they are reliable and valid) but they can take up about a half hour to complete. Employers should be wary of self-report instruments that are much shorter as they are less likely to have the necessary validity and reliability; although job applicants might prefer the shorter test-taking time! Table 2.3 provides you with a chance to score yourself on a shortened version of the Big Five.

Another advantage of self-report inventories in the recruitment process is that they are standardised, and norm referenced. This is important when making a selection decision from a pool of candidates. For example, as a manager you must decide between three candidates for one position. Imagine that one of these candidates could not make the assessment day and

reliability refers to the extent to which a measure is consistent or repeatable.

validity refers to the extent to which a measurement tool measures what it purports to measure.

predictive validity is the extent to which a measurement tool accurately predicts future job behaviour or performance.

Table 2.3 Measure yourself on the Big Five

Below are words associated with each of the Big Five factors. Read the words at both ends of the scales and place yourself where you think you actually are, not where you'd like to be. Then ask a friend or family member who knows you well to do the same thing. Are your impressions the same?		
Open to new experience, complex	|_|_|_|_|_|_|_|	Conventional, uncreative
Dependable, self-disciplined	|_|_|_|_|_|_|_|	Disorganised, careless
Extrovert, enthusiastic	|_|_|_|_|_|_|_|	Reserved, quiet
Sympathetic, warm	|_|_|_|_|_|_|_|	Critical, quarrelsome
Anxious, easily upset	|_|_|_|_|_|_|_|	Calm, emotionally stable

Source: Adapted from Gosling et al. (2003).

offered to take the test at home. Could you assume that this test is comparable to the other candidates who took the test on assessment day? Not really. Standardisation means that the testing process and candidates are the same. They receive the same test, at the same time, are given the same instructions before and after test taking and the test is conducted in the same quiet environment. This way, you are controlling for any disturbances or distractions that may influence a candidate's assessment. It's also important that candidates' scores are compared not just against each other and the job description, but also against scores taken from groups of people for whom the measure is designed, for example, accounting graduates or army cadets. This is called norm referencing and it allows you to see where candidates fall in line with others in the same profession who have taken the same test previously. As you can imagine, this is important as some professions have different requirements than others, for example the emotional stability criteria for an accountant would not be the same as those for an army recruit!

CAN A PERSON HAVE TOO MUCH PERSONALITY?

Highly **conscientious** people are more motivated, organised and persistent, therefore they are more likely to reach their goals and performance targets. However, recent research has questioned whether too much conscientiousness may be detrimental (Le et al., 2011). Highly conscientious people may be compulsive perfectionists who are overly rigid and become focused on the minutia rather than the big picture. Sticking too close to plans and goals may make them unable or unwilling to change direction and/or acquire new knowledge and skills. Similarly, very low and very high levels of neuroticism might also be more detrimental to performance. Feeling a certain amount of stress and anxiety is useful for performance, but certainly very high levels can be crippling and lead to deterioration in performance.

As it happens, Le found that the high/low relationship is not linear but rather curvilinear, and more is better but only up to a point. After that point, high levels of conscientiousness and low levels of neuroticism were associated with lower levels of task performance and citizenship behaviour and higher levels of counterproductive work behaviours. Also, because of extroverts' tendency to express enthusiasm, confidence and dominance they are perceived to be highly competent at the outset and often get selected for leadership positions ▶See Chapter 6◀. As time goes by, extroverts seem to disappoint fellow group members by not delivering on what was initially expected. It's not clear whether the extroverts 'promised' too much or whether their fellow group members simply expected too much.

IN REALITY

We know that a good first impression is important. The 'halo effect' is a cognitive bias in which overall impressions of a person influence how we think and feel about their character. So much so, it has even been said that employees know within the first 30 seconds or less whether the person has a chance at getting hired. In an interview a candidate can give a socially desirable or fake version of themselves in order to be more attractive to the employer.

You could get candidates to complete a personality test to assess their personality and compare it with interview answers. However, some candidates may be well versed in the testing procedure and know what questions to respond to in order to give off a certain impression; they are very sociable and outgoing (extroverted – tick), they are detail orientated and love planning (conscientious – tick), and love problem-solving and being involved in different projects (open to experiences – tick). This is called 'faking-good' or socially desirable responding and is typically defined as the tendency to give positive self-descriptions (MacCann *et al.*, 2012). The issue with faking-good is that in high-stake situations (e.g. job recruitment) it can affect the rank order of individual job candidates (Morgeson *et al.*, 2007). Certain formalities, however, are incorporated into personality testing to inhibit faking-good from occurring.

This topic has been debated extensively by academics because of the implications for employee selection. On one hand, we want to use validated measures to select the best employee and we know that interviews have poor predictive validity. On the other hand, if well validated psychometric tests and self-report instruments can be faked, then they're not any better. Hogan *et al.* (2007) provide strong evidence that faking isn't as much of a problem as once thought. While the study is highly sophisticated, it found that people who were given a second chance to take personality assessments six months after being rejected for a job they had applied for because their scores did not meet the required threshold, did not do any better the second time around. Even though these applicants were motivated to improve their scores, any attempt at faking or managing impressions did not lead to better scores. Since well validated instruments were used, faking may not be the concern that many think it is.

THE FUTURE OF PERSONALITY IN THE WORKPLACE. THE OK. THE BAD. THE UGLY

INCLUSIVITY IN THE WORKPLACE AND PERSONALITY TESTING

Here's a new term for you, 'homosocial reproduction'. It refers to the tendency of people to select incumbents who are socially similar to themselves. Selection on social similarity such as views, backgrounds or even physical appearances plays a crucial role in shaping the demographic composition of organisations, as well as the structure of opportunity within them. So how can personality play a role in this?

One theory, called personality–environment fit theory, suggests that every organisation and individual has certain personality traits, and if the individual is compatible with the organisation

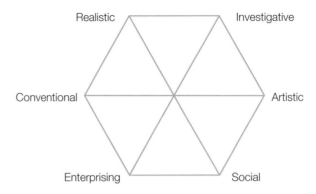

Figure 2.5 RIASEC personality types

Source: Reproduced by special permission of the Publisher, Psychological Assessment Resources (PAR), 16204 North Florida Avenue, Lutz, FL 33549, from Holland, J.L. Making Vocational Choices, 3rd edition. © 1973, 1985, 1992, 1997 by PAR. All rights reserved.

this may result in higher productivity, less stress and higher satisfaction. John Holland's Theory of Career Choice (RIASEC) states that when choosing a career, individuals prefer jobs where they can be around others who are like them. Individuals search for jobs that are compatible with their skills, abilities, values, etc. Holland's theory is centred on the idea that most people fit into one of six personality types: Realistic (R), Investigative (I), Artistic (A), Social (S), Enterprising (E) and Conventional (C). His model has been very influential in career counselling.

Personality testing is a great asset to organisations, but it also has some drawbacks. One concern with personality testing in the workplace, specifically in recruitment and selection, is that it may generate the belief that only individuals with specific traits will succeed in an organisation, just like homosocial reproduction. This has issues for inclusion and diversity, as people who don't fit the perceived mould fail to advance or may leave the company. The downside of using personality tests to weed out job candidates is that when an employer has a fixed personality criterion for a job position, they can overlook qualified candidates. Furthermore, can personality be measured and interpreted reliably across the world? Validity outside of Western, educated, industrialised, rich and democratic (WEIRD) populations has produced mixed results.

PERSONALITY AND TECHNOLOGY

You've heard the saying 'The eyes are the window of the soul'? Well now researchers are interesting in determining if eyes can also indicate our personality! Hypothetically, the way in which humans move their eyes is influenced by their personalities, so that individuals with similar traits move their eyes in similar ways. For example, individuals high in openness are found to spend longer fixating and dwelling on locations when watching abstract animations (Rauthmann *et al.*, 2012). In a study conducted by Hoppe and colleagues (2018), eye movement was measured using a state-of-the-art head-mounted video-based eye tracker with a group of Finnish University students. Students were asked to walk around campus for 10 minutes and then fill out a personality inventory. They found that an individual's level of neuroticism, extroversion, agreeableness, conscientiousness and perceptual curiosity can be predicted from eye movements. Could you envision eye tracking as part of HR in the future?

There has also been a surge of technological developments that make online personality testing a more attractive avenue for organisations (see Ihsan and Furnham, 2018, for a review). The reliability of these assessments is yet to be reported. Controversial approaches to online personality assessment come from online social media platforms such as LinkedIn and Facebook. According to the website Statistica, over 3 billion people in 2019 alone used some form of social media. This opens new possibilities for personality profiling but also concerns. Social media profiles allow companies to gather information about a potential applicant's personality and other attributes, based on the information individuals are putting on their profiles. This is more cost effective than paying for commercial personality tests, particularly if you are a small company. Facebook and personality profiling have a notorious history (google 'Cambridge Analytica scandal') yet there is some research into how self-presentation is linked with personality traits.

DARK TRIAD OF PERSONALITY

Researchers are interested in understanding more about negative aspects of organisational life and identifying and understanding toxic individuals. There are three maladaptive personalities that have received attention in the literature recently: Machiavellianism, narcissism and psychopathy (Spain *et al.*, 2013). Machiavellianism is the manipulative personality; narcissism is the superiority personality; and psychopathy is the highly impulsive, thrill-seeking personality that includes low levels of empathy. These three personality traits have several features in common, including self-promotion, emotional coldness, aggressiveness and deception. Not surprisingly, all three of these personality traits correlate significantly and negatively with the Big Five dimension of agreeableness (Wu and LeBreton, 2011). These are not characteristics you would want in your friends, bosses or co-workers.

Machiavellian types are scheming, planning and manipulative. Adam Grant would call them 'takers' rather than 'givers' (read more in Adam's book *Give and Take: Why Helping Others Drives Our Success*). They are playing a game in which everyone is under their control. They form strategic friendships that last only if they are useful. They thrive on conflict and make sure that they are two steps ahead of everyone else ▶See Chapter 6◀. Narcissists use conversation tactics to make everything about them. They take credit even when others do all the work and they promote themselves at every opportunity. For anyone working with a psychopath, the combination of lack of empathy and thrill-seeking is dangerous. They will happily walk all over others, not caring about the consequences, and they do it for the thrill! Your misery makes them happy.

It's not surprising, in fact it's reassuring, that research has found negative workplace consequences for people with these dark personality traits (Judge *et al.*, 2006; Spain *et al.*, 2014). People who are high on these dark traits tend to receive lower performance appraisal ratings from their boss. Machiavellianism is also negatively associated with citizenship behaviour and positively linked to unethical decision-making in organisations. They also respond less well to leadership training and development, in part because their overconfidence makes them less likely to take on board negative feedback. While narcissists claim to be very creative, the evidence suggests that they are no better at creative performance than others. All three of the dark triad traits have been linked with counterproductive work behaviours.

One area of concern is that individuals with Machiavellian and/or narcissistic traits can make very good first impressions which might help convince employers to hire them. Narcissists tend to be talkative and good at self-promotion, both of which are advantageous at interviews. Machiavellian types seem to be more willing to engage in faking; they also seem to be better at it. However, researchers have argued that these initial good impressions wear off pretty quickly and others soon see them for what they are (Spain *et al.*, 2014).

⟨ETHICAL⟩ BEHAVIOUR IN THE WORKPLACE

When McCrae *et al.* (2005) administered the Big Five personality instrument to university students in over 50 countries, they found country differences. On average, people in some countries are more agreeable/extrovert/etc. than people in other countries. For example, Europeans and Americans scored higher on extroversion than Asians and Africans. Do you think there is any danger that this type of research would reinforce national stereotypes? Do you think there is any merit in hiring people from certain countries because they are reported to be high in certain desirable traits without conducting in-house assessments? Do you think that culture/nationality influences employees' perception of one another in the workplace and does this influence group work?

OTHER CLASSIFICATIONS OF PERSONALITY CHARACTERISTICS

core self-evaluation (CSE) is a broad trait that includes four specific traits: internal locus of control, emotional stability, self-esteem and generalised self-efficacy.

Core self-evaluations (CSE) as a collective emerged around 2000, which makes it quite a new addition to the personality literature. CSE is a basic, bottom-line set of evaluations that individuals make about themselves in determining their own self-worth (Judge *et al.*, 2003). It is made up of four traits that are closely linked to one another and are well established in the psychology literature. Those who are higher in CSE tend to appraise situations more positively, have greater confidence in their ability to influence the world in a positive way, and generally feel pretty good about themselves. This self-belief and self-confidence mean they have higher levels of motivation. See Table 2.4 for explanations of each of these concepts and some sample questions. There is some overlap with the Big Five in that both include emotional stability (i.e. neuroticism), but in general the emphasis of this personality lens is quite different.

Research (e.g. Kacmar *et al.*, 2009) found that these four dimensions are collectively very good at predicting many important organisational outcomes such as performance and satisfaction. The people with a high score have more successful careers (e.g. earn more) and experience lower levels of stress and conflict. They are good at capitalising on opportunities and they cope well with setbacks. They persist more at job searching when unemployed and experience reduced levels of work–family conflict. Researchers are enthusiastic about CSE as a way of looking at individual differences because it explains behaviour within (and outside of) organisations beyond what is explained by the Big Five.

Table 2.4 The meaning and self-assessment of core self-evaluations

CSE Dimension	Meaning of CSE Dimension	To what extent do you agree with the following sample statements? (1 = strongly disagree and 5 = strongly agree)
Internal locus of control	Beliefs about the causes of events in one's life – internal locus is when individuals see events as being the result of their own behaviour (rather than luck or external circumstances)	1 My life is determined by my own actions. 2 When I get what I want, it's usually because I worked hard for it.
Emotional stability	Tendency to have a positive belief/style and focus on the positive aspects of oneself	1 Too often, when things go wrong, I get discouraged and feel like giving up. (R) 2 I often feel inferior to others. (R)
Self-esteem	Overall value that one places on oneself as a person	1 I feel that I have a number of good qualities. 2 I feel that I am a person of worth, at least on an equal basis with others.
Generalised self-efficacy	Evaluation of how well one can perform across a variety of situations	1 If something looks too complicated, I will not even bother to try it. (R) 2 When I make plans, I am certain I can make them work.

(R) These questions are what are called 'reverse coded' items. They're negatively worded whereas the others are positively worded. You therefore need to reverse the scoring such that 5 = strongly disagree and 1 = strongly agree for these items.

Source: Judge et al. (2003).

CORE SELF-EVALUATIONS: HEXACO

We have discussed the Big Five, but have you heard of the Big Six? Even more recently in the world of personality, the HEXACO model of personality (Ashton and Lee, 2007) added a sixth factor: honesty-humility. The six factors, or dimensions, together include Honesty-Humility (H), Emotionality (E), Extroversion (X), Agreeableness (A), Conscientiousness (C) and Openness to Experience (O). Persons with very high scores on the Honesty-Humility scale avoid manipulating others for personal gain, feel little temptation to break rules, are uninterested in lavish wealth and luxuries, and feel no special entitlement to elevated social status. Conversely, persons with very low scores will flatter others to get what they want, are inclined to break rules for personal profit, are motivated by material gain and feel a strong sense of self-importance.

Extroversion, Conscientiousness, and Openness to Experience factors of the HEXACO model are like those of the Big Five. Agreeableness and Neuroticism have some overlap. Agreeableness and Emotionality from the HEXACO model represent rotated variants of their Big Five counterparts, for example, as characteristics related to a quick temper are associated with Neuroticism in the Big Five framework, but with low Agreeableness in the HEXACO framework. Therefore, the Big Five Agreeableness and HEXACO's Agreeableness are not identical. Furthermore, some characteristics of Honesty-Humility are incorporated in the Big Five Agreeableness.

MANAGERIAL TAKEAWAYS

This chapter has shown that individuals differ quite significantly in several ways. As a manager, it's important to note how these differences influence the way employees think, feel and behave at work. They also influence their productivity and happiness. Research shows that while environmental factors are important, genes also play a very important role in

BrewCo

Tom Singh has recently been appointed HR manager of BrewCo, a young and promising micro-brewery in Oregon, USA. While completing his undergraduate degree in business, Tom did part-time bar work and was actively involved in clubs and societies. After graduating, Tom worked as an Assistant Manager for a local bar and restaurant for three years then completed a master's degree in HRM.

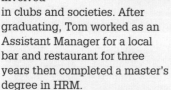

OB IN PRACTICE

Tom is looking forward to working with this growing company. He is the first person they have hired to work in HR. His first challenge is devising a plan for a recruitment drive. BrewCo is expanding into new markets and needs to hire for several positions. He hasn't received any guidance from the Senior Managers at BrewCo about how to do this, except from Jonathan Geary, who is BrewCo's co-founder.

We want people who are as passionate about our craft as we are, and that craft is making awesome beer and breaking down any walls of tradition in the process. The more walls we break – the better!

BrewCo projects an image of a rebellious, non-conventional organisation with an almost rock star attitude. Jonathan Geary heads the influential Culture Management Team, whose job it is to ensure that BrewCo stays true to its values and that its culture remains strong, as the company grows.

Although Tom has experience in management and the adult beverage industry, this organisational structure and culture is new to him. Despite this, he is adamant on doing a good job and making a good impression. He recognises the importance of working with the Culture Management Team as he develops his recruitment plan. They have a good point about not wanting to dilute BrewCo's values and culture as the company grows. When employees all share the same assumptions about 'how things are done around here', things run more smoothly. It's easy to see that someone who doesn't fit into the organisation's culture would struggle to be effective. They would probably also be quite unhappy and would therefore leave. These are things that Tom wants to avoid. However, he also recognises the importance of hiring people with the right knowledge, skills and abilities (KSAs) to do the job they are hired to do. He worries that the Culture Management Team might want him to emphasise organisational fit more than job competencies.

There is a second issue: BrewCo has received a lot of publicity lately and the organisation is highly attractive to potential job applicants. Tom worries about how they will manage the barrage of applications they anticipate after the online announcement of job listings is made. He's considering screening applicants using psychometric testing. Only those who are successful will be invited for interviews.

Questions

1 When hiring new employees, do you think Tom should give priority to the KSAs deemed necessary for the specific positions or to applicants who fit with BrewCo's culture?

2 Tom has to recruit an accountant. He has done some research on the personality traits of effective accountants and found that they tend to be detail-oriented, introverted, logical and structured. They also prefer stability over change. Do you think it's possible for Tom to find someone with these traits that will also fit into BrewCo's culture? Is it crucial that BrewCo's accountants fit

CREDIT: PHOTO BY RADOVAN ON UNSPLASH

the mould set in place by BrewCo's CEO?

3 Tom also needs to hire Sales Reps. Research on the Big Five has found that successful Sales Reps tend to be extroverted and conscientious. A potential candidate with an excellent sales track record makes it to interviews; upon interviewing, the candidate appears shy and reserved, yet in the group role play, there is no question s/he is a natural. Why might this be the case?

determining personalities, and that personality is stable over time. As a manager, you can't change a person's personality, but you can use it to understand them better. The Big Five inventory is a useful tool for understanding employee personality traits. You can use it to compare similarities and differences between potential candidates and the job description, or as a developmental tool for understanding how and why different employees are effective in different work situations.

An important issue that came up throughout this chapter was around fit. While having the right fit for a job, work colleagues and organisation is important, we must ask ourselves: is fit more important that having the right knowledge, skills and abilities? You also need to think about adequate training in psychometric testing if you think your organisation should utilise these 'tests' in the selection process. The cost of hiring the wrong candidate can be quite expensive!

As we look toward the future of personality in the workplace, there will be more advanced technological tools coming onto the market; it is important that we don't let a computer guide the testing process, ignoring the importance of the human aspect to testing. Finally, personality isn't all about the bright side and there are several personality traits, beyond the Big Five, that managers, employees and HR practitioners need to understand because of their potentially toxic influence in the workplace.

 CHAPTER REVIEW QUESTIONS

1 After reading the chapter, what is your understanding of the term 'personality'? Is it important for HR practitioners and line managers to understand personality?

2 What is the nature–nurture debate and why is it important to our understanding of personality?

3 What are the two main perspectives in personality theory? Which has better application in the workplace and why?

4 What are the five domains that make up the Big Five? List the traits that are associated with each of the five domains. Can you name the sixth HEXECO trait?

5 Your team at work is experiencing interpersonal conflict and you feel it's because of personality differences. You think it would be useful to have a team-building session using personality as a way of discussing how and why the team members approach things differently. Would you use the Big Five or the MBTI, and why?

6   List some advantages and disadvantages of utilising personality testing in the workplace.

7   Why and where should personality testing be used in the workplace?

8   What characteristics are associated with the dark triad? How might you deal with a work colleague who displayed some of these characteristics?

 FURTHER READING

Ashton M.C. and Lee, K. (2007) Empirical, theoretical, and practical advantages of the HEXACO model of personality structure. *Personality and Social Psychology Review*, 11(2), 50–66.

Colquitt, J.A., Lepine, J.A. and Wesson, M.J. (2012) *Organizational Behavior: Improving Performance and Commitment in the Workplace*, 3rd edition. New York: McGraw-Hill Irwin.

Hogan, J., Barrett, P. and Hogan, R. (2007) Personality measurement, faking, and employment selection. *Journal of Applied Psychology*, 92(5), 1270–1285.

Judge, T.A., Klinger, R., Simon, L.S. and Yang, I.W.F. (2008) The contributions of personality to organizational behavior and psychology: Findings, criticisms, and future research directions. *Social and Personality Psychology Compass*, 2(5), 1982–2000.

 USEFUL WEBSITES

http://www.ted.com/talks/susan_cain_the_power_of_introverts

Susan Cain presents a thoughtful reflection on the struggles of introverts in what she perceives to be an extroverted world. As you watch this TED Talk, you might think about your own experiences and times when you felt like you didn't fit into a situation or with others' expectations of you. You might also reflect on times when you thrived because you did fit in. How much of this fitting in or not fitting in had to do with your personality?

http://www.bbc.co.uk/science/humanbody/mind/index.shtml?personality

The BBC provides a great deal of information about personality including a number of personality assessments. One of the assessments you can access from this website is based on the Big Five, while others focus on careers and even on the relationship between personality and food preferences.

http://www.youtube.com/watch?v=z11DeKK13vM

This is a short video clip originally shown on ABC television in America. It discusses the Barnum Effect and shows how easily we can be fooled into believing horoscopes or mind readers. Personality assessments that are not designed and validated by experts can also take advantage of Barnum types' statements, resulting in people mistakenly believing that the assessment they are given is a true reflection of their personality. Barnum is the man who is credited with saying, 'There is a sucker born every minute.'

http://www.careersportal.ie/

Most universities offer their students access to online career advice and resources. Some of these websites, like the Irish one whose link is provided here, are hosted at the national level. These websites offer students access to a wide range of resources including personality assessments.

http://www.123test.com/personality-openness/
123test® is a Dutch-based, privately owned company that creates and publishes psychometric tests online. They provide a wide number of tests covering IQ, personality, and career assessment.

http://www.personal.psu.edu/~j5j/IPIP/
Professor John A. Johnson at Pennsylvania State University set up a website in which anyone can find out how they score on the Big Five. You can take the long or short version of the IPIP-NEO, which is the International Personality Item Pool representation of the NEO PI-R™.

Online Resources

Visit bloomsbury.pub/organisational-behaviour to access additional materials to support teaching and learning.

3 PERCEPTION

Ashley Bamberg and Jennifer Hennessy

LEARNING OUTCOMES

BY THE END OF THIS CHAPTER YOU SHOULD BE ABLE TO:

- Define perception.
- Discuss the perception process.
- Identify common perceptual distortions.
- Explain the link between perception, attribution, and behaviour at work.
- Explain the importance of perception in organisations.

THIS CHAPTER DISCUSSES...

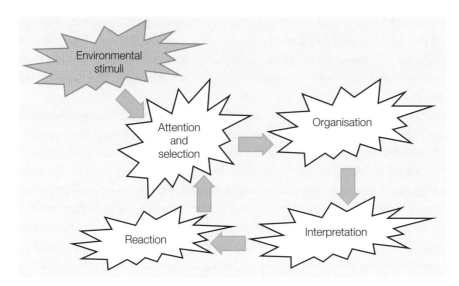

Figure 3.1 The perceptual process

INTRODUCTION

Perception is the unique psychological process of how individuals make sense of the world around them. Knowledge of this process is critical to our understanding of how and why individuals within an organisation behave the way they do. Everyone brings their own perceptions to the workplace and as we will discuss, this can provide a distorted understanding of reality and can influence behaviour. Figure 3.1 is a visual representation of the perceptual process. This chapter provides an understanding of the perceptual process, the errors that might occur within the perceptual process, and the significance of perceptions in organisations.

The chapter begins by defining perception, noting the power of perception, and how perception is a sense specific to individuals. The factors which might influence an individual's perceptions are then outlined before the chapter provides a detailed explanation of the stages within the perceptual process. In the perceptual process, we identify how individuals detect stimuli from their environment and the actions that occur in response to a given stimulus. As perceptions are unique to an individual, and represent their version of reality, errors can occur. We discuss common perceptual errors and how these errors might appear in organisational settings. We conclude the chapter by highlighting how our perceptions influence our behaviour at work.

THE NATURE OF PERCEPTION

The five senses of sight, smell, touch, taste and hearing enable individuals to take in information from the environment and through a complex process, filter and organise that information in order to create meaning. Perception relates to how individuals process and interpret the world around them. This is important to understand, as how individuals perceive the world around them can have significant outcomes. A good illustration on the power of perception is Milgram's well-known obedience experiment. Milgram (1974) wanted to test how much pain individuals would inflict on another individual (through shocks), simply because they were ordered to do so by a figure of authority. In this study, shocks were not actually administered to the other person and no harm was done, but the research participants were unaware of this. Interestingly, Milgram (1974) found that individuals

perception
originally comes from the Latin term 'perceptio', meaning comprehension, or literally, 'a taking in'.

(albeit reluctantly) administered these perceived levels of dangerous electric shocks to another person because they were told to by the scientist in charge of the experiment. This experiment demonstrates the lengths individuals were willing to go to because of the perception of authority ▶See Chapter 8◀. This experiment was replicated on a French television documentary called 'The Game of Death' in 2010 and similar results occurred.

In an organisational context, perceptions can have significant outcomes as well. For example, a manager might set a number of goals for an employee who recently asked about career development opportunities in the organisation. The manager perceives these goals as motivational and a welcome challenge for the employee, whom they hope to develop within the organisation. The employee, however, perceives these goals as unrealistic and unattainable. In turn, the employee then becomes demotivated, questions the manager's intentions, and starts to apply for other positions in a competing company. Failure to acknowledge these differences in perception can cause potential conflicts at work or lead to detrimental outcomes for an organisation, such as the loss of a valuable employee.

As illustrated, how an individual perceives a situation does not necessarily represent a true or accurate reflection of reality; however, what an individual perceives, is what they believe reality to be. In a recent 'Public Perceptions' survey by Ipsos MRBI, a global marketing research agency, the public perceptions of key global issues across 40 countries were explored. One of the questions asked participants to rate their population's happiness. Surprisingly, all countries thought their population was less happy than they actually were. In Great Britain alone, only 47% of British people perceived the population to be rather happy or very happy, when in fact, 92% of British people had rated themselves as rather happy or very happy. These survey results demonstrate that people's perceptions influence their understanding of reality; however, the reality they perceive isn't always an accurate reflection of what is actually going on.

IN REALITY

Have you ever heard the saying, 'what you see is what you get'? We tend to think that our perceptions are relatively stable and unfaltering and that what we see closely matches reality. However, in reality, our perception can often be manipulated to change what we experience. Many companies significantly invest in marketing and advertising resources to try and create a certain perception of their product. In a study conducted by researchers at Columbia University and MIT, participants in a pub were asked to evaluate regular beer and an 'MIT brew' to which a few drops of balsamic vinegar had been added (Lee *et al.*, 2006). The researchers discovered that disclosure of the additional ingredient of balsamic vinegar significantly reduced people's preference for the MIT brew *only* when the disclosure took place prior to tasting. This suggests that participants' perceptions changed enough to influence how they experienced the subsequent taste of the beer. What is also interesting is the fact that the addition of the balsamic vinegar can actually enhance the flavour of the beer, yet people's perception of the taste of vinegar produced a negative connection to its taste in the beer. This connection was strong enough to alter subjects' perceptions of what the beer would taste like!

This experiment demonstrates how our perception can be influenced to such a degree that it can change our subsequent experience of an event. Our perception of an event or experience is therefore subject to various influences and is not as objective as the common saying above would lead us to believe.

It is important that we acknowledge that individuals perceive the world in their own, unique way. Oscar Wilde once noted, 'We are all in the gutter, but some of us are looking at the stars.' In this sense, your perception of the world can be very different from other people's. For example, if you view the picture in Figure 3.2, what do you see?

Figure 3.2 'My Wife and My Mother-in-Law' illusion

This is a well-known image by British cartoonist William Ely Hill. It was introduced into psychological literature by Edwin Boring, whose subject of expertise was visual perception. Some people perceive a young girl when they see this image, whereas others perceive an old woman. How difficult is it for you to perceive both?

Having learned a little about what perception actually is and the significance it can have, we now need to explore how perception actually takes place. Let's now look at the actual process of perception in more detail. We will begin by first looking at the factors which have the ability to influence perception.

FACTORS INFLUENCING PERCEPTION

As demonstrated in Figure 3.3, there are a number of factors which influence perception. These include characteristics of the perceiver, the object or target being perceived, and the context of the situation in which perception occurs. We will now explore these factors before turning our attention to the process of perception.

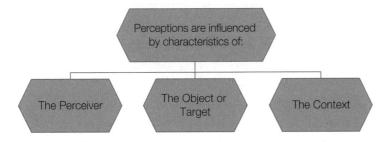

Figure 3.3 Factors influencing perception

THE PERCEIVER

perceptual set
means a set of
internal factors
that influence what
stimuli individuals
select and pay
attention to.

An individual's attention to and selection of stimuli is influenced by their perceptual set, which includes their personality, goals and motives, prior learning and experiences, emotions and attitudes (Mullins, 2007).

BUILDING YOUR EMPLOYABILITY SKILLS

Perceptual Sets in Organisations

Think about the personalities, goals, experiences and emotions of the people in your classroom or even in your own home. How do you think their perceptual set influence how they perceive college? How they perceive life? Think about how their perceptual set might influence how they perceive things in an organisational setting. How might this compare with your perceptual set and how you might perceive things in an organisation? Think about things like pay equity, benefits offered, development opportunities, etc.

Let's explore how these factors might influence what stimuli an individual selects and pays attention to.

- **Personality** The personality traits an individual holds may predispose the individual to attend to, and react to, stimuli in different ways ▸See Chapter 2◂. For example, a company's social committee organises a holiday work party. An employee who typically scores high in extroversion might perceive this social event as exciting and fun. Alternatively, an employee who tends to score high in introversion might perceive this social event as awkward and may feel apprehensive about attending.

- **Goals and Motives** An individual's motivational needs can also influence what they pay attention to. An employee who is interested in advancing their career might be more percep-tive to internal job vacancies sent through the company's e-mail than an employee who is reaching retirement age. The employee reaching retirement age is probably giving more attention to e-mails about pension performance. An important feature of motivation, the salience or importance of one's motivational need ▸See Chapter 5◂, may impact the level of attention paid to a stimulus. In our example, the employees have different salient needs and each employee pays more attention to the stimulus that is more important to them.

- **Learning and Experience** In regards to the prior learning and experiences of an individual, an employee working in a senior accounting role for over 20 years might notice more quickly an error made in the company spreadsheets than a junior colleague only in their role for six months. The senior accountant's knowledge gained from association in the role might prompt attention to the error in the company's spreadsheets faster than would be the case with the junior accountant, who has gained less insight from their position.

- **Emotions and Attitudes** Our emotional and attitudinal state can also influence what we pay attention to in certain situations. An employee who is worried and nervous about the security of their job may pay little attention to a manager providing a motivational speech on teamwork. Likewise, an employee with a negative attitude towards their organisation may perceive the company as poor to work for, ignoring the positive aspects of the organisation, such as their generous compensation and benefits package ▸**Chapter 4**◂.

THE OBJECT OR TARGET

External factors also influence the way in which individuals perceive things. These factors relate to the nature of the stimulus itself. There exists a number of characteristics a stimulus may have that could influence the level of attention we pay to it. These may appear individually, or as a combination of elements, and include:

- **Size** Individuals tend to notice larger objects, which is why, for example, a billboard advertisement will often catch our attention.

- **Intensity** Individuals notice stimuli which have a greater intensity. For example, fire alarms produce a high intensity noise to gain your attention.

- **Contrast** People tend to be more aware of stimuli which are contrasting. The McDonald's 'M' sign is yellow, which contrasts and stands out from its environment.

- **Degree of Motion** Individuals pay more attention to objects that are moving. Advertisements on webpages often move up and down in order to attract your attention.

- **Level of Repetition** A stimulus that is repeated is noticed more. For example, in a busy train station, an announcement that is repeatedly played over the messaging system is more likely to be received by commuters.

- **Novelty** Something which is different, or new, stands out more to people. An unknown visitor to the workplace will attract attention, as will a new notice board put on the wall of the company entrance.

- **Familiarity** People are more likely to notice something familiar to them in a situation where most objects are unfamiliar. For example, we can easily pick out a familiar face in a photograph when we don't know anybody else in the picture.

CONTEXT

The context or situation in which the stimulus is observed should also be considered, as it can influence what individuals pay attention to. For example, employees who are called in to a meeting knowing the company has been performing very poorly may have a different perception of what will occur in the meeting, than employees who are unaware of the company's performance. When studying perceptions, qualitative researchers will often include context in their investigation in order to gain a deeper understanding of what is happening.

Culture and language are two specific contextual factors which should be paid attention to with regards to their influence on perception. These dimensions will now be explored.

- **Culture** Culture can predispose us to react in different ways to certain stimuli. A study by Jack *et al.* (2012) demonstrated that people from different cultures perceive facial expression in different ways. Their research found East Asians and Western Caucasians differed in the recognition of various facial expressions such as happiness, surprise, fear, disgust, anger and sadness. Culture may also influence perceptions with regard to food and table manners. In England, for example, people are usually expected to finish the food on their plate; however, if a person clears their dish in China, the hosts may perceive the individual as questioning their generosity and will place more food on their plate. These examples reflect how people in different cultures perceive the environment in different ways. Hofstede (2011) has conducted research exploring cultural differences, developing a categorisation scheme for exploring cultural dimensions ▸See Chapter 12◂.

Culture might also predispose individuals at work to react in different ways. HSBC's (Hong Kong and Shanghai Banking Corporation) advertisements illustrate variations in cultural perceptions at work. In one of their advertisements, it is noted that some American management consultants believe it is better to have meetings standing up in an effort to save time, which is perceived as precious. In Japan, however, company chairmen perceive it important to contemplate what has been discussed in a meeting and would prefer to sit down. In another example from HSBC, an advertisement demonstrates how in America, if you hit a hole-in-one golfing, you are expected to buy your partners a drink; however, in China, you are expected to buy everyone expensive gifts. These advertisements demonstrate how the culture of the work environment might predispose an individual's behaviour at work. For example, an American expatriate working as a manager for a company in Japan might observe that Japanese employees prefer to sit down for meetings, and would also sit down during meetings, therefore changing their behaviour based on the perceptions of their environment.

◂ETHICAL▸ BEHAVIOUR IN THE WORKPLACE

A common question for organisations, particularly in the field of organisational behaviour, is 'does a bad cultural environment lead to bad ethical behaviour?' When we think about perceptions, and the factors which influence perception, such as culture, it would suggest that the culture of the work environment could influence an employee's perceptions of how to behave. This is depicted in the 2013 film *The Wolf of Wall Street*, about investment banker Jordan Belfort's Stratton Oakmont company. The film is not necessarily an accurate depiction of Jordan Belfort or the Stratton Oakmont company in reality; however, it does demonstrate how unethical corporate culture could lead to unethical behaviour of employees. In the movie, Jordan Belfort's employees were trained to be unethical, taught from the beginning how to scam the system and make the most profit. Through leadership, and the behaviour of others, the company's culture became a host for unethical behaviour. As we know, culture can influence our perception of a stimulus, such as a work environment, and our view of that stimulus will produce a response, such as believing in unethical actions or partaking in unethical behaviour. Thinking about what you know about factors influencing perception, if you were hired by Stratton Oakmont as depicted in the movie, do you think you might also have participated in an unethical way?

- **Language** Language and how we use it also has an important impact on the way in which we perceive the world. Our language enables us to recognise stimuli and identify their role. For example, in Alaska, there are many different variations for the word 'snow', enabling Alaskans to perceive many different types of snow. In English-speaking countries, there is just the one English word for snow, so we don't tend to perceive these variations. Some researchers interested in discourse analysis actually study the way in which we construct words, sentences and phrases in order to understand the meaning of people's discourse.

Now that we have a better understanding of the factors which influence perception, let us look at how perception actually works.

THE PERCEPTUAL PROCESS

We will examine the stages in the perceptual process (see Figure 3.1) and look at each of these elements in turn. It is important to remember that the meaning we extract from what we perceive is unique to us, as individuals. Perception is an active process; we process everything that we see, smell, touch, hear and taste and these senses allow us to take in information about the world around us. It is through the process of perception that we select stimuli from the environment, make sense of it, create meaning from it and react to it. It is important to be aware of all of the senses; however, this chapter predominantly focuses on the sense of sight.

process of perception means the process of how we attend to, organise, interpret and respond to stimuli.

ATTENTION AND SELECTION

The first stage in the perceptual process is attention and selection. Since our senses are constantly bombarded with stimuli, individuals must find a way to choose the information they need to attend to, filtering out the irrelevant information to avoid their senses being overloaded. This process is known as selective attention. For example, an employee who is immersed in a work project on their computer may not notice the noise made by the airconditioning unit. There must be certain levels of a stimulus present before our senses will register its presence. People's sensory thresholds vary with regard to the amount of sensation they need present before they pay attention to it, the level of sensation they are comfortable with, and the impact sensory deprivation has on them.

selective attention is the process through which we attend to certain stimuli and select out others.

BUILDING YOUR EMPLOYABILITY

Selective Attention

Close your eyes. Imagine that you are working as a checkout operator in a large grocery store. Imagine the pictures and sounds you could potentially see and hear? What visuals and sounds do you think you would particularly note? These images and sounds are reflective of your selective attention in action and will influence what you pay attention to in your role.

Sensory deprivation is sometimes used as a technique by military forces to interrogate prisoners. Brian Keegan, who was kidnapped by Islamic Jihad in Beirut, wrote of his experiences in his book *An Evil Cradling* (1992), where he stated, 'you are in the dark, there are no windows, you can't see. But, tiny and oppressive as it is, you find in your mind ways to push the walls back.' This quote illustrates his ability to attend to certain stimuli and select out others in order to survive in captivity, even under extreme conditions of sensory deprivation.

We now know that we select certain stimuli to attend to, and from earlier in the chapter, that what we decide to pay attention to is influenced by various internal, external and contextual factors. Let's now look at the next stage in the perceptual process.

ORGANISATION

The next stage of the perceptual process is organisation. The Gestalt School of Psychology, established in the early 20th century, developed a number of principles which they suggest individuals use to help organise and give meaning to information they have attended to and selected. These principles are applicable in an organisational context and are discussed below.

FIGURE-TO-GROUND EFFECT

The first principle, the figure-to-ground effect, suggests that figures are better seen against a background. For example, as I am typing on my keyboard the black letters stand out from the white background; however, sometimes this is not as straightforward as it seems. In Figure 3.4, what do you see?

Figure 3.4 Rubin's (1915) vase illusion

Did you see a vase or two faces? Most people tend to attend to one part of the picture at a time, either the figure (in this case the faces), or the background (the vase), but not both at the same time. In the workplace people use the principles of organisation to identify the key parts of their job, so as not to become overwhelmed.

GROUPING

In trying to make sense of what we perceive, we tend to group stimuli together rather than viewing them as separate entities. This is based on the Gestalt principle that the whole is greater than the sum of its parts. Wertheimer (1923) developed a number of laws to illustrate the principles underpinning these processes, the most common of which are described in Table 3.1.

Table 3.1 Examples of grouping principles

Principle	Example
Proximity: when things are close together we tend to think of them as a group.	When we see a group of people sitting together in an office we assume that they are part of the same department.
Law of Continuity: we perceive items that appear to have a continuous form as making a pattern.	In a manufacturing plant, we may perceive that a row of machines together on the factory floor produce the same element, when in fact they all produce different parts.
Similarity: we tend to group elements together that have similar characteristics.	A manager might think that payroll should be part of the finance function because the payroll section works with figures; however, the person working in payroll might feel better placed in the HR department because of the people aspect of the payroll job.
The Law of Closure: we tend to close off or finish any objects that we perceive as being incomplete.	The IBM logo is comprised of a number of lines which do not actually connect, but in our mind we join up the lines to create the logo.

INTERPRETATION

The third stage of the perceptual process is interpretation. During this phase of the process we interpret the information that we have attended to and organised in order to create meaning. We use information that we have already processed and stored to make sense of the new information that we receive. This process is very subjective, as we use pre-existing schemas and scripts to help us interpret information. A schema is a unique mental representation of the world around us and is based on information from our memories. For example, why do you dress up for an interview? This is a representation of a schema; you know from experience that it makes you look professional and like a more qualified candidate. We also hold schemas about ourselves, which are called self-schemas; for example, we may view ourselves as intelligent, caring or funny (or even all three). Correspondingly, cognitive scripts are like predetermined steps in our mind that we follow to help us know how to behave in a certain situation. A candidate entering an interview has a pre-existing script as to what will take place and how they should act in the situation, such as shaking hands and introducing themselves to the interviewers.

The schemas and scripts we create in our minds are unique to each of us and our prior experiences influence how we construct them. Returning to our example, a person who previously had a very negative interview experience may have developed a very different cognitive script for future interviews from that of a person whose past experience with interviewing was positive. However, these schemas and scripts can change, as new information and experiences are gathered. It should be noted that our pre-existing schemas and scripts also influence the information that we attend to in the first stage of the perceptual process. Although schemas and scripts help us to structure and make sense of our world, we must be also aware that they can increase our tendency to make perceptual errors, such as stereotyping, because we are making assumptions based on pre-existing thought patterns.

> schema is a unique mental representation of the world around us and is based on information from our memories.

> cognitive scripts are like predetermined steps in our mind that tell us how to behave in a certain situation.

RESPONSE

The final stage in the process of perception is where our interpretation of a stimulus elicits a response. Our response may manifest as an internal reaction, such as feeling a particular emotion, or as an external behaviour, or as a combination of both. For example, in an organisational context, an employee who perceives that she is likely to receive a promotion

SPOTLIGHT ON SKILLS

Awareness of Confirmation Bias

The concept of perception is very important for managers within an organisation. It influences them in their selection of employees through the interview process, and they have to be careful not to let perceptual errors taint their judgement. Later, when successful candidates become employees of the organisation, the manager has to try and ensure that these employees have a positive perception of the organisation.

1 Have you seen other interviewers making any perceptual errors when carrying out interviews in the organisation?

2 As a manager, how do you try to ensure that employees in your company have a positive perception of the organisation?

To help you answer these questions, visit bloomsbury.pub/organisational-behaviour to watch the video of Gavin Connell from the University of Limerick talking about perception.

may feel worried about the extra responsibility that she will be asked to take on (internal reaction), or she might go and talk to another employee who previously carried out the role to learn more about the position (external behaviour), or she may do both. As we know, in an organisational setting, not all responses will be positive. For example, that same employee may have perceived she was likely to receive the promotion, but did not get the promotion. She might feel frustrated and angry about not getting the promotion (internal reaction) and may start to come into work late and put less effort into the duties of her job description (external behaviour).

The perceptions and reactions of an individual in a given situation will of course be influenced by their personality, past experiences, social context, etc. It is important that leaders in an organisational setting understand how people's perceptions influence their attitudes and behaviour ▶See Chapter 6◀. Managing organisational activities that influence perceptions helps to shape the attitudes and behaviours of employees at work. Many of such activities are carried out by the organisation's HR function, such as staffing, compensation and benefits, etc. ▶See Chapter 4◀. HR departments often attempt to gauge the perceptions of their employees through surveys. Some organisations develop their own surveys and others use external consultants to design data collection instruments. The Great Place to Work Institute administers a Trust Index Assessment which evaluates employees' perceptions of trust in their organisation. Once the organisation gains an understanding of employees' perceptions, they can take actions (manage organisational activities) to change or keep employees' perceptions (attitude) and actions (behaviour) as positive towards the organisation.

Marwood

Marwood is a manufacturing plant located in Kenya. The company is aware that the key to their survival is to be able to provide a low-cost, high-quality product to their customers. Their strategy is twofold; firstly, to contain costs through constant innovation, and secondly, to respond to their customer needs faster than their competitors. The company's 400+ employees are seen as a key contributing factor to their business success. A number of organisational and functional initiatives reflect the company's commitment to its employees. One initiative, which seems to have had a particular impact on company culture and employees' perception of the organisation, is the continuous improvement process.

The company has implemented a process of continuous improvement since 2015. The company has used various continuous improvement tools such as value stream mapping, total productive maintenance, 5S, visual management systems, and demand smoothing, to increase efficiencies. The company management team has tried to push a continuous improvement culture in the organisation where the employees themselves are the drivers of improvement initiatives. Bi-monthly director meetings are held, where directors provide information on company performance, new initiatives, and any relevant operational and strategic issues that employees need to be aware of. Employees are encouraged to ask questions and make suggestions at these meetings. Some employees are transferred onto continuous improvement projects to examine ways in which work processes can be improved, but even employees who are not working on specific projects consider it important to look for ways of making improvements to the way in which they carry out their work.

Supervisors in the plant are rotated through continuous improvement roles and there is a focus on internal promotion. Approximately 60% of the supervisors and team leaders in the plant have been promoted from within the organisation. Employees go through a performance appraisal and are evaluated on both their performance and their behaviour. The company has a set of 10 standards of behaviour which all employees are expected to adhere to. Employees are recognised for high performance or suggestions which lead to cost savings or an improvement in work processes. Sometimes this takes the form of a luncheon voucher, but more often a simple thank you card is regarded as sufficient recognition. The HR director states that when people start with the organisation they come with their 'hands and the head', and if you look after them, the 'heart will follow'. Initiatives should, as those outlined above, drive a continuous improvement culture and employees will have a good attitude towards their work environment and also have a positive perception of the organisation. One team leader noted, 'you are in tune with what's going on in the organisation, and they are in tune with what you are doing as well'. A member of staff working in a support function noted, 'you do feel a part of something when you come in, which was lovely'.

OB IN PRACTICE

CREDIT: PHOTO BY REMY GIELING ON UNSPLASH

Questions

1 Can you think of examples which might change employees' positive perceptions of the work environment?
2 Why do you think the continuous improvement initiative has created such positive employee perceptions of the organisation?
3 What other types of initiatives might the company introduce to create a positive response from employees?
4 In class exercise: think of a specific event for your university/college that could be held for all staff and students to encourage a positive perception of the organisation.

We have now outlined the perceptual process, understanding how we pay attention to and select stimuli, organise and interpret the information received, and react to it in some way. Yet this process is often flawed and we will now explore some of the ways in which our perception can be obscured.

PERCEPTUAL DISTORTIONS

perceptual distortions are the errors that people make in their perception of others and events.

As previously noted in the chapter, how people perceive events is not a perfect representation of reality, allowing for errors in the perceptual process. Perceptual distortions occur when people misinterpret the information they have received, taking mental shortcuts in order to speed up the perceptual process. As the perceptual process can affect the attitudes and behaviours of people at work, perceptual distortions also influence the behaviour of, and the interaction between, people in organisations. This is quite common and there are many different types of perceptual distortions that can occur. These perceptual distortions can have detrimental effects on employee performance and might also lead to workers being discriminated against ▶ See Chapter 10◀. Managers must be particularly cognisant of the dangers of perceptual errors with regard to the recruitment and selection process and when conducting performance appraisals. It is important that organisations are aware of these shortcuts and work on trying to reduce these errors. Common perceptual distortions include:

CONTRAST EFFECT

The contrast effect is the comparison of two stimuli, as opposed to assessing them independently on their own merits. This is frequently used in marketing and sales, in the hopes of upselling an item. For example, a car dealer might know what type of car you are looking for and your budget. The first car they show you is lovely, but way over your budget. The next car they show you is just as lovely and only a little over your budget, so you end up thinking it is a good deal in comparison with the first car. Rather than assessing each car as independent entities, the second car was assessed in contrast to the first. Contrast effect occurs in organisational settings as well. Take for example a manager doing performance reviews. The first performance review the manager conducts is with an employee who is performing poorly in their role, has high absenteeism and is rude to co-workers. The manager then has a performance review with an employee who is frequently late; however, after the review with the first employee, the manager ignores the lateness of this employee and instead, praises them for performing well in their role, consistently showing up for work and being friendly with co-workers.

HALO/HORNS EFFECT

This is where we tend to focus on either one positive or negative aspect of an individual and use that characteristic to evaluate the person as a whole. For instance, a panel of interviewers may view a candidate as friendly and, because of this, evaluate that candidate as a highly skilled employee who works well in teams. This is an example of the halo effect, as the panel, without any evidence of the candidate's skills or experience working in teams, perceive the candidate's friendliness as a sign of their abilities. In a study by Turnipseed (2002), individuals who were perceived as being 'more ethical' were also perceived as being more productive than those who were considered 'less ethical', demonstrating the existence of the halo effect. In contrast, an example of the horns effect might be that an employee who is often late for work is generally regarded as being difficult and troublesome by the manager, although there is no evidence from the employee's last performance appraisal to suggest this. To avoid the halo or horns effect, particularly when assessing employees, a manager must try to evaluate each employee across a range of preset criteria and to examine each criterion independently of the others.

STEREOTYPING

We tend to assign a set of characteristics to a group of people or to an individual; however, more often than not, these perceptions are inaccurate assumptions and are not reflective of the true characteristics of others. For example, we may perceive all Japanese to like sushi and all Americans to like burgers; however, you may have a friend who is Japanese who hates sushi or an American friend who doesn't like burgers. We can actually discriminate against people because of the stereotypes we assign to them. For instance, a hiring manager at a hospital who stereotypes nursing as being a female profession might not hire many male nurses. People who feel negative judgement by a stereotype label may feel more pressure to perform particularly well. This pressure can potentially have the opposite effect, causing a person to underperform or not be able to perform at all.

stereotyping is a preconceived belief that suggests that all members of a particular category share a set of characteristics.

Steele and Aronson (1995) conducted the first experiments demonstrating stereotype threat weakening intellectual performance. Their study explored the college entry exam performance of black and white students in the United States. The first part of their study found that stereotype threat negatively influenced the performance of black participants. The rest of their study established that this stereotype threat could be diminished through a change in instructions (describing the test as a simple problem-solving exercise rather than a measure of intellectual ability), in turn, positively influencing the performance of black participants. Since stereotypes, and subsequent stereotype threats, have the ability to negatively impact individuals, employment equality legislation is there to help protect some of the most commonly stereotyped groups against discrimination (i.e. The Employment Equality Acts (1998–2015), which in Ireland prevent discrimination on the basis of gender, marital status, family status, age, disability, membership of the traveller community, race, religious views or sexual orientation).

Age Discrimination

A recent issue discussed in the media, age discrimination demonstrates how perceptions can negatively influence an organisation's actions. As age is one of the first characteristics we perceive (Bamberg *et al.*, 2019), the Irish Human Rights and Equality Commission (IHREC) predicts organisations will face an increase in age discrimination cases (Miley, 2018). Supporting their prediction, a recent survey by the American Associations of Retired Persons (AARP) revealed that 61% of people had seen or experienced age discrimination at work, and of those, 38% thought it was common practice (Perron, 2018). Age discrimination

 IN THE NEWS

CREDIT: PHOTO BY AHSANIZATION ON UNSPLASH

can be defined as making organisational decisions based on age-related stereotypes (McCarthy *et al.*, 2019).

Although age discrimination is illegal under the Employment Equality Acts (Miley, 2018), age-related stereotypes have been widely accepted (Bamberg *et al.*, 2019; Posthuma and Campion, 2009). For example, older workers have frequently been labelled as poor performers, resistant to change, low in learning ability, and high in turnover (Posthuma and Campion, 2009). These are largely negative characteristics, which have not been supported by empirical evidence (Bamberg *et al.*, 2019); thus, representing a stereotype, or a perceptual distortion, that does not necessarily reflect reality. Due to age discrimination being a stereotype, it could

lead to stereotype threat and hinder individual performance. Geber (2019) noted that individuals who perceive ageing positively, behave differently from those who perceive it as negative. Studies have actually demonstrated that those with a positive perception of ageing are more likely to take care of themselves, have higher resilience, do better on memory tests, and live up to about 7.5 years longer (Geber, 2019).

These age-related stereotypes pose a problem for organisations, as although they may not be reflective of reality, they have been used to make decisions at work (Bamberg *et al.*, 2019; Posthuma and Campion, 2009). Google recently made international headlines through the loss of an $11 million age discrimination lawsuit (Kelly, 2019). Over 200 applicants, aged 40 and above, sued the company for making hiring decisions based on age (Kelly, 2019). Google is now required to train employees on age bias and has been instructed to form an age diversity committee that will aid in the recruitment and selection process (Kelly, 2019). Other major organisations, including Facebook, IBM, Verizon Communications, and Goldman Sachs, have also been involved in age discrimination cases (Kelly, 2019).

Questions

1 List some consequences organisations might face when perceptual distortions play a role in decision-making.
2 Can you think of other stereotypes or perceptual distortions that might occur in organisational decision-making?
3 How do you think organisations could avoid perceptual distortions in decision-making?

Sources

Bamberg, McCarthy and Heraty (2019). See RTE: https://www.rte.ie/brainstorm/2019/0204/1027384-stop-talking-about-my-generation-the-problem-of-ageism-at-work/

Geber (2019). See Forbes: https://www.forbes.com/sites/sarazeff-geber/2019/07/15/ageism-a-moral-and-personal-dilemma-for-our-ti-me/#ee0d01c1dd18

Kelly (2019). See Forbes: https://www.forbes.com/sites/jackkelly/2019/07/23/google-settles-age-discrimination-law-suit-highlighting-the-prolifera-tion-of-ageism-in-hiring/#38c9bd8d5c67

McCarthy, J., Heraty, N. and Bamberg, A. (2019). Lifespan perspectives on age-related stereotypes, prejudice, and discrimination at work (and beyond). In B.B. Baltes, C.W. Rudolph and H. Zacher (eds), *Work Across the Lifespan* (pp. 417–435). London: Academic Press.

Miley (2018). See: https://www.rte.ie/news/ireland/2018/0430/959143-em-ployers-could-face-surge-of-age-dis-crimination-ca/

Perron (2018). See AARP: https://www.aarp.org/research/topics/economics/info-2018/multicultur-al-work-jobs.html

Posthuma, R.A. and Campion, M.A. (2009). Age stereotypes in the workplace: Common stereotypes, moderators, and future research directions. *Journal of Management*, 35, 158–188.

PREJUDICE

Prejudice is a feature of stereotyping and is defined as holding a positive or negative impression about a group of people which has no foundation. For instance, the Nazis held extremist views about the behaviours and preferences of Jewish people, based not on facts but on hatred. Not all prejudice is as obvious or extreme as this, it can also be subtle; nevertheless, it can still be very damaging. Research conducted in the US by Harrison and Thomas (2009) found skin-tone prejudice in regards to job selection. Their results indicated that among black candidates, applicants who were lighter skinned received significantly higher selection ratings than their darker skinned counterparts. They described this prejudice as 'colourism'.

PROJECTION

This perceptual distortion is where we perceive others as feeling or thinking in a similar way to ourselves. In other words, we project our perception of the world onto another person, assuming they see the world as we do. In an organisational setting, the HR department might perceive training as valuable and then perceive that all employees value the training provided; when in fact, many of the employees may find the training disadvantageous to their working day. Successful organisations, and managers, recognise that employees have different perspectives on certain matters, pay attention to these alternative viewpoints, and consider different options for addressing these matters.

SIMILAR-TO-ME BIAS

We tend to have a preference for individuals who are most similar to ourselves. For example, in a performance review meeting, a manager may rate employees with a similar work style to their own, higher than employees with different work styles, even though they are equally performing workers. In another example, a hiring manager might show preference for applicants who have a similar educational background, work experience or hobbies to themselves. A manager must try to put their personal preferences aside when recruiting, hiring and evaluating staff.

SELF-FULFILLING PROPHECY

This is based on Merton's (1957) premise that because we make a prophecy, it is more likely to come true. In other words, we predict something, do things that reinforce the prediction, then when the prediction happens, the prophecy is validated. For example, in a work environment, employees who feel that their organisation is going to close may become demotivated and put very little effort into their work. In turn, productivity levels go down, affecting profitability, and the company is ultimately forced to shut down. The employees have unwittingly contributed to the self-fulfilling prophecy. It is important individuals in an organisation take responsibility for their actions and are aware of the potential outcomes of their actions.

IMPACT OF TECHNOLOGY ON BEHAVIOUR

LinkedIn is an online professional networking platform that helps employees and organisations in the recruitment and selection process. Organisations are able to build their brand through a profile, post job advertisements and share news; candidates are able to build their name and connect to networks through a profile, view job advertisements and apply for the roles if they so wish. Due to LinkedIn's ability to provide organisations with a large number of globally diverse candidates, it is seen as the new frontier in the hiring process. However, as with any form of social media, a profile picture and the ability to build your profile so others perceive you in the way that you wish, comes into play. In this sense, self-fulfilling prophecy could occur. Say a company had narrowed down to two candidates on the basis of their CVs, for interviews. Candidate A has a LinkedIn profile and Candidate B does not. Before the interview, the panel views Candidate A's LinkedIn profile. Candidate A has a lot of experience on their profile, and is connected with important members within the organisation. The panel immediately views Candidate A as a better fit for the role. Neither candidate has been interviewed, but when the candidates are interviewed, Candidate B does better. However, the panel chooses Candidate A for the role, as the information from the online profile suggests that that candidate is the best choice, demonstrating how technology might allow perceptual errors in hiring to occur.

PERCEPTUAL DEFENCE

perceptual defence is discounting information in order to defend an existing perception.

As individuals, we don't like to be wrong or faced with information that challenges our existing view of things. Perceptual defence is where an individual discounts any information that might threaten their existing perception of a stimulus. An example of this might be if a manager perceives a particular employee to be very diligent but the employee forgets to do something, the manager would downplay this in order to preserve their opinion about that employee.

CONFIRMATION BIAS

confirmation bias is a tendency to seek out information in line with expectations and existing knowledge and to assign more weight to evidence which confirms these beliefs, undervaluing evidence to the contrary.

Confirmation bias is where we actively seek out information to support our initial hypothesis, even when all the evidence suggests this hypothesis is incorrect. For example, during interviews, one of the HR managers in the hiring panel declares that the next candidate interviewed is going to be the best candidate for the customer-service role. The candidate has come highly recommended by a friend of the HR manager. The HR manager then asks the candidate simple questions regarding customer-service experiences and is encouraging, probing the candidate to provide stronger answers to the questions asked. When the interview is over, the HR manager strongly suggests the customer-service role go to this candidate. This phenomenon is also useful for understanding and explaining why people continue with a course of action and seek out information to support them in their endeavours, even when all of the indicators suggest that their chosen path is not the right one. In such situations, it is useful to play devil's advocate and challenge the decisions being made.

FUNDAMENTAL ATTRIBUTION ERROR

Fundamental attribution error is where individuals tend to attribute external factors to the causes of their own behaviour and attribute internal factors to the causes of others' behaviour. In an organisational context, for example, you might have a colleague who has been consistently late. You might perceive their tardiness as them being a lazy disorganised person (internal factors); however, when you are late the next day, you attribute it to your car needing fuel or your husband accidentally taking your car keys (external factors). Another example would be that if you had performed poorly on a performance evaluation, you might attribute this to having a poor evaluator or difficult work environment (external factors), whereas, when a co-worker performs poorly, you may attribute this to their poor performance and lack of work ethic (internal factors). We do this in order to maintain our existing perspective and to support our own perceptions. We don't like making adjustments to how we think about things and we will do what we can to preserve our viewpoint. Having an awareness of our tendency to preserve our self-belief can help us determine whether our viewpoint on a particular matter is relatively accurate, or is potentially skewed.

fundamental attribution error is where individuals attribute external causes to their own behaviour and internal causes to the behaviour of others.

ATTRIBUTION THEORY

Individuals like to be able to make sense of their world and to have answers for things. **Attribution theory** enables us to understand how perceptual errors might occur, particularly, fundamental attribution error, as well as explore how people form explanations regarding the behaviour of themselves and of others. One of the original researchers of attribution theory was Heider (1958), who suggested that behaviour in a particular situation is primarily attributed to either personal attitudes (internal forces) or situational factors (external forces). Managers, for example, must constantly assess employee behaviours, making sense of these behaviours by attributing the employee's behaviour to an internal cause, such as a lack of ability, or to an external factor, such as a lack of training. Kelley (1967) developed attribution theory with the co-variance model, which explained how people make attributions about the behaviour of others depending on different circumstances. He suggested that there are three variables which influence the explanations that people make about the behaviour of others (Kelley, 1967). These variables are consensus, consistency and distinctiveness, and can be linked together in different compositions. Let's look at what these terms mean:

attribution theory is used to describe the processes that individuals engage in to develop explanations for behaviours.

- **Consensus:** Whether the person's behaviour is similar to that of other people in the same situation.
  Example: An employee stands to eat lunch. If all employees stand while eating lunch, that employee's consensus is high. If only that employee stands to eat lunch, the employee's consensus is low.

- **Consistency:** Whether the person's behaviour is the same across time.
  Example: If an employee eats a salmon bagel for lunch every day, then that employee is high in consistency. If that employee only eats a salmon bagel for lunch on special occasions, then the consistency is low.
- **Distinctiveness:** Whether the person's behaviour is the same across situations.
  Example: If an employee only shows up late for work once, which is 'out of character' for them, then distinctiveness is high. If an employee shows up late for work often, then distinctiveness is low.

There are a number of different ways that these variables can be organised and the way in which they are organised can lead people to attribute behaviours to internal or external factors.

Let's look further at how attribution theory can help assist in explaining people's behaviour at work. We will explore two different scenarios using the same example of an employee who has received a poor result in a performance evaluation from their supervisor (see Figure 3.5).

Scenario One:

Low Consensus, High Consistency, Low Distinctiveness = Internal Factors

Scenario Two:

High Consensus, Low Consistency, High Distinctiveness = External Factors

Figure 3.5 Patterns of attribution elements

SCENARIO ONE

The supervisor has noted that the employee's job behaviour is usually poor (*high consistency*), other workers doing the same job and working in the same area as the employee have not performed poorly in the evaluation (*low consensus*) and the employee has again received a low rating on the performance evaluation sheet (*low distinctiveness*). The supervisor may then attribute the employee's poor performance to a lack of effort and a poor attitude at work (internal factors).

SCENARIO TWO

The supervisor is aware that the employee usually performs well in the performance evaluation (*high consistency*), other workers doing the same job and working in the same area have also performed poorly in the evaluation (*high consensus*), the employee's poor performance score is very unusual and the individual usually works well in any work environment (*high distinctiveness*). The supervisor may then attribute the employee's poor performance to a scoring error on the performance evaluation sheet (external factors).

As you can see, depending on the pattern of variables, behaviour in a given situation can be attributed to internal or to external factors. It is important managers and employees try to be objective when it comes to understanding the behaviours of others; rushing to judgement and overlooking external causes can lead to perceptual distortions ▶See Chapter 7◀.

Fundamental attribution error as mentioned earlier is where individuals tend to attribute external causes to their own behaviour and internal causes to the behaviour of others. People do this to preserve their self-beliefs. For instance, if an employee doesn't finish a project on time, a manager may attribute this to the employee being lazy (internal factor); however, if the manager doesn't himself finish a project on time, he may attribute this to a very busy work schedule (external factor). This is particularly useful to understand in a work context, not only with regard to how managers attribute explanations to the behaviour of employees, but also how co-workers attribute explanations to the behaviours of others and how employees attribute explanations to the behaviour of management.

MANAGERIAL TAKEAWAYS

In this chapter we have explained what perception is and how the process of perception works. We explored the concept of attention and how people select and attend to some environmental stimuli and not others, how they organise and interpret that material, and finally how they react to what they have taken in and processed. As individuals differ in how they perceive things, managers must remain aware of the different factors which might influence perceptions, such as an employee's personality, goals and motives, and culture. We also explored the possibility of error in the perception process and identified some of the common perceptual distortions that might occur in an organisational setting. It is important managers are aware of these common perceptual distortions. Recognising and being aware of their own biases can help them identify when a perceptual error is occurring. Playing devil's advocate or considering the reason behind their perceptions also might help to reduce perceptual distortions in decision-making. Last, we discovered how attribution theory helps clarify how individuals proccess and explain the behaviour of others and themselves. Here we shed light on causal attribution theory, which assists in making sense of how individuals attribute the behaviour of others, either through internal causes or external factors. As attribution theory demonstrates how fundamental attribution error can occur, it is necessary that managers, and even employees, do not rush to judgement or make assumptions about the behaviour of others. A common saying, 'put yourself in their shoes', might be a simple way to think about the realities of the situation at hand. Perception should be noted as an important psychological phenomenon at work. How individuals interpret and provide meaning to their reality or environment can affect an organisation, as it impacts people's experiences within the organisation, as well as their attitudes and behaviours at work. Managers should have knowledge of how the perceptual process works, and the common perceptual errors that might occur, to better understand how and why people might react or behave in certain ways at work.

 ## CHAPTER REVIEW QUESTIONS

1 How would you explain the concept of perception to an engineering student?
2 Why is understanding perception important to the study of organisational behaviour?
3 Can you explain the process of perception and the factors that are included in our perceptual set?
4 Can you explain the concept of a schema? Can you give an example of a schema?
5 What is a script? How does a script influence how we perceive things?
6 What is a perceptual error?

7   Can you provide examples of perceptual distortions that might occur in a work context?

8   How does attribution theory assist in explaining behaviour at work? What is fundamental attribution error?

 FURTHER READING

Bradley, L.M. (2006) Perceptions of justice when selecting internal and external ob candidates. *Personnel Review*, 35(1), 66–77.

Fiore, R.A. and Lee, L.W. (2017) Improving strategic decisions: Insights from multinational attributions to organizational outcomes. *Proceedings of the Northeastern Business and Economics Association*, 103–107.

Hentschel, T., Heilman, M. and Peus, C.V. (2019) The multiple dimensions of gender stereotypes: A current look at men's and women's characterizations of others and themselves. *Frontiers in Psychology*, 10(11), 1–19.

Mullins, L.J. (2007) *Management and Organisational Behaviour*. London: Pearson Education.

Ng, T.W.H., Yam, K.C. and Aguinis, H. (2019) Employee perceptions of corporate social responsibility: Effects on pride, embeddedness, and turnover. *Personnel Psychology*, 72(1), 107–137.

USEFUL WEBSITES

https://www.youtube.com/watch?v=8BL9uRJpTqY

A presentation which explores the relationship between perceptions and reality and how to 'mind the gap' between them.

http://video.ted.com/talk/podcast/2009G/None/BeauLotto_2009G-light.mp4

A TED Talk on perception that teaches us what we see is not always representative of reality.

https://www.youtube.com/watch?v=dfcnlADSuQ4

A presentation which helps explain the perceptual proccess and the research on perceptions and culture.

http://www.greatplacetowork.ie/

Check this website out and explore their Employee Trust Survey, which examines employees' perceptions of satisfaction with their work environment.

Online Resources

Visit **bloomsbury.pub/organisational-behaviour** to access additional materials to support teaching and learning.

4 ATTITUDES AND JOB SATISFACTION

Ultan Sherman

LEARNING OUTCOMES

BY THE END OF THIS CHAPTER YOU SHOULD BE ABLE TO:

- Understand what is meant by the term 'attitude'.
- Analyse the process of attitude formation.
- Assess how attitudes and behaviour are connected.
- Decide what is meant by the term 'job satisfaction' and explain why it is an important concept in the organisational behaviour literature.
- Distinguish between important work-related attitudes and analyse the implications they have for the organisation.

CREDIT: PHOTO BY IESHOOTS.COM ON UNSPLASH

THIS CHAPTER DISCUSSES ...

INTRODUCTION

When applying for a job in the past you may have noticed in the person specification that the employing organisation was looking for candidates who have 'a positive attitude'. Indeed, organisations often make important decisions regarding an employee based on their attitude (e.g. *she has the right attitude for this project so let's bring her onto the team*'). But what do we actually mean by the term 'attitude'? Is it a behaviour in the sense that you can observe an attitude in action? Is it a mind-set where one consciously perceives the world in a certain way? To answer these, and other questions, this chapter draws on contemporary research in work-related attitudes and provides real-life examples of how exploring attitudes can contribute to our understanding of behaviour in organisations. In particular, we focus on 'job satisfaction', one of the most widely researched topics in the organisational behaviour field, and assess its practical value to employers and organisations alike. Overall, we discuss the contribution of 'attitude theory' to how we understand behaviour in the work environment.

IN REALITY

Do you know the generation to which you 'belong'? You might be a 'Millennial' (born between 1980 and 1990), a 'Baby-Boomer' (born between 1946 and 1965), or some of you might be members of the latest cohort 'Generation Z' (born after 2000). Research on generational differences has been a long-standing feature of Organisational Behaviour with many scholars arguing that the generation to which you belong shapes your relationship with your job (e.g. De Hauw and De Vos, 2010). For instance, studies in this area suggest that Millennials are more creative at work than previous generations (e.g. Graham, 2014) or that Generation Xers (born between 1965 and 1979) have a stronger work ethic (Barnett, 2017). Consequently, many organisations believe that exploring generational differences at work allows them to gain a competitive advantage in terms of how certain employees should be managed or developed accordingly. Indeed, 'generation consultants' are increasingly being hired by leading organisations as a means of better understanding their workforce. However, research by Constanza and colleagues (2012) has called attention to what they call the 'myth' of generational differences. In a meta-analysis of existing generational research, they found little if any difference across contrasting generations regarding important work-related attitudes such as job satisfaction or organisational commitment. The authors argued that any differences found could be explained by 'age' rather than 'generation'. This, and related studies highlighting the confusion over the date ranges of particular generations, for instance, challenge universally held truths that employee behaviour can be explained by the generation to which they belong and raises important questions about the value of generational research to our understanding or organisational behaviour.

EXPLAINING THE TERM 'ATTITUDE'

The eminent social psychologist Gordon Allport wrote, almost 90 years ago:

> '*The concept of attitudes is probably the most distinctive and indispensable concept in ... social psychology*' (Allport, 1935, p. 798).

His statement is no less true today as exploring attitudes allows us to understand how others view the world. The term 'attitude' has entered our everyday vernacular. We have different attitudes towards our families, friends, work, music, and so on which direct how we behave in relation to each one of them. Some of you might *believe* that Taylor Swift is the greatest pop star in the world. As a result, you may have bought all her albums and attended some of her concerts. Others might *feel* she is overrated and *change* the song when they hear her music on a playlist. So, what is an attitude? If we examine the words italicised above it suggests that attitudes are beliefs or feelings or behaviours. Like many concepts within the organisational behaviour field there are competing theories drawn upon to define the term 'attitude', although Allport is arguably the father of attitude research, and most subsequent research is congruent with his definition. We define attitudes as evaluative judgements relating to people, events or objects.

attitudes are evaluative judgements relating to people, events or objects.

There is much debate as to what constitutes an attitude. Some theorists prefer a one-component attitude model, specifically the *affective* component (e.g. Thurstone, 1931). Other theorists propose a two-component attitude model, incorporating a *cognitive* component into the one-component model (e.g. Petty and Cacioppo, 1986). They argue that exploring the cognitive underpinnings of attitudes can tell us something different about how they function in a way that the affective component cannot. A third approach is the three-component model incorporating a *behavioural* component. Therefore, there are potentially three different components of an attitude:

1 **Cognitive component:** This refers to the values and beliefs that the individual holds about a particular person or thing. The idea here is that an individual will perceive and make sense of the world in a way that is unique and subjective ▸**See Chapter 3◂**. For example, a first-year student at the National University of Singapore may hold particular values and beliefs about her new university. One belief may be that she is now studying at one of the world's most prestigious academic institutions. This is likely to be a source of pride for the student – the underlying value supporting the belief.

2 **Affective component:** This points to the feelings and emotions arising from an evaluation of the two elements in the cognition component. An individual making sense of an object, event, situation, etc. evokes an emotional or affective reaction. For instance, the Singapore student would typically develop feelings about the university related to the inherent beliefs and values she holds about it. For example, she might have a great sense of accomplishment for having been accepted into the university. However, she might also feel greater pressure in terms of her academic performance given the high standards expected of Singapore students. The affective component of attitude structure tends to be learned from our environment (this is discussed below).

3 **Behavioural component:** This is about the behavioural outcome of the process. This behaviour stems from the affective component of the model. The affective reaction will dictate the subsequent behaviour or action. Again, using the Singapore student as an example, she may make an extra effort at her studies given the expectation of success for Singapore students. Of course, the cognitive and affective components can change over time, which in turn results in a change in behaviour. She could, perhaps, lose interest in her course, resulting in a change in behaviour (for example, she might change her course or drop out of the university).

These three components have a profound influence in our everyday life. They essentially make up the ABCs of attitudes. Reich and Adcock (1976) argue that if attitudes refer to phenomena that are not directly observable but only inferred, then the behavioural component of an attitude by itself cannot fully illustrate the attitude. Broadly speaking, the cognitive, affective and behavioural components need to be assessed together to fully understand the dynamics of the attitude itself.

ATTITUDE FORMATION

As discussed above, our attitudes are a manifestation of cognitive, affective and behavioural processes. However, it is important to examine how these attitudes are created in the first place. Many philosophers believe that we are born with a 'tabula rasa' (Latin for 'blank state'), effectively without any mental content. Our knowledge and perception come from experience as we develop. The argument here is that our attitudes are formed as we develop, with new experiences shaping how we view the world. This developmental process is complex with a number of competing theories often cited to explain it. We will examine the main theories put forward in the literature to explain how our attitudes are created.

1 **Dispositional characteristics:** It is generally accepted that underlying personality predispositions influence attitude formation. Our personality is relatively stable but can change over time with the onset of new experiences. A number of studies have shown how different personality traits affect behaviour (for example, 'extroversion' and public speaking; 'conscientiousness' and adhering to rules; 'emotional stability' and staying calm under pressure) ▶See Chapter 2◀. In the work environment, behavioural manifestations of inherent personality characteristics can be easily observed. For example, air stewards are expected to be knowledgeable about the rules and regulations concerning air travel and to adhere to them at all times. They are also expected to be stoic when interacting with the passengers. For this reason, conscientiousness and emotional stability are two personality dimensions that are sought in candidates when airlines are recruiting for these positions. Their attitude towards established procedure must be unwavering, even in challenging situations.

2 **Direct experience:** Many of the attitudes that people hold are the result of direct experience with attitude objects. Attitude objects are the 'things' in our environment with which we directly interact (for example, school, friends, pensioners). People tend to have positive or negative experiences with these objects, which can go some way to influencing their attitudes. A jobseeker after a number of unsuccessful interviews may view future interviews in a pessimistic light. A famous example from psychology is the Little Albert case. Albert was an infant participating in an experiment investigating associations between different stimuli. In the experiment, Albert played with a pet rat and displayed no visible signs of fear or panic. Later, when loud, frightening noises were repeatedly made whenever Albert played with the rat he began to cry. Eventually, just seeing the rat (no longer paired with the loud noises) aroused feelings of panic and fear in the infant. Accordingly, due to his unpleasant encounter Albert formed a very negative attitude towards the rat. In a broader sense, this experiment investigated classical conditioning, an important concept in learning and behaviour. Classical conditioning emphasises the role of direct experience in shaping an attitude and associated behaviour.

classical conditioning happens when, through repeated association, a formerly neutral stimulus can elicit a reaction that was previously elicited only by another stimulus.

3 **Social learning:** While direct experience certainly plays a significant role in the construction of attitudes, another approach views attitude formation solely as a social learning process. The actions of other people in our social environment shape our attitudes too. For an infant, parents are arguably the most important source of information in attitude formation. Often, we follow a similar career path to those of our parents. However, Connell (1972) found that, although a positive correlation existed between the specific attitudes of parents and their children towards a given issue, it is also a rather weak relationship. Beyond a family context, wider socio-cultural factors influence how we view the world. Bandura (1986) developed a social learning theory whereby people learn by observing the behaviour of other people in their social environment. He has also likened attitude formation to a process of modelling whereby one person models their behaviour on a referent other. His famous 'Bobo' Doll experiment neatly captured this modelling process. Children watched adults attacking an inflatable doll and receiving encouragement and positive feedback for their actions. Later, when children were alone in the room with Bobo, many attacked him in a similar way to the adults. To most children, adults are seen to be significant models on which to base behaviour. While parents have a powerful influence on the child, adults are also shaped by the behaviour of others in their social environment. In a work context, new recruits model their behaviour on what Morrison (1993) refers to as 'organisational insiders'. Many new recruits are assigned a mentor upon organisational entry in the hope that they will acquire important information, understand the culture of the organisation, and learn the 'right' attitude from their more experienced counterpart. Indeed, co-workers pass on social cues to the new entrant throughout the socialisation process, resulting in a broad 'homogenisation' of the workforce ▸See Chapter 11◂. For example, if a new employee notices that his first 'staff night out' is very well attended by the employees, then this will be perceived as a cue to guide future behaviour. It is likely that the new recruit will continue to attend future staff events in light of this newly acquired information. Many organisational factors play a role in attitude formation, such as leadership style ▸See Chapter 6◂, organisational culture ▸See Chapter 12◂ and work design.

> socialisation is the process of learning how to think, feel and behave by conforming to and imitating influential others within social settings.

These three factors have informed a lot of research into work-related attitudes. For instance, affective events theory (AET) is often drawn upon by researchers to make sense of behaviour in organisations. This theory encapsulates the idea that our attitudes stem from individual characteristics and from our interactions with and observations of the social environment (Brief and Weiss, 2002). Specifically, it suggests that the work environment and work events can evoke an emotional reaction in an employee depending on their dispositional characteristics, which influence how they react and subsequently behave. Let's say, following a meeting with senior management about future redundancies in the firm (see the 'Impact of Technology on Behaviour' feature), an emotionally stable employee believes that if he achieves a high level of performance, he will be kept on. Accordingly, he is more likely to put in a bigger effort and work harder. A less emotionally stable person may react differently to news of the redundancy, resulting in contrasting behaviour. Underpinning AET is the idea that human behaviour is guided by both cognitive and emotional elements.

In an overall sense, the source of our attitudes originates from our interaction with our social environment, through direct experience and vicariously through observation and modelling. We can now say that our attitudes are shaped by and shape our interaction with the world.

IMPACT OF TECHNOLOGY ON BEHAVIOUR

The film *Up in the Air*, starring George Clooney and Anna Kendrick, introduces the idea of making people redundant using online telecommunications. That is, an employee is told they are being made redundant by a stranger on screen. Of course, more and more organisations are outsourcing their HR operations to outside firms for issues relating to payroll, benefits administration and layoffs.

While these external firms often have long-lasting relationships with the hiring organisation it raises questions about the appropriateness of being made redundant by someone who is not your manager or direct superior. Does it matter how an employee is ultimately let go? Would it change your attitudes towards your job, knowing that the organisation would prefer that a stranger or maybe even an AI robot told you that you were losing your job?

CREDIT: GETTY IMAGES/CULTURA RF

CONNECTING ATTITUDES AND BEHAVIOUR

Attitudes and behaviour are closely linked, but it is a complex relationship. Simply holding an attitude towards an object does not predict behaviour in relation to that object. For example, an employee may feel that team-building exercises are a waste of time. However, this does not mean that she will refuse to participate in any such activity. There are other factors at play. Ajzen (1991) has developed an important model capturing this association (see Figure 4.1). His theory of the planned behaviour model posits that attitude towards the behaviour, subjective social and environmental norms (discussed above) and perception of behavioural control (the extent to which the person believes they are in control of the situation) lead to the formation of a behavioural intention. Behavioural intention then predicts behaviour.

So, this model highlights that holding an attitude towards a specific object does not directly predict that a person will behave in a corresponding way towards that object. Social norms and behavioural control beliefs mediate the relationship between attitudes and behaviour. Let's say an employee is thinking about applying for an internal position within the organisation. She may view this post as an exciting opportunity (attitude toward the behaviour). If she believes she has a good chance of being successful (perceived behavioural control) and if the organisation is one that encourages internal promotion (subjective norms) then it is likely that she will intend to apply for the position. Again, the ABC model of attitudes is at the core of this theory. Ajzen's research in this domain has been particularly helpful in understanding and predicting behaviour in a wide variety of contexts.

Indeed, people are often very inconsistent in their espoused attitudes and beliefs and how they subsequently behave. For example, people often value their health, yet they smoke. How

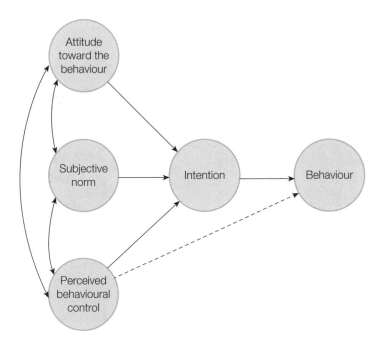

Figure 4.1 Theory of planned behaviour

Source: Adapted from Ajzen (1991).

many of you believe using your mobile phone while driving is reckless, but still do it? Festinger (1957) developed the concept of cognitive dissonance to explain the often complicated relationship between the different components of attitude structure. Cognitive dissonance is an unpleasant cognitive state that motivates an individual to resolve perceived conflict among beliefs, attitudes and behaviours. The dissonance is an uncomfortable or stressful feeling that one often experiences with perceived inconsistency between cognitions and behaviour. For example, a director of an environmental charity who regularly takes first-class flights around the world may experience dissonance as a result of the conflict between her travel patterns (i.e. a high carbon footprint) and the values of the organisation she leads (protecting the environment) (see the 'Ethical Behaviour in the Workplace' feature). However, if an attitude is not particularly important to the individual, then the incongruent behaviour creates relatively little dissonance.

Of course, different contexts will lead to different levels of dissonance. This unpleasant feeling can be resolved by changing one element of the structure to restore consonance, for example, changing your view of the object, in this case cigarettes (cognitive), giving up smoking (behavioural), rationalising that smoking light cigarettes is less harmful (belief). Recently, many schools in Britain found themselves under the spotlight for the nutritional content of the food provided to their students. Both parenting groups and the media questioned how a school could, on the one hand, espouse the principles of science yet, on the other, neglect to educate their students on the values of healthy dietary habits. As a result of this negative press, many of these schools removed vending machines containing sugary snacks and ensured canteens served more nutritious food for the students. Cognitive dissonance is an important concept in organisational behaviour as it furthers our understanding of the link between cognition, emotions and behaviour.

cognitive dissonance is an unpleasant cognitive state that motivates an individual to resolve perceived conflict among beliefs, attitudes and behaviours.

◀ ETHICAL ▶ BEHAVIOUR IN THE WORKPLACE

In recent years the phenomenon of 'whistleblowing' has gained considerable attention from both academics and practitioners alike. Whistleblowing is when an individual or group of individuals discloses in-group (see below) wrongdoing to an external agency (Anvari *et al.*, 2019). For instance, many people consider Edward Snowden a hero for exposing the National Security Agency (NSA) in the

CREDIT: GETTY IMAGES

United States and their attempts to obtain private information about people all around the world. Whistleblowing touches on the notion of cognitive dissonance in that whistleblowers often experience dissonance before they act. Reflecting on your own work experience, are you likely to be a whistleblower if you witness corruption or wrongdoing in your firm? Remember, most people say and do nothing in these instances. In the context of managing organisations, what can firms do to ensure whistleblowing is encouraged and supported?

ATTITUDE CHANGE

Earlier in the chapter we examined the environmental forces that influence the creation of attitudes. Similarly, there are myriad factors that are responsible for bringing about attitude change. From a management perspective, an organisation needs to mould and shape new recruits into participating members of the firm as quickly as possible. This often requires a change in attitude and behaviour ▶See Chapter 11◀. As discussed, social norms help shape the new recruit to align with the culture of the organisation. When an employee joins an organisation, they bring with them a belief system that has been constructed and developed over time with experience. This belief system dictates how they view the new work environment. Studies have shown that employees adjust their attitude and behaviour in accordance with the information that they have received. Thus, those of new employees are likely to change towards those of experienced insiders as they become accepted as an integral part of the company (Thomas and Anderson, 1998).

There are many other organisational forces that can bring about attitude change, such as punitive procedures, rewards, and so on, but it is important to directly examine how the change itself occurs. Consider the scenario described in 'Building Your Employability Skills: Conflict Management', where a change in attitude may be required from both parties:

BUILDING YOUR EMPLOYABILITY ▚▚▚▚ SKILLS

Conflict Management

Imagine you are the human resource director in a small medical supplies company with 205 employees. You are a smoker and, like some other employees at the firm, you regularly use the designated smoking areas. One day you receive an e-mail from an employee with a petition containing signatures of over 150 non-smoking employees asking for smoking to be prohibited from all areas of the organisation. How do you resolve this issue?

Certainly, the process of attitude change is a matter of great interest to managers and those in positions of authority. Hovland *et al.* (1953) were among the first researchers to explore the factors that contributed to attitude change. For Hovland and his colleagues, the key issue in their study was understanding the principles of persuasion. Persuasion is a form of learning, so the underlying theoretical mechanism of their study was learning theory. Any factor that influenced the learning of a message was considered central to understanding attitude change. They divided these factors into three separate categories: the communicator; the audience; and the communication. A credible source of communication was predicted to produce persuasion because it was believed to be more rewarding to agree with someone who is more likely to be perceived as correct (Crano *et al.*, 2010). However, the researchers found that less credible sources were often more persuasive in certain circumstances, undermining their proposition. The audience were assumed to affect the persuasion process through their attention levels. The study found that the persuasiveness of the message was associated with how well the audience attended to it. Finally, the message itself was examined in terms of its content (e.g. the strength of the inherent argument). This too had an effect on the level of persuasiveness. While the scientific merit of this study has been questioned by certain researchers (Wanous, 1990) it is an important milestone in attitude change research as it highlights the multiple factors at play in bringing about a change in attitude.

In attempting to examine the factors that influence persuasion, the Hovland study calls attention to the reasons explaining why and how people change their attitudes. Arguably, the most dominant theory to explain the attitude change process is Cognitive Response Theory. A Cognitive Response is a thought created in response to persuasive communication. Often the thoughts generated trigger an attitude change. An individual interprets the message using pre-existing thoughts they already hold about the subject. An attitude is then changed (or not changed) depending on the degree of incentive to generate their attitude in the first place (Greenwald, 1968). For example, during a presidential election campaign a voter with a slight preference for one candidate may change her mind upon hearing a rallying speech by the opponent. On the other hand, a staunch supporter of one candidate is unlikely to change their mind under any circumstances. Cognitive Response Theory highlights the importance of initial thoughts (cognition) to a message in triggering an attitude change.

Other factors influencing this persuasion process have been examined in the literature. For example, Popovich and Wanous (1982) highlight how the *medium* through which the message is delivered is an important factor influencing persuasion. Indeed, *how* important information is communicated to the employee influences their response. If an organisation is forced to make a number of their staff redundant, the medium through which the message is communicated takes on greater significance. Informing a staff member that they are to be sacked through a text message or via Twitter is likely to evoke a much more negative reaction (think about the fact that more and more football managers appear to learn of their dismissal through unofficial sources before they hear from the club itself, and the impact this must have not only on the manager but on the remaining staff too). Taken together, these, and other studies, highlight the multiple ways through which an attitude can change.

'Forced contact' has been shown to decrease racial prejudice (Deutsch and Collins, 1951). The contention here is that forced interaction will 'normalise' relations between different groups of people. Relating this to an organisational example, a teacher may 'relocate' an errant student to an area in the class where he or she will interact with more diligent students, with the intention that this 'forced contact' will bring about a change in that student's attitude and subsequent behaviour. All of these studies highlight both the multiple causes accounting for attitude change but also the cognitive activity intrinsic to the change process.

Winning the Lottery

In June 2006, high-school janitor Tyrone Curry (56) won $3.4 million in the Washington State lottery. To celebrate his victory, he went bowling with his friends that evening at the local alley. The following morning his alarm sounded at 4 am and he headed into work, just as he did every morning. Today, Tyrone still works at the same high school.

OB IN THE NEWS

When asked why he kept up his job, he replied 'You need to be doing stuff. That's my philosophy.' For Tyrone, it seems that his job at the high school means more than simply a way to pay the bills. Tyrone viewed 'work' in a different way.

If you were in Tyrone's position, would you continue to work? Trying to predict how a person would answer this question is difficult. There is a wide range of factors that could influence their response. For example, age is likely to be a relevant factor in the decision. A person close to retirement may be more likely to quit their job than someone in their thirties. The occupation itself is likely to be an important variable affecting the decision. If someone is working in a job perceived to be particularly unpleasant then it is reasonable to assume that they would not continue to work, or that they'd certainly change their job. However, in November 2014, George Kinghorn (60) won £1 million in the European Union lottery. However, when asked if he would give up his gruelling offshore oil rig job, he insisted that 'he would carry on working'. In George's case, winning the lotto did not change his perception of his job. Both of these examples clearly demonstrate that there is more to work than simply money.

Arvey et al. (2004) examined the post-award work behaviour of lotto winners. They found that the size of the jackpot as well

CREDIT: PHOTO BY DYLAN NOTTE ON UNSPLASH

as the level of 'work centrality' determined their decision to continue working. Work centrality is an important concept in work-related attitudes and it refers to the general importance of work in an individual's life compared with other activities such as leisure, spending time with friends or family (Kanungo, 1982). When someone attaches a significant degree of importance to their employment, they are likely to behave in a certain way in and around their job. Indeed, understanding a person's level of work centrality allows us to better predict their behaviour in the work environment. Work centrality is just one of many work-related attitudes assessed in the organisational behaviour field.

Questions

1 How big a jackpot would convince you to never work again? How would you fill your time? Do we need 'to be doing stuff'?

2 Besides the financial reasons, what does an individual gain from working? Are these factors important?

3 Is age an important issue when understanding an individual's relationship with their job?

Sources

http://www.dailymail.co.uk/news/article-2012235/Lottery-winner-works-school-janitor-Tyrone-Curry-won-3-4m.html

https://www.pressandjournal.co.uk/fp/news/north-east/415759/north-east-couple-scoop-1million-on-euromillions/

PREJUDICE, STEREOTYPES AND DISCRIMINATION

Earlier in the chapter we explained how certain social factors influence how attitudes are formed. A significant concept in this area is that of 'in-groups' and 'out-groups'. Attitudes towards members of both groups are one of the most widely researched topics in the field. Broadly speaking, we have a preference for people similar to ourselves (i.e. members of the in-group) over those considered dissimilar (i.e. members of the out-group). Accordingly, inter-group attitudes are particularly prone to irrational, affective distortions (Allport, 1954). There is an affective element pervasive in intergroup relations, and interaction with the in-group and out-group can evoke positive and negative emotions respectively. Affect (or emotion) is thus likely to influence intergroup judgements both through the information processing strategies used and the way further information is selected and used (Forgas *et al.*, 2007). When an individual encounters an out-group, their level of anxiety is heightened, which reduces their capacity to process information objectively. For this reason, the individual resorts to stereo-typing ▸**See Chapter 3◂**. The tendency to see all out-group members in stereotypical ways can be observed in a variety of contexts (for example, 'salespeople are exploitative and aggressive', 'Irish people have a drink problem', and so on). While stereotypes can exist about people as well as things, this chapter solely addresses stereotypes about people in a work context.

Stereotyping is a mental shortcut that helps individuals to make sense of another person or a group of people. It allows us to 'fill in the blanks' on an individual about whom we know very little. Often, this can lead to benefits. In the work environment stereotyping allows us to categorise employees into groups. For example, those entering an organisation from college or university often join as part of a graduate programme. The underlying notion being that every graduate (and the organisation itself) will be best served by the various processes of this programme (i.e. induction, training, mentoring). Such a programme supposes that each graduate requires a comprehensive introduction to the work environment given their assumed lack of work experience. It is argued that this socialisation process can have a positive effect in reducing turnover among new entrants (e.g. Feldman, 1981). However, stereotyping can also

in-groups are social groups to which an individual believes he or she belongs.

out-groups are social groups to which an individual believes he or she does not belong.

lead to problems for organisations. It is likely that one may overlook the array of differences and level of individuality of people being stereotyped. For example, an organisation may not select a female candidate for a position on the assumption that she plans on having children in the near future, thus creating a future short-term vacancy. This, of course, limits the applicant pool for the organisation, and can result in the best candidates being overlooked.

Stereotyping often has an enduring quality. Even in the face of contradictory information, people can go to great lengths to sustain the original stereotype. They seek out information that supports and protects the established view and ignore information that may refute it. Thus, confirmation bias is closely linked with stereotyping. For example, when a line manager is rating an employee's performance as part of the performance management process they may focus on incidents where the employee performed poorly and ignore instances of high performance in line with their existing negative view of the employee.

prejudice can be defined as a negative attitude towards members of a specific group and can be either explicit or implicit.

When an individual holds a stereotyped view of certain types of people, they are often accused of being prejudiced. The concept of 'prejudice' falls neatly within the attitude domain. It can be considered to be an example of an extreme attitude. Prejudice can be defined as a negative attitude towards members of a specific group and can be either explicit or implicit. Prejudicial attitudes can be consciously or unconsciously held. Prejudice can be either explicit and conscious (e.g. critical remarks about a person based on their race) or implicit and unconscious (e.g. believing it is important to show female employees the crèche facilities on site during induction but not the male employees). In line with the ABC structure of an attitude, to be prejudiced against someone implies that we feel, behave and think about that person in a negative way (Reich and Adcock, 1976).

SPOTLIGHT ON SKILLS

You are the HR manager in a small call centre. The work is repetitive and monotonous. Labour turnover is high. In fact, less than 50% of your staff have more than one year's service with the firm. Starting salary for operators is €22,000 per annum.

What can you do to ensure operators hold positive attitudes towards their work?

How important is job design in shaping an individual's work-related attitudes?

To help you answer these questions, visit bloomsbury.pub/organisational-behaviour to watch the video of Melissa Challinor from Which? talking about attitudes.

As we saw above, prejudice tends to endure even in the face of conflicting evidence. For example, a successful encounter with a builder may not dispel the view that all builders are lazy and unscrupulous. The prejudiced person is capable of rationalising the incident in such a way (e.g. 'this was a one-off') that the stereotype prevails. In a famous study of anti-Semitism among female university students, Frenkel-Brunswik and Sanford (1945) found that those women who held deep-rooted prejudice against Jews displayed repressed hatred and suspicion of parental figures. In effect, the students were projecting on the Jews their entrenched attitudes that would be normally directed at their parents. This is a good example of how innate factors, stemming in this case from the students' relationship with their parents, can shape how we see the world.

While stereotyping is a belief and prejudice is an attitude, discrimination is an act. Believing all female employees are too emotional in the workplace is a stereotype. Resenting them for this perceived characteristic is prejudice. Actively overlooking them for a position because of their group membership is discrimination. As we have discussed, behaviour does not always follow attitude and discrimination is not an inevitable consequence of prejudice. An employer may be prejudiced against men but she may not act upon her negative attitude for fear of the consequences. Nevertheless, discrimination is a significant issue in the work environment. Many countries have established legislation that protects employee rights in terms of workplace discrimination. Sex, age, ethnicity, religion and sexuality are all grounds against which an individual can be discriminated. As the workplace becomes increasingly diverse, the threat of discrimination becomes more apparent. In response to this, organisations invest significant time and money in ensuring all work practices are free of discrimination. Important decisions involving, for example, recruitment and selection, promotion, and so on, should not be made on grounds that may be perceived to be discriminatory.

discrimination is unjustified negative behaviour towards a group or its members.

Of particular relevance to a work context is the issue of positive discrimination. The argument here is that in order for minority groups to receive the same opportunities as the majority group, some form of discrimination must occur. A famous example is the 'Rooney Rule' in American football (named after former US ambassador and former chairman of the Pittsburgh Steelers football team, Dan Rooney). National Football League (NFL) teams are required to interview minority candidates for high-ranking coaching and operation positions in the team. In almost 80 years before the Rooney Rule was established in 2003, only six non-white head coaches had been appointed. In the 17 years since, 14 have been hired. Had this rule not existed it is unlikely that these coaches would have been given such an opportunity.

positive discrimination is preferential discriminatory treatment of members of a minority group over a majority group.

WORK-RELATED ATTITUDES

Many different work-related attitudes have been examined by researchers. For the purposes of this chapter, we will explore the attitudes that have received the most attention in the literature. First, job satisfaction is a type of work attitude. It is one of the most widely researched measures in organisational behaviour literature due to the much hypothesised view that it has a direct effect on important workplace outcomes. Job satisfaction, according to Locke (1976), is a pleasurable or positive emotional state resulting from the appraisal of one's job or job experiences. When an employee has a high level of job satisfaction, they tend to view their job in a positive light. When dissatisfied with their job they tend to hold a negative attitude towards it. There are an unquantifiable number of factors that influence job satisfaction and researchers agree that it is difficult to develop a comprehensive model of its antecedents. We next explain three perspectives on job satisfaction, with each approach offering a unique insight into the origins of this attitude (Baker, 2004):

job satisfaction is a positive emotional state occurring as a consequence of appraising one's job and job experience.

1 **Task characteristics approach:** This perspective proposes that certain task characteristics are related to employee attitudes. Five key dimensions have been identified that influence levels of job satisfaction: (1) autonomy; (2) job feedback from the job; (3) job variety; (4) task identity; and (5) task significance. Consequently, this argument contends that if an

employee is in a job where these criteria are being fulfilled there is an increased likelihood of reported job satisfaction.

2   **Social information processing approach:** This situational approach has been proposed as an alternative to the task characteristics approach (Salancik and Pfeffer, 1978). As has been discussed, job attitudes are shaped by social cues processed from the work environment. A number of studies have found that certain socio-organisational factors impact upon job satisfaction, for example leadership (Lok and Crawford, 2004); organisational culture (Egan *et al.*, 2004); and teamwork ▶**See Chapter 7◄** (Griffin *et al.*, 2001).

3   **Dispositional approach:** This perspective indicates that the individual possesses dispositional characteristics that impact upon levels of job satisfaction. Studies show support for intrinsic motivation (e.g. Schonfeld, 2000); positive/negative affectivity (such as happiness/anxiety (e.g. Simmons *et al.*, 2001), and self-efficacy (e.g. Judge and Bono, 2001). Self-efficacy is an important concept in organisational behaviour (Bandura, 1977). In the context of work-related attitudes, it shapes how an individual views their employment, and their likely behaviour in the workplace. For example, an employee with high self-efficacy is likely to view an upcoming project or task with optimism, confident that they will be able to perform effectively.

self-efficacy refers to an individual's judgement of their capacity to execute behaviours necessary to produce specific performance attainments.

Therefore, we can view job satisfaction in three ways: as a function of (1) the characteristics of an employee's job; (2) information sourced from referent others in the organisation; or (3) a person's dispositional characteristics.

MEASURING JOB SATISFACTION

Since attitudes are not directly observable, they can only be measured indirectly. This presents a number of methodological difficulties for researchers. The most obvious approach is to simply ask people, and the majority of research has adopted this line of enquiry.

Typically, attitude questionnaires ask respondents to indicate whether they agree or disagree with a series of 'belief' statements about an attitude object. Questionnaires, or 'instruments' as they are known, are designed using 'factor analysis' (a common scientific method to reduce a large set of variables into a smaller set). The technique ensures the instrument has the correct number of statements that best capture the variability of the attitude being measured. Each statement is referred to as an 'item'. The number of items in an instrument varies markedly depending very much on the type of attitude being measured. For example, a job satisfaction questionnaire might ask candidates to what extent they are happy about their current career opportunities in the organisation, or their current level of salary. Regardless of the number of items used, the final statements included in an instrument need to be carefully selected. Each item should represent a different and independent perspective on the attitude being measured. Factor analysis is helpful in this regard in identifying the most significant items. Building on the work of Thurstone (1928), Likert (1932) developed an effective technique to measure attitudes. A number of attitude statements are presented to respondents. They are then asked to determine the extent of their agreement or disagreement with these statements using a 5-point scale, with the two poles typically labelled '*strongly agree*' and '*strongly disagree*'. There are other techniques used to measure attitudes, such as *Guttman's Scalogram Method* and *Osgood's Semantic Differential*, but the Likert Scale has been the dominant methodological approach used in modern questionnaires.

Work Centrality Scale (see above)

Respondents specify their agreement ranging from strongly agree (5) to strongly disagree (1) to the following six items:

1 The most important things that happen in life involve work.

2 Work is something people should get involved in most of the time.

3 Work should be only a small part of one's life (reverse scored).

4 Work should be considered central to life.

5 In my view, an individual's personal life goals should be work-oriented.

6 Life is worth living only when people get absorbed in work.

The higher the score, the higher the level of work centrality.

Source: Arvey et al. *(1996).*

There are of course a number of problems to be considered when measuring attitudes in general. Participants' responses can be affected by a wide variety of biases which render the outcome of the instrument invalid. For example, in an effort to portray a socially acceptable view of the world, the participant may not answer truthfully. This is known as social desirability. Or a respondent holding a prejudiced view against a certain group of people (e.g. women) would run counter to a prevailing norm (e.g. equality). Often attitude measurement suffers from definitional and operational difficulties, which goes some way to explaining why the field of attitude measurement often contains conflicting results. For instance, job satisfaction can be measured in a number of different ways, such as surveys, interviews and critical incident technique. Each method for measuring job satisfaction has its own limitations and it is recommended that a mixed-methods approach be used, to more accurately measure the concept, such as combining both an interview and a questionnaire approach.

JOB SATISFACTION AND PERFORMANCE

The big question in research on job satisfaction concerns its consequences. Does job satisfaction predict job performance? The 'human relations' movement in the middle of the 20th century called attention to the positive outcomes of job satisfaction, such as higher levels of performance and productivity. Empirical support for this notion is, however, somewhat weak. For example, Vroom (1964) found a correlation of .13 between overall job performance and overall job satisfaction, which represents a very tenuous relationship between the two. A similarly weak relationship has been found in a number of subsequent studies (e.g. Riketta, 2008; Podsakoff and Williams, 1986). Judge *et al.* (2001) outline six possible ways in which job satisfaction and job performance are linked (see Figure 4.2).

The oft-cited expression 'happy workers are productive workers' is a good example of the assumptions that people make about the association between attitudes and behaviour. As we can see in Figure 4.2, the relationship is a lot more complex than simply cause and effect. The Judge *et al.* (2001) research above is seen to be a landmark study in this area. Their findings suggest a modest relationship between satisfaction and performance. However, the multi-faceted nature of job satisfaction and job performance presents methodological difficulties for researchers investigating the causal link between these concepts. Universal measures of both concepts lack scientific value. It is a much more valid approach to investigate the relationship between specific components of satisfaction and specific components of performance. More attention needs to be paid to the shaping role of third variables, such as rewards, as outlined in Model 4 and Model 5 in Figure 4.2. For example, do satisfied employees with a salary of 80,000 dollars perform better than satisfied employees with a lower salary level? Answering questions like this will further our understanding of the relationship between job satisfaction and job performance.

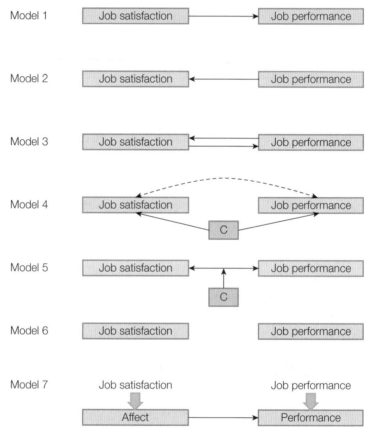

Figure 4.2 The relationship between job satisfaction and job performance

Source: Judge et al. *(2001).*

ATTITUDES TOWARDS THE ORGANISATION: CONTINUANCE, NORMATIVE AND AFFECTIVE COMMITMENT

organisational commitment is an individual's comparative strength of identification and involvement with an organisation.

The concept of organisational commitment has received considerable attention from researchers over the last 30 years. Most employers seek commitment from their employees as a means of ensuring that goals and targets are met and of achieving overall strategic roles. However, a sense of organisational commitment can be difficult to engender in the workforce.

There are many variables that influence it. One such variable is job security. However, in recent years job security is no longer as readily available and stable as it once was. The upheaval caused by the financial crisis has seen millions of people around the world lose their jobs. How can an organisation gain commitment from the employees if their job may not exist in six months? For this reason, employees now seek security from their profession and no longer from the organisation. The idea here is that the employee will remain committed to the organisation as long as the employer increases their level of employability, for example through upskilling and providing educational opportunities. If the employee is then made redundant, they know that they are likely to find new opportunities elsewhere because of this higher level of employability. This 'new deal' has characterised the employment relationship over the last quarter century (Guest, 2004). It is important to understand the context in which the employment relationship plays out. As explained earlier, socio-economic factors can also shape an employee's commitment to the firm. Job security is just one of many antecedents of organisational commitment and there are many possible reasons, besides the security inherent in the job itself, as to why employees commit their future to an organisation.

Similar to job satisfaction, commitment does not guarantee a higher level of work performance. Also, it is generally accepted to be a multi-faceted construct. For example, Allen and Meyer (1990) have distinguished between different types of commitment:

1 **Affective commitment:** Concerning the individual's emotional investment with their organisation.
2 **Continuance commitment:** Concerning an individual's perception of the risks involved in leaving the organisation. Two factors are likely to influence the perception process: the personal sacrifice in leaving and the alternatives sources of employment available.
3 **Normative commitment:** An individual's perceived moral obligation to remain with the organisation.

Let's say an employee has been made an offer for a position in another company. They may perceive this role as more attractive in terms of salary and benefits (continuance commitment) but because of their emotional ties to the organisation (affective commitment) and the fact that they are overseeing a major project for the firm (normative commitment) they decide to stay and commit to the company. It is clear that this model is founded on the tri-dimensional model of attitudes, that is, affective, behavioural and cognitive. While the validity of the model has been criticised by some researchers (Solinger et al., 2008), it has served as a very useful guide to investigate commitment. It is also important to consider what exactly constitutes the organisation. Who represents the organisation? Indeed, Rousseau (1995) has highlighted how individuals will feel numerous commitments at work, such as to their line manager, their colleagues and their subordinates. Organisations consist of many different groups of people, each with their own goals and ambitions, and the relationship the individual has with these groups shapes that sense of commitment. This is one of many reasons why organisational commitment is a contentious issue.

Wasti and Can (2008) found that commitment to the organisation predicted outcomes such as increased turnover, whereas commitment to the supervisor predicted extra role behaviours like staying at work late. Oftentimes, the employee willingly goes above and beyond the agreed terms of the employment relationship. This type of behaviour has been termed organisational citizenship behaviour (OCB) and refers to individual behaviour that is discretionary, not

organisational citizenship behaviour (OCB) is voluntary behaviour from the employee that is likely to have positive consequences for the organisation.

explicitly recognised by the formal reward system, and that promotes the effective functioning of the organisation (Organ, 1997).

Similar to job satisfaction, commitment is generally measured using Likert scaling such as the Organisational Commitment Questionnaire (OCQ) developed by Mowday *et al.* (1979) (see Figure 4.3). Again, the important issue within the literature on organisational commitment is the relationship with job performance. Does the committed employee perform better than the less committed employee? Again, it is difficult to answer this question as organisational commitment is a multi-faceted construct. Broadly speaking there is modest support linking both variables (e.g. Harrison *et al.*, 2006), but there is more robust evidence supporting the idea that organisational commitment is a predictor of an employee's intention to leave a job (e.g. Solinger *et al.*, 2008).

Organisational Commitment Questionnaire (OCQ)

Instructions

Listed below are a series of statements that represent possible feelings that individuals might have about the company or organisation for which they work.
With respect to your own feelings about the particular organisation for which you are now working, please indicate the extent to which you agree or disagree with each statement below ranging from strongly agree (5) to strongly disagree (1)
(R = Reversed Score)

1 I am willing to put in a great deal of effort beyond that normally expected in order to help this organisation be successful.
2 I talk up this organisation to my friends as a great organisation to work for.
3 I feel very little loyalty to this organisation. (R)
4 I would accept almost any type of job assignment in order to keep working for this organisation.
5 I find that my values and the organisation's values are very similar.
6 I am proud to tell others that I am part of this organisation.
7 I could just as well be working for a different organisation as long as the type of work was similar. (R)
8 This organisation really inspires the very best in me in the way of job performance.
9 It would take very little change in my present circumstances to cause me to leave this organisation. (R)
10 I am extremely glad that I chose this organisation to work for over others I was considering at the time I joined.
11 There's not too much to be gained by sticking with this organisation indefinitely. (R)
12 Often, I find it difficult to agree with this organisation's policies on important matters relating to its employees. (R)
13 I really care about the fate of this organisation.
14 For me this is the best of all possible organisations for which to work.
15 Deciding to work for this organisation was a definite mistake on my part. (R)

Figure 4.3 Organisational commitment questionnaire

Source: Mowday et al. *(1979).*

Job satisfaction and organisational commitment are important concepts in understanding how attitudes manifest in the work environment. As has been explained, a conclusive model capturing the inter-relationship between these variables and job performance has yet to be developed. However, given that they do indirectly impact upon how an employee behaves in the work environment, there is a considerable need for employers to understand their causal factors.

WORK-RELATED ATTITUDES AND BEHAVIOUR IN ORGANISATIONS

How work-related attitudes manifest in the organisation will be of particular interest to those in managerial positions. Indeed, understanding the attitudes held by employees can allow managers to better predict how workers are likely to behave. In recent years, there has been a great deal of interest in employee engagement. Organisations seek to have employees engaged in the workplace as engagement is associated with a number of desirable behaviours such as intention to stay with the firm and organisational citizenship behaviours (see above) (Saks, 2006). Research suggests that engaged employees are more alert, more efficient in their jobs and achieve a higher level of task performance (see Rich *et al.*, 2010). Disengaged employees, on the other hand, are lethargic, inefficient and tend to perform worse on task performance. Let's say two employees working for the same organisation have similar jobs and salary. The reason that one employee is outperforming the other could be attributed to their level of engagement. Of course, there may be other viable explanations for their work performance but increasingly organisations are trying to understand the antecedents of engagement. Again, there are myriad factors that shape engagement, such as job rewards and job content. Research in this area highlights the central role of supervisors and leaders in influencing levels of engagement. For example, Schaufeli and Bakker (2004) suggest that engagement levels improve when the supervisor adopts a coaching approach to developing the employee. Indeed, investing resources in the employee in this way can often lead to benefits for the worker and the organisation. However, Gruman and Saks (2011) caution against adopting a universal or best practice approach to managing employee engagement. They highlight the importance of recognising the individual needs of each employee and being aware that what works in one organisation may not work in another. The general point here is that there are both individual and organisational factors that influence levels of engagement and that the nuances of each employment relationship must be understood before managers or leaders attempt to address the challenge of engagement.

> employee engagement is the degree to which an individual is attentive and absorbed in the performance of their role.

Again, it is important to emphasise the interconnectivity between the concepts explored in the chapter so far. For example, job satisfaction and organisational commitment are also associated with the level of engagement (see Harter et al., 2002; and Saks, 2006), emphasising the importance of engagement in the organisational behaviour field.

Another widely studied concept in this area is job involvement. Once again, job involvement has been linked with organisational outcomes such as performance and attendance and is shaped by many factors including leadership and personality (see Brown, 1996, for a comprehensive review of job involvement). It may seem that many of the terms examined in this section are relatively similar from a definitional perspective but it is important to

> job involvement is the extent to which an employee psychologically identifies with their job.

recognise that each concept is distinct from the others. Each tells us something different about an employee's relationship with their work (see Hallberg and Schaufeli, 2006, for an in-depth discussion of this issue).

pro-social behaviours are those that benefit another party.

The behaviours explored so far in this chapter can all be broadly described as pro-social. Within the context of the organisation, these behaviours benefit the organisation in that they result in positive outcomes for the organisation. Of course, not every behaviour will be pro-social. Employees often hold attitudes towards the firm that result in behaviours at odds with the goals of the organisation. In the literature, these behaviours are often referred to as deviant. Many of these behaviours may seem inconsequential if they only happen very occasionally. While not encouraged by the employer, the consequences to the organisation of one employee calling in sick to take a three-day weekend is relatively minor. However, if many employees (or the same employee) repeatedly fake illness, then this can cause great disruption to the organisation. Call centres are organisations that typically experience higher levels of 'voluntary absenteeism'. Many researchers point to the repetitive, monotonous nature of this work as a primary reason to explain this behaviour. Again, this explanation highlights the shaping role of organisational factors on employee behaviour. Sometimes employees view their job in a negative way and have high turnover intentions. Assembly line workers often have high turnover intentions (see Bakker *et al.*, 2003), which, again, may be explained by the repetitive nature of the work.

deviant behaviours are those that are counterproductive to an organisation.

turnover intentions are an employee's self-reported intentions to leave their job.

On the other hand, not every counterproductive behaviour can be traced back to a negative attitude. Recently, both employers and researchers have directed their attention to the concept of 'presenteeism'. Being ill is a legitimate reason not to turn up to work. However, many of you will be able to remember times when you have gone to work or attended an important lecture despite feeling under the weather. While this behaviour can be seen as admirable or even necessary for one-off occasions (for example, a sales pitch to important new clients or a mid-term exam), attending work while ill for a prolonged period creates a number of difficulties for the organisation. For instance, an employee suffering from depression is likely to make poorer decisions, be less productive and experience relationship difficulties in their personal life. Of course, these problems do not disappear when in the work environment. If this worker decides to attend work and not take time off, the consequences of these difficulties can be considerable for the organisation such as decreased productivity and interpersonal conflict. As this is an under-developed area within organisational behaviour research, we have limited insight into the causes of presenteeism. There is evidence that suggests the economic climate plays an important role. It seems likely that a temporary employee fearing for her job would be more likely to attend work in spite of illness when compared with a permanent member of staff (for a detailed study of the causes and consequences of presenteeism, see Johns, 2010).

presenteeism refers to attending work while suffering with illness.

While we have already explored the relationship between attitudes and behaviours in this chapter, it is clear that important workplace behaviours can, to some extent, be attributed to work-related attitudes. The consequences of these behaviours for organisations can be significant and managers need to understand their root causes. A recurring theme in this chapter is the shaping role of organisational factors on the various attitudes and behaviours discussed. This suggests that the organisation can go some way towards influencing employee behaviours. Decisions concerning pay, work design, autonomy and other work-related factors will have considerable bearing on how employees interact with the organisation.

BUILDING YOUR EMPLOYABILITY SKILLS

Managing Relationships

You have just hired an employee on a six-month fixed-term contract. While this is a very important role for the organisation it is unlikely that the contract will be extended. The employee is aware of this. Can you expect the employee to be committed to the organisation during the six months? If so, how do you bring about this commitment?

WORK VALUES

Values are different from attitudes. For example, most of us would prefer to work for an organisation that is socially responsible. However, some of us would *only* work for an organisation that is committed to corporate social responsibility (CSR). For these people, ethical behaviour is fundamental to their career choice. Therefore, we can say that social responsibility is a value they hold regarding their job. Simply, values are the degree of importance underpinning our attitudes. However, like attitudes, a person's value system is shaped by social factors such as the values of their parents, teachers and friends, and the cultural influences they are exposed to. The resulting values developed often endure throughout our lifetime. Therefore, when a person enters the work environment for the first time, they bring with them relatively stable expectations.

> values refer to the degree of importance an individual ascribes to a particular belief they hold about an object.

Our values reflect how we view ourselves. Indeed, our identity and our self-concept determine how we are likely to behave in the workplace. For instance, if an employee views herself as a leader, then she is likely to value opportunities in the workplace where she can demonstrate her leadership, and would certainly pursue a career where she would be in a leadership position. Relatedly, recent research by Greco and Kraimer (2019) found that when an employee identifies with many aspects of their profession, they place greater importance on work and career goals that reinforce their standing in the profession. For example, a lawyer who strongly identifies with the prestige of the legal profession may seek a position where they are well-paid but also where they have the opportunity to do meaningful pro-social work. How we view ourselves determines our values and our relationship with our job.

According to James and James (1989) these work values serve as a filter through which individuals interpret their work environment. They help the individual to make sense of the environment. Individuals' work values determine the meaning that work, their career and the organisation have for them. Work values are defined by Super and Šverko (1995) as the general and relatively stable goals that people try to reach through work. They are expressions of more general human values in the context of the work setting. The central idea put forward in the domain of work values is that they lead individuals to seek jobs or organisations that are characterised by certain attributes (Rentsch and McEwen, 2002). For example, work–life balance has emerged in the last two decades as a value that many employees particularly seek. The option of, for example, beginning work at a later time or working three-day weeks are all flexible work arrangements that were largely unheard of a quarter of a century ago. That these options are available to employees reflects the changing societal needs and values that have emerged during this time (Guest, 2004). Employees with young families require flexible work practices and they seek employment opportunities in organisations where such arrangements are valued and practised.

> work values are identified as the general and relatively stable goals that people try to reach through work.

Of course, people's values can also change over time for a variety of reasons such as the life-stage they are at and the different experiences they encounter through their lives. In terms of work–life balance, a nineteen-year-old employee with no children will typically have a very different value system from that of a middle-aged employee with four children. Indeed, employees often search for an organisation whose cultural values are congruent with their own value system. De Vos *et al.* (2005) found that employees new to an organisation constantly seek information that directly relates to the fulfilment of their values. For example, an employee who values personal development in their job will explicitly seek out information from the employer regarding issues like training opportunities and development plans.

Work values play an important role in helping an employee to identify a suitable organisation and also in how the employee behaves after organisational entry. However, as we have discussed already, the organisation can deliberately shape the employee through socialisation tactics as a means of ensuring greater alignment between values ▶**See Chapter 11◀**. While an individual's values often remain stable over their lifetime, the effect of socialisation can influence how employees view their work. Like attitudes, our experience at work is shaped by and shapes our values.

Pulsate

Pulsate is a well-established Chinese franchise that has its headquarters in Beijing, from where it directs the operations of its 16 sites across Asia. It is one of the leading 'home entertainment' brands in Asia, specialising in high-definition televisions and smart devices. It employs over 350 people across four countries. Last week, Pulsate bought Phonic – a large independent trader in home entertainment based in Seoul, with over 50 employees. Within five months they expect the transition from Phonic to be completed and for the Seoul office to be operational as the 17th site of Pulsate. To speed up this process, a number of senior managers from their Beijing and Shanghai sites are to be temporarily transferred to Phonic to oversee day-to-day operations during the changeover.

Phonic has been well served by its loyal staff for over 25 years, many of whom have been with the company from its very first day. Five years ago, Phonic had a sterling reputation in its field. However, recently the company has 'fallen behind' the technological advancements that are now considered an integral part of 21st-century home entertainment. While Phonic pride themselves in their customer service, the actual goods and services on offer are both limited and dated. As a result, they have seen some of their customers move to more 'modern' service providers. However, they still have a large pool of customers, which Pulsate believe can be significantly grown with the introduction of more desirable goods and the provision of a better service. Pulsate's stores are designed to minimise the number of shop assistants on the floor by using an in-house catalogue ordering system. Customers shop in Pulsate because the service provided is efficient and the average length of time spent by a customer in a Pulsate store is nine minutes. The majority of Pulsate's staff, therefore, work in the warehouse next to the shop floor, obtaining the customer's product.

Pulsate were surprised to learn of Phonic's persistence in selling outdated goods and customer service. For Pulsate, it

OB IN PRACTICE

CREDIT: PHOTO BY STEVE JOHNSON ON UNSPLASH

is essential that every employee is technologically proficient with both modern technology (e.g. tablets, HD televisions) and also the functioning of the catalogue system. However, they also see the value in 'face to face' interaction with customers and will continue to offer this service, albeit to a lesser degree. The company wants to minimise redundancies and believes a role can be found for each of the 51 employees at Phonic but will not prevent anyone from leaving. They feel this acquisition will cement their position as the Asian leader in home entertainment.

Understandably, Phonic's employees have been a little apprehensive about the takeover. Firstly, they have heard whispers of large scale redundancies with many consultants losing their jobs to the new catalogue service. They fear being replaced by younger, technologically savvy employees, the perceived profile of a typical Pulsate employee. They believe that a failure to upskill in the necessary areas will result in their exit from the company. Some of the employee representatives have voiced their concern over the uncertainty that surrounds the takeover, and they are still awaiting the director's response. Ultimately, they believe abandoning existing services will jeopardise the long-term relationship with established customers.

You are the Director of Phonic and you will assume a similar position within Pulsate in the coming weeks. You are concerned about how the employees have welcomed the news of the takeover.

Questions

1. How would you describe Phonic employees' attitude to the takeover? How is this likely to affect their behaviour over the coming months?
2. Is it possible to change the employees' attitude to be more positive about the takeover? If so, how can this be achieved?
3. Has technology changed employees' attitudes towards their job in this case? Explain your answer.

MANAGERIAL TAKEAWAYS

It is clear that the concept of attitudes can help us understand behaviour within the organisation. In assessing attitudes, it is important to understand their tri-dimensional structure. Certainly, the cognitive, affective and behavioural components of attitudes need to be explored together to fully understand the dynamics of the attitude construct itself. As explained, it is critical for managers to understand where work-related attitudes come from and identify the organisational forces at play in attitude formation. For instance, significant work-related attitudes like job satisfaction, employee engagement and organisational commitment are shaped by multiple workplace factors. From a practical perspective, an in-house survey might help the manager to identify that staff morale is low due to wages, uncertainty over the firm's future or even work demands, for example. Having this knowledge allows managers to make the necessary changes to the organisation, leading to more positive attitudinal outcomes. Another particular strategy increasingly employed by organisational leaders to impact the attitudes held by staff is to invest a significant deal of time into how they socialise new recruits into organisations ▶See Chapter 11◀. The early stages of the employment relationship are particularly formative in attitude development. If managers want their staff to think and behave in certain ways there is a great opportunity to help achieve this with sound investment in their onboarding process (e.g. training, mentoring, coaching, etc.) Relatedly, attitude change is at the heart of organisational communication ▶See Chapter 14◀. If an organisation decides to move in a new direction it needs to have the support and buy-in of its staff. The starting point of this is changing how employees view their jobs and their roles within the firm. As explained, managers need to be effective communicators in gaining the support of the team for any change initiatives they wish to introduce.

Overall, much of our behaviour at work can be explained by attitude theory. Of course, this is just one lens through which organisational behaviour can be understood. Given that attitudes influence how we view and behave in the world, it is critical for the managers to understand the attitudes held by their employees towards the organisation.

CHAPTER REVIEW QUESTIONS

1 What is the difference between a 'good' attitude and a 'bad' attitude?
2 What are the key factors that influence a person's attitude? In what way can an organisation influence the attitude formation process?
3 Explain the association between attitudes and behaviour. Can the organisation predict an employee's behaviour in the workplace?
4 Why is job satisfaction such a complex issue for organisations? Is there any merit in measuring it?
5 What is 'positive discrimination'? What are your thoughts on the criticism that it restricts the recruitment process to find the best candidate?
6 Is it easy to change an attitude? Can a person learn to be prejudiced? Can a person unlearn their prejudice?
7 Can you explain what is meant by the term 'the ABCs' of attitude formation?
8 How are values different from attitudes? How do they influence behaviour in organisations?

FURTHER READING

Albarracín, D., Johnson, B.T. and Zanna, M.P. (eds) (2014) *The Handbook of Attitudes*. Mahwah, NJ: Psychology Press.

Burnes, B., Patterson, F., Robertson, I.T., Silvester, J., Cooper, C.L. and Arnold, J. (2004) *Work Psychology: Understanding Human Behaviour in the Workplace*. Harlow: Financial Times Prentice Hall.

Currivan, D.B. (2000) The causal order of job satisfaction and organizational commitment in models of employee turnover. *Human Resource Management Review*, 9(4), 495–524.

Kowske, B.J., Rasch, R. and Wiley, J. (2010) Millennials' (lack of) attitude problem: An empirical examination of generational effects on work attitudes. *Journal of Business and Psychology*, 25(2), 265–279.

Sutton, R. and Douglas, K. (2013) *Social Psychology*. London: Red Globe Press.

USEFUL WEBSITES

www.cipd.co.uk

This is a useful website for students. The CIPD is the governing body of human resources in Britain and Ireland. Here you will find real-life examples of how organisations manage attitudes in the workplace.

http://dop.bps.org.uk/

This is the Division of Occupational Psychology within the British Psychological Society. Here you will find information on how psychologists work with organisations to better understand workplace attitudes and behaviour.

www.pearnkandola.com

Pearn Kandola is a firm of psychologists who work closely with employees and organisations on issues relating to attitude and behaviour. They have regular blogs and examples of how real-life organisational problems are tackled.

https://www.shl.com/

SHL are one of the world's leading occupational testing firms. Here you will see a broad range of attitude surveys used by contemporary firms to help address a variety of workplace issues such as recruitment, organisational change and leader development.

Online Resources

Visit bloomsbury.pub/organisational-behaviour to access additional materials to support teaching and learning

5 MOTIVATION AND REWARDS

Colette Darcy and T.J. McCabe

LEARNING OUTCOMES

BY THE END OF THIS CHAPTER YOU SHOULD BE ABLE TO:

- Explain why motivation is important in the workplace.
- Understand how motivation processes influence behaviour at work.
- Explore how managers use knowledge of motivation theories to influence behaviour at work.
- Distinguish between need theories of motivation and process theories of motivation.
- Understand the difference between extrinsic and intrinsic sources of motivation.

CREDIT: PHOTO BY CHARLOTTE KARLSEN ON UNSPLASH

THIS CHAPTER DISCUSSES...

INTRODUCTION

Motivation is a set of forces that energise, direct and sustain behaviour, and hence makes people behave in certain ways (Steers *et al.*, 2002; Hitt *et al.*, 2014). It is an important concept in the workplace as the challenge for managers is to maximise the likelihood of staff using their energy, to work hard so that the organisation achieves its goals. A recent poll showed that 70% of employees are 'not engaged' or 'actively disengaged' at work (Seppala, 2016). Employee disengagement is estimated to cost US corporations in the region of $450 billion to $550 billion per year (Hewlett *et al.*, 2017). On any given day an employee may choose to work as hard as possible, or work just hard enough to avoid a reprimand. Human Capital Theory recognises individuals as cognitive and emotional beings who possess free will (Wright *et al.*, 2001). It is the employee who decides what behaviours they will engage in. The employee owns their knowledge, skills and abilities, not the organisation they work for. Therefore, it is the individual who makes a conscious decision whether or not to invest their knowledge, skills and abilities for the strategic benefit of the firm. If an employee lacks ability, it could be argued that a development plan could be put in place to tackle this deficit. If resources are lacking, again a manager could intervene to correct the problem by making these available, but if motivation is lacking, the problem for the manager becomes more complex. The idea of discretionary effort (MacDuffie, 1995) is really at the heart of the challenge of motivating employees. How do we get our employees to maximise their discretionary effort for the benefit of the organisation and its goals? What factors positively influence this discretionary effort and what factors have a negative impact?

> **motivation** is a set of forces that energise, direct and sustain behaviour and hence make people behave in certain ways.

> **discretionary effort** is the level of effort people could give if they wanted to, but above and beyond the minimum required.

While it is often relatively easy to motivate someone in the short term, to achieve a short-term goal for example, it is often much more difficult and complex to motivate someone for longer periods of time. Motivation and the ability to motivate an individual and groups of workers has, therefore, been the focus of much research. If an organisation, or managers within an organisation, can master the skills which allow them to motivate their staff, then they are likely to witness higher performance from individuals (Locke and Latham, 1990), greater team cohesiveness (Evans and Dion, 1991), lower absenteeism (Mowday *et al.*, 1982), greater job satisfaction (Judge *et al.*, 2001) and a strong positive organisational culture (Milne, 2007) ▶See Chapter 12◀. You can see therefore why organisations are so keen to understand what drives their employees and equally why anyone with people responsibility within an organisation should have a fundamental understanding of what motivates and drives individual performance. This chapter begins by looking at the drivers of individual performance and how these impact upon motivation. Several theories of motivation are relevant when it comes to work settings, with three main groups of theories identifiable: needs theories, process theories and situational factors that influence motivation.

WHAT DRIVES INDIVIDUAL PERFORMANCE?

Individual performance is generally determined by three things: motivation (the desire to do the job); ability (the capability to do the job); and the work environment (the resources needed to do the job) (Griffin, 2014) (see Figure 5.1).

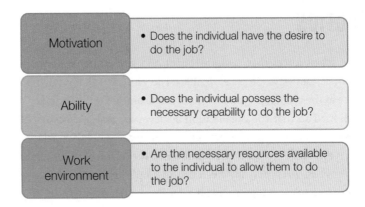

Figure 5.1 What drives individual performance?

Without all three in place simultaneously the chances of the individual successfully performing a job to the optimal level are drastically reduced. Consider an individual who might be highly motivated to become a doctor. Since a very early age, all they have ever wanted to be is a doctor. Yet, when it came to completing the final state school examinations, they were unable to achieve the points required to gain access to an undergraduate medicine course. They were highly motivated *but lacked the ability* to achieve their desired outcome.

Take another example. Within a fictional college there is a lecturer who is a world-recognised expert in entrepreneurship. This lecturer has published her research in top academic journals and has written numerous books. However, the lecturer does her best to avoid having to teach and when she does, her students report that it is a disastrous experience. The lecturer clearly has the ability, yet *lacks the motivation* to teach. Her interests lie elsewhere in terms of getting her work published and she finds teaching an unnecessary distraction.

Equally, we could have a highly motivated and capable employee who wants to launch a new product onto the market. The product they have developed has a clear selling point and initial studies have confirmed that customers would be willing to buy it. Yet the senior management team are reluctant to invest in a national marketing campaign to launch the product. In this case the individual is highly motivated and has clear ability but due to the work environment and specifically a *lack of organisational support* for the marketing campaign, is unlikely to be successful in launching the new product.

From a management perspective, therefore, it not sufficient to simply recruit capable individuals – that is just the first step. We must ensure that when we recruit these capable individuals we convince them to invest their ability and skills in their work to achieve the organisational goals, and make sure that we provide them with the necessary resources to do that successfully. This chapter is therefore concerned with not only what motivation is, but *how* managers can leverage theories of motivation to convince their employees to use their skills to best effect in the workplace.

WHAT IS MOTIVATION?

Motivation can be thought of as the set of forces that energise, direct and sustain behaviour (Hitt *et al.*, 2014). Much of the literature focuses on the initial galvanisation of employees in order to motivate them to take on a particular task and to focus this energy in order to complete it. In one way this is the easy piece of the jigsaw. It is the ability to sustain the initial burst of motivation that is difficult for managers.

These forces can come from the person, the so called *'push' internal forces*, or they can come from the environment that surrounds the person, the so-called *'pull'* of *external forces*. We are going to concentrate on the push, or internal forces, first. As the name suggests, these forces are internal to the individual, so in essence they are the forces within an individual which cause them to act in a certain way.

Psychologists typically categorise motivation theories as they relate to individuals, into two types:

1 *Need theories*, which focus on what needs a person is trying to satisfy and on what features of the work environment seem to satisfy those.

2 *Process theories*, which focus on the way different variables or factors combine to influence the amount of effort people are willing to make in order to gain some outcome.

NEED THEORIES

Need theories of motivation therefore focus on the personal needs that workers attempt to satisfy while also taking account of the features in the work environment that satisfy their needs. In this way managers can design work to meet these needs and hence elicit appropriate and successful work behaviours. There are three main content theories, namely Maslow's Need Hierarchy, Herzberg's Two-factor Theory and McClelland's Acquired Needs Theory.

MASLOW'S NEED HIERARCHY

Most people have heard of Maslow's hierarchy of needs and are familiar with its basic premise. The theory argues that people are motivated to satisfy five need levels, starting with the most basic first (such as physiological needs like hunger) and then, once those are satisfied, to move

'push' internal forces are motivational forces which come from the person.

'pull' external forces are motivational forces which come from the environment that surrounds the person.

need theories focus on the needs that motivate people: the internal drive that motivates specific behaviours in an attempt to fulfil the needs.

process theories focus on how people decide what actions to choose to engage in to meet their needs, and decide if these actions were successful.

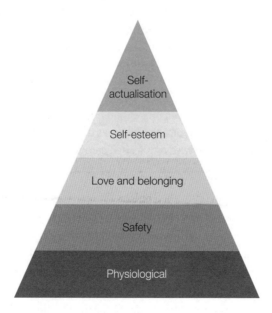

Figure 5.2 Maslow's hierarchy of needs theory

Source: Maslow (1943), published by APA. Reprinted with permission.

to the next level, which includes their safety needs, then the third stage, which is a need for a sense of belonging, then on to the level concerning need for self-esteem, and the final step, which is the need for self-actualisation (see Figure 5.2). The theory was not developed specifically with the work environment in mind but it is worth considering how each of these five levels might relate to a work setting.

Try and think of what needs might fall into each level of Maslow's Need Hierarchy. To start you off, an example of a physiological need in a work-based setting might be an adequate basic salary. Now it is your turn.

Maslow's need level	Work-based example
Physiological	Adequate basic salary
Safety	
Love and belonging	
Self-esteem	
Self-actualisation	

Possible answers

Safety needs could relate to a safe work environment with good job security – you could include fringe benefits here in relation to sick pay and pension, which provide for the current and future well-being of the individual. A sense of belonging is quite a powerful desire within an organisational context as individuals strive to be accepted by their peers, to feel part of work teams and have relationships with their co-workers and managers which are positive, respectful and mutually beneficial. Self-esteem needs actually comprise two different sets of needs, one internal and one external. The one internal to the person is the need for a positive self-image and self-respect, while the external one focuses on the need for recognition and respect from others. The need for internal self-esteem is met when an individual feels that they have the level of recognition and high status they desire in relation to their work. The need for external self-esteem can be met with increased responsibilities and a sense that the individual is climbing up the career ladder. At the very top of the hierarchy are the self-actualisation needs. Within a work context these are considered to have a significant impact on motivational levels of individuals. These involve realising one's potential for continued growth and individual development and fulfilling the desire for challenging and stimulating work. You would typically find opportunities for training, advancement, growth and creativity considered within this need category.

According to this theory only an unsatisfied need is a motivator and only when the individual's most basic needs have been met will they be able to concentrate on satisfying higher-order needs. Interestingly, the theory would argue that should a lower-order need come under threat despite an individual having previously satisfied this need and moved on to higher-order needs, they would likely revert to focusing on the need under threat and decrease their efforts to satisfy higher-order needs until such time as this threat has passed. However, recent research based on Maslow's theory has found little evidence for the ranking of the needs that Maslow described, or even for the existence of a definite hierarchy at all, indicating that all the needs may be important all the time.

EXTENSION OF HIERARCHY OF NEEDS – A MANAGER'S PERSPECTIVE

Recently researchers have become increasingly interested in the idea of 'psychological safety', which builds on Maslow's idea of physiological needs. A renewed interest in this concept of psychological safety is particularly relevant in today's workplaces. Psychological safety allows both individuals and teams to face challenges in an open and honest manner, allowing for a more complete and effective response. Where employees feel they cannot raise an issue, or in doing so, they are likely to face negative consequences for their self-image, status or career (Kahn, 1990), then they are likely to back away or hide their true feelings (Gallo, 2014). Essentially, as managers, we want our employees to feel psychologically supported in work. Where they feel this support is present, they are more likely to be productive members of the team and also more likely to commit to the organisation in the longer term.

psychological safety refers to the ability of someone to show their true self without fear of negative consequences to self-image, status or career.

HERZBERG'S WHY MOTIVATION MUST COME FROM WITHIN

According to Herzberg (1966), at work individuals are not content with the satisfaction of lower-order needs as set forth by Maslow, but rather, individuals look for higher-level psychological needs to be satisfied through their work such as a sense of achievement, recognition, advancement and the nature of the work itself.

HERZBERG'S TWO-FACTOR THEORY OF MOTIVATION

Having established in theory that motivation must come from within, Herzberg set out to further his work by now considering the notion that the presence of one set of job characteristics or incentives leads to worker *satisfaction* at work, while another and separate set of job characteristics leads to *dissatisfaction* at work. What is most interesting is that Herzberg was convinced that satisfaction and dissatisfaction were not opposites of one another, at either end of a continuum, but rather completely separate phenomena. Herzberg's real breakthrough was to argue that managers really need to focus on both the motivators and hygiene factors to ensure that satisfaction is increased while dissatisfaction is minimised.

Herzberg interviewed 200 accountants and engineers in an attempt to understand the factors associated with satisfaction and dissatisfaction. He asked participants to recall occasions when they had been satisfied and motivated and occasions when they had been dissatisfied and unmotivated. His Two-factor Theory of Motivation was the result, by which he attempted to distinguish between factors that increase job satisfaction (motivators) and those that can prevent dissatisfaction but cannot increase satisfaction (hygiene factors).

Unsafe working conditions will cause people to be dissatisfied, but an improvement in working conditions such that they are deemed safe, will not lead to a high level of motivation. Hygiene factors are therefore the minimum required to allow employees to avoid feelings of dissatisfaction. Motivators, however, must be in place before employees will be highly motivated to excel at their work. Motivators influence the level of satisfaction gained from individual experiences, and so are the intrinsic factors that are directly related to the *doing* of a job. They focus on achievement, recognition, responsibility, the work itself and elements of personal growth directly received by performing the work. Hygiene factors are extrinsic to

motivators influence job satisfaction based on fulfilling higher-level needs such as achievement, recognition, responsibility.

hygiene factors focus on lower-order needs and involve the presence or absence of job dissatisfiers, such as working conditions and pay.

directly performing the job. They are associated with conditions *surrounding* the job such as pay, company policies and interpersonal relationships. When hygiene factors are poor, work is dissatisfying.

So, the factors involved in producing job satisfaction and motivation are separate and distinct from the factors that lead to job dissatisfaction – this is the key to understanding Herzberg's Two-factor Theory of Motivation. Unlike movement, true motivation has longer lasting effects over a longer period of time. Because the reward is intrinsic, focused on personal growth and satisfaction, employees don't need to be rewarded incrementally.

BUILDING YOUR EMPLOYABILITY SKILLS

Employee Motivation

There is increasing recognition among managers, of the importance of employee recognition given the difficulties associated with using pay as a motivator. In economically difficult times, how do you motivate employees if you have no financial rewards to offer? Or if you do offer employees financial rewards, do you simply keep paying more and more to continue to motivate them? Is there a limit to the amount of money available to motivate staff? If there is a limit to how much you can offer them, what happens when you reach the maximum? How do you motivate those employees who previously were in receipt of financial only rewards?

IMPLICATIONS OF HERZBERG'S TWO-FACTOR THEORY OF MOTIVATION FOR MANAGERS AND JOB DESIGN

What does this all mean for managers attempting to motivate their workers? The model proposes a very simple message: to motivate employees, focus on improving how the job is structured and what the individual is asked to do. Providing hygiene factors will remove employee dissatisfaction but will not motivate workers to high achievement levels. On the other hand, recognition, challenge and opportunities for personal growth are powerful motivators and will promote high levels of satisfaction and performance.

However, as with all theories, this one is not without its critics. It has been claimed that the model is overly simplistic; for example, is it always possible to distinguish hygiene factors from motivational ones? Supervision would be classed as a hygiene factor in Herzberg's theory, but we know that the type of supervision an individual receives can potentially increase motivation to perform at a higher level as well reduce their dissatisfaction (Locke and Latham, 1990). In this case, the division of factors into those that impact on *doing* the job and those concerned with the conditions *surrounding* the job, while appealing, falls down.

One of the main contributions of Herzberg's Two-factor Theory was the increased emphasis it placed on how jobs are designed, for example how different tasks and skills should be combined into jobs, so as to maximise the motivation of the individual to perform them. Designing jobs in such a way as to give employees greater feelings of responsibility, accomplishment and achievement can affect their individual motivation.

⟨ETHICAL⟩ BEHAVIOUR IN THE WORKPLACE

You manage a small team of project managers. Over the past three years you worked hard to recruit and train up all of your project team and have achieved considerable success as a result. The last five large projects the team have completed have been delivered on time and within budget. One of your star performers, Anna, approaches you to tell you that she has stagnated in terms of her learning and would like more challenge in her role with perhaps a move into a different role within the company. You are aware that there is such a role about to become available within a different team but putting Anna forward for this role would mean losing your star performer and unsettling the whole team, which you have spent so long building up.

CREDIT: PHOTO BY AMY HIRSCHI ON UNSPLASH

Questions

1 Should you tell Anna about the upcoming position in another functional area?

2 Should you keep quiet and hope this is a passing phase and that some reassurance from you and perhaps a bonus or salary increase will be sufficient?

3 What can organisations do to ensure that managers do not 'block' employees from promotional opportunities, to preserve their own teams?

JOB CHARACTERISTICS MODEL

The work of Herzberg has become fashionable again in recent years despite criticisms levelled against it. Its implications for job design, and in particular the idea of job enrichment, have seen a resurgence of late.

job enrichment is increasing the complexity of a job to provide a greater sense of responsibility, accomplishment and achievement.

The Job Characteristics Model developed by Hackman and Oldham (1976) (see Figure 5.3) emphasises three components which are the focus of how one might go about designing enriched jobs with high potential for increased motivation:

- Core job characteristics – the level of skill variety, task identity, task significance, feedback and autonomy.
- Critical psychological states – the level of experienced meaningfulness of the work, the experienced responsibility for outcomes of the work, and knowledge of the actual results of the work activities.

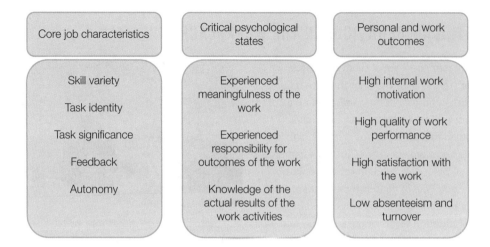

Figure 5.3 Job Characteristics Model

Source: Adapted from Hackman and Oldham (1976).

- Expected outcomes – high outcomes would result in internal work motivation, growth satisfaction, work effectiveness and general job satisfaction.

Skill variety, task identity and task significance tend to influence the employee's psychological state of experienced meaningfulness of work. This essentially means that the employer can ensure that the work itself is satisfying and provides opportunity for intrinsic rewards for the employee. If work can be designed in such a way as to provide workers with situations where they are required to use different skills, to achieve an identifiable piece of work which has a visible outcome and has a meaningful impact on the lives of other people within the organisation, then it is likely to be highly motivational.

Autonomy influences workers' experience of responsibility. This speaks to the degree to which an individual has freedom and discretion to decide the scheduling of the work and determine the approach or procedures used to carry it out. The greater the level of autonomy an individual has, the more likely it is to be motivational. Finally, the job characteristic of feedback provides the worker with knowledge of actual results. The employee thus knows how he or she is doing and can change work performance to increase the likelihood of achieving desired outcomes.

Not all employees will seek out more responsibility or more challenging work, but many do, particularly over time. Who wants to go to work day after day, week after week and undertake the same tasks, using the same skills while having little if any say in how, when, where or why things are done in the way they are? Who would not rather work in an organisation where every day you get to do different things, where you are faced with different problems or challenges and have to use different problem-solving skills to get results? More and more organisations are therefore paying attention to the motivational content of their employees' jobs and thinking about how they can structure roles in such a way as to maximise their motivational content for the person charged with undertaking them. The job characteristics model states that the more the five core characteristics can be designed into a role, the higher the employee's motivation and performance, quality of work and overall job satisfaction.

HR at Google

Google's People Operations unit (essentially what Google calls HR) was tasked with using data to find out what makes a Google team effective. Using over 200 interviews with employees looking at over 250 individual attributes, they arrived at five key dynamics that, they say, make for effective teams. Interestingly they found that *who* was a team member was less important than *how* the team members interacted, structured their work and viewed each other's contributions. The five key dynamics for effective team performance identified by Google were:

1 **Psychological safety** – see above.

2 **Dependability** – knowing that you can rely on team members to get things done on time and to a high standard.
3 **Structure and clarity** – team members need to have clear roles, plans and goals.
4 **Meaning** – the work the team members are tasked with must be meaningful to them personally.
5 **Impact** – the team members need to be able to see how their work contributes to the overall goal, how it matters and creates change.

It is interesting to see these findings against the backdrop of the theories we have been discussing.

CREDIT: PHOTO BY ANNIE SPRATT ON UNSPLASH

Questions

1 Taking each of the theories discussed, how do they relate to Google's findings?
2 Do you see an overlap between the theory and Google's findings?

See: https://rework.withgoogle.com/blog/five-keys-to-a-succesful-google-team/

MANAGERIAL IMPLICATIONS OF THE JOB CHARACTERISTICS MODEL

The Job Characteristics Model highlights a number of important considerations for managers. In creating or redesigning roles, the more managers can include elements of the core job characteristics into the role, in terms of skill variety, task identity and significance with feedback and high levels of autonomy, the more likely those roles are to motivate the individual tasked with completing them. Having input in to *how* and *when* you do certain parts of your job are important motivating factors for individuals. As is the ability to see how that particular job fits into the broader fulfilment of the goals of the team or organisation. A sense of 'my job matters' and I understand how it contributes is a very powerful motivator for most employees. For managers looking at implementing the insights from this model, a good rule of thumb is to try to make the roles of those who report to them more like their own!

IMPACT OF TECHNOLOGY ON BEHAVIOUR

Carl Frey and Michael Osborne from the University of Oxford estimate that 47% of US jobs are at risk from robotics and AI. This is an incredible statistic based on rigorous research. The implications of this for job design and the nature of work as we know it, are profound. If nearly half of all jobs are going to be done by robots and artificial intelligence, then what does that mean for companies and the types of employees they are going to need, now

and in the future, to achieve their goals? What does this mean for how we train and educate our young people? What roles should we be preparing them for?

Sources

Frey, C. and Osborne, M. (2017) The future of employment: How susceptible are jobs to computerisation? *Technological Forecasting and Social Change*, 114, 254–280.

https://www.hrmagazine.co.uk/article-details/gratton-why-the-future-of-work-is-so-fascinating

https://www.youtube.com/watch?v=6Z6L7iZlC9o

ACQUIRED NEEDS THEORY

David McClelland (1985) adopted a similar but slightly different approach to factors which influence individuals' motivation. He argued that certain types of needs are acquired during a person's lifetime. Individuals have very different life experiences and the learned, or acquired, needs which come from these become 'enduring predispositions', which are almost like personality traits ▸See Chapter 2◂ that can be activated by certain cues in the environment. The three key needs he identified are:

● Need for achievement – the drive to accomplish something difficult, surpass others, and master complex tasks.
● Need for affiliation – the desire to form close personal relationships and avoid conflict.
● Need for power – the desire to influence or control others and have authority over them.

Individuals with a high need for achievement tend to prefer work which has a moderate level of task difficulty, have a preference for personal responsibility for their actions, like taking moderate risks and desire specific and concrete feedback on their performance. The need for achievement has received the most widespread attention of researchers and it appears to be present in all cultures, although the percentage of those with a high need for achievement varies from country to country (Erez and Earley, 1993). Individuals with a high need for affiliation seek to resolve conflicts, make decisions and interact with others in the organisation in a positive, collaborative manner. They seek to enhance their relationships with others and develop a common understanding. These individuals are concerned with being liked and respected by their supervisors, peers and subordinates in the workplace.

Finally, the desire for power is a tremendous source of motivation. Not only does power determine an individual's standing within an organisation, but it is also a reflection of the individual's importance to that organisation. McClelland argued that some individuals actively seek to gain and use power. Having power to influence decisions or other people can be a source itself of great personal satisfaction. A high need for power has been associated with aggressive reactions as well as with managerial success (McClelland, 1985). McClelland suggested that a high need for power, if unrestrained, can lead to actions indicative of a desire to dominate others and to triumph, particularly at someone else's expense.

To recap, need theories of motivation are those theories which focus on what needs a person is trying to satisfy and what features of the work environment appear to satisfy those needs. So, Need Theories focus on both the particular needs of the individual, which are internal to them and act as a source of motivation, and the external forces, which need to be in place to satisfy the individual's needs. We move on now to look at process theories of motivation.

PROCESS THEORIES

Process theories of motivation focus on the way different variables combine to influence the amount of effort people are willing to put into something. Where content theories of motivation focus on *which* variable affects motivation, process theories focus on *how* the variable affects it. Three process theories will be discussed in this section, namely Equity Theory, Expectancy Theory and Goal-Setting Theory.

EQUITY THEORY

Equity theory was developed in the early 1960s by Stacy Adams and emphasises the social aspect of motivation. This focus on the social dimension of motivation is a recognition that individuals do not work in a vacuum; they work with people in various different social networks. The theory proposes that individuals are motivated to change their effort levels in response to comparisons of their own situation with that of others. So, in essence, the theory assumes that individuals are fully aware of the kind of effort and skill they put into their jobs and the level of outcomes, for example salary and promotions, they expect to receive in return. The theory also assumes that individuals are likely to compare whether the amount of effort they put into their job makes sense given the level of outcomes they receive; in other words, they evaluate whether the amount of effort they expend is worth the outcome they receive as a result. In addition, the individual will also look around to see what effort others expend and what outcomes *they* receive as a result. By comparing these situations an individual determines whether they feel fairly treated.

So, what does this look like in reality? Suppose that you have a job working in a supermarket. Part of your role is to restock the shelves and you agree to do this for a rate of €8 per hour. You

equity theory is a process based motivational theory that focuses on how individuals compare their circumstances with those of others and attempts to explain how such comparisons may motivate certain kinds of behaviour.

feel that €8 an hour is a reasonable rate of pay for this task. It is not the best paid job in the world, so you take a view that you are not prepared to go above and beyond what is required. You will do what you can, within the time you are there. Honestly, you could probably do more but you feel that for the level of pay that is on offer you are not prepared to exert yourself more than necessary, and you see this as a reasonable trade off. You begin your first week of work and something surprising happens. You talk to your co-workers and they tell you something very interesting: they are being paid €11 an hour, which is €3 per hour more than you! You feel that they work no harder than you and that they expend no more effort than you. You stack as many shelves as them, in the same way as them and in the same time period. Why should they get €3 more? You think this situation is grossly unfair and so you reassess your situation, about which you are pretty angry. It *feels* unfair. Why should you get paid less than the others for the same work? The options available to you are straightforward: you can quit your job, you can approach your boss and ask to be paid the same as your work colleagues, or you might decide that a pay rise is unlikely and that you need the job even though it isn't fair that you get paid less for doing the same work as others. In this case, you could decide to decrease your level of effort to reflect the amount of pay you receive.

Alternatively, you could take a slightly different approach and try to rationalise why you are paid less than the others. You might decide not to compare yourself with this group at all but instead with your university friends (referent group), who all earn the same as you, making you feel that perhaps this is a fair rate for the work. You could also re-evaluate the individuals you work with in terms of their experience or skill set and decide that they bring something else to the role which merits them getting paid more than you. They may have worked there longer, or have an additional responsibility attached to their role. In this way you can re-evaluate your sense of unfairness about the situation. All these scenarios are summarised in Table 5.1.

But what happens if, rather than perceiving yourself to be disadvantaged, you perceive yourself as having an advantage? What happens if you are the one being paid €11 when someone else is being paid €8? In this case the theory suggests that the individual would increase their inputs or decrease outputs to realign the balance between effort and return. That is to say, you would work harder to justify your extra pay or seek a reduction in your pay to regain balance. In reality, however, common sense suggests that people would be happy to be paid more and just take the cash and run!

The difficulty with equity theory is that it doesn't help us to predict which method people will use in which specific setting or situation – it doesn't indicate who will quit, who will reduce their efforts or who will change their comparison group. What the theory does do, however, is emphasise that it is the individual's *perception* of equity when compared with others' circumstances which is so powerful and has such a magnified impact upon motivation. The important lesson for managers from equity theory is the ability to recognise that not all employees will be motivated in the same way or react in the same way. It is their perception of fairness, whether based in reality or not, which will ultimately influence how they react.

expectancy theory is a process based theory of motivation that focuses on the thought processes people use when choosing among alternative courses of action and their anticipated consequences.

EXPECTANCY THEORY

'Expectancy theory' focuses on individuals' thought processes as they choose between alternative actions in the workplace (Vroom, 1964). In deciding how much effort to put into a task,

MOTIVATION AND REWARDS 105

Table 5.1 Basics of equity theory explained using the example of a job in a supermarket

If		is		then		and I am motivated to	
If	the ratio of my outcomes to my inputs	is	equal to the ratio of the others' outcomes to inputs	then	I am satisfied	and I am motivated to	do nothing
If	the €8 an hour I am paid for the work	is	perceived by me to be equal to the pay and effort of my colleagues	then	I am happy with my pay and the work I am asked to do	and I am motivated to	do nothing
HOWEVER							
If	the ratio of my outcomes to my inputs	is	less than the ratio of the others' outcomes to inputs	then	I am dissatisfied (inequity)	and I am motivated to	increase my own outcomes by either: • decreasing my own inputs, or • re-evaluating the others' inputs, or • changing the referent, or • leaving the situation
If	the €8 an hour I am paid for the work	is	perceived by me to be less pay for the same effort of my colleagues doing the same work	then	I am really annoyed. I am seriously unhappy that I get paid less	and I am motivated to	either: • quit my job, or • put in less effort, or • re-evaluate why I am paid less by considering my colleagues may have other responsibilities, or • rationalise it by looking at my university friends who are all paid €8 an hour

individuals first perform an internal assessment or calculation inside their head. The first thing they consider is the effort to performance ratio – the probability that a certain amount of effort on their part will lead to a certain level of performance. For example, if I were to do 100 stomach crunches a day for a year, I would have a reasonable expectation that after a year my stomach would be flat and toned. The second thing people consider is the probability that a particular level of performance will lead to particular outcomes. So, if I have a flat stomach my chances of getting a new boyfriend are greatly increased! From a work perspective the answer to these internal questions in relation to effort and outcome will result in an employee being motivated to perform a certain task at a certain level or to be demotivated to undertake such a task.

valence is the extent to which an individual values a particular outcome.

The third point they consider is what is referred to in the theory as the valence of a particular outcome – the anticipated value that a person attaches to it. In our example this would be that I would love to have a new boyfriend as I haven't had one in over three years (high valence), or I already have a boyfriend who I deeply love and respect (low valence). If the valence of rewards offered is high, there is potential for increased motivation. Equally if the anticipated value of the reward is low or the offered rewards are not relevant to the individual, motivation is likely to be weak.

$$\text{Effort} = (E{\rightarrow}P) \times (P{\rightarrow}O) \times V$$

Where:

$E{\rightarrow}P$ = effort to performance

$P{\rightarrow}O$ = is the probability that a particular level of performance will lead to particular outcomes

V = the anticipated value a person attaches to an outcome

IMPLICATIONS FOR MANAGERS ARISING FROM EXPECTANCY THEORY

This theory has been widely embraced by both academic researchers and managers in organisations. One of the reasons for its popularity with managers is because it suggests explicit ways to improve workers' performance. If managers can improve workers' confidence in their performance ability by increasing training to improve skills, or by mentoring or providing feedback, then it is likely that employees will be more motivated because they will believe that their increased ability to perform will result in some sort of reward. Managers should be consistent in their application of rewards and positive feedback to facilitate this. They should also think carefully about what rewards and outcomes are really valued by their employees. There is little point in offering an employee a reward that is of little perceived value to them personally. A good example of this is offering employees very generous retirement benefits when perhaps younger employees would place more value on the cash equivalent or additional days of annual leave. Organisations have a habit of assuming they know what employees value, yet they rarely do a sense checking exercise to see if this is really true. Managers need to know their employees and understand what it is that they value in order to make whatever rewards and outcomes they offer have high valence for that individual.

IN REALITY

People are naturally loss averse, that is, they hate to lose! But did you know that in terms of motivation, people's preference for avoiding loss far outweighs acquiring equivalent gains? In a 2016 study, scientists asked a group of study participants to walk 7,000 steps a day for six months. Half the participants were paid $1.40 for each day they achieved their goal of walking 7,000 steps, while another group were told they would lose $1.40 for each day they failed to reach 7,000 steps. What the scientists found surprising was that the second group, who stood to lose $1.40 for each day they failed to hit their target, actually achieved the target of 7,000 steps a day 50% more often!

Perhaps even more interesting was the finding that participants were more likely to be motivated when the financial incentive was given to them up front and then reduced or taken away when they failed to achieve their target, rather than being given to them at the end of the experiment. In terms of this experiment, participants were given $42 up front but it was reduced if they didn't meet their step goal. This was seen as more effective than giving participants the full $42 at the end of the experiment.

In addition to being loss averse, people are more motivated when there is an element of risk to the reward. People work harder, investing more effort, time and money, to qualify for a 50% chance of getting either $150 or $50 than they would for a certain reward of say $100. Scientists believe the reason for this is to do with the first being viewed as more challenging and hence exciting. Many companies have adapted this motivational approach in the form of gamification for work-related activities; however, care does need to be taken to ensure that challenging and competitive doesn't become an aggressive winner-takes-all mentality.

Sources

https://penntoday.upenn.edu/2016-03-24/research/prospect-losing-money-pushes-people-achieve-fitness-goals

Fishbach, A. (2018) How to keep working when you're just not feeling it. *Harvard Business Review*, Nov/Dec.

GOAL-SETTING THEORY

The third process theory is goal-setting theory, which emphasises the importance of conscious goals and intentions in directing human behaviour (Locke, 1968). The idea is that if managers can influence employees' goals and intentions then they can directly influence performance. What is critical to the success of this approach is an understanding of the importance of the *level* at which the goals are set and the *commitment* of individuals to the goals. We know that the more challenging (higher or harder) goals result in more effort than easier goals, although only if the individual accepts and commits to the goal achievement (Nicholson, 2003). General or vague goals are less effective (Fishbach, 2018). Equally, goals that are perceived as too easy will not result in any additional effort and so it is unlikely that they will be perceived as motivational. Specific and clear goals are more likely to result in higher levels of effort (Britt, 2003).

goal-setting theory emphasises the importance of conscious goals and intentions in directing human behaviour.

Most people have heard of SMART goal setting – that goals should be Specific, Measurable, Achievable, Realistic and Time-bound. Crucially, it is important that goals are not set so high as to make them unachievable, but also, when setting goals managers must work hard to get employee buy-in and commitment to their achievement, otherwise the goals quickly become pointless. There is little point to setting a goal which is unachievable, and in doing so you are likely to demotivate employees. The 'Goldilocks' principle needs to be applied to the setting of goals – not too high, not too low but just challenging enough to stretch individuals while ensuring that, when the goals are achieved, they are appropriately recognised.

IMPLICATIONS FOR MANAGERS ARISING FROM GOAL-SETTING THEORY

For managers it can be difficult to correctly assess whether or not a goal is set too high for an individual. Vague or unclear goals, such as 'do your best', are less effective than something more concrete such as secure 10 new contracts each month for the next six months (Fishbach, 2018). In the workplace it is often the case that individuals are tasked with more than one goal and so the balancing act becomes more complex as more goals are added to the mix. Most organisations use goal setting as part of their performance-management system. Without clear performance goals and feedback, most people are not committed to work and are not inclined to give their best effort (Locke and Latham, 2002). As above, participation in the goal-setting process is likely to lead to greater employee acceptance of the goal and therefore higher motivation to achieve it, but again this is challenging for managers to balance. What happens when you have 15 subordinates reporting to you directly and each has six goals? How much time do you spend working through the goal-setting phase, let alone the measurement of their success? It can very quickly become a time-consuming process and particularly where the goals have to be documented, in a performance management system, for example.

Finally, feedback on the achievement of goals is a very important aspect of the critical success of goal-setting theory. The more feedback an individual receives about how they are doing in terms of achieving the goals set, the better. There is little motivational value in waiting until 12 months after the goal was set, only to inform a person that they have failed to achieve it. Regular feedback in terms of how the individual is doing against the target is more likely to result in increased effort and/or continued high performance. It is just as important to recognise high performance among staff as it is to tackle poor performance.

To recap what we have just learned in the first two sections of this chapter, need theories are those which focus on what needs a person is trying to satisfy and on what features of the work environment seem to satisfy those. On the other hand, process theories are those which focus on the way different variables combine to influence the amount of effort people are willing to make in order to gain some outcome. Although these two sets of theories offer us insights into what, how and when people are likely to be motivated, we must also consider what happens to an individual following the action they have taken, that is to say, what the consequences of the behaviour were. The consequences can be positive (in terms of reward for desired behaviour) or negative (in terms of punishment for undesirable behaviour). The use of reinforcement theory in this way provides managers with another set of tools to use to motivate their employees to engage in behaviours which help the organisation as a whole to achieve its goals.

The Influence of Organisational Culture on Motivation at Netflix

Netflix has been a real success story in the US and is rapidly expanding across the globe. This success has attracted a lot of attention from rivals in the industry, academics and practitioners alike. The fact that during 2013 alone the stock price for Netflix more than tripled, and by the end of 2020, Netflix had over 73 million US subscribers, is likely to explain some of this interest. So what is it about Netflix and its approach which is so compelling? Firstly, the company set out to 'craft a culture of excellence'. This is evident in everything they do, but particularly in relation to their people management practices. At Netflix they believe that the best thing you can do for current employees is to hire only the best new colleagues to work alongside them. This sentiment is captured beautifully in the statement that at Netflix 'adequate performance gets a generous severance package!' This means that they do not tolerate people who only perform to a passable standard and where they recruit an individual who turns out not to be a true

OB IN THE NEWS

high performer, they let them go albeit with a generous payment.

They also do not conduct any formal reviews. The organisation believes that performance should be discussed on an ongoing basis, all year round. They strongly advocate that managers be as honest as possible with their subordinates about how they are doing and, where an employee is not up to standard, that they let them go. They do not believe in performance improvement plans for low performers, on the basis that it just prolongs the inevitable. If someone isn't a good fit for the organisational culture, then they should let them go. This approach is very different from that of other organisations where there are formal review systems in place and a lengthy process to deal with underperformance issues, including providing employees with time to improve or address short-comings. The approach advocated by Netflix appears harsh, yet the logic is hard to argue with, particularly if the underperforming employee receives a generous severance package on leaving.

Furthermore, Netflix don't pay bonuses because they believe they are unnecessary if you hire the right person in the first instance. A bonus is unlikely to motivate the 'right' person to work harder or smarter; if they are committed to the company and believe in its values then they will work to their absolute best all the time and a bonus isn't going to make them more motivated. Compared with other high-tech companies, the reality is that the financial reward or pay that they do offer their employees is likely to be as good as, if not higher than, competitors, which allows them to recruit the best people in the first place. But a decision not to pay bonuses is a brave one given the fact that they are the norm in other organisations. Yet Netflix has a reputation for this strong culture and those that go to work there appear to embrace it.

This strong organisational culture is built around a clear understanding of how the company operates and what drives the business. This, they believe, is the key to motivating employees. Even when you have recruited well you need to clearly communicate how the company makes money and what behaviours will drive its success. In doing this you demonstrate to employees the direct link between the impact of their actions and the success of the organisation. Netflix also acknowledge that not all employees are the same and that within any company there are subcultures that need to be managed differently. The employees who work in the company call centre are very different from those who work at the company headquarters. Awareness of the different subcultures, and what makes

CREDIT: PHOTO BY PHILLIP GOLDSBERRY ON UNSPLASH

each tick, is the key to good leadership ▶See Chapter 6◀.

Questions

1 Do you think this non-traditional approach to the management of people is likely to be effective in all organisations? Do you think you would find it motivating

if you were an employee of Netflix? Explain your answer.

2 Paying bonuses is typical in most high-tech companies, particularly in the US. Why do you think Netflix has been so successful in attracting and retaining talented staff despite this fact?

3 What dangers, if any, can you see with having such a strong

dominant organisational culture?

4 Reading through the Netflix case, what theories of motivation do you recognise as being deployed by the organisation?

Source

McCord, P. (2014) How Netflix reinvented HR (cover story). *Harvard Business Review*, 92(1/2), 70–76.

WHAT ROLE DO SITUATIONAL FACTORS PLAY IN INFLUENCING MOTIVATION?

There is more to motivation than simply looking at individual behaviour. What role, if any, does the situational context have in motivating behaviour? People do not work in a vacuum. According to the Gallup 2018 State of the American Workplace report, only 49% of employees in the US are actively engaged. For the 51% who are not engaged, they represent a risk to the business. A non-engaged employee is more likely to negatively influence their co-workers, take sick days while not actually sick, provide poor customer service or, at the most extreme, sabotage the organisation by ignoring problems. Many employees who are not engaged, however, *want* a reason to be inspired (Gallup, 2018). It is clear that while there are individual factors which influence motivation (push factors), which are internal to an individual, there are also those pull factors whose operation is external to an individual, which have the potential to influence motivation. This section will take a closer look at three of those factors, namely the influence of co-workers, supervisors and the organisation's culture.

INFLUENCE OF CO-WORKERS

One of the biggest situational factors which impact upon individual motivation is the influence of the immediate work group. The ability of groups to strongly influence the motivation of individual members cannot be underestimated. This influence can be either positive or negative but equally as powerful in either direction. The ability of groups to influence individual behaviour depends on there being a strong group identity, an in-group, with established norms which have been developed over time, and whose members seek the approval of the rest of the group ▶See Chapter 7◀. Where such a strong in-group identity exists, the group's influence will almost certainly impact on the level of effort or motivation a person exhibits.

Consider this example. John began working as a porter in a children's hospital. His job required him to collect patients from wards and departments and bring them to other areas of the hospital for various appointments and procedures. One of the most important aspects of the role was ensuring that patients were brought down to the surgical units on time so as not to delay the surgical list. John was enthusiastic and keen to make a good impression when he began his new job. He went about his work as quickly and efficiently as possible and believed he was doing a good job. He managed to get through all his allocated tasks quickly and without fuss. Over lunch one day, however, a colleague of John's told him he needed to slow down because his fast-paced work was making them look bad. To John the message was clear: if you want to be 'one of us' you need to toe the line. John strongly wanted to get the approval of his work colleagues and did not want to be excluded, so he subsequently altered his behaviour to bring it into line with their expectations. He worked slower and as a result maintained his position as one of the in-group but at the expense of the organisation he worked for.

INFLUENCE OF SUPERVISORS

In the same way that co-workers and the desire to be a part of an in-group can drive motivational levels either positively or negatively, so too can the influence of supervisors ▶**See Chapter 7◀**. Supervisors, as we know from the earlier section, have within their power the ability to reward or punish employees. They equally have the ability to set expectations around what is, and is not, acceptable behaviour. However, as with rewards, the ability of supervisors to motivate performance varies from individual to individual. The same supervisor can be a source of increased motivation for some employees, while having the opposite effect on others. The potential impact of the supervisor on subordinates is heavily dependent on the one-to-one interpersonal relationship they have developed over time.

Consider this example. When managing a football team, the coach needs to pay attention to what motivates each individual player. There are always the players who require gentle handling, a quiet word in their ear and encouragement, to drive on their performance. There are others who respond better to the side-line calls and shouted demands for better performance. The key to getting the very best out of each player from a coaching perspective is to know each player and what motivates them.

It is a mistake to think that talented employees are so skilled and motivated that they don't need supervisor attention. The reality is that superstar performers need as much, if not more, of their manager's attention. High performers want their manager to track their performance, to recognise their efforts and give them rewards for those efforts. They crave feedback on a job well done and want to be seen to be doing a good job. Often high performers are looking to develop and move to the next level in terms of challenge. The role of a supportive, motivational manager is to recognise this need in their star performers and to ensure these opportunities for development and stretch are available to them to maintain this level of high performance.

SPOTLIGHT ON SKILLS

Given what you know about motivation, how would you approach the challenge of motivating a group of your classmates to get involved in training for four months for a charity 10k fun run?

1 What factors would you emphasise to motivate them? What measures would you put in place to monitor and track their performance?

2 What action would you take if someone was not motivated over the stretch of the four months?

3 Why do you think that people are motivated initially towards a goal or objective, but then find it hard to maintain this over the long term?

To help you answer these questions, visit bloomsbury.pub/organisational-behaviour to watch the video of Clare Hodder, a freelance rights consultant, talking about motivation.

INFLUENCE OF ORGANISATIONAL CULTURE

O'Reilly (1989) talks about culture as a form of social control. By this, he argues that individuals who work together and share a common set of expectations will try to live up to the expectations of their colleagues if they agree with them. This idea is often more effective than formal control systems. Culture is often defined simply as 'how we do things around here' ▶See Chapter 12◀. The beliefs that such a culture nurtures result in norms that powerfully shape the behaviour of individuals and groups. Norms are expectations about what are appropriate and inappropriate attitudes and behaviour. Where a strong culture exists within an organisation these acceptable norms are very evident and send strong messages to employees.

MONEY AS A MOTIVATOR – A SPECIAL CASE

Organisations use money to attract, motivate and retain employees. It is used to reward good performance, to motivate work to be done, and withheld from those who have not performed as expected in their work. Yet we know that a reward that effectively motivates one individual doesn't necessarily work for another, and we also know that there are other problems associated with offering financial rewards to employees to motivate them, yet despite this, most organisations persist in using money as their primary motivational tool. So let's take a closer look at the arguments against using monetary rewards to motivate employees.

Money or financial incentives are often criticised as motivators. They tend to have a short-term focus and are, by their very nature, temporary. Once you receive the reward you are no longer motivated by it. In this way there is a danger that they become the focus and that the employee loses interest in the actual work. For example, imagine you are a sales representative in a mobile phone shop and you have been told that if you achieve your target of selling a certain number of phones in the coming two months you will receive a 20% bonus. You achieve your target after only one month. Where is the motivation or incentive for the remaining month of the target period? What is the likely impact? Would you work as hard as you had been for the previous month or do you think you might take your foot off the pedal?

In some organisations the setting of specific targets like this can have a negative impact upon performance, as the employee is only interested in achieving the target set and is not incentivised to go beyond it. Worse still, by setting targets like this you may even be incentivising an individual to delay their performance so as to increase their chances of achieving their target the following month, or to avoid the target being increased to a level that they will find harder to achieve. This doesn't just apply in a sales environment, but across organisations. The achievement of a target or goal can mean that better ways of working and serving clients' needs may go undiscovered as there is no incentive to improve the process if the target can be achieved.

Financial rewards assume that people are motivated by lower-level needs. While money is important, and we all need a certain amount of it, it would appear that it is no substitute for higher-level needs. It is these higher-level needs that, when met, have a much more long-lasting effect. When an individual is so focused on the achievement of a particular extrinsic goal it often comes at the expense of intrinsic rewards. Let's take the example again of our sales representative in the mobile phone shop. What if rather than a 20% bonus for achieving a target of selling a certain number of phones in any given period, they were told that those sales representatives who consistently performed above expectation would be in line for promotion to store manager. What do you think would be the likely impact of this incentive over pure financial incentives for the sales representative? Do you think they would be more, or less, motivated? Do you think they would be likely to focus on long- or short-term goals? Do you think they would be more, or less, likely to engage in mis-selling products to customers knowing they were not what the customer needed? Why do you think this might be?

MANAGERIAL TAKEAWAYS

We can see that motivation in the workplace, while offering enormous potential benefits to both the organisation and the individual, is a highly complex phenomenon. Motivation influences people's decision to actively choose to undertake a task and to persist at that task over time until it is complete. If managers understand the theories of motivation, they offer the potential of a highly motivated and engaged workforce who are likely to drive higher performance. For the individual, being highly motivated is likely to lead to greater job satisfaction, greater sense of achievement and a more fulfilling career. The difficulty, however, is that individuals are all unique and what motivates one, may not motivate another. The ability of managers to understand the sources of motivation, in terms of both internal individual factors which drive motivation and the external situational factors which motivate, are key in organisational life.

 ## CHAPTER REVIEW QUESTIONS

1   Why is an understanding of motivation so important to the success of any organisation?
2   What are 'push' and 'pull' motivational forces? Provide some examples.
3   How can managers affect motivation by changing the content of a job?
4   What are some of the characteristics of an individual with a high need for achievement?
5   According to Equity Theory, what would happen if an individual felt they were being paid less for the same effort as colleagues doing the same work? What options would be opened to the individual to address the imbalance?
6   According to Expectancy Theory, how can managers influence employees' level of motivation?
7   What role do situational factors play in influencing motivation?
8   How important is money in motivating individuals?

 ## FURTHER READING

Britt, T.W. (2003) Black Hawk Down at work. *Harvard Business Review*, 81(1), 16–17.

Clark, R.E. (2003) Fostering the work motivation of individuals and teams. *Performance Improvement*, 42(3), 21–29.

Kalleberg, A.L. (2008) The mismatched worker: When people don't fit their jobs. *Academy of Management Perspectives*, 22(1), 24–40.

Kehoe, M. (2013) *Make that Grade: Organisational Behaviour*, 2nd edition. Dublin: Gill & Macmillan.

McCord, P. (2014) How Netflix Reinvented HR (cover story). *Harvard Business Review*, 92(1/2), 70–76.

Nicholson, N. (2003) How to motivate your problem people. *Harvard Business Review*, 81(1), 56–58.

 USEFUL WEBSITES

http://hbr.org/magazine

Harvard Business Review magazine website is useful for short, up-to-date and easy to read management insights into all areas.

http://www.ted.com/talks/dan_pink_on_motivation

This TED Talk on motivation contains some very interesting ideas.

http://www.motivate.com.au/

This website covers all aspects of motivation from workplace motivation to student motivation.

Online Resources

Visit bloomsbury.pub/organisational-behaviour to access additional materials to support teaching and learning.

PART 2
MANAGING BEHAVIOUR AT WORK

OVERVIEW

Managing a group of people brings a new set of challenges. This part of the book identifies some of the key
issues involved in managing behaviour at work. Given
the impact of Covid-19 on all our lives we have included
a new chapter which focuses on health and well-being
at work. The impact that work has on our well-being
is very important to understand. In this new chapter
we deal with managing emotions at work, stress in the
workplace, resilience and positive psychology. We have
also included a new chapter on managing diversity at
work. Although diversity can present a number of challenges if not managed correctly, the benefits it brings
to organisations far outweigh the few potential issues.

- Chapter 6: Leadership
- Chapter 7: Groups and teams in the workplace
- Chapter 8: Management control, power and authority
- Chapter 9: Managing healthy workplaces
- Chapter 10: Managing diversity

 Visit bloomsbury.pub/organisational-behaviour to play an interactive simulation that will allow
you to practise what you have learned about managing behaviour at work. The simulation puts
you in the role of a manager acting out the decision-making process.

6 LEADERSHIP

Ronan Carbery and Nuala Ryan

LEARNING OUTCOMES

BY THE END OF THIS CHAPTER YOU SHOULD BE ABLE TO:

- Define leadership and understand the differences between leaders and managers.

- Distinguish between trait, behavioural and contingency leadership theories.

- Recognise the new leadership theories – specifically what is meant by transformational, charismatic and distributed leadership.

- Recognise the nature of good leadership and the darker side of leadership.

- Explain the issues that need to be considered when deciding whether a leader can be developed, why organisations invest in leader development, and show an awareness of the different approaches used to develop leaders.

CREDIT: GETTY IMAGES/ISTOCKPHOTO

THIS CHAPTER DISCUSSES...

INTRODUCTION

Leaders are important in organisations because they drive the development of an organisational culture ▸See Chapter 12◂ and manage organisational change, two key aspects of organisational life ▸See Chapter 13◂. While Bennis (2007, p. 3) asserts that a 'handful of people have changed millions of lives and reshaped the world', there is also a debate as to how influential these leaders really are. Some writers believe they are key to organisational success. Day and Lord (1988) suggest that up to 45% of the variance in organisational performance can be explained by leadership within the organisation, 'It is when an organization must be changed to reflect changes in technology, the environment and the completion of programs, it's leadership is critical in completing that process' (Bass, 2008, p. 15). Leaders develop a vision for the future along with strategies for producing the changes needed to achieve that vision. They articulate this vision to employees in order to get their commitment to its achievement and motivate these individuals to keep them moving in the right direction by appealing to basic but often untapped human needs, values and emotions. Successful leaders who have done this at various times in history include Mary Robinson (Irish President and UN High Commissioner for Human Rights), Barak Obama (US President), Hillary Clinton (former US Secretary of State), Elon Musk (Tesla and SpaceX) and Mother Teresa (Founder of the Missionaries of Charity).

This chapter examines the concept of leadership and considers the importance of effective leadership in organisations. We look at the leadership under three main headings, Classical leadership theories, which includes Trait, Behaviour, Contingency, and Leader–Member Exchange; Contemporary leadership theories including Transformational, Charismatic, and Distributed; finally, central topics of leadership including Gender, Dark Side of Leadership and Ethics, Leadership Development, and Leader Identity.

WHAT IS LEADERSHIP?

leadership is the ability to lead, guide and inspire a group of followers.

The study of leadership can be traced as far back as the early part of the 20th century. However, a scientific approach to studying leadership did not fully emerge until the early 1930s (House and Aditya, 1997). Investigations into what constitutes leadership effectiveness began in earnest over the next several decades at various centres for research on leadership such as at Iowa during the 1930s and at Michigan and Ohio States in the 1940s to 1950s. According to Bass (1990), 'The study of leadership rivals in age the emergence of civilization, which shaped its leaders as much as it was shaped by them. From its infancy, the study of history has been the study of leaders – what they did and why they did it' (p. 3). The study of leadership has been characterised by not only a significant amount of research, but by shifting interpretations of what it means to be a leader and what leadership actually involves. Over 60 years ago, Bennis (1959) suggested: 'Of all the hazy and confounding areas in social psychology, leadership theory undoubtedly contends for top nomination. And, ironically, probably more has been written and less is known about leadership than about any other topic in the behavioral sciences' (pp. 259–301). In more recent times, thankfully, a more cohesive overview of the nature of leadership has emerged.

Defining leadership in a concise manner isn't an easy task, with Fiedler (1971) highlighting that 'there are almost as many definitions of leadership as there are leadership theories – and there are almost as many theories of leadership as there are psychologists working in the field'

(p. 1). Broadly however, leadership can be characterised as the nature of the influencing process that takes place between a leader and followers, and how this influencing process is affected by the leader's dispositional characteristics, their behaviours, followers' perceptions and the context in which the influencing process takes place.

It is important to differentiate leadership from power and management, because these concepts are often confused with leadership. Power ▶**See Chapter 8◀** refers to the means leaders have to potentially influence others; for example, referent power (i.e. followers' identification with, or respect for, the leader), expertise or the ability to reward or punish performance. In terms of a comparison between leadership and management, leadership is more purpose driven, resulting in change based on values, ideals and emotional exchanges compared with the more objectives-driven approach of management, resulting in stability based on bureaucratic means, and the fulfilment of contractual obligations.

LEADERS VERSUS MANAGERS: ARE THEY THE SAME OR DIFFERENT?

There is considerable debate as to how a leader is different from a manager. A critical understanding of how these individuals are defined is important as it underpins organisational systems of support such as development and talent management practices. Cunningham (1986), for example, identifies three different viewpoints on the relationship between leadership and management. The first position assumes that leadership is one competence among a range required for effective management. A second position advocated by Bennis and Nanus (2003) suggests that the two concepts are separate but related, whereas the third position sees both concepts to be partially overlapping. There are, however, some who view leaders and managers as fundamentally different individuals differing in their world views. Zaleznik's (1977) award winning article argued that managers look to solve problems quickly to re-instate order and control whereas leaders will tolerate risk and chaos to delay closure until the deep problems are understood and rectified. Leaders 'have more in common with artists, scientists, and other creative thinkers than they do with managers' (Zaleznik, 1977, p. 74). There is evidence among academics that there is a need to conceptually distinguish leadership from management, often at the expense of the latter. Management as an activity and concept is often viewed as a 'second class citizen', something which is very transactional in nature.

Kotter (1988) has argued that leaders and managers are distinct in their roles and functions. He considers management to be concerned with planning and organising whereas leadership is concerned with creating, coping with change and helping organisations to adapt in turbulent times. Other contributions have similarly emphasised that these concepts are different. Boydell *et al.* (2004) consider management to be about implementation, order, efficiency and effectiveness. They define leadership as concerned with future directions in time of uncertainty. Boydell *et al.* (2004) argue that management may be sufficient in an organisation in times of stability; however, it is insufficient when organisational conditions are characterised by complexity, unpredictability and rapid change. Research suggests that how well a leader influences his/her followers is related to self-confidence. This self-confidence is derived from the leader's ability to influence. However, in order to be an effective leader, it is also important to have the capacity to motivate. Judge and Bono

Narcissistic Leaders

What happens when a group is without a leader? Research suggests you can often count on a narcissist to take charge (Brunell *et al.*, 2008). Academics at Ohio State University found that people who score high in narcissism tend to take control of leaderless groups. Narcissism is a trait in which people are self-centred, exaggerate their talents and abilities, and lack empathy for others. While this sounds like a recipe for disaster when it comes to leadership, not only do narcissists generally rate themselves as leaders, but other group members also see them as the people who really run the group.

Senior executives often appear to behave in destructive and chaotic ways. Many abuse and insult employees and use fear, bullying and chaos as tools for managing their workforce. Others cheat, lie and abuse positions of trust to enrich themselves and to move up the corporate ladder. Others engage in sexual harassment on an almost routine basis. While the desire for power is what really drives narcissists to seek leadership positions, how do people with such characteristics end up as leaders in many organisations?

Psychologists have a set of three personality characteristics (narcissism, Machiavellianism and psychopathology) which make some people particularly successful in manipulating others, and there is a lot of evidence indicating that these traits are indeed linked to career advancement. One explanation for the surprising prevalence of psychopathology, narcissism and Machiavellianism in the ranks of executives is that these are the very traits that make them successful, at least in the short term.

Individuals who score highly on these personality characteristics are often charming, highly confident, ruthless, highly motivated to succeed, willing to take extreme risks, identifying their opponents' weaknesses, and willing to do what is necessary to succeed, even if it is not honest, ethical or legal. These same individuals are often drawn to power, and skilled at skirting social norms and rules to attain it. All of these character flaws help managers and junior executives to climb the ladder to the top of organisations.

And what happens when they get to the top? Evidence suggests that organisations led by narcissistic CEOs experience significant downsides, including evidence of increased risk taking, overpaying for acquisitions, manipulating accounting data, and even fraud. O'Reilly III *et al.* (2018) found that the effects of the narcissistic behaviour of CEOs subject their organisations to undue legal risk because they are so overconfident about their ability to win these cases, and less concerned about the financial costs to their organisations of such lawsuits.

Questions

1 Why don't organisations detect narcissists before they reach the top?
2 What can organisations do to prevent hiring individuals with narcissistic tendencies?
3 What strategies would you employ if you were dealing with a narcissist at work?

OB IN PRACTICE

CREDIT: GETTY IMAGES/ISTOCKPHOTO

(2000), for example, found that warmth, trustworthiness and altruism are the strongest and most important predictors of leadership. Other studies have found that effective leaders are less critical and aggressive than non-leaders. Leaders are often characterised as having the ability to 'move people' or the ability to inspire others with a vision of the future to which they can aspire. To express this vision with enthusiasm, leaders are expected to be optimistic and energetic.

The ability to provide effective leadership is one of the most important skills that a manager can possess and it is increasingly recognised that all managers, including first-line supervisors, need at some level to be leaders and to understand the concept of leadership, albeit the higher the organisational level, the more complex leadership becomes and the more it is concerned with broader and long-term aims. In some organisations people may be senior professionals such as doctors or scientists but not defined as managers (at least in terms of the formal organisational hierarchy). It would be naïve, however, not to think of them as leaders or potential leaders.

CLASSICAL THEORIES OF LEADERSHIP

TRAIT THEORIES

Early leadership theories focus on the leader's traits or behaviours, with employee work performance or commitment as outcomes of interest (Gibb, 1947) ▶**See Chapter 2**◀. Early research on leadership prior to the 1950s was based on the psychological focus of the day, which was that of people having inherited characteristics or traits. Attention was focused on discovering these traits, often by studying successful leaders, but with the underlying assumption that if other people could also be found with these traits, then they, too, could become great leaders.

Stogdill (1974) identified a number of traits and skills as critical to leaders, including being adaptable to situations, being alert to the social environment, being ambitious and achievement-orientated, demonstrating assertiveness, creativity, and being diplomatic and tactful.

McCall and Lombardo (1983) identified four primary traits by which leaders could either succeed or fail:

- **Emotional stability and composure:** The ability to be calm, confident and predictable, particularly when under stress, is crucial for leadership success.
- **Admitting error:** Owning up to mistakes, rather than putting energy into covering them up, is an important determinant of leadership ability.
- **Good interpersonal skills:** Being able to communicate and persuade others without resorting to negative or coercive tactics is necessary for effective leadership.
- **Intellectual breadth:** Successful leaders are able to understand a wide range of areas, rather than having a narrow area of expertise.

These traits are broadly similar to Richard Branson's three most important leadership principles, which he suggests are listening (interpersonal skills), learning (intellectual breadth) and laughter (composure), which he outlines in his book *The Virgin Way: Everything I Know About Leadership* (2014).

There have been many different studies of leadership traits and they agree only in the general honourable qualities needed to be a leader. One of the major criticisms of trait theory is its simplistic approach; that it fails to take account of other factors that will influence the development of a successful leader, such as the situational and environmental factors we mentioned briefly earlier. A more significant issue regarding trait theories is that few traits seem to correlate strongly with leadership efficacy. Trait leadership theory usually only focuses on how this is perceived by followers rather than a leader's actual effectiveness (Judge *et al.*, 2009), for example, in the financial performance of the organisation they lead.

IN REALITY

'Some are born great,
some achieve greatness,
and some have greatness thrust upon 'em'
Shakespeare, *Twelfth Night* (1602)

The above quotation from Shakespeare's play *Twelfth Night*, touches upon the issue as to whether people are born leaders or whether it is something that can be developed. We often assume that those who make good leaders possess some attributes that allow them to excel in this role, that the rest of us simply do not have. But are leadership qualities innate or acquired? Researchers are fascinated by the links between personality and leadership, hoping to better understand what differentiates leaders from everyone else. Trait theories of leadership identify the specific personality traits that distinguish leaders from non-leaders. They are based on the premise that leaders are 'born, not made'. But while early research focused on the relationship between personality and leadership, it reported little supporting evidence. Nevertheless, research interest in this area still continues, with Judge and Bono (2004) reporting that 12% of all leadership research published between 1990 and 2004 included both 'personality' and 'leadership'. Behavioural genetics has provided a useful tool to investigate the often-debated question of whether leaders are born or made. A 2013 study looking at brain functions in 103 US Army officers found that neural networks in the frontal and prefrontal lobes of those deemed 'leaders' were different from those who were not (Hannah *et al.*, 2013). These areas of the brain are associated with self-regulation, decision-making and memory. Closely related to trait theory, biological theories of leadership, one of the oldest schools of leadership theories, is making a comeback and is set to be an area of significant research over the next decade. This research has provided evidence to support the heritability of leader emergence (Ilies *et al.*, 2004), identified genes associated with leader emergence (De Neve *et al.*, 2013) and outlines the effects of physical appearance on leadership outcomes (Antonakis and Dalgas, 2009; Antonakis and Eubanks, 2017).

What are the implications of this? It could potentially revolutionise how organisations assess and develop leaders, with brain scans being used to identify those with the 'leadership gene' early and then training being given them accordingly.

Interestingly, research by De Neve *et al.* (2013) may take us full circle back to the inheritability argument, as it suggests the possibility that a 'leadership gene' exists. De Neve *et al.* (2013) identified a specific DNA sequence associated with the tendency for individuals to occupy a leadership position, and estimate that a quarter of the difference between how effective and ineffective leaders behave can be explained by genes passed down from their parents.

BEHAVIOURAL THEORIES OF LEADERSHIP

From the late 1950s onwards, there was a move away from the belief that leaders are born, towards a desire to determine the types of behaviours that specific leaders displayed. Behavioural theories of leadership are based on the premise that certain behaviours differentiate effective leaders from non-leaders. Seminal behavioural theories of leadership were proposed by studies in Ohio State University (Stogdill and Coons, 1957) and the University of Michigan (Likert, 1961). We will look next at both of these studies and also at the concept of participative leadership.

OHIO STATE STUDIES

In the 1950s and 1960s a series of studies carried out by researchers at Ohio State University identified two factors related to leader effectiveness: consideration and initiating structure. The initiating structure leadership style focuses on the extent to which a leader defines and structures their role, and the roles of their followers, in achieving organisational goals and objectives. The consideration leadership style is essentially the same as an employee-centred leadership style; it focuses on meeting people's needs and developing relationships.

Because a leader can be high or low on initiating structure and/or consideration, four types of leadership styles were developed: low structure and high consideration; high structure and high consideration; low structure and low consideration; and high structure and low consideration. The results of the research demonstrated that leaders who were rated high in both initiating structure and consideration were more likely to achieve greater performance among their followers.

UNIVERSITY OF MICHIGAN STUDIES

A second set of studies adopting a behavioural approach to leadership was done in Michigan University, starting in the 1950s under the general direction of Rensis Likert. The focus of the Michigan studies was to determine the principles and methods of leadership that led to productivity and job satisfaction. The University of Michigan Leadership Model identifies two leadership styles: the production-centred style and employee-centred style. Production-centred style refers to the extent to which the leader takes charge of technical aspects of the role to get the job done. Employee-centred style looks at the extent to which the leader focuses, similarly to the consideration style mentioned above, on meeting the needs of employees while developing relationships. Unsurprisingly, employee-oriented leaders consistently achieved higher levels of both productivity and job satisfaction. It should be noted, however, that the technical aspects of the role cannot be ignored. Truly successful leaders who adopted an employee-oriented approach reported that production was one of their primary responsibilities.

THE MANAGERIAL GRID

Recognising that leaders need to be concerned for their people while also having concern for the work to be done, Blake and Mouton (1962) built on the Ohio State and Michigan studies by looking at how much attention they pay to one or the other, and developed the Managerial Grid (see Figure 6.1). The grid is similar to both the Ohio State studies and Michigan studies in that its two axes – Concern for People and Concern for Production – link to Ohio's initiating structure and consideration, and Michigan's production-centred style and employee-centred style.

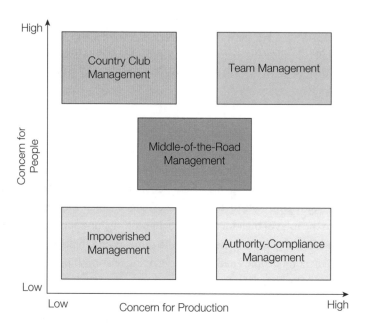

Figure 6.1 The Managerial Grid

Source: Adapted from Blake and Mouton (1962).

The grid identifies five key styles:

1 Impoverished management: Minimum effort to get the work done. A basically lazy approach that avoids as much work as possible.
2 Authority-compliance: Strong focus on task, but with little concern for people. Focus on efficiency, including the elimination of people wherever possible.
3 Country Club management: Care and concern for the people, with a comfortable and friendly environment and collegial style. But a low focus on the task may give questionable results.
4 Middle of the road management: A weak balance of focus on both people and the work. Doing enough to get things done, but not pushing the boundaries of what may be possible.
5 Team management: Firing on all cylinders: people are committed to the task and the leader is committed to people.

Many other similar models and variants have appeared since this was proposed in 1962. The dimensions presented here are a useful starting point for understanding aspects of leadership, but as other models point out, there is more to leadership and management than this.

CONTINGENCY THEORY

In the 1960s several scholars argued that the style of leadership that would be most effective depended upon the situation. In this approach, the leader's ability to lead is contingent upon various situational factors, including the leader's preferred style, the capabilities and behaviours of followers and also various other situational factors. This is also often referred to as Situational Theory. Contingency theories are a type of behavioural theory that argue that there is no one best way of leading and that a leadership style that is effective in some situations may not be successful in others.

> contingency theories present a belief that there is no one best way to lead.

Contingency theory is similar to situational theory in that there is an assumption of no simple one right way to do things. The main difference is that situational theory tends to focus more on the behaviours that the leader should adopt given situational factors such as how followers behave, whereas contingency theory takes a broader view that includes contingent factors about leader capability and other variables within the situation. Two of the main contingency theories are Fiedler's Contingency Model and House's Path Goal Theory.

FIEDLER'S CONTINGENCY MODEL

Fiedler's (1971) situational contingency theory suggests that group effectiveness depends on an appropriate match between a leader's style and the demands of the situation. Fiedler started from the premise that anyone appointed to a leadership position should have a certain standard of technical knowledge, therefore he wanted to determine what aspects of leadership behaviour influence how well groups work together. Fiedler believed that situational control (the extent to which the leader can control what their group is going to do) was a significant factor in determining the effectiveness of leadership behaviour. He first proposed a contingency model, which was a dynamic model where the personal characteristics and motivation of the leader are said to interact with the current situation that the group faces.

Fiedler and Chemers (1974) then identified the Least Preferred Co-Worker (LPC) scoring for leaders by asking them first to think of a person with whom they worked that they would like least to work with again, and then to score the person on a range of scales between positive factors (friendly, helpful, cheerful, etc.) and negative factors (unfriendly, unhelpful, gloomy, etc.). A high LPC leader generally scores the other person as positive and a low LPC leader scores them as negative. High LPC leaders tend to have close and positive relationships and act in a supportive way, even prioritising the relationship before the task. Low LPC leaders put the task first and will turn to relationships only when satisfied with how the work is going.

Three factors are then identified about the leader, the member and the task, as follows:

- **Leader–member relations:** The extent to which the leader has the support and loyalty of followers, and relations with them are friendly and cooperative.
- **Task structure:** The extent to which tasks are standardised, documented and controlled.
- **Leader's position-power:** The extent to which the leader has authority to assess follower performance and give reward or punishment.

The best LPC approach depends on a combination of these three. Generally, a high LPC approach is best when leader–member relations are poor, except when the task is unstructured and the leader is weak, in which case a low LPC style is better.

Leadership Principles at Amazon

IN THE NEWS

With revenues of over a quarter of a trillion dollars in 2019, Amazon is the world's largest internet company and the second largest private employer in the USA. The company has a unique culture of hiring and developing leaders with a focus on 14 Amazon Leadership Principles that have guided and shaped the company's decisions and its distinctive culture. These Amazon leadership principles were set in stone to build a strong entrepreneurial and highly execution-based culture. Every Amazon employee is expected to adhere to these principles, and the firm tests all hires on the same criteria.

At Amazon's headquarters, in Seattle, the Leadership Principles are painted on walls, posted in bathrooms, printed on laminated cards in executives' wallets. They urge employees to 'never say "that's not my job"', to 'examine their strongest convictions with humility', to 'not compromise for the sake of social cohesion', and to commit to excellence even if 'people may think these standards are unreasonably high'.

Jeff Bezos, the founder, CEO and President of Amazon, believes the company is successful not because of any asset or technology but because of the Leadership Principles which underpin the organisational culture. Bezos refers to the company's management style as Day One Thinking: a willingness to treat every day as if it were the first day of business, to constantly re-examine even the most closely held beliefs. In his first letter to Amazon shareholders in 1998, Bezos declared that it was 'Day 1 for the internet, and if we execute well, for Amazon. com'. By this, he meant that the company, which was already four years old, should always think of itself as being at the beginning of its journey. Nineteen years later in a 2017 letter to shareholders, Bezos wrote 'Day Two is stasis, followed by irrelevance. Followed by excruciating, painful decline. Followed by death. And that is why it is always Day One.'

The culture within Amazon strongly forbids doing anything that is considered to slow the company down. As another Leadership Principle articulates, 'Speed matters … Many decisions and actions are reversible and do not need extensive study. We value calculated risk taking.'

This culture has, however, led to a great deal of criticism. The *New York Times* published an article portraying Amazon as a tough employer that places innovation and company performance above the well-being of its people. Reports of unreasonably high standards, colleagues sabotaging one another, and managers who deal unsympathetically with workers enduring family tragedies and serious health problems, were immediately refuted by Bezos, who wrote a memo to all 180,000 workers in Amazon saying that

CREDIT: GETTY IMAGES

'The article doesn't describe the Amazon I know or the caring Amazonians I work with every day.' In response to continued criticism, however, in October 2018, Bezos announced that Amazon would pay all of its US-based employees $15 an hour for their work. Nonetheless, its leadership principles have remained constant and a recent survey of Amazon warehouse workers in England by the group Organise found that 74% were afraid to go to the toilet during a shift out of fear of missing productivity targets.

Questions:

1 How are culture and leadership related?
2 Given the success of Amazon, can it be argued that their approach to leadership is appropriate?
3 Look at the full list of Leadership Principles – can they be applied to any organisation?

Sources

Amazon Leadership principles
https://www.amazon.jobs/en/principles

Is Amazon unstoppable?
https://www.newyorker.com/magazine/2019/10/21/is-amazon-unstoppable

Inside Amazon: Wrestling Big Ideas in a Bruising Workplace
https://www.nytimes.com/2015/08/16/technology/inside-amazon-wrestling-big-ideas-in-a-bruising-workplace.html

'I worked in an Amazon warehouse. Bernie Sanders is right to target them'
https://www.theguardian.com/commentisfree/2018/sep/17/amazon-warehouse-bernie-sanders

SITUATIONAL LEADERSHIP THEORY

Another popular leadership model that has its roots in the Ohio State leadership studies is the Hersey and Blanchard (1972) theory of Situational Leadership. This suggests that leaders should match their leadership style to the development level of the person, or group of people, being led. In their leadership model they describe development level in terms of the follower's competence (ability) and commitment (willingness). According to this theory, there are no good and bad styles, only those that are appropriate for the given situation of the task and people who are being led.

Hersey and Blanchard (1972) proposed four leadership styles (S1 to S4) that match the development levels (D1 to D4) of the followers. The four styles suggest that leaders should put greater or less focus on the task in question and/or the relationship between the leader and the follower, depending on the development level of the follower. Figure 6.2 presents their model of situational leadership.

S1: Directing

Follower: D1: Low competence, low commitment / unable and unwilling
Leader: High task focus, low relationship focus

When the follower cannot do the job and is not motivated, then the leader takes a highly directive role, telling them what to do and without a great deal of concern for the relationship. The leader may also provide a working structure, both for the job and in terms of how the person is controlled.

This is taking a particularly managerial stance, using whatever legitimate coercive power the leader has to make the person do the job that they do not want to do. The relationship is less important here, first because the person may be replaced if they do not perform as required.

The lower maturity of the person also is assumed to lead to an attitude that does not respond well to a relationship-based approach.

S2: *Coaching*

Follower: D2: Some competence, low commitment / unable and willing
Leader: High task focus, high relationship focus

When the follower wants to do the job but lacks the skills or knowledge, the leader now turns on the charm more, acting in a friendlier manner as they persuade and help the follower to complete the task.

S3: *Supporting*

Follower: D3: High competence, variable commitment / able and unwilling
Leader: Low task focus, high relationship focus

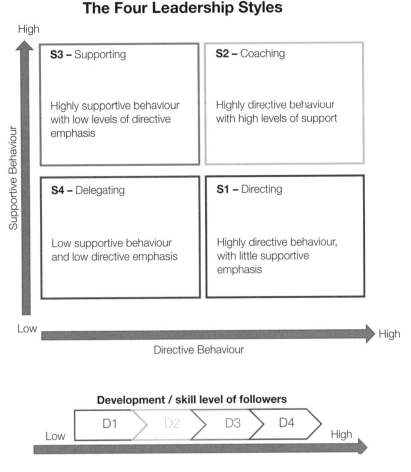

The Four Leadership Styles

Figure 6.2 Situational leadership styles

When the follower can do the job, but is refusing to do it, the leader need not worry about showing them what to do, and instead is concerned with finding out why the person is refusing and thence persuading them to cooperate.

S4: Delegating

Follower: D4: High competence, high commitment / able and willing
Leader: Low task focus, low relationship focus

When the follower can do the job and is motivated to do it, then the leader can basically leave them to it, trusting them to get on with the job.

One thing to note is that the assumptions that the model is based on can be challenged, for example the assumption that at the 'telling' level, the relationship is of lower importance.

LEADER–MEMBER EXCHANGE THEORY

Another relatively recent leadership theory concerns relational theories. Relational leadership theories focus on the relationship between two parties and reflect the influence process that occurs through the strength of a relationship. The most well-known of these, Leader–Member Exchange Theory, also called LMX or Vertical Dyad Linkage Theory, is a social exchange leader–follower approach that investigates the quality of the relationship experienced between and leader and follower (Graen and Uhl-Bien, 1995). LMX focuses on followers and describes how leaders in groups maintain their position through a series of unspoken exchange agreements with their members. In particular, leaders often have a special relationship with an inner circle of trusted assistants and advisors, to whom they give high levels of responsibility, decision influence and access to resources. This 'in-group' essentially pay for their position. They work harder, are more committed to task objectives, and share more administrative duties. They are also expected to be fully committed and loyal to their leader. Individuals not in this group, on the other hand, are given low levels of choice or influence. This can put constraints upon the leader. They have to nurture the relationship with their inner circle, balancing giving them power with ensuring they do not have enough to strike out on their own. These relationships, if they are going to happen, start very soon after a person joins the group and follow three stages.

1 **Role taking** The member joins the team and the leader assesses their abilities and talents. Based on this, the leader may offer them opportunities to demonstrate their capabilities.
2 **Role-making** In the second phase, the leader and member take part in an unstructured and informal negotiation whereby a role is created for the member, and the often-tacit promise of benefit and power in return for dedication and loyalty takes place.

3 **Routinisation** In this phase, a pattern of ongoing social exchange between the leader and the member becomes established. Successful members are thus similar to or compatible with the leader in many ways (which perhaps explains why many senior teams are all white, male, middle-class and middle-aged). They work hard at building and sustaining trust and respect. To help this, they are empathetic, patient, reasonable, sensitive, and are good at seeing the viewpoint of other people, especially that of the leader. Aggression, sarcasm and an egocentric view are keys to the out-group wash-room. The overall quality of the LMX relationship varies with several factors. Curiously, it is better when the challenge of the job is extremely high *or* extremely low. The size of the group, financial resource availability and the overall workload are also important.

BUILDING YOUR EMPLOYABILITY SKILLS

Demonstrating Leadership

Rosenberg *et al.* (2012) highlight that leadership skills, management skills, interpersonal skills, critical thinking skills and a strong work ethic are among the most essential for graduate employment. Leadership skills and information technology skills have also been identified as the strongest predictors of employee career advancement (Heimler *et al.*, 2012).

When interviewing for jobs after you graduate you will likely be asked how you exhibited leadership skills in your educational environment. Identify those you have developed over the course of your studies to date.

CONTEMPORARY LEADERSHIP THEORIES

DISTRIBUTED LEADERSHIP

distributed leadership is the idea that leadership of an organisation should not rest with a single individual, but should be shared or 'distributed' among those with the relevant skills.

Moving on from the relationship between leaders and groups, distributed leadership is a relatively new approach to leadership which has encouraged a shift in focus from the attributes and behaviours of individual 'leaders' as promoted within traditional theories of leadership discussed earlier, to a more systemic perspective, where collaborative working is undertaken between individuals who trust and respect each other's contribution ▶See Chapter 7◀.

Spillane and Diamond (2007) outline the way that distributed leadership roles are played by multiple individuals, whether in formal or informal positions. Distributed leadership is neither a top-down nor a bottom-up approach but recognises that leadership roles are played by different people at different times. Under distributed leadership, everyone is responsible and accountable for leadership within his or her area. Good ideas come from throughout the University, and many people cooperate in creating change. A central goal of the distributed leadership approach is for individuals to succeed in a climate of shared purpose, teamwork and respect.

This approach has become popular in educational institutes, but Bolden *et al.* (2008) found that a distributed leadership approach may be most powerful as a rhetorical device, and be used by those in positions of real power to disguise power differentials, offering the illusion of consultation and participation while disguising the methods by which decisions are reached and resources distributed.

CHARISMATIC LEADERSHIP THEORIES

In the early 1980s a number of prominent academics expressed considerable disillusionment with the state of leadership theory. Out of this negativity emerged a number of 'positive' approaches, which shared some common features, which Bryman (1992) referred to as the 'new leadership'. The new leadership approaches focused on symbolic leader behaviour, visionary, inspirational messages, emotional feelings, ideological and moral values, attention, and intellectual stimulation, in contrast to more traditional leadership models which emphasised leader–follower exchange relationships, the provision of direction and support, and reinforcing behaviours. Emerging from these early works, charismatic and transformational leadership theories have turned out to be the most frequently researched theories over the last two decades.

Charismatic leadership is characterised by leaders who have what is commonly referred to as a special gift for doing exceptional things, charisma. When we think of charismatic leaders, names like Gandhi, John F. Kennedy and Nelson Mandela come to mind. Charismatic leaders, with their personal abilities and personal power, are capable of having profound and extraordinary effects on their followers (Conger and Kanungo, 1987) by using articulation and impression management skills to formulate their visions. In 1976, Robert House published the theory of charismatic leadership, and since then it has received a large amount of attention from researchers trying to understand its importance and place in leadership theory. House (see Hunt and Larson, 1977) listed four main personality characteristics of a charismatic leader (dominance, self-confidence, the desire to influence and strong moral values) and several behaviours (a leader articulates clear goals and communicates high expectations, displays as a strong role model, shows competence and expresses confidence in the follower, and arouses motives). House suggests that, combined, these characteristics and behaviours produce followers that: trust and give unquestioned acceptance of the leader's ideology; develop affection for and, obedience to, the leader; and develop heightened emotional goals, emotional involvement and increased confidence. These outcomes suggest the importance of charismatic leadership in terms of follower effectiveness.

TRANSFORMATIONAL LEADERSHIP

A person with vision and passion can achieve great things and it may be easier to get things done by injecting enthusiasm and energy into followers.

Transformational leaders transform their followers' values, needs and beliefs and inspire them to go beyond their own self-interests for the good of the team by engaging in behaviours that elicit admiration and respect in their followers. Transformational leadership

transformational leadership is a leadership style that can inspire positive changes in those who follow.

starts with the development of a vision, a view of the future that will excite and convert potential followers. This vision may be developed by the leader, by the senior team, or may emerge from a broad series of discussions. The important factor is that the leader is fully committed to it. The next step is to constantly sell the vision. This takes energy and commitment, as few people will immediately buy into a radical vision, and some will join the show much more slowly than others. A transformational leader thus takes every opportunity and will use whatever works to convince others to climb on board the bandwagon. In order to create followers, the transformational leader has to be very careful in creating trust, and their personal integrity is a critical part of the package that they are selling. In effect, they are selling themselves as well as the vision. In parallel with the selling activity is seeking the way forward. Some transformational leaders know the way, and simply want others to follow them. Others do not have a ready strategy, but will gladly lead the exploration of possible routes to achieve a specific vision.

One example of a transformational leader is Martin Luther King, an American pastor, activist, humanitarian and leader in the African-American Civil Rights movement. Dr King was an inspiring orator who motivated followers to have the level of courage required to practise nonviolent protest in the service of justice. He also had the capacity to keep a network of activists, both black and white, organised, while he worked to gain wider support through challenging Americans outside the movement to live up to the fundamental American principle that all citizens are created equal with rights to 'life, liberty, and the pursuit of happiness'.

The transformational approach is often contrasted with the transactional leadership approach. Transactional leadership styles are more concerned with maintaining the status quo. Transactional leadership can be described as 'keeping a steady ship'. Transactional leaders use disciplinary power and an array of incentives to motivate employees to perform at their best. The term 'transactional' refers to the fact that this type of leader essentially motivates subordinates by exchanging rewards for performance (Bass, 1985).

transactional leadership is a leadership style that focuses on managing and supervising employees.

CURRENT TOPICS IN LEADERSHIP

GENDER AND LEADERSHIP

Women are significantly under-represented when it comes to leadership positions in organisations. Among Fortune 500 companies in 2020, women held only 7.4% of CEO positions. This means that 37 of the largest 500 corporations in the USA are run by females. While this is a record (for perspective, in 2000, women ran two corporations), and it beats the previous high of 33 female CEOs in 2019), the overall numbers highlight a slow progression. While it makes sense to address this disparity from an equality and moral perspective, it also makes business sense. UK organisations with more women on their boards were found to outperform their competitors, with a 42% higher return in sales, 66% higher return on invested capital and 53% higher return on equity (Davies, 2011). So why do women struggle to obtain leadership positions? According to Eagly (2013), there are a number of reasons for this. Firstly, leadership stereotypes tend to be more 'masculine' (for example, highlighting traits such as assertiveness) than 'feminine' (for example, prioritising more communal, supportive traits).

Women experience a strong gender bias when being evaluated for promotions on both their level of performance as well as their potential impact. Research shows that women have to work harder to be perceived as equally competent as men (Khattab *et al.*, 2020). In addition, unfortunate assumptions are sometimes made about women's ambitions and abilities. Research by DDI (Development Dimensions International, 2009) shows that women do not excel sufficiently in their career due to assumptions regarding their perceived lack of ambition and a lesser company commitment due to family responsibility. However, women and men rarely differ in their ambitions (Eagly *et al.*, 2020). Furthermore, women struggle with so-called second-generation gender biases, which are 'powerful yet often invisible barriers to women's advancement that arise from cultural beliefs about gender, as well as workplace structures, practices, and patterns of interactions that inadvertently favour men' (Ely *et al.*, 2011, p. 4).

It may be no surprise that males get selected for leadership positions more frequently than women ▸See Chapter 3◂ – people making selection decisions are likely to be strongly influenced by leadership stereotypes. Secondly, in order to succeed in leadership roles, many women leaders may need to live up to masculine (be tough) and feminine (be nice) stereotypes – a difficult challenge. In addition, the perceived demands placed on leaders at senior levels may be seen as a deterrent to women. As a result, women either 'fall off the track' to the top, have to take time out to have children, or forgo having children in order to have top-level leadership careers. There are often deep-seated prejudices from those in power, usually men, which prevent women from attaining leadership positions.

When women do get selected for leadership positions, they are often precarious positions. In 2005 Michelle Ryan and Alexander Haslam developed the term 'Glass Cliff' to describe how women are commonly promoted into leadership positions when organisations are in a crisis, leading to a much riskier and precarious role. Clear examples of this phenomenon can be seen, for example, when Ann Mulcahy took over the Xerox Corporation as it was about to go into bankruptcy, or British Prime Minister Theresa May, when she took over the Brexit negotiations. The 'Glass Cliff' phenomena show the often invisible and immense hurdles women must scale in these leadership positions, which are then used to evaluate their capability.

THE DARK SIDE OF LEADERSHIP AND ETHICS

Most scholars working in the area of leadership place ethics and moral values at the core of leadership. However, to ignore or not consider the leadership in history that has emerged through leaders that were both unethical and highly destructive would be remiss ▸See Chapter 8◂. Ciulla (1995) calls it the 'Hitler problem', where some scholars maintain that leaders who are destructive bullies are not leaders; however, Hitler was a leader albeit a terribly immoral one. Other than the obvious emotional response these leaders evoke, recent studies have provided academic evidence that supports the negative economic influences of these leaders in organisations. Schyns and Schilling (2013) showed that there was a strong relationship between destructive leadership and: followers' attitudes to their leader; followers' attitudes to their job; followers' attitudes to the organisation; and increased occupational stress of the follower.

Padilla *et al.* (2007) provide a construct of toxic leadership (Figure 6.3) that divides it into three main areas: destructive leaders characterised by charisma, power and coercion for personal gains; susceptible followers who are conformers based on unmet needs, or colluders based on their desire to advance or profit from the outcomes; conducive environments which are characterised by instability, possible threats, common values and a lack of checks and balances in the institution.

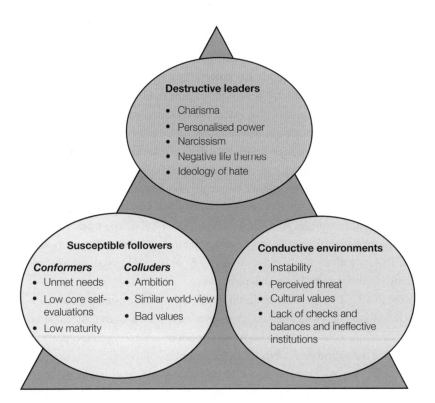

Figure 6.3 The toxic triangle

Adapted from Padilla et al. *(2007).*

When trying to understand and unearth the issues that arise in this type of leadership, the concept of ethics or ethical leadership theory is often considered. This theory is used to understand the nature of good and bad leadership as it relates to ethics or morality. Bennis and Nanus (1985) state that managers do things right while leaders do the right things, implying that the term 'leader' means morally good, which, as we know, is not always the case. We can, however, understand *good* leadership in terms of whether or not these leaders are ethical or moral. The choices and decisions that leaders make are informed by their ethics. Ethical leaders are leaders who are honest, caring individuals who make clear and balanced decisions setting clear standards of conduct while acting as proactive role models (Brown and Treviño, 2006). Ciulla (2005) identifies three categories for the moral assessment of leaders:

1 The ethics of leaders themselves – the intentions of leaders and the personal ethics of leaders.
2 The ethics of how a leader leads (or the process of leadership) – the means that a leader uses to lead (the ethics of the relationship between leaders and all those affected by his or her actions).
3 The ethics of what a leader does – the ends of leadership (Ciulla, 2005, p. 332).

BUILDING YOUR EMPLOYABILITY SKILLS

Ethical Leadership

While ethics is central to leadership and supports an organisation's value base, ethical leadership is not always clear cut. Walzer (1973) calls it the 'dirty hands problem' where leaders in some situations cannot be both ethical and effective, and sometimes they must do the wrong thing for the right reason. Is there a case for leaders making decisions where the end justifies the means? Do we hire leaders to make difficult decisions and, when they do, do we criticise them? Is leading a morally dangerous occupation?

◁ ETHICAL ▷ BEHAVIOUR IN THE WORKPLACE

In December 2018, Deloitte became the first of the Big Four accountancy firms to publicly announce the number of senior staff that were fired due to inappropriate behaviour in the workplace. Deloitte's chief executive, David Sproul, told the *Financial Times* that around 20 UK partners left the firm between 2014 and 2018 over behaviour that included bullying and sexual harassment. Reiterating the company's stance, Sproul said: 'We will fire people for any inappropriate behaviour, no one is protected.'

The move came as the #MeToo movement exposed the pervasive sexual harassment of women at work across multiple industries. Deloitte also reinforced existing guidance on appropriate conduct in response to the #MeToo movement, such as the rules on socialising with colleagues after work. These efforts were made to address cultural issues that had long prevented women from rising to leadership positions.

Deloitte also created 'respect and inclusion ambassadors' to provide employees with a 'safe route' to voice concerns and signpost them to sources of support. Initially, these were partners and directors, but the move is now being piloted at more junior grades. Deloitte's existing ethics hotline was broadened, refresher training sessions took place in 2018 and digital training has been rolled out across its 18,000 employees world-wide.

Top-down support from senior management has had a significant impact from a gender perspective. In 2014, only 13% of the auditor's partners were female. As of 1 June 2019, that figure had jumped to 21%. Of the 78 partners promoted in the UK, 41% were female. This is three times the number of women promoted to partnership in 2018 and Deloitte's work in this area earned it the Gender Equality Award at the 2019 Business in the Community's Responsible Business Awards.

DEVELOPING LEADERS

The importance of leadership in today's changing world makes it imperative that we understand how to effectively develop leaders. Yet, research in leader development has not given us a definitive model with evidence to support its application. Current research predicts a shortage of leaders in North America within the next decade, due to the retirement of talent, the problems caused by downsizing, and the reduction in the number of middle managers (Hogan and Benson, 2009). For example, Boeing in 2011 predicted that 70% of its senior to middle-level leaders would retire in the next five years (Avolio and Vogelgesang, 2011). There are signs in every business communication that we are in an era where demand currently exceeds the supply of leaders, suggesting that the leadership pipeline is drying up (Charan et al., 2010). Also, 'the increasing mobility of workers and a shrinking world market are predicted to have a negative impact on organisational leadership' (Avolio and Vogelgesang, 2011, pp. 179–204).

Currently, organisations are investing significantly to provide development opportunities to their leaders, as a way of ensuring their companies' longevity in today's economy. DeRue and Myers (2014) state that in 2009, almost a quarter of the $50 billion spent by US organisations on learning and development was spent on leadership development: that is, $12.5 billion (Day, 2014). Gurdjian et al. (2014) put the annual spend on leadership development in the US alone as high as $14–15 billion. However, are all these interventions providing a good return on investment for the organisation? Some well-documented studies would say that the return on investment is low and that people taking part in these learning systems make very little change to themselves or to the organisation.

A recent meta-analysis had a more optimistic view, suggesting that leadership training is indeed more effective than anticipated, leading to improvement in participant reactions, learning, transfer, and results for both organisational outcomes and subordinate outcomes (Lacerenza et al., 2017). In particular, this study highlights the importance of an individual approach for leader development effectiveness (Lacerenza et al., 2017, p. 1686). The overarching goal of leadership development in organisations is the development of individuals' capacity to be effective in leadership roles. For leadership development to be effective, it must be closely aligned with the organisational context including its strategy and culture, and also the specific needs of individual leaders. Leadership development competencies are frequently used by organisations to ensure that their leadership development practices are effectively aligned in this way. Competency models are considered an effective way of ensuring that leadership development practices contribute to the bottom line (Kapp and O'Driscoll, 2010).

Numerous definitions exist concerning what is meant by the term 'competencies'. The Society for Human Resource Management (2010) defined competencies as 'the knowledge, skills and abilities required to perform a specific task or function' (p. 18). Swiercz and Lydon (2002) classified leadership competencies into two sets: (a) functional competencies, and (b) self-competencies. However, Quinn et al. (2003) identified them in terms of the roles that leaders were expected to perform. GlaxoSmithKline, for example, have six core values and 21 leadership competencies. They emphasise thinking strategically, being a change champion, leading courageously, managing execution and fostering enthusiasm and teamwork.

The Centre for Creative Leadership propose a 70:20:10 development mix, where they consider lessons learned by successful and effective leaders are roughly:
- 70% from tough jobs (on-the job development)
- 20% from people (coaching, mentoring and networking)
- 10% from courses and reading (formal learning).

It is beyond the scope of this chapter to detail all of the practices that can be used but organisations have a large number of choices when it comes to selecting the optimal methods for

leadership development comprises activities and practices that enhance the ability of leaders to work as part of a team to develop relationships with organisational stakeholders.

competencies are the practical applications of knowledge, skills, attitudes, motivation, values, beliefs, cognitive style and personality that enable an individual to work effectively and autonomously in a clearly defined context.

developing leadership competencies. These include job assignments, formal coaching and mentoring, action learning, peer networks, job shadowing and technology-enabled practices.

SPOTLIGHT ON SKILLS

When it comes to selecting individuals for leadership development, organisations often start with the most basic of questions: How 'developable' is the individual? Given the investment in resources required to develop a leader, this represents the most fundamental question. It can be answered using a systematic leader assessment process that focuses on three key criteria:

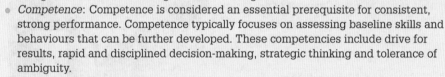

- *Self-confidence*: It is well established that developable leaders possess strong self-confidence. They project confidence in their interactions with others. However, they are not arrogant. Arrogance is considered a significant derailing factor.
- *Competence*: Competence is considered an essential prerequisite for consistent, strong performance. Competence typically focuses on assessing baseline skills and behaviours that can be further developed. These competencies include drive for results, rapid and disciplined decision-making, strategic thinking and tolerance of ambiguity.
- *Emotional intelligence*: Emotional intelligence consists of both self- and social awareness components and includes interpersonal skills, conflict management, influencing, and relationship management components.

Careful attention to these characteristics when selecting leaders for development will significantly enhance the chance of future leadership success. With this in mind, how can organisations identify and assess these criteria? What can individuals do to ensure that organisations know that they possess these criteria?

To help you answer these questions, visit bloomsbury.pub/organisational-behaviour to and watch the video of Joanna Moriarty from Green Park Interim and Executive Search discussing her experience recruiting senior leaders for charities and social enterprises.

LEADER IDENTITY DEVELOPMENT

Lord and Hall (2005) argue that developing leadership skills is facilitated by viewing oneself as a leader. The terms 'self-concept', 'self' and 'identity' can be interchanged. The activated portion of the self-concept is referred to as the 'working self-concept', which is the enactment of deferent identities, based on the arena we are in (van Knippenberg and van Knippenberg, 2005). A leader's identity is defined as who we are as a leader and, as a result, what leadership role we play. Leader identity has received growing attention in theory and empirical support, as it is critical to understanding leadership effectiveness and development. Reicher *et al.* (2005)

characterises leaders as entrepreneurs of identity. Leader identity is considered important because developing an understanding of who you are as a leader affects how you feel, think and act as a leader. This in turn provides the motivational force for seeking out leadership roles, development opportunities and experiences (Day *et al.*, 2009). Day and Harrison (2007) propose that 'Identity is important for leaders because it grounds them in understanding who they are, their major goals and objectives and their personal strengths and limitations' (Day and Harrison, 2007, p. 366). Because of this, the role of identity in the leader development process has gained much traction in the last decade, leading to novel theoretical and empirical studies on the topic (Epitropaki *et al.*, 2017). Lord and Hall (2005) argue that the development of a leader's self-conception as a leader is one of the most important parts of advanced leadership

IMPACT OF TECHNOLOGY ON BEHAVIOUR

CREDIT: PHOTO BY HANSON LU ON UNSPLASH

Machine learning (ML) and artificial intelligence (AI) applications are thriving in the corporate world. Algorithms sort through CVs to identify suitable candidates, monitor performance at work, and in some cases determine if people should be fired, without any human involvement or oversight. With business decisions increasingly more automated and data-driven than they were in the past, it raises the question of what leadership will look like in this context.

In April 2017 United Airlines forcibly removed a man from a fully boarded sold out flight. The incident was captured on video by other passengers and the story went viral on social media. An initial apology from United appeared to justify the removal of the passenger, indicating that they were simply 're-accommodating' him. The story went global overnight, sparking outrage and within 24 hours United Airlines had suffered a drop in stock price.

The decision to remove this particular passenger was not random. United Airlines used a customer value algorithm to determine the value of each passenger based on frequent flyer status, the price of the ticket, connecting flights, etc. The customers with the lowest value to United were flagged for removal from the flight. The CEO, Oscar Munoz, praised his employees for following the corporate algorithm and for not backing down. It took 48 hours for another apology to be issued that absolved the passenger from any blame. The situation ultimately cost the CEO a planned promotion to Chairman of United Airlines. It is important that leaders do not hide behind machine learning and AI, and demonstrate positive human qualities such as wisdom, empathy and trustworthiness over the prioritisation of data.

development. It is suggested that important motivational consequences can occur when there is a gap between our current view of self and possible selves. In particular, where the possible self is considered, a significant motivation to develop may be inspired (van Knippenberg and van Knippenberg, 2005). Over time, and with experience, the development of a leader identity occurs, as a view of oneself as a leader solidifies and becomes more critical.

Many organisations accept that leadership development is a sound investment for organisations to make for their future, therefore the focus of any leadership development activity should be on ensuring the fit of leadership development with organisational goals. Organisations that invest in human capital development, which inevitably includes leadership development, will achieve significant advantages in terms of business performance. Leadership development is a multi-billion-euro business world-wide and the costs of leadership development continue to increase. However, many organisations have moved past questioning the worth of this investment to questioning which approach brings the best results and is most effective in impacting the bottom line. It is estimated that leadership development can have significant pay-off for organisations in terms of creating a sustained competitive advantage (Day *et al.*, 2009). Specific organisational benefits highlighted also include productivity and financial performance.

MANAGERIAL TAKEAWAYS

In considering leadership and management, we can identify characteristics that distinguish effective leaders. It is important to understand the distinction between different theories of leadership so that we can both recognise leaders and place them in an appropriate position within the workplace. Selecting the right leaders for the right jobs has a significant impact on organisational performance. Gender equality in terms of leadership offers significant benefits for organisations, not least in financial terms. Leadership strength represents an important source of competitive advantage and organisations can use a variety of leadership development strategies to develop this human resource pool. Investment in leadership development is driven by the belief that it confers significant benefits to both individual leaders and organisations.

 CHAPTER REVIEW QUESTIONS

1 What do leaders actually do in organisations?
2 How does management really differ from leadership?
3 Distinguish between trait and behavioural theories of leadership.
4 Highlight the main criticisms of trait theories of leadership.
5 What is meant by transformational, charismatic and distributed leadership?
6 Do you believe gender has an impact on leadership behaviour?
7 Discuss the 'dark-side' of leadership.
8 What are the main approaches to leader development?

 ## FURTHER READING

Billsberry, J. (2009) *Discovering Leadership*. London: Palgrave.

Kotter, J.P. (2001) What leaders really do. *Harvard Business Review*, 71(11), 3–11.

Lord, R.G., Day, D.V., Zaccaro, S.J., Avolio, B.J. and Eagly, A.H. (2017) Leadership in applied psychology: Three waves of theory and research. *Journal of Applied Psychology*, 102(3), 434.

Sinek, S. (2019) *The Infinite Game*. New York: Penguin.

 ## USEFUL WEBSITES

www.ccl.org

Centre for Creative Leadership: A very useful website that provides interesting articles, white-papers and blogs on contemporary leadership development issues.

https://www.mckinsey.com/quarterly/overview

Published by consultancy firm McKinsey, the *Quarterly* combines insights from McKinsey with ideas from other world-leading experts and practitioners on thought leadership.

https://www.gartner.com/en/human-resources/role/human-resources-leaders

The Gartner website includes a variety of resources on contemporary leadership development topics.

https://www.strategy-business.com

Strategy & Business is the award-winning management and leadership magazine for decision makers published by PwC.

Online Resources

Visit **bloomsbury.pub/organisational-behaviour** to access additional materials to support teaching and learning.

---

7 GROUPS AND TEAMS IN THE WORKPLACE

Christine Cross and Caroline Murphy

LEARNING OUTCOMES

BY THE END OF THIS CHAPTER, YOU SHOULD BE ABLE TO:

- Consider the role of groups in organisations.
- Outline how groups develop and the factors that impact on performance.
- Discuss some key group decision-making dynamics such as cohesiveness, conformity, groupthink, and social loafing.
- Consider the key differences between groups and teams in the workplace.
- Identify the characteristics of an effective workplace team.

CREDIT: PHOTO BY MICHAŁ PARZUCHOWSKI

THIS CHAPTER DISCUSSES...

INTRODUCTION

It is likely that you have been assigned to a group or a team to work on a project in college. How did you feel about that? Some of you may be delighted to have the opportunity to learn from others, while some of you may be less enthusiastic, concerned that others will not work as hard or smart as you which might negatively impact your grades. The rationale for asking you to work in groups at college is to help you develop the skills needed for working in groups in organisations. The reality of working life is that each one of us will be part of a group or a team. For many organisations the amount of time employees spend engaged in collaborative work – in meetings, on phone calls, or answering e-mails – has increased roughly 50% and takes up 80% or more of their time (Cross *et al.*, 2016). We are on twice as many teams as we were five years ago (Wright, 2018). The ability of teams to deliver innovative ideas and solutions is also well documented, hence why organisations are keen to develop high functioning teams (Fay *et al.*, 2015). Working in groups and teams is seen as a way for organisations to deal with the fact that work has become more complex. The way in which group members share knowledge, and pool complementary knowledge and ideas, is seen to be key to organisational success. Groups are also a mechanism for individuals to satisfy their social needs. In this chapter we consider both groups and teams and their popularity in workplaces. Teams are essentially a special type of group. Working together can be energising and rewarding, but it can also be complicated,

IN REALITY

Virtual teams are on the rise in organisations as a result of significant technological advances. Being a member of a virtual team means you are part of a group of individuals who work across time, space and organisational boundaries and use communication technology to interact, so as to achieve an organisational purpose. In the 'war for talent', virtual teams allow organisations to attract talent across geographic boundaries. The benefit for organisations is that it can also reduce their operating costs and expand their business hours by using the different time zones of virtual team members. For employees, it offers the freedom and flexibility to attain a healthy work–life balance. In this type of team, you would rarely meet face to face with other members of the team. So the results should be very positive for both employee and employer. Sounds like it should be a real winner for all. However, a study in MIT Sloan Management Review reported that only 18% of the 70 global business virtual teams assessed were found to be highly successful. That means over 80% did not achieve their goals. So what are the reasons for this? How would you feel if you never met the other members of your team face to face? This lack of contact in a virtual team seems to create problems around building trust and establishing relationships between team members. A *Harvard Business Review* article found that remote employees are more likely to report feeling that colleagues mistreat them and leave them out. Specifically, they worry that co-workers say bad things behind their backs, make changes to projects without telling them in advance, lobby against them and don't fight for their priorities (Grenny and Maxfield, 2017). The idea behind a global virtual team might sound better than it is in reality.

time consuming and does not always lead to positive outcomes. Struggles to communicate, to agree and to coordinate mean that groups are not always efficient or effective, and at times may not feel comfortable places to be. We will deal with these issues later in the chapter; now we will move on to a discussion of different types of groups. We begin by discussing how groups develop and move on to examine the difficulties that arise in groups and the impact of group dynamics such as group development, roles, and patterns of group behaviour. Finally, we consider the differences between groups and teams, the characteristics of effective teams, and the implications for their support and management in the organisation.

WHAT ARE GROUPS?

There is a well-known saying that 'many hands make light work'. This saying captures one of the promises of social life – that with social organisation people can fulfil their individual goals more easily through collective action (Latane *et al.*, 1979, p. 822). When there are many hands, people do not have to work as hard as when they are on their own. This is not really a surprise, since both collaboration and competition are deeply rooted behaviours within the natural and social world. We are in effect 'social animals' (Aronson, 2007) and often need to be able to interact with others in order to function individually. Sometimes it is about shared interests, or pooling resources and getting things done. Sometimes it is rooted in identification, such as the need to belong, the need to interact with those who share our outlook and to feel solidarity with them (McKenna, 2012). It can also be about attraction. Groups serve a major purpose in that they support *collective action*, which is getting things done through shared effort and knowledge or making larger tasks manageable by breaking them down into specialist roles and responsibilities (Carr and Walton, 2014).

groups are two or more people who interact together to achieve a common objective and are interdependent.

The potential for synergy within groups is what makes them so important for organisations. A group is perhaps best understood by what it is *not*, for instance, a group is not just a collection of people occupying the same space or sharing something such as having red hair. It is only when something connects people and causes them to develop that they take on the internal identity of a group. For example, people waiting in a queue would not be classified as a group as they are not working towards achieving a common objective. Schein's definition of a group (1980, p. 145) assists us with this classification process: 'any number of people who interact with each other and perceive themselves to be a group'. At the core of a group is interdependence. If a group does not have a sense of interdependence it will have to work much harder to stay together as it has little real incentive to collaborate beyond a superficial level.

synergy is where the effect of combining efforts leads to more creative or effective outcomes than would have been achieved had each individual operated alone.

The idea of belonging is central to our being and a basic human need ▸See Chapter 5◂. Interestingly, social psychologists have found that when we become part of and belong to a group, we consciously or unconsciously tend to be influenced by the beliefs, expectations and actions of the other people in the group. This is the dynamic of group conformity, where group members may feel pressurised to agree with the opinions and ideas of other groups members. Put more simply: we sometimes come to think, feel or behave differently in a group than we might do if we are working alone. We will explore this further when we examine group formation later in the chapter.

group conformity is the tendency of group members to consciously or unconsciously align their beliefs and behaviours with the apparent beliefs and behaviours of the group.

Social identity theory (Tajfel, 1979) tells us that we divide the world into 'us' (known as our in-groups) and 'them' (known as out-groups) in a process of social categorisation. People who we believe share our particular qualities are in our in-group, and those who do not are in our out-group. We exhibit what is referred to as in-group bias. Indeed, Tajfel (1979) states that the in-group will discriminate against the out-group to enhance their perception of themselves ▶See Chapter 3◀. This distinction is one that is used a lot in the sports arena. Rivalry between certain teams is seen as a way to drive group performance. The creation of a 'them' and 'us' approach, where a strong identification is made with your own team, the in-group, over the other team, the out-group, is commonplace in team sports such as football, cricket and basketball.

TYPES OF GROUPS

You might currently be a member of a group project for some of your subjects, a member of the organising committee for a sports club activity, or perhaps at work you are part of a new group working on product development or a member of the Finance Department. Also, you are likely to be working as part of more than one group at the same time. You might be working in a Finance Department and you may simultaneously be working on a cross-departmental project which means you are working with people from outside your department. Membership of a group can be self-selecting or organisationally defined, and range from nominated structures such as committees and boards, to organisational principles such as departments, occupational groupings and staff categories. They can also arise through shared interests, such as trade union membership, sports and social groups. Groups are normally categorised as formal or informal. Formal groups are to be found in every organisation. They are deliberately formed in order to allow the organisation to achieve its objectives. Membership of these groups is usually determined by those in authority in the organisation and they also set out the rules of operation. Formal groups can also be classified as command or task groups. Command groups are permanent formal groups that are formed as a result of organisational structures. From the example above, the new product development group and the Engineering Department fall into this category. Task groups are temporary groups designed to deal with specific issues and are dismantled once the task is complete. An example would be the group at Macmillan publishers consisting of marketing managers, editors, IT systems executives and project managers brought together to launch the company's new website.

The second type of group is an informal group which emerges in the organisation from the informal interaction of people at work. Their membership and rules of engagement are internally rather than externally defined. Group membership often crosses the boundaries of the formal groups. The people we normally have lunch with or see socially after work are members of our informal group. These groups can often be a source of concern for management, as they have no control over group membership. As the Hawthorne Studies (Roethlisberger and Dickson, 1939) famously revealed, informal groups can be powerful and have a significant effect on what gets done in the workplace ▶See Chapter 1◀. This 'below the surface' dynamic is often forgotten about in the formal structures of organisations, but is one of the reasons why the study of groups is interesting and insightful. Have you ever worked anywhere where the informal group was able to impact either negatively or positively on the organisation?

---

in-group bias is the process where members of a group favour members of their own group over members of other groups.

formal groups are officially established, usually as a result of the organisation's structure, with a specific purpose.

command groups are permanent formal groups that are formed as a result of organisational structures.

task groups are temporary groups designed to deal with specific issues and are dismantled once the task is completed.

informal groups are those which develop naturally in the workplace in response to our need for belonging.

IMPACT OF TECHNOLOGY ON BEHAVIOUR

The Covid-19 pandemic has changed the way people work. There is no question about that. Staff who never thought their jobs could be done remotely are working remotely. Technology has been the key to the successful pivot that took place to allow groups and teams to continue to communicate with each other and to work together. Tools such as Zoom and Microsoft Teams have allowed live meetings to take place, which allows groups and teams to continue to function in much the same way as they did in an office setting. Indeed, some organisations such as Twitter have
announced that all staff can work remotely forever and there is no need for them to go into the office (https://www.irishtimes.com/business/technology/twitter-says-employees-will-be-allowed-to-work-from-home-forever-1.4252310). This is because for many staff they have enjoyed the flexibility provided by working from home and the feared drop in productivity has not materialised. The key here is that technology platforms have made it easy for people to work together and collaborate in an effective way in groups.

THE DEVELOPMENT OF GROUPS

When we try to understand why some groups work well together and others do not, Tuckman's (1965) seminal work indicates that groups pass through a number of clearly defined stages of development (see Figure 7.1). His work provides us with a commonly used framework that can actually help us better understand why things are happening in the groups we are part of. In the first stage, *forming*, individuals are getting to know each other and finding

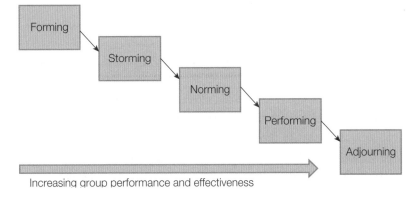

Figure 7.1 Stages of group development

out about each other's attitudes and backgrounds. There is often an excited anxiousness associated with this stage as individuals are assessing one another and trying to make a good first impression. When the group meet for the first few times, they are confronted with both the advantages of becoming a group, and equally, the challenges. Questions people often have include will I fit in? Will everyone work to get the job done? What will I do if there are people who do not do their share of the work? There is a high level of uncertainty in the early stages of forming a group and for most of us uncertainty is uncomfortable. In general, members will take a low stakes approach, rather than offering immediate commitment to the group. The more confident or experienced members of the group may push forward to suggest how the group might work and offer route maps, but everyone knows that this early stage is critical and full of judgements. If you have ever watched a reality TV show you will have seen how most people are reticent to reveal much of themselves when they initially meet the others or how they try to put forward an image of themselves that can sometimes be later revealed to be untrue.

The second stage, *storming*, is where the group members are getting to know each other better. People begin to settle into the group and this is the stage when the most conflict arises between group members. It may be that more than one person wants to be identified as the leader of the group, or that differences in personal motivations are revealed. There may be considerable disagreement over group roles and work allocation. People may be less polite in this stage than in the previous stage and they may express their frustration about issues that are slowing the group's progress. The reality of completing the task becomes real and here personalities might clash. Group members might let everyone know if they feel the task is not being completed in the right way or they may question the authority of the group leader. This stage is critical to group development as a group can end up 'stuck' here for a considerable amount of time.

Once the group members have developed ways of working together the group identifies who will do which tasks and how they will be done. The third stage, *norming*, identifies the norms within the group. They govern behaviour of members of the group (Blau, 1995). These norms have a strong effect on group behaviour and can be difficult to change (Feldman, 1984). For example, everyone will be punctual to meetings and there will be time after the meetings for some social chat, but not during the meetings. Street gangs and prison gangs have been a useful source of information on the study of group norms as their norms are often very obvious to outsiders, for example gang tattoos and clothing (Skarbeck, 2012). The same is true for prisoners in a prison setting (Bondeson, 2017). Norming is a comforting process of converging so that there is less need to question and more agreement, and goals and roles are relatively clear to each member. This phase travels the interesting tightrope between cohesion and conformity, which we discuss in more detail shortly.

The final stage, *performing*, relates to the effective performance of the group. Here the group has developed effective productive methods of working and the group is meeting its goals. Not all groups make it to this stage, however, as many get stuck in a cycle of moving between earlier stages. In Figure 7.1 we see a further stage called *adjourning*. This is the stage where the group disbands, either because it has achieved the group task or because the members have left the group. For a high-performing team this stage can bring feelings of sadness as they will no longer be working together as a group. This stage was added to the

group roles are patterns of behaviour expected of group members.

norms are the unwritten and unspoken rules and expectations of behaviour that apply to a group's members.

group development process some 10 years after the original model was developed (Tuckman and Jensen, 1977).

While this group development process may look linear, it is often the case that groups move from one stage to the next and back again, before moving forward once more. The 'punctuated equilibrium' view, for example, observes a group may move back and forth through these stages as new things happen (such as the arrival of a new member, or a significant change in group context or task). In the reality TV programme example, the group may find it difficult to move out of the storming stage depending on the motives of the individual group members. They may move from the storming to the norming stage and back to the storming stage on a cyclical basis until some 'difficult' members of the group are voted out of the house.

Benne and Sheats (1948) have identified three broad types of roles people play in small groups: task roles, building and maintenance roles, and self-centred roles. *Task roles* focus on completing the group objective, for example, taking minutes of a meeting. *Building and maintenance roles* focus on building interpersonal relationships, for example, someone who offers encouragement by providing positive feedback. *Self-centred roles* focus on preventing the group from achieving its goal, for example the person who does not pull their weight. This issue is known as social loafing (Karau and Williams, 1993) and people who engage in social loafing often think others in the group do not notice their lack of contribution. We have all been part of a group where one person does not contribute an equal amount and yet expects to benefit from membership of the group in the same way as those who have fully contributed. It happens when individuals feel other people will 'pick up the slack' and thus, they do not have to do their share of the work (Latane *et al.*, 1979). It is an aspect of group work that is of particular concern where individual contributions are not specifically measured.

> social loafing is where a group member exerts less effort in the group than if they were working alone.

BUILDING YOUR EMPLOYABILITY SKILLS

Managing Conflict

Put yourself in the shoes of a store manager in a retail outlet. You have five people who work together in the storeroom and their work is critical to ensuring stock is always available for customers on the shop floor. However, they seem to be unable to get along together and are always fighting and arguing. How can you apply Tuckman's group development model to this situation to improve the functioning of the group?

CHARACTERISTICS OF GROUPS

There are many variables which affect overall group performance such as roles, size, cohesiveness and conformity. Group dynamics such as these have been the subject of a significant amount of research which has resulted in a number of theories (Lewin, 1948, 1951; Campion *et al.*, 1993; Channon *et al.*, 2017). In this section we deal with some of the key properties and processes that impact on the performance of groups, both positive and negative.

GROUP SIZE

The size of the group has a direct impact on group performance and productivity. The larger the group the more ideas and knowledge the members can share, which may lead to more success-ful outcomes in terms of ideas and problem solving. However, it also makes sense that the larger the group the more difficult it is to have clear lines of communication and to coordinate tasks. Jeff Bezos has a rule at Amazon, that if a team cannot be fed by two pizzas, then that team is too large. The reasoning is quite straight forward. More people means more miscommunication, more bureaucracy, more turmoil. Research highlights that beyond a certain point an increase in numbers does not deliver additional productivity (Wheelan, 2009; Johnson and Johnson, 2009). Conversely, where the number of group members is small and the task is complex, there may not be enough resources to complete the task. In a small group of three people, issues like social loafing are more easily visible and communication within the group is more intimate. For example, research from Seijts and Latham (2001) highlights that individual performance in seven-person groups was significantly lower than individual performance in three-person groups. However, research evidence varies in relation to the optimal size of a group, with some indicating that seven is the optimal number (Blenko *et al.*, 2009). In general, the appropriate group size is dependent on both the task and the context in which the group operates.

GROUP COMPOSITION

When we talk about group composition here, we are talking about homogenous and hetero-geneous groups. Homogeneity exists when the prolife of the members is similar, for example, gender, education, age, nationality. In a heterogeneous group the members are dissimilar. Studies, however, have reached conflicting conclusions about whether homogeneous or heterogeneous team composition provides stronger results. It is a common belief that like-minded individuals who share similar backgrounds and interests lead to the most effective groups because the common experiences among their members promotes greater group cohesion and communication. However, research has shown that groups with more diverse members are more innovative and creative (Chamorro-Premuzic, 2017) and facilitate better more productive intra-term processes (Hamilton *et al.*, 2012). This is particularly evident when the team includes female members. Studies from MIT, Carnegie Mellon, and Union College have found that the teams which were best at collaborating and demonstrating effective problem-solving in an efficient time frame were the teams with the highest numbers of women (c.f. Engel *et al.*, 2014). These studies showed that the more women on the team, the better it performed. This was attributed to women being found to have higher levels of emotional intelligence (EI). In essence, it may mean that in the absence of female team members, the opinions of individuals in the team are less likely to be fully explored and conflict may arise from the failure of others to notice early cues of, for example, disagreement or distress.

The Rugby World Cup 2019

When we look at the issue of homogenous and heterogeneous groups there are so many examples to choose from in the sporting arena. There was much debate during the 2019 Rugby World Cup about the composition of some of the teams. Take for example, the host side's team. Japan were captained by Michael Leitch, of mixed New Zealand and Fijian heritage. One of the best players on the team was Kotaro Matsushima, a South African-born winger with a Zimbabwean father and Japanese mother. In all, the Japanese 31-strong squad included 16 players originally from seven countries. Seven of the 15 men who started for Japan in their first match were born overseas. For some, this is evidence of the need for national teams to select the best available players. For others, however, Japan's multiracial side is simply an example of how teams are exploiting the three-year residency requirement for drafting foreign-born players into national squads. Criticism of rugby's relaxed attitude towards eligibility was questioned during the tournament.

IN THE NEWS

Rugby has traditionally been seen in the UK as a white middle-class sport. Yet more than a third of the players in the squad for the World Cup were from Black, Asian, Minority, Ethnic (BAME) backgrounds. The question for us here is do culturally homogenous groups perform better than culturally heterogeneous groups. This is important in organisational life because, as global virtual teams become more common, the need to better understand how groups composed of individuals from different cultural backgrounds perform has never been more pressing.

Questions

1 Do you believe cultural diversity can make a positive contribution to team performance?
2 In what ways do you think cultural diversity can both positively and negatively impact on team performance?

Sources

https://sloanreview.mit.edu/article/the-trouble-with-homogeneous-teams/

https://www.rugbyworldcup.com/

https://www.theguardian.com/sport/ng-interactive/2019/sep/09/rugby-world-cup-2019-japan-team-guide

https://www.theguardian.com/sport/ng-interactive/2019/sep/14/rugby-world-cup-2019-england-team-guide

CREDIT: PHOTO BY HANSON LU ON UNSPLASH

GROUP ROLES

All members play a particular role in a group. If we take the example of the well-known TV programme the Big Brother house, people will take responsibility for cooking, or cleaning the house, or for being the 'mother' of the group, or the 'entertainer' of the group. The roles people take on have an important impact on the group's development and its effectiveness. In life we have many roles, such as sister/brother, friend, waitress/waiter, student and girlfriend/boyfriend, many of which may conflict with each other. For example, if your work as a waitress/waiter interferes with your work as a student, but you need to earn money to pay for tuition fees, you are experiencing *role conflict*. It arises when a person performs more than one role and performance in that role makes performance in another more difficult (Peterson *et al.*, 1995). This also happens when two or more *role expectations* (the way other people believe you should act in a given context) are contradictory. There are five types of role conflict (Kumar *et al.*, 2013) identified: intra-role conflict, inter-role conflict, intra-sender conflict, person-role conflict and role overload (Sell *et al.*, 1981). Role conflict can lead to negative outcomes for the individual such as stress ▶See Chapter 9◀. One of the most interesting studies on roles was conducted by Philip Zimbardo and his colleagues from Stanford in the US. Seemingly normal and well-adjusted Stanford students were recruited to participate in this landmark 1971 study about the psychology of imprisonment. The results showed that students took their role-playing as prisoners and guards to extremes, with the 'guards' turning power-hungry, violent and occasionally sadistic, resulting in the shutting down of the experiment after only six days. You can see this experiment on the big screen now as a movie called *The Stanford Prison Experiment* which is based on the study. You can see a YouTube clip that gives an overview of the experiment, at: https://www.youtube.com/watch?v=760lwYmpXbc.

GROUP COHESIVENESS

group cohesiveness is the force that binds a group together.

Group cohesiveness can be thought of as the glue that binds the group together and represents a form of solidarity between group members (Beal *et al.*, 2003). In a cohesive group, members place a value on being part of the group and interpersonal relationships are strong. Group cohesiveness is identified as a key factor in successful sports teams (Carron *et al.*, 2002). The main factors that influence group cohesiveness are:

- group size
- members' similarity
- entry difficulty
- group success
- external competition and threats.

As it is easier for smaller groups to coordinate their activities, they are often more cohesive than larger groups. The more group members are similar to each other on various characteristics the easier it is to reach cohesiveness. As discussed earlier, we know from Social Identity Theory (Tajfel, 1974) that people feel closer to those who they perceive as similar to themselves ▶See Chapter 3◀. In addition, coming from a similar background makes it more likely that members share similar views. In a recent survey of 500 hiring managers, 74% reported that their most recent hire had a personality similar to theirs. This is not necessarily a good thing, however. The study interviewed professionals from elite investment banks, consultancies and law firms about how they recruited, interviewed and evaluated candidates, and concluded that among the most important factors driving their hiring recommendations were shared leisure interests. As explained by one attorney, 'The best way I could describe it is like if you were going on a date. You kind of know when there's a match' (see http://www.theatlantic.com/magazine/archive/2013/12/theyre-watching-you-at work/354681/).

Entry difficulty to the group also creates a sense of exclusivity. The more elite the group is perceived to be, the more prestigious it is to be a member in that group. Consequently, the more motivated members are to belong and stay in it. This is particularly true where the group is successful. Group rivalry, in the form of external threats, is often used to encourage competition and stimulate performance levels, particularly in sales.

Group diversity has been found to be an important factor impacting group performance. Diversity among employees can create better performance when it comes to creative tasks such as product development, and managers have been trying to increase diversity to achieve the benefits of innovation and fresh ideas (Northcraft *et al.*, 1996). And cohesiveness sounds like an ideal situation, and in many cases it is. However, strongly cohesive groups can also cause problems. They can become defensive of their group membership and output and make it difficult for new members to join the group. They can resist change and become overly protective of their decisions. This can lead to issues of group conformity and groupthink, both of which are discussed below.

GROUP CONFORMITY

A seminal study by Solomon Asch (1951) highlights the pressure that group members feel to conform to group norms. In his classic experiment he showed a group of volunteers a line and asked them to say aloud which of three other lines matched it in length (see Figure 7.2). However, only one of the subjects was a real volunteer. The others were planted by Asch and were told to give an incorrect answer to the question. In almost one third of cases the volunteer went along with the incorrect answer, even though it was very obviously incorrect. This study demonstrated how difficult it is to go against the opinions of others even when you know their opinion is wrong. There is a strong social pressure to conform when among our peers. Can you think of a time when you have found yourself in a situation like this? How did you feel and what did you do?

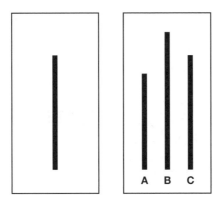

Figure 7.2 The Asch experiment

GROUPTHINK

Groupthink is similar to the concept of conformity and, as a term, was created by social psychologist Irving Janis. It occurs when a group makes faulty decisions because group pressures lead to a deterioration of 'mental efficiency, reality testing, and moral judgment' (Janis, 1972,

groupthink occurs where maintaining group conformity is more important than critically evaluating alternative viewpoints, even if it means actively discouraging dissenting opinions.

p. 9). Janis noted that high levels of group cohesiveness can lead to groupthink, and identifies eight symptoms of this phenomenon:

- Illusion of invulnerability – this creates excessive optimism that encourages extreme risk-taking.
- Belief in inherent morality – members believe in the rightness of their cause and therefore ignore the ethical or moral consequences of their decisions.
- Collective rationalisation – members have a collective mind-set and discount warnings.
- Stereotyped views of out-groups – negative views of the 'enemy' make effective responses to conflict seem unnecessary.
- Direct pressure on dissenters – members are under pressure not to express disagreements with any of the group's views.
- Self-censorship – doubts and deviations from the perceived group consensus are not expressed.
- Illusion of unanimity – the majority view is assumed to be unanimous.
- Self-appointed 'mindguards' – members protect the group and the leader from information that is problematic or contradictory to the group's cohesiveness, view, and/or decisions.

One of the key ways to avoid groupthink occurring is for the group to encourage its members to voice their opinion and to actively critically evaluate the group's decisions. Another technique is to appoint someone to the role of devil's advocate. Much of the analysis of the Global Financial Crisis points to the possibility of groupthink having played a role in the collapse of some financial institutions.

⟨ETHICAL⟩ BEHAVIOUR IN THE WORKPLACE

CREDIT: PHOTO BY JONAS LEUPE ON UNSPLASH

You will most likely work as part of a group or a team when you start working. So, you will have lots of interaction with others on a daily basis and will get to know them well, even becoming friends with some of them. The question is, if you saw your colleagues or friends behaving in an unethical way in the workplace would you report them to your manager? Let's look at an example, that is, misusing time in the workplace. What about if your colleague asks you to cover for them as they will be late back from lunch as they have to do their grocery shopping and know there will be queues, which will make them late back after lunch. How would you feel about doing that for them? Do you see this as behaving unethically at work?

'Cyberslackers' or 'cyberloafers' are terms used to identify people who surf the Web when they should be working. It has become a really significant problem for companies due to the wasting of company time. If you knew members of your group or team were doing this during working time, would you report them to your manager? Who would have thought checking Twitter could be classed as unethical behaviour?

GROUPS AND TEAMS – HOW DO THEY DIFFER?

In this chapter so far, we have discussed groups in detail, including what they are, their different types, their purpose and how they develop. But how exactly does a group differ from a team? Before you read further, think about how you would answer this question based on your own experiences and views. For some people there is a clear distinction between a group and a team, for others there is no clear difference to be found. It is true that the terms are often used interchangeably in popular discourse. In an organisational behaviour context a team is defined as a group of people working together with a defined purpose in order to achieve a common goal. While individuals who have some relationship with one another or who share similar traits may be part of a group, a team essentially means that all members are involved in the same activity. Unsurprisingly then, organisations develop teams to achieve goals that are considered too complex, lengthy or challenging to be completed by individuals working alone. Hence, one of the fundamental differences between workplace groups and teams is that while individuals who are part of a group will often share knowledge and expertise with each other, this is primarily to help others in the group achieve their own individual aims rather than to complete an overarching task together, which is the aim of a team. Table 7.1 outlines some of the core differences between groups and teams.

> **team** refers to a group of people working together with a defined purpose in order to achieve a common goal.

> Great things in business are never done by one person; they're done by a team of people. – Steve Jobs, Founding CEO of Apple, quote from his biography

> The leaders who work most effectively, it seems to me, never say 'I'. They don't think 'I'. They think 'we'; they think 'team'. They understand their job to be to make the team function. They accept responsibility and don't sidestep it, but 'we' gets the credit. – Peter F. Drucker, 1990 (Managing the Non-Profit Organization, 2011, p. 14)

Table 7.1 Differences between groups and teams

Characteristic	Groups	Teams
Purpose	Knowledge and information sharing between group members. The aims of groups are generally broad and reflect the main aims of the organisation.	The achievement of a common goal by all individuals in the team. Team aims can be specialised and clearly defined for each member as part of the organisation's objectives.
Skills and task orientation	Group members can possess a diverse range of skills and no coordination of task completion among the members is required.	Members possess a range of skills which complement each other and the allocation and achievement of tasks within the team is tightly coordinated.
Accountability	Accountable for individual performance only.	Both individually and mutually responsible for team performance.
Size	Unlimited	Limited – optimum number of individuals is between 5 and 9 (Schein, 1965).
Synergy	Neutral	Positive, with group performance greater than the sum of individual efforts.
Leadership	Since groups are not established with a shared specific goal to achieve, a single leader is generally appointed in a role much like a chairperson, to speak on behalf of the group rather than coordinate tasks.	An official team leader is appointed whose role may be shared or the role may rotate among members.

A vast array of management research now exists which clearly shows that, in general, teams outperform individual efforts. As the quote above from management guru Peter Drucker quite clearly shows, to be a successful manager in modern organisations requires the ability to manage a team effectively. The strong belief in teamwork can be seen too in the quote from Apple founder Steve Jobs. From an organisational perspective, teams have been found to: improve levels of overall productivity; strengthen the competitive advantage of the organisation over its rivals; lead to advances in innovation and creativity; improve quality; and improve job satisfaction, motivation and commitment to the organisation among employees (Parker, 1990). As such, teams (of many different forms) are now a standard feature of most modern organisational structures. The way in which individuals and groups are structured and coordinated in terms of the task they perform within the organisation, and the way in which the structural aspects are configured, are key elements in the success of an organisation ▸**See Chapter 1**◂. An understanding of team processes and structure is therefore an essential part of a manager's role. An interesting movie worth watching that reinforces the idea of becoming a team is *Remember the Titans* (2000) starring Denzel Washington.

TYPES OF TEAMS IN ORGANISATIONS

Teams can serve a variety of functions in organisations. However, depending on the task to be achieved or the working environment in which it is to be completed, different types of teams with varying structures can be developed. In today's globalised and competitive business environment, traditional corporate structures aren't always best placed to deliver fast, efficient results to business needs and therefore must be reviewed. This often results in the creation of various types of teams in the organisation. In this section we will discuss five types of teams commonly found in organisations: cross-functional; self-managed; problem solving; virtual; and management teams.

CROSS-FUNCTIONAL TEAMS

cross-functional teams are those which have members from a range of functional departments within the organisation, working towards a common goal.

A cross-functional team draws on members responsible for varying tasks in the organisation and brings them together to achieve a specific purpose. The bringing together of a cross-functional mix of members ensures that a range of diverse skills and talents are present in the team, for example a cross-functional team in a manufacturing setting will have members from product development, production management, engineering, sales and marketing when designing a new product. Taking part in one of these cross-functional teams is often referred to as *boundary spanning*. Large organisations, particularly those in the automobile sector, have been utilising cross-functional teams for decades. Toyota, for example, use this type of team design in complex projects and in product development. While the great benefit of cross-functional teams is the varying insights and perspectives brought to them by so many different backgrounds, some drawbacks can also be found. The development of a cross-functional team can take some time; also, with so many differing perspectives, achieving agreement and consensus decision-making can be difficult. Sobek II *et al.* (1998) found that in the case of Toyota a dilution of knowledge within each functional level was a problem because individuals were spending too much time away from their core roles on other projects. This is an important difference between a cross-functional team and the creation of a new division entirely;

the premise of a cross-functional team is that members maintain substantial contact and links with their own departmental area, for example an engineer working on a new product design may be part of a cross-functional team drawing on designers, engineers and marketers but, ultimately, he/she is still part of the engineering department. Despite the clear advantages of cross-functional teams, a result from Deloitte's Insights Survey (2019) found that only 6% of organisations rated themselves very effective at managing cross-functional teams, illustrating the need for HR to address this in many organisations.

SELF-MANAGED WORK TEAMS (SMWT)

Self-managed work teams (SMWT) can also be referred to as *self-directed teams*. SMWTs often perform tasks traditionally completed by managers (Orsburn *et al.*, 1990). The development and origin of SMWTs arose largely from the Socio-Technical Systems approach and the Quality of Work Life movement, hence such teams strongly feature elements associated with job enrichment ▶See Chapter 5◀ (Polley and Ribbens, 1998). During the 1990s, SMWTs were commonly found to exist in product environments where TQM (Total Quality Management) and JIT (Just in time) manufacturing processes were also present (Proença, 2010). The role of the SMWT in such settings is believed to enhance the quality of goods produced and reduce costs while simultaneously leading to improvements in the levels of job satisfaction and motivation among employees. For example, the introduction of a SMWT in a work setting where an assembly line style of production existed could serve to improve job satisfaction by giving members of the team more control over their work and reduce monotony in the process. However, while there are many advantages to such teams, a number of problems can also arise. Research has shown that SMWTs can be prone to conflict between members regarding individual levels of productivity (Proença, 2010). It has also shown that employees on self-managing work teams can display higher rates of absenteeism and turnover, despite also supporting the view that employees in autonomous work groups report more favourable work attitudes than their counterparts in traditionally designed jobs (Cordery *et al.*, 1991). Cordery *et al.* (1991) argued that these are complex behaviours and, as previously suggested by Nicholson and Johns (1985), are caused by diverse reasons often beyond the organisational sphere. Gill *et al.* (2018) also point to the importance of team member roles with self-managed teams, emphasising the importance of social dynamics within the team. Examples of self-managed work teams can be found in a variety of industries, and given the desire for individuals to have more autonomy at work, are likely to feature in even more organisations in the future. For example, Federal Express has utilised the concept with positive results. Also cited as an example of an organisation embracing the self-managed team idea is the food chain Taco Bell. Organisations may even be able to reduce the number of management positions in a number of areas by encouraging teams at various sites to increase their levels of independence and accountability.

self-managed work teams consist of a small number of employees who have been given autonomy to plan and manage their team's day-to-day activities with relatively little supervision.

PROBLEM-SOLVING TEAMS

Typically, such teams may be formed to find solutions to problems regarding quality, costs and efficiency that are identified as needing to be addressed in the organisation. Similar to cross-functional teams, a problem-solving team created to solve a strategic level issue is likely to draw individuals from different sectors of the organisation so as to facilitate a wider array of perspectives on the problem and identify an appropriate

problem-solving teams are formed specifically to find a solution to an existing problem.

solution. At an operational level, a problem-solving team will generally consist of a small number of employees (fewer than 12) who will discuss how processes and methods can be improved. Problem-solving teams do not always have the autonomy or resources to implement the recommendations they decide upon. The motor manufacturer Ford is one organisation who have championed the use of problem-solving teams. The organisation operates a process known as 8D (eight disciplines of problem solving) which involves the identification of the problem, its symptoms, the creation of a team and the design of permanent corrective and preventative actions. An article featured in the *Harvard Business Review* (2018) highlighted the importance of creating what is referred to as 'psychological safety' in a team environment; this essentially means creating a feeling within the team that everyone's contributions will be respected, and avoiding unwarranted criticism of individual contributions. In a problem-solving team where delivering solutions is key, this is fundamentally important.

VIRTUAL TEAMS

virtual teams are those where the team members are dispersed geographically and where the team communicates and collaborates together through the use of a variety of electronic systems.

This type of team may never need to meet face to face in a traditional sense to achieve their aims. The presence and use of virtual teams have increased vastly since the 2000s as technological advances have made it possible for more organisations to adopt such work practices. The virtual team has a great number of advantages for both organisations and employees themselves. Cascio (2000) highlights some of these benefits as savings in time and expenses, since access to experts in a variety of locations through electronic collaboration reduces the need for travel within and between organisations. In addition, Cascio (2000) points out that virtual teams allow organisations to draw on a wider pool of talent when selecting team members as they are no longer restricted by geographical location. For employees, working as part of a virtual team can be beneficial in terms of gaining expertise through collaboration with a diverse group, and from a work–life perspective cut down on travel and potentially facilitate a remote working or working from home option. However, in spite of the many advantages virtual working creates, drawbacks also exist with regard to communication style. In a virtual team, many of the non-verbal signals and cues between members are neglected ▶**See Chapter 10◀**. Furthermore, Mann (2013) shows that it can be challenging for managers to develop and foster a sense of trust between team members in a virtual setting. Virtual teams are now used in a wide variety of settings within and beyond the technology sector; take, for example, the university or college in which you are studying. It is very likely that the researchers and lecturers you meet on a daily basis work in virtual teams on international research projects. For many virtual teams the challenge is operating without a clear management structure and this is a challenge which the team members may have to negotiate for themselves in some instances. According to the *Sloan Management Review* (Sharon Hill and Bartil, 2018) a paradox exists whereby, in dispersed teamwork, trust is more critical for effective functioning – but also more difficult to build – than in more traditional teams. This is something the leader of a virtual team must endeavour to address early on. However, in some instances there is little alternative other than a virtual team, as was the case when the Covid-19 pandemic took hold globally in the spring of 2020. Rice *et al.* (2007) argued that to ensure that virtual teams can adapt rapidly to situations, members must have completed adequate training on the technology and the work processes afforded by the technology they use. This certainly was the case amid the pandemic, where teams who previously may have only worked in a virtual capacity on an ad hoc basis found themselves in the situation where they had no choice other than to utilise all available technology in order to work virtually. Waizenegger *et al.* (2020) argue that all formal and social communications that began to take place through digital channels during the pandemic allowed remote workers, or in this case those in virtual teams, to be socially and professionally integrated in a more successful manner than before the pandemic.

MANAGEMENT TEAMS

A management team is usually one which is ongoing and does not end or disband with the completion of a specific task or project. One of the fundamental roles of a top management team is to effectively coordinate the efforts of interdependent work teams at lower levels in the organisation. These managers also serve a coaching role and offer guidance for those in the teams they coordinate. Top management teams often experience problems in working effectively as a team due to the characteristics of high-powered individuals within the team who may find it difficult to share resources or adapt to being part of a team rather than a leader (Hart, 1996).

management teams consist of individuals with managerial roles in different areas of the organisation who coordinate the work of their respective teams.

SPOTLIGHT ON SKILLS

Teams are accepted as a feature of working life, whether we enjoy this aspect of work or not. How would you help a team in your organisation to be effective? Would you utilise training such as team roles analysis? Why, or why not? If you would, how would you use it? Would you use team building? If you would, what would you do and how would you measure or perceive its effects?

To help you answer these questions, visit **bloomsbury.pub/organisational-behaviour** to watch the video of Doug Howlett, a former rugby player who has played for the All Blacks (New Zealand) and Munster.

team roles are patterns of behaviour or sets of characteristics displayed in the way one team member interacts with another when serving to progress the performance of the team towards its aims.

TEAM ROLES

As discussed earlier, for any team to perform effectively a sense of cooperation among its members has to exist. We pointed out that one of the key differences between groups and teams lies in the sense of purpose they have, in other words that teams have a clearly

Table 7.2 Belbin's nine team roles typology

Role Type	Description
Plant (PL)	The first role identified was the Plant. The title derived from the fact that one such individual was 'planted' in each team who tended to display creative qualities and who was skilled at problem-solving in unusual ways.
Monitor Evaluator (ME)	The Monitor Evaluator role describes a team member who is logical and impartial in their judgements. This individual is capable of assessing a team's available options in a calm, unemotional manner.
Coordinator (CO)	This role fulfils the requirement of focusing on the team's objectives and delegating tasks accordingly based on each person's expertise.
Resource Investigator (RI)	The Resource Investigator role describes a team member who is an extrovert, skilled at making contacts and ensuring that the team has identified clearly its challenges with respect to competitors and its future opportunities.
Implementer (IMP)	Implementers create practical plans and strategies of work to ensure that tasks are completed efficiently.
Completer Finishers (CF)	Individuals displaying this role type display their talents most effectively at the end of a task when quality and attention to detail are required before completion of a project.
Teamworker (TW)	Teamworkers help the team to work together by being versatile, identifying tasks and completing them for the team.
Shaper (SH)	Shapers are viewed as challenging individuals who are skilled at sustaining the momentum of the team and helping others to focus on the task at hand.
Specialist (SP)	The final category of team member to emerge is the Specialist. This role represents in-depth knowledge of a key area essential to team success.

Source: Based on information in the Belbin Team Report from http://www.belbin.com/rte.asp?id=8.

defined sense of purpose while that of the group is broad and less clearly defined. In order for teams to work cooperatively to achieve their goals, members must fulfil different roles. According to Belbin (1993), for a team to cooperate successfully members need to perform a variety of functions and roles which complement each other rather than overlapping, in which case conflict is likely to occur or possible aspects of the task could be overlooked. In the 1970s, management psychologist Dr Meredith Belbin conducted research studies which sought to identify certain patterns of behaviour in teams which could in turn be used to predict the success of teams in a variety of different projects. Belbin used the basic psychological personality types ▸**See Chapter 2**◂ to divide participants across simulated teams. Belbin identified nine commonly found team roles. These roles are described in Table 7.2.

Belbin's investigation showed that the difference between successful and unsuccessful teams was less dependent on factors related to intelligence and experience but primarily related to behaviour within the team; the way team members made decisions and cooperated with each other; and finally, how each individual applied their abilities to reach the team goal (Batenburg *et al.*, 2013, p. 902). The Belbin model continues to be extremely popular and is used by many FTSE 100 companies in team development. However, there has been some criticism of the model, particularly regarding the validity of the psychometric measures and instruments used to determine each of the role types (Broucek and Randell, 1996). Furnham *et al.* (1993) in examining the Belbin Team Role Self-Perception Inventory (BTRSPI) found the predictive or construct validity to be unimpressive. Belbin (1993) responded to this criticism of the tool's validity, pointing out that had Furnham *et al.* (1993) not adopted the recommended method of use for the BTRSPI insisting that the tool was designed to intimate to individuals what their team roles might be.

BUILDING YOUR EMPLOYABILITY SKILLS

Team Building

You have been promoted to team leader within a financial services call centre and are now in charge of a group of eight call centre agents in the loan defaults division, where contacting clients in order to recoup debts and create new payment plans is the core function. The work can be very stressful for agents as they are often dealing with emotional situations in client interactions. Having come from a different division of the business, you have only a limited understanding of this yourself. How would you approach the first day and your first meeting with the team? What steps would you take to gain the respect of your new team? How would you convey your commitment to supporting, motivating and managing your new team?

Guidance

The *Harvard Business Review Guide to Leading Teams* (find it at: https://hbr.org/product/hbr-guide-to-leading-teams/an/13906E-KND-ENG) by Mary L. Shapiro provides guidance and advice for managers in leading teams. The guide advocates six important facets in managing teams effectively. Firstly, choosing the right team members for tasks and cultivating their skills accordingly. Secondly, setting clear goals for the group. Thirdly, fostering a sense of camaraderie and cooperation among a team. Fourthly, holding individuals accountable for their actions and setting expectations for individual and team behaviour. Finally, maintaining team focus and motivation until tasks are accomplished. Shapiro also highlights the importance of the initial stages of meeting a new team. She states that a priority must be 'to get to know your team members and to encourage them to get to better know one another', and to 'resist the urge to immediately start talking about the work and the task outcome'. Team activities and icebreaker techniques are often suggested as really useful ways to foster this approach.

Source

Reynolds, A., and Lewis, D. (2018) The two traits of the best problem-solving teams. *Harvard Business Review*, 2 April.

Visit http://humanresources.about.com/od/icebreakers/a/my-10-best-ice-breakers.htm for ice breaker and team activity ideas.

CHARACTERISTICS OF HIGH-PERFORMING WORK TEAMS

Throughout this chapter we have emphasised that groups and teams possess a kind of synergy that is greater than the sum of individual efforts. However, it is important to bear in mind that this is only the case where they function successfully and achieve results which reflect those efforts. Naturally, in business, just as in sport, no team can be successful and win 100% of the time. Where a team's failure can be put down to strong external competition, lessons can be taken from that for future performance. However, when a team is unsuccessful due to internal factors such as a lack of cooperation between members, insufficient resources from management or the presence of factors such as groupthink, then the organisation must look at how team structures can be improved.

Although there are many attributes of high-performing work teams, Nelson (2010) has identified the following seven key characteristics which capture most of these elements. These include: purpose, empowerment, relationships and communication, flexibility, optimal productivity, recognition and appreciation, and morale (see Table 7.3).

While Table 4.4 outlines the value of each of the characteristics of high-performing teams from an organisational perspective it is also important to focus on what this means for individual and team behaviour in the workplace. Take, for example, an individual working in a healthcare setting: an understanding of the sense of purpose of the organisation and of each individual within it is vital, so ensuring quality healthcare not just in medical interventions

Table 7.3 Characteristics of high-performing work teams

Characteristic	Value
Purpose	All members are aware of the team's mission and why it is important. They have a precise understanding of the aim that needs to be achieved and they develop mutually agreed upon goals that relate to that aim. Clear action strategies are created and each member understands his/her role.
Empowerment	Mutual respect within the team enables members to share responsibilities, support each other and take initiative, providing personal as well as collective power. Sets of rules and processes exist to enable members to do their jobs more easily.
Relationships and Communication	An atmosphere of trust and acceptance is created through open communication, and differences of opinion are valued. Methods for managing conflict are established. Members provide honest and constructive feedback to each other.
Flexibility	Members are flexible and perform different functions as needed. Members recognise that change is inevitable and are willing to adapt to changing conditions.
Optimal Productivity	High-performing teams display a commitment to high standards. Effective decision-making and problem-solving methods result in optimal task accomplishment.
Recognition and Appreciation	Both individual and team accomplishments are regularly acknowledged by the leader, the other team members and the organisation as a whole.
Morale	Members share a sense of pride in being part of the team and a strong sense of team spirit exists.

Source: Adapted from Nelson (2010), pp. 10–13.

but in all other functions from administration to cleaning and maintenance. Furthermore, if we look at empowerment and flexibility, we see the importance of each individual being able and having the authority to take on alternative roles and work within a team in order to deal with issues such as absenteeism or employee turnover on a day-to-day basis. Previously in this chapter we discussed how 'groupthink' can be detrimental to decision-making. The collapse of Swiss Air is often cited as an example of groupthink in an organisation. Strong communication channels and good working relationships between team members is essential in avoiding situations of groupthink or poor decision-making if people on the team are in a position to voice opposition to ideas ▶**See Chapter 14**◀ . From a management perspective, providing recognition for work and fostering a sense of pride in team achievements is hugely important to task achievement. This is true even in a voluntary setting; take, for example, the success of the London Olympics, much of which was attributed to the successful management of thousands of volunteers in the event.

As with leadership, a key determinant of the success or failure of team structures is the context. Does the context support and empower team operation? Teams are often presented as a kind of universal solution to organisational problems, but of course, this is unrealistic. Teams, no more than anything else, can only thrive if they are well matched to their environment. Fundamentally, teams are a much more integral part of the organisational landscape than they have been in the past. However, this is not always comfortable or effective. With justification, a lot of effort goes into team-building activity in organisations – giving teams the chance to bond, the structural and cultural support to thrive, and the knowledge to understand potential group difficulties and how to overcome them.

TEAM EFFECTIVENESS

In any situation, the success of a team is typically judged by how effective it is in meeting its aims. Cohen and Bailey (1997) conducted a review of numerous types of teams, resulting in a generalised model of the factors (both external and internal) that contribute to team effectiveness. Although the focus of their study was on organisational teams such as those that produce goods or deliver services, their model of team effectiveness can be applied to many different types of teams. For example, a team of students working to produce a college assignment! Cohen and Bailey categorised team effectiveness in three different ways: the performance effectiveness of the team in terms of the quantity and quality of their outputs, attitudes (e.g. satisfaction, commitment, trust) and behavioural outcomes (e.g. turnover). Cohen and Bailey argued that to reach effectiveness in those three categories, a number of factors needed to be examined. These included environmental factors (e.g. organisational or industry characteristics), design factors (size and composition of the team, team member autonomy), processes (e.g. how conflict is managed in the team) and finally the psychosocial traits of the team (e.g. shared beliefs). Consider how different teams you have been involved in during college may have experienced different outcomes in terms of their effectiveness. It is likely that some of those differing outcomes could be accounted for in looking at the environmental factors, design factors, processes and psychosocial traits.

Teamwork at Madame Chu's: A Case of Too Many Cooks?

Madame Chu's is an almost infamous Asian restaurant based in the coastal city of Brighton (around 50 miles south of London). Its popularity has grown not only because of its excellent reputation for good quality Asian cuisine at reasonable prices but also for being one of the most 'Instagrammable' restaurants in the south of England due to its flamboyant interior décor.

OB IN PRACTICE

From humble beginnings to huge success
The restaurant first opened in the late 1970s. It was opened by the Chu family, who had emigrated from China to England earlier that decade. The business was run by Jeremy and Mary Chu, and also employed in the business were their two sons, Dylan and Tony, and their daughter Claudia. Over the 1980s and 1990s the restaurant expanded from a 30-seater evening restaurant to a 120-seat restaurant with two evening sittings, lunchtime and breakfast trade. In the late 1990s, Jeremy and Mary retired and

the ownership of the business was passed on to their three children, who effectively became business partners. Each of them plays a differing, yet significant role in the business, with Dylan running the kitchen, Claudia managing front of house and guest bookings, while Tony essentially manages the financial, marketing and regulatory requirements of the business. Profits (which have remained remarkably high for a business in the hospitality sector, largely due to its strong reputation) have always been shared equally between the three partners. Each of the partners have had families of their own and, growing up, their children worked part-time in the restaurant among the other waiting and kitchen staff. On reaching adulthood, only two showed any long-term interest in the business. Dylan's son Jeff went on to become a chef and now works alongside his father as sous-chef in the business, earning a salary of £35,000 per year. The other is Claudia's daughter Lianne, who completed a degree in marketing and event

management at college; she also now works in the business and has played a key role in using 'influencers' and 'bloggers' to raise the profile of Madame Chu's to a national level. She has a salary of £30,000 but also negotiated a share of profits from the private dining and corporate event catering elements of the business, which she initiated two years ago. This part of the business has proved profitable, resulting in Lianne's salary reaching over £50,000 last year.

Trouble in the team
Madame Chu's employs more than 100 staff across catering, kitchen and floor staff. They pay just over the minimum wage. This has never caused a problem since the customers' tips are shared equally among all staff. However, problems have begun to emerge over the last few months. On Claudia's insistence, Tony has allowed Lianne to take on a more influential role in the running of the business. While he feels she is still a little naïve when it comes to certain aspects of the business (for instance, her people management skills have been questionable – at times she was witnessed 'barking orders' at staff, and she seems to lack understanding of the finances), yet he couldn't deny that some of her ideas have reaped rewards. After nearly 40 years in the business, it is time he feels to step back a little anyway. Dylan, however, is hugely unhappy with Lianne's level of involvement. Her plans seem to revolve around having Madame Chu's acquire a Michelin star, appearing in Condé Nast, and by association appealing much more to the 'corporate London crowd' than to traditional holidaymakers and locals. One of the first

actions Lianne took was to hire a new Michelin star chef for the restaurant. Dylan had assumed his son would become head chef one day; this no longer seems to be the case as this new sous-chef is already being paid more! Even Tony questioned how they could afford this additional high salary but was told that his reputation and plans for new menus would pay off in the long run. Within weeks, new 'Asian Fusion' menus were introduced. The kitchen staff have not responded well to the changes as the new menus, as they see it, are unduly complicated and emphasise 'style over substance'. Further to that, Lianne took to switching some of the staff roles, moving many of the long-serving waiting staff to kitchen and clearing roles while hiring a dozen new, young and attractive waiting staff many of whom simultaneously work in modelling or sports-related roles. While the restaurant never prioritised hiring staff of

Asian origin in the past, it just happened to be the case. None of the new staff are of Asian background. There have been tensions in the kitchen and on the floor, with new staff viewed as a clique. The situation is not helped by the fact that Claudia and Dylan are no longer seeing eye to eye either. Breakdowns in communication between the floor and kitchen have led to longer customer waiting times, mistakes in orders, and a few unhappy customer reviews on TripAdvisor!

The end of an era?
Things reached an all-time low last week when the entire kitchen staff threatened to 'walk off the job' after Lianne announced that customer tips would no longer be shared equally among all staff. Instead, there was to be a service charge for groups of eight or more but all discretional tips would remain with the waiting staff. An irate

Dylan phoned Tony, who was on holiday at the time, and told him 'either she goes or I do!' Tony is concerned that if that were to happen the entire business would have to be sold as neither he nor Claudia have the capital required to buy Dylan out of his share of the business. Moreover, the breakup of the business would be devastating news for his parents, for whom Madame Chu's had been their life's work.

Questions

1 Having read the case, list the different groups and teams that you can identify.
2 Identify what you feel are causes for the breakdown in teamwork in Madame Chu's.
3 Assume the role of a management consultant. If Tony were to hire you to advise him on how to resolve the issues that are now facing Madame Chu's, what action would you advise him to take?

MANAGERIAL TAKEAWAYS

The material in this chapter has highlighted the importance of groups and teams in contributing to all aspects of organisational requirements from operational to strategic-level tasks. For management, the development and fostering of effective teams is vitally important; in fact, many organisations consider being a team player, contributing to team effectiveness, and even building great teams, to be core competencies among employees. But how can managers, particularly middle managers who are often bound by both time and budgetary constraints, facilitate the development of strong team work capabilities among their staff? According to Inc.com, one of the key ways a manager can enhance their team is by encouraging transparency. The premise of the idea is that teams need to be able to work together with autonomy and without the constant involvement of the manager. However, it is when something goes wrong that management involvement is crucial in ensuring that the process gets back on track without allowing blame to damage the team. Managers should seek to bring together those who aren't getting along, to help them work through their concerns. For a manager, the primary job on the team is to help other team members understand each other better. For more strategies on building better teams visit https://www.inc.com/eric-v-holtzclaw/5-things-smart-managers-know-about-building-teams.html.

All in all, the reality of today's world is that every one of us will be part of a group or a team at some point during our working lives. While a distinction is made between groups and teams in this chapter, this difference is not always as obvious. For most organisations the aim of group work is to achieve the results of a high-performing team. In this chapter we have identified that synergy and interdependence can create high levels of performance. However, as we have seen, group work is fraught with difficulties, such as social loafing and groupthink. In order to help us achieve the ideals of teamwork, a number of characteristics and team roles have been identified. The point to remember is that teams, generally, need a lot of support and investment for their potential effectiveness to be optimised.

CHAPTER REVIEW QUESTIONS

1 Discuss a fundamental difference between a group and a team.
2 Reflect on the characteristics of each stage of group development – why is each stage important?
3 What are the challenges and advantages of working in a group, from your own experience?
4 What is group conformity? Discuss and assess the dynamics of conformity using the Asch studies as a reference point.
5 Each of Belbin's team roles can be placed in the category of either people-oriented, action-oriented or problem-solving oriented. Place each of these team roles within one of those categories in Table 4.2.
6 List three features of high-performing work teams and outline how these features might differ in an underperforming team.
7 Critically evaluate the advantages for organisations in using virtual teams over traditional teams based in a central location.
8 Identify two drawbacks of (a) self-managed teams, and (b) cross-functional teams.

FURTHER READING

Bond, M. (2014) *The Power of Others: Peer Pressure, Groupthink and How the People Around Us Shape Everything We Do.* London: Oneworld Publications.

Cain, S. (2012) The Rise of the New Groupthink. *The New York Times*, 12 January. Available at: http://www.nytimes.com/2012/01/15/opinion/sunday/the-rise-of-the-new-groupthink.html?pagewanted=all&_r=0 (accessed 25 January 2021).

Duhigg, C. (2016) What Google learned from its quest to build the perfect team. *The New York Times Magazine*, 26, 2016. Available at : https://theaxelagroup.com/wp-content/uploads/2019/01/What-Google-Learned-From-Its-Quest-to-Build-the-Perfect-Team.pdf

Sennet, R. (2012) *Together: The Rituals, Pleasures and Politics of Cooperation.* Boston, MA: Yale University Press.

Wheelan, S.A. (2010) *Creating Effective Teams: A Guide for Members and Leaders.* Thousand Oaks, CA: Sage.

USEFUL WEBSITES

https://www.huddle.com/blog/team-building-activities/

Huddle creates systems that allow teams to collaborate to share, discuss and work on their content. On the Huddle site, they also provide descriptions of some easy-to-replicate team-building activities that can be used in multiple types of organisational settings.

http://www.tavinstitute.org/

The Tavistock Institute of Human Relations applies social science insights to contemporary issues and problems. It promotes learning culture, and helping groups, organisations and individuals to think and reflect. Their website is an interesting source of research, historical background and case studies, looking at organisations and groups through the lens of socio-technical systems.

http://www.belbin.com/

Belbin Associates is a company founded by Meredith Belbin and others to promote knowledge about Belbin's team roles. While this is a commercial site, it is a useful resource for locating information about the history, sample reports, research and contemporary insights relating to the team roles inventory.

https://www.youtube.com/watch?v=3boKz0Exros

Watch this TED Talk where business school professor Amy Edmondson studies 'teaming', where people come together quickly (and often temporarily) to solve new, urgent or unusual problems. Recalling stories of teamwork such as the incredible rescue of 33 miners trapped half a mile underground in Chile in 2010, Edmondson shares the elements needed to turn a group of strangers into a quick-thinking team.

Online Resources

Visit bloomsbury.pub/organisational-behaviour to access additional materials to support teaching and learning.

---

8 MANAGEMENT CONTROL, POWER AND AUTHORITY

Lorraine Ryan

LEARNING OUTCOMES

BY THE END OF THIS CHAPTER YOU SHOULD BE ABLE TO:

- Understand the importance of management control in organisations and detail different forms of control.

- Discuss the importance of power and politics in organisational life.

- Outline the different sources of power.

- Explain how people translate power into action (power tactics).

- Differentiate between power, authority, influence and leadership.

- Discuss the ethical issues associated with the use of power and control at work.

CREDIT: IMAGE BY FREE-PHOTOS FROM PIXABAY

THIS CHAPTER DISCUSSES ...

IN REALITY

Who is the boss around here? Spend time in any organisation and you would think you could easily identify who the people with power are. Managers may have assigned offices, name plates, even designated parking spaces, and the organisational chart will give an outline from the top down of the leaders or key people in each department. Traditional views of power in organisations typically see it as the authority held by those in particular positions which give them the ability to direct others. However, power is a much more complex concept than that. Research by French and Raven in 1959 identified five different power bases, which recognised that power is more than simply the position a person holds in the organisation. These are: legitimate, reward, coercive, expert and referent power. Of course, managers have power that is associated with the position they hold in the organisation. This is known as legitimate power. Other sources of power may also be gained from holding legitimate power including the ability to provide resources (reward power) or withhold them (coercive power). However, some sources of power relate more to the characteristics of a person, which may not be held by all of those who have legitimate power and may in fact be held by those without a position of power. These include power that comes from having knowledge (expert power) and power associated with being likeable and respected (referent power). Consider the following scenario – the boss in a department has an important upcoming meeting next day and has accidentally lost her presentation. She is sure it is backed up somewhere on her PC but has no idea how to retrieve it. Her meeting is first thing in the morning and it's almost close of business. She knows she needs help from her junior colleague who knows a lot about technology. However, it might take some time to retrieve the presentation, which will involve staying late after work. Her legitimate power may not enable her to get what she needs – she cannot insist her colleague stays on after work. However, if her colleague likes and respects her (referent power) he may be willing to stay on to help her out. In this situation her junior colleague also has power stemming from the knowledge of technology he holds (expert power).

INTRODUCTION

Have you ever wondered why some people panic if they find themselves late for work, or fear 'getting into trouble' if they make a mistake in their job? In most other aspects of life, people are relatively free to make choices about what they do and how they act. So why do people conform, often unquestioningly, to orders from management about what to do, what to wear, how to speak and how to organise their time? Why do management have control over people at work? Part of the role of management is to maintain control and ensure things are done as planned in line with organisational objectives. There are numerous factors that influence who has the power to get others to behave in a particular way. Much of what occurs in organisational life can be explained by understanding key concepts relating to power, control and influence at work. This chapter begins by discussing (1) management control in the workplace, and examining some of the theoretical roots of control as a management function. It then discusses (2) sources of power in organisations, exploring what types of power management have and why. Building on this understanding of power, (3) other sources of power at work are identified. You have possibly heard of the term (4) 'office politics', which relates to how people get and use power to influence behaviour at work. The (5) links between power and politics are explored and the (6) ethical issues concerning the use of power and control at work are discussed, including key contemporary issues such as using technology to monitor employees.

MANAGEMENT CONTROL

The word 'control' can evoke negative thoughts if we associate it with dominance, manipulation, order and obedience, but imagine an organisation without any control. What would it look like? Does it seem like a place you would like to work? Control is one of the essential features of management's role and is necessary for organisations to operate in an orderly and efficient way. Control offers individuals predictability and certainty in their day-to-day working lives and many workers like knowing what is expected of them and being given clear direction and feedback. Indeed, role ambiguity where certainty, direction and control are absent is often a source of workplace stress (Kahn *et al.*, 1964; Jackson and Schuler, 1985). Control is a multi-faceted concept and in studies of management and organisational behaviour control can have positive as well as negative connotations. Essentially control is about ensuring the organisation meets its objectives by directing, measuring and correcting the use of the organisation's resources including people (Snell, 1992). Management control is a management function aimed at achieving organisational objectives through setting standards, measuring actual performance against standards and taking corrective action where necessary.

management control is a management function aimed at achieving organisational objectives through setting standards, measuring actual performance against standards and taking corrective action where necessary.

CLASSICAL THEORISTS AND CONTROL

Early Classical studies of management theory in the 20th century ▸See Chapter 1◂ were strongly focused on efficiency and control. Organisations were typically bureaucratic top-down arrangements where managers did the thinking and workers were expected to do as they were told. F.W. Taylor's work on Scientific Management emphasised the breakdown of work into specialist tasks, and used time and motion studies to measure how each task could be made most efficient. It also used payment by piece rates to motivate workers to operate as efficiently as possible ▸See Chapter 5◂. For Taylor, management control was a critical component of the 'best way' to manage an organisation. Another key influential management thinker was French engineer Henri Fayol. His administrative theory identified five key managerial functions:

1 **Forecasting and planning** – part of management's job is to decide the future direction of the organisation and plan for this. Think about organisations' mission statements, target setting or project planning. They are developed as a result of information gathering and analysis about the environment, competitors and consumers in an effort to plan for the organisation's best future.
2 **Organising** – in order to achieve the organisation's goals, management must arrange the structure of the organisation and utilise its resources, processes and procedures in the best way possible.
3 **Coordination** – organisations are complex systems of different departments, functions and people. Part of management's job is to coordinate all the different elements of the system to ensure they work together and achieve synergy where possible.

4 **Command** – management must provide direction and leadership in the organisation so that resources can be organised and coordinated.

5 **Control** – once objectives have been set, management must ensure that they are met. Control means ensuring that instructions and rules are followed, and performance is translated into desired results.

McLean (2011) argues that control could be seen as the underpinning function of management because without it, carrying out the other four functions would be difficult. Organisations have been compared to machines comprised of different parts that operate together to make the machine work. The role of management is to design and put together the machine, ensure it runs as best it can in a smooth manner, and to try to prevent the machine from breaking down.

BUILDING YOUR EMPLOYABILITY SKILLS

Management Control ...

Think about the following activities in a modern organisation:

- Taking minutes at a department meeting
- Sharing those minutes with other departments in the organisation
- Developing a strategic plan
- Conducting performance and development reviews with staff
- The use of time cards for clocking in and out
- Limiting staff's internet use during working hours
- Organising a team building day off site
- Providing an employee handbook.

Which of Fayol's management functions do you think they represent? How many of them fall under the function of management control?

While management must control all of the resources in an organisation, our concern when studying organisational behaviour focuses on management control and people at work. The Classical management studies were criticised for neglecting the human element of work. Workers do not like to be controlled to the extent that they feel they are being treated like cogs in a machine. The Human Relations approach ▶See Chapter 7◀ which emerged in the 1920s began to recognise the importance of individual attitudes, personalities and human behaviour in groups, core concepts that you are studying as a student of organisational behaviour ▶See Chapters 2 and 7◀. That is not to say, however, that the writings of Classical theorists such as Taylor, Fayol and others are not relevant to organisations today, particularly in relation to management control. Much of the ideas put forward by these early management thinkers influenced subsequent theoretical approaches to the study of organisation behaviour, structure and management. Think about organisations such as McDonald's or Ryanair. Can you see evidence of the breakdown of tasks, of time and motion efficiency in the way workers complete their tasks and of strict management control? Are they successful and profitable organisations?

Thus, modern-day organisations and managers are still very much concerned with control; however, the methods used to exercise control over workers have become more sophisticated over time. Indeed, management control is more difficult to recognise when it is not as overt as the form of control we might imagine when we consider early factory work of the 20th century (see 'OB in the News'). Think of organisations that have developed cultures of long working hours and strong employee identification with the company ▶See Chapter 12◀. Is this a form of employee control?

CONTROL AND RESISTANCE

Earlier we noted that control can have both positive and negative connotations. While it can be positive to have order, certainty and cohesion in an organisation the human element of relationships means that control over people in organisations can never be absolute or indeed desirable. If complete control over employees was exercised in an organisation, then there would be little scope for independent thought, innovation and creativity. It could negatively impact employee motivation ▶See Chapter 5◀. It may also give rise to resistance from workers, who would find ways to escape control mechanisms, either individually or collectively and cause workplace conflict or even industrial sabotage. In fact, Taylor recognised that workers engage in 'soldiering' whereby workers approach orders at the slowest rate that goes unpunished and that all workers work at the rate of the slowest among them. Tight control over employees does not therefore necessarily result in the greatest productivity. Direction and control need to take into consideration employee motivation and commitment ▶See Chapter 5◀. While Fayol is often categorised as being similar to Taylor, it is suggested that closer examination of his work shows a management thinker with a sophisticated understanding of the necessity of integrating the requirements of authority, order and control with a consideration for the welfare and morale of employees, equity and the value of enabling employees to take part in decision-making (Parker and Ritson, 2005, p. 1350).

BUILDING YOUR EMPLOYABILITY SKILLS

Exercising Managerial Control

You work as a manager in CoffeeCo, an exclusive and upmarket coffee house and bistro that has recently opened in a busy area in Hong Kong. There are 15 baristas/waiting staff and three kitchen staff working there, most of whom are good workers committed to the organisation and who identify strongly with the CoffeeCo brand. They are proud to work there. However, there is a small number of staff who you feel you have no control over. They are frequently late for shifts, take long breaks and seem to invent their own recipes for drinks instead of sticking to the prescribed CoffeeCo guidelines. Their interactions with customers are in your view much too informal even though CoffeeCo has clear directions in the employee handbook on appropriate greetings, including recommended phrases to use. You make sure you watch them closely whenever you are around but that just doesn't seem to be working – they tend to do as they please. You have overheard them laughing about you and your rules and you know it is that group who keep hiding your CoffeeCo manager badge! Worse still, you have noticed other workers are starting to adapt to their ways. It is difficult for you to complain to the owner though because sales are up and customers keep coming back. You just wish all the workers would stick to the rules.

1 What efforts at exercising managerial control can you identify in CoffeeCo? Are they successful? What might you change?

2 What sources of power do you have? How useful are they?

IMPACT OF TECHNOLOGY ON BEHAVIOUR

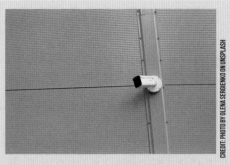

It is critically important to consider how technology can have an impact on behaviour in the workplace given the unprecedented acceleration in technological advancement across the globe. A key consideration for this chapter is the possibilities for management control offered by new technologies. Information relating to employees' hours of work, pay, performance, etc. has long been collected and used by organisations. However, given the pervasiveness of technology in our lives and work environments, employers are now able to gather vast amounts of data on employees. This could be through CCTV monitoring, measuring keystrokes, GPS tracking, biometrics (such as fingerprints and facial recognition) and providing employees with fitness tracking devices, or even implanting a digital chip in employees' wrists (see Spicer, 2017). The result is employers have greater access to employee data than ever before. This includes data not just relating to location, calendars, time spent on tasks or in meetings, online activity and social media, but data relating to heart rate, sleep, emotions, hormone levels and brain activity. The availability of such data means that certain organisational decisions can be made by algorithms with little human intervention. It also means that employers can literally know every step we take and every move we make.

CREDIT: PHOTO BY OLENA SERGIENKO ON UNSPLASH

Having considered the concept of management control we can begin to understand just how complex organisations and working relationships can be. Control is necessary for an organisation to fulfil its planned objectives, but control can also result in resistance and low motivation. We know that the purpose of control is to encourage people to behave as we want them to in order to fulfil organisational objectives. This can be done in numerous ways, and of critical importance is who has the ability to get people to behave in a particular way. Therefore, we now consider the concept of power in organisations. In the opening segment of this chapter, we saw how management power is only one source of power in the workplace. The concept of power in organisations is quite complex and there are numerous factors that dictate who has power and how they use it.

POWER IN ORGANISATIONS

Philosopher Michel Foucault suggested that 'power is everywhere' and can be wielded from many directions. In organisations, power is important – those who have it want to keep it and those who don't have it often want to get it. Yet power is a difficult concept to identify and is often confused with other concepts such as authority and leadership. A manager may find it difficult to get employees to do what he wants them to do, even though he is in a position of authority. Someone else in the organisation may easily persuade others to do as she wants, but is not 'the boss'. So, who has more power in these two situations? Where does power come from and why are some people in organisations powerful, while others aren't? How do people in organisations use their power? To answer these questions, we must first understand what power is.

WHAT IS POWER?

power exists where person A can get person B to do something that B would not otherwise do.

Dahl's (1957) famous definition of power asserts that it exists where person A can get person B to do something that B would not otherwise do. A closely related concept to power is influence. Power often refers to the *potential* of one person to cause another to act in accordance with their wishes, whereas influence refers to the *actual* behaviour of that person (Somech and Drach-Zahavy, 2001). Power is the 'what' and influence is the 'how'. Definitions of power typically assume that the person with power and the person subject to it have incompatible objectives; influence, however, can be exerted collaboratively where goals are not mutually exclusive (Tjosvold *et al.*, 1992). The essence of power, therefore, may be *control* over the *behaviour of others* or the ability to influence others. This may be achieved by bringing about change in others' beliefs or attitudes or having the capacity to reward or punish others. In an organisational context, power can stem from those who have control over resources and the ability to make decisions to allocate those resources to others. Power can come in many different forms, but importantly, power is not absolute.

The extent of power is dependent on the amount of resistance to it. When discussing management control, it was noted that people generally do not like to feel they are being controlled. Therefore, person A has more power over person B if they can get B to do something without B 'putting up a fight' or resisting doing it. The extent to which people will resist power or succumb to influence depends on a number of factors including personality ▸See Chapter 2◂ and culture. The cultural values of a society have a tremendous impact on the extent to which people readily accept people in positions of power. Hofstede's (1991) well-known model of culture identified power distance ▸See Chapter 12◂ as reflecting the extent to which employees welcome the idea that people in organisations rightfully have power. Japan typically has a high level of power distance, meaning people readily accept the role of management as power holders. Other Western cultures have lower power distance, meaning that they do not accept management power as readily and value individuality and diversity. This makes them less susceptible to power influence. Dependency is also important when examining power relationships. The more dependent one party is on another, the more they may be influenced by them.

BUILDING YOUR EMPLOYABILITY SKILLS

Powerful Leaders

Think about a person you would consider as a powerful leader, such as Jeff Bezos, CEO of Amazon, or Joe Biden, President of the United States, or Kim Jong-un, Leader of North Korea. What is it about them that makes them powerful?

WHERE DOES POWER COME FROM?

At the beginning of this chapter, we identified a number of different sources of power in organisations that can relate to the person as an individual (informal or personal power) or to the position a person holds within the organisation (formal power) **▶See Chapter 4◀**. Some sources of power may be negative, for example an employee will do something because they feel they *have to*, while other sources may be positive, for example they will do something because they *want to*. Which do you think would be more effective? Research has shown that positive sources of power are the most important to acquire (Robbins and Judge, 2012). Think back to our opening scenario in this chapter, about the boss who can't retrieve her presentation. One of the most commonly used classifications of power in organisational behaviour literature is French and Raven's (1959) model. They identify five power bases or sources of power, three of which relate to the position a person holds (formal power) and two that relate to the person as an individual (informal or personal power).

Table 8.1 Sources of power

FORMAL POWER / POSITION POWER		
Someone in a position of authority has:	**Legitimate Power**	Typically determined by the organisational hierarchy and identifiable through titles such as Senior Manager.
Someone who has control over resources has:	**Reward Power**	Power wielder must be able to confer valued material rewards such as pay increases or promotions. The target of this power must value the rewards.
Someone who can punish or withhold rewards has:	**Coercive Power**	Power wielder can threaten and use their position to force others to take action. The target of the power must value the rewards and fear having them withheld.
INFORMAL POWER / PERSONAL POWER		
Someone who others want to be like has:	**Referent Power**	Charisma, interpersonal skill and personal attraction of an individual. This power is dependent on the target wanting to identify with the individual, perhaps someone you 'look up to'.
Someone who has knowledge or expertise that others don't has:	**Expert Power**	Their knowledge and expertise must set them apart from others. This power is determined by the extent to which others attribute knowledge and expertise to the power holder.

Source: Adapted from French and Raven (1959).

French and Raven's model still remains relevant today both within and outside organisations. Think of the power social media influencers have over the things we buy because we want our lives to look like theirs (Referent Power). Or the power an IT specialist has over a customer who knows nothing about technology (Expert Power). A manager has power over workers if the manager can determine who gets monetary bonuses (Reward/Coercive Power), and whoever holds the office of President of the United States is one of the most powerful people in the world

(Legitimate Power). The strength of these sources of power depends on the characteristics of those the power holder is trying to influence. There are also limitations to how many of these sources can be used at the same time. If, for example, a manager used coercive power towards a group of workers, they would be unlikely to identify closely with that manager and so he or she may not expect to use referent power. Sources of power also depend on the perceptions of others ▸See Chapter 3◂. For example, you may be an expert in something but unless others perceive this expertise as important, then this may not be a source of power. Power therefore is often 'in the eye of the beholder'.

French and Raven's model views power as something that is dependent on relationships between individuals and groups in organisations. In other words, one party only holds power over another because of the relationship between them. If the relationship ends or changes, then so does the power. Other views see power as something that is possessed, something that you have or can accumulate. Pfeffer (1981) identified sources of power and, similar to French and Raven's model, classified these into *structural* and *personal* sources of power. Structural sources of power include formal position and authority, access to and control over information and resources, and being irreplaceable, for example as held by a manager. Personal sources of power include talent, energy, endurance and stamina, and emotional intelligence, for example Lionel Messi. While power can be viewed as something that is possessed, something that relates to position or personal factors, or something dependent on relationships, power is also context dependent. A number of factors can shape or change sources of power and these include the structure of the organisation, formal and informal networks, factors in the external environment ▸See Chapter 1◂, and sources of knowledge or information. Access to information has always been a source of power, which has become particularly influential in this current digital age. Think about management control and all the ways that management attempt to restrict the use of information by those in certain positions. These can include systems designed to limit the sharing of data, and regulations relating to financial information. The considerable increase in external regulations on organisations' use of data, particularly personal data such as GDPR (General Data Protection Regulation) in recent times, shows just how important access to information can be as a source of power. Other theories can also provide insight into power in organisations. Negotiation theory tells us that power can come from having alternatives, that is, the more and better alternatives available to you, the less pressure you are under to agree to what's on the table. In fact, the idea of knowing your BATNA (Best Alternative to a Negotiated Agreement) developed by Fisher and Ury (1981) has long been recognised as a critical source of power for negotiators. A good BATNA means you have other options and will not be compelled to agree to terms that are not in your interest to accept.

HOW IS POWER USED?

We have identified what power is and where it comes from but how do people use power in organisations? Does power even have to be used to be effective? Maybe it is enough that others know you have power. Power in the workplace is more complex than simply something you have or do not have. Power tactics describe the ways in which people use their power. The choice of power tactic used will depend on the person using it (power holder) and the person they are trying to influence (power target). Other relevant factors include why the person is exercising power, the choice of power sources they have, the power sources they believe the

power tactics are the ways in which power bases are translated into actions.

other party has, the expected outcomes and beliefs about how targets will react. For example, a manager may have coercive power and the ability to dismiss an employee; however, such an action may result in backlash from other employees. So they choose another power tactic instead. Some examples of power tactics are outlined in Table 8.2.

Table 8.2 Power tactics in organisations

Tactic	Example
Rational persuasion	Explain to someone the logical arguments as to why they should do what you want.
Ingratiation	Try to get the other party to like you so they will do what you want. Can involve use of praise or flattery.
Coalition	Get others to support your ideas, especially those in positions of authority.
Exchange	Create obligations based on the principle of reciprocity. I do something for you, you must do something for me.
Personal Appeal	Appeal to friendship and loyalty to gain support.
Inspirational Appeal	Use values, beliefs or emotions to gain enthusiasm.
Consultation	Involve someone to participate in decision-making to gain their support.
Legitimating	Use formal authority or appeal to a higher authority for support.
Pressure	Use demands, threats or warnings, or intimidation to get others' support.

Elias (2008) notes that French and Raven intended their original classification of sources of power would be developed and built upon by other scholars. The sources of power were not to be seen as a complete explanation of social power. Different factors combine to determine if and how individuals will use different sources of power to influence others. Such factors include: the reason the person is trying to use power – is it to achieve an organisational goal or is it because the individual wants to be powerful? Is the use of this type of power acceptable within the context where it is being used or would it be frowned upon? What are the different options of power sources available? How does the individual think others will react? Figure 8.1 shows the relationships between these factors, that is, the power of a person (agent power), the influencing tactics they use, the content factors, and how these shape influence outcomes.

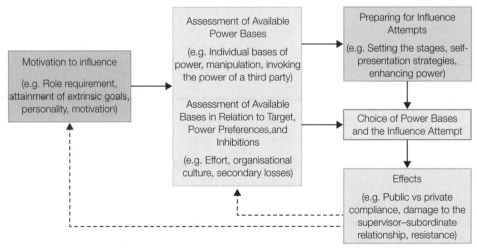

Figure 8.1 The power/interaction model

Source: Raven (1993).

POWER AND THE EMPLOYMENT RELATIONSHIP

Power is a critical factor in the employment relationship and studies in employment relations and Human Resource Management examine the structural determinants of power in the workplace from a societal or class perspective (see Townsend *et al.*, 2019). Some perspectives view power and authority as a right of management whereas others maintain that power should be shared in the organisation with workers, for example through involving them in decisions that affect their working lives. Employment relations scholars have long emphasised the *imbalance of power* that exists between management and workers in capitalist organisations (Dundon and Rollinson, 2011; Fox, 1966; Wallace *et al.*, 2013). Although management typically has more power than workers in an organisation, that is not to say that workers have no power. Workers do not usually have legitimate or position power over management, but they may have access to power sources of their own such as tacit knowledge over a work process, in other words only they know how something is done. There may also be powerful elements of moral persuasion around issues of fair treatment of workers in the workplace. That is, management should treat workers fairly because it is the right thing to do. A recent trend has been the use of 'zero-hours contracts' where employees are not guaranteed hours of work but have to be available when an employer offers hours (Adams *et al.*, 2015). This is a very visible use of management power and the use of such contracts is increasing across many organisations including fast-food outlets, retail stores, hotels and restaurants, and universities. Due to the imbalance of power in this employer–employee relationship there is little employees can do to improve their working conditions. One way in which workers can try to increase their power is by joining trade unions to represent their interests and negotiate with management on their behalf. The principle behind trade union joining is 'power in numbers'.

POWER PATHWAYS

Power and influence do not just occur where management seek to make employees behave in a particular way. Although power typically comes from those in positions of authority to influence those below them, it is also possible for power to be used in other directions. Power can be downward (managers' influence over workers); upward (workers' influence over managers) or lateral (workers' influence over other workers or managers' influence over other managers). Many organisations are no longer characterised by typical hierarchical bureaucratic structures. They have changed and become 'flatter', emphasising more lateral relationships. Power tactics depend on the direction of power; for example, management may use certain tactics to influence and/or control workers but workers may use different power tactics to influence management or other workers.

EMPOWERMENT

empowerment
is a process
where managers
delegate power to
employees, who
use it to make
decisions affecting
both themselves
and their work.

No discussion of power in modern-day life is complete without identifying the concept of empowerment. As a result of flatter organisational hierarchies there has been a move to transfer power to employees. There is an expectation in contemporary organisations that managers empower their employees and that those empowered employees make decisions without seeking supervision (Wilkinson, 1998). Moss Kanter's (1977) Structural Theory of Power in Organisations identifies that structures important to the growth of empowerment are access to information, being provided with the appropriate resources and support to perform required tasks at a high level of achievement, and having access to programmes that will enable individuals to develop and enhance their work experience. This approach is grounded in trust, commitment and cooperation within and across self-organised units/teams.

The goal in empowering employees is to create a work environment in which people have a degree of autonomy, are productive, contributing, motivated and happy, and in which the speed of decision-making is improved, all of which contribute to organisational success (Wilkinson, 1998). The philosophy behind empowerment is based on the idea that if employees are empowered to take control and make decisions, they feel more confident, capable and motivated to work more effectively and efficiently. As a result, employees become more productive. Toyota has been associated with embracing the concept of employee empowerment. Toyota believes that every employee should take ownership of their work by identifying quality defects and ways to improve efficiency. This philosophy helped established the company as a quality champion and one of the world's largest car-makers. Empowered employees engage in a number of behaviours, such as taking the initiative, applying critical thinking skills, offering judgements and identifying and acting on opportunities to improve systems. Empowerment is also associated with becoming stronger and more confident in personal areas of life and giving individuals the freedom to take control. Empowerment tends to have positive connotations but Hyman and Mason (1995) suggest that in the context of increased decision-making and responsibility, empowerment is a euphemism for work intensification.

It is worth noting here the differences in cultures in terms of perceptions of empowerment. In Scandinavian countries there is an expectation that managers will involve workers in decision-making processes. A directive manager would not be well accepted by workers in a Swedish organisation. Yet, in countries such as India, Singapore and Hong Kong, workers value the directive use of power and they see a directive manager as powerful and a consultative one as having little power.

Control or Empowerment?

OB IN THE NEWS

In recent years many giant tech companies including Apple, Facebook and Google have introduced a somewhat controversial new health benefit 'perk' for female employees – egg freezing, a procedure which enables women to delay child bearing by freezing their eggs until a time they choose, without the constraints of their 'biological clock'. Facebook became one of the first major employers to cover egg freezing for non-medical reasons as part of its health insurance plan, and Apple, Google and others soon followed suit. The procedure, which costs thousands of dollars per employee for the initial process and subsequent storage of eggs, is said to offer female employees empowerment by enabling them to have greater choice over when to start a family. An enduring challenge for many organisations is how to ensure women remain in the organisation if they choose to have children. Many (often talented and highly valuable) women leave the workforce when the demands of balancing work and family just don't balance. Even if women don't leave the organisation, there are few who break the 'glass ceiling' and lack of female representation in top management positions is a problem across organisations in numerous occupations, sectors and countries (ILO, 2015). This has negative consequences for individuals and organisations. Issues relating to this organisational conundrum have been extensively researched and organisations continually search for policies that provide an answer. For women, their 20s and early 30s, which is the biological norm for having children, coincide with the time when many women, particularly career-driven women, want or need to devote time to their careers and work their way up the corporate ladder. In many cases progressing your career during these years means long hours at work, frequent travel and extensive social networking, tasks that are not compatible with having a young family. In providing a solution to the pressures of balancing career and motherhood, egg freezing might seem like an attractive option allowing women to delay motherhood until they have achieved success in their career. Yet the move was met with criticism from some, who suggest

that nature and biology cannot (or should not) be controlled in this way. Although egg freezing is only one of a range of family-planning 'perks' for employees, critics suggest that the principal beneficiaries of this are the companies, not employees. Commentators suggest that egg freezing is a quick fix which does not address the underlying barriers in employment that prevent women from successfully combining work and motherhood. It has been suggested that offering such 'perks', rather than simply offering women more choice, is a subtle form of control that pressurises women to delay motherhood and devote themselves to their career and the organisation. In an article for *The New Yorker*, Rebecca Mead asks: 'rather than being a means of empowerment whereby a young woman is no longer subject to the ticking of her biological

clock – is freezing one's eggs merely a surrender to the larger, more invisibly pervasive force of corporate control?'

Questions

1 Do you think companies that offer egg freezing for female employees are giving them empowerment? Or do you think this is another example of organisations trying to exert control over their employees?

2 How do you think you would feel as a female employee who didn't avail yourself of the option of delaying motherhood in this way? Do you think it would impact on your career?

3 What are the implications for society of initiatives like these from organisations? Do they help to foster equality between male and female employees? Consider the ethical implications of organisations offering this perk.

Sources

Mead, R. (2014) Cold comfort: Tech jobs and egg freezing. *The New Yorker*, 17 October.

Moore, S. (2017) It's not a perk when big employers offer egg-freezing – it's a bogus bribe. *The Guardian*, 26 April.

Weller, C. (2017) What you need to know about egg-freezing, the hot new perk at Google, Apple, and Facebook. *Business Insider*, 17 September.

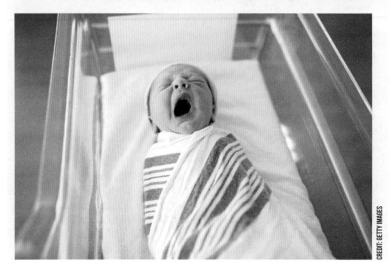

CREDIT: GETTY IMAGES

AUTHORITY AND LEADERSHIP

When studying power in organisations it is important to understand a number of other concepts which are closely linked to power. 'Authority', 'leadership' ▸See Chapter 6◂ and 'power' are terms often used to describe the same thing but there are differences between these concepts and it is important to be able to distinguish between them. Authority relates to the concept of management's prerogative or right to manage. There is an expectation from those in authority that others will conform and there is generally acceptance from others that authority is legitimate. Authority is sometimes unquestioned by subordinates and obedience follows as a matter of course, as we identified in our opening discussion about management control. In a now famous experiment, Yale University psychologist Stanley Milgram showed just how much people were willing to obey those perceived to be in authority (Milgram, 1963). His experiment involved participants administering electric shocks to volunteers if they got answers to questions wrong (no shocks were actually administered but the participants did not know this and believed they were inflicting pain on another person). Although they expressed various levels of discomfort in administering the shocks, a surprisingly large number inflicted the highest voltage of shock because the person 'in authority' told them it was OK to do so. This was despite hearing sounds of distress from those they were administering electric shocks to!

> **authority** typically refers to positional power and relies on the assumption that others are willing to obey.

Reading our definitions of power ▸**See Chapter 8**◂ and leadership ▸**See Chapter 6**◂ we can identify similarities between them. The link between power and leadership is a complex one. Packard's (1962) perspective on leadership maintains it is the art of getting others to *want* to do something that you are convinced should be done. This suggests that leadership is different from power as followers willingly do what the leader wants, whereas power might result in others doing something because they *have* to. If you ever watch a reality TV show (e.g. *The Apprentice*), notice how certain people assume leadership roles in the group. When leadership roles are not assigned or based on formal authority there are other ways in which individuals exert their power or become leaders. Maybe someone in the group has a dynamic personality or desirable skills or talents that others look up to. Recent research shows that employees' trust in business leaders has been seriously eroded following numerous scandals, such as the downfall of Enron and Lehman Brothers (Qu *et al.*, 2019). Leadership scholars have therefore emphasised the importance of *authentic* leadership where leaders are led by their true values which they do not compromise in response to external pressures (Gardner *et al.*, 2011). It is suggested that this type of leadership will result in positive outcomes for employees and organisations (Hirst *et al.*, 2016). However, critics suggest it is possible for leaders to be 'authentic jerks' (Qu *et al.*, 2019) in that their behaviour can match their values but those values are not necessarily good. This leads us to consider the ethical dimension of behaviours and the use of power in organisations.

Controlling the behaviour of workers while at work has always been a key concern of management. Employees have been subject to direct supervision by a manager since organisations began, but the advent of technology has allowed for significantly greater and tighter supervision of workers. Employee surveillance refers to an organisation's ability to monitor, record and track employee performance, behaviours and personal characteristics through technology.

> **employee surveillance** refers to an organisation's ability to monitor, record and track employee performance, behaviours and personal characteristics through technology.

◀ETHICAL▶ BEHAVIOUR IN THE WORKPLACE

Imagine you work as a supervisor in the deli section of a large supermarket. The employer has recently introduced discreet video surveillance without employees' knowledge or consent. The employee handbook clearly states that theft (of money or food products) is an offence punishable by dismissal. Food not sold by the end of the day is routinely dumped.

There are two employees who during their shift regularly eat a few chicken pieces and sausages when it's quiet (they're actually both trying to stick to a diet but the food smells so good!). Would you tell the workers who report to you about the surveillance? What are the ethical issues involved in a situation like this? Who is in the wrong here – the employer or the employees?

Source

Deegan, G. (2014) Dunnes has to pay worker €8,000 after spy camera catches her eating deli food. *The Independent*, Friday 23 August. Available at: https://www.independent.ie/irish-news/courts/dunnes-has-to-pay-worker-8000-after-spy-camera-catches-her-eating-deli-food-30209450.html

POWER, POLITICS AND ETHICAL BEHAVIOUR

Lord Acton once famously said that 'power tends to corrupt and absolute power corrupts absolutely'. By this he meant that the more powerful a person becomes, the fewer morals they seem to have, and the less concern they have for others around them – an idea demonstrated perfectly by George Orwell in his seminal novel *Animal Farm*. In studying power, therefore, it is important to consider the concept of ethics. Ethical behaviour refers to the extent to which it is seen as right or wrong to use power in any given situation. Ethics are codes that reflect our values and moral principles and drive our decisions and behaviours with respect to what is right and wrong, good and bad. Ethics is a normative concept that refers to how we *should* behave in our dealings with others and is underpinned by notions of fairness and justice. However, within organisations there are many different groups or stakeholders and it is not possible to 'please all of the people all of the time'. Many of our ideas about ethical behaviour are that actions should be determined based on whatever results in the greatest good. However, the use of political behaviour in organisations is often focused on self-interest regardless of the cost to others. For example, getting promoted, securing a bonus or finding favour with the boss regardless of the impact on others. Typically, political behaviour is unethical when the political tactics do not serve the organisation's goals or the goals of a larger group of people than the single political actor, and when using power and political behaviour violates another person's rights (Mingers, 2011). Such behaviour in organisations might include accepting bribes, avoiding taxes or taking credit for work that is not yours. These actions usually relate to power in some way. For example, a manager with decision-making authority may be bribed to decide things

ethics are codes that reflect our values and moral principles and drive our decisions and behaviours with respect to what is right and wrong, good and bad.

Power, Control and Ethics at Amazon

Amazon is one of the most profitable companies in the world, generating billions of dollars every year in revenue and returns to shareholders. The company that originally started out selling books is now a global phenomenon and the world's largest online retailer. Amazon's mission is to be 'the Earth's most customer-centric company' and provides TV, music, cloud computing, groceries and famous products such as its voice recognising smart speaker Alexa, to millions of customers every day. Its CEO Jeff Bezos' wealth is estimated to be worth over 100 billion US dollars. However, the company has been subject to its fair share of controversy in the media. One aspect of Amazon's activities that has received considerable negative attention in the press is undercover documentaries and worker websites which detail its treatment of warehouse employees. While much of Amazon's commercial activities are online and virtual, the activities in its warehouses require much physical human input from workers, whose job it is to find the products to match customer orders and get them processed and delivered to customers as quickly as is humanly possible.

OB IN PRACTICE

How does Amazon ensure that workers operate at their most efficient levels? The company uses strict control and surveillance of workers' activities using computer generated targets, timers and arm monitors to track the movement of each 'Amazonian' worker. Each warehouse worker, known as a 'picker', has to pick up to 400 items per hour, targets described as impossible and unrealistic by workers. Given that items are located across the floors of the company's vast warehouse, this is a task which could involve walking (or running) up to 11 miles during a shift. Strenuous physical work, boring and monotonous environments, continuous beeping from monitors, no natural light, long shifts, low pay and constant monitoring by supervisors are part of the management control systems reported across Amazon's warehouse locations. Workers who do not meet set targets are given warnings through a points system and points are also accrued for being late or taking time out sick. Disciplinary action or dismissal follows once a certain number of points have accrued. Media reports give details of workers suffering physical and mental breakdowns as a result of the incessant control and the unrealistic targets, with reports of ambulances being regularly called to warehouses to treat employees. In a statement during a push to organise a union, one picker said: 'I feel like all the company cares about is getting their products out to the customers as quickly as is humanly possible, no matter what that means for us workers in the end.'

Questions

1   What is your view of the methods of employee control in Amazon?

2   If you were appointed to a senior role in Amazon, what steps do you think you could take to promote a more ethical form of control over warehouse workers?

3   Do you think customer behaviour is impacted by perceptions of unethical treatment of workers at Amazon?

CREDIT: IMAGE BY THAM YUAN YUAN FROM PIXABAY

a certain way. Colleagues fighting for a promotion which will increase their power may take credit for others' work to 'get ahead'. It may be argued that whether or not behaviour is ethical is strongly dependent on context, and politics are a natural feature of organisational life. Do you think unethical behaviours or 'playing politics' are more acceptable if 'everybody does it' or if 'you have to look out for number one' or 'the end justifies the means'?

SPOTLIGHT ON SKILLS

A group of workers are discussing their country's upcoming semi-final match in the World Cup next week over their tea break. This is the first time the country has reached this stage of the competition for 20 years. The entire country will come to a standstill to see if the team might manage to beat Brazil and qualify for the final for the first time ever!! The game starts at 3 pm and the workers are due to finish their shift at 4.30. They decide to approach management and see what the options are. There's no way any of them are going to miss the big game. Anyway, they've just finished a huge order where they worked overtime and things have quietened down a bit now. Surely management will be reasonable and anyway they'll probably be watching the match on the big screen they have in the company boardroom (this screen is used for presentations to clients and it is fantastic quality).

1 If you were in management's position, what approach would you use to resolve this issue and why choose that approach?

2 What do you think might be the benefits of the approach you choose?

3 What might be the disadvantages of adopting a different approach?

To help you answer these questions, visit bloomsbury.pub/organisational-behaviour to watch the video of Declan Deegan from Milford Hospice talking about conflict resolution.

ORGANISATIONAL POLITICS

Power and politics are inextricably linked in organisations. Politics is an inherent feature of organisations as people try to get others to behave in a particular way through using power. One of the most well-known definitions of organisational politics is that it 'involves those activities taken within organizations to acquire, develop, and use power and other resources to obtain one's preferred outcome in a situation where there is uncertainty or dissensus about choices' (Pfeffer, 1981, p. 7). While DuBrin (2001, p. 192) defined organisational politics as 'informal approaches to gaining power through means other than merit or luck'. Both these definitions help us identify that political activity in the workplace results from the conversion of power into action. Political behaviour occurs in organisations for numerous reasons such as competition for scarce resources, incompatible goals, uncertainty and organisational change.

political behaviour is the conversion of power into action.

Such behaviour in organisations can influence salary outcomes, hiring decisions, promotion opportunities and other rewards and is often seen as a negative but necessary facet of organisational life. Political behaviour is based on influence tactics used to further personal and/or organisational interests. Kapoutsis *et al.* (2012) outline how influence tactics can be classified as legitimate (sanctioned) or illegitimate (non-sanctioned) depending on their social desirability. Legitimate political tactics are those that are openly accepted or encouraged to promote personal or organisational objectives. Illegitimate tactics, however, are those that we associate as being conducted 'behind closed doors' as their use may hurt others in the bid for self-interest. The following are some examples of legitimate and illegitimate political tactics:

Legitimate political tactics

Persuasion – sometimes viewed as a soft interpersonal tactic, this involves convincing others of things you want them to believe.

Use of expertise – if someone is an expert in a particular topic their opinion holds quite a lot of weight and so they may be able to get others to agree with them and behave in a particular way.

Image building – such behaviour includes drawing attention to your own (and others') successes and developing a reputation for qualities seen as important in the organisation. Image building might also be viewed as an illegitimate tactic if the behaviour involves taking credit for the ideas or work of others.

Networking – networking is a critical behaviour in most organisations and involves developing relationships with others both internal and external to the organisation. It can include *forming coalitions* (groups of people with similar interests).

Illegitimate political tactics

Manipulation – seeking to win another party over to your point of view through distortion of reality or misrepresentation of intentions.

Control of information or lines of communication – this might include keeping certain information from key stakeholders or creating an information overload so that key information gets lost.

Blaming or attacking others – making others look bad instead of taking responsibility when things go wrong. This may also involve devaluing the work of others. (See also Zanzi and O'Neil, 2001.)

You may have noticed that some of these political tactics overlap with ways of increasing power as discussed earlier in the chapter, further illustrating how power and politics are linked in organisational life.

Suppose your organisation is undergoing major structural change and you hear from someone in your network that new top management posts are going to be introduced. You have this information before it is made available within your organisation. In a bid to develop your reputation and position yourself for one of the new roles, you organise meetings with key influential people in relation to a new project. You remind them of your past successful projects (and hint at others' failures). You also spend some time highlighting the work you're doing on this new project on social media, enhancing the profile of the organisation. When a new role is advertised you feel you are in a great position to be chosen for it. Do you think such behaviour is ethical? Is it fair to those who didn't have the information at the same time as you?

MANAGERIAL TAKEAWAYS

In this chapter we have examined a number of key concepts relating to management control, power, politics and ethics in the workplace. As well as expanding your theoretical knowledge of organisational behaviour, consider how this knowledge might be useful to you in your career when you are dealing with people in organisations. You have learned that control is an important management function in ensuring organisations fulfil their objectives, but that control can never be absolute and may be resisted. You might therefore consider strategies that encourage commitment and participation rather than try to strictly dictate to others what to do. In this way control may not negatively impact on motivation and morale while ensuring organisational activities occur as needed. Approaching control in this way may also increase your referent power. In learning about sources of power you can understand that the power that typically comes from being in a managerial position in an organisation is limited and that there are other sources of power. This could help you not only to identify potential sources of power you could acquire for yourself, but also to recognise who around you might possess power and how that might affect your behaviour towards them. You should be able to recognise power tactics and political behaviour in organisations so that you can respond as appropriate to them. You may also have identified strategies you can use yourself in the workplace if you think they are appropriate. Above all, your knowledge of ethics in the workplace is intended to help you to consider the impact of your behaviour and decisions on others. You should use this knowledge to ensure that your behaviour, in as much as is possible, is directed towards the good of the organisation and the people who work there.

 CHAPTER REVIEW QUESTIONS

1 Why is management control an important function for organisations?
2 Outline the different sources of power in organisations. What sources of power do you have?
3 Identify four different power tactics that people in organisations use and give an example of a work situation where each tactic might be most appropriate or effective.
4 Is there a difference between power, authority and leadership?
5 What impact has technology had on the possibilities for management control?
6 How do you feel about politics in the workplace? Would you engage in office politics? What would you do if a colleague used political tactics against you?
7 What are the possible negative outcomes of using political tactics in your job?
8 Why is ethical behaviour important in organisations? Do you think it is possible to always behave ethically at work? Why or why not?

FURTHER READING

Angrave, D., Charlwood, A., Kirkpatrick, I., Lawrence, M. and Stuart, M. (2016) HR and analytics: Why HR is set to fail the big data challenge. *Human Resource Management Journal*, 26(1), 1–11.

Elias, S. (2008) Fifty years of influence in the workplace: The evolution of the French and Raven power taxonomy. *Journal of Management History*, 14(3), 267–283.

Qu, Y.E., Dasborough, M.T., Zhou, M. and Todorova, G. (2019) Should authentic leaders value power? A study of leaders' values and perceived value congruence. *Journal of Business Ethics*, 156(4), 1027–1044.

USEFUL WEBSITES

www.mindtools.com

This website aims to help you learn the practical, straightforward skills you need to excel in your career. It has sections on dealing with office politics at work, negotiation, persuasion and influence, and understanding power.

www.managementstudyguide.com

Management Study Guide is an educational portal with the vision of providing students and corporate workforces worldwide with access to rich, easy to understand, frequently updated instruction on many management related topics. There is a useful section on office politics.

www.hbr.org

The *Harvard Business Review* has many excellent articles on power, politics and conflict at work.

http://www.thenation.com/article/178696/can-germany-reform-american-labor-relations

This article identifies how German corporations respect worker rights and considers whether they may have an influence on future US development.

Online Resources

Visit **bloomsbury.pub/organisational-behaviour** to access additional materials to support teaching and learning.

---

9 MANAGING HEALTHY WORKPLACES

Deirdre O'Shea, Paolo Yaranon and Clodagh Butler

LEARNING OUTCOMES

BY THE END OF THIS CHAPTER, YOU SHOULD BE ABLE TO:

- Develop an overview of what well-being means in workplace contexts.
- Develop an understanding of stress in the workplace and ways to manage emotions to combat stress.
- Consider ways in which organisational contexts have an impact on workplace well-being.
- Understand the impact that the move towards positive occupational health psychology has had on our understanding of workplace well-being.
- Develop awareness of skills that are beneficial for sustaining workplace well-being.

CREDIT: PHOTO BY VLADIMIR FEDOTOV ON UNSPLASH

THIS CHAPTER DISCUSSES...

INTRODUCTION

As adults, we spend a very large proportion of our waking lives working. As such, the impact that work has on our well-being is very important to understand. In this chapter we deal with managing emotions at work, stress in the workplace, resilience and positive psychology. The trend to focus on health and well-being at work in organisations is identified and explained. We focus on how theory can be applied to well-being in the workplace to investigate the empirical evidence for and against solutions to improve well-being. Taking such an evidence-based approach ▶See Chapter 1◀ means that we can help workers in need and we do not implement untested methods. Just as you would not want a doctor to treat you with unproven treatments, we must take the same approach to address well-being in workplace contexts.

We begin by taking a look at what well-being means in the context of work. We focus specifically on one model of well-being that emphasises the importance of affect or emotions. We then consider the ways in which stress can develop, what it is about the work environment that can cause stress and we look at coping strategies for dealing with stress. We explain the job demands-job resources model to understand how the work environment can have both a positive and negative effect on our well-being. The interactions we have at work can also impact our well-being and so we also look at issues such as incivility. Finally, we consider the potential of positive psychology and its related concepts (e.g. resilience) to changing the way in which we conceptualise well-being and evaluate the merits of such approaches.

WELL-BEING IN THE WORKPLACE

Subjective well-being includes happiness, life satisfaction and positive affect (Diener, 1984), and refers to the experience of feeling good as well as the experience of fulfilment and purpose (Sonnentag, 2015). In workplace contexts, we are most often considering the psychological health of an individual, rather than their physical health. Of course, the two are related but in this chapter, we focus primarily on the psychological aspects of health and well-being that can be impacted. Physical health can be affected in a number of ways in workplace settings and most countries have health and safety legislation which regulates the work environment for the physical safety requirements of different industries. Ergonomics is a related area of study which focuses on ensuring that work areas and workspaces do not have a health cost to a worker (for example, how a desk and computer are positioned can cause musculoskeletal problems for workers).

> subjective well-being refers to the extent to which individuals experience happiness, life satisfaction and positive affect.

Subjective well-being is broader in scope than mental health, which typically only considers mental illnesses or disorders such as clinical levels of depression and anxiety, and their consequences (Hasin et al., 2018). A mental disorder is a 'clinically significant disturbance in an individual's cognition, emotion regulation, or behaviour that reflects a dysfunction in the psychological, biological, or developmental processes underlying mental functioning' (American Psychiatric Association, 2013). While workers are not immune from having a mental illness, they can experience impaired well-being without necessarily experiencing a mental illness. Oftentimes, such impaired well-being stems from some form of stress.

Subjective well-being has both an emotional and a cognitive component (Diener *et al.*, 2003), which means that it is about how we feel and think. In the work domain, subjective well-being reflects how employees' feelings and thoughts about their working life influence their lives in general (Ilies *et al.*, 2015). Thus, work-related subjective well-being is experienced when a person is satisfied with their job and experiences positive emotions more frequently than negative emotions at work (Bakker and Oerlemans, 2011; Ilies *et al.*, 2015). Subjective well-being has some very important outcomes which make it important for both individuals and organisations to pay attention to it. People who feel satisfied and experience positive feelings have higher productivity, live longer and behave differently than those who are unhappy (Diener, 2013). Furthermore, people with higher subjective well-being have been shown to earn higher incomes later in life and be less likely to experience unemployment (Diener, 2013).

THE MODEL OF AFFECTIVE WELL-BEING

affective well-being is the emotional or affective component of well-being, which can be described in terms of the level of pleasure (or displeasure) combined with the level of arousal.

A very important component of subjective well-being is a general experience of feeling 'good' or feeling 'bad'. To this end, Warr (1990) developed a model of affective well-being in the workplace, which was subsequently updated by Warr *et al.* (2014). These models draw on the concept of core affect (Russell and Barrett, 1999), which describes feeling good or bad, energised or tired, and influences our thoughts and behaviour (Russell, 2003). Core affect has a two-dimensional structure. Labelling our emotions as either positive or negative refers to the *valence* of an emotion. The second dimension, the level of activation, refers to the extent to which an emotion energises or prompts us to take action. For example, consider a rugby fan who is at a final – this person will likely encounter highly active emotions, which will be positive (e.g. excited) if their team is winning and negative (e.g. upset) if their team is losing. We can also experience less active emotions such as when we feel calm and relaxed (positive) or depressed and fatigued (negative). Core affect forms a circle around these two bipolar dimensions (Niedenthal *et al.*, 2006); this model is often referred to as the **Circumplex Model of Core Affect**.

core affect is momentary, elementary feelings of pleasure or displeasure and of activation or deactivation.

Warr (Warr, 1990; Warr *et al.*, 2014) drew on the Circumplex model of core affect in developing the four aspects of affective well-being in the workplace (see Figure 9.1). These four aspects are:

- **High activation pleasant affect (HAPA)** which includes emotions such as feeling enthusiastic, excited, inspired and joyful.
- **Low activation pleasant affect (LAPA)** is indicated by feelings of being at ease, calm, laid-back and relaxed.
- **High activation unpleasant affect (HAUA)** includes emotions such as feeling anxious, nervous, tense and worried.
- **Low activation unpleasant affect (LAUA)** is associated with emotions such as feeling dejected, depressed, despondent and hopeless (Warr *et al.*, 2014).

As one would expect, positive affect indicates better well-being while negative affect suggests poorer well-being. However, the activation level is also important as it differentiates the impact that experiencing pleasant or unpleasant affect has on our subsequent workplace behaviours. For instance, Warr *et al.* (2014) demonstrated that *high-activation pleasant affect* predicts more

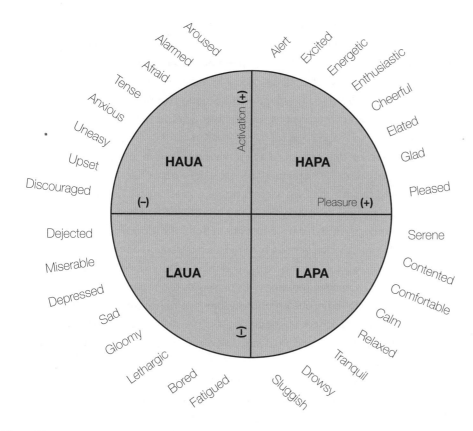

Figure 9.1 Four quadrant model of affective well-being

Source: Warr et al. (2014).

discretionary positive workplace behaviours (e.g. proactivity, extra-role contribution, workplace advocacy, voice, taking charge, strategic scanning, problem prevention) and higher job proficiency. In contrast, *low-activation unpleasant affect* is associated with a range of negative workplace behaviours, such as withdrawal (i.e. putting less effort into one's tasks and social relationships at work), minor theft, and also lower discretionary behaviours and work proficiency (Warr *et al.*, 2014). Interestingly, experiencing *high-activation unpleasant activation* does not seem to have such a wide range of negative effects, although it is associated with effort withdrawal. What we can conclude from this is that affective well-being is important to consider in the workplace as it has a substantive effect on various aspects of our work performance.

WORKPLACE STRESS

'Stress' is a term that is frequently used in the context of work. Employees often refer to being stressed out (e.g. about the pressure of meeting a deadline or about a negative encounter with a customer). But what do we mean when we say we are stressed? Psychological stress is a normal everyday experience which is simply an awareness that we are not able to cope with the demands of the situation we are currently in and this raises a concern for us (Folkman and Lazarus, 1986). We then perceive this as a threat and experience negative emotions. So, the experience of stress and the experience of negative emotions go hand in hand. Psychological

stress is a relationship with the environment that the person appraises as significant for his or her well-being and in which the demands tax or exceed available coping resources.

stress is defined as 'a relationship with the environment that the person appraises as significant for his or her well-being and in which the demands tax or exceed available coping resources' (Lazarus and Folkman, 1986, p. 63). Stress is an important experience for human beings as it has a role to play in our survival. It places us in a mode of information processing where we can assess information very quickly, respond to the situation we are in rapidly and ignore information that is not relevant to a threat we are facing. It is linked to the fight-or-flight response (https://www.health.harvard.edu/staying-healthy/understanding-the-stress-response), which is a physiological reaction that developed as a survival mechanism to allow us to react quickly to life-threatening situations. For example, at some stage we have likely all had the experience where we have tried to cross the road without properly checking for traffic and have stepped out in front of an oncoming vehicle. Typically, this is preceded by a lack of awareness or attention to our surroundings, which led us to step out in front of the oncoming vehicle in the first place. However, this quickly changes to a hyper-focus of attention on the threat facing us (i.e. the oncoming vehicle), which is prompted by something in the environment alerting us to the danger (e.g. a car horn, someone shouting to us to alert us to the danger). Once we realise the danger we have put ourselves in, our attention becomes completely focused on the threat and how to get ourselves out of danger, our bodies react very quickly (we may jump back from the road or quickly break into a run) and afterwards, we may feel weak or jittery. This is very similar to an acute stress response.

Acute stress occurs when we experience a short-term demand – it may be a life-threatening situation like the one described above, or it may just be a short-lived situation that we have to deal with (e.g. an irate customer). If the situation is seen as a threat, it can manifest itself in terms of short-term emotional disturbances (e.g. anxiety, worry, frustration, rumination) and physical issues (e.g. fatigue, a change in blood pressure, rapid heart rate, dizziness, headaches, muscle tension, jaw pain, back pain; Jamieson *et al.*, 2013). This fight-or-flight type response increases our chances of being able to cope effectively with this type of situation. Once we have successfully dealt with it (we have gotten ourselves out of danger of the oncoming vehicle, or we have satisfied the demands of the irate customer), we shift out of this stressful state and back to our habitual way of behaving. Ideally, we learn to avoid similar situations in the future or learn strategies to deal with them if they are likely to reoccur.

Episodic stress includes the criteria for acute stress but it occurs frequently, consistently and in multiple episodes (Colligan and Higgins, 2006). For example, episodic stress may occur when an individual takes on multiple tasks and becomes overwhelmed with high demands. Episodic stress symptoms include aggressiveness, low tolerance, impatience and a sense of time urgency. Along with the symptoms listed in the acute stress section, episodic stress increases the risk of heart disease, chest pain, asthma, hypertension and persistent headaches (Lazarus, 2000). If we don't learn to cope with situations we find threatening or stressful, we start to experience **chronic stress**, where stress becomes our normal state rather than a state we switch into for dealing with emergencies. Chronic stress is persistent, long-term stress, and it occurs in situations that are unpredictable and uncontrollable by the person experiencing them. This includes experiencing unemployment, job dissatisfaction, job insecurity, lack of control over decision-making, and lack of social support (Karasek, 1990). Unfortunately, our workplaces can sometimes create such unpredictable and uncontrollable environments. Consider a situation where an employee has been given goals to meet but the ways to accomplish these goals are unclear and there are consequences for not achieving them (e.g. losing one's job). As such, chronically elevated stress responses can produce chronic heart disease, burnout and depression (Maslach *et al.*, 2001).

IMPACT OF TECHNOLOGY ON BEHAVIOUR

CREDIT: PHOTO BY KAMIL S ON UNSPLASH

Having the feeling that one is being constantly monitored at work ▶See Chapter 8◀ can be experienced as stressful. Wearable monitoring devices are increasingly being used to enhance performance and decrease injury in professional sportspeople. Such wearable devices and sensors can be very effective in monitoring training loads, and their utility and efficacy are increasingly being investigated in sports medicine. Indeed, it is not only elite sports performers who are using such devices – many of us now have Garmins, Fitbits and Apple watches (or similar) that monitor our sleep patterns, heart rate, movement patterns, daily steps as well as exercise regimes.

Increasingly, employers are beginning to offer workplace wearables (for free or at a subsidised price) as a job perk or as part of their workplace health promotion efforts. However, there are some considerations for whether workplace wearables are a positive or negative development in the workplace. First and foremost, we need to consider whether or not they have an impact on worker well-being or health, and if they do, in what occupations? For example, there is a clear rationale from sports performance for why they could be beneficial in very physical jobs (e.g. to ensure the correct position while lifting, to alert workers to load bearing positions that could cause injury) but is there justification to use them in more sedentary occupations?

In a 2018 news article, the *South China Morning Post* reported that workers in factories, transports and some state-owned companies wear hats or helmets with brain surveillance devices to monitor brainwaves, which can be used to adjust the pace of production and redesign flows. Employers need to consider the potential unintended effects of such initiatives. Choosing to wear a watch that provides information on one's heart rate, activity, steps and so on for one's information or use is very different from being required to do so by one's organisation or having this information available to an employer! Removing choice or privacy is what can make such things a stressor.

For a view on this topic, see the following articles:

https://www.siliconrepublic.com/careers/workplace-wearables-privacy

https://www.scmp.com/news/china/society/article/2143899/forget-facebook-leak-china-mining-data-directly-workers-brains

HOW BIG AN ISSUE IS STRESS?

When not managed effectively, high levels of workplace stress lead to an array of issues, the harmful consequences of which not only affect employees' health and well-being but also organisational functioning. Occupational stress is linked to negative personal outcomes such as anxiety, depression (Park and Bernstein, 2008), burnout (Ozkan and Ozdevecioğlu, 2013), as well as performance outcomes such as lack of engagement (Adriaenssens *et al.*, 2015; Beattie and Griffin, 2014). In 2018, a report from the Economic and Social Research Institute (ESRI; Russell *et al.*, 2018) concluded that the most common stress reactions are psychophysiological in nature (e.g. fatigue, sleep disturbances) and that stress, anxiety, depression and musculoskeletal disorders account for between 18% and 50% of work-related illnesses, respectively. Psychosocial risks, including emotional demands and time pressures, were the highest reported stressors (see also Kahn and Byosiere, 1992). In a survey by the American Psychological Association (2018), the most common work stress factors reported by working Americans were low salaries, lack of opportunity for growth, heavy workload, role ambiguity and unrealistic job expectations: one in five employees (18%) stated that mental health problems made job challenges more difficult to handle, and 21% reported cynicism and negativity during the workday. Over half (52%) said that their employer did not provide sufficient resources to help manage their stress, while 58% stated that not enough resources were provided to necessarily meet their mental health needs (on resources, see Halbesleben *et al.*, 2014). More than a third of working Americans (37%) said they experience chronic work stress. Thus, it is clear that stress is a substantial issue for many employees, stemming from a variety of workplace characteristics (e.g. high demands, unclear roles, not enough resources). Moreover, stress not only negatively impacts individuals and organisations through reduced performance, it can eventually lead to a high cost for society as well.

Occupational stress produces negative organisational outcomes such as performance deficits, absenteeism and turnover (Goetzel *et al.*, 2004; Michie and Williams, 2003). In relation to economic costs, the European Agency for Safety, Health and Work reported that work-related stress is estimated to cost the economy of the European Union €20 billion per year. Similar trends are evident across the globe; in America stress accrues a cost of $300 billion, while in Hong Kong the annual estimated economic cost of occupational stress is estimated to be HK$550–860 million (Siu *et al.*, 2020). These costs include loss of potential labour supply, unemployment, absenteeism, reduced productivity in the workplace, premature mortality, and unpaid work (O'Shea and Kennelly, 2008). Additionally, there are significant indirect financial and non-financial costs of job stress, such as spillover into family life and relationships (Dembe, 2001) greater conflict and deterioration of relationships within organisations, and higher job turnover (Tziner *et al.*, 2015).

BURNOUT – THE END STATE OF STRESS

Burnout is characterised by feelings of exhaustion, cynicism towards one's job, and reduced work efficacy (https://www.who.int/mental_health/evidence/burn-out/en/), and can result if we experience stress for long periods of time and ineffectively deal with it. It is considered an end state of stress. Although burnout is not classified as a medical condition, it has now been

stressors are events or conditions encountered by an individual that evoke strain.

resources are anything perceived by an individual to help attain their goals.

burnout is a phenomenon in the work context that is derived from ineffectively managed chronic workplace stress.

recognised by the World Health Organization (WHO) as an occupational phenomenon. The WHO consider burnout to be a syndrome that results from chronic workplace stress that has not been successfully managed. It is characterised by three dimensions (https://www.who.int/mental_health/evidence/burn-out/en/):

1 Feelings of energy depletion or exhaustion.
2 Increased mental distance from one's job, or feelings of negativism or cynicism related to one's job.
3 Reduced professional efficacy.

People who experience burnout may withdraw from social situations, be less able to regulate the expression of their emotions, experience lower morale, be less efficient, show poorer performance and eventually be absent from work (Ahola *et al.*, 2009; Gorgievski and Hobfoll, 2008).

The 'Always On' Culture and Employee Well-Being

OB IN THE NEWS

Working too hard and not having sufficient rest and recovery from work can lead to burnout. One of the key aspects of recovery is the ability to psychologically detach from work (i.e. not think about work when not at work). With the advent of smartphones and tablets, workers often have their work e-mail set up on their personal mobile devices. Although it should be a simple task to just ignore any e-mails that are sent outside of work time, it seems that we, as humans, are not good at resisting temptation and so, increasingly, reply to e-mails whether we receive them during working time or not. This means that workers are often not detaching from work as they should, which can have a negative effect on their well-being.

This was initially recognised as a problem for individual workers themselves and several apps have been developed to help employees switch off and avoid the temptation of checking e-mail outside of working time. For example, a Berlin-based company, Offtime (https://offtime.app/the-app.php), in collaboration with Humboldt University Berlin, developed an app designed to help individuals unplug without missing urgent matters. For example, users can whitelist contacts (e.g. spouse or children) who can pierce through the self-selected downtime, but otherwise it shuts down apps, calls, texts and e-mails.

Some countries have developed specific laws concerning the right to switch off. In 2017, France was the first country to introduce a law mandating companies with more than 50 employees to develop a charter defining employees' right to switch off and setting out the hours when staff are not supposed to send or answer e-mails. Italy was the first country to associate this right to disconnect with remote work, and Chile and Argentina quickly introduced similar measures.

Questions

1 In your opinion, where does responsibility lie with regard to switching off? Should workers just have some self-control?
2 Can organisations really influence the behaviour of workers outside of working time?
3 Think about your own behaviour when you e-mail someone working in an organisation. How quickly do you expect a response? Are your expectations reasonable?

Source

https://techcrunch.com/2014/10/01/a-new-app-called-offtime-helps-you-unplug-without-missing-out/

CREDIT: PHOTO BY VICTORIA HEATH ON UNSPLASH

COGNITIVE FACTORS IN STRESS

The way in which we evaluate a situation is at the core of whether we experience it as stressful or not. Think about the following situation – let's say you and a friend of yours are visiting Australia during your summer holidays. You are staying a few nights in the Australian outback and as you are about to get into bed one evening, you notice something move, out of the corner of your eye. It is a massive spider! You are petrified of spiders, and you scream, jump on the bed and this is where your friend finds you as she runs into the bedroom after hearing you scream. She is not scared of spiders (and has also read up on what to do if finding one, given that it is not an unlikely event on your trip). She promptly gets a glass, puts this over the spider, places a sheet of cardboard under the spider and the glass, and moves the spider outdoors.

You and your friend were in the same situation, but while you found it extremely stressful, she was not stressed at all. There are a number of reasons for this. Firstly, you felt fear and she did not. Secondly, she knew what to do in that situation (she had what is referred to as a behavioural script) whereas you did not. We experience situations as stressful when we appraise them as threatening and do not know how to deal with the situation.

COPING WITH STRESS

Coping is a process where an individual tries to orient their thoughts and behaviours in such a way as to protect themselves against stress and/or remove the source of the stress (Lazarus, 1993). We can distinguish two broad categories of strategies that individuals use to cope with stress – strategies that are problem-focused and strategies that are emotion-focused. *Problem-focused coping* relates to efforts to overcome or reduce the effect of an undesirable situation, and often involves planful actions to change the person–environment relationship by directly acting on the environment or oneself (Carver, 1997). *Emotion-focused coping*, on the other hand, is aimed at minimising distress triggered by stressors by using cognitive strategies to master, reduce or tolerate an undesirable situation (Carver and Connor-Smith, 2010). It alters only what is in the mind, either by attention deployment (changing what one chooses to focus on) or by changing the meaning of the relationship (e.g. denial or distancing) (Lazarus, 1991). Table 9.1 provides some examples of different problem-focused and emotion-focused coping strategies.

BUILDING YOUR EMPLOYABILITY SKILLS

Coping with Stress

Being a student can be quite stressful. It can be hard to balance your studies with your social life, and potentially job or family responsibilities also. Reflecting on your college experience, what coping strategies help you during demanding periods such as before exams or assignment deadlines? Do you tend to use problem-solving coping or emotion-focused coping?

Problem-focused coping strategies are adaptive strategies, and hence, may be more effective in terms of attaining goals. Although emotion-focused coping has generally been found to be less adaptive than problem-focused coping, Baker and Berenbaum (2007) suggest that these results need to be qualified by considering the type of goal and the type of emotion-focused strategy. These authors focus on a subset of emotion-focused strategies, which they collectively call emotion-approach coping. Such strategies focus on actively identifying, processing and expressing one's emotions, which can provide information about one's goal status (Baker and Berenbaum, 2007). Secondly, they found that different approaches to coping (problem-focused versus emotion-approach) were differentially effective depending on whether the situation was an achievement context or an interpersonal one. Problem-focused coping resulted in lower levels of positive affect if individuals were not clear about their emotions, suggesting that problem-focused coping can be less effective if one hastily decides on a particular strategy without using one's emotions as a guide to help solve the problem (Baker and Berenbaum, 2007).

Table 9.1 Coping strategies identified by Carver *et al.* (1989)

Coping Strategy	Description
Problem-Focused Coping	
1 Active coping	Taking active steps to try to remove or circumvent the stressor or to ameliorate its effect. Active coping includes initiating direct action, increasing one's efforts, and trying to execute a coping attempt in a stepwise fashion.
2 Planning	Thinking about how to cope with a stressor. Planning involves coming up with action strategies, thinking about what steps to take and how best to handle the problem. This strategy differs conceptually from a problem-focused action and occurs during secondary appraisal.
3 Suppression of competing activities	This means putting other projects aside, trying to avoid becoming distracted by other events, and letting other things slide if necessary to deal with the stressor.
4 Restraint coping	Refers to waiting until an appropriate opportunity to act presents itself, holding oneself back and not acting prematurely. This is an active strategy in the sense that the focus of behaviour is on dealing effectively with the stressor, but is also a passive strategy in the sense that using restraint means not acting.
5 Seeking instrumental social support	Seeking advice, assistance or information.
Emotion-Focused Coping	
6 Seeking emotional social support	Getting moral support, sympathy or understanding.
7 Positive reinterpretation	Coping aimed at managing distressing emotions rather than dealing with the stressor. Construing a stressful situation in positive terms should intrinsically lead the person to continue or to resume active, problem-focused coping actions. Also termed positive reappraisal.
8 Acceptance	This is argued as a functional coping response, in that a person who accepts the reality of a stressful situation would seem to be engaged in an attempt to deal with the situation. Acceptance of a stressor as real occurs in primary appraisal, but acceptance of a current absence of active coping strategies relates to secondary appraisal. The opposite of denial.
9 Denial	Reports of refusal to believe that the stressor exists or of trying to react as though the stressor is not real. A response that sometimes emerges in primary appraisal. It has been suggested that denial can be useful in that it minimises distress and therefore facilitates coping. On the other hand, denying the reality of an event allows the event to become more serious and makes it more difficult for coping to occur.

Coping Strategy	Description
10 Focus on and venting of emotions	The tendency to focus on whatever distress or upset one is experiencing and to vent these feelings. Such a response may sometimes be functional, but focusing on these emotions, particularly for long periods, can impede adjustment.
11 Behavioural disengagement	Reducing one's effort to deal with the stressor, perhaps giving up the attempt to attain goals with which the stressor is interfering. Behavioural disengagement is also reflected in phenomena such as helplessness.
12 Mental disengagement	A variation on behavioural disengagement, hypothesised to occur when conditions prevent behavioural disengagement. Mental disengagement occurs via a wide variety of activities that serve to distract the person from thinking about the behavioural dimension or goal with which the stressor is interfering. Tactics that reflect this strategy include using alternative activities to take one's mind off a problem, daydreaming, escaping through sleep or escape by immersion in TV.
13 Turning to religion	The tendency to turn to religion in time of stress, for example, to pray, attend church services, engage in prayerful meditation, visit sites of religious significance.

Adapted from Carver et al. (1989).

BUILDING YOUR EMPLOYABILITY SKILLS

Your coping strategies

Charles Carver and colleagues (Carver *et al.*, 1989) developed a way of assessing the strategies that individuals prefer to use to cope with stress – the COPE inventory. You can access this inventory at:

http://local.psy.miami.edu/faculty/ccarver/sclCOPEF.phtml

Complete this inventory and see what your preferred coping strategies are. Do you tend to prefer problem-focused or emotion-focused strategies, or a mixture of both? Reflect on which stressful situations your preferred coping strategies may be particularly useful for and when they may not.

STRATEGIES FOR MANAGING EMOTIONS ASSOCIATED WITH STRESS

As individuals, we can learn ways of managing our emotions, which can help us manage the emotions associated with stress. Two of the most common ways of doing this are to either reappraise or suppress our emotions. The strategy we use to manage our emotions can also have an impact on our well-being. *Reappraisal* is a form of cognitive change and begins with the idea that no situation in and of itself generates an emotion. It is the individuals' appraisal of the situation that does so, just like the appraisal processes in stress. Hence, reappraisal involves changing a situation's meaning in a way that alters its emotional impact (Gross and Thompson, 2007). *Suppression*, in contrast, refers to inhibiting the expression of emotion (Gross, 1999). It requires individuals to exert effort to manage emotional expressions as they arise, and this effort may consume cognitive resources that could otherwise be used to optimise performance (Gross and John, 2003).

Comparing the effectiveness of these two strategies, Gross (1998) found that reappraisal is more effective than suppression. People who reappraise cope by thinking about the situation in a different way, which can help to reduce worry and manage the negative emotions associated with stress. Furthermore, reappraisers tend to experience and express greater positive emotion (Gross and John, 2003). In contrast, suppressors cope with adversity by 'battening the hatches' (Gross and John, 2003, p. 355) and hence feel inauthentic and do not vent their true feelings. They tend to evaluate their emotions in negative terms, and the lack of clarity they experience around their emotions is associated with a lower ability to repair their mood, lower estimates of their own ability to regulate negative mood, and increased rumination.

BUILDING YOUR EMPLOYABILITY SKILLS

Learning to reappraise your emotional reaction to negative events

Reappraisal can be a powerful tool to help us use our emotions more effectively for both students (Pogrebtsova *et al.*, 2018) and employees (Hülsheger *et al.*, 2013). Recent research has even shown that reappraising one's bodily reactions to stress can significantly reduce its negative effects (Jamieson *et al.*, 2013). Dr Kelly McGonigal talks about how to do just this in an interesting Ted Talk:

http://www.ted.com/talks/kelly_mcgonigal_how_to_make_stress_your_friend.html

Watch this talk and make a list of how you can build your skills in reappraising stress. What impact do you think this would have in the workplace?

WORK-RELATED CAUSES OF STRESS

There are many aspects of our work that can cause stress. We can distinguish between broad, global issues, such as economic recessions, and narrower, job-specific reasons. For example, experiencing stress because one is afraid of losing one's job is referred to as job insecurity. This is a major source of stress for many employees as the concept of a 'job for life' is fading rapidly, being replaced by short-term contracts, project-based employment and zero-hours contracts. This is an example of a broader issue that is not unique to one organisation or one job. Demands in the workplace that cause people to experience stress are called stressors. Stressors in the workplace are actual or perceived threats to the individual that cause strain (Kahn and Byosiere, 1992).

JOB INSECURITY

The global economic crisis that began in September 2007 was one of the worst economic recessions in several years (Briscoe *et al.*, 2012). It raised an interesting question about macro-economic influences on employee well-being. This economic crisis led to increased levels of unemployment, underemployment, job insecurity and financial concerns, collectively considered economic stressors (Probst *et al.*, 2018). An economic recession may impact the career attitudes and job satisfaction of employees ▶See Chapter 4◀. In a study of employees in the early stages of their career, work design features such as skill variety were positively related to job satisfaction when such employees had a strong preference for organisational mobility. However, for those with a strong self-directed career attitude, work characteristics such as skill specialisation and autonomy were more important for their job satisfaction (O'Shea *et al.*, 2014). The economic recession also led to much higher levels of immigration, often by well-educated people, many of whom subsequently worked in jobs that they were over-qualified for in their new country. In a study of Italian immigrants in Germany, perceived overqualification was associated with higher levels of depressive symptoms and lower levels of life satisfaction (Wassermann and Hoppe, 2019). However, this relationship was weaker for more optimistic immigrants.

◁ETHICAL▷ BEHAVIOUR IN THE WORKPLACE

'For some reason, people think working long hours means being successful and productive. It doesn't' – according to Professor Cary Cooper, a renowned expert in workplace wellness, in a BBC interview talking about how job insecurity can lead people to work longer and longer hours, working into the evening and experiencing reduced well-being as a result. This seems likely to increase in the future as it is becoming more common for organisations to offer contracts of employment that do not offer job security.

CREDIT: GETTY IMAGES

To deal with job insecurity, workers often feel that they have to be constantly performing above and beyond what is expected, potentially placing workers in a state of chronic stress. Besides issues such as absenteeism associated with stress, a 2018 survey by the Chartered Institute of Personnel Development (CIPD) reported that two-thirds of workers in the UK have observed a concept called *leaveism* in the previous 12 months. Hesketh and Cooper (2014) describe leaveism as a set of practices whereby:

- employees utilise time off, such as annual leave entitlements, flexi hours banked, re-rostered rest days and so on, to take time off when they are in fact unwell,
- employees take work home that cannot be completed in normal working hours, or
- employees work while on leave or holiday to catch up.

Leaveism means that not only are employees stressed in their jobs, but they are also not taking the appropriate time to recover from work.

This poses ethical issues which organisations need to deal with. Discuss some of these issues. For example, do workers have the right to a secure contract of employment? How do organisations deal with seasonal and irregular demand if they don't offer these types of contracts? Shouldn't jobs be designed so that the workload is manageable, or are workers just taking on this additional out-of-hours work themselves?

Sources

https://twitter.com/bbcbreakfast/status/966949234242076672?lang=en
https://www.bbc.com/worklife/article/20190718-leaveism

THE JOB DEMANDS–RESOURCES (JD-R) MODEL

To understand factors in the workplace that can result in stress or conversely buffer the effects of stress, Demerouti *et al.* (2001) developed the job demands, job resources model. Work features can be classified into two categories. **Job demands** relate to any physical, mental, social or organisational elements of a job that require persistent physical and/or psychological effort (Demerouti *et al.*, 2001). Job demands include hazardous working conditions, work overload, irregular shift patterns, rude colleagues, demanding clients, and so forth. **Job resources** are the physical, psychological, social and organisational features of the job that (a) are functional and facilitate achieving work goals, (b) lessen job demands and the related physiological and psychological costs, and (c) encourage personal growth, learning and development. Moreover, job resources may be found at the organisational level (e.g. wages, commissions, learning opportunities), interpersonal level (e.g. support from colleagues or supervisors), within the job (e.g. role clarity, inclusion in decision-making), and at the level of the task (e.g. autonomy and performance appraisal, Demerouti and Bakker, 2011). Lots of job resources mean that employees are better able to dedicate their skills and abilities towards their work, and to complete their work goals (Demerouti and Bakker, 2011).

The JD-R model assumes that the health and well-being of an employee depend on the balance between the demands of a job and the resources available to meet those demands. When demands are high, more effort is required to achieve work goals and to prevent the decline of performance (Schaufeli and Taris, 2014). The additional effort that an employee must exercise to meet these demands can be taxing and may have psychological and/or physiological costs, such as the experience of fatigue, stress or, eventually, even burnout.

Figure 9.2 shows the relationships between resources and demands. Job demands are related to work strain, while job resources are linked to motivation (Bakker and Demerouti, 2008). When both demands and resources are high, we can expect employees to develop strain

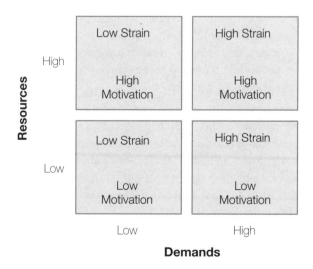

Figure 9.2 Relationships between motivation and strain in the Job Demands–Resources Model

Source: Bakker and Demerouti (2007).

and experience low motivation. In contrast, when both are low, we can expect the opposite. Employees in a scenario where the demands are high and resources are low are described as unhappy and demotivated. In this kind of working environment, we would expect to see issues such as health problems leading to high rates of absenteeism. Finally, work environments characterised as high in resources and low in demands should result in low strain and highly motivated employees.

IN REALITY

From what you have learned in this chapter, it is evident that well-being in organisations is very important to consider. Many organisations recognise this and have put in place initiatives to try to encourage and help their employees to maintain their well-being both within and outside of work. For example, in the USA, workplace wellness programmes have been reported to be an $8 billion industry (https://www.governing.com/topics/health-human-services/khn-workplace-wellness-study.html). However, there is mixed evidence concerning their effectiveness. In a recent study, Song and Baicker (2019) evaluated a workplace wellness programme conducted in a large multistate warehouse retail company in the USA which included almost 33,000 employees. Approximately 4000 took part in the wellness programme on nutrition, physical activity, stress reduction and other topics. The researchers then compared employee-reported health and behaviours collected from surveys and clinical health measures among 20 work sites with wellness programming, and 20 others without it. They also compared healthcare spending, use and employment outcomes among 20 sites with wellness programmes, with 140 sites without. Findings suggest that worksites with wellness programmes have higher rates of employees reporting more regular exercise and actively managing their weight. However, after 18 months, they found no significant differences in clinical measures such as their cholesterol levels, blood pressure and BMI, and employment outcomes such as absenteeism, job tenure and performance.

In reality, would you conclude that workplace wellness programmes like the one described by Song and Baicker (2019) are worth the cost? Are they effective in addressing the job demands and resources available to employees? Is it reasonable for employers to expect that such initiatives would have the ability to lower healthcare costs and improve employee health and productivity?

A further issue worth considering is the rates of participation and uptake for health promotion programmes. Toker *et al.* (2015) investigated this issue, discovering that 50–75% of employees chose not to participate in health promotion programmes when offered the opportunity to do so. The barriers to participation reported in their survey pertain to resource availability (e.g. age, health status) and valuation (i.e. low value placed on making a lifestyle change). Given this information, what solutions would you suggest, to reduce non-participation?

INTERPERSONAL RELATIONSHIPS AND WORKPLACE WELL-BEING

Work relationships are typically described as a collaboration of two or more members for the purpose of achieving a common objective (Ferris *et al.*, 2009); they can be characterised according to their quality (e.g. positive or negative) and the product of the partnership (Heaphy *et al.*, 2018). People spend much of their workday engaged in interdependent tasks, and so, maintaining positive working relationships with colleagues is essential for employee well-being. For example, having a colleague whom one can ask for advice (particularly if new to an organisation) can help a worker to achieve their tasks. More broadly, working in an organisation where individuals are generally willing to help a colleague when in need gives employees a feeling of being cared about in their place of work, and promotes an overall 'good' feeling in an organisation.

Healthy relationships can be created through support and sharing knowledge. Both social support from supervisors and perceived support from one's organisation have a positive effect on the employees' willingness to share their work knowledge and skills with others (Chiaburu *et al.*, 2010). Additionally, positive working relationships lessen the likelihood of employees leaving their job (Madden *et al.*, 2015). Good working relationships can be viewed as part of a social exchange process whereby employees exchange resources, which can be used either as a coping mechanism to overcome adversities at work or as learning tools for professional and career advancement (Colbert *et al.*, 2016; Feeney and Collins, 2014). Although research has highlighted the positive aspects of having a harmonious working atmosphere, antisocial behaviours exist, and this is an ongoing challenge faced by both employees and organisations.

Antisocial employee behaviour is an umbrella term that describes any behaviour that creates harm to the organisation and its employees (Andersson and Pearson, 1999). These behaviours have a damaging effect, but they vary according to intensity and intentions. For example, *aggression* is associated with overt physical and verbal harm resulting in damage and injuries, while *violence* is the intensified form of physical aggression (Baron and Neuman, 1996). *Bullying* refers to the persistent and systematic form of mistreatment that makes a victim upset, humiliated and threatened, to which prolonged exposure can leave the target in an inferior position and cause severe psychological problems (Einarsen *et al.*, 2011), whereas *incivility* is characterised as subtle, disrespectful and rude acts with unclear intention to cause harm (Andersson and Pearson, 1999). All of these concepts violate the mutual norms of respect in a workplace. Cortina *et al.* (2011) found that women, and employees who were of ethnic minorities, were more susceptible to experiencing uncivil treatment at work. This would suggest that incivility may mask covert forms of gender and racial discrimination (Cortina *et al.*, 2011) ▶**See Chapter 10**◀.

Deviant workplace relationships can have a detrimental impact on the overall well-being of an employee as they increase negative emotions, which can have a disadvantageous bearing on task performance and work engagement (Chen *et al.*, 2012; Giumetti *et al.*, 2013). These rude interactions can also intensify feelings of isolation and embarrassment of employees (Hershcovis *et al.*, 2017), leading to psychological distress and eventual withdrawal from work (Adams and Webster, 2013; Sliter *et al.*, 2012).

THE MOVE TOWARDS A POSITIVE OCCUPATIONAL HEALTH PSYCHOLOGY

Positive psychology is an umbrella term for the study of positive emotion, positive characteristics and enabling institutions (Seligman *et al.*, 2005). Until the start of the 21st century, occupational health and well-being focused on the negative aspects of work on health and well-being, considering how to help sick employees return to work, reduce absenteeism and provide training to 'fix' employees (Bakker and Derks, 2010). Following the publication of a seminal article by Seligman (2011), work-related well-being research and practice started to address more positive aspects of well-being, including work engagement and thriving (Sonnentag, 2015). More recently, there has been a surge in popularity of well-being interventions based on positive psychology, which has also reached the workplace.

WORK ENGAGEMENT

Work engagement is experienced as a positive, fulfilling, work-related state of mind (Schaufeli *et al.*, 2002). Schaufeli and Bakker (2004) identified three core components of work engagement, namely vigour, dedication and absorption.

- Vigour is characterised by experiencing high levels of energy and mental resilience while working, the willingness to invest effort in one's work and persisting even in the face of difficulties.
- Dedication refers to experiencing a sense of significance, enthusiasm, inspiration, pride and feeling involved in one's job.
- Absorption refers to being able to fully concentrate and become engrossed in one's work.

In early research in this area, work engagement was considered the antithesis of burnout (Gonzalez-Roma *et al.*, 2006), and the three components of engagement were considered opposites of the three components of burnout. Individuals who experience high levels of engagement in their work are less likely to become burned out – they still get tired from work but experience it differently and see themselves as able to deal with the demands of their jobs (Bakker and Demerouti, 2008; Schaufeli *et al.*, 2006). They also generate their own positive feedback, are engaged outside of their work, and want to do things other than working (Schaufeli *et al.*, 2001).

POSITIVE PSYCHOLOGY INTERVENTIONS

In keeping with the rise in popularity of positive psychology, there is an increasing trend of using positive psychology interventions in the workplace. However, research evidence for the effectiveness of such interventions has lagged behind their implementation. We review the evidence for positive thinking and mindfulness interventions, which are two of the more popular interventions.

The 'three good things' activity is a very popular positive psychology activity based on positive thinking. This activity asks individuals to write down three things that went well each day and the cause or explanation for why it occurred. Research indicates that practising this exercise can lead to higher levels of happiness (Seligman *et al.*, 2005). There have been studies which examined whether this type of activity might be beneficial in workplace settings. For example, Bono *et al.* (2013) found that both naturally occurring positive work events and a brief, end-of-workday positive thinking reflection intervention were associated with reduced stress and improved health in the evening after work. Clauss *et al.* (2018) examined the impact of a daily intervention which was a modification of the three positive things exercise, which asked care workers to recall one good thing that happened to them at work each day and to consider the meaning of this event. They found that those who completed the intervention had lower emotional exhaustion and fatigue. Combined, this suggests that there are some benefits to positive work reflections.

Mindfulness refers to a state of mind that when cultivated regularly promotes an experience of the present moment (Marianetti and Passmore, 2010) and can be used to help individuals disengage from automatic thoughts, habits and unhealthy behaviour patterns (Brown and Ryan, 2003). It is conceptualised as more than meditation, as a unique quality of consciousness associated with enhanced self-awareness, and attention, that is distinct from other modes of mental processing (Brown and Ryan, 2003). Hülsheger *et al.* (2013) conducted two studies to investigate the role of mindfulness in the workplace. In their first five-day diary study, they found that mindfulness was negatively related to emotional exhaustion and positively related to job satisfaction. The second study looked at the impact of a mindfulness intervention. They randomly assigned participants to either a control condition (no intervention) or the mindfulness condition. Those who were in the mindfulness condition experienced lower emotional exhaustion and higher job satisfaction than those in the control condition.

There is some evidence that mindfulness can also be beneficial in managing the boundary between work and home. Michel *et al.* (2014) found that those who practised a mindfulness intervention (compared with a control group who did not) experienced less strain-based work –life conflict and more psychological detachment and satisfaction with work–life balance. Hülsheger *et al.* (2014) also found that mindfulness was associated with a higher level of psychological detachment from work, resulting in better sleep quality. So, it would seem that mindfulness may be particularly useful if used to detach from our work.

Thus, there appears to be some evidence to suggest that mindfulness can be beneficial for promoting well-being in work contexts. However, Hülsheger (2015) cautions that this should not be used as a quick-fix solution, nor as a panacea to fix well-being, motivation or performance-related problems in organisations. Mindfulness takes time to successfully develop and needs practice. Furthermore, it is not necessarily the case that mindfulness will have benefits for an organisation even if it has benefits for an individual.

More broadly, positive psychology has become extremely popular and there are many apps and websites that provide tools to access freely available activities. However, there is always a need to ensure that all types of psychological interventions, whether positive psychology activities or otherwise, have been researched and shown to be effective. For example, while a recent meta-analysis of positive psychology interventions (White *et al.*, 2019) confirmed that there is a positive relationship between positive psychology interventions and well-being, this effect is quite small.

RESILIENCE

Have you ever wondered why some employees, even though they are all exposed to the same stressors at work, are able to keep working through demands, deadlines and unexpected challenges while others struggle and fail to respond? The answer may lie in the concept of resilience.

resilience is the ability of a person to recover, re-bound, bounce back, adjust or even thrive in the face of adversity

In its simplest form, resilience refers to 'the demonstration of positive adaptation in the face of significant adversity' (Britt *et al.*, 2016; and see Garcia-Dia *et al.*, 2013). Resilience is a dynamic process by which individuals successfully use personal resources to protect themselves against the negative consequences of stressful experiences, while promoting the ability to overcome, steer through and bounce back from stress (Richardson, 2002). Resilience as a topic has received a lot of attention over the last number of decades in academic journals, books, business practice and even the popular press. In the beginning, some scholars argued that resilience was a rare and uncommon trait within individuals – in other words, resilience was something you either had or did not have (Rutter, 1987). Nowadays, resilience is considered a fairly common phenomenon that is developed as part of normal human adaptions to life situations (Masten, 2001). While some individuals may have more resilience capabilities than others, resilience is seen as a capacity that can be developed over time. Employees must work on developing their resilience capabilities, but dealing with stressors in the workplace is likely also to play a role in this development.

RESILIENCE IN THE WORKPLACE

The organisational context can encourage or discourage the emergence of resilience at work. One strategy that managers can use to ensure that employees feel challenged but not threatened by their work is through support and by providing a challenging yet manageable working environment. When employees view work as a threat it is harmful and paralysing. Employees experiencing workload that is unmanageable, over time become less engaged, have reduced creativity, more presenteeism and are less productive. On the other hand, when work is viewed as a challenge it is perceived as an opportunity for individual growth and goal attainment and contributes to occupational well-being. This is in line with research looking at the distinction between challenge stressors and hindrance stressors. Gonzalez-Morales and Neves (2015) show that although challenge stressors tend to be positively related to performance, this is not always the case and depends on one's appraisal. They are only related to performance when they are appraised as opportunities.

Resilience is important for the mental health and well-being of employees. Employees high in resilience are also more likely to demonstrate lower levels of anxiety, distress and burnout, better quality of life, optimistic thinking, positive work attitudes and job satisfaction (Fletcher and Sarkar, 2013; Seligman, 2011; Waugh *et al.*, 2008). Resilience is also associated with performance benefits that demonstrate progression, such as an increase in goal attainment, productivity, organisational citizenship behaviour, observed behavioural performance and organisational commitment (Robertson *et al.*, 2015; Shin *et al.*, 2012).

STRATEGIES TO ENHANCE INDIVIDUAL RESILIENCE IN THE WORKPLACE

Resilience does not prevent stress from occurring, but rather it increases our ability to with-stand stress and develop preparedness for future stress. There are various ways that resilience may be enhanced – you can try out the strategies below to help with your college life!

- Embrace failure. Failure = First Attempt in Learning.

In our daily life, we come up against setbacks when pursuing goals. It is important to see setbacks as learning curves and opportunities for growth. Using a piece of paper, write down some positive and negative past experiences you have experienced and the sources of personal strength that helped you get through those times. Looking back over these experiences can help you learn about what strategies for building resilience work for you best. It's also impor-tant to celebrate your successes, even the small ones! Take time to review what went well and congratulate yourself. This helps trains the mind to look for success rather than dwelling on negativity and failure.

- View stress as a challenge, not a threat.

Unfortunately, experiencing stress at work is inevitable. Some of this stress will be controllable and some will be uncontrollable. For stress that is controllable, we can choose how we interpret and respond to that stress. Looking at stress as a challenge increases our performance-related behaviours.

- Set some goals, and anticipate future barriers to those goals.

Develop some SMART goals: goals that are specific (S), measurable (M), achievable (A), realistic (R) and time-bound (T). Set yourself some realistic but also challenging targets for a given day or week. While you envision and plan those goals, anticipate any barriers that might hamper you from achieving your goal (such as not getting through all your to-do list for that day). Use IF/THEN statements to plan alternative action. IF I don't clear my to-do list … THEN I will …

- Seek and surround yourself with social support.

Relationships in work can create trust, provide role models, offer encouragement and reassur-ance. It is also important to seek social support and not just wait for it. Broaden your network and be open-minded to making new connections.

- Create and develop personal resources.

Some of the key personal resources that have been reported to help build resilience include the following. Self-efficacy: develop confidence in your ability to take on new tasks and overcome any stress that may come your way. Optimism: accept the reality of a situation and maintain a positive and desirable attitude about the future. Hope: in times of stress, hope motivates us to envision a positive future, take risks and initiate action.

Check out the Penn Resiliency Programme (PRP) developed at the University of Pennsylvania for more on developing resilience skill sets within occupational settings: https://ppc.sas.upenn.edu/resilience-programs/resilience-skill-set.

The Vulnerable Heroes of the Pandemic

Since the World Health Organization (WHO) declared the coronavirus outbreak as a public health emergency of international concern (PHEIC), it has affected people in different walks of life in many ways across the world. In particular, the healthcare sector was under immense pressure. Classified as frontline workers, they worked tirelessly to ensure the safety and protection of the public. Consequently, the public depicted them as heroes due to their efforts despite the anxieties and uncertainties.

Governments' main challenges world-wide were to ensure that their frontline workers were safe and well prepared to battle this virus. This was a significant concern in China, where the outbreak began. Reports from the National Health Commission of China indicated that the virus infected nearly 2000 healthcare workers within the first month and a half. There was a call among local agencies for government to focus on providing sufficient medical facilities and essential equipment for healthcare workers. Additionally, enough food and rest were suggested, paving the way for converting hotels near hospitals into recuperating hubs for healthcare workers.

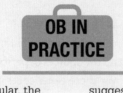

OB IN PRACTICE

While all of these recommendations were arranged, the National Health Commission also highlighted the impact of this virus on the healthcare workers' overall emotional well-being. The threat that Covid-19 posed was extraordinary and unprecedented. Indeed, nurse managers of Covid-19 facilities found it extremely challenging to operationalise their role. First, while infection control policies and measures were in place to guarantee staff safety, nurse managers were continuously bombarded with concerns from their team, mainly the fear of being infected due to insufficiency in personal protective equipment (PPE). In addition, hospital systems became overwhelmed and staff were required to work extremely long hours, which became further exacerbated by staff shortages as healthcare workers themselves contracted the virus and were unable to attend work. As the upward trajectory of new cases and deaths became uncontrollable, hospital administrations had to very quickly develop and implement new policies and measures.

Secondly, the surge of transmission and mortality rates meant that staff stress was also on the rise. Healthcare workers had an acute awareness of the severity of the threat that the virus posed, and substantial fears of acquiring it, which, combined with the strain on the healthcare system and dealing with very sick patients, led to a detrimental effect on their well-being. The threat elicited tension, anxiety and fatigue leading to depleted energy and burnout. Nurse managers were confronted with a dilemma in safeguarding employees' well-being while maintaining acceptable staffing levels.

Finally, nurse managers had to deal with the fractured interpersonal relationships of their workers. The impediments, the insuppressible daily morbidity and mortality rates, and Covid-related absences of healthcare staff were catalysts for a stressful workplace characterised by uncivil behaviours, misunderstandings and arguments at work. Recent reviews have indicated that healthcare workers are experiencing mental health problems such as insomnia and depression (Spoorthy et al., 2020), and stressed that these maladaptive reactions could be enduring (Preti et al., 2020).

The pandemic highlighted some positivity in the workforce. For instance, the shortage of PPE during the initial stages of the outbreak meant that healthcare workers had to find alternative ways to protect themselves. Their resilience and dedication to their service led to innovation, where healthcare workers transformed raincoats as PPEs.

Healthcare professionals were provided with PPE and eventually

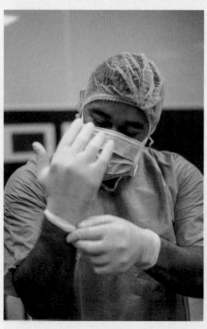

CREDIT: PHOTO BY MAGDIEL LAGOS ON UNSPLASH

a vaccine to shield themselves from the virus's devastating effects. However, more attention will need to be devoted in the coming years to the psychological repercussions of dealing with the virus first-hand. One can argue that as a healthcare manager, it is taxing to be involved in this situation. You have to consider the welfare of your patients and the protection of your frontline workers' well-being.

Questions

1 What kind of stress is being experienced as a result of the Covid-19 pandemic in healthcare workers?

2 Earlier in the chapter, you read about the problem- and emotion-focused coping strategies. Which of these two coping strategies are more beneficial to use among healthcare workers in this situation, and why?

3 As a nurse manager, how would you maintain harmonious interpersonal relationships in this stressful setting?

Sources

Preti, E., Di Mattei, V., Perego, G., Ferrari, F., Mazzetti, M., Taranto, P., Di Pierro, R., Madeddu, F. and Calati, R. (2020) The psychological impact of epidemic and pandemic outbreaks on healthcare workers: Rapid review of evidence. *Current Psychiatry Reports*, 22(8), 1–22.

Si, C. (2020) Central government demands better conditions for medical workers. *China Daily*, 14 February. Available at: http://www.chinadaily.com.cn/a/202002/14/WS5e4658c8a310128217277a5a.html

Spoorthy, M.S., Pratapa, S.K. and Mahant, S. (2020) Mental health problems faced by healthcare workers due to the Covid-19 pandemic – A review. *Asian Journal of Psychiatry*, 51, 102119.

Zhang, M. (2020) Protecting the healthcare workers in China during the coronavirus outbreak. *The BMJ Opinion*, 14 February. https://blogs.bmj.com/bmj/2020/02/14/min-zhang-protecting-healthcare-workers-china-coronavirus-outbreak/

SPOTLIGHT ON SKILLS

1 What effects has Covid-19 had on employee wellness in the workplace?

2 What can organisations do to create a healthy workplace for employees post-pandemic?

To help you answer these questions, visit bloomsbury.pub/organisational-behaviour to watch the video of Marcus Kelly from Analog Devices talking about healthy workplaces.

MANAGERIAL TAKEAWAYS

There are a number of important takeaway messages from this chapter. First, chronic stress is associated with unpredictable and uncontrollable situations, and so while it can be minimised, it is unlikely it can ever be avoided completely. However, some efforts to reduce the impact of stress is important so as to avoid burnout, which is an end state of stress. Second, managers need to carefully consider the off-job demands placed on employees (e.g. checking mail outside of work). This can increase stress and reduce well-being and so managers need to be aware that technology presents opportunities and also threats for worker well-being. Finally, many typical workplace wellness initiatives have little effect. Positive psychology interventions hold some promise but only address individual responses to stress. They cannot address issues of work design or work demands, so should be used in combination with organisational level interventions.

 CHAPTER REVIEW QUESTIONS

1   What is subjective well-being?
2   Is well-being different from mental health?
3   Does everyone experience stress in the same way?
4   What are the different ways of coping with stress?
5   What role do social relationships play in workplace well-being?
6   Are positive psychology interventions effective?
7   Is resilience a trait (something we have or not) or a state (something we can learn)?
8   Why is recovery from work important?

 FURTHER READING

Bakker, A.B. and Derks, D. (2010) Positive occupational health psychology. In S. Leka and J. Houdmont (eds), *Occupational Health Psychology*. Chichester: Wiley-Blackwell.

Bryan, C., O'Shea, D. and MacIntyre, T. (2019) Stressing the relevance of resilience: A systematic review of resilience across the domains of sport and work. *International Review of Sport & Exercise Psychology*, 12(1), 70–111.

Jamieson, J.P., Mendes, W.B. and Nock, M.K. (2013) Improving acute stress responses: The power of reappraisal. *Current Directions in Psychological Science*, 22(1), 51–56.

Linley, P.A., Harrington, S. and Garcea, N. (2009) *Oxford Handbook of Positive Psychology and Work*. New York: Oxford University Press.

Provenzano, D.M. and Heyman, R.E. (2006) Harry Potter and the resilience to adversity. In N. Mulholland (ed.), *The Psychology of Harry Potter: An Unauthorized Examination of the Boy who Lived*. Dallas, TX: BenBella Books.

Setti, I., van der Velden, P.G., Sommovigo, V., Santa Ferretti, M., Giorgi, G., O'Shea, D. and Argentero, P. (2018) Well-being and functioning at work following thefts and robberies: A comparative study. *Frontiers in Psychology*, 9, 168.

Sonnentag, S. (2015) Dynamics of well-being. *Annual Review of Organizational Psychology and Organizational Behavior*, 2, 61–93.

 USEFUL WEBSITES

http://www.eaohp.org

European Association of Occupational Health Psychology (EAOHP)

https://campaign.curtin.edu.au/future-of-work-institute/

Future of Work Institute (and associated Thrive at Work website) at Curtin University

https://www.thriveatwork.org.au

https://ppc.sas.upenn.edu

Positive Psychology Center, University of Pennsylvania

https://www.who.int/mental_health/in_the_workplace/en/

World Health Organization – Mental health in the workplace information sheet

---

Online Resources

Visit **bloomsbury.pub/organisational-behaviour** to access additional materials to support teaching and learning.

---

10 MANAGING DIVERSITY

Maeve O'Sullivan

LEARNING OUTCOMES

AFTER READING THIS CHAPTER, YOU SHOULD BE ABLE TO:

- Define organisational diversity.
- Distinguish between affirmative action and diversity management programmes.
- Describe the demographic changes taking place globally and how these are likely to have an impact on the workplace.

- Discuss the barriers to effectively managing a diverse workforce.
- Explain what discrimination is and how it manifests in organisations.
- Understand how organisations can successfully manage diversity.

CREDIT: PHOTO BY SHARON MCCUTCHEON ON UNSPLASH

THIS CHAPTER DISCUSSES...

INTRODUCTION

The successful management of an increasingly diverse workforce has become a strategic driver of organisational performance in the modern workplace (Barak, 2016). Societies and organisations are becoming more diverse as a result of several factors including changing demographics, consumer trends and globalisation. Most developed countries are experiencing ageing populations due to greater longevity and declining fertility rates. In contrast, unprecedented population growth is a feature of many developing nations. These demographic changes, combined with the introduction to the workplace of Generation Z, continued employment of older workers and the growth in labour force participation of women and workers with disabilities, point to increasingly diverse workforces in the future. In addition, the growth of the service sector and increased globalisation will require greater management of diversity within organisations to maintain competitiveness. The aim of this chapter is to unpack these issues by firstly examining what diversity and diversity management mean in an organisational context. We then examine the benefits to both organisations and individual employees of effective diversity management. The challenges posed are discussed before we highlight specific actions taken by firms to encourage and manage diversity. Discrimination in the workplace is then explored in terms of why it occurs, which forms of discrimination are most prevalent at work and what actions employers can and must take to prevent discrimination at work. The chapter concludes by summarising the key points from the chapter before highlighting some managerial takeaways for managing diversity in the workplace.

Generation Z means those born between 1993 and 2005.

WHAT IS DIVERSITY?

Diversity in its simplest form refers to all the ways in which people differ. In reality, any characteristic that impacts upon a person's identity and how they view their surroundings should be taken into account when defining diversity. According to Casper *et al.* (2013), diversity can be divided into several dimensions. Surface-level diversity speaks to differences in physical characteristics of workers, such as age, gender, ethnicity, race and disability, whereas deep-level diversity refers to characteristics which are not as easily observed, for example educational attainment, work experience, values and opinions. Other important dimensions of diversity include religion, sexual orientation, personality ▶See Chapter 2◀, social class and geographical origin.

diversity involves more than one characteristic being present among a group of people.

DRIVERS OF DIVERSITY IN THE WORKPLACE

Over the past few decades, greater diversity in societies and organisations is evident due to changes such as shifting population demographics, the increased importance of the service sector, globalisation and the need for greater organisational productivity. Significant workforce changes have occurred globally due to immigration, worker migration and the demand for equal rights based on gender, religion, race, sexual orientation and disability. In addition to a changed global workforce, the world's population continues to increase albeit with considerable variations regionally. Indeed by 2050, the United Nations (UN) predicts that almost one third of the working age population in developed countries will be over 50 years of age (Armstrong-Stassen and Schlosser, 2011). In contrast, developing nations are witnessing extraordinary growth with the population of sub-Saharan Africa predicted to double by 2050

(United Nations, 2019). Gender differences in the workforce are also taking place, with female labour force participation having grown steadily in recent decades, especially in Western societies. In 2018 according to the World Bank (2019), 67% of women in the EU aged between 16 and 64 were in employment, compared with a global rate of 48%.

In addition to changing global demographics, service sector employment (which includes information, investment and professional services, healthcare, warehousing and transportation) is growing as a result of more women and ethnic minorities entering the workforce. Approximately two thirds of US economic activity occurs in the service sector. Other countries have also experienced exponential growth in the value of the service sector to the economy. In 2018, this sector was worth US$6.2 trillion to the Chinese economy, US$2.1 trillion to the UK economy and US$1.5 trillion to the Indian economy (Chappelow, 2019).

The US Bureau of Labor Statistics (2019) predicts that service sector employment in the US is set to grow faster than industry and goods-producing employment, projected to result in 137 million jobs in this sector by 2028. A recent report by Hunt *et al.* (2018) found that, compared with less diverse organisations, firms having greater gender and ethnic/cultural diversity at executive team level are, respectively, 21% and 33% more likely to be more profitable.

Globalisation ▶See Chapter 1◀ has increased due to the opening up of new markets, increased communication and a growth in large organisations having a global footprint. Bartlett and Beamish (2018) suggest that large organisations have different perspectives on managing their employees in a global context. Multinational organisations engage with customers world-wide and employ several thousand workers outside their home countries, thus requiring competent management of culturally diverse individuals. Research by Urwin *et al.* (2013) found that in addition to women and racio-ethnic minorities preferring to work for inclusive organisations, they may also prefer to be customers of such organisations.

MANAGING DIVERSITY IN ORGANISATIONS

managing diversity requires the ability to harness the attributes of a diverse workforce to foster a productive environment which celebrates and nurtures differences.

In recent times, firms have devoted much attention to increasing and effectively managing diversity to meet strategic objectives. In its simplest form, according to the CIPD (Chartered Institute of Personnel and Development), workplace diversity is about recognising differences, acknowledging the benefit of having a range of perspectives in decision-making, and the workforce being representative of the organisation's customers. The three largest companies in the world in 2019 by market value define diversity in the following ways:

Apple Inc: *At Apple, inclusion and diversity means bringing everybody in. We welcome all voices and all beliefs.* (Apple Inc, 2019)

Microsoft: *Our mission is deeply inclusive: empower every person and every organization on the planet to achieve more. We expect each of us – no matter what our level, role or function is – to play an active role in creating environments where people of diverse backgrounds are excited to bring all of who they are and do their best work.* (Microsoft, 2019)

Amazon: *Diverse and inclusive teams have a positive impact on our products and services, and help us better serve customers, selling partners, content creators, employees, and community stakeholders from every background. We are constantly learning and iterating, whether through central programs or work within our business teams, through programs that are local, regional, and global.* (Amazon, 2019)

In order for workforce diversity to contribute to the organisation's strategic goals, it must be effectively managed. Similarly, corporate leaders need to recognise the importance of justice and equality in the work place and put measures in place to avoid 'us' versus 'them' situations (Yang and Guy, 2006). The literature in this area highlights two distinct viewpoints in inclusive management practices: promoting equal employment opportunities (EEO) and managing diversity in the workplace.

BUILDING YOUR EMPLOYABILITY SKILLS

Building Inclusive Teams

Your boss has asked you to give a presentation to a group of supervisors/team leaders outlining specific actions they can take to develop more inclusive work teams. Which actions would you include and why?

EQUAL EMPLOYMENT OPPORTUNITIES

The equal employment opportunities approach (EEO) is associated with an individual's rights. This approach stems from the social justice perspective which views diversity within the wider context of fairness and decency in society. EEO promotes tolerance and is focused on increasing the proportion of minority groupings in firms and fostering equality of opportunity across the organisation. Grounded in equality legislation, this perspective seeks to develop policies and procedures to overcome discrimination and value diversity along a variety of dimensions. Equality of outcome, on the other hand, can be described as equalising where people end up rather than where or how they begin. In many organisations, EEO is implemented through Affirmative Action Programmes (AAPs) to ensure that equality of opportunity is translated into equality of outcome (Gagnon and Cornelius, 2000). These programmes originated in the United States as a means of tackling deeply rooted, systematic discrimination in employment policies, and any company doing business with the US Government must implement an AAP. According to Hitt *et al.* (2009), key features of AAPs include an analysis of the proportion of women and minorities recruited and their position in the organisation, specific goals and timelines for reversing discriminatory practices, and detailed actions to recruit, retain and develop disadvantaged groups in organisations. These programmes also tend to be temporary and are no longer required once appropriate representation of minority groups is achieved.

DIVERSITY MANAGEMENT PROGRAMMES

In recent times, equal opportunity initiatives in organisations have focused more on a diversity management approach. Diversity management programmes aim to improve organisational performance by changing the culture ▶See Chapter 12◀ of the organisation to become more inclusive so as to enable all employees to achieve their potential. As these programmes have different objectives, they are distinct from Affirmative Action Programmes in several ways, as highlighted in Table 10.1. Managing diversity is one of the key challenges facing corporate leaders both now and in the future, according to Barak (2016). It requires organisational buy-in

equal employment opportunities approach (EEO) is an approach that promotes, through the development and implementation of policies and procedures, the fair and equitable treatment of individuals in the workplace irrespective of gender, age, race, ethnicity and other attributes.

equality of opportunity is the idea that people should be able to compete on equal terms, or on a 'level playing field', for opportunities and positions.

Affirmative Action Programmes (AAPs) are specific measures taken by organisations to prevent or counter discrimination.

diversity management programmes are programmes targeting organisational productivity and profitability through a culture that fosters diverse cultural backgrounds and values.

Table 10.1 Differences between Affirmative Action Programmes and diversity management programmes

	Affirmative Action	Diversity Management
Purpose	To prevent and/or remedy discrimination	To create an inclusive work environment where all associates are empowered to perform at their best
Assimilation	Assumes individuals will individually assimilate into the organisation; individuals will adapt	Assumes that managers and the organisations will change (i.e. culture, policies and systems foster an all-inclusive work environment)
Focus	Recruitment, mobility and retention	Creating an environment that allows all associates to reach their full potential
Cause of diversity problems	Does not address the cause of problems	Attempts to uncover the root causes of diversity problems
Target	Individuals identified as disadvantaged (usually racial and ethnic minorities, women, people with disabilities)	All associates
Time frame	Temporary, until there is appropriate representation of disadvantaged groups	Ongoing, permanent changes

Source: Adapted from Hitt et al. (2009).

to recruit, retain, develop and appropriately compensate workers from diverse backgrounds and requires a cultural shift so that differences are celebrated.

BENEFITS OF MANAGING A DIVERSE WORKFORCE

Much, but not all, previous research highlights the benefits to organisations and individuals of having a more inclusive and diverse workforce. Studies have found that as well as being the right thing to do morally, encouraging diversity in organisations can lead to improved organisational performance (Cho *et al.*, 2017; Pitts, 2005; Richard *et al.*, 2013; Ely and Thomas, 1996; Opstrup and Villadsen, 2015), greater innovation and creativity (Richard *et al.*, 2013), improved corporate image (Cox, 1994), the ability to recruit and retain key talent (Armstrong *et al.*, 2010) and better group performance (Roberge and Van Dick, 2010). A recent report from Hunt *et al.* (2018) found that companies with the most ethnically/culturally diverse executive teams – not only in terms of absolute representation, but also of the variety or mix of ethnicities – were 33% more likely to outperform their peers on profitability.

BUILDING YOUR EMPLOYABILITY SKILLS

Women in the Workforce

How might an organisation benefit from employing more women? A *Harvard Business Review* survey of 7280 leaders found that women outperformed men at every level in the company. These highly gender-diverse organisations generally had 50% more customers and above-average profitability and market share (Ye, 2017). Have you ever worked in a place where there were only a small number of women in senior positions? What made you notice this? What could your employer have done about it?

Despite this, other studies have found negative consequences arising from greater organisational diversity, such as a decline in profits, increased training and development costs, the inability to retain employees, claims of reverse discrimination, inter-personal conflict and lack of cohesion among staff (Gonzalez and Denisi, 2009; Mamman *et al.*, 2012; Sacco and Schmitt, 2005; Chatman and Spataro, 2005). An example of how stated intentions towards a more inclusive workforce can be hampered by organisational practicalities is highlighted in a recent study by Moore *et al.* (2018) on inclusive recruitment practices in a large Australian retailer. Their research found that despite intentions to the contrary, trends such as technical changes to the recruitment process, greater productivity demands and the availability of suitable roles were likely to reduce employment opportunities for people with intellectual disabilities such as learning difficulties. Diagnosing autism, as distinct from intellectual disabilities, continues to be challenging.

INDIVIDUAL-LEVEL OUTCOMES

From the individual's perspective, having a more diverse workforce can lead to heightened organisational commitment and job satisfaction (Giffords, 2009; Acquavita *et al.*, 2009; Pitts, 2009). On the flip-side, research from Hicks-Clarke and Iles (2000) found that under-represented groups such as ethnic and racial minorities, women and people with disabilities are less positive towards their roles, careers and organisations when they believe their firms to be less open to diverse and inclusive practices. On this point, Colquitt *et al.* (2001) reviewed 25 years of organisational justice research and found that employees who feel they have been unfairly treated or discriminated against can under-perform and seek retribution in work or through litigation.

Take, for example, age diversity in the health sector. Nurses of different ages can bring greater perspectives and connect better with patients of different ages. Despite this, newly-qualified nurses will likely have been trained differently, have varying degrees of technical competency and use different communication methods compared with those with many years' work experience. These differences in a highly pressurised environment can lead to increased stress-levels, have negative consequences for well-being ▸**See Chapter 9**◂ and reduce overall performance (Lehmann-Willenbrock *et al.*, 2012).

IMPACT OF TECHNOLOGY ON BEHAVIOUR

3 ways AI can support gender equality at work

The following are ways in which AI can present solutions to typical employment issues.

Gender pay gap reporting

There is clear potential for AI to assist employers to make pay gap reporting accurate, thereby helping employers to better analyse data to resolve problems. AI can also help authorities with the collection and presentation of data.

Encouraging gender diversity

In tackling gender discrimination, AI can be used to identify, learn from and prevent bias within organisations. Textio, an 'augmented writing' platform, analyses job

intellectual disabilities are a significantly reduced ability to understand new or complex information and to learn and apply new skills.

autism is defined primarily by social difficulties, communication issues and repetitive behaviours.

AI is the study of how to produce machines that have some of the qualities that the human mind has, such as the ability to understand language, recognise pictures, solve problems and learn.

descriptions and suggests alternative wording to ensure gender balance and elimination of unconscious gender bias. Textio uses a 'tone meter' to help companies spot when certain words or phrases are imbalanced and alert them to combinations of words and phrases that can impact which gender applies for jobs. They explain that seemingly harmless words such as 'exhaustive' and 'enforcement' can create a gender imbalance in job descriptions.

Maintaining engagement

It is widely acknowledged that family life has an impact on career engagement and progression. AI can be used to undertake tasks that usually require employees to be in the workplace. For example, *The Irish Times* recently reported on a Swiss bank that has 'cloned' its regional chief investment officer so that he can give briefs to clients and staff in a digital format. The 'clone' appears on a screen and is programmed to answer questions and give advice on specific areas.

---

disability employment gap means the difference in employment outcomes for people with and without disabilities.

Turning to employment opportunities for people with disabilities, a recent report shows that the disability employment gap in the UK stands at 29%. Despite the fact that almost one in five of the UK's working age population report having a disability, just over half were in employment, compared with 80% of those with no disability.

BUILDING YOUR EMPLOYABILITY SKILLS

A colleague who has a disability has told you that they were subjected to harassment the other day but don't want to make 'a big deal of it'. As a colleague, what advice would you give them?

BARRIERS TO INCLUSIVE WORKPLACE MANAGEMENT

horizontal and vertical segregation is the concentration of men and women in different economic sectors and occupations.

Despite the benefits to both individuals and organisations of fostering inclusive workplaces, such initiatives face many challenges from work colleagues, such as inherent stereotyping, prejudice and discrimination. Other structural barriers include power struggles, horizontal and vertical segregation and communication issues.

Stereotypes enable those who hold them to reduce uncertainty about what people or groups are likely to want and how they are likely to behave. These generalisations tend to be rigid, often inaccurate, and act as a heuristic or mental 'short-cut' in evaluating the traits of an individual belonging to a group. For example, a recent study by Ng and Feldman (2012) found the following to be the most common stereotypes associated with older workers: (a) less motivated, (b) generally less willing to participate in training and career development, (c) more resistant and less willing to change, (d) less trusting, (e) less healthy, and (f) more vulnerable to work–family imbalance. Interestingly, these researchers found evidence to support only one of these stereotypes, unwillingness to train.

stereotypes are generalised, pre-established expectations about the characteristics of a group of people.

The main issue with using stereotypes is that they ignore the fact that individuals within a group are just that: individuals rather than a homogenous group. Changing stereotypes can be challenging for a number of reasons. We tend to think of a person's behaviour which differs from this view as being the exception rather than the norm. Using the common stereotype of older workers being less open to change, if we witness an older colleague who is flexible in their work patterns, we are likely to ignore this fact and view this worker as being an exception or we may simply forget about this instance. Furthermore, stereotypes can lead to confirmation bias, which influences the information we seek, process and recall in order to support our beliefs about this group. If we believe that all accountants are boring, then when meeting an accountant, we will actively seek information that confirms this, such as social awkwardness, and ignore any information to the contrary.

IN REALITY

In March 2013, Nottinghamshire Police Service in the UK had Black and Minority Ethnic (BME) officer representation of 4% against a population figure of 11.2%. Despite a recruitment process held in February 2013 that attracted over 2000 applicants, only 149 of these were BME, and only six were ultimately successful in the process.

From previous experience and based on an analysis of the success of previous BME candidates at different stages in the recruitment process, they identified three key areas that needed to be addressed:

1 attracting the right candidates

2 supporting those candidates through the process

3 adapting the process to meet the needs of the candidates.

Initiatives taken

Attracting the right candidates

The chief constable met leaders from diverse faith groups and invited them to identify and propose members of their communities who they felt had the potential to be the future of policing in Nottinghamshire. The Positive Action Coordinator worked in partnership with these faith leaders to deliver an event that would attract intelligent and talented individuals from within their communities. Personal invitation packs to a recruitment seminar, to be held in the community, were then sent out to these individuals. A programme was designed to explain the recruitment process and the support from the Positive Action Team that would be available to candidates.

positive action involves actions taken in order to achieve equality for group members who are economically and/or socially disadvantaged.

Out of this event, 50 individuals who had never before considered a career in the police service, chose to embark on this journey.

Supporting those candidates through the process

To support the candidates and to provide them with the best opportunity for success, the following measures were put in place.

- Support sessions – fortnightly evening sessions, two and a half hours in length, were organised for candidates to attend. These were followed by a 'walk-through' of the first three sections of the application form so that candidates would be clear on the information required.
- Candidates then received sessions relating to the competency-based questionnaire and these were followed by a two-day training session.

- To ensure ease of access and to provide revision materials, sessions delivering new information were audio-recorded and forwarded to candidates via an e-mail link to Dropbox. Additionally, the Corporate Communications Team worked with the Positive Action Team to video-record sessions and post these on a secure YouTube link.
- Mentors – early in the process, mentors were allocated to each candidate. Both police officers and staff volunteered, on an agreed 50:50 duty time basis, to act as buddies and provide extra guidance and support throughout the process. To help them do this, they were provided with mentoring training and awareness sessions and they were invited to attend the evening support sessions along with their candidates.

Adapting the process to meet the needs of the candidates

At the request of our local community and faith leaders, Nottinghamshire Police Service brought the in-force interview stage forward to the first stage of the recruitment process to test the qualities of the candidates aspiring for a career in policing. Community members were also invited to sit in on the interviews so that they could observe what was taking place.

The Head of the Vetting Unit asked all the usual questions. He responded to the candidates directly, informing them of any next steps they needed to take to ensure a smooth security check should they reach the end of the process. In addition, the police force worked in partnership with Nottingham City Council, using their facilities to deliver support sessions, ensuring that wherever possible these were held within the community rather than on police premises.

The results

- Improvements were seen at all points in the recruitment process. Overall, 9% of applicants were successful through the whole process compared with just 5% of BME applicants and 8% of white applicants in the 2013 recruitment process.
- The police service has maintained contact with those who failed the previous stages and is working to support them should they wish to apply again.

Prejudice includes feelings, beliefs and inclination to act, and tends to be resistant to reason and experience. According to Pettigrew and Meertens (1995), prejudiced attitudes tend to form ideological clusters of beliefs that justify discrimination. Ageism, sexism and racism are all examples of prejudice, often leading to negative emotions such as fear, anxiety and hate. Blatant or explicit prejudice can take the form of discriminatory remarks: 'immigrants should go back to their home country' or 'all Muslims are terrorists' but prejudice can also be subtle or covert such as excluding certain people from social events. This deep-rooted, automatic prejudice is more likely to occur when we know that these attitudes (such as racism) are wrong, and the covert nature of our behaviour frequently serves to protect ourselves from this realisation.

social identity theory describes a person's sense of who they are based on their group membership(s).

Modern examples of prejudice include the assumptions that men are more intelligent than women, all black people are athletic, and people with disabilities are helpless. So, what underpins prejudice? These attitudes can be formed based on several factors including the tendency to justify entitlements when competing for scarce resources such as housing or employment, social identity theory and being oblivious to our privileges. Sources of prejudice can include social inequalities, family socialisation, that is, being raised by a family with definite attitudes towards certain groups, and institutional supports from our schools, governments and the media. A recent study by Meleady *et al.* (2017) found that prejudice against immigrants from the EU was a significant deciding factor in how people intended to vote in the Brexit referendum of 2016.

Having discussed expectations (stereotypes) and attitudes (prejudice) ▸**See Chapter 4**◂ as challenges to creating inclusive workplaces, we now focus on the behavioural manifestation of these attitudes. Discrimination results in unequal treatment of individuals based on their group membership. Prejudice and discrimination differ in that prejudice refers to what people think whereas discrimination is what they do (adapted from Surbhi (2016)).

EXAMPLES OF DISCRIMINATION AT WORK

Examples of discriminatory work practices include:

- Racism – firing, demoting or disciplining someone based on their race.
- Unequal pay – the persistent gender pay gap, which is also evident in part-time employment (O'Sullivan *et al.*, 2019).
- Ageism – introducing a mandatory retirement age of 65 without just cause.
- Lack of appropriate access to employment – failure by organisations to make appropriate accommodations for employees or prospective employees with disabilities.
- Bogus self-employment – the successful bid in 2016 by Uber drivers in the UK to be recognised as 'workers' and not self-employed.
- Discriminatory advertising – recruitment advertising that might reasonably be understood as indicating an intention to discriminate based on nationality or age. Examples include job adverts seeking applications from 'recent graduates' or 'US-passport holders'.

Prejudice and discrimination can hinder the effective management of diversity in organisations according to Dipboye and Colella (2005) and can be costly to both workers and firms. Employees who fall victim to prejudice and discrimination can feel stressed, perform poorly, have reduced organisational commitment and feel a sense of injustice. Organisations who fail to effectively deal with these issues can experience reputational damage and financial loss through fighting costly litigation.

Gender Quotas

OB IN THE NEWS

In an attempt to counteract the slow progress made towards achieving gender balance in senior executive positions, many national governments have introduced gender quotas for boards, while others are considering doing so. In 2008, Norway was the first country requiring a 40% quota for female directors of listed companies. Despite the population in most countries being evenly split between genders, females represent the majority of all graduates in most developed countries but make up a decreasing share of the workforce, the further up the corporate ladder they go. Less than 7% of the CEOs on the 2019 Fortune 500 list were women (Dah *et al.*, 2020). In Canada for example, despite implementation of a 'comply or explain' disclosure regime to facilitate gender diversity on boards of directors, a report from the Ontario Securities Commission (2015) found that 45% of companies in 2016 still had no women on their boards. Even some positive action policies, such as requirements to fill candidate pools with underrepresented minorities without setting hard quotas, have failed to resolve the issue of female representation. Because of this, the introduction of gender quotas at board of director level is firmly back on the agenda.

A number of leading academics in this field met at the University of Toronto in 2017 to present research-led evidence to debate the pros and cons of introducing gender quotas as a means to achieve gender parity. They summarised reasons why gender quotas may be unsuccessful as follows:

- **Illegality or perceived injustice** – these quotas may be illegal in some countries and may lead to a sense of unfairness by men (Shteynberg *et al.*, 2011).
- **Potential stigma** – women who are placed on these boards may be seen as less qualified, thus undermining their ability to effectively contribute to board business (Leslie *et al.*, 2014).
- **Reduced employee engagement and negative job attitudes** from males, potentially leading to men being less supportive of diversity initiatives in organisations (Dobbin *et al.*, 2015).
- **No trickle down** – introducing gender quotas of 40% at board level in Norway did not have the effect of making organisations as a whole more gender balanced (Bertrand *et al.*, 2018).
- **Failure to address underlying discrimination** – quotas may not tackle the deep-rooted issues of discrimination. In the Norwegian example, a small number of women called the 'golden skirts' held board positions in several organisations. While quotas require a certain number of women to be employed in the organisations, they don't measure impact.

On the flip-side, other research suggests reasons why quotas might work:

- **Fears not realised** – evidence suggests that there is hostility towards the idea of quotas in countries that don't have them and an acknowledgement that increased representation by women on boards in Norway actually improved governance and decision-making (Dhir, 2015).
- **No pipeline problem** – male board members surveyed explained the under-representation of women on boards as arising from a lack of female candidates, whereas female board members attributed this gap to bias and closed male networks.
- **No stigma** – evidence from Norway suggests that since the introduction of the 40% quota, few female board members felt marginalised or stigmatised.

- **Positive effects** – studies show that achieving a critical mass of female representation on boards leads to more thorough discussions, less groupthink, better risk management, more systematic work and higher quality management oversight (Dhir, 2015).
- **A much-needed shock to the system** – gender biases are deep-rooted in many organisations and in the human psyche, such as unconscious biases, stereotypes and seeking to associate with others who are similar. The quota system provides a clear and consistent charter to counteract these unconscious biases and overcome discrimination.

Questions

1 If gender quotas were introduced widely, what specific actions could organisations take to avoid negative consequences?
2 Should promotion/ representation be based purely on merit? If so why, if not, why not?
3 Introducing quotas for other under-represented minorities would not work. Comment/ discuss.

Sources

Bertrand, M., Black, S.E., Jensen, S. and Lleras-Muney, A. (2018) Breaking the glass ceiling? The effect of board quotas on female labour market outcomes in Norway. *The Review of Economic Studies*, 86, 191–239.

Dah, M.A., Jizi, M.I. and Kebbe, R. (2020) CEO gender and managerial entrenchment. *Research in International Business and Finance*, 54, 101237.

Shteynberg, G., Leslie, L.M., Knight, A.P. and Mayer, D.M. (2011) But affirmative action hurts us! Race-related beliefs shape perceptions of White disadvantage and policy unfairness. *Organizational Behavior and Human Decision Processes*, 115, 1–12.

OTHER STRUCTURAL BARRIERS TO DIVERSITY AT WORK

Despite the introduction of equality legislation in many countries and workplaces generally becoming more inclusive, structural challenges prevail which hamper diversity initiatives linked to power, the glass ceiling and communication.

POWER STRUGGLES

Groups and individuals in organisations do not have equal power. Individuals typically gain power through their human capital, the position they occupy in the organisation or how irreplaceable they are (Hitt *et al.*, 2009). Depending on the type of organisation, some departments, such as the finance or sales departments, may have more, or less, power compared with other departments. Sidanius and Pratto (2003) describe how, in society, groups have ascribed status. This status has typically translated into the workplace with the consequence of developing power differentials between traditionally high-status, that is white males, and low-status groups such as people with disabilities, racial and ethnic minorities and women. Previous research by Kalkhoff and Barnum (2000) found that high-status individuals are more likely to speak up and use strategies to influence others, compared with low-status individuals. In addition, employees belonging to groups tend not to mix with individuals from other groups with different levels of power or status, according to Konrad (2003). This lack of integration can result in cliques being formed which are resistant to diversity efforts.

LACK OF STRUCTURAL INTEGRATION

The term **glass ceiling** is frequently used to explain how women tend not to progress beyond certain levels in an organisation. Other scholars, such as Ní Léime *et al.* (2015), extend this categorisation to highlight the fact that many women are not only vertically segregated into mid/lower occupational categories but also horizontally segregated into poorly paid jobs. These forms of segregation can also hold for members of racial and ethnic minority groups. In 2005, General Electric faced a lawsuit for discriminating against managers of colour. The suit accused the company of paying Black, Asian and Minority Ethnic managers less than white, denying them promotions and using offensive terms to describe people of colour. The company settled the lawsuit in 2006. Minority Ethnic employees may face other disadvantages in progressing their careers, such as not having studied at the 'right' schools or not being as well connected as their Caucasian colleagues.

COMMUNICATION ISSUES

Problems with communication arising from employees being unable or unwilling to converse and communicate in the main language of employment can arise for several reasons. These reasons include a lack of language fluency, communication misunderstandings, different cultural norms and groups of employees who speak the same mother tongue excluding others. It is, however, important not to stereotype or make assumptions about communication

glass ceiling means an invisible barrier that inhibits women's and minorities' advancement through the managerial hierarchy, which is more pronounced further along one's career.

human capital is a combination of a person's qualifications, skills, competencies and relevant work experience.

ascribed status is the status assigned by cultural norms, dependent on group membership.

tendencies based on background. Hitt *et al.* (2009) state that African Americans, Hispanics and Asians tend to be less likely to speak freely during meetings, compared with Anglo-Americans. Gestures can also have different meanings than what was intended depending on cultural differences. For example, showing the sole of your shoe is considered rude in Arab cultures.

SPECIFIC MEASURES TO MANAGE DIVERSITY IN ORGANISATIONS

Despite the many obstacles faced by organisations to fostering inclusive and multi-cultural work environments, there are many strategies which can be adopted to overcome these barriers. Comprehensive compliance with employment equality legislation is a bare minimum in this regard. Other strategies, according to Hitt *et al.* (2009), include achieving buy-in from senior management in addition to all employees and making diversity a key strategic, measurable goal.

Gender Discrimination

In October 2019, a school in Ireland was ordered to pay a deputy principal €93,498 compensation after it discriminated against her because she was a woman in a contest with a male colleague for a school principal's post. In the case, the Workplace Relations Commission (WRC) ordered the Board of Management (BOM) of the school to pay Pamela Brennan €93,498. Employed at the school in question, Ms Brennan had superior academic qualification and more relevant teaching experience than the successful male candidate for the post.

WRC Adjudication Officer, Emer O'Shea, noted that the award – equivalent of 78 weeks' pay – is a sanction that is required to have a real deterrent effect and be effective, proportionate and dissuasive. Ms Brennan complained at the WRC in her case, taken under the Employment Equality Act, that she first heard that she didn't get the job via local chat on the golf course.

In her findings relating to the male candidate beating Ms Brennan to the job through obtaining a higher score at interview, Ms O'Shea said: 'I find on the balance of probabilities that the process was tainted with discrimination on gender grounds.' Ms O'Shea said that the school Board of Management had not provided a convincing and transparent rationale for their scoring at interview. Ms Brennan scored 249 marks at interview while the successful candidate scored 273. Ms O'Shea said that she found the evidence of the chairman of the interview/selection panel 'to be unconvincing and inconsistent'. She said that the interview panel chairman altered Ms Brennan's marks to her detriment by two points and could not recall the basis for doing so.

The Adjudication Officer also found that the interview chairman took significantly more notes of the successful candidate's answers and recorded three words with respect to Ms Brennan – Leadership, Administration and Vision. Ms O'Shea said that she was satisfied that Ms Brennan had superior academic qualifications and

OB IN PRACTICE

CREDIT: GETTY IMAGES

more relevant experience than the male candidate for the position of School Principal. She noted that Ms Brennan had an Honours B. Ed Degree and a Higher Diploma while the successful candidate had a BA in English and Philosophy and a Higher Diploma. She said that Ms Brennan had 12 years' accredited service as a teacher while the successful candidate had 10 years according to his CV. Ms O'Shea further noted that Ms Brennan had five years' experience as a Deputy Principal while the successful candidate acted as Deputy Principal from January 25, 2018, to February 2018 and shared acting Principal duties for around four months to 5 June 2018, when Ms Brennan returned prematurely from maternity leave.

In her direct evidence at hearing, Ms Brennan asserted that there was no justification for the marking by the selection board, given her qualifications and experience, and questioned how the successful candidate could have scored higher than her in 9 of the 10 criteria adopted by the Board. Ms Brennan said that when she asked for an explanation as to how the appointed candidate outscored her at interview, 'I did not receive one'.

In response, the school BOM contended that the successful candidate performed better at interview than Ms Brennan and that gender was not a consideration and a fair assessment was carried out. In his direct evidence, the BOM Chairman submitted that he had been conducting interviews since 1973 and that he treated all candidates equally.

Questions

1 If you were the Chairperson of an interview panel, what steps would you take to prevent discrimination in the selection and recruitment process?

2 Why might interview panel members be reluctant to take notes during interviews?

3 When and how should a HR manager inform unsuccessful candidates of the recruitment and selection process?

EQUALITY LEGISLATION IN EMPLOYMENT

Despite national governments enacting legislation which obliges employers to treat employees and prospective employees equally, discrimination in the workplace persists (Cohn, 2019). Equality legislation varies by country and tends to be influenced by factors such as political ideology, and social and historical issues. In the EU, the Employment Equality Directive (2000), enacted by all 28 Member States, prohibits discrimination on grounds of religion and belief, age, disability and sexual orientation and covers employment and occupation, vocational training, and membership of employer and employee organisations. In the USA, the Equality Act (2010) aims to adopt a single approach by combining 116 pieces of equality legislation regarding sex, race, disability, sexual orientation, religion or belief.

The EU's Employment Equality Directive (2000) defines four types of discrimination, namely direct and indirect discrimination, harassment, and instruction to discriminate. In addition, many European countries prohibit victimisation. How do these discriminatory practices differ?

- Direct discrimination – is where your employer says he/she will not promote you because you're 'too old'/gay/disabled, belonging to a certain religion/race/ethnic group.
- Indirect discrimination – where the manager of a Jewish employee changes her work roster, requiring her to work every third Saturday.
- Harassment – where colleagues make offensive jokes about your age/religion/disability/sexual orientation/ethnicity/race.
- Instruction to discriminate – for example, where the HR manager is told not to hire any people of a certain religion.

discrimination is unjustified negative behaviour towards a group or its members.

Direct discrimination discrimination that is obviously contrary to the terms of equality legislation, such as explicitly excluding people over 50 from applying for a job.

indirect discrimination is an apparently neutral provision, criterion or practice which puts members of specific groups at a particular disadvantage compared with others.

<table>
</table>

harassment is unwanted conduct that takes place with the purpose or effect of violating the dignity of a person and of creating an intimidating, hostile, degrading, humiliating or offensive environment.

instruction to discriminate refers to telling or making someone discriminate against another person.

victimisation refers to negative consequences suffered by a person in reaction to her/his complaint about discrimination, or because of being a witness in a discrimination case.

● Victimisation – being passed over for a promotion that you would otherwise have been given, after making a witness statement supporting a colleague's complaint of sexual discrimination.

In an attempt to counteract unfair treatment of people based on discrimination, the concept of positive discrimination has become topical. Proponents argue that because certain groups have been systematically discriminated against over protracted periods, employers should positively discriminate in favour of employees or prospective employees from under-represented minority groups. This, they argue, is essential to bring about equality in the workplace and to ensure that an organisation's workforce is reflective of the wider societal population. This form of discrimination is generally illegal except when a statutory exception exists or in relation to disability discrimination. An example of workplace positive discrimination (which in this instance is unlawful in many countries) is when a law firm seeks to address the low numbers of women partners by interviewing all women regardless of whether they meet the criteria for partnership.

SPOTLIGHT ON SKILLS

1 What measures need to be included in diversity programmes in order to be effective?

2 What challenges if any does social media usage by employees at work pose in successfully managing diversity in organisations?

To help you answer these questions, visit bloomsbury.pub/organisational-behaviour to watch the video of Lucile Kamar from ITN talking about diversity at work.

Positive action, on the other hand, seeks to enhance the employment prospects of certain disadvantaged groups rather than discriminate in favour of individuals from these groups. It also differs from positive discrimination in that it is lawful. In particular, employers can take positive action measures in relation to gender balance, older workers, people with disabilities and members of under-represented racial or ethnic groups. Despite 'positive action' initiatives being facilitated under EU law, Member States adapt these measures to varying degrees. For example, the Cypriot Supreme Court developed a practice of declaring void and unconstitutional any law introducing positive action in employment which is challenged (Tymowski, 2016).

In order to develop an effective diversity management programme, a top-down approach must be taken, with the organisation's senior leaders being fully committed to developing and communicating a vision of inclusivity. Specific actions include:

● Starting with the CEO, develop and implement strategic goals for diversity and inclusion, leading by example.

- Senior leadership executives need to communicate regularly and through various channels to support training, awareness and all inclusion initiatives.
- Hold managers and supervisors accountable for championing diversity initiatives at every level in the organisation.
- Include and measure employee engagement by developing a variety of methods to get buy-in from employees, such as discussion groups, employee satisfaction surveys, cultural diversity audits and informal feedback channels.

More recent research by Deloitte (2017) suggests that CEOs must take ownership and drive accountability for diversity to bridge the gap between what companies say and the actual impact of their diversity and inclusion initiatives. Table 10.2 distinguishes between previous and more recent initiatives which organisations must take to foster diverse and inclusive workplaces. These 'new rules', according to Deloitte, will require a novel focus on process change, data-driven tools, experiential learning, accountability and transparency.

Procter & Gamble is a company which has deeply embedded a commitment to diversity and inclusion within its culture. Between 2010 and 2017, the company spent US$2 billion annually to develop a broad diverse supplier base which includes 1500 businesses owned by women and people from minority groups (Procter & Gamble, 2015). Developing women leaders through a leadership development strategy ▸See Chapter 6◂ is another initiative undertaken, resulting in increases in female representation at manager and VP level. This company has also developed a 'reverse mentoring' programme enabling senior staff to witness some of the daily obstacles faced by employees with disabilities, with funding to support accommodations being centrally allocated. In addition, 10% of senior executive bonus pay is linked to the achievement of diversity goals, evaluated during performance appraisals.

Table 10.2 Diversity and inclusion: Old rules vs new rules

Old rules	New rules
Diversity is considered a reporting goal driven by compliance and brand priorities.	Diversity and inclusion are a CEO-level priority and considered important throughout all levels of management.
Work–life balance is considered a challenge for employees to manage, with some support from the organisation.	Work–life balance, family and individual wellness are all considered part of the total employee experience.
Companies measure diversity through the demographic profile of designated groups defined by attributes such as gender, race, nationality or age.	Companies measure inclusion, diversity and lack of bias in all recruitment, promotion, pay and other talent practices.
Diversity is defined by gender, race and demographic differences.	Diversity is defined in a broader context, including concepts of 'diversity of thought' also addressing people with autism and other cognitive differences.
Leaders are promoted on 'merit' and experience.	Merit is unpacked to identify built-up biases; leaders are promoted on their ability to lead inclusively.
Diversity and inclusion are a programme of education, training and discussion.	Diversity and inclusion go beyond education to focus on de-biasing business processes and holding leaders accountable for inclusive behaviour.
Companies regularly report progress on diversity measures.	Companies hold managers accountable for creating an inclusive culture, using metrics to compare them against each other.

Source: Adapted from Deloitte University Press 2017. Diversity and Inclusion; The Reality Gap. (2017). Available at: https://www2.deloitte.com/us/en/insights/focus/human-capital-trends/2017/diversity-and-inclusion-at-the-workplace.html

The key priorities for effectively managing diversity include:

- Ensuring that top leadership understands the importance of diversity and holding them accountable through specific measures and transparent reporting with regard to recruitment, promotion, retention and compensation.
- Using technology to identify and measure problem areas and progress.
- Moving beyond HR – diversity and inclusion must be embedded in the organisation and practised by all employees, with line managers being held accountable.
- Taking into account regional differences – global organisations must accommodate regional differences in diversity challenges and bespoke solution development.

◁ETHICAL▷ BEHAVIOUR IN THE WORKPLACE

Abercrombie's Classic American Look

Clothing retailer Abercrombie & Fitch made headlines in 2003 after being sued for discriminating against African Americans, Asian Americans, and Latinos. In particular, Latinos and Asian Americans accused the company of steering them to jobs in the stock room rather than on the sales floor because Abercrombie & Fitch wanted to be represented by workers who looked 'classically American'.

CREDIT: GETTY IMAGES

Minority employees also complained that they'd been fired and replaced by white workers. A&F ended up settling the lawsuit for $50 million. 'The retail industry and other industries need to know that businesses cannot discriminate against individuals under the auspice of a marketing strategy or a particular "look". Race and sex discrimination in employment are unlawful.' Equal Employment Opportunity Commission lawyer Eric Drieband stated, upon the lawsuit's resolution.

Questions

1 If you were the hiring manager in Abercrombie & Fitch, what specific measures would you take to ensure that recruitment and selection procedures did not breach anti-discrimination legislation?

2 Should all employees in an organisation be required to attend diversity training irrespective of their willingness to do so?

3 Apart from participating in diversity training programmes, what other initiatives can organisations foster to promote ethical behaviour and an ethical culture in the workplace?

MANAGERIAL TAKEAWAYS

With the increase in globalisation, greater workforce diversity and ever-changing demographic population shifts, the need to promote and embrace diversity in organisations has never been greater. Leading organisations now see diversity and inclusion as a comprehensive strategy embedded in every aspect of the talent life cycle to enhance employee engagement, improve brand image and drive performance. This chapter has examined the concepts of diversity and its management in organisations by highlighting its benefits both to organisations and to individuals. Organisations face many challenges in creating more inclusive environments. These challenges can and must be overcome to improve performance, create a positive brand image and harness the potential of a diverse workforce in an environment of transparency and respect.

- Organisational diversity can be defined as differences among employees. Common diversity attributes include gender, race, ethnicity, disability and sexual orientation.
- Populations in developed countries are ageing and becoming more diverse, whereas population growth is taking place in other world regions. In addition, the increased importance of the service sector economy and greater globalisation are other 'push' factors driving diversity management.
- Diversity management programmes seek to develop more inclusive work cultures whereas affirmative action programmes aim to achieve fair representation.
- Effective diversity management can lead to greater organisational productivity, better brand image and superior talent acquisition and retention. From the employee perspective, these initiatives can lead to greater job satisfaction and organisational commitment.
- Failure to comprehensively manage diversity in organisations can lead to a decline in profits, increased training and development costs, the inability to attract and retain employees, claims of reverse discrimination, inter-personal conflict and lack of cohesion among staff.
- Issues such as stereotypes, prejudice, discrimination, power struggles, lack of effective structural integration and communication problems can negatively impact on managing a diverse workforce.
- Today's successful diversity management in organisations requires leadership from the top of the organisation to set, monitor and champion goals which are strategic to the organisation and embedded in the company's culture.

 CHAPTER REVIEW QUESTIONS

1 What is diversity?
2 How does diversity management differ from affirmative action programmes?
3 What changes are taking place globally which make effective diversity management important?
4 What are the key differences between prejudice and discrimination?
5 Are there any situations where it is appropriate to discriminate against a specific group of people? Please explain your answer.
6 How should complaints of harassment at work be handled?
7 How can organisations promote cultural awareness among employees?
8 Should diversity training be compulsory in organisations?

 FURTHER READING

Barak, M.E.M. (2016) *Managing Diversity: Toward a Globally Inclusive Workplace*, 4th edition. London: Sage Publications.

Cox, T.H. and Blake, S. (1991) Managing cultural diversity: Implications for organizational competitiveness. *Academy of Management Perspectives*, 5, 45–56.

Eslie, L.M., Mayer, D.M. and Kravitz, D.A. (2014) The stigma of affirmative action: A stereotyping-based theory and meta-analytic test of the consequences for performance. *Academy of Management Journal*, 57, 964–989.

 USEFUL WEBSITES

https://www.siop.org/
Society for Industrial and Organizational Psychology
https://www.cipd.co.uk/
Chartered Institute of Personnel and Development (CIPD)
https://www.ilo.org/global/topics/future-of-work/lang--en/index.htm
International Labour Organization
http://centreforglobalinclusion.org/
The Centre for Global Inclusion
https://www.eeoc.gov/
US Equal Employment Opportunity Commission
https://humanrights.gov.au/
Australian Human Rights Commission
http://english1.english.gov.cn/2005-10/02/content_74185.htm
Chinese Ministry of Labor and Social Security

Online Resources

Visit **bloomsbury.pub/organisational-behaviour** to access additional materials to support teaching and learning.

PART 3
ORGANISATIONAL PROCESSES

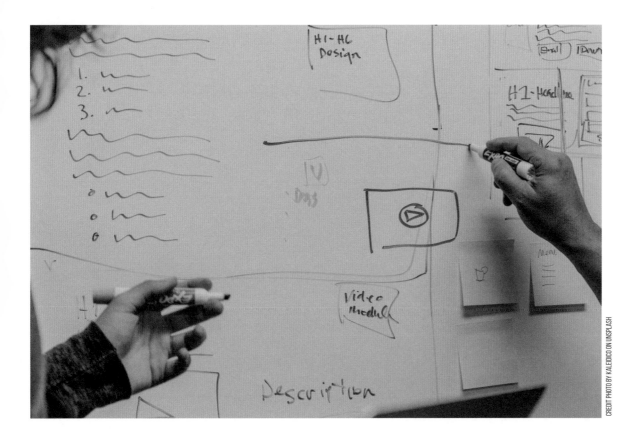

OVERVIEW

People's behaviour can impact many areas of the organisation, from organisational performance to organisational change. For that reason, organisational processes are a main focus for managers, HR professionals and others who want to ensure the optimal function of the organisation. This part of the book includes activities that establish the business goals of the organisation and develop processes which will help to achieve business goals.

- Chapter 11: Organisational socialisation
- Chapter 12: Organisational culture
- Chapter 13: Managing organisational change
- Chapter 14: Communication in the workplace

 Visit **bloomsbury.pub/organisational-behaviour** to play an interactive simulation that will allow you to practise what you have learned about organisational processes. The simulation puts you in the role of a manager acting out the decision-making process.

11 ORGANISATIONAL SOCIALISATION

Ciarán McFadden

LEARNING OUTCOMES

BY THE END OF THIS CHAPTER YOU WILL BE ABLE TO:

- Understand the concept of organisational socialisation.
- Appreciate why organisational socialisation is a topic of growing importance in organisations today.
- Differentiate between the various stages in the process of organisational socialisation.

- Critically discuss the different outcomes that can result from an effective organisational socialisation process.
- Evaluate the different tactics companies may use in socialising their new employees.
- Explore examples of various organisational socialisation programmes in different companies.

CREDIT: PHOTO BY SMARTWORKS COWORKING ON UNSPLASH

THIS CHAPTER DISCUSSES...

INTRODUCTION

organisational socialisation is the process by which an organisational outsider gains the social knowledge and skills necessary to become a participating, effective and accepted member of an organisation.

This chapter deals with the process of organisational socialisation, or, the way in which an employee enters the workplace (or, indeed, a new department or role) and becomes a fully-fledged, accepted and productive member of the organisation. In this chapter, we will look at the stages of this process; the various strategies organisations take to adapt this process to their own context; the outcomes, both positive and negative, of effective or ineffective socialisation; and the roles that a co-worker, group or team and organisation itself play in this process.

Every organisation has its own values, regulations, way of working, set of traditions, norms and practices. A workplace therefore develops its own organisational culture ▶See Chapter 12◀ that helps to distinguish it from others, and gives it its own identity. A workplace can differ from another even if it's in the same industry, the same geographic location or part of the same organisation. With such distinct workplace cultures at play, employees who move from one organisation to another risk experiencing a type of culture shock – where they might feel confused, disoriented or anxious as a result of a sudden change in the way that things are done. For example, imagine you worked in the more casual, open environment common to Silicon Valley companies like Google, and then changed to a job in the more traditionally conservative London financial sector. Your comfort levels, and most likely your productivity as an employee, might differ significantly.

Organisational socialisation is a way of helping employees acclimatise to a new work environment and culture. It is a process that involves the individual's own motivation ▶See Chapter 5◀ and needs, the involvement of co-workers and the influence of the organisation and its structures. The main goal of organisational socialisation is to ensure as smooth a transition as possible for an employee entering a new workplace culture. Socialisation has become an increasingly important topic, particularly because employees now spend less time in the same role as in years before; they are therefore exposed to a number of different organisations within their career, and organisations will recruit new employees more frequently. It is therefore in the individual's and organisation's joint interest that a new employee can 'hit the ground running' and get settled in as soon as possible.

This chapter offers an overview of how new employees can be inducted into the social aspects of the organisation, and shows why the socialisation process is now a critically important topic within organisational behaviour. However, because organisational socialisation involves many different factors, we must first look at defining the term more closely.

WHAT IS ORGANISATIONAL SOCIALISATION?

Broadly speaking, organisational socialisation is the route through which employees 'learn the ropes' when they join an organisation, or when they move to a very different new role within an organisation. A key author on the topic of organisational socialisation, Daniel Feldman, defines it as 'the process by which employees are transformed from organisation outsiders to participating and effective members' (1976, p. 309). This definition offers a few key elements that can help us understand the term better. Firstly, organisational socialisation is a *process*; that is, not a one-time event or something that can happen overnight. Feldman (1976) himself discusses what happens within that process – see the next section below. Secondly, we can see in his definition two sets of people – the *organisation outsiders* and the *members*: the former are not part of 'the club', while the latter are seen as being accepted members of it. A third key element of the definition is the use of the verb *transformed* – the member has become, and been made, different from the outsider as a result of the process. Lastly, Feldman's use of *participating* and *effective* in describing a fully socialised member gives some clues as to the overall aim of the process – productivity and efficacy in one's role is a key outcome of organisational socialisation.

Van Maanen and Schein (1979, p. 3), another two important authors on the topic, offer a slightly different definition – 'organizational socialization is the process by which an individual acquires the social knowledge and skills necessary to assume an organisational role'. In contrast to Feldman's definition, this one is not specifically in reference to a new employee entering the workplace; it could also refer to an *existing* employee entering a new role, such as a staff member becoming a manager for the first time, or someone moving from the manufacturing department to the sales department. This definition also highlights that the organisational socialisation process involves not just the formal, job-related aspects such as your new tasks, assignments and projects, but also the informal, relationship-based aspects of connecting with a new culture and new colleagues. Both Feldman's and Van Maanen and Schein's definitions discuss a slightly different aspect of socialisation; we will therefore combine their definitions to obtain a fully rounded explanation of the process.

When new employees enter the workplace for the first time, organisational socialisation is often known as 'onboarding' in companies, and within many larger companies onboarding usually refers to a pre-defined programme of activities, meetings and interactions to help introduce the new recruit to the organisation (and often vice-versa). New employees might have seminars to get them up to speed with the latest projects in the company, have social events designed to allow more interpersonal introductions, and usually have a less focused, more slow-paced couple of weeks. Larger companies can spend a lot of time, energy and resources in introducing their new employees to the organisation; for an example, look at the description of Twitter's onboarding programme, called 'Yes-to-Desk', below.

> onboarding is the more modern, corporate definition of the process of socialising a new employee into an organisation.

Organisational socialisation will look different in different companies, industries and countries, due to the differences in organisational and national culture. However, by keeping in mind these definitions, we can track the process and aims of socialisation, no matter what the context.

BUILDING YOUR EMPLOYABILITY SKILLS

First Week at Work

You are a line manager responsible for a new employee beginning employment in your organisation. What do you think are the most important things they need to know in their first week?

THE PROCESS OF ORGANISATIONAL SOCIALISATION

We have already seen that organisational socialisation is described as a process. Let's now look at the stages within that process. Feldman (1976, 1981) proposed a classic model (shown in Figure 11.1) that breaks down the process of organisational socialisation into three distinct stages, shows the activities involved in each stage, and describes some outcomes of a successful socialisation process. His model was influenced by earlier work by theorists such as Porter *et al.*

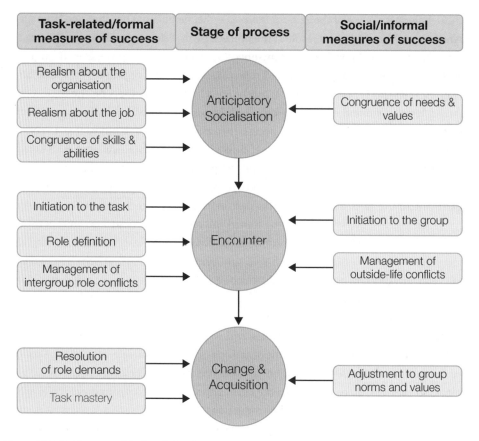

Task-related/formal measures of success	Stage of process	Social/informal measures of success
Realism about the organisation		
Realism about the job	Anticipatory Socialisation	Congruence of needs & values
Congruence of skills & abilities		
Initiation to the task		Initiation to the group
Role definition	Encounter	
Management of intergroup role conflicts		Management of outside-life conflicts
Resolution of role demands	Change & Acquisition	Adjustment to group norms and values
Task mastery		

Figure 11.1 Feldman model of socialisation

Source: Feldman (1981).

(1975) and Schein (1964, 1968). It's helpful to look at the process as a combination of formal, task and work-related issues, and informal, interpersonal and cultural factors – both of these types of factors are involved in making the outsider a 'participating and effective member'.

Each stage refers to a specific time in the new employee's relationship with their new organisation, from before even entering the workplace until they are fully settled in. Although they are presented as three distinct stages, in reality there may be some overlap across them. Feldman (1981) also discussed some key variables that indicate how well the stage is going; in other words, how successfully the individual is progressing through the socialisation process.

Anticipatory Socialisation how individuals prepare themselves to occupy a job within an organisation.

The first stage, Anticipatory Socialisation, refers to what one knows and learns about the organisation before entering it. Imagine you are about to graduate and are looking for potential jobs. Your first look at an organisation may be at a careers fair, where current employees will give you some information about applying for a job there, what type of graduates they want to apply, and their own experiences of working there. You would probably also look at the organisation's social media or website, particularly their careers page, where photos, videos and personal profiles will give you a sense of what it's like to work there, what the dress-code is, what the tone of the workplace is, and how people interact with each other. When you have an interview at an organisation, you will also consciously and subconsciously gather information about the organisation and its culture.

Hopefully, by the time you enter the organisation (and begin the next stage of the socialisation process, below), you have a good picture of what it is like to work there. Feldman (1976, 1981) identified various factors that indicate how well this stage has gone, which we can group under the headings of *realism* and *congruence*. Realism refers to how accurate your idea of what the organisation is like is – have you done your research on the organisation and what it's like to work there? This is known as *realism about the organisation*. Is the job what you expected, and are the duties and tasks involved what you thought they were? This is known as *realism about the job*. Conversely, has the organisation made available enough information to fully inform prospective employees? If someone isn't fully educated about the workplace, they may find upon entry that it is not what they expected, and the socialisation process may be more difficult or even impossible. Congruence in this context refers to how good a match you and the organisation are – does this look like somewhere you want to work? Do the organisational values, norms, and the work itself, address what you are looking for and want – is there *congruence of needs and values*? On the other hand, are you a right fit for the organisation in terms of your capabilities; that is, is there *congruence of skills and abilities* with your new role? While one could argue that the interview is supposed to clarify the latter question, the former question is up to the individual and their personal attitudes, goals and aspirations. Again, if there is a lack of congruence between the organisation and the individual, it may be more difficult or impossible to successfully socialise an employee, because there will be an inherent misfit between what the organisation thinks is important and what the new employee values.

> **realism** is the extent to which individuals gain a full and accurate picture of what life is really like in an organisation.

> **congruence** refers to the extent to which there is a match between the needs and skills of the person and the requirements of the job.

IMPACT OF TECHNOLOGY ON BEHAVIOUR

CREDIT: PHOTO BY PROXYCLICK VISITOR MANAGEMENT SYSTEM ON UNSPLASH

In the same way that companies advertise their products to certain demographics and markets, organisations also design their recruitment materials and platforms to attract certain preferred types of candidate, expertise and education. Have you ever looked at the careers webpage of an organisation? What was it like? If not, take a look now at the careers webpage or social media platform of a company that you know. What impression are they trying to communicate to you about the company? Does it look like a place you would like to work at? Why/why not? How do they communicate what it's like to work at their company? What type of employee do you think they are targeting with their choice and design of social media platform, website and recruitment material? Reflect on these questions with reference to Feldman's (1976) Anticipatory Socialisation stage of the organisational socialisation process. Technology has allowed organisations to more effectively communicate with potential employees about the type of organisational culture they have, and the type of person they are hoping to recruit.

The second stage, **Encounter** (called *Accommodation* in earlier work), occurs when you have actually become an employee within the organisation. You have not yet become a fully-fledged member of the organisation, but are perhaps not considered an organisation outsider either. In Feldman's terms, you are in the middle of the 'transformation'. At this stage of the process, you are learning what tasks you are to complete and how to do them; clarifying your own role and responsibilities within the broader organisation, establishing organisational and interpersonal relationships with your co-workers, subordinates and bosses; and working out how well you are doing in your new role. At this point in the process, you will be learning about the work-related tasks involved in your new job, but also figuring out the internal politics of the organisation; who is good friends with whom, who doesn't like whom, who the cliques are, etc. This is something that can't really be known before you enter the workplace, but is still an important part of learning to navigate a new organisation.

Feldman (1981) argues that there are five key variables that will help define how successful you are during this stage of the socialisation process: *Initiation to the task*, *Initiation to the group*, *Role definition*, *Management of outside-life conflicts*, and *Management of intergroup role conflicts*. **Initiation to the task** refers to how well you have learned how to do the work you're supposed to do in your new role, as well as how accepted you feel as a qualified member of the team. This might take a while as you're learning a new system, new ways of doing things and new work relationships, and you might feel a little out of your depth at first. Assuming that you have chosen the job that's right for you, however (in the Anticipatory Socialisation stage above), it shouldn't be long before you find your feet. **Initiation to the group** is the more informal counterpart to the last variable. This refers to how well you feel accepted by your new colleagues and that you've formed good interpersonal relationships with them. No matter how good you are at your work-related tasks, it would be hard to feel happy or successful at a company where you didn't get along with your colleagues, or felt that you had very different values from theirs. **Role definition** considers how clear you are about your new role, the associated tasks and responsibilities, the priorities and the resources involved. Ostensibly, your new workplace should clarify all of this for you, but there will probably be some things that you have to find out for yourself. **Management of outside-life conflicts** refers to how well you can achieve your preferred work–life balance. This correlates with the *realism* and *congruence* factors discussed at the anticipatory socialisation stage above – the more educated you are about the organisation, the job and its associated requirements, and the more congruent those are with your own needs and desires, the more likely it is that you will be able to manage any conflicts between your personal and work life. Lastly, an individual may be included in a number of groups as part of their role, and will therefore have several, possibly competing interests, demands and priorities to manage. **Management of intergroup role conflicts** refers to how successfully that conflict is addressed. If it is not managed successfully, the individual may find themselves pulled in many directions and unable to focus on one task at hand.

The third stage of the socialisation process, **Change and Acquisition**, once called *Role Management*, starts when the employee begins to show some proficiency in their new role and begins to adjust to the group and the organisation. They are completing their change from an 'organisational outsider' into a fully-fledged 'participating and effective member'. As a result of the information that they have sought out and been given, the new employee has begun to alter their behaviour somewhat to resolve any incongruence between their initial behaviour and the culturally ingrained, explicitly and implicitly desired behaviours of an organisational member. According to Feldman (1981), the three key measures of success at the Change and Acquisition stage are *task mastery*, *resolution of role demands*, and *adjustment to group norms and values*. **Task mastery** refers to how well one has learned how to do the tasks and duties associated with one's new role, as indicated by consistently good performance evaluations and one's own feeling of self-efficacy. **Resolution of role demands** refers to the conflicts identified in the Encounter stage, where the varying, competing demands from the employee's personal life and between different groups in the organisation are finally balanced. One's role is therefore more well defined and acceptable to the individual and relevant others. **Adjustment to group norms and values** concentrates on the informal, social aspect of the organisation, and is concerned with how well the new employee fits in with and is trusted by their work group and the organisation. If the socialisation process has gone successfully, the new employee has absorbed the group culture and helps to reproduce and communicate it themselves.

GOALS AND OUTCOMES OF ORGANISATIONAL SOCIALISATION

One key question concerning the organisational socialisation process arises when we consider the changing nature of careers. In the past, employees joined an organisation and generally stayed there for a much longer time than today. The US Bureau of Labor Statistics reported in 2018 that the average job tenure was just over four years. Hall (1996) argues that many employees now believe that moving organisation relatively quickly can help them gain competitive advantage in their careers, because they will be exposed to a variety of settings and be able to practise different skill sets. This raises the question: is investment in organisational socialisation really worth it, if the employee might be leaving in a few years? Why should employers engage in this process at all? Our questions can be answered by looking at an overview of the main aims and outcomes of a well-managed, effective organisational socialisation process, which can affect both the individual and the organisation.

BUILDING YOUR EMPLOYABILITY SKILLS

Learning from Others

You have joined a new company and have been there for six weeks on a graduate management programme. You notice that people leave at 4.30 pm on a Friday even though your contract says to work until 5 pm on a Friday. You are wondering what to do? Do you follow the others, or do you continue to stay until 5 pm?

INDIVIDUAL OUTCOMES

Feldman (1981) argues that socialisation leads to three main categories of outcomes – the *acquisition of appropriate role behaviours*, the *development of work skills and abilities*, and the *acquisition of group norms and values*. The **acquisition of appropriate role behaviours** refers to how quickly and well an employee works out what is really required of them in their role, how they should prioritise tasks, and other responsibilities that they have in relation to their work. One (perhaps extreme) example of an enforced role behaviour can be found in Apple. Apple employees, and the company itself, are famously secretive about their products, designs and processes – and this is a standard that is introduced at Day 1 for each employee. While even the exact onboarding process itself is Apple's secret, author Adam Lashinsky (2013) was able to pick up some details, and reports that one of the first people new employees will meet is the head of security. The security chief tells all new recruits that anyone knowingly or accidentally divulging company secrets will be fired immediately. Feldman (1981) also argued that a successful socialisation process would lead to the **development of work skills and abilities** essential to one's new role. More recent research (Bauer *et al.*, 2007) has looked at the relationship between organisational socialisation and performance, and found that a combination of the organisation's involvement and the individual's own information-seeking tendencies were positively related to performance, specifically because they helped clarify the employee's role, resulted in increased self-efficacy, and led to the employee being more accepted socially. Lastly, Feldman (1981) argued that a successful socialisation process would lead to the **acquisition of group norms and values**. Every organisation has its own norms and values, and within the organisation, every department and subgroup might differ in their own norms and values. When continually communicated by its visible figures and leaders, and repeated by staff members, the organisation's norms and core values become embedded. When a new employee starts at the organisation, therefore, socialisation can lead to the transmission of these norms and values, through both task-based and interpersonal factors. In addition to these more task-focused outcomes of socialisation, individual outcomes at the personal level have also been identified. Ashforth and Saks (1996) find that organisational socialisation has a number of positive effects on the individual employee; any ambiguity or conflict one might have concerning one's role is lessened, while work stress also decreases.

ETHICAL BEHAVIOUR IN THE WORKPLACE

CREDIT: PHOTO BY GOOD FACES ON UNSPLASH

Could organisational socialisation be experienced differently for new employees from marginalised groups, such as female, LGBTQ or minority ethnicity employees? Ostensibly, structured, formal parts of an organisational socialisation process can be similarly designed for all employees, but the more informal and interpersonal aspects could lead to varying degrees of success for certain employee groups. If the current organisational insiders seem to all be of a heterogeneous profile, this could send a negative message to minority newcomers, and could affect their adjustment to a new role. In addition, 'old boys networks', comprised of high status white men, often exclude women and ethnic minorities from social activities and interpersonal conversations (Kanter, 1977), job leads (McDonald, 2011), and other forms of social capital (McDonald and Day, 2010) that could help one's knowledge of and success within a new role. How would you, as a manager, ensure that newcomers from marginalised/minority groups are supported before and after joining an organisation?

ORGANISATIONAL OUTCOMES

As discussed above, Bauer *et al.* (2007) find that socialisation is positively related to individual performance. As well as being an individual-level outcome, we can see how this is also a positive outcome for the organisation, which benefits from increased productivity and performance from its staff. Another key aim of socialisation that is of core importance for the organisation is to ensure that employee turnover is minimal. Employee turnover is costly to an organisation, because they must use resources to search for, interview, hire and socialise new employees to replace the departing staff. Previous research has shown that ineffective socialisation is often cited as a reason for unwanted turnover (Bauer *et al.*, 1998), while multiple studies show that socialisation leads to more organisational commitment (Allen and Meyer, 1990; Ashforth and Saks, 1996; Baker, 1992; Baker III and Feldman, 1990).

> **employee turnover** is the replacement of employees who have left the organisation with new employees. A high turnover rate can be costly to an organisation.

As we have seen, there are multiple positive outcomes, for both the organisation and the new employee, associated with a successful socialisation process. Importantly, research by Taormina and Bauer (2000) suggests that, despite differences in national culture, the positive effects of socialisation can be found across countries, which has implications for multinational organisations operating in different parts of the world. We have also established that the social-isation process is a process that involves the organisation and the individual new employee. We will now look deeper at the roles that both the organisation and the individual play in the socialisation process.

THE ORGANISATION'S ROLE IN THE SOCIALISATION PROCESS

We have looked at the process of organisation socialisation and seen that it can be broadly divided into three main stages. However, within those stages is a lot of potential for creativity and variation, and the culture, size and type of organisation could have an effect too. For exam-ple, do you think socialisation would look different in a supermarket chain, compared with in an engineering company? One of the primary duties an organisation has in socialisation is to design and implement an appropriate, effective and relevant process.

Van Maanen and Schein (1979) proposed that there were a number of factors (which they referred to as 'tactics') that are involved when an organisation designs and conducts their socialisation process. The six tactics are shown in Figure 11.2. Note that each tactic exists on a spectrum, reflecting the complexity of the process. Thus, one part of the process might look different from another part, depending on the activities involved and the particular role, organisation or industry.

1 **Collective vs Individual**

This tactic relates simply to whether new employees are socialised into the organisation in groups or individually. For an example of collective socialisation, think about your first day at college – your class, or groups within a class, would probably have gone through some introductory activities together. Another example would be a graduate recruit-ment scheme, where a set of new graduates starts at a company at the same time. The socialisation events, such as talks, meetings and informal gatherings, would be offered to

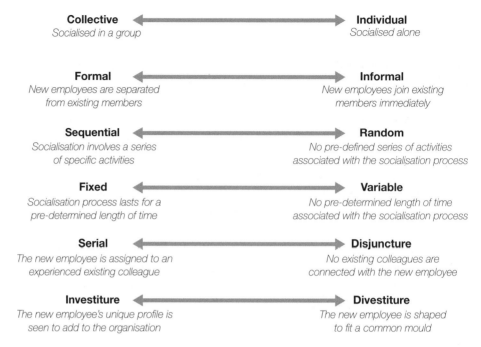

Figure 11.2 Socialisation tactics

Source: Adapted from Van Maanen and Schein (1979).

everyone in the group, and would most likely be somewhat similar for everyone. Individual socialisation takes place when one person enters the organisation and goes through the process on their own, and would most likely be unique and customised to the new employee and their particular role. We can presume that a collective socialisation process would probably take place only in larger companies, where the resources are in place both to hire a new group of employees at the same time and to offer them a group orientation. In contrast, individual socialisation could reasonably take place in both small and large companies, both when a new employee enters the organisation and when an existing employee enters a new department or a new role.

2   Formal vs Informal

A formal socialisation process is one where the new employee(s) is/are somewhat separated from other employees while they are being introduced to and learning about the organisation – for example, if a set of new employees were to attend presentations and do activities and projects that didn't include the existing organisational members. Here, the newcomers might specifically be referred to as the 'new recruits' or a similar term (for example, Google refers to new employees as 'Nooglers'). In contrast, an informal socialisation approach is when the new employees enter the organisation and join their new colleagues immediately, learning as they go along with minimal singling out. The new employees would be seen as a similar, if newer, part of the team to everyone else. Van Maanen and Schein (1979) argue that a formal process could be important where the new employee has to learn very exact ways of thinking and doing in the organisation, such as in the police force or in the medicine profession. However, a potential downside to this could be that the new employee's special and separate status could hinder their efforts to socialise on an interpersonal level with new colleagues during this time, which may have to be delayed until after the formal socialisation. On the other hand, an informal socialisation process would allow interpersonal relationships to be made immediately, but it's possible that the newcomer could start to replicate the 'bad habits' of the existing staff, which could be troublesome in a profession where exact standards are needed.

3 Sequential vs Random

In some companies, there are a series of steps involved in the socialisation process that new employees must go through before being considered a fully-fledged member of the organisation. Van Maanen and Schein (1979) refer to this as 'sequential socialisation', that is, a sequence of events and activities is involved. At the other side of the spectrum is random socialisation, where the steps involved in socialisation are not pre-defined in terms of order, scope or content. Take a look at the 2020/2021 sales graduate management programme for the supermarket chain Lidl, pictured in Figure 11.3, which is a good example of a sequential organisational socialisation process. Graduates wishing to pursue a career in management in Lidl must go through a number of steps before they can become managers. This programme of rotations exposes the graduates to various different functions within the business within the first year, and they then become trainee store managers in the second year. While new employees will learn about the task-related aspects of managing each function, and see the connections between the different parts of the company, the socialisation process will naturally also involve the interpersonal aspects.

While a sequential socialisation process might be useful to teach employees about the organisation in a logical order, a random process may be more helpful when the organisation needs an employee to start quickly, and flexibly get involved in key areas as and when they are needed. Ultimately, the size and scale of the company, plus the key tasks they are facing at the time of hiring, may determine how random or sequential their socialisation process is.

4 Fixed vs Variable

This tactic refers to whether the socialisation process has a particular timetable associated with it or not. In some organisations (e.g. Lidl's graduate programme shown in Figure 11.3), new employees have a certain, fixed amount of time within which they are socialised into the workplace. A variable socialisation process occurs when the length of time is not determined beforehand. Although seemingly simple, the length of time the process takes may be harder to determine than the others tactics we discuss here. As we have discussed above, although organisational socialisation is often centred on the task and job-related factors that a new employee must learn about, interpersonal, social and cultural factors are also involved. So, while a company's 'official' socialisation process might be fixed (i.e. specifically time-limited), the 'unofficial' socialisation may continue long after the end of the formalised process (Van Maanen and Schein, 1979). While a fixed socialisation process may be more useful from a planning and management perspective, a variable socialisation process can more flexibly adapt to the particular needs and abilities of the individual employee, with each moving at their own pace.

5 Serial vs Disjunctive

A serial socialisation process, in Van Maanen and Schein's (1979) terms, is one in which an experienced colleague acts as a form of role model to the new employee. These role

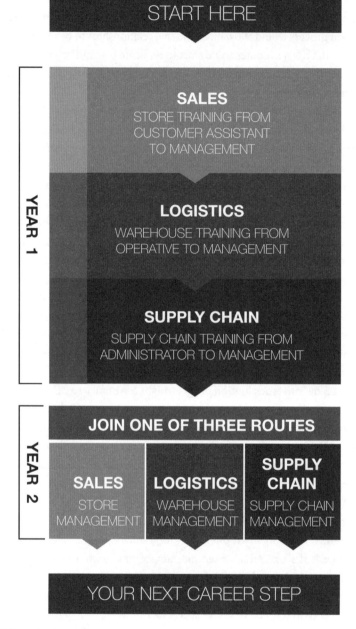

Figure 11.3 Lidl graduate programme

Source: Available at: https://careers.lidl.co.uk/statics/career-lidl-uk/ds_img/assets_382_x/RGMP%20Overview%20
382x310.jpg. *Used with permission.*

models are usually involved in the same area of work as the new recruit. Depending on the seniority of the colleague and the style and length of the formal relationship, this could be referred to as a buddy-system, a coaching session or a mentorship. The serial approach to socialisation can be seen in the police force, where new recruits are often partnered with experienced officers (Van Maanen and Schein, 1979).

A disjunctive socialisation process is one where there are no role models or experienced colleagues assigned to the new employee. A common feature of Apple's onboarding process requires new employees to set up their new computer and connect it to the organisation's network by themselves. While this might be seen as a test of IT-related knowledge, it also requires the new employee to begin engaging with the relevant people on the team and in the organisation, and in this way forces the individual to take a more active part in the socialisation process.

6   Investiture vs Divestiture

Some organisations are happy to accept the new employee as they are, and aim to make use of their personal characteristics, skills and attitudes. This is known as an investiture socialisation process, and is a common tactic among larger professional organisations that wish to capitalise on their recruits' varied backgrounds, traits and abilities. For example, companies like Deloitte and EY will consider taking in graduates with a degree in any discipline. Having a variable set of backgrounds on a team can counter common organisational problems such as groupthink, where people in a group attempt to achieve consensus and in doing so make poorer decisions (Janis, 1972).

Other organisations and professions take a divestiture approach to socialisation, with each requiring new employees to somewhat change their personal identities in order to fit into its own particular culture and procedures. In a divestiture approach, the organisation attempts to break the new employee's 'bad habits' (e.g. behaviour that was common in previous organisations but not desirable in the current one) (Ashforth, Harrison & Sluss, 2014). While this type of socialisation might seem somewhat harsh or unappealing, it may be useful in situations where a high degree of conformity and predictability is needed – such as in the military. However, having a divestiture approach may negatively impact upon efforts to diversify the workforce, leading to a homogenous group and/or homogenous thinking. Identity scholars Ashforth *et al.* (2014) discuss how organisations often use a type of *identity narrative* during the socialisation process. These are stories which are shared with newcomers to the organisation that relate to someone else in the organisation demonstrating the organisation's values and ideals – a sort of fable that is used to 'informally' share the organisation's culture ▶**See Chapter 12◀** but also to establish (either implicitly or explicitly) what is expected of its members. These narratives are designed to appeal to the newcomer because they offer a pathway towards personal growth (in one's career, self-esteem, identity) but are, of course, centred around the desired behaviours and goals of the organisation itself.

A critic might argue that divestiture is, at its worst, a sort of attack on the new employee's identity and their ways of thinking and doing – a method of those in power ▶**See Chapter 8◀** enforcing conformity among employees at the very beginning of their tenure in the organisation, when they are less able to resist it. Therefore a 'good' onboarding programme may be seen as such by those in power within the organisation, because it leads to desired employee outcomes, but may be resented by those who go through it, because it quashes individuality and creativity.

As we can see above, although organisational socialisation appears at first quite a linear, one-dimensional process, there are indeed multiple aspects that can lead to variation and customisation. An organisation has therefore quite a lot of elements to consider when designing an onboarding programme for new employees. The exact style that they take will depend on factors such as the size of the organisation, the number of new employees, the organisational culture and the type of job and level involved. The 'In Reality' feature discusses the design and outcomes of socialisation processes in different organisations, and how the process is not as clear cut as it seems at first.

IN REALITY

As discussed above, the average amount of time an employee stays with an organisation has decreased dramatically over the last few decades. Because the recruitment and training of new employees is costly, encouraging organisational commitment is an important aspect of the HR manager's and line manager's role. We also saw above that organisational socialisation is linked to organisational commitment (Allen and Meyer, 1990; Ashforth and Saks, 1996; Baker, 1992; Baker and Feldman, 1990); however, the exact mechanisms through which this relationship happens are relatively unknown. While one might intuitively think that a well-structured, comprehensive formal onboarding process might result in more well-adjusted and loyal employees, more recent research has examined the role played by the informal aspects of the organisational socialisation process (Filstad, 2011; Korte and Lin, 2013). Filstad (2011), researching newcomer socialisation within two large government organisations in Norway, found that the degree of formality and the timing of organisational socialisation activities had no effect on the newcomers' affective organisational commitment (or how emotionally attached an employee is to their organisation, leading to more commitment and desirable work behaviour). Instead, newcomers' higher affective organisational commitment was found to be significantly related to the *social* dimensions of the organisational socialisation process, such as the provision of role models or support from experienced colleagues. Similarly, Korte and Lin (2013), in a study of newly hired engineers in a manufacturing organisation, found that the quality of the relationships that the newcomers formed affected how well they fitted into their workgroup and the quality of their learning and performance on the job. A key message to take from this research is that, although a formalised organisational socialisation process may lead to positive task-related outcomes (as discussed by Feldman, 1976, 1981), the social relationships and interpersonal factors that an organisational newcomer is exposed to have just as important effects on their commitment to the organisation and their intentions to stay there or not. Although an HR department can carefully design a comprehensive formalised onboarding process, this research highlights that the cultural and social aspects of the organisation (which are a lot more difficult, or perhaps impossible, to design or control) make the difference for the long-term adjustment and success of new employees.

THE NEW EMPLOYEE'S ROLE IN THE SOCIALISATION PROCESS

Until this point, most of the focus of our discussion has been on the role of the organisation and its policies and procedures in welcoming and socialising a new employee. However, research also shows that the individuals themselves have a role to play in the process, and can affect

Table 11.1 Ashford and Black's (1996) proactive behaviours for new employees

Proactive Behaviour	Description
Information seeking	The individual looks for information that will help them know about the organisation and do their job better. There are multiple sources from which an individual can gather information; see 'Sources of Information' below.
Feedback seeking	The individual specifically asks for feedback on tasks, assignments and projects that they've completed, from colleagues, supervisors and managers. This allows them to adjust their behaviour accordingly in an effort to improve.
Positive framing	The new employee attempts to interpret an event or situation in a positive light, in order to increase their self-confidence and sense of self-efficacy.
Negotiation of job changes	One challenge that may arise in the early stages of one's job is the struggle to adapt one's job to suit one's needs and expectations. This proactive behaviour surrounds the negotiation of what tasks, responsibilities and procedures the new employee has, and how they must accomplish them.
Networking	The new employee engages in purposeful behaviours to form a positive working relationship with their colleagues, such as asking a colleague to lunch or dropping by at their desk.
Building relationship with boss	The new employee attempts to build a positive relationship with their boss and managers.
General socialising	The new employee attends functions and generally tries to be sociable with other members of the organisation.

Source: Ashford and Black (1996).

how successful it is (Bauer and Green, 1998). Namely, the more *proactive* an individual is, the more quickly and successfully the socialisation process will go (Ashford and Black, 1996; Bauer and Green, 1998). Proactive behaviour in this context refers to self-initiated behaviour that is focused on future results, and aims to make change through the employee taking control. In other words, the more active employees are in the socialisation process, the better they will adjust to the organisation and become effective members.

But what type of proactive behaviours will help an employee hit the ground running when they've just joined an organisation or started a new role? Two important authors on this topic, Ashford and Black (1996), identified seven such behaviours – information seeking, feedback seeking, networking, negotiation of job changes ▸**See Chapter 13◂**, positive framing, general socialising and building a relationship with their boss. Different combinations of these behaviours were found to be associated with increased job performance and job satisfaction ▸**See Chapter 4◂**. Table 11.1 gives an overview of these behaviours.

SOURCES OF INFORMATION

When an individual enters a new organisation or a different role, they do not simply receive all the necessary information from the organisation. As discussed above, scholars have identified the individual's own 'information-seeking behaviour' as a key factor in the success of the organisational socialisation process. In other words, the onus isn't only on the organisation to ensure a smooth transition for the employee! There are quite a number of places where an employee can find information relevant to their new role, job or project. For simplicity, Table 11.2 shows the three main levels where information can be found – from other individuals,

proactive behaviour is a self-initiated behaviour that is focused on future results and aims to make change through the employee taking control.

information-seeking behaviour is a proactive behaviour an individual engages in to find relevant information useful to the execution of their tasks and job.

Twitter's 'Yes To Desk' Onboarding Programme

We have looked at the theory behind organisational socialisation and how workplaces can ensure new employees transition well into their new job. Feldman's  IN THE NEWS model provides a step-by-step breakdown of the process. Now let's look at a real-life socialisation, or onboarding, programme, at Twitter. The company has 35 offices including their main headquarters in San Francisco and EMEA headquarters in Dublin. They have a highly commended, 75-point process of making sure that their newly hired employees hit the ground running, from the 'Yes' outcome of their interview to when they're first at their desk. Unlike many other companies, which start the onboarding process on the employee's first day, Twitter's programme starts before the employee begins their new role.

CREDIT: PHOTO BY MIKA KORHONEN ON UNSPLASH

The Culture

Twitter, like every company, partly transmits their culture through the style of their office. Theirs is an open-plan, casual and fun workspace, with foosball (table football) tables, video-game consoles, free food, and informal breakout areas. New hires therefore get a sense of the vibe the company is trying to convey before they've even begun work there. In addition, each new employee gets a 'swag-bag', with branded merchandise and a bottle of wine. Induction sessions often include introductions to the more informal parts of the company, such as inside-jokes, traditions and office superstitions.

The People

Joining a new company and learning the names and roles of dozens of new people can be anxiety-inducing, so Twitter intentionally links a new hire up with key managers and co-workers before they've even started work. In addition, new hires have lunch with their team in those first few weeks, so they don't have to worry about who to sit with, or whether they'll be sitting alone! Work desks are also arranged so the new employee will be sitting next to key people that they'll be working closely with on projects. Within the first week, senior managers within the company will host a happy-hour or breakfast with the new employees. The 'Yes to Desk' programme consists of intentional discussions and meetings not just with the usual recruitment and HR team, but also with managers, IT and Facilities.

The Role

Twitter has many employees covering a lot of different areas of expertise, from software engineers to recruiters to data-scientists and accountants. Learning and settling into this new system of roles can be complex and daunting, so before the new employee's first day, Twitter provides a set of documents that clarifies their place within the company, the role expectations and their new responsibilities. On their first day, the new employee will already have their new laptop set up with the tools they'll be using and a functioning e-mail address, and their tasks for the next 12 weeks, so there's less waiting around, ambiguity and anxiety. Over the first few weeks, there will be 30-minute presentations every Friday covering the corporate structure, current projects, and the type of tools the employees use internally.

Questions

1 What elements of Feldman's (1981) model of organisational socialisation can you see in Twitter's 'Yes to Desk' onboarding programme?
2 Look again at Van Maanen and Schein's (1979) tactics of organisational socialisation. How would you describe Twitter's approach in terms of these tactics?

Table 11.2 Where information can be found in an organisation

	Formal Information Sources	**Informal Information Sources**
Individual Level	Role Model/Mentor/Coach, Manager, Colleague	Interpersonal relationships, the 'grapevine'
Group Level	Group/team/ departmental meetings, projects	Group culture, social events
Organisation Level	Organisational programmes, memos, meetings	Organisational culture – norms, values and traditions

from the group, team or department, and from the organisation itself. The type of information ranges from more formal, official information, to more informal, unofficial information. Gathering information from a variety of sources, and ensuring that one is keeping abreast of the official details while still 'keeping an ear to the ground', will make the adjustment to a new organisation or new role much easier.

INDIVIDUAL-LEVEL INFORMATION SOURCES

As discussed above, the organisation may pair the new employee with an experienced co-worker, role model or mentor to act as a guide to the new role and/or organisation. Depending on the particular relationship and its tone, an experienced colleague can provide formal and informal information to help the new employee settle into their role. Formal information can help the new employee with their tasks and duties, while informal information allows the new employee to know about the organisational politics and social issues, such as who to avoid, who doesn't like whom, etc. The 'grapevine', used to describe the informal word-of-mouth rumour spreading among colleagues, is also a key source of information, with De Mare (1989) estimating that around 70% of all communication within organisations happens 'through the grapevine'.

grapevine is a metaphor used to describe the informal communication and gossip that occurs in an organisation. The metaphor was originally used to refer to the telegraph lines used in the American Civil War.

GROUP-LEVEL INFORMATION SOURCES

At the group level (e.g. a team or department), the new employees can access formal and informal information that is more local to their particular role or workspace. In formal terms, this might be procedures or practices particular to that department, or methods of communicating and working that the team prefers to use.

Informally, a group or department-level culture might exist, which can differentiate the group from others in the organisation. Other members of staff are an important source of information, and can informally transmit some aspects of the workplace culture that aren't communicated by the 'official' organisational introduction. Social events such as happy hours or lunches can be a valuable source of informal information for a new employee.

New employees who are socialised at the same time as other employees have an extra source of information to help them adjust – their fellow new recruits. At Google, a mailing list called 'Noogle Engineers Helping Engineering Nooglers' allows new engineers in the organisation to ask seemingly trivial or simple questions that they may feel embarrassed to ask a more experienced colleague (Johnson and Senges, 2009).

ORGANISATION-LEVEL INFORMATION SOURCES

At the organisation level, the most obvious source of information for new employees is from people like the HR manager or the recruitment team, who will communicate the role and its responsibilities, and the relevant policies and procedures. They will most likely be the assigned 'go-to' person for a new employee if they have questions. Other information that affects all members of the organisation is most likely to come from all-staff e-mails and memos, or all-staff meetings. Town-hall meetings, where the organisation's leaders give information and answer questions from staff members, are increasingly popular.

Of perhaps more importance to an organisation and its communication is the role of organisational culture ▶See Chapter 12◀. The values, norms and traditions that make up the organisation's culture will convey to new employees key information about the way in which the organisation likes to conduct business, how it views its employees, and what is seen as acceptable and unacceptable behaviour.

The OB in Practice feature gives you the chance to test out your knowledge on organisational socialisation, by designing a graduate programme of your own.

town-hall meetings are meetings involving many, if not all, employees in an organisation, which are usually relatively informal in nature, wherein a leader/leaders convey(s) information to employees and asks for feedback, questions and discussion; the expression originates in politics.

Designing a Graduate Programme

You are the Vice President of HR for Tech/Soc, a consulting company with offices based in London and Paris. While relatively small (700 employees), the company has begun to be seen as the 'friendly alternative' to the larger consulting firms, and for that reason attracts many SME clients across Europe and Asia.

OB IN PRACTICE

Since its inception as an early 2000s start-up, the organisation has had a very relaxed culture. The staff adopt a casual dress code, the organisational structure is relatively flat with little separation across departments, and communication is mostly friendly and informal. While both offices have a similar organisational culture, there are naturally some variations arising from the different geographical locations and the differences across national cultures. Turnover in the company is particularly low, which the senior executives put down to their careful selection methods.

Recently, the company has won a number of government contracts based around the integration of technology into civil engineering projects, and is thus entering a stage of rapid growth. To cater for these new projects, Tech/Soc is expanding the staff in both offices by implementing its first graduate scheme. They plan to hire 120 new graduates across a variety of functions (Technology, People, and Strategy). Although the new employees will be divided according to function and location, the President hopes that the friendly cross-communication that is characteristic of the company will remain in place. As VP of Human Resources, it is part of your job to design the graduate programme, and you are particularly tasked with

CREDIT: GETTY IMAGES

maintaining the organisational culture. You need to ensure that the graduate programme:

a Finds capable, skilled candidates who can become accustomed to the organisational culture and fit in well;

b Provides a running start for the new employees, to make sure that they quickly become integrated into the company and its projects;

c Provides both structural and interpersonal supports for the new employees;

d Considers improving the diversity ▶See Chapter 10◀ of new employees, and particularly how to support those from different cultures as they adapt to working in a new country.

The President, also a co-founder, has seen the evolution of the company from a couple of employees to the hundreds it has today, and is worried that the structured graduate programme may risk disrupting the previous organic growth and casual culture. In short, she doesn't want Tech/Soc to become like its overly-corporate, stuffy competitors, and lose its unique, friendly approach and image.

Questions

1 How will you ensure that the company finds the right type of candidate for the programme, and how will you convey the company's particular organisational culture, both before, during and after the recruitment and selection stage?

2 What behaviours would you look for in a candidate that would tell you they'll be proactive in learning the ropes in their first few weeks as an employee?

3 How will you design the graduate programme to meet the aims discussed, and what will a new employee's first few weeks at Tech/Soc look like? Refer to Van Maanen and Schein's (1979) tactics framework and your own experiences, preferences and knowledge.

4 How will you communicate information to new employees?

5 How will you measure whether the socialisation part of the graduate programme has been

SPOTLIGHT ON SKILLS

1 What does your organisation's process of onboarding new employees look like?

2 What are the important things that an employee should know and do in their first few weeks at an organisation?

To help you answer these questions, visit bloomsbury.pub/organisational-behaviour to watch the video of Lavinia Duggan from VHI talking about employee socialisation.

MANAGERIAL TAKEAWAYS

This chapter has defined and discussed the process of organisational socialisation, and explored the role of the organisation and the role of the individual. A successful socialisation process will have benefits for the individual, including better engagement with their work and personal well-being, and for the organisation, such as less employee turnover and a more productive workforce. There are a number of proactive behaviours that can help the individual in adjusting to their new role and workplace, and the organisation can tailor their socialisation process specifically to the type of role, the particular culture, and the industry they're in. Managers have a key role to play in organisational socialisation, as the person who will often provide necessary information, transmit the organisational culture and be involved in structuring and managing the process. When setting up an organisational socialisation process, they must reflect on the outcomes they want for the new employee and the organisation, and adjust the process accordingly. They must also ensure that the process is appropriate for the industry and fits the tone of the company's culture, and perhaps try to find out what their competitors are doing!

CHAPTER REVIEW QUESTIONS

1   Outline the concept of organisational socialisation.
2   Describe the three stages of the organisational socialisation process identified by Feldman (1976).
3   What are the overall aims of organisational socialisation?
4   When are the potential consequences for the individual and the organisation if the organisational socialisation process does not go well?
5   What seven proactive behaviours did Ashford and Black (1996) argue were associated with increased job performance and satisfaction?
6   From where can an individual seek information when they first enter a workplace? Discuss with reference to the organisational levels.
7   What are the differences between formal and informal information?
8   Discuss how the organisational socialisation process can differ across companies, using Van Maanen and Schein's (1979) tactics framework as a guide.

FURTHER READING

Allen, N.J. and Meyer, J.P. (1990) Organizational socialization tactics: A longitudinal analysis of links to newcomers' commitment and role orientation. *Academy of Management Journal*, 33, 847–858.

Ashford, S.J. and Black, T.S. (1996) Proactivity during organizational entry: The role of desire for control. *Journal of Applied Psychology*, 81(2), 199–214.

Feldman, D.C. (1981) The multiple socialization of organization members. *Academy of Management Review*, 6(2), 309–318.

Van Maanen, J. and Schein, E.H. (1979) Towards a theory of organisational socialisation. In B.M. Staw (ed.) *Research in Organisational Behaviour*, vol. 1. Greenwich, CT: JAI Press, pp. 209–264.

 USEFUL WEBSITES

https://www.cipd.ie/news-resources/practical-guidance/factsheets/induction

The CIPD website is a great source of information on all areas related to the management of people at work. This link examines the induction process and its purpose.

https://resources.workable.com/remote-employees-onboarding-checklist#:~:text=How%20 to%20onboard%20remote%20employees%201%20Send%20new,scan%20and%20email%20 all%20...%20More%20items...

Workable is an organisation that helps companies find and hire the right people. They have some useful information on how to onboard employees remotely.

https://www.shrm.org/resourcesandtools/hr-topics/talent-acquisition/pages/new-employee-onboarding-guide.aspx

SHRM is an excellent website for all those involved in HR. They have a really useful section on how to onboard new employees.

Online Resources

Visit **bloomsbury.pub/organisational-behaviour** to access additional materials to support teaching and learning.

12 ORGANISATIONAL CULTURE

Caroline Murphy and Jean McCarthy

LEARNING OUTCOMES

BY THE END OF THIS CHAPTER YOU SHOULD BE ABLE TO:

- Understand the concept of organisational culture and explain the nature of culture within an organisational context.
- Identify and discuss both the visible and invisible elements of organisational culture.
- Understand how organisational culture is formed, transmitted, reinforced and changed by

management, groups and individuals.

- Outline the linkage between organisational culture and organisational type.
- Demonstrate the benefits and drawbacks of strong organisational cultures.
- Describe the interplay between organisational culture and work performance.

CREDIT: GETTY IMAGES

THIS CHAPTER DISCUSSES...

INTRODUCTION

Culture is one of the first things we notice about organisations, perhaps without even realising it. When you walk into a department store, what do you notice? When you visit your local library, gym or coffee shop, what do you see? What does the environment look like? Is it colourful, comfortable, friendly or otherwise? How are people dressed? Is the atmosphere formal or informal? What kinds of behaviour do you observe? What kind of behaviour is expected of you? What signs or signals do you receive to tell you to behave in this way? Think of an organisation that you visited recently, and answer these questions. Your answers will highlight aspects of this organisation's culture. Just as when you visit a different country you notice and observe aspects of the national culture, so too do you notice and observe aspects of organisational culture when you visit an organisation.

Culture is part of everyday life, evident in the people we meet and the places we go; it can be viewed as a pattern of learned assumptions about our thoughts, behaviour and actions, which are shared and transmitted among individuals in society. Just as cultures vary across different countries, organisational cultures vary across different organisations. Cultural processes underlie much of what happens in modern organisations, prescribing some forms of behaviour while discouraging others. The values, beliefs, and norms adopted by members of an organisation have an impact on the behaviour of individuals and groups at work. An organisation's culture, therefore, has a significant impact on those working in the organisation, as well as on those who interact with the organisation, such as customers, clients, suppliers and other stakeholders.

values and beliefs can be defined as basic convictions or ideals about desirable behaviour and outcomes.

This chapter explores the ways in which organisational culture is formed and transmitted, and its impact on organisational performance. It also addresses how an organisation might go about changing its culture.

IN REALITY

Organisational culture is considered one of the most difficult things for an organisation to change since it takes a long time to develop (as we will explore later in this chapter). However, from time to time some organisations will go to great lengths to change aspects of their culture. One such case is ANZ Bank, the fourth largest bank in Australia. Financial incentives and bonus pay have become almost synonymous with working in the banking and financial services sector. However, following the global financial crisis of 2008, many countries took steps to increase regulation within the financial sector, and much more scrutiny was paid to how organisations reward and incentivise their employees. For example, the link between bonuses and high-pressure sales tactics was identified by the UK's Financial Conduct Authority, which fined Lloyds Banking Group £28 million for failing to control sales incentive schemes. Internationally, this has led to more organisations taking steps to review their own processes. In 2019, ANZ bank announced that it was abolishing individual performance bonuses for most employees in response to concerns the payments incentivise misconduct and lead to disservice for customers. The move was described in the *Financial Times* as a 'cultural shift in an industry in which banks typically rely on bonus payments linked to the performance of individuals or the business unit they work in to motivate and retain key staff'.

Source

https://www.ft.com/content/c2c262b8-b7e9-11e9-8a88-aa6628ac896c

WHAT IS ORGANISATIONAL CULTURE?

The concept of 'culture' is difficult to define. It is derived from the field of anthropology (the study of humans), and broadly represents the transmission of the beliefs and behaviours of one group, or generation, to another. From an anthropological perspective, culture is seen as something which individuals are either consciously aware of, or which exists without their recognition, but that impacts on their behaviour and actions regardless. When we look to the concept of 'culture' from an organisational perspective, we define organisational culture as the basic pattern of shared assumptions, values, beliefs and practices that govern behaviour in an organisation; these assumptions, values, beliefs and practices are transmitted (and sometimes adapted) from one generation of employees to the next, and observed by all new organisational members. The notion of culture in organisations is derived from both Durkheim's and Weber's interpretations of the anthropological concept of culture, applied to organisations. They viewed organisations as

organisational culture is the basic pattern of shared assumptions, values, beliefs and practices that govern behaviour in an organisation.

entities characterised by a particular system of collective values, beliefs and symbols which are transmitted throughout the organisation, and which govern the behaviour of those within the organisation. The term 'organisational culture' (also termed 'organisation culture' and 'corporate culture') became popular in the 1980s, when a number of managerial, practitioner-orientated books were published on the topic. What followed was a burgeoning interest among academics in the topic of organisational culture as a way of understanding and explaining collective behaviour in organisations, as well as a tool for examining the ways in which organisations operated differently, and were distinct from one another. Perhaps the most familiar writer on the topic is psychologist and former Massachusetts Institute of Technology professor, Edgar Schein. Schein (1985) defined organisational culture as a set of beliefs, values and assumptions that are shared by members of an organisation. Smircich (1983) introduced the idea of organisational cultural as a 'root metaphor', in other words the core idea that culture is something an organisation 'is', as opposed to being something an organisation 'has'. Core to the idea of thinking about organisational culture as a 'root metaphor' is the belief that patterns of logic and ways of thinking are shared among organisation members. This in many ways is reflected in the way that Deal and Kennedy (1982) define culture. A common definition still utilised by many practitioners today, simply, 'the way we do things around here' (Deal and Kennedy, 1982, p. 4). Table 12.1, presents the various ways in which culture has been defined through the years.

Table 12.1 Defining culture through the years

'a set of beliefs, values, and assumptions that are shared by members of an organisation'. Schein (1985)
'the way we do things around here'. Deal and Kennedy (1982, p. 4)
'[Culture] is the collective programming of the mind which distinguishes the members of one group or category of people from another.' Hofstede (1994, p. 5)
'... the set of attitudes, values, beliefs, and behaviors shared by a group of people, but different for each individual, communicated from one generation to the next'. Matsumoto (1996, p. 16)
'Although there are a variety of meanings and connotations about organizational culture (Ostroff, Kinicki, & Tamkins, 2003), researchers conceptualize organizational culture as being shared among members (Glisson & James, 2002), existing at multiple levels (e.g., group and organizational levels; Detert, Schroeder, & Mauriel, 2000), influencing employees' attitudes and behaviors (Smircich, 1983), and consisting of collective values, beliefs, and assumptions (Schein, 2004).' Hartnell *et al.* (2011, p. 657)

IMPACT OF TECHNOLOGY ON BEHAVIOUR

For many organisations, issues of organisational culture and diversity are interlinked. This is particularly pertinent in the technology sector where public scrutiny has placed pressure on many organisations to diversify their workforce, which have predominantly been white, Asian and male, particularly at senior levels (Marcus, 2015). One of the first things senior management need to do to address this is to assess their culture, including looking at the potential that discrimination in pay and hiring practices exists in the organisations. Technology and advanced analytics allow an organisation to do this in multiple ways. For example, through analysing performance review data to determine if gender was a factor in the feedback or award provided to employees, conducting pulse surveys with employees to determine satisfaction with organisational practices, and in ensuring that recruitment and selection processes are operating effectively through a review of the applicant tracking systems. However, it should be noted that technology is not a golden bullet to resolve cultural or diversity issues in organisations. It has been suggested that bias can be counteracted in recruitment and promotion processes through the use of automated decision-making. However, it has also been shown that these software programs can in fact have built-in bias from the design phase. For example, Amazon found that a piece of software it used produced biased results by using word analysis based on gender, even where the creators had no deliberate intention of it doing so (Dastin, 2018). If technology results in errors that affect employees, or the integrity of the organisation, it's vital that senior management adopt the appropriate behaviour to address it, for example by committing to a corrective action plan.

Sources

Dastin, J. (2018) Amazon scraps secret AI recruiting tool that showed bias against women. Available at: https://www.reuters.com/article/us-amazon-com-jobs-automation-insight/amazon-scraps-secret-ai-recruiting-tool-that-showed-bias-against-women-idUSKCN1MK08G? (accessed 18 January 2021).

Marcus, B. (2015) The lack of diversity in tech is a cultural issue. Available at: https://www.forbes.com/sites/bonniemarcus/2015/08/12/the-lack-of-diversity-in-tech-is-a-cultural-issue/?sh=3c53bdb579a2

ORGANISATIONAL CULTURE AND ORGANISATIONAL CLIMATE: DIFFERENT OR THE SAME?

The terms 'organisational culture' and 'organisational climate' have come to be used interchangeably by some; however, subtle differences exist between the two. Interpersonal relationships between employees and between employees and managers are core to the development of an organisation's climate. Given the impact of interpersonal relations on climate it is prone to more variability across the organisation, with climate varying between different subsidiaries, departments or units; climate is also therefore viewed more subjectively by employees. Both culture and climate affect employee behaviour at work through their impact on the context, environment and social interactions in the workplace. Organisational culture envelopes the ethos, values and behavioural norms of the organisation, which often take years of tradition to cultivate and refine and are therefore considered to be very difficult to change in a short period of time. Organisational climate, however, is viewed as more malleable and immediate in terms

organisational climate relates to 'how it feels' to work in the organisation, while organisational culture refers to 'the way' in which tasks are completed.

of its impact on employees since it is defined by current situations, performance and group interactions. Since organisational climate has a more immediate impact on employees and is something which can be adjusted more easily than organisational culture, an understanding of employees' perceptions of their own organisational climate is a valuable tool for organisational leaders and managers. An analysis of employee perceptions of their work setting through, for example, a survey or focus group, is referred to as a 'climate study'.

Just as culture has an impact on employees and organisational performance so too does climate. A healthy organisational climate, where support, cooperation and democratic decision-making are strong, contributes towards greater work effectiveness. In contrast, stressful organisational climates are characterised by limited participation in decisions, use of punishments, conflict avoidance and non-supportive group and leader relations (Rousseau, 2011).

A variety of dimensions have been found to impact on employees' perceptions of organisational climate; these include:

- Support – the perception of the degree to which superiors in the organisation value the employees' contribution and care about their well-being.
- Fairness – the perception of the degree to which organisational policies are non-arbitrary and are operated on a fair and equitable basis.
- Autonomy – the perception of the degree to which individuals can assume control over their work.
- Recognition – the perception of the degree to which employees' contributions to the organisation are acknowledged.
- Trust – the perception of the degree to which the organisation communicates with integrity with its employees and takes decisions in the best interests of all.

SCHEIN'S MODEL OF CULTURE

In 1985, Schein (1985, p. 14) wrote that 'Organisation culture is the pattern of basic assumptions which a group has invented, discovered and developed in learning to cope with its problems of external adaption and integration, which have worked well enough to be considered valid, and therefore to be taught to new members as the correct way to perceive, think and feel in relation to problems ... culture is not the overt behaviour or visible artefacts that one might observe if one were to visit the company. It is not even the philosophy or value system which the founder may articulate or write down in various "charters". Rather it is the assumptions which lie behind the values and which determine the behaviour patterns and the visible artefacts such as architecture, office lay out, dress codes and so on.'

As such, Schein proposed that there are three 'layers' or 'levels' of organisational culture: first, there is the visible layer, what he termed 'surface manifestations'; second, there are 'organisation values and beliefs', located beneath the surface, and although this level is not visible, individuals in the organisation can be made aware of it; third, there are the 'basic assumptions' which underpin both the first and second layers, which are invisible, but are what Schein sees as true organisational culture. This model is explicated in Figure 12.1.

Some have likened Schein's model to an apple. The first layer, the surface level manifestations, is viewed as the skin of an apple, which you can see. The second layer, the organisation values and beliefs, is viewed as the pulp – visible once the skin has been peeled away. The final layer, the basic assumptions, are viewed as the core of the apple, which holds the apple

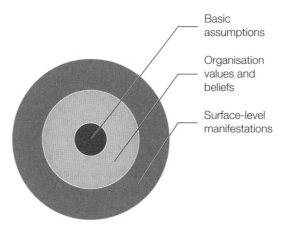

Basic
assumptions

Organisation
values and
beliefs

Surface-level
manifestations

Figure 12.1 Schein's model of organisational culture

Source: Schein (1985).

together, but needs to be deeply rooted out in order to be observed. Another way people have attempted to explain Schein's model is to use an iceberg as a metaphor. The tip of the iceberg (the visible part) represents the surface level manifestations of culture while the organisational values and beliefs, and the basic assumptions, lie beneath the water and are large and deep.

◀ETHICAL▶ BEHAVIOUR IN THE WORKPLACE

The B Corp is a completely new 'for-profit' legal entity,
which explicitly works to balance profit maximisation with social and environmental mission. The B Corp certification legally requires organisations to evaluate and enhance their outcomes for employees, community and the environment, and to adhere to higher than typical standards of purpose and transparency. The significance of the B Corp is that it institutionalises the first structural, legal and moral alternative to the primacy of shareholder value – and represents a radical shift away from capitalist organisational culture.

Patagonia, the outdoor and adventure-wear brand, is one such certified B Corp. Their mission is to strive to make the best product, cause no unnecessary harm (make products with the least impact possible), and inspire and implement solutions to the environmental crisis. Patagonia belongs to both the Sustainable Apparel Coalition and 1% For The Planet, and went as far as discouraging customers from purchasing too many of their products with their 'Don't buy this jacket' campaign: https://eu.patagonia.com/gb/en/stories/dont-buy-this-jacket-black-friday-and-the-new-york-times/story-18615.html.

What arguments do you think the CEO of Patagonia may have put forward to convince shareholders on the utility of this particular campaign? Visit https://bcorporation.net/ to help you answer.

LAYER 1: SURFACE LEVEL MANIFESTATIONS

Surface level manifestations in Schein's model are the visible elements of an organisation's culture. Schein does not view these elements as organisational culture itself; rather, he sees these elements as manifestations of the culture. These include:

1 **Artefacts:** These are physical, tangible manifestations of an organisation's culture such as furniture, appliances, tools, and clothing. Some examples include McDonald's 'Ronald McDonald' statues and the new uniforms provided to staff at Zara, a large European clothing retailer, every season, which display their new trends.

2 **Symbols:** These are visuals that represent the organisation, usually in the form of company logos. Some examples include Nike's swoosh, McDonald's golden arches and Apple's bitten apple. Symbols may be used to convey a message about the company, for example, the FedEx logo contains an arrow between the 'e' and the 'x' to represent precision, while NBC's logo displays a peacock with six feathers to represent the six divisions of the organisation.

3 **Norms:** Norms are expected behaviours that are demonstrated by members of the organisation. For example, employees greeting each other on arrival at the office in the morning, employees having lunch together, and the style of dress adopted by organisational members.

4 **Ceremonials and Rituals:** Activities that express and reinforce the values and assumptions of an organisation's culture. Examples would be the concept of 'casual Fridays', where some organisations allow employees to dress more informally on Fridays – this often reflects an organisation which values creativity, autonomy and flexibility; annual award ceremonies, which reflect the value an organisation places on hard work and good performance; family days reinforce an organisation's belief in work–life balance; and charity events instil the importance of corporate social responsibility.

5 **Language:** This can refer to e-jargon or more technical vocabulary which is used to express and reinforce an organisation's culture. For example, McDonald's staff are known as 'crew', not employees, reflecting the value placed by the organisation on teamwork, and Google's staff are known as 'googlers', to instil a sense of identity with the organisation and to reflect what the organisation does.

6 **Mottos and Slogans:** These are phrases used in organisations that manifest an organisation's culture. For example, McDonald's 'I'm loving it', Nike's 'Just do it' and Pepsi Max's 'Live life to the max'.

7 **Stories:** Stories are narratives which can contain elements of both truth and fiction, and are based on real-life events that often have shaped the organisation, or focus on decisions made by individuals which helped to steer the success of the organisation (often referred to as 'heroes'). For example, there is the now famous story about the founders of Snapchat (a popular photo messaging app) who turned down an offer of $3 billion from Facebook to buy the company, so that they could retain creative control aligned with their vision. Obviously, Snapchat founders value commitment to their ideals.

8 **Physical Layout:** This is the way in which an organisation chooses to organise its office space, floor space or store space and is another manifestation of its culture. For example, in every Subway food outlet the ordering station starts with choosing a bread, then a meat, then salads and sauce, before finally reaching the cash register – this is a surface level manifestation of the culture aligned with Subway's basic assumptions about how they make their product.

LAYER 2: ORGANISATION VALUES AND BELIEFS

Schein believes that the above-mentioned surface level manifestations are underpinned by the organisation's values and beliefs, and while values and beliefs are intangible, and invisible, organisational members can be made aware of them. These values and beliefs usually hold meaning to the founders or senior management, and are typically based on moral principles (Huczynski and Buchanan, 2001). Just like surface level manifestations, Schein does not believe the organisation's values and beliefs are organisational culture itself, rather they are manifestations which can be articulated and transmitted throughout the organisation. They are often articulated in an organisation's mission statement, or values statement, and can be incorporated into employee handbooks, company policies and procedures, as well as employee induction programmes and other forms of organisational training and development. For example, Accenture, an international consultancy firm who, in 2013, were ranked among the top 50 companies in the world for valuing diversity, include the following statement in their employee handbook: 'inclusion and diversity are fundamental to our culture and core values, fostering an innovative, collaborative and high energy work environment. Having a diverse workforce of people with different capabilities, cultures, and experiences enables Accenture to compete effectively in the global marketplace' (Accenture, 2013).

BUILDING YOUR EMPLOYABILITY SKILLS

Measuring Culture in Organisations

Every educational institution, college or university has its own unique culture. Think about the culture where you study. Complete the following template to assess the culture in this institution:

Alone, or in groups, list the surface level manifestations of culture, the values and beliefs, and the basic assumptions present in your institution/organisation.

1 Surface level manifestations of culture (e.g. artefacts, stories, mottos, physical layout, etc.)	2 Values and beliefs (e.g. check out the mission statement and the strategy statement of your institution, what values and beliefs are contained here?)	3 Basic assumptions (taken for granted understandings about behaviour)

This exercise has been used to successfully measure culture in many organisations (Schein, 1990).

LAYER 3: BASIC ASSUMPTIONS

In Schein's view, true organisational culture lies within the basic assumptions that individuals hold about the organisation and how it should function. Huczynski and Buchanan (2001, p. 633) describe basic assumptions as 'invisible, preconscious and "taken for granted" under-standings held by individuals with respect to aspects of human behaviour, and the nature of reality'. Indeed, the strength of an organisation's culture is based on how homogenous the basic assumptions of all organisational members are. For example, in a hospital setting, the overall objective of the organisation is to provide high quality patient care, therefore if the basic assumptions and behaviour of all healthcare staff match this belief, then the organisational culture can be said to be strong.

HOW IS ORGANISATIONAL CULTURE FORMED?

Now that we know what organisational culture is, we move on to explain how it comes to be. The formation of an organisation's culture begins with its founders. The personal assumptions, beliefs and values of the organisational founder(s) shape the development of organisational culture. As an organisation grows in size, these assumptions, values and beliefs are passed on to every new employee. This process may be conscious or unconscious. Founders and senior level management may consciously set out to 'design' an organisation's culture, or it may form organically as a response to the business environment. Some organisations train their employ-ees on 'the way we do things around here', draw up extensive mission and value statements, and pay particular attention to the surface level manifestations of the espoused basic assumptions held by senior level management. Later in this chapter, we will consider how different types of organisational culture can exist, and how they can vary from each other.

SOCIALISATION

We have just discussed how organisational culture is formed. Socialisation is the process through which organisational culture is reinforced among employees. Socialisation is a term used to 'describe the process in which an individual acquires the attitudes, behaviors and knowledge needed to successfully participate as an organizational member' (Wesson, 2005, p. 1018). Induction and socialisation are also typically referred to as assimilation, transition, orien-tation, alignment, organisational entry, integration and onboarding. It has also been suggested by Schneider and Rentsch (1988) that a socialisation process can be considered effective when newcomers understand and accept the organisation's key values, goals and practices. Ashkanasy *et al.* (2000) suggest that if socialisation is implemented correctly within an organisation it can ensure that both the organisation's and the newcomer's expectations are met. Van Maanen and Schein's (1979) work on socialisation theorised about the tactics that organisations employ to socialise employees, and defined them as ways in which the experiences of individuals in transition from one role to another are structured for them by the organisation.

According to Feldman (1976), three phases occur during socialisation: the anticipatory phase; the entry/encounter phase; and the change/metamorphosis phase. At the anticipatory stage the organisation should have created a realistic set of expectations for the individual before they take up a role there. This can be achieved through, for example, a comprehensive job description in recruitment and a realistic job preview in selection. The individual, on accepting the position, then enters the encounter phase, which really represents their initial induction period, the formal process of placing an individual in a new role. The final stage of change/metamorphosis focuses on the ability of the new employee to master tasks, resolve problems and 'fit in' with the organisational culture as well as sustain working relationships.

When it comes to filling a vacant position, many organisations will look at their internal candidates first. According to Werner and DeSimone (2006) the existing employee may have some advantages over new external hires. These include:

- Accurate expectations of the organisation, its culture, staff and reward systems.
- An existing knowledge-base of products/services that the organisation provides, knowledge of internal systems, and even minor items such as locations and directions.
- Relationships with others in the company that can be built on to form internal synergies.

TYPES OF ORGANISATIONAL CULTURE

As stated earlier, culture varies from one organisation to another. In some organisations, the culture has a significant influence on the manner in which employees complete their tasks; in other organisations, the impact of culture is less obviously felt. A strong organisational culture is viewed as one in which widespread agreement with respect to the core elements of the culture exists, making it possible for culture to exert major influences on the way people behave (Greenberg, 2011, p. 514). In a strong culture, members exhibit greater levels of commitment to the core values of the organisation, which in turn impacts

strong culture means one in which the company values are widely held and felt by all members of the organisation.

Table 12.2 Characteristics of strong and weak organisational cultures

Strong Culture	Weak Culture
A clear philosophy with regard to how the business is operated.	No clear philosophy exists to guide how the business should operate.
Emphasis on the communication of core values and beliefs of the organisation.	Core values are not clearly defined or well communicated.
The existence of statements, symbols and traditions which explicitly describe the values of the organisation.	Few if any indicators of the values and traditions of the organisation.
A shared sense of values and norms of behaviour exists among members.	Only limited or no evidence of alignment between the way things are done and the espoused values of the organisation.
Attention is paid to the importance of maintaining organisational culture when recruiting new employees, for example, selection of new members involves screening to ensure they fit with the culture.	No efforts are made to retain organisational culture and there is a greater need for procedures and policies in order to achieve desired results.

Source: Based on information in Greenberg (2011).

on everyday behaviour. In the long term this has the effect of reducing employee turnover through building cohesiveness and loyalty (Robbins and Judge, 2010, p. 256). In contrast, a weak organisational culture is defined as one in which there is limited agreement with respect to the core elements of the organisation's culture, and where the culture as a whole has little impact on the way people behave (Greenberg, 2011, p. 514). Maintaining a strong organisational culture becomes increasingly difficult as organisations grow and expand. This is mainly due to the diffusion of culture across larger organisations with greater numbers of employees. A further issue in larger organisations is that the leadership and values of the original founder are less widely felt by employees, who are in daily contact with management teams rather than the person who initiated the culture and ethos ▶See Chapter 6◀. Indeed, some organisations, for example Walmart, have taken steps to ensure that the values and ethos of the original founder, Sam Walton, continue to be understood by employees today by instilling 'the Walmart way' of doing business (you can read find about this in the Further Reading section at the end of this chapter).

weak organisational culture means one in which the values of the company are not widely held by members of the organisation.

SUBCULTURES

subcultures are those which hold the core assumptions of the dominant culture, as well as supplementary assumptions unique to members of that particular section of the organisation.

In addition to an overarching organisational culture, a number of subcultures can also exist, beyond that system of shared meaning held by all organisational members. Subcultures tend to develop in different sections of the organisation, for example, different departments or geographic locations, and reflect common issues faced by members of those sections. As discussed earlier, the larger an organisation grows, the more diffused the culture becomes and this typically results in more subcultures. Within a large organisation that values promotion based on performance, an example of a subculture would be a department where a manager promotes members of his team based on seniority rather than performance, and this is accepted as the norm is this department.

What's Really at the Core of Apple?

Apple Inc. is an American multinational corporation which designs, develops and sells computer software, personal computers, and consumer electronic goods all over the world. It is widely recognised as one of the most successful organisations of the 21st century, with *Forbes Magazine* naming it the world's 'Most Admired Company' every year from 2008 to 2014. Since its beginnings in 1976, Apple has credited its success with its focus on creating a culture of innovation within

 **OB IN THE NEWS**

the company. On their official website, Apple state that '*we expect creative thinking and solutions from everyone here, no matter what their responsibilities are. Innovation takes many forms, and our people seem to find new ones every day. Ask anyone here. It's hard work. It means forever asking, "Why is it this way?" and "How can it be better?" It means rethinking every customer experience until the clutter has fallen away – until all that remains is what's essential, useful, and beautiful.*' Indeed, Apple's culture of innovation has

been described as 'as distinct as its products are ground-breaking' (Business Insider, 2011). Speaking at a Goldman Sachs Conference in 2013, Tim Cook, current CEO of Apple, stated that Apple's culture of innovation has 'never been stronger. Innovation is so deeply embedded in Apple's culture … There's that word "limit". We don't have that in Apple's vocabulary … The boldness, ambition, belief there aren't limits, a desire to make the very best products in the world. It's the strongest ever. It's in the DNA of the company.'

But what is it really like inside the apple? Here's what some former employees had to say:

Apple is a pretty divided mix of typical corporate red tape and politics mixed in with start-up level urgency when the direction comes from Steve [former CEO, Steve Jobs]. If you have a project that Steve is not involved in, it will take months of meetings to move things forward. If Steve wants it done, it's done faster than anyone thinks is humanly possible. The best way to get any cross-departmental work done was to say it's for Steve and you'd probably have it the same day.

CREDIT: PHOTO BY JASON LEUNG ON UNSPLASH

Paranoid management, disrespect, constant tension, and long hours sum up most of the real culture in operations ... Most of the people in SDM [supply demand management] see it as something they need to suck up for a few painful years after b-school so they can move on to a better gig with the Apple brand on their resume. Like the investment banking of tech. Culture here is strictly top down: any attempt to streamline, impact change, or even discuss a better way to do anything is strictly frowned upon when it comes from the bottom. Work longer/harder, don't complain or try to fix any of the myriad broken systems or processes, and don't forget that there are 10 people lined up outside to take your spot (your manager won't forget). Work here at your own risk. On the upside, cafe food is pretty good and dress is casual.

Questions

1 Compare and contrast what Tim Cook says about Apple's organisational culture with those of the employees quoted above.

2 What issues do you think might arise when the espoused organisational culture is different from reality? Do you think this often happens in organisations? Can you think of any examples?

3 Whose perceptions of organisational culture matter most, do you think, the senior level managers', or the employees'? Provide a reason for your answer.

Sources

www.apple.com

http://money.cnn.com/magazines/fortune/most-admired

http://www.businessinsider.com/10-ways-to-think-different-inside-apples-cult-like-culture-2011-3

http://appleinsider.com/articles/13/02/12/cook-apples-culture-of-innovation-refuses-to-recognize-limits

http://macdailynews.com/2013/10/11/what-former-employees-say-about-apples-corporate-culture-the-food-the-secrecy-and-the-control/

http://www.businessinsider.com/what-apple-employees-say-about-the-companys-internal-corporate-culture-2013-10

FORMS OF ORGANISATIONAL CULTURE: THE COMPETING VALUES FRAMEWORK

The Competing Values Framework (CVF) developed by Cameron and Quinn (1999) provides a tool for identifying and comparing cultures across organisations. The basic premise of the CVF is that organisational cultures differ with regard to two sets of values, namely Organisational Focus, as represented in a contrast between internal and external focus; and Organisational Structure, as represented in a contrast between an interest in flexibility and change or an interest in stability and control. Figure 12.2 presents this framework.

Based on this framework, four unique types of organisational culture can be identified: hierarchy, market, clan and adhocracy.

1 **Hierarchy culture**

Organisations which have a hierarchy culture (those that have an internal focus, and demonstrate a strong interest in maintaining stability and control) are characterised by formalisation, structures, policies and procedures. Effective leaders within such a culture are those who display strong coordination and organisational skills. This type of culture is highly associated with a bureaucratic structure. Public sector bodies, government agencies and very large organisations often fall into this category. Advantages of this type of culture are the existence of clear reporting relationships, clear communication channels and recognition of authority. Disadvantages include a potential lack of innovation and creativity, as well as resistance to change given the formalised nature of this type of culture.

2 **Market culture**

The core assumptions of an organisation with a **market culture** are competitiveness and productivity. These assumptions result in a strong emphasis on external positioning and control. Leaders in this type of culture tend to be goal oriented and emphasise the achievement of measurable targets. ▸**See Chapter 6**◂. A good example of an organisation with a market culture would be the European low-cost airline, Ryanair.

3 **Clan culture**

Typical characteristics of an organisation with a **clan culture** are teamwork, employee involvement programmes and corporate commitment to the employee. These organisations are usually paternalistic environments where the leaders or heads of the organisation are viewed as mentors. Loyalty, tradition and emphasis on development are strong. According to *L&D Daily Advisor* (https://lddailyadvisor.blr.com/2018/04/4-distinct-types-corporate-culture), companies such as Google and Zappos represent examples of clan culture.

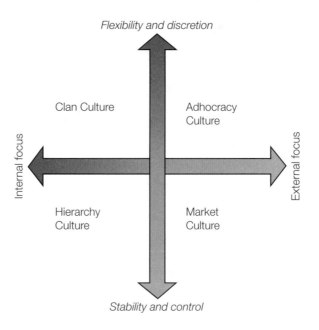

Figure 12.2 The competing values Framework

Source: Cameron et al. (2011).

4 **Adhocracy culture**

The major goal of an adhocracy culture is to foster adaptability, flexibility and creativity so as to produce innovative products and services and adapt quickly to new opportunities. Leaders in this type of culture are considered to be risk takers ▶See Chapter 6◀. For example, Richard Branson's Virgin Group is widely recognised as one which responds quickly to market changes, and adapts its products and services to meet market preferences.

THE IMPACT OF ORGANISATIONAL CULTURE ON ORGANISATIONAL PERFORMANCE

As we have seen above, there are many different types of organisational culture and organisations often go to great lengths to form and preserve their culture, but why is it so important? The culture of any organisation affects the performance of that organisation through its impact on individuals and teams at work. Maintaining a positive organisational culture is therefore an important aspect in sustaining strong organisational performance over time. Sustained business success has as much to do with company values and vision as with market forces, competitive positioning and resources. Siehl and Martin (1990) state that organisational culture influences employee attitudes ▶See Chapter 4◀ and these attitudes in turn, impact organisational effectiveness. Organisational culture should guide employees to form attitudes and consequently behave in ways that are consistent with its values and beliefs. In addition to impacting on employee attitudes and behaviour, research indicates that organisational culture also impacts overall organisational performance and profitability. For example, Kotter and Heskett (1992) conducted research detailing the corporate cultures of 200 companies to determine how each company's culture affected its long-term economic performance. Their research found that strong corporate cultures facilitated change (which we discuss later in the chapter), and were associated with strong positive financial results. A common feature of the strongest performing companies was cultures that encouraged leadership but also empowered everyone in the organisation, thus facilitating change and adapting new practices to meet the new needs.

The Society for Human Resource Management (SHRM) outlines four major cultural traits identified in research by Denison and Mishra (1995) that correspond to high performance and overall organisational effectiveness, which are involvement, consistency, adaptability and mission. Dennison and Mishra's (1995) research studied 764 organisations. Their results found that involvement and adaptability are indicators of flexibility, openness, responsiveness, and were strong predictors of growth in organisations. The consistency and mission were found to be indicators of integration and of profitability. All four of the traits were shown to significantly predict other effectiveness criteria such as quality, employee satisfaction, and overall performance. While the research studies highlighted above show that a link exists between culture and performance (the C-P link), there has been debate as to the nature of this causal link, that is, whether culture causes performance or if indeed performance causes culture. Research by Sackman (2011) and Boyce et al. (2015) indicates that culture 'comes first, with performance levels to follow'.

However, while a positive organisational culture can enhance business performance it can never supersede the effects of a flawed business model (Stanford, 2010; Mullins, 2013).

Moreover, according to Sørenson (2002), who examined the relationship between the strength of organisational culture and business performance, strong cultures contributed to successful business strategy in a stable operating environment, but in scenarios where market or economic conditions were volatile, businesses with strong cultures tended to be *less* successful. Sørenson suggested that this was due to the fact that strong cultures, which tend to be stable over time, were less adaptable in a rapidly changing environment. This is due to the fact that in a strong culture, members exhibit greater levels of commitment to the core values of the organisation, which results in very well established ways of behaving that are hard to change.

PROMOTING CREATIVITY AND INNOVATION THROUGH CULTURE

innovation in business refers to the process of developing inventions or ideas into marketable goods, services or processes that customers want.

As you have seen in the example of Apple discussed earlier, creating an environment where an employee can nurture and develop their own creative ideas makes sense from a business perspective as it can help foster innovation. There are risks, however, associated with high levels of innovation. For one, innovation can prove costly where technology and expertise are required to refine a good before it can be produced cost effectively. Secondly, there is a greater risk of failure involved in developing new ideas, for example that they will not be well received by consumers. Nonetheless, Ekvall (1996) found a positive relationship between climates or cultures emphasising creativity and innovation, and their overall profitability. So, how do organisations develop a culture of innovation and creativity? Oldham and Cummings (1996) identify a number of conditions which organisations can create in order to foster an environment conducive to innovation. These are:

- **Autonomy:** employees are more likely to display creative qualities when they are given a degree of freedom over the way in which they work, rather than feeling as though they are being constantly micromanaged by a supervisor.
- **Empowerment:** enabling workers to set their own goals and take responsibility for problem solving liberates employees and allows creativity to flourish.
- **Encouraging diversity:** organisations employing people from diverse ethnic and cultural backgrounds benefit from the existence of a greater range of viewpoints and ideas about how to solve problems and create new products/services.
- **Top level support for creativity:** encouragement from managers, leaders and top executives is a fundamental part of an innovative culture. Employees are far less likely to exercise their creative flair and risk failure if they fear criticism and reprisal from superiors for doing so.
- **Making tasks intrinsically motivating:** the idea behind this is that individuals will be more creative and put more effort into tasks that they actually *want* to be involved in. This may be because the individual has a personal interest in the task, because they find it interesting or even fun to be involved in.
- **Resources:** innovation and creativity usually require time and finances; if organisations are to develop a culture of innovation, employees cannot be expected to operate in a vacuum without the necessary resources to bring their ideas to fruition.

SPOTLIGHT ON SKILLS

Mergers and acquisitions are a staple part of business life across all industries in the modern, globalised marketplace. A merger happens when two or more companies come together to form a new company, while an acquisition occurs when one company purchases another company. What aspects of business operations and functions could contribute to a potential 'culture clash' during a merger or an acquisition? How can an organisation manage this issue, or indeed, avoid this issue altogether? How can management ensure a uniform culture is created and maintained once an acquisition or merger has occurred?

To help you answer these questions, visit bloomsbury.pub/organisational-behaviour to watch the video of Michéal Clancy from AMCS Group talking about their experience of the issue of 'culture clash' during mergers and acquisitions.

CULTURE CHANGE

In general, most theorists agree that organisational culture is difficult to change, or at the very least, that cultural change takes a long time to achieve. The previous section explored the interplay between organisational culture and performance. A performance enhancing culture is unlikely to be in need of change; however, a culture which is toxic or unethical and therefore damaging to either the organisation's performance or its reputation does need to be altered. Similarly, an organisation which may have been highly successful may need to change to adapt to market conditions, new competitors, and technological, political or social changes in the external environment.

Mergers, the joining of two companies on a relatively level footing, and acquisitions, the purchase of one organisation by another, are two key drivers of organisational cultural change. The respective culture of each organisation is often ignored during the initial merging or takeover process; however, internal cultural differences often emerge quite quickly as one of the major obstacles to successful business functioning afterwards. This process is referred to as 'culture clash'. Kotter (2008 p. 4) outlines how cultural change at this level is extremely challenging 'because group members are often not even aware of the values that bind them together'.

The dynamic nature of both organisational culture and organisational change ▶See Chapter 13◀ means that the two concepts are inextricably interlinked. Naylor (2004) points out that while organisational changes affect the culture of the organisation, the existing culture also affects or constrains the process and impact of any changes.

As discussed at the beginning of this chapter, culture is developed, transmitted and reinforced through a system of rituals, communications, symbols and values. These facets of an organisation are deep rooted and therefore require enormous effort to change. Meek (1988) argues that culture is not something an organisation 'has' but rather culture is what it 'is'.

cultural change the process of changing mind-sets, behaviour and practices in an organisation, is a long process which cannot be achieved effectively in a short time frame.

Indeed, so strong is the belief of some theorists in the prevailing strength of organisational culture that they argue organisations should adopt market strategies to match existing culture rather than attempt to alter their values and ethos (Schwartz and Davis, 1981). Take for example Apple's long-established culture of innovation; while the mobile phone development trend was towards smaller, lighter handsets, Apple pursued its strategy and launched the iPhone in 2007, which subsequently revolutionised the market. However, not all organisations take such an approach to maintaining their ethos and cultures. Some organisations have opted, or been forced, to change their organisational culture in reaction to market forces or to combat internal problems. A number of approaches are described below that they have taken to achieve this.

APPROACHES TO CULTURE CHANGE

Ashleigh and Mansi (2012) have identified the following different approaches to achieving cultural change in an organisation:

1 Changing employees' values and beliefs – achieved through development, such as training, education and effective communication of the organisation's new mission and values.
2 Altering the composition of the workforce – achieved through recruitment, selection and human resource interventions to retain only those employees who share the new values and beliefs of the organisation.
3 Altering the organisational climate – achieved through changes in policies, procedures and routines which result in changes in employee behaviour.
4 Behaviour change – achieved through organisational restructuring where through new roles, responsibilities and relationships employees are compelled to learn new behaviours. Altered beliefs, values and attitudes follow from a change in behaviour.

Hope and Hendry (1995) compared a range of different approaches to culture change and found behaviour change to be the most effective.

EMPLOYEE RESPONSES TO CULTURAL CHANGE

Piderit (2000) outlines three types of negative responses to cultural change: affective (where employees become emotional or anxious about the impact of change), cognitive (feelings of resentment toward management with regard to how the change was introduced) and behavioural (collective industrial action, reduction in performance, damaging the organisation in some way). Achieving employee 'buy-in' and commitment to new practices and new ways of doing things can be one of the most challenging aspects of an organisational change process. Even when top level managers are dedicated to introducing a cultural change they may inadvertently revert to old patterns of behaviour since the existing culture is so engrained. For example, in attempting to introduce a culture that is more environmentally aware, a manager produces a glossy report that is distributed to each member of the organisation. ▸See Chapter 13◂.

BUILDING YOUR EMPLOYABILITY SKILLS

Checking your Culture in light of #MeToo

Reinforcing and communicating organisational culture is a critical requirement of management. You are the director of a public relations organisation in a large city. The #MeToo movement has received widespread attention across social media. You are aware that some of the organisations that you work with have been embroiled in allegations of harassment and unequal treatment of female employees. In light of the reports, what actions could you take to ensure that the culture of your organisation is doing enough to ensure that everyone is treated in a respectful manner?

Visit the World Economic Forum for ideas: https://www.weforum.org/agenda/2019/01/how-improve-your-corporate-culture-metoo-era-sexual-harassment/

NATIONAL AND INTERNATIONAL CULTURES

Values, language, education, political and legal systems vary widely from country to country, and these practices in turn impact on the culture within organisations. It is important to recognise that even in the initial design of an organisation's structure, national culture plays a role. Basic theories on how work should be organised reflect the different cultural backgrounds of the theorists. For example, Fredrick Taylor's principles of scientific management are regarded as reflecting an American work ethic and culture; the bureaucratic model of work espoused by Max Weber is considered to fit with the norms of German society; and Henri Fayol's administrative model is viewed as mirroring a French approach to work organisation.

An appreciation of cultural difference is imperative in international business in understanding how best to accomplish organisational goals effectively. Hofstede's Cultural Dimensions Theory describes the effects of a society's culture on the values of its members, and how these values relate to behaviour. Hofstede's work was based on the results of a world-wide survey of employee values at IBM in the 1960s and 1970s. The theory was one of the first to explain observed differences between cultures. The original theory proposed four dimensions along which cultural values could be analysed: individualism–collectivism; uncertainty avoidance; power distance and masculinity–femininity. These are explained in detail below.

Individualism–collectivism: this relates to the extent to which societies reflect an individualistic or a collective ethic. In individualistic societies, great importance is placed upon personal achievement, competition and individual rights; in contrast a collectivist society is one which favours members acting in a cohesive fashion. The USA, Britain, Canada, France and Spain are all considered to be highly individualistic societies in contrast with India, Hong Kong, Portugal, Greece and much of Latin America, which hold more collectivist values.

Uncertainty avoidance: this dimension reflects how members of a society cope with ambiguity. It examines the extent to which members attempt to minimise or avoid uncertain situations. Societies with high uncertainty avoidance tend to exhibit more rules, laws and regulations in order to carefully plan their way through changes. France, Spain, Germany and Latin America display high uncertainty avoidance. In contrast, low uncertainty avoidance countries tend to have fewer laws and often cope with change more easily; the Netherlands and Scandinavia are examples of low uncertainty avoidance.

Power distance: this relates to the extent to which members of society (or within organisations) accept that power is distributed unequally, and this manifests in individuals' interactions with hierarchy and management. Cultures that endorse low power distance demonstrate social relations that are more consultative or democratic in nature; Germany, Australia and the United States exhibit low power distance cultures.

Masculinity–femininity: this dimension refers to a continuum between characteristics assumed to be masculine in nature such as assertiveness and competition, at one end, and characteristics assumed to be feminine such as care and concern, at the other. In masculine cultures, the differences between gender roles are more dramatic than in feminine cultures. Scandinavia and the Netherlands reflected feminine cultures whereas the United States, Germany and Britain were found by Hofstede to have more masculine cultures.

Hofstede's work has been extremely influential in the organisational behaviour field. With regard to the interaction between national culture and organisational cultures, however, Hofstede's work has been questioned with regard to its applicability across cultures since it explores only national level characteristics and ignores variations that may exist at regional level, which can be quite significant in some countries. Furthermore, some theorists question whether the findings have the same relevance in today's society where many nations have experienced significant changes, in particular with regard to the individualism–collectivism dimension. More recently, Project GLOBE has become more prevalent in discussions about national culture. GLOBE is a long-term research effort designed to explore the complex effects of culture on leadership, organisational effectiveness, and the economic competitiveness of societies (House *et al.*, 2004). Project GLOBE developed nine cultural dimensions, extending Hofstede's work (Shi and Wang, 2011), which make it possible to capture the similarities and/or differences in norms, values, beliefs and practices among societies (Table 12.3).

Table 12.3 Project GLOBE

Dimensions	Definitions
Power Distance	The degree to which members of an organisation or society expect and agree that power should be shared unequally.
Uncertainty Avoidance	The extent to which members of collectives seek orderliness, consistency, structure, formalised procedures, and laws to cover situations in their daily lives.
Institutional Collectivism	Level at which a society values and rewards collective action and resource distribution.
In-Group Collectivism	Level at which a society values cohesiveness, loyalty, and pride, in their families and organisations.
Humane Orientation	Ideas and values, and prescriptions for behaviour, associated with the dimension of culture at which a society values and rewards altruism, caring, fairness, friendliness, generosity, and kindness.
Performance Orientation	Level at which a society values and rewards individual performance and excellence.
Assertiveness	A set of social skills or a style of responding amenable to training or as a facet of personality.
Gender Egalitarianism	Level at which a society values gender equality and lessens role-differences-based gender.
Future Orientation	The extent to which members of a society or an organisation believe that their current actions will influence their future, focus on investment in their future, believe that they will have a future that matters, believe in planning for developing their future, and look far into the future for assessing the effects of their current actions.

Source: Adapted from House et al. *(2004) and Shi and Wang (2011).*

According to Thrive Global (an organisation formed in 2007 whose purpose is to help organisations and people understand the link between well-being and performance), cultural awareness is learned. This means that when working in international settings or with members of international teams, it can take time to appreciate and understand cultural nuances that influence behaviour. Thrive Global's (2019) research has shown that when team members from various different cultural backgrounds are all speaking to each other, ensuring they use the same direct, simple and familiar language increases efficiency and the likelihood of success. This is something which organisational leaders can seek to foster and develop over time.

CULTURE MANAGEMENT

According to the *Harvard Business Review* (2019), compared with some other activities of business leaders, such as hiring the right talent and setting strategy, changing corporate culture can be especially challenging. The argument made for this assertion is the amorphous nature of organisational culture, which means that there are no simple and direct levers for changing a culture in one direction or another. For organisational leaders, being aware of cultural management is more important than ever before, with CEOs now putting a higher priority on this aspect of leadership than in the past. Mistakes can be a valuable learning tool and in order to illustrate how leaders should and should not approach cultural management, research from Gartner featured in the *Harvard Business Review* identified three things that leaders should avoid doing in relation to culture. These included: using simple adjectives and buzzwords to describe the organisation's culture, trying to measure culture with data from things like employee surveys alone, and finally, failing to adapt organisational policies to support organisational culture. This is particularly important in organisations where there is a strong culture present. This is something many organisations strive for, but it needs to be managed and maintained in order to avoid the development of unintended or negative consequences. For example, the Future for Work Institute (2017) points out that strong cultures can have negative effects such as hindering the integration of people from different cultural backgrounds or negatively impacting the cognitive diversity of their members because such differences are not viewed as meeting the cultural norms of the organisation.

NEW APPROACHES TO MEASURING AND MANAGING ORGANISATIONAL CULTURE

In order to measure an organisation's culture, we generally tend to focus on surveys or questionnaires with employees. Surveys, however, are only a snapshot at one point in time, and often fail to capture the link between organisational culture and employee behaviour over time. Corritore *et al.* (2020) focused on a new method of measuring organisational culture: they used big data to mine pervasive 'digital traces' of culture in electronic communications. Their research examined the diversity of thoughts, ideas and meaning expressed by team members in a number of organisations and then measured whether it was beneficial or detrimental to team performance. In doing so, they were able to analyse the language and discourse of conversations to measure how organisational culture influences thoughts and behaviour. They also partnered with employer-review website Glassdoor to explore how employees talk about their organisations' culture in anonymous reviews, in order to examine the effects of cultural diversity on organisational efficiency and innovation. Their research found that a high level of cultural fit led to more promotions, more-favourable performance evaluations, and fewer people leaving. Cultural adaptability, however, turned out to be even more important. Employees who could quickly adapt to cultural norms as they evolved over time were more successful than employees who exhibited high cultural fit when first hired. These results suggest that the process of cultural alignment does not end at the point of hire; so it's important that managers and all organisational decision-makers are mindful about cultural adaptability throughout the work lifespan, and that cultural alignment forms part of all employment-related decisions, from hiring, to learning and development opportunities, and beyond.

Encountering a Culture Clash

OB IN PRACTICE

Tecqson Inc. is the world leader in the manufacture of semi-conductor technologies for use in both large and small electronic based consumables. The organisation was established as a medium sized manufacturing company in Baltimore, Maryland, in 1972 but has since grown into a publicly traded multinational corporation employing 6000 people world-wide across 11 countries. The organisation is widely recognised as the leader in the market both in terms of the quality of items produced and of the excellent service it provides to its corporate customers. The company is valued at over $3bn USD. While the main manufacturing sites for the organisation have traditionally been US and European based, in 2010 Tecqson purchased a large-scale manufacturing facility in Shenzhen, China. This action was in line with the organisation's strategic plan to increase sales in the Asian market where they were struggling to compete on price with other manufacturers. By 2013, the facility was operational with a workforce of almost 800 people. Unlike the European and US plants, production workers in the new facility have very little autonomy in their roles, a strong hierarchal culture exists, and there is limited sharing of information between management and staff. Yet, despite these differences, the facility has so far had excellent production numbers and this has contributed to rising sales in the Asian market.

Tecqson operates a state-of-the-art quality system in all its operations, utilising quality management processes such as 5S, Lean Technology and Six Sigma practices, which are systems designed to increase production efficiency. While each manufacturing operation has its own internal quality and reliability teams, the main quality function is based at company headquarters in Baltimore. A culture of accountability and learning is encouraged at Tecqson and employees have always been encouraged to admit mistakes rather than cover things up.

The quality office is made of three main teams: the Internal Quality Processes (IQP) team, the Product Reliability and Test (PRT) team, and the Defective Product and Customer Returns (DPCR) team. The quality function in Baltimore employs approximately 50 people mainly from engineering, science and technology backgrounds. The quality function is led by the Quality Director Greg Shaw, who has been employed by Tecqson since 1999. Greg and the three other team managers travel to each of the manufacturing sites on an annual basis but beyond that keep in touch with local level quality teams via teleconferencing, e-mail and online virtual meetings.

Since the end of the second quarter in 2013 the Defective Product and Customer Returns (DPCR) teams have noted an unacceptably high level of customer returns based on products from the Shenzhen site. This has led to some internal conflicts in the Baltimore office between the DPCR team and the IQP and PRT teams. The leader of the DPCR team, Harry Peterson, has made it clear that he feels it is unfair that his team should have to deal with so many returns, which clearly wouldn't have occurred if the other teams had been liaising effectively with the local level quality team in Shenzhen. The other team leaders responded in kind by informing Greg Shaw, the Quality Director, that the quality teams in Shenzhen were extremely 'difficult to deal with'. For example, the IQP team noted that they routinely failed to supply documentation of quality processes on time. In addition, the PRT team reported that the Shenzhen team regularly delayed or cancelled vital system shutdowns which were required as part of the reliability check process, choosing instead to use the time to increase production levels in the factory. Greg was aware that there were some issues to iron out with the new facility such as the level of information sharing. However, until now he had not acted upon anything; since the top management team had been so impressed with the impact of the new facility on sales, he felt it unwise to bring up problems prematurely and planned instead

to go and visit the site in the coming months.

In the first quarter of 2014, just before Greg's planned visit to Shenzhen, an unexpected crisis occurred. One of the micro-imaging engineers in the DPCR team discovered that the part which had been returned was in fact not produced by Tecqson at all. The part, which has the company trademark, was in fact counterfeit. An investigation by the quality team as a whole revealed that this counterfeit part had been installed in at least 100,000 units and perhaps countless more. To have produced such a part, the company making the counterfeit must have had a high level of knowledge of the processes and material used by Tecqson, not to mention who the potential customers for such goods might be. The team immediately pointed to a lack of tight quality controls at the Shenzhen plant and a failure of the employees there to keep certain patents and plans confidential.

The presence of counterfeit goods in the market

alone has the potential to cost Tecqson millions in lost sales, not to mention the costs associated with the numerous customer returns, from products containing actual Tecqson parts produced in China. The top management team have pointed the finger firmly at Greg and his team and told him to 'sort this mess out'.

Greg has been tasked with forming a taskforce of eight people from within his own team in Baltimore, who will basically spend the next eight weeks (or as long as it takes) to sort out the problems in Shenzhen. As yet, he has no idea where to start. To him it's clear that the issues here are much more engrained with cultural issues and an understanding of the business than anything to do with personality or team issues on an individual level. How can he make top management see that this issue doesn't have an overnight solution?

Questions

1 Assume the role of Greg. Using Hofestede's model (or alternatively the GLOBE framework) and/or other sources, create a presentation outlining key differences between Chinese and American national cultures and the implications of this.

2 The problem-solving task force will not only need to identify problems but also implement changes at the Shenzhen plant. Identify a variety of actions that will be required to ensure the start of a successful intervention over the eight-week period.

MANAGERIAL TAKEAWAYS

The focus of this chapter has been on the nature of organisational culture, something which has an impact on individuals who work in an organisation, or those who interact with an organisation, either consciously or unconsciously. We have discussed the emergence of organisational culture as a concept within the field of management. Moreover, we have outlined how organisational culture, in reality, is formed, transmitted and reinforced by organisations. We have examined the differences that exist between organisational culture and organisational climate, and also we have looked at how a subculture can differ from an organisation's dominant culture. Throughout the chapter we have shown how organisational culture can impact on both employee and organisational performance; the types of organisational culture that exist can impact on this profoundly. Further, we have discussed the issue of cultural change, and varying national cultures. We have also discussed the important question of whether organisational culture impacts on organisational performance, a question which most managers continually seek to answer.

 CHAPTER REVIEW QUESTIONS

1 What is organisational culture?
2 Does organisational culture have a purpose?
3 How is organisational culture formed, transmitted and reinforced?
4 Discuss the visible and invisible aspects of organisational culture.
5 Does culture impact on organisational performance?
6 How can we tell if an organisation has a strong culture?
7 Are there different types of cultures in organisations?
8 Describe how organisational culture can be changed.

FURTHER READING

Barney, J.B. (1986) Organizational culture: Can it be a source of sustained competitive advantage? *Academy of Management Review*, 11(3), 656–665.

Grant, A.M. (2017) The third 'generation' of workplace coaching: Creating a culture of quality conversations. *Coaching: An International Journal of Theory, Research and Practice*, 10(1), 37–53.

Koss, L. (2012) The impact of recession on culture: And what it means for organizations and leaders, ONTOS Global. Available at: http://ontosglobal.com/2012/04/the-impact-of-recession-on-culture-and-what-it-means-for-organizations-and-leaders/

Levering, R. (2010) *Transforming Workplace Cultures: Insights from Great Place to Work Institute's First 25 Years*. São Paulo: Primavera Editorial.

Lok, P. and Crawford, J. (2004) The effect of organisational culture and leadership style on job satisfaction and organisational commitment: A cross-national comparison. *Journal of Management Development*, 23(4), 321–338.

Naranjo-Valencia, J.C., Jiménez-Jiménez, D. and Sanz-Valle, R. (2011) Innovation or imitation? The role of organizational culture. *Management Decision*, 49(1), 55–72.

Rafaeli, A. and Pratt, M.G. (eds) (2013) *Artifacts and Organizations: Beyond Mere Symbolism.* Mahwah, NJ: Psychology Press.

Schneider, B. and Barbera, K.M. (eds) (2014) *The Oxford Handbook of Organizational Climate and Culture.* Oxford: Oxford University Press.

Soderquist, D. (2005) *The Wal-mart Way.* Nashville, TN: Thomas Nelson.

 ## USEFUL WEBSITES

https://hbr.org/2018/01/the-culture-factor

The Culture Factor package at *Harvard Business Review* provides an essential guide to determining an organisation's current culture and shaping it to fit its strategy.

www.greatplacetowork.ie

Great Place to Work Institute is a global research, consulting and training organisation which focuses on helping organisations identify, create and sustain high-trust organisational cultures. Their website's publication and events section contains lots of interesting information on their work and their research findings.

www.worldatwork.org

This is a non-profit human resources association for professionals. The website's 'resource center' has lots of stimulating information for anyone interested in learning more about organisational culture, and people management more generally.

http://www.huffingtonpost.com/vala-afshar/100-tweetable-business-cu_b_3575595.html

Go to this link from the Huffington Post blog to read '100 Tweetable Business Culture Quotes from Brilliant Executives', and see what top business executives have to say about organisational culture.

Online Resources

Visit **bloomsbury.pub/organisational-behaviour** to access additional materials to support teaching and learning.

13 MANAGING ORGANISATIONAL CHANGE

Gráinne Kelly

LEARNING OUTCOMES

BY THE END OF THIS CHAPTER YOU SHOULD BE ABLE TO:

- Demonstrate an understanding of the nature of organisational change.
- Explain the forces of organisational change.
- Discuss the planned approach to change management.
- Identify why employees resist change, and recognise strategies for overcoming resistance.
- Explain the role of leadership in organisational change.
- Discuss the field of organisational development (OD) critically.

THIS CHAPTER DISCUSSES...

IN REALITY

'A change is as good as a rest', or so the saying goes. We all generally associate change with something welcome, a fresh start or a new challenge. In contemporary business environments, managers have to consider many factors involved in complex and dynamic situations before making decisions about implementing changes that will positively influence the effectiveness, efficiency and ultimately the sustainability of their organisations. Yet, does it not depend on what the change is, the size of the change effort, the actual and perceived change(s) and who the change affects? Some people may be more deeply affected than others by the change. Dahl's (1957) research illuminates the potentially negative outcomes of change at the level of the employee. His study of 92,860 employees working in 1,517 of the largest Danish organisations found that organisational changes are associated with significant risks of employee health problems. Change has been equated with high levels of stress among employees. During periods of constant change, employees may encounter stress when they don't have sufficient time to adjust to the change. ACAS recommends that employees' emotional well-being is taken into account when managing change by including the following within every change process:

- Create a vision.
- Lead the change.
- Consult with employees.
- Engage employees.
- Reflect on the change process.

INTRODUCTION

Organisational change is an inevitable consequence of organisational life. Almost every organisation must adjust to a global marketplace, demographic changes, immigration and technological advances. There is general agreement that the rate and pace of change facing organisations are greater now than they have ever been (Black, 2014; Hayes, 2018; Kotter, 2007). External factors such as those that we looked at in Chapter 1 ▸See Chapter 1◂, coupled with internal pressures to raise productivity and develop more effective and sustainable ways of working ▸See Chapter 9◂, are leading organisations to revise their strategies, structures and processes, all of which require them to manage change (Clegg and Walsh, 2004). This is especially true in the wake of the major global shock (Covid-19) that has led to changes the vast majority of the population have never experienced before, and completely transformed our way of life and patterns of work. In this chapter we will learn about the nature of organisational change and discuss which forces act as simulants to change. We will consider some of the work changes that have occurred as a result of the pandemic. We will describe what factors contribute to and influence employees' resistance to change. We will also learn about the planned approaches to change management and outline the key insights to effective implementation offered by the field of organisational development (OD).

THE NATURE OF ORGANISATIONAL CHANGE

Organisational change occurs when a company makes a transition from its current state to some desired future state. It has been defined as 'a comprehensive, collaborative, and planned process of solving problems through altering foundational assumptions and beliefs of individuals in order to improve work content, structures and relationships in organisations' (Rusaw, 2007, p. 349). Change management can be described as an integral part of all managerial work that '(a) copes with the changing patterns of resource input and knowledge available to work organisations and the shifting demands made by the parties with which they deal, and (b) initiates change that managers perceive to be in the interests of those who employ them' (Watson, 2002, p. 418). Today's business environment requires companies to undergo changes frequently if they are to remain competitive. Factors such as the internationalisation of markets and growth in technology force businesses to be proactive in order to survive.

Theories of change have a long history and draw on organisational behaviour concepts, including learning theory, motivation theory, organisational culture theory and theories of leadership and strategy. In order to understand organisational change, it is important to remember that there are many types and levels of change. Such changes may be relatively minor – as in the case of installing a new software program or removing a major section or practice – or quite major – as in the case of refocusing an overall production strategy. Change also occurs when an organisation evolves through various lifecycles. In organisational settings, change is often understood in terms of specific techniques to manage it, but change can also occur at a broader level and be less structured if it is unplanned or the result of unforeseen events. When this happens, organisations often use a discrete piecemeal approach in order to respond to the change as it emerges.

TYPES OF ORGANISATIONAL CHANGE

Change can be categorised as planned, unplanned, emergent, incremental or quantum. Lewin (1951), who we will discuss further in this chapter, first made the distinction between planned change and unplanned or emergent change. Child (2005) provides a useful framework for differentiating between incremental and quantum or radical change. Incremental change is usually targeted at fixing specific departments of the organisation, or specific problems such as changes agreed in staff performance plans, while quantum or radical change involves a more generic organisation-wide change programme, such as business process engineering (BPR). By its very nature, planned change is likely to be either quantum or incremental, while unplanned change is more likely to be emergent.

Yet despite this emphasis on the need for change, for a number of organisations change is not part of their strategic plan and, in some cases, change is not even something that is viewed as desirable. In these cases, change is occurring as an unplanned response to external or internal events beyond the control of the organisation that make it necessary for organisation survival. As an illustration, we can consider organisational changes following the 9/11 terrorist attacks in the US, when, among other things, the travel industry experienced a decline in business. At this point, airlines and hotels across the US and Europe were forced to engage in unplanned, incremental and emergent change, including lay-offs, as they looked for ways to cope with the

planned change is change that an organisation consciously thinks about and decides to engage in, which is designed to specifically change organisational outcomes.

unplanned or emergent change is change that the organisation did not initiate or had no control over planning.

incremental change is a small change aimed at achieving certain goals.

quantum or radical change is change that affects the entire organisation.

crisis. We can also see an example of quantum change at airports, which had to introduce new security regulations and train staff in safety procedures to combat further terrorist attacks.

Global shocks such as Covid-19 are a quantum change that require a complete reappraisal of how organisations operate and manage employees. For example, socially distanced working was introduced by many companies, such as manufacturing companies, where changes included the re-design of their production lines, separate entrances for different groups of workers, regular cleaning of work areas and toilets, and protective equipment. Also, furloughing became a common feature of work in Ireland and the UK. '**Furloughing**' is a term used in the United States for many years when an employee is temporarily laid off either because of a government shutdown or where an organisation wishes to retain its staff without pay or on reduced terms rather than make them redundant. Many employers have also shifted to a remote working or a home working business model, with advances in technology making it easier for employees to log in from home and take part in virtual meetings via MS Teams and Zoom or other platforms. This approach to working in a blended or a remote environment may become the norm for many employees in the future, for example, those employed by Twitter (see Fung, 2020).

LEVELS OF ORGANISATIONAL CHANGE

As well as the type of change, it is important to understand the different levels within the organisation where change can occur. At the broadest organisational level change usually centres on restructuring and reorganising. This can mean the introduction of new policies and rules that affect the entire organisation. At this level, different strategies can be planned, which are then transformed into two other levels which are more specific and detailed. We can take the example of Total Quality Management (TQM), which is a management approach that centres on quality and customer satisfaction, based on the participation and commitment of an organisation's workforce. At the group level, change is aimed at altering work processes, including the introduction of new technologies to accomplish the work. This would be the stage at which entire work processes would be changed by implementing TQM initiatives. Finally, at the individual level, changes attempt to alter the behaviours, attitudes, norms and perceptions of the employees in the organisation to bring them in line with the new values and cultural context ▸**See Chapter 12**◂.

CONTENT-DRIVEN CHANGE

While it may be assumed that all organisational change occurs at various levels, it is useful to explore patterns of change in terms of content- and process-driven types. Content-driven change is a programmatic change in which specific interventions are used as the driver for change. Examples include lean manufacturing, which seeks to eliminate activities that do not add value from the perspective of the customer, and agile development, which consists of a process for product development based on collaborative cross-functional team effort. To help understand content-driven change, we can identify a set of characteristics that are common across particular change efforts – change that:

- serves as the building block for stimulating change throughout the company unit or department.
- is directed by top management.

- relies on standardised, off the shelf solutions.
- is practised in a uniform manner across the organisation.

PROCESS-DRIVEN CHANGE

A process-driven approach to change works from the opposite direction to content-driven change. Process-driven change emphasises the methods of conceiving, introducing and institutionalising new behaviours, and uses content as a reinforcer rather than a driver of new behaviours. An example involves the use of a process model for developing new applications. Process-driven change seeks to foster a cultural context and climate in which employees at all levels of the organisation engage in a mutually collaborative way to achieve the strategic goals of the organisation. It is clear from the literature that there are various types and levels of organisational change. However, ultimately the type of change an organisation engages in is dependent on forces that are both within and beyond its control. It is to these forces that we now turn.

FORCES FOR CHANGE

External and internal forces have been responsible for driving change in relation to work for centuries, with one of the most significant examples being the Industrial Revolution, which changed the nature of work. Internal forces for change include employee dissatisfaction and industrial conflict, both of which are important factors in highly collectivised environments characterised by a strong trade union presence. Other internal forces are new leadership, new strategy, new structures, the redesign of jobs and the installation of new technology. External forces for change include the growth in the knowledge economy, which has stimulated the increasingly knowledge-intensive nature of work (Kase *et al.*, 2009) and the need for more autonomous and collaborative work designs (Foss *et al.*, 2009). In addition, since the 1990s societal and political pressures such as the fall of communism, increased global competition, privatisation and deregulation, and the growing influence of EU directives on employment relations, have played a role in the changing nature of the organisational environment. Below we identify some of the major external forces for change:

- **Technological innovations:** Organisations are being transformed by the presence of faster, cheaper and more mobile computers, the growth of social media and the rise in e-commerce.
- **Socio-economic forces:** Since 2008, the housing and financial sectors have experienced economic shocks and organisations have had to cope with a recessionary climate.
- **Market competition:** Competition now occurs on a global scale.
- **Social trends:** Organisations must constantly adjust product and market strategies in light of changing social trends. For example, in 2015 Apple faced a growing number of competitors in the sale of tablet computers, due to the new social demand for these devices. As a result, Apple needed to continually update and innovate to keep ahead of market competitors such as Samsung, and aimed to achieve this through a focus on the attraction and retention of a talented staff.

internal forces are motivational forces which come from the person.

external forces are motivational forces which come from the environment that surrounds the person.

Figure 13.1 Kotter's integrative model of organisational dynamics

Source: Adapted from Kotter (1980, p. 282).

- **Global politics:** There is ongoing growth in the interdependency of economies and opening of trade across EMEA (Europe, the Middle East and Africa).

These elements do not occur in an isolated manner. Rather, the changes to any one of the external or internal elements of an organisation's system will cause changes to other elements. We will now discuss two frameworks that provide insight into the interaction between the external and internal organisational environments affecting change events. The first model, by Kotter (1980), is presented in Figure 13.1.

The primary organisational processes in Kotter's framework consist of information gathering, communication and decision-making. More specific processes include the market research process, the product development process and the manufacturing process. Kotter's framework describes six structural dimensions:

- The external environment involving the political and government systems.
- Employees and other tangible assets such as buildings, plant and inventories.
- Formal structure, job design and operating systems.
- Social systems involving organisational culture and social structure.
- Technology.

● Dominant coalition embracing the objectives and strategies of those who control policy-making.

Kotter's process perspective on change management provides a useful framework for managers leading a change, and highlights, in terms of leadership, what needs to be done to ensure success for each element. For instance, an organisational leader needs to identify and remove obstacles that can prevent employees acting to implement the organisational vision. Some of these obstacles might include organisational processes, such as reward systems that penalise valued behaviour, restrictive rules and regulations or inflexible organisational structures.

THE MCKINSEY 7S FRAMEWORK

The McKinsey framework was developed in the early 1980s by Peters and Waterman, two consultants working at the McKinsey & Company consulting firm. The basic premise of the model is that there are seven internal aspects of an organisation that need to be aligned if it is to be successful with a change event. The McKinsey 7S model involves seven interdependent factors, which are categorised as either 'hard' or 'soft' elements. Hard elements are easier to define or identify and management can directly influence or direct them through strategy statements, organisation charts and reporting lines, and formal processes and IT systems. Soft elements are less tangible and more influenced by culture, and include employee skills and shared values. The model in Figure 13.2 depicts the interdependency of the elements and indicates how a change in one area affects all the others.

We can illustrate this interdependency with the example of the introduction of digital technology into an organisation. The modification of organisation structure to support digital

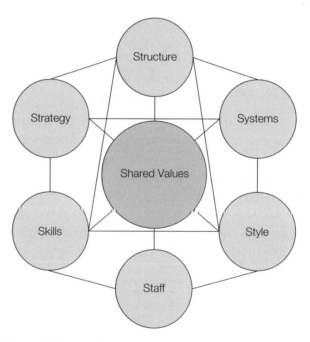

Figure 13.2 The McKinsey 7S framework

Source: Adapted from Peters and Waterman (1982).

business may require cross-functional teams or steering groups, and decisions around insourcing or outsourcing. The development of specific systems, processes and information technology to support digital business could consist of the choice of internal or external integrated technology solutions. Staff considerations involve those around recruitment, and training and development, and exploring employee skills in specific areas such as project management or e-marketing campaigns. Managerial style focuses on the manager's vision for the introduction of the technology in light of achieving the organisational objectives. Shared values are at the core of the framework and they involve the leader fostering perceptions of the importance and effectiveness of digital business among senior managers and staff. These beliefs and assumptions underpin the development of a climate in which people believe in the value of their roles and are confident that they have the support of senior staff to make changes.

The elements of the model can be explained as follows:

- **Strategy:** the plan devised to maintain and build competitive advantage over the competition.
- **Structure:** the way the organisation is structured and who reports to whom.
- **Systems:** the daily activities and procedures that staff members engage in to get the job done.
- **Shared values:** the core values of the company that are evidenced in the corporate culture and the general work ethic.
- **Style:** the style of leadership adopted.
- **Staff:** the employees and their general capabilities.
- **Skills:** the actual skills and competencies of the employees working for the company.

Peters and Waterman's (1982) research emphasises the management of culture ▸**See Chapter 12**◂ and employee behaviour as critical interventions for sustaining organisational capability to manage long-term change and improve performance. For example, it emphasises the importance of training and developing people using organisational learning methods to develop the skills they need to carry out their new roles.

THE PLANNED CHANGE PROCESS

At some point in time, all organisations have desired to change some facet of how they operate and have taken deliberate, planned rational steps to accommodate this change. Leaders seeking to implement organisational change are often surprised by the degree of complacency and lack of interest they face from their employees. They are perplexed as to why their employees want to retain the status quo and continue with the same behaviours – often even in the face of declining organisational performance. How can managers overcome this? Some adopt a strategy whereby they announce the need for change and present a rational argument around the importance of the change for improving organisational performance. They tell employees how they need to adjust their behaviours and work together in new ways in the interests of the organisation. However, studies indicate that this will not motivate behavioural change and often weak organisational performance will not create an urgent need to change within an organisation. An explanation for this was provided by Kurt Lewin, who suggested the need for an approach which would 'unfreeze' the existing situation. The planned approach to organisational change assumes that change strategies are intentional and rational processes which rely on analysis, forecasting and planning, thus resulting in the logical and rational implementation of change within the organisation (Hayes, 2018).

Changes in the Retail Sector

There have been many stories of big retail companies who are what we would call brick and mortar retailers moving into new

markets and finding new customers as a result of new business strategies. In 2018 the large American retailer Walmart made one of its biggest deals ever when it spent $16 billion to acquire Indian e-commerce business Flipkart. It acquired approximately 77%, becoming the largest shareholder. While in the short term the company expects the acquisition to lead to lower profits, its long-term play is for market dominance in India, which is a top developing country for

retail investment and a major battleground in the fight against Amazon.

Questions

1 Consider what has happened in the retail industry since the arrival of Covid-19. Does this acquisition now look like a good deal?
2 What changes do you think this acquisition will bring to the US organisation?

Source

https://www.retaildive.com/news/7-retailers-that-made-pivotal-deals-in-2018/541107/

We have highlighted the planned nature of change events in organisations. In the next section we will study a seminal approach by Lewin in the field of organisational change.

LEWIN'S CHANGE MODEL

In the mid-20th century, psychologist Kurt Lewin identified three stages of change that are the basis of contemporary approaches to change management. In the aftermath of the Second World War, Lewin published two essays, 'Behaviour and Development as a Function of the Total Situation' (1946) and 'Frontiers in Group Dynamics' (1947) (see Lewin, 1951), which made important contributions to our understanding of organisational change and development. First, he highlighted the role that context plays in shaping individual behaviours. Second, he argued that the only way to motivate an individual to change his or her pattern of behaviour is to create a sense of disequilibrium or dissatisfaction with the status quo within the individual. Lewin suggested that successful change requires a three-step procedure that involves the stages of unfreezing, moving and refreezing (see Figure 13.3).

- **Unfreezing** is the first stage of the change process and consists of unlearning past behaviour. Lewin emphasised that announcing the need for change or presenting a rational argument for how the changes will improve performance will not motivate behavioural change among employees. This is because existing behaviours are often ingrained in shared expectations or norms of how organisational members ought to behave. Organisational membership instils a positive sense of belonging to members and a shared understanding; they like being part of the group, accept the group's norms, and are pleased with what the group has been able to achieve in the past as a result of a collective effort. The literature suggests that the more individuals assign positive value to group membership and group norms, the greater the resistance on the part of the individual group members to any change in those norms ▶See Chapter 7◀. To break the social habits that support existing patterns of behaviour, a leader needs to initiate unfreezing or create dissatisfaction with the status quo by alerting organisational members to the need for change. This is brought about by the leader creating a vision of the future desirable state and communicating this vision, which instils a sense of urgency and reduces any restraining forces.

- **Moving** is where the change actually occurs and the organisation moves to a desired state. During this stage, new policies, procedures, structures, behaviours and attitudes are developed. A key part of Lewin's model is the notion that change, even at the psychological level, is a journey that unfolds over time rather than a single event. Employees must be involved and participate in the change process. Old customs and norms that reinforce the old ways of doing things must be replaced with norms that reinforce the new ways. For example, if the organisation is developing teams and moving away from functional departments, then teamwork across departmental boundaries should be emphasised and a suitable team-based reward structure should be considered, to reinforce the moving process.

- **Refreezing** is the final stage of the change process and involves reinforcing and measuring behavioural change. Once change has been implemented, in order to be successful, the new situation must be refrozen so it can be sustained over time. Without this last step, change is likely to be a brief event and employees will attempt to revert to the previous equilibrium state. Here it is critical that the appropriate organisational systems such as reward structures and social support are implemented to strengthen the development of new behaviours. Training must be provided to ensure that employees understand and can perform their roles in the change process. After the training requirements are defined, the reward system, reporting relationships, performance management and development systems need to be adjusted. These aspects are critical to help people and the organisation internalise or institutionalise the changes.

Figure 13.3 Three-step model of change

Adapted from Lewin (1997).

BUILDING YOUR EMPLOYABILITY SKILLS

Understanding Resistance to Change

Your organisation has decided to introduce a new performance management system. As a section manager you have been asked for your views on likely employee attitudes for and against this change initiative. What are the likely impacts of this type of change in the organisation? How can these be anticipated and planned for?

An example of what these three stages might look like when put into practice is that of an insurance company which has been receiving poor customer evaluations over the last three months. The organisation realises that good customer service is essential for success in the industry and wishes to become more customer focused. New competitors are emerging and the company is concerned over losing its market share. Managers in the firm survey its customers and the findings suggest that customers feel disengaged from the agents they speak with on the telephone and that the waiting time to speak to a representative is quite long.

The application of Lewin's three-step model of change might look like the following:

- **Unfreezing:** Managers hold a meeting with all telephone representatives. During the meeting, the customer survey results are presented and discussed. Additionally, lost customer estimates are translated into financial terms so that telephone representatives can see how poor customer service results in overall poor company performance.
- **Moving:** After the meeting, telephone representatives are provided with customer service training that involves role-playing, group discussions and peer-based learning. This allows them to experience poor versus good service. Representatives are instructed to take their time with calls and to exhibit active listening techniques. In addition, more staff are trained and moved into the customer service section to provide feedback and support.
- **Refreezing:** The organisation needs to examine its existing compensation system, which rewarded representatives based on the quantity of calls made per hour. To support the desired behavioural changes, representatives will be paid an hourly rate and can receive a bonus based on improvements in customer satisfaction surveys.

Several researchers have built on Lewin's model. Lippitt (1958) have expanded the moving stage in relation to managing change for people, groups, organisations and communities. They differentiate three dimensions which are important to achieving the change:

- Clarification or diagnosis of the problem.
- Examination of alternative routes and goals, and the establishment of goals and intentions for action.
- Transformation of intentions into actual change efforts.

Research by Egan (1996) focused on both the unfreezing and moving stages of Lewin's model. He identified the importance of the assessment of the current scenario (diagnosis), mapping out the preferred scenario (visioning) and the movement from the current to the preferred scenario (planning for change). The dimensions of each of these three stages can be described as:

- **The current scenario:** assessing problems and opportunities, developing new perspectives, and choosing high-impact problems or opportunities for attention.
- **The preferred scenario:** developing a range of possible futures, evaluating alternative possibilities to establish a viable agenda for change, and gaining commitment to the new agenda.
- **Strategies and plans for moving to the preferred scenario:** brainstorming strategies for getting there, choosing the best strategy or best-fit package of strategies, and turning these strategies into a viable plan.

To summarise the planned change approach, it is apparent that change requires significant individual and organisational commitment before, during and after the change event. Lewin's model considers the organisation's environment in a holistic manner, and recognises the need for employee receptiveness to change before it occurs and support for change by management once it has occurred. In addition, Lewin's model suggests that the most effective way to manage behavioural change among employees is to devote attention to changing the group's norms ▶**See Chapter 7◀** before adjusting individual behaviours. Surprisingly, the literature suggests that organisations frequently neglect to focus on these areas when attempting to implement change initiatives. Employees are often asked to accept change initiatives without a clear understanding of the need for the change or any involvement in the decision-making processes. In addition, employees often don't receive the support they need to maintain the change, aspects which are explored further in the next section.

EMPLOYEE RESISTANCE TO CHANGE

As mentioned in the In Reality box at the start of this chapter, individuals can undergo a traumatic experience when they are personally confronted with major organisational change. It is suggested in the literature that most employees go through four phases: initial denial, resistance, gradual exploration and eventual commitment. In this section we will focus on resistance. Resistance occurs along a continuum, ranging from passive withdrawal from change initiatives to actively sabotaging them to make them fail (Bacharach and Bamberger, 2007). Each of these reactions to change shapes the behaviour of individuals and, ultimately, the success of the change event. Resistance is a natural part of the change process and occurs because change involves going from the known to the uncertain. Change appears threatening to many people, which makes it difficult to gain their support and commitment to implementing changes. Resistance to change can have a significant impact and influence upon the success of an organisational change project. The results of a survey of 1,536 executives involved in a wide variety of minor and substantial change initiatives indicated that only 38% had accepted these initiatives and deemed them to be successful, and just 30% thought they had contributed to the sustained improvement of their organisations (Isern and Pung, 2007).

resistance refers to action, overt or covert, exerted on behalf of maintaining the status quo.

A study by Meaney and Pung (2008) also reported employee resistance as the most common problem faced by management in implementing change. Given that resistance to change can be a very real problem for those leading change, focus has been directed in the literature around change attitudes and in particular individual and organisational change readiness (Bouckenooghe, 2010). Individual change readiness reflects an individual's beliefs, attitudes and intentions regarding the extent to which changes are needed, and the organisation's capacity to successfully undertake those changes (Armenakis *et al.*, 1993).

According to Jones *et al.* (2005) the reasons why employees resist change include the following:
- Satisfaction with the status quo.
- Perception of change as a personal threat.
- Viewing the cost of change as outweighing the benefits.
- Belief that management is mishandling the process.
- Belief that the change effort is not likely to succeed.

A useful framework for gaining a broader understanding of why the resistance is happening was proposed by Dijk and Dick (2009). They discuss two individual sources of resistance to change. The first, person-orientated resistance to change, involves an employee's fear of a loss of status, loss of pay or concern that the change has or will have a negative impact on their job security. The second source, principle-orientated resistance, centres on employee beliefs that the proposed or enacted change carries more costs than it does benefits for the organisation. By studying these elements, we can see how often employee resistance can be understood in part as a natural and expected outcome of implementation. Given the issues just explained, we will now outline some strategies for managing resistance to change.

BUILDING YOUR EMPLOYABILITY SKILLS

Resistance to Change

Have you ever worked anywhere where they brought in a change to the way people carried out their daily work? What could they have done to anticipate and avoid employee resistance to that change?

IMPROVING EMPLOYEE REACTIONS TO CHANGE

Although it appears that employee resistance to change is inevitable, managers need to understand whether change interventions are being implemented as intended and are producing the desired outcomes. Just as management practices have a powerful effect on employees' work experiences and performance, the way changes are managed can influence employees' attitudes towards the change and their level of receptiveness and commitment ▶See Chapter 8◀. According to Kotter and Schlesinger (1979) there are six methods that managers can draw upon to facilitate change and overcome resistance, and we look at these in turn below.

EDUCATION AND COMMUNICATION

It has been argued that the reason so many change efforts encounter resistance can be traced back to the absence of any attempt by the organisation to communicate with employees at both individual and team levels (Alas and Sharifi, 2002). As a result, some literature has pointed to the need for understanding change readiness at the collective level, involving the individual and group change processes. According to Weiner (2009) the concept of organisational change readiness refers to organisational members' change commitment and self-efficacy to implement organisational change. Kim *et al.* (2011) define change in supportive behaviours in this context as actions employees participate in which facilitate and contribute to a planned change initiated by the organisation. They state that trust and social support are integral to good employee relations and maintaining the outcomes of change initiatives. Empirical research has indicated that high communication increases acceptance, openness, and commitment to change (for example, Bordia *et al.*, 2004; Jones *et al.*, 2005) ▶See Chapter 14◀. Individuals need to know what is happening, why it is happening and how it will impact them. Indeed, as we discussed earlier, one of the reasons for a failed change event is that management invests in the planned change strategy but fails to communicate, train and follow up with staff as the change process progresses.

SPOTLIGHT ON SKILLS

You are working as a manager in Novetal, an organisation which is a privately owned world-wide manufacturer of metal cans, operating in 21 countries, with 8000 employees and turnover of €1.6 billion in 2006. The corporate culture centres on trust, transparency and teamwork. Novetal is based in the Netherlands but has a head office in Paris, and operates primarily throughout Europe. Its strategy is to be one of the best metal-can manufacturers as opposed to the most profitable or biggest, and it places great emphasis on values surrounding operational excellence. The company is considering an acquisition strategy in order to meet company objectives.

1 Assess how the company could approach the change using Kotter's checklist.

2 Consider whether the leadership of change always happens from the top of the organisation.

To help you answer these questions, visit bloomsbury.pub/organisational-behaviour to watch the video of Simon Shaw from Eurostar talking about organisational change.

PARTICIPATION AND INVOLVEMENT

Employees are unlikely to resist a change decision in which they have participated. Their participation is critical for obtaining commitment and increasing the quality of the change decision. The success of implementing change is generally associated with those who facilitate the change process. It is thus important to view the change process through the eyes of the participants who are most critical to the process – that is, the managers themselves, the people who establish priorities, devise strategies, control resources and manage performance ▸**See Chapter 3**◂. In this respect, managers constitute internal change agents who shape the conditions for change. A change agent is generally a person from inside or outside the organisation who helps an organisation transform itself by focusing on such matters as organisational effectiveness, improvement and development. Such change agents may be senior line managers or those specifically charged with managing the processes of organisational development and cultural change in the organisation. They act as a champion for employees, representing employee concerns to senior management and working to increase employees' commitment to the organisation and their ability to deliver business results.

change agent refers to a manager who seeks to reconfigure an organisation's roles, responsibilities, structures, outputs, processes, systems, technology or other resources in the light of improving organisational effectiveness.

NEGOTIATION AND AGREEMENT

Literature on the management of change has frequently indicated that the first step to achieving lasting organisational change is to deal with the resistance; that is, to identify resistance as an obstacle to be overcome and to select a change strategy that will minimise or eliminate it. However, this underplays the political dimensions which shape organisations' and their members' decisions and conduct ▸**See Chapter 8**◂. Indeed, the change agent has to find a balance between being the technical expert (the person assumed to have the answers on all matters relating to the change) and the process facilitator (the person with the techniques to allow the organisation to find its own answers). This is challenging given the diversity of values and interests, politicised and value-driven decision-making processes and the subjective interpretation of information in change efforts. In addition, some employees see change programmes as just another task to do in addition to the tasks which are central to their individual roles.

MANIPULATION AND CO-OPTATION

Manipulation refers to covert ways of influencing employees. For example, if management threatens to close a plant where employees are resisting an across-the-board pay cut, but the threat is actually untrue, management are using manipulation. In contrast, co-optation combines manipulation and participation. It strives to pay off the leaders of a resistance group by giving them a key role, seeking their advice so as to get their approval, and emphasising the value placed on their opinions.

SELECTING PEOPLE TO LEAD CHANGE

The literature suggests that proactive, open-minded managers embrace change willingly as it offers additional opportunities to help their organisations grow, to generate more sales and deliver more value to customers. Models of change have been criticised for implying a top-down approach to initiation and implementation of change. However, as we have discussed, employee involvement and participation are critical for ensuring employees' commitment to and ownership of the change process.

EXPLICIT AND IMPLICIT COERCION

Kotter and Schlesinger (1979) define coercion as the application of direct threats or force on the resisters. Examples of this strategy include threats of transfer, loss of promotions, negative performance evaluations and a poor letter of recommendation.

LEARNING HOW EMPLOYEES RESPOND TO THE CHANGE

One way in which the organisation can review the success of a change event is by studying employee perceptions of the way the changes were managed and the effect it had on their experience of work. A useful framework in this regard is the change management indicator proposed by Hayes and Hyde (1998), which provides managers with an insight into employee attitudes towards the change and the issues they encounter. This is presented in Figure 13.4.

This diagnostic change tool can be used by management to promote an open discursive culture around the change initiative. It can also be used to capture employees' opinions over time and to assess employee experiences in different departments, functions and organisational levels. Managing change involves helping an individual, group or organisation to change their existing behaviour and providing feedback that signals the effectiveness of new behaviours, with incentives that reward new levels of performance to help embed new practices.

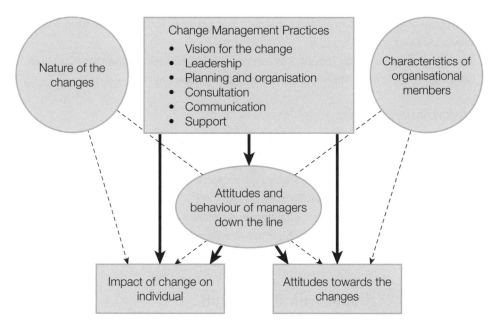

Figure 13.4 Factors affecting employee responses to change

Source: Hayes (2018).

LEADERSHIP AND ORGANISATIONAL CHANGE

Leadership is widely regarded as the primary enabler of the change process, in which a strong vision can make a valuable contribution to the success of an initiative. Reflecting on the role of the leader as a critical change agent is a central theme in the literature on change processes. Leadership can be understood as a set of activities or behaviours that mobilise adaptive behaviours on the part of members of the organisation.

Within the literature, focus has been directed on differentiating between transactional and transformational types of leadership ▸**See Chapter 6**◂. The Ohio State studies, Fielder's model, and path–goal theory describe transactional leaders who guide their followers towards established goals by clarifying role and task requirements. Transformational leaders inspire followers to transcend their self-interest for the good of the organisation and can have an extraordinary effect on their followers.

CHARACTERISTICS OF TRANSACTIONAL AND TRANSFORMATIONAL LEADERS

According to Bass (1999), and discussed in more detail in Chapter 6 ▸**See Chapter 6**◂, transformational leaders can be differentiated from transactional leaders as follows:

Transactional leader

- Contingent reward: emphasises the exchange of rewards for effort; promises remuneration for good performance; recognises accomplishments.

- Management by exception (active): watches and searches for deviations from rules and standards; takes corrective action.
- Management by exception (passive): intervenes only if standards are not met.
- Laissez-faire: abdicates responsibilities; avoids making decisions.

Transformational leader

- Idealised influence: provides vision and sense of mission; instils pride; gains respect and trust.
- Inspirational motivation: communicates high expectations; uses symbols to focus efforts; and expresses important purposes in simple ways.
- Intellectual stimulation: promotes intelligence, rationality and careful problem-solving.
- Individualised consideration: gives personal attention; treats each employee individually; coaches and advises.

IMPACT OF TECHNOLOGY ON BEHAVIOUR

The impact of Covid-19 has resulted in a significant change in the way people work across the world. Employees had to pivot to remote working and are continuing to work remotely while the vaccinations are being rolled out. In effect, remote working presents an opportunity for organisations to change their way of working over the longer term. However, many employees have reported that they miss the social interaction of going into the office. New research has found that almost half of employees are finding working from home much more difficult physically, mentally and emotionally. The issue of isolation was mentioned by many respondents; nearly a third (28%) of employees said that their mental health had declined as a direct result of the pandemic. Despite the difficulties associated with working from home, a significantly large proportion (86%) said they would be happy to work from home more frequently than before Covid-19. This raises really interesting questions around how organisations will manage this hoped for change after the pandemic is under control and employees are free to return to the office.

CREDIT: PHOTO BY SURFACE ON UNSPLASH

KOTTER'S CHANGE MODEL AND LEADERSHIP

John P. Kotter is a Harvard Business School professor and leading thinker and author on organisational change management. Kotter believes that organisational change can be managed by a leader using a dynamic, non-linear 8-step approach. Each stage acknowledges a key principle identified by Kotter relating to people's response and approach to change. Kotter's 8-step change model is summarised below.

1   Establish a sense of urgency by creating a compelling reason why change is needed.

2   Form a coalition with enough power to lead the change. Kotter indicates that unless those who recognise the need for change can build a team to direct the process, the change event is unlikely to build momentum.

3   Create a new vision to direct the change, and strategies for achieving the vision. Kotter (1996) identifies six criteria for an effective vision – it needs to be: imaginable (conveying a picture of what the future will look like); desirable (appealing to the long-term interests of employees, customers and stakeholders); feasible (comprising realistic, attainable goals); focused (clear enough to provide guidance in decision-making); flexible (general enough to allow individual initiatives and alternative responses in light of changing conditions); and communicable (easy to communicate).

4   Communicate the vision throughout the organisation.

5   Empower others to act on the vision by removing barriers to change and encouraging risk-taking and creative problem-solving.

6   Plan for, create and reward short-term wins that move the organisation toward the new vision.

7   Consolidate improvements, reassess changes and make necessary adjustments in the new programmes.

8   Reinforce the changes by demonstrating the relationship between new behaviours and organisational success.

Kotter (1996) organises each of these steps into three distinct phases. The first phase, creating a climate for change, includes steps 1, 2 and 3. The second phase, engaging and enabling the whole organisation, consists of steps 4, 5 and 6. The final phase, implementing and sustaining the change, encompasses steps 7 and 8.

ORGANISATIONAL DEVELOPMENT

In the last section we learned that leading change is a form of management control through the application of techniques that involve assisting employees to achieve a desired future, with defined performance outcomes in line with the organisational strategy. Organisational development (OD) is an approach to organisational effectiveness that draws on behavioural and social sciences for understanding planned change efforts. French and Bell (1978) described organisational development as the long-term effort to improve an organisation's problem-solving and renewal processes. This improvement should occur through fostering the development of a more collaborative organisation culture characterised by team working arrangements and supported by a change agent and the use of applied behavioural sciences, including action research. OD offers a systematic framework on how and why people behave and organisations operate. Below, we identify 10 key perspectives and assumptions that underpin the field:

organisational development (OD) refers to the concern for the vitalising, energising, actualising, activating and renewing of organisations through technical and human resources.

1   **Systems perspective:** Outstanding performance depends on interactions between and among the multiple elements of the organisation; between the people, processes, structure and values of the organisation, and between the organisation and its external environment.

2   **Alignment perspective:** The effectiveness of organisations will be determined by a state of congruence between people, process, structure, values and environment.

3 **Participation perspective:** People will become more committed to implementing solutions if they have been involved in the problem-solving process.
4 **Social-capital perspective:** To achieve outstanding performance, organisational leaders seek to create a network of interdependent relationships that provides the basis for trust, cooperation and collective action.
5 **Teamwork perspective:** Accepting a shared purpose and responsibility for interdependent tasks enhances coordination, commitment and creativity, and supports outstanding performance.
6 **Multiple stakeholder perspective:** Outstanding performance requires the organisational leaders to balance the expectations of multiple stakeholders: shareholders, employees, customers, suppliers, host community, labour unions, trade associations, governments and so on.
7 **Problem-solving perspective:** Conflicts over task issues can increase the quality of decisions if they occur in an environment of collaboration and trust.
8 **Open communications perspective:** Open and candid communication, especially upward in the hierarchy, creates the opportunity for learning and development while building trust and collaboration.
9 **Evolution/revolution perspective:** Organisations must develop the competence to engage in both incremental (evolutionary) and fundamental (revolutionary) change.
10 **Process facilitation perspective:** Individuals who reside outside of the organisational hierarchy can become both facilitators and teachers of effective implementation processes in partnership with organisational members.

ETHICAL BEHAVIOUR IN THE WORKPLACE

At this stage of the chapter, you are now aware of the pressures that organisations are regularly under to change in order to stay competitive and increase both efficiency and effectiveness.

A lot of change initiatives depend on employees being able to implement the changes. And this is where we often find resistance. As humans we generally like routine at work as it makes us feel safe and comfortable. Research tells us that if we have been doing our work in the same way for some time, then it becomes difficult for us to see how a change can be good for us as individuals. Change brings uncertainty. This often leads to employee resistance to change. If an organisation wants to lead change efforts with integrity, ethics must be instilled into the approach taken to change management. Keeping ethical approaches to the fore, what initiatives do you think would be important, to overcome employee resistance to change?

DEFINING AND EXPLAINING ORGANISATIONAL DEVELOPMENT

French and Bell (1978) identified several characteristics that differentiate OD from more traditional change interventions. These consist of an emphasis on group and organisational processes, the work team as the key unit for learning more effective modes of organisation, the collaborative management of work-team culture, the use of employees as change agents, and a view of the change effort as an ongoing process. French and Bell (1978) also indicated the key assumptions of OD. These centred on assumptions that employees are motivated if provided with an environment that is both supportive and challenging. In addition, it supposes that employees wish to be accepted and to interact cooperatively and that the interplay of the dynamics of work teams has a powerful effect on the attitudes and behaviours of people. In particular, the leadership style and the climate of the team are powerful in the change effort. Finally, organisational development efforts need to be sustained by corresponding changes in the appropriate compensation, training, staffing, task and communications system.

Organisations can draw on a number of OD techniques or interventions for bringing about change. We will outline three of these.

1 **Survey feedback approach.** This tool assesses the attitudes possessed by organisational members. For this approach, employees are usually asked to complete a question-naire about their perceptions and attitudes on a range of topics. Such topics include decision-making practices, communication effectiveness, coordination among units, and satisfaction with the organisation, job, peers and immediate supervisor.

2 **Team building.** Team building is an approach which focuses on goal setting, the development of interpersonal relations among team members, role analysis to clarify each member's role and responsibilities, and team process analysis to increase trust, improve coordinative efforts and accomplish work tasks.

3 **Appreciative inquiry.** This approach seeks to identify the unique qualities and special strengths of the organisation, which members can build on to improve performance. The approach consists of four steps: discovery, which sets out to identify what people think are the organisation's strengths; dreaming, where employees use information from the discovery phase to speculate on possible futures; design, where participants find a common vision of how the organisation will be in the future; and destiny, which involves writing action plans and developing implementation strategies.

MANAGERIAL TAKEAWAYS

There are a number of key forces driving organisations to adjust their strategies, including factors such as globalisation, technology and global shocks, and this has led to a lot of research aimed at understanding what makes change processes work. The three key phases of the planned change theory of Kurt Lewin are one of the most well known. Research has also highlighted that the success rate of major change initiatives within organisations has been less than expected. To understand this issue, we focused on the question of why employees resist change in their organisations, and discussed the ways in which organisations can manage this resistance. We drew attention to the importance of a leader who develops a vision for change. We emphasised the central role of management practices involving communication, participation and consultation, planning and organisation, and an awareness of the personality types of the people involved and their level of receptivity towards the change. Finally, we presented the key assumptions and themes characterising the field of organisational development.

Change at ChemCo

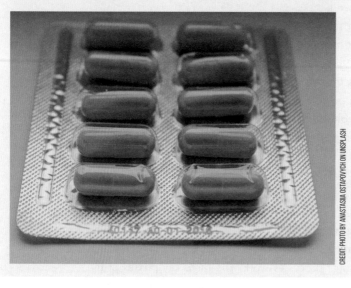
OB IN PRACTICE

ChemCo is a global organisation which distributes pharmaceutical products throughout Europe, the Middle East and recently in Indonesia. Despite a long history of growth through acquisition, some of the company's recent acquisitions, which have been led by a relatively new top team, have not delivered the anticipated level of benefit. The company faces increased external pressures from changes in the legal, technological and economic environments in which it operates. As part of a strategy to grow its share of the specialist pharmaceuticals market in

Asia, the company has recently finalised a deal to acquire a local distributor, MedicalCo, which dominates the pharmaceuticals market in large parts of Asia. The CEO has turned to you, the HR Manager, for advice about the management of the current acquisition.

This acquisition will involve operating in a completely foreign business environment characterised by poor infrastructure due to a lack of public infrastructure investment and endemically high levels of corruption. In addition, approximately 80% of the population count themselves as

Muslims, but it is also one of the most ethnically diverse. More than 500 languages are spoken in the country, and separatists are active in a number of provinces.

MedicalCo has four distribution depots in the country and two of these depots will have to be closed to ensure operational efficiencies. This will result in a reduction in the number of depot staff. In addition, there will be some overcapacity of middle managers. The focus after the acquisition will centre on consolidating existing sales and jointly developing new products and services to secure future business.

Questions

Imagine that you have been asked as part of your role as HR Manager to advise ChemCo about how to manage the integration of MedicalCo in Asia.

1 Outline what you see as issues which may act as barriers to the change process.
2 What advice would you give to the CEO regarding strategies to tackle the issues?
3 Which theories and concepts of managing change would inform the advice you would offer?

 ## CHAPTER REVIEW QUESTIONS

1 Outline the different types of organisational change.
2 How can a manager analyse the change context?
3 What are the considerations for organisations when deciding upon the nature and type of change, and how change should take place?
4 What are some of the potential forces acting for and against a change initiative? Use Lewin's model as a guide.

5   How can organisational development (OD) improve organisational performance through managing change?

6   A significant feature of Kotter's model is the role of leadership in the management of change. Discuss this statement.

7   To what extent can the HR function act as a change agent during the change process?

8   Why do employees resist change efforts?

 FURTHER READING

Black, S. (2014) *It Starts with One: Changing Individuals Changes Organizations*, 3rd edn. Upper Saddle River, NJ: Pearson.

Buchanan, D., Fitzgerald, L. and Ketley, D. (2007) *The Sustainability and Spread of Organizational Change*. London: Routledge.

Clegg, C. and Walsh, S. (2004) Change management: Time for change? *European Journal of Work and Organizational Psychology*, 13(2), 217–229.

Hayes, J. (2018) *The Theory and Practice of Change Management*, 5th edn. London: Red Globe Press.

Kotter, J. (2007) Leading change: Why transformation efforts fail. *Harvard Business Review*, 85(1), 96–103.

LaScola, M. (2017) Employee involvement in change can be messy – But it's necessary. *People Management*. Available at: http:// www.peoplemanagement.co.uk/voices/comment/employee-involvement-change

USEFUL WEBSITES

www.shrm.org

The Society for Human Resource Management provides relevant and current information on HR topics such as managing organisational change.

www.peoplemanagement.co.uk

The CIPD website has a number of articles on organisational change:

https://www.peoplemanagement.co.uk/voices/comment/post-covid-company-not-exist-create-together

https://www.peoplemanagement.co.uk/experts/advice/employee-relations-during-organisational-change

https://www.cipd.co.uk/knowledge/fundamentals/emp-law/health-safety/coronavirus-factsheet

This 2020 CIPD factsheet explains the role of HR as a change agent during and after the pandemic and explains how HR practices could help protect their workforces.

Online Resources

Visit bloomsbury.pub/organisational-behaviour to access additional materials to support teaching and learning.

14 COMMUNICATION IN THE WORKPLACE

Vivienne Byers and Lindsay Harrison

LEARNING OUTCOMES

BY THE END OF THIS CHAPTER YOU SHOULD BE ABLE TO:

- Understand the importance of communication in the workplace.
- Describe the process of communication, both verbal and non-verbal.
- Identify the different communication channels and barriers to effective communication.

- Outline elements of effective organisational communication.
- Demonstrate how changes in technology have affected communication within and between organisations and their employees.
- Explain how to overcome potential problems in inter-cultural communication.

CREDIT: ALAMY STOCK PHOTO

THIS CHAPTER DISCUSSES...

INTRODUCTION

All individuals, groups and organisations communicate by sharing 'meaning' between each other. This meaning is conveyed through information and ideas, which can be constructed effectively, as outlined in the following feature. Communicating is not just about transferring this meaning, but is a two-way process as it is also about being understood and belonging to a group. The study of communication employs concepts basic to an understanding of human behaviour. Thus, an understanding of the process of communication and how the use of different communication channels can impact on the messages delivered and received is at the centre of most organisational activity. This chapter identifies the key factors involved in organisational communication and explains how changes in technology have affected communication within and between organisations and their employees. Communication as an organisational behaviour topic has become a specialist sub-discipline in its own right (Buchanan and Huczynski, 2020). Bringing people together with common goals in an organisation cannot be done without communication (Thompson, 2013, p. 14). According to Boone and Kurtz (2010) managers spend about 80% of their time in direct communication with others, whether on the phone, in meetings, via e-mail or in individual conversations. Communication and organisational success are directly related. Good communication can have a positive and mobilising effect on employees. Poor communication can lead to negative or unintentional consequences, such as distortion of goals and objectives, conflict, loss of motivation and poor performance.

communicating is sharing or exchanging information.

IN REALITY

Communication techniques are used by both governments and businesses globally. One communication technique or tool that has gained significant attention is 'nudging'. The term 'nudge' was coined by Richard Thaler (Nobel Prize in Economics winner, 2017) and his colleague Cass Sunstein. They define nudging in their seminal book published in 2008 as '... any aspect of choice architecture that alters people's behavior in a predictable way without forbidding any options or significantly changing their economic incentives' (Thaler and Sunstein, 2008, p. 6). Essentially, it communicates options or choices by structuring their context, timing and presentation to 'nudge' the employee or the citizen to make a decision. It can be used as a tool or approach for an organisation seeking to innovate, through guiding employees' behaviour, as well as influencing potential prospects or customers externally. It has been used by governments worldwide to influence citizen's behaviour.

Nudging is rooted in the study of behavioural economics and behavioural science and is utilised in over 70% of the world's governments, with the formation of 'behavioural insights teams' or 'nudge units' (Deloitte Insights Report, 2019) The theory underpinning this approach is that when making a decision, individuals do not consider all the possible options available to them, but instead 'satisfice' by reverting to familiar shortcuts or heuristics to process information (Simon, 1965). This can be due to reasons such as limited attention or a lack of consideration of the consequences of a decision for the future. Research recognises that decision-making is also influenced or constrained by the role of social norms and routines, including the importance of society and fairness.

To expand individual awareness of positive choice options, nudging has been used to communicate warnings in relation to smoking or waste management, reminders for tax payers, obligations to conserve energy. It also has been used to communicate social norms by sharing what most of the population does – for example, nine out of ten hotel guests reuse their towels – in order to facilitate choices. It can be described as a gentle push by intervening in the choice architecture of individuals. Thaler and Sunstein (2008) describe it as the deliberate design of the individual's environment, where the designer is aware of the choices people usually make in that context, such as in retail environments where healthy foods are shelved at eye level. According to Dianoux *et al.* (2019) it is a flexible tool, quickly adaptable and modifiable, with low implementation cost, in order to change current individual behaviour by promoting appropriate actions. This is achieved through construction of the choice architecture, using communication that leaves the individual free to behave as they choose, that induces behaviour that is beneficial for the individual, the community or the planet, and where the cost of implementation is low, but the consequences for behaviour change are positive.

Sources

Deloitte (2019) Government trends 2020: What are the most transformational trends in government today? *Report from Deloitte Center for Government Insights*. Available at: https://www2.deloitte.com/us/en/insights/industry/public-sector/government-trends/2020/government-nudge-thinking.htm (accessed 4 October 2019).

Dianoux, C., Heitz-Spahn, S., Siadou-Martin, B., Thevenot, G. and Yildiz, H. (2019) Nudge: A relevant communication tool adapted for agile innovation. *Journal of Innovation Economics Management*, 1, 7–27.

Samson, A. (ed.) (2018) *The Behavioral Economics Guide 2018*. Available at: http://www.behavioraleconomics.com (accessed 4 October 2019).

Simon, H.A. (1965) *Administrative Behavior*, 2nd edn. New York: Free Press.

Sunstein, C.R. (2014) Nudging: A very short guide. *Journal of Consumer Policy*, 37(4), 583–588.

Thaler, R.H. and Sunstein, C.R. (2008) Nudge: Improving decisions about health, wealth, and happiness. New Haven, CT: Yale University Press.

WHAT PURPOSE DOES COMMUNICATION HAVE IN AN ORGANISATION?

People have always needed to communicate to live in social groups and to plan and coordinate activity. No group or organisation can exist without sharing meaning in some way between its members. When we communicate with others, we are usually trying to influence other people's understanding, behaviour or attitudes.

Core to most organisational activity is an understanding of the process of communication and how the use of different communication channels can impact on the messages delivered and received. Mintzberg (1990) describes the purpose of communication with others in the workplace as being able to inform, instruct, motivate or seek information. His seminal study of the work of senior managers points out that managers don't often leave meetings or hang up the telephone to get back to work, as communication *is* their work. From a top management perspective, the purpose of organisational communication is to achieve coordinated action. The members of the organisation will not have a focus if they are not involved in effective communication with one another. Employers expect employees to be effective communicators and rate employees for their communicative performances. A study in the US reported that employers ranked communication skills among the top three most valued skills, but rated new graduates at all levels as largely deficient in this area (Association of American Colleges and Universities, 2013). However, many organisations see organisational communication as a problem. It has been cited as a key issue that impacts on planning effectiveness, organisational change ▶**See Chapter 13**◀ and implementation (Kotter, 1995; Jones *et al.*, 2004; Lewis and Seibold, 2012; Carlström and Ekman, 2012). How often do we hear 'what we need around here is good communication'? (Cai and Fink, 2009, p. 425). It is pivotal to dealing with people and the workplace and is fundamental to organisational success. Therefore, it is important that managers and employees are aware of the systems and techniques of communication that are in place for their organisation and use them well.

WHAT ARE ELEMENTS IN THE COMMUNICATION PROCESS?

Communication in organisations is crucial; it may be direct in terms of a verbal instruction, an e-mail or a written report, or indirect in terms of information sharing through internal IT platforms or apps. It also may be more casual in terms of a chat at lunch, or it may be

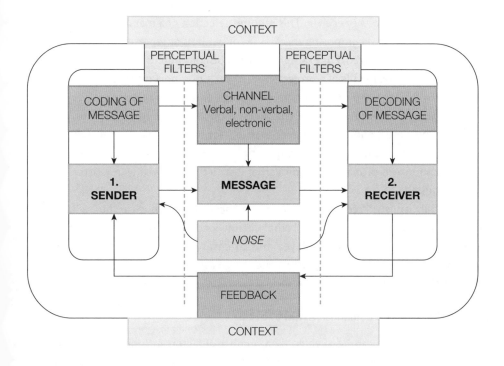

Figure 14.1 The communications process

Source: Developed and adapted from Shannon (1948), and Buchanan and Huczynski (2020, p. 225).

unintentional in terms of body language or posture observed at a meeting. The most basic form of human interpersonal communication can be described as a process by which ideas, information, opinions and attitudes – the message – are conveyed between one person or one group and another.

To explore this idea further we can look at the key components in the communication process, which are illustrated in Figure 14.1. This model is adapted from the work of mathematician Claude Shannon (1948); his original model was designed to accommodate any form of communication rather than just human interpersonal communication.

However, the model of communication illustrated here includes a number of additions, which will be described in this section, including a feedback loop, perceptual filters and the context in which the communication takes place – all of which are very important in interpersonal human communication. The basic elements of the model include: (1) the source or sender (a person who is responsible for encoding an intended meaning into a specific message), and (2) the receiver (the intended person who decodes the message into a perceived meaning). This process may appear to be very basic but it is not quite as simple as it looks. Hence, we need to examine it further to identify the other elements at work, their sequencing and the weaknesses and barriers that can arise and lead to communication problems or distortions.

HOW IS INFORMATION TRANSMITTED?

encoding is the process of designing a message, represented as a set of symbols to be sent that makes sense to the receiver.

Thus, the communication process commences with the encoding of the message to be transmitted or sent to the receiver. This requires selection of a message from a number of potential messages and composing this as a set of symbols or representations of the meaning that can be transmitted. For example, this can be communicating with an employee to instruct them on the details of a project. Therefore, it is important that these instructions are clear and make sense to them. The next stage entails the selection of a channel for the transmission of this message. A channel is a medium through which the message is delivered. There are a number of choices available for transmission: verbal, written or electronic. In the case of a project brief or for a student assignment or continuous assessment, communication will probably include verbal instructions as well as a written outline of what is required.

decoding is the process of deciphering and interpreting a message received, to make sense of it.

A carefully constructed e-mail may make the instructions clear but a face-to-face meeting can utilise verbal and non-verbal channels not only to clarify the details but to encourage and motivate the employee and to ensure they have received the message. Once the content has been transmitted, the receiver needs to pick up the message, which will require decoding.

noise is any factor, either external or internal, that interferes with transmission of the message, through creation of static or interference in the communication process.

WHAT IS NOISE IN THE COMMUNICATION SYSTEM?

The signal or message can be affected by a number of factors including noise. If this is too strong the message may become garbled or fail to reach the receiver at all. This can be as simple as not being able to decode a telephone conversation due to a lot of external factors such as background noise in an office or static on the line. It could also refer to distractions caused by internal factors such as hunger, fatigue or headaches that affect how we process the message.

The message can also be affected by perceptual filters ▶**See Chapter 3◀**. For example, does the receiver perceive the message in a way that is consistent with the sender's intention? This can be affected by cultural and language differences when the words themselves are not mutually understood. The message is also affected by the context; communication style will vary if the boss and employee are in a very formal situation in the workplace, such as when the employee is called to the boss's office, as opposed to outside of the workplace in a social context. The context can also be affected by relations between both sender and receiver.

The model allows for a feedback loop where the receiver can send back what they have understood by the message. This can be done using non-verbal cues, such as a nod, or by requesting clarification verbally. Frequently, this feedback loop does not operate effectively and the sender may not be sure that the message has been received. Therefore, the process of communication is not as simple as you would think, as messages are not always perceived as intended (Kikoski, 1998, cited in Bowditch and Buono, 2005). Communication accuracy can be affected by the perceptual filters already mentioned, as they can play a large part in the deciphering of a message. People can associate different meanings with certain concepts and ideas due to their differing experiences and backgrounds, and this needs to be taken into account when communicating with others. The process becomes even more complicated when working in a culturally diverse workplace (we will discuss this in more detail later). To recognise the errors that can occur in communication in the workplace we must consider six factors (adapted from O'Reilly and Pondy, 1979, cited in Bowditch and Buono, 2005, p. 105):

1   Who is communicating to whom in terms of the roles they have in the organisation (for example, boss and subordinate)?
2   Are the language or symbols being used to communicate understood by both parties?
3   What communication channel is being used?
4   What is the content of the communication? (Is it familiar or unfamiliar information?)
5   What are the personal characteristics of the sender (for example, personality or appearance can lead to assumptions or judgements by the receiver based on experience) and the relations between the sender and receiver (do they trust one another)?
6   What is the context in which the message is being sent, such as the structure of the organisation, the physical space and social surroundings?

Therefore, this means that as a sender or communicator, if you want to get your message across accurately, you need to consider:
- The message;
- The audience or receiver; and
- How the message is likely to be received.

This model assumes that communication is intentional. However, in many cases our body language or non-verbal communication may transmit a message that we never consciously meant to transmit. These non-verbal signals and communication will be dealt with later in the chapter.

perceptual filters are personal characteristics or perceptions that influence the way individuals take in and make sense of information, which can interfere with transmitting or receiving messages.

INTERPERSONAL COMMUNICATION AND ACTIVE LISTENING

A number of issues arise in attempting to communicate successfully with others. In the workplace it is crucial that we get our message across; whether it is in a job interview, a work presentation or instructing an employee about an important project or task. It is important to establish good open communication through taking care not only to encode and deliver clear messages but also to be able to receive the messages that are returned and really take on board what the other person is saying. Effective usage of the feedback loop in the communication process (see above) will help to ensure that the communication is successful. Listening is a large part of the communication process and its importance is often underestimated. How well you listen has a major impact on job effectiveness and on relationship quality with others. It is used not only to receive the message and obtain the information but to understand it and to learn from it.

active listening
is a process of
making a conscious
effort to sense,
process and
respond actively to
a communicated
message.

This can be achieved through active listening. Often we are only marginally listening; distracted, uninterested or already processing what we are going to say in response. This often happens when you are introduced to a group of new people and you are too busy introducing yourself to actually keep track of their names. Active listening in this case would require that you sense (receive the message, for example a name in an introduction), process (assign a meaning to the information transmitted) and then respond (clarifying what you have heard). In the case of introductions, that may simply be repeating the person's name, for example *'Pleased to meet you, Mary.'* Active listening is not only consciously engaging in listening and being encouraging but it also requires deferring judgement, letting the sender complete their point before asking questions. It is also appropriate to be respectful and understanding, as that way you will get the best out of the communication exchange.

COMMUNICATION CHANNELS

Revisiting the key components in the communication process (see Figure 14.1), the choice of channel to communicate a message is very important to achieve understanding in the exchange. The organisation or workplace is a network of information and communication channels. Traditionally, there have always been formal and informal communication channels but the electronic age has added a third category – quasiformal channels (French *et al.*, 2015). Managers now have tools such as intranets and web-based technologies to establish organisation-wide communication channels. All managers and employees should understand and be able to use each of the multiple channels for communication within their organisation.

FORMAL COMMUNICATION CHANNELS

These formal channels are officially defined pathways that follow the chain of command or hierarchy in organisations. These channels, being official and holding authority, are used to send letters, e-mails, policy statements or announcements. They are an important part of organisational life but they are only one part of a manager's communication skill set.

INFORMAL COMMUNICATION CHANNELS

Informal channels do not follow the chain of command. They are represented by interpersonal networks. For example, groups with similar interests form to exchange information. This networking cuts across chains of command and can come about, for example, as employees meet at the water cooler, or in the canteen at work. Some managers use these informal networks to facilitate formal communication channels or to gather information. Management by Walking Around (MBWA) (Peters and Waterman, 1982) can be seen as a way of cutting across the usual formal channels by visiting the staff as well as customers to find out what is happening at the front line. Managers who spend time walking around can reduce the 'distance' that might be perceived between themselves and their employees and enable them to engage in more meaningful communication. It can result in better information and communication exchange. This information will help inform senior strategic decision-making and the decisions will have more relevance for the front-line staff. Additionally, this participatory approach to communication and decision-making can influence levels of employee engagement and motivation. However, the 'walking about' option needs to facilitate genuine engagement by senior managers rather than looking like an opportunity to check up on employees' activities.

WHAT IS THE GRAPEVINE?

Informal communication can take a number of forms, such as unofficial networks that supplement the formal channels, and the grapevine. The grapevine functions as a major informal channel in organisations. Employees rely on it as an invaluable source of information. The grapevine arises from social interactions, therefore it is as dynamic and varied as the people involved. There are some drawbacks to its use in that information can become distorted along its pathways or channels and it can be used to spread rumour and negativity. However, it can also be used to disseminate important information along informal lines. Management sometimes uses the grapevine deliberately to transmit information that it may not wish to transmit formally, or even to 'sound out' employees in respect of an initiative that may prove unpopular.

Van Hoye and Lievens (2009) showed that the grapevine and information communicated by peers had a strong influence on whether a potential applicant applied for a job in a company. A good manager should be aware of the information circulating in this unofficial communication channel and should take measures to prevent the flow of false information. In order to combat rumours in organisations it is important to promote healthy, accurate communications and to avoid concealing bad news. It is also important to maintain open communication channels so that employees can voice their concerns and to encourage their ideas and suggestions.

Gossip is another informal source of information in an organisation. It is the idle talk or snippets of information about people and events that are passed along informal communication channels. It can be damaging and dangerous, but it can also fulfil a function as a source of socialising and developing group norms ▸See Chapter 7◂, as well as allowing employees to feel they belong to informal groupings and thus, the organisation. In this way it can also be a morale booster, and a means to express employee concerns.

QUASIFORMAL CHANNELS

QUASIFORMAL CHANNELS

Quasiformal channels are planned communication connections between holders of various positions within the organisation. They are defined as being almost, or partly, formal and add additional channels between the formal and informal channels. Thus, managers can have access to information on an authorised basis and these channels can form a useful part of the company's overall management system. These systems using structures such as project teams or product committees are often used to help encourage innovation rather than through formal structures and formal communication processes. This approach has been extended by the information age, which has provided organisations with new opportunities to link managers effectively through e-mail, intranet and other electronic media tools.

HOW DOES ORGANISATIONAL STRUCTURE AND DESIGN IMPACT ON COMMUNICATION?

Utilising the communication channels outlined above, one may assume that information is flowing both upwards from the employees and downwards from management. Direction of communication is important and is influenced by the structure and design of the organisation. Facilitating flows of communication in an organisation is important as communication must also be able to move laterally to be effective (see Figure 14.2).

DOWNWARD COMMUNICATION

downward communication flows from one level of an organisation to a lower level.

Downward communication is used to implement plans and goals, explain policies and procedures, offer feedback on performance and give directions or instructions regarding job specifications and duties. In traditionally structured hierarchical organisations, this is seen as the primary direction for an organisation's information flow. It is important to

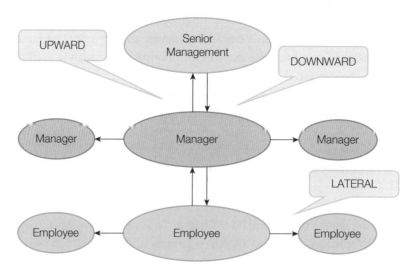

Figure 14.2 Direction of communication flows

gain employee commitment especially in times of organisational change, so that they are fully informed about the reasons behind any changes. There may be reasons why certain information is withheld, such as commercial sensitivities, but this has to be balanced with the need to involve and motivate employees ▶See Chapter 5◀. Another key issue in respect of effective communications is that of trust in management. If employees feel they are being left out of the information loop this can undermine their feelings of trust and belonging to the organisation and affect the psychological contract (Dries and De Gieter, 2014). They may even feel that management is out of touch and has no plan. Middle managers can also help in interpreting and explaining information coming from top management to lower-level staff (Floyd and Wooldridge, 1997). Neeley and Leonardi (2011) found that many managers repeated their communications a number of times to lower-level employees utilising different media, as this made the message more effective and ensured it was getting through. Blocks to downward communication can include managerial style, the organisational culture ▶See Chapter 12◀, which may be closed/secretive, or that the organisation has a tall or overly bureaucratic structure.

UPWARD COMMUNICATION

Upward communication is used to provide information to management about what is happening at an operational level. It is important for a number of reasons, in that it facilitates feedback regarding performance and progress of plans and goals, it notifies management of problems or potential problems and it passes on complaints, but it is also important in providing a channel to facilitate ideas or suggestions. Upward communications from front-line and middle-level management have been found to be very important in terms of developing innovations and implementing change management (Floyd and Wooldridge, 2000). Middle managers can interpret and relate information from the front line to the organisation as a whole in what is referred to by Swanson *et al.* (1997) as a communicative role. The story of the Post-it® – the self-attaching note that sticks – is an example of how Spencer Silver, its creator, used standard channels of communications both upwards and laterally to communicate his idea without success. It was only when he used informal channels to garner interest that he achieved a breakthrough (Glass and Hume, 2013). It is the staff, who are experiencing the day-to-day reality of the organisation, and its customers who are best placed to provide feedback to senior management on what is working and what is not. This inclusive communication approach also has benefits for staff, with upward communication reported to increase employee motivation and commitment (Kalogiannidis, 2020). Barriers to upward communication include a lack of facilitation of an upward communication channel and culture, as well as the employees' fear of admitting to mistakes or that their ideas might be taken on board without due credit. Management can facilitate effective upward communications with an 'open door' policy and by enabling and acting on encounters for the receipt of feedback and information. An organic organisational structure and open climate facilitates commitment to communication. See also the 'changes in technology' impact section later in this chapter for further details on communication flows.

upward communication flows from a lower level of an organisation to a higher level.

LATERAL COMMUNICATION

lateral communication flows between members or employees in the same work group or department, or managers at the same level.

Lateral communication is communication between members or employees in the same work group or department, or between managers at the same level. Lateral communications serve an important function to facilitate coordination of the work undertaken. They also allow sharing of information and ideas, as well as expertise and best practice. Lateral communication flows are seen in flatter organisational structures. Barriers to lateral communication can be the protective self-interest of groups or departments, as well as increased specialisation, and thus, problems with language used such as different 'jargon' that is not widely and easily understandable.

BUILDING YOUR EMPLOYABILITY SKILLS

Communication Strategy

The Business Insider (Edwards, 2019) reported that countless Metro Bank customers queued to withdraw their money and valuables following a false rumour circulating on WhatsApp suggesting that the bank was on the verge of collapse through bankruptcy. Shares in Metro Bank hit a low despite efforts to shut down the social media rumours. As a line manager of Metro Bank, and given your understanding of the direction of communication and the communication process (Figure 14.1), what communication strategy would you implement to reassure customers and assist staff?

ARE THERE DIFFERENT TYPES OF COMMUNICATION?

How do members of an organisation communicate or transfer meaning between and among each other using the channels and information flows already described? Standard approaches are oral communication, written communication and non-verbal communication. With the development of multiple media tools there is an ever-expanding range of approaches that managers and employees can use. Some approaches can be more useful than others depending on the context.

ORAL COMMUNICATION

The main means by which we communicate with one another is through speaking. This can include conversations, group discussions and presentations, as well as using the grapevine to pass information by 'word of mouth'. The advantages of the oral communication approach are instant feedback and speed. You can gauge by body language whether your message has been understood or not, especially in a one-to-one situation. Now, thanks to communications technology, we can use video-conferencing or voice-over-IP services such as Skype or Zoom. A

Forbes Insights/Zoom global survey of 333 executives found that 92% of respondents believe that expanded use of video conferencing has a positive impact on their performance (Forbes Insights, 2017). However, there can be difficulties in communicating with a wider more disparate audience and the message can be lost altogether as it becomes distorted, if it is passed along the grapevine. To counteract any distortions or confusion and to be effective in getting a message across, Neeley and Leonardi's (2011) study showed that managers often repeated messages or instructions to employees by giving a verbal or oral message and backing it up with an e-mail repeating the same instruction.

Presentations are an important part of work life. They facilitate both upward and downward communication. If you are employed as a senior manager you will have to make presentations to your staff, to your shareholders or to potential clients. You may have to motivate your staff as you engage in an organisational change programme. Working as an employee you will need to be able to present results or progress in your work or that of your team. You may have to be able to convince management about a new way of doing things or new ideas or concepts that you or your team have developed. According to Dixon and O'Hara (2013) there are a number of basic steps you need to take to enable an effective presentation: the first is to establish a *strategy or plan*, that is, to understand your purpose and role and formulate a plan for communicating to, and understanding, the specific audience; then develop a *structure* to the presentation so that it flows; then you must put together the material with a good presentation *style*, making sure that you are aware of minimising distractions; and finally respond confidently to questions and challenges. It is important to remember that how you present is as important as the content that you present.

WRITTEN COMMUNICATION

Written communications include letters, e-mails, instant messaging, magazines or e-zines, and notices (including on electronic notice boards). A written communication can be useful to make sure the message is clear and verifiable. It can be stored and is available for reference. Taking time to draw up a concise yet detailed letter can be useful in order to gather your thoughts clearly and carefully. Written communications can be given if the instructions required are complex and lengthy. It is used to transmit plans and strategies as it can be used as a continuous reference point by which to measure progress. The only drawback to the approach is it can be time consuming and lacks an immediate feedback mechanism.

NON-VERBAL COMMUNICATION

Verbal literally means 'in words', therefore non-verbal communication is communication achieved by not just using words. It is the process of coding or conveying meaning through behaviours such as facial expressions, gestures and body posture. We can never 'not' communicate non-verbally as even an absence of response can convey some meaning. When we interact with others we are constantly sending and receiving messages via signs and gestures, use of space, as well as vocal tone. This is often referred to as 'body language'.

Body language can convey two important messages: the first is interest in another person and their views; and the second message is the perceived status between sender and receiver. Body language can add to a verbal message or complicate it. If you use gestures that are encouraging and open, and smile when delivering praise to a colleague, the message is augmented. If in contrast you are saying something positive but your facial gesture is negative, this can cause confusion.

SPOTLIGHT ON SKILLS

You have been selected as a communication consultant to support a restructuring of work teams in your organisation. This is part of an organisation-wide strategy to shake up people and develop innovation through teamwork. You need to put together an internal communications plan for this change initiative in your organisation.

1 Advancing technology is a regular feature of modern work environments. How has your understanding of channel transmission in the context of the communication process enabled you to ensure effective communication in a workplace environment with new and advancing mediums?

2 Explain how your understanding of the direction of communication within your workplace enabled you to encourage and develop innovation within the company.

To help you answer these questions, visit bloomsbury.pub/organisational-behaviour to watch the video of Gina London talking about internal communication strategies.

WHAT ARE THE BARRIERS TO EFFECTIVE COMMUNICATION?

Communication is not always perfect. Earlier in the chapter we looked at the process of communicating and identified two barriers to communication: noise and perceptual filters. Noise is anything that interferes with the message, idea or information we are trying to convey in the process of communication. A number of factors can cause noise in the system including tension or emotions, conflict, confusion, haste, cultural differences, gender differences or the setting itself (Thompson, 2013). The perceptual filters refer to the characteristics or perceptions of the individual that can interfere with transmitting or receiving messages. They include filtering and selective perception ▸See Chapter 3◂. Filtering can refer to purposely changing or manipulating information so you can present the best case possible and the receiver will respond positively. This can happen when you have made an error in the workplace and you want to explain it away in the most favourable light. Selective perception refers to how the receivers in the communication process will be influenced by their past experience, motivation, interest and expectations as to how they decode the message being conveyed by the sender. This is due to all of us interpreting reality in line with our experience and beliefs. We need to actively listen and read and not be held back by preconceived beliefs and thoughts. A study reported in *BusinessWeek* in 2006 found that participants only decoded e-mails' intent and tone correctly about 50% of the time (Brady, 2006).

Other barriers to communication include information overload. The developments in information and communications technology mean that communication is more frequent and faster and yet still needs management. For instance, the number of e-mails has increased exponentially. Brustein (2013) reported that 30% of all work time is now spent reading and sifting through e-mails. Another barrier to effective communication is the use of language itself. There is no need to confuse your listener or receiver by using a lot of jargon, technical language or abbreviations. Finally, the problem of effective communication can involve the sender. Communication apprehension or fear of communicating is a major factor which inhibits a sender's willingness to communicate and thus affects their capability to develop effective communication skills. Byrne *et al.*'s (2012) study assessed first year business students and showed that varying levels of communication apprehension existed among the students. It was influenced by perceptions of peer evaluation, prior experiences of communicating with new people, and how prepared the students were.

STRATEGIES FOR EFFECTIVE COMMUNICATION

Barriers to communication can be overcome through face-to-face communication, by checking decoding, by paying attention to context and by taking the other person's perspective through listening. Buchanan and Huczynski (2020) outline a range of different questioning techniques, conversation controls and listening skills to facilitate effective communication. Questioning techniques enable us to get the information we are looking for through the use of closed, open ended, reflective and probing questions. Conversational controls are described as lubricators, bridges and pauses. These controls can facilitate understanding and reciprocal communication. Lubricators are phrases to encourage further communication from a communication partner. Bridges allow links to conversation topics you want to reach. Pauses in terms of small gaps in conversations can facilitate further conversation. However, if they are longer than three seconds, they can either give a conversation partner time to think or, in a more threatening context, they can be seen as pressure to respond. Effective communication through effective listening is important and something many of us do not utilise. Active listening (see the discussion earlier, p. 304) conveys interest and attention to the other person. Giving constructive feedback employs a wide range of skills including listening skills and feedback skills.

DO WE ALL HEAR THE SAME THING IN A MESSAGE?

Researchers have identified a number of language difficulties that can arise when people are communicating cross-culturally. The communications process model in Figure 14.1 above doesn't fully account for cultural differences between the sender and receiver, other than through perceptual filters. Inter-cultural communication leads to possible communication barriers that need to be anticipated. A study reported by McShane (2006) of cultural diversity in some of Toronto's major hotels found that language barriers made it difficult for managers to give non-English speaking employees effective feedback.

Some of these language barriers include:

- Semantics – differences in meanings of words to different people.
- Differences in non-verbal symbols and signals.
- Word Connotations – words imply different things in different languages.
- Tone Differences – in some cultures tone changes, depending on context.
- Differences in Perception – different world views.

As a manager, you need to be sensitive to the fact that cross-cultural barriers may exist. You have to show respect for all workers. You should use language that is clear without any clichés or colloquialisms and speak slowly and clearly. You should remain alert to cultural differences in customs and behaviours. Do not let style, accent or grammar affect your perceptions and interpretation of the communications you are involved in.

Working in multi-cultural teams requires good communications. Professor Martha Maznevski has carried out extensive work on leading diverse teams globally (Maznevski, 2007). Her guide to building diverse teams provides invaluable insights to developing effective inter-cultural communication (see the video clip link in Useful Websites at the end of the chapter). She notes that diverse or multi-cultural teams need to do three things: mapping, bridging and integrating. Mapping requires drawing a picture of the similarities and differences in the team. You can then map the differences in culture among different team members, as well as the differences in personality, and all of the different perspectives that people bring to the team that can be useful. The second step is bridging. Bridging is communicating effectively; taking those differences into account, speaking, and listening to the other person. You need to decentre, or put yourself in the other person's place and speak and listen from their point of view. Thereafter, you need to re-centre and find commonalities, develop common norms, common definitions of the situation and common objectives. The third part of the process is integrating, which involves using the differences to create new ideas to build on, to increase participation, to resolve conflicts and to foster innovation.

BUILDING YOUR EMPLOYABILITY SKILLS

Communicating Using Technology

How much time do you think you spend communicating with other people via your mobile phone every day? Do you think you use a different form of communication when doing this than if you were communicating with those people face-to-face? Why is this?

HOW HAVE CHANGES IN TECHNOLOGY AFFECTED COMMUNICATION WITHIN AND BETWEEN ORGANISATIONS AND THEIR EMPLOYEES?

As we have seen, a large amount of business communication is now being done electronically. Communications technology is an important part of information technology infrastructure. The significant components of this technology include networking, internet access and website development in order to easily exchange, transfer and provide information through a network (Patra, 2017). A key purpose of communications technology is to facilitate effective communication between individuals or groups that are physically distant from each other, as well as providing it by cheaper and more efficient means.

The ever-expanding development of communications technology has enabled new forms of working patterns to evolve that include working from home and other locations. Working from home is made possible as employees can communicate with their colleagues, managers and customers via internet, e-mailing, Skype, instant messaging and other related technologies. PricewaterhouseCoopers, one of the larger business consultancy companies, has adopted this practice. Bohlander and Snell (2009) cite significant cost savings for both company and employees as one of the main advantages of the practice, as well as increased levels of performance.

As information travels faster and faster and the barrier of distance disappears, organisations are outsourcing many jobs overseas. Outsourcing refers to the practice of hiring employees who work outside the company or remotely, even many thousands of miles away. Ernst & Young (EY) utilises cross-country teams to improve organisational performance, which are enabled by using a set of communication technologies such as video-conferencing, e-mails and company-specific communication technologies. Video-conferencing has proved very effective in terms of cost savings through cutting down on travel and other costs.

Instant messaging is seen as a key communication tool in the business world and will replace e-mails more and more over time as it is faster and allows for an instant response. Airlines such as KLM are using apps such as WhatsApp to update customers on flight details. Many companies are using e-mail as a primary means of communication with their customers. E-mail, though one of the 'older' of the new technologies, has had a major impact on personal communication as it has replaced speaking on the phone and many personal conversations. In comparison with those modes of communication, e-mail is unaffected by distance and time. It has also linked many people to leaders and senior managers directly through the simple click of the 'send' button. However, it has had another impact in that it encourages indiscriminate sending of often unimportant or unsolicited information. The volume of messages that managers as well as employees and customers receive has increased. Due to e-mail always being accessible and not being regulated by business hours, a culture has been created where senders expect an instant response. At times that can occur, with e-mail responses being returned in the 'heat of the moment'. The French government recently introduced a new labour agreement in April 2014 with an obligation to 'disconnect communications tools' after an employee has worked a 13-hour day.

IMPACT OF TECHNOLOGY ON BEHAVIOUR

Computer-mediated communication has been used positively to connect people. However, in the workplace, communications technology can result in employees being over-connected and can have an impact on users' mental and physical health. Recent studies have identified anxiety disorders as among the most common mental health problems in younger people, with the numbers affected steadily rising. Core to this is the overstimulation of the Generation Z due to the large amount of time they spend online with no allowance for downtime. Excessive use of technology releases stress hormones and increases the arousal of the central nervous system. This reduces time available to switch off, with a growth in sleep disturbances. A recent longitudinal study has reported that adolescents who spend more than three hours a day using social media may be at heightened risk for internalising problems. The researchers recommend that future research should look at the effects of setting limits on daily social media use, increasing media literacy, and redesigning social media platforms to reduce mental health problems. In the workplace this problem has begun to be recognised by introducing technology-free times and zones, which improves sleep and has a role in alleviating anxiety. French law giving workers the ability to negotiate the responsibility to check e-mails outside standard working hours has resulted in 'the right to disconnect'.

THE IMPACT OF SOCIAL MEDIA ON COMMUNICATION

Social media is termed 'social' for a reason, as it enables communication (King, 2012). Using social media tools by 'friending', 'liking', linking and following gives organisations direct access to their customers. Many large organisations such as Tesco, BP, Barclays and British American Tobacco maintain their own dedicated Facebook pages. Prospective and current customers of these businesses can 'Like' the company page on Facebook to receive any status updates by the business. Marks and Spencer use Twitter to send messages to its followers and the messages are used to market products, services and offers. The result of this in terms of communication is that companies have access to your e-mail address, Facebook and Twitter accounts among others, and can utilise your preferences to monitor your buying, leisure and lifestyle habits to target you with specific ads online. Free 'Wi-Fi' is now being provided by cities across the globe as internet connectivity has shifted from our desks to our hands in the form of handheld smart phones. Recent statistics from StatCounter GlobalStats show that more than half of global internet usage was mobile: 52.5% compared with desktop at 44.5% (StatCounter GlobalStats,

2019). Evidence now shows that young people are highly reliant on their smartphones and this reliance is beginning to change the face of communication significantly, now and into the future.

As a tool for communication, social media has a number of characteristics according to Adler *et al.* (2012). These include:

- **Message richness** – Messages transferred in face-to-face communication have traditionally been seen as rich due to the ability to use multiple cues (Reichwald *et al.*, 1998, cited in Meissner, 2005; Cameron and Webster, 2005). Dennis *et al.* (2008) argue that the 'richest' medium is that which best provides the set of capabilities needed by the situation: the individuals, tasks and social contexts in which they interact. They conclude that online communication can be at times as 'rich' as face-to-face communication. The information or message transferred via social media can utilise text, chat, visual images and links to ensure communication success.

- **Hyperpersonal communication** – Text-based computer-mediated communication lacks physical and social cues, which may foster less inhibited behaviour as well as impeding the development of socio-emotional bonds (Sproull and Kiesler, 1991). Thus, Walther (1996) argues that the social media environment can create 'hyperpersonal' relationships, where the individual experiences a level of closeness above that gained in a face-to-face context, since the absence of social cues enhances sharing and openness, and idealisation of the other communicator. This idealisation can occur for both individuals in the dialogue as each sender can selectively self-represent by editing messages and images before sending. Then through the feedback loop there can be an interplay of idealisation and thus, the self-presentation becomes a dynamic process and creates a self-reinforcing cycle

- **Asynchronous communication versus synchronous communication** – Synchrony refers to whether or not the sender and receiver are communicating in real time. Some media are used synchronously, so that all participants are communicating at the same time (e.g. instant messaging, Skype, video conference, Snapchat). Others are used asynchronously so that participants do not communicate at the same time (e.g. messages on Facebook). Some media can be used either synchronously or asynchronously depending upon how they are set up (e.g. discussion forums) (Walther, 1996). During synchronous communication, multiple exchanges are completed in rapid succession. By contrast, asynchronous communication, such as posting messages, limits the process to only small portions of an exchange at any given time. Synchronous communication facilitates the 'give and take' that is required to understand each other and solve issues or problems (Moyer and Katz, 2007).

- **Permanence of digital messages** – Messages can be stored by both senders and receivers. Images, videos and tweets are transferable and can go viral in the social media space. Removing an image from a social media account may be too late as it already has transferred beyond the creator's control. This happened with Snapchat, where images usually self-destruct after a short period of time but were found to have been leaked to the internet and kept on a database (Grieg, 2013).

◄ETHICAL► BEHAVIOUR IN THE WORKPLACE

Communication is an important tool for an organisation. Communications with employees, customers and vendors can involve promotions, job offers, contract negotiations and wider discussions. This requires a sense of responsibility on the part of the communicator to adhere to ethical guidelines. Ethical dilemmas can occur when as a communicator you have a choice between possible moral options. Working in an organisation, there are accepted principles in terms of how to behave drawn from wider society but essentially adhering to ethical principles such as fairness, care and justice. Ethical communication means including relevant information, is not deceptive and recognises the rights and sensitivities of others. Unethical communication includes passing ideas of others off as your own, withholding or misrepresenting information or failing to respect privacy or the need for information security. Blogging is a way for employees to communicate on a personal basis and often about the organisation. However, you've recently seen very personal comments, as well as criticism of some managers in an employee's blog. Should this be allowed and what can organisations include in their social media policies to guide employees?

Authentic Communication in the 21st Century: The 'Greta Thunberg' Effect

Computer-mediated communication is now impacting our behaviour both in terms of lifestyle and at work (Trenholm, 2017). In the current global and political landscape, the capacity of traditional political leaders, experts including environmental activists, and academics, to influence and even mobilise the public has been declining. Partially this was due to key figures being associated with particular vested interests. Now Twitter, YouTube and blogging are being used to communicate science-related issues such as climate change by very young activists with infinitely more success.

Jamie Margolin founded the group Zero Hour in Washington, in 2017, when she was 15 years old. Greta Thunberg has urged younger audiences to protest against current political inactivity in the face of recognised global warming, utilising the communicative dynamics of technology. At the age of 15, she missed school to strike for climate action outside the Swedish parliament in Stockholm. She has mobilised thousands of children across the planet to strike against climate change, garnering significant support. An estimated 1.6 million children in 125 countries took to the streets to protest in March 2019; followed by a global youth-led demonstration in September, which is probably the largest climate protest ever. Since then, Greta has addressed the UN General Assembly during the Climate Action Summit in New York where she delivered a short speech, which gained significant recognition globally, including a backlash from President Trump.

The UN special envoy on El Niño and climate, Mary Robinson, spoke of how Greta and her generation are humanising the issue of climate change, which moved her to tears during the UN address.

In contrast, President Donald Trump refuted that climate change exists utilising Twitter. This use of technology communicating personal opinion is now displacing traditional media, which communicate authoritative scientific expert opinion. Now, in social media communication, authenticity rather than expertise is regarded as crucial. Tweeters, bloggers and YouTubers are mobilising behaviour change more effectively than established experts. In terms of communicating a key scientific message neither Donald Trump nor Greta Thunberg can establish credentials in fully understanding the science and facts of the subject matter of climate change.

However, there a number of factors at play. These include that young climate protesters don't represent someone else's agenda and their message can be seen to be direct and not influenced by personal gain. Matthew Nisbet, an expert in environmental communication at Northeastern University in Boston, wrote an article recently pointing out that young protestors are not as constrained by careers or responsibilities and say things that older activists don't or can't say. However, the real attraction of Greta Thunberg's call to younger audiences has to do with the communicative dynamics of contemporary media (Bucchi, 2019). The proof of expertise, certified competence and celebrity that were seen as standard elements to establish the authority and appeal of public figures in traditional media contexts holds less sway than what is seen as the authenticity of young bloggers and YouTubers, who provide science-related content with enthusiasm and zeal. The message they convey is seen as more important, as recipients perceive them as more accessible and believable than established experts. In turn, this movement has led to a change in how governments and governmental organisations across the globe are dealing with the issue of carbon emissions.

Questions

1 Why do you think people believe and trust more in what they see and hear via social media regarding climate change?

2 Are social media more successful at generating negative messages compared with positive messages?

3 How convinced are you that social media are driving how organisations and teams work, achieve their goals and get their message across?

Sources

Harris, E. (2019) Why the world is watching young climate activists: Researchers break down why the movement and its message are gaining ground. *Nature, News in Focus*, 573, 471–472. Available at: https://www.nature.com/magazine-assets/d41586-019-02696-0/d41586-019-02696-0.pdf (accessed 17 October 2019).

Trenholm, S. (2017) *Thinking through Communication: An Introduction to the Study of Human Communication*, 8th edn. London: Routledge.

Bucchi, M. (2019) The 'Greta Thunberg Effect': Some reflections on communication. *ESOF2020, Euroscience Open Forum*. Available at: https://www.esof.eu/en/news-reader/the-greta-thunberg-effect-some-reflections-on-communication-427.html (accessed 12 September 2019).

Everuss, L., Carvalho, M., Casanova, J.L., Chaffee, D. and Lever-Tracy, C. (2017) Assessing the public willingness to contribute income to mitigate the effects of climate change: A comparison of Adelaide and Lisbon. *Journal of Sociology*, 53(2), 334–350.

Clark, R.P. (2019) What I learned about writing from reading Greta Thunberg's speech to the UN. *Poynter*. Available at: https://www.poynter.org/reporting-editing/2019/what-i-learned-about-writing-from-reading-greta-thunbergs-speech-to-the-u-n/ (accessed 17 October 2019).

MEDIATED COMMUNICATION AND RELATIONAL QUALITY

Earlier studies have suggested that mediated communication such as through social media channels is less effective than other means of forming and sustaining strong social relationships (Cummings *et al.*, 2000). Research shows that although using phrases such as 'online community', many social media users feel lonely and feel that their social media use discourages community.

A study examined the profiles and activity of 608 female Facebook users and found that half described themselves as 'lonely' and as a result tended to overshare personal information (O'Callaghan, 2014). Dr Ethan Kross and his colleagues of the University of Michigan, in 2013, concluded that although on the surface Facebook provides an invaluable resource for fulfilling the basic human need for social connection and communication, it may actually undermine rather than enhance well-being (Kross *et al.*, 2013). Since then, Facebook has faced further criticism for spreading misinformation and encouraging online harm, as well as not protecting users' privacy (Reuters Institute, 2019). Thus, communication can become less like an exchange and more like a passive and unpoliced observance of the lives of others.

In order to mitigate the downside of social media use, Adler *et al.* (2012) suggest a number of strategies to employ in order to communicate competently. Firstly, always be careful of what you post and be considerate of others in your online community. They warn to keep your tone civil and watch for disinhibition. There is also a need to balance socially mediated communication with face-to-face time. To conclude, social media can be used to enhance the communication experience by increasing opportunities, as well as improving connections. This has led to an overall facilitation of the communication experience in what McLuhan (1964) famously termed the 'global village', where he foresaw that members of every nation would be connected by communications technology.

The internet has become the most powerful driver of innovation the world has ever seen. One result has been to change the structure of the communications industry, shifting the focus of innovation toward young hothouses and start-ups. Another has been to drive forward communications technology at a formidable pace. Instagram and messaging apps are now becoming more relevant to communicate news (Reuters Institute, 2019). Through the internet, new products can be developed and launched relatively inexpensively, potential customers and investors can be targeted, and markets can be quickly identified and tested. No other mechanism provides such instant communication links between investors and their customers.

Communication in the Health Sector

The Health Service Executive (HSE) is the public health service provider in Ireland and is responsible for delivering health services across hospitals and communities nationally. The HSE is the largest national employer. It has 67,000 direct staff and a further 35,000 employed in externally funded agencies covering a population of 4.9 million people. There have been media reports of a waiting list crisis across health services in recent times. In response to growing waiting lists, which reached 707,000 in May 2018, the HSE established the National Centralised Validation Unit

OB IN PRACTICE

(NCVU). The NCVU decided that a suitable strategy for managing the waiting lists was to tackle the number of non-attendances for scheduled appointments (479,000 in 2018). They developed a communication strategy in the form of a waiting list validation process to ensure that people on hospital waiting lists were ready and able to attend for treatment. The strategy involved hospitals writing every six months to patients who were on a waiting list for three or more months, to determine if they still required their appointment. Patients were asked to respond to this letter within a two-week period via

a freepost envelope to indicate whether they wished to remain on the waiting list. Should the hospital receive no response within this timeframe, they, as well as their General Practitioner (GP), were then informed that they had been removed from the waiting list. If the patient or their GP considered that their hospital appointment was still needed, they were asked to contact the hospital manager to request that the patient be reinstated to the waiting list. This communication strategy added an extra workload across all stakeholders. Not only did it increase administrative tasks for already overburdened hospital services and for GPs, it further obliged potentially vulnerable patients to receive

CREDIT: PHOTO BY GREG ROSENKE ON UNSPLASH

and return letters within the short, specified time frame and failing this, to navigate the large healthcare organisation in order to re-establish their place on the waiting list. Therefore, the strategy avoided addressing the core reasons for the waiting list problem in the first place and could be seen to shift the burden of responsibility from the HSE onto the people under its care. It is unsurprising that the communication strategy was not well-received across stakeholders. Following the national implementation of this strategy, there was a critical response from the National Association of General Practitioners Ireland (NAGPI). The association's president described the programme as a 'political ploy'. His main complaint about the communications programme was the short response period for patients, arguing that some people may be away or have moved address and may not have received their letter. He added that the process was difficult for at-risk groups, including people with reading problems, the elderly, non-native

English speakers and other groups. An article in the *Irish Medical Times* pointed out that it redirected accountability from the hospitals back onto the GP that referred the patient. This resulted in patients having to navigate a complex health system to get back onto the waiting list. A representative for the NAGPI has called upon the Irish Health Minister to address their concerns about the strategy. However, this representative reported that the association had been largely 'ignored', and that a scheduled meeting to discuss the waiting list issue was cancelled with no reason given. In response to these concerns about the strategy, the HSE released a statement on their website which noted that '*validation exercises on waiting lists across all Hospital sites … [was] to ensure that patients still require their outpatient appointment. This helps improve the overall use of resources and access times for patients.*'

Questions:

1 What message transmission channels are utilised in the communications strategy? Consider why these channels may have been selected and how they may impact on stakeholder perceptions of the strategy.

2 What stakeholders are involved and affected by this communication strategy and how does the relationship between the stakeholders impact on the validation programme's implementation and success?

3 You have been tasked with reviewing the hospital

waiting list communications strategy in light of recent criticisms. Given your understanding of the communication process, what steps will you take in your management of this review?

Sources:

Bowers, F. (2018) GPs criticise HSE over hospital waiting lists validation. Raidió Teilifís Éireann (RTE), 18 July. Available at: https://www.rte.ie/news/health/2018/0718/979524-health-waiting-lists/ (accessed 10 October 2019).

Hanley, R. (2018) Rage against waiting lists validation. *Irish Medical Times*, 28 November. Available at: https://www.imt.ie/opinion/rage-waiting-lists-validation-28-11-2018/ (accessed 9 October 2019).

Health Service Executive (2018) HSE Statement RE: Outpatient Waiting List Validation. Available at: https://www.hse.ie/eng/services/news/media/pressrel/hse-statement-re-outpatient-waiting-list-validation.html (accessed 9 October 2019).

Health Service Executive (2019a) About human resources. Available at: https://www.hse.ie/eng/about/who/hr/ (accessed 9 October 2019).

Health Service Executive (2019b) Who we are, what we do. Available at: https://www.hse.ie/eng/about/ (accessed 10 October 2019).

National Treatment Purchase Fund (2019) Waiting list validation. Available at: https://www.ntpf.ie/home/Waiting_List_Validation.htm (accessed 10 October 2019).

O'Neill, K. (2019) Irish population rises by 64,500 bringing it to almost 5m. *The Irish Medical Examiner*, 28 August. Available at: https://www.irishexaminer.com/breakingnews/ireland/irish-population-rises-by-64500-bringing-it-to-almost-5m-946672.html (accessed: 9 October 2019).

O'Reilly, L. (2018) Health Waiting Lists: Motion. Dáil Éireann debate, 20 June. Available at: https://www.oireachtas.ie/en/debates/debate/dail/2018-06-20/32/ (accessed 10 October 2019).

MANAGERIAL TAKEAWAYS

In this chapter we have described how understanding the process of communication is core to most organisational activity and how the use of different communication channels can impact on how messages are delivered and received.

An increasingly global and disparate workforce places pressure upon organisations to favour indirect communication channels over face-to-face contact. As evidenced through the practical examples in this chapter, mediated communication can be prone to increasing misunderstandings across stakeholders. As a manager you need to protect against false impressions and enhance communication within and across organisations by highlighting common communicative pitfalls to your employees, as well as supporting in-person meetings where possible. Barriers to communication can arise in the communication process, such as noise, perception and information overload; these can be overcome by checking decoding of the message, paying attention to context and taking the other person's perspective through listening. Employees need to be made aware of the potential difficulties, as well as advantages to the use of social media.

Communication is a central feature of organisations and people management. To be successful in our jobs we need to make the most of our communications skills. Communication isn't only about ourselves though; it's a careful balancing act requiring us to balance the needs of senders and receivers. When communicating in the workplace we need to always be careful of the content, manner and timing of our communications, actively listen, and make the best use of the channels and modes of communication open to us.

 ## CHAPTER REVIEW QUESTIONS

1 If communication is central to organisations, why do managers often fail to communicate effectively to their employees?

2 What are the key advantages of face-to-face communication in modern organisations? Explain where this strategy would be best used.

3 What contribution can a competent communications strategy make to an organisation's sustained competitive advantage?

4 Identify and describe common barriers to effective communication.

5 Outline the key elements to supporting effective communication.

6 Do technological advances in communication make it easier for members of an organisation to communicate with each other and with people outside the organisation?

7 Outline and describe the causes of potential problems in cross-cultural communication.

8 How can non-verbal communications techniques be used to enhance the delivery of important messages?

 FURTHER READING

Blaschke, S., Schoeneborn, D. and Seidl, D. (2012) Organizations as networks of communication episodes: Turning the network perspective inside out. *Organization Studies*, 33(7), 879–906.

Heath, R.G. and Isbell, M. (2015) Broadening organizational communication curricula: Collaboration as key to 21st-century organizing. *Management Communication Quarterly*, 29(2), 309–314.

Koschmann, M.A., Kuhn, T.R. and Pfarrer, M.D. (2012) A communicative framework of value in cross-sector partnerships. *Academy of Management Review*, 37, 332–354.

Mishra, K., Boynton, L. and Mishra, A. (2014) Driving employee engagement: The expanded role of internal communications. *International Journal of Business Communication*, 51(2), 183–202.

USEFUL WEBSITES

https://www.shrm.org/resourcesandtools/tools-and-samples/toolkits/pages/managingorganizationalcommunication.aspx

The Society for Human Resource Management (SHRM) has many resources on their website for both students and managers in practice. By accessing this page on managing organisational communication you will find an accessible overview of communication strategy and practical advice on how to build your own successful communication strategy. While on the page, you may decide to follow one of its many links. These will lead you to a range of other articles within the subject of organisational communication.

https://www.ioic.org.uk/

The Institute of Internal Communication (IoIC) is a UK based professional body dedicated to promoting high quality internal communication within organisations. Their website has continuous professional development (CPD) resources for management professionals interested in internal communication. The knowledge hub provides access to IoIC-generated research, blogs and webinars, as well as the IoIC competency framework. This resource outlines the core communicative skills, knowledge and behaviours professionals should seek to build as they navigate their career.

https://instituteforpr.org/organizational-communication-research/

The Institute for Public Relations is a non-profit foundation which aggregates research in public relations and corporate communication to promote its use in practice. Their organisational communication research centre in the research section allows access to summaries of academic articles in the field, including change communication, culture and values and leadership communication.

https://www.youtube.com/user/mattkoschmann/videos

Dr Matthew A. Koschmann, a professor in the Department of Communication at the University of Colorado Boulder (CommProf Productions), has developed a range of innovative videos to support communication education. The videos seek to aid understanding of organisational communication concepts through the use of dynamic animations, as well as access to lectures.

https://thebusinesscommunication.com/

The Business Communication is a blog about business communication. Its articles span internal communication within companies, oral and written communication and traditional and modern communication. The website is a useful resource for those new to the field of organisational communication.

http://video.ft.com/62063401001/IMD-Leading-diverse-teams/Management

The *Financial Times* website offers a business school section which presents video clips of experts discussing issues in management and communication. This is an interesting clip (IMD: Leading diverse teams Part 3) presented by Professor Martha Maznevski on how to get the best performance from diverse teams through facilitating their communication.

Online Resources

Visit bloomsbury.pub/organisational-behaviour to access additional materials to support teaching and learning.

GLOSSARY

Active listening is a process of making a conscious effort to sense, process and respond actively to a communicated message.

Affective well-being is the emotional or affective component of well-being, which can be described in terms of the level of pleasure (or displeasure) combined with the level of arousal.

Affirmative Action Programmes (AAPs) are specific measures taken by organisations to prevent or counter discrimination.

AI is the study of how to produce machines that have some of the qualities that the human mind has, such as the ability to understand language, recognise pictures, solve problems and learn.

Ascribed status is the status assigned by cultural norms, dependent on group membership.

Attitudes are evaluative judgements relating to people, events or objects.

Attribution theory is used to describe the processes that individuals engage in to develop explanations for behaviours.

Authority typically refers to positional power and relies on the assumption that others are willing to obey.

Autism is defined primarily by social difficulties, communication issues and repetitive behaviours.

Burnout is a phenomenon in the work context that is derived from ineffectively managed chronic workplace stress.

Change agent refers to a manager who seeks to reconfigure an organisation's roles, responsibilities, structures, outputs, processes, systems, technology or other resources in the light of improving organisational effectiveness.

Citizenship behaviour is discretionary behaviour that is often not formally recognised or rewarded by organisations but benefits the organisation and/or its members.

Classical conditioning happens when, through repeated association, a formerly neutral stimulus can elicit a reaction that was previously elicited only by another stimulus.

Cognitive dissonance is an unpleasant cognitive state that motivates an individual to resolve perceived conflict among beliefs, attitudes and behaviours.

Cognitive scripts are like predetermined steps in our mind that tell us how to behave in a certain situation.

Command groups are permanent formal groups that are formed as a result of organisational structures.

Communicating is sharing or exchanging information.

Competencies are the practical applications of knowledge, skills, attitudes, motivation, values, beliefs, cognitive style and personality that enable an individual to work effectively and autonomously in a clearly defined context.

Confirmation bias is a tendency to seek out information in line with expectations and existing knowledge and to assign more weight to evidence which confirms these beliefs, undervaluing evidence to the contrary.

Contingency approach suggests that organisational and individual behaviour is contingent, or depends, on a number of interacting factors.

Contingency theories present a belief that there is no one best way to lead.

Core affect is momentary, elementary feelings of pleasure or displeasure and of activation or deactivation.

Core self-evaluation (CSE) is a broad trait that includes four specific traits: internal locus of control, emotional stability, self-esteem and generalised self-efficacy.

Counterproductive work behaviour is any intentional behaviour by an employee that is seen to be contrary to the organisation's interests.

Cross-functional teams are those which have members from a range of functional departments within the organisation, working towards a common goal.

Cultural change is the process of changing mind-sets, behaviour and practices in an organisation; it is a long process which cannot be achieved effectively in a short time frame.

Decoding is the process of deciphering and interpreting a message received, to make sense of it.

Deviant behaviours are those that are counterproductive to an organisation.

Disability employment gap means the difference in employment outcomes for people with and without disabilities.

Discretionary effort is the level of effort people could give if they wanted to, but above and beyond the minimum required.

Discrimination is unjustified negative behaviour towards a group or its members.

Distributed leadership is the idea that leadership of an organisation should not rest with a single individual, but should be shared or 'distributed' among those with the relevant skills.

Diversity involves more than one characteristic being present among a group of people.

Diversity management programmes are programmes targeting organisational productivity and profitability through a culture that fosters diverse cultural backgrounds and values.

Downward communication flows from one level of an organisation to a lower level.

Employee engagement is the degree to which an individual is attentive and absorbed in the performance of their role.

Employee surveillance refers to an organisation's ability to monitor, record and track employee performance, behaviours and personal characteristics through technology.

Employee turnover is the replacement of employees who have left the organisation with new employees. A high turnover rate can be costly to an organisation.

Empowerment is a process where managers delegate power to employees, who use it to make decisions affecting both themselves and their work.

Encoding is the process of designing a message, represented as a set of symbols to be sent that makes sense to the receiver.

Equal employment opportunities approach (EEO) is an approach that promotes, through the development and implementation of policies and procedures, the fair and equitable treatment of individuals in the workplace irrespective of gender, age, race, ethnicity and other attributes.

Equality of opportunity is the idea that people should be able to compete on equal terms, or on a 'level playing field', for opportunities and positions.

Equity theory is a process based motivational theory that focuses on how individuals compare their circumstances with those of others and attempts to explain how such comparisons may motivate certain kinds of behaviour.

Ethics are codes that reflect our values and moral principles and drive our decisions and behaviours with respect to what is right and wrong, good and bad.

Evidence-based practice means basing decisions on the best presented scientific evidence.

Expectancy theory is a process based theory of motivation that focuses on the thought processes people use when choosing among alternative courses of action and their anticipated consequences.

External forces are motivational forces which come from the environment that surrounds the person.

Formal groups are officially established, usually as a result of the organisation's structure, with a specific purpose.

Fundamental attribution error is where individuals attribute external causes to their own behaviour and internal causes to the behaviour of others.

Generation Z means those born between 1993 and 2005.

Glass ceiling means an invisible barrier that inhibits women's and minorities' advancement through the managerial hierarchy, which is more pronounced further along one's career.

Goal-setting theory emphasises the importance of conscious goals and intentions in directing human behaviour.

Grapevine is a metaphor used to describe the informal communication and gossip that occurs in an organisation. The metaphor was originally used to refer to the telegraph lines used in the American Civil War.

Group cohesiveness is the force that binds a group together.

Group conformity is the tendency of group members to consciously or unconsciously align their beliefs and behaviours with the apparent beliefs and behaviours of the group.

Group roles are patterns of behaviour expected of group members.

Groups are two or more people who interact together to achieve a common objective and are interdependent.

Groupthink occurs where maintaining group conformity is more important than critically evaluating alternative viewpoints, even if it means actively discouraging dissenting opinions.

Harassment is unwanted conduct that takes place with the purpose or effect of violating the dignity of a person and of creating an intimidating, hostile, degrading, humiliating or offensive environment.

Hierarchy culture has an internal focus, and demonstrates a strong interest in maintaining stability and control.

Hindsight bias refers to the tendency, after an event has occurred, to overestimate our ability to have foreseen the outcome.

Horizontal and vertical segregation is the concentration of men and women in different economic sectors and occupations.

Human capital is a combination of a person's qualifications, skills, competencies and relevant work experience.

Hygiene factors focus on lower-order needs and involve the presence or absence of job dissatisfiers, such as working conditions and pay.

Idiographic refers to an approach which describes personality in terms of traits that are unique to the individual.

Incremental change is a small change aimed at achieving certain goals.

Indirect discrimination an apparently neutral provision, criterion or practice which puts members of specific groups at a particular disadvantage compared with others.

Individual differences are psychological ways in which people differ from each other, and include factors such as intelligence, personality and emotionality.

Informal groups are those which develop naturally in the workplace in response to our need for belonging.

Information-seeking behaviour is a proactive behaviour an individual engages in to find relevant information useful to the execution of their tasks and job.

In-group bias is the process where members of a group favour members of their own group over members of other groups.

In-groups are social groups to which an individual believes he or she belongs.

Innovation in business refers to the process of developing inventions or ideas into marketable goods, services or processes that customers want.

Instruction to discriminate refers to telling or making someone discriminate against another person.

Intellectual disabilities are a significantly reduced ability to understand new or complex information and to learn and apply new skills.

Internal forces are motivational forces which come from the person.

Job enrichment is increasing the complexity of a job to provide a greater sense of responsibility, accomplishment and achievement.

Job involvement is the extent to which an employee psychologically identifies with their job.

Job satisfaction can be defined as a positive emotional state as a consequence of appraising one's job and job experience.

Lateral communication flows between members or employees in the same work group or department, or managers at the same level.

Leadership is the ability to lead, guide and inspire a group of followers.

Leadership development comprises activities and practices that enhance the ability of leaders to work as part of a team to develop relationships with organisational stakeholders.

Management control is a management function aimed at achieving organisational objectives through setting standards, measuring actual performance against standards and taking corrective action where necessary.

Management teams consist of individuals with managerial roles in different areas of the organisation who coordinate the work of their respective teams.

Managing diversity requires the ability to harness the attributes of a diverse workforce to foster a productive environment which celebrates and nurtures differences.

Motivation is a set of forces that energise, direct and sustain behaviour and hence make people behave in certain ways.

Motivators influence job satisfaction based on fulfilling higher-level needs such as achievement, recognition, responsibility.

Need theories focus on the needs that motivate people: the internal drive that motivates specific behaviours in an attempt to fulfil the needs.

Negative affectivity is a dispositional tendency to experience negative moods such as nervousness, annoyance and hostility.

Noise is any factor, either external or internal, that interferes with transmission of the message, through creation of static or interference in the communication process.

Nomothetic means an approach which describes personality in terms of specific dimensions that vary across people.

Norms are the unwritten and unspoken rules and expectations of behaviour that apply to a group's members.

Objective career success is career success that can be assessed by a third party, and is usually measured by the hierarchical level reached, salary attained and/or number of promotions received.

Onboarding is the more modern, corporate definition of the process of socialising a new employee into an organisation.

Organisational behaviour is a field of study that seeks to understand and improve organisational effectiveness by examining factors about individuals, teams, and organisational culture and structure and the way they interact.

Organisational citizenship behaviour (OCB) is voluntary behaviour from the employee that is likely to have positive consequences for the organisation.

Organisational climate relates to 'how it feels' to work in the organisation, while organisational culture refers to 'the way' in which tasks are completed.

Organisational commitment is an individual's comparative strength of identification and involvement with an organisation.

Organisational culture is the basic pattern of shared assumptions, values, beliefs and practices that govern behaviour in an organisation.

Organisational development (OD) refers to the concern for the vitalising, energising, actualising, activating and renewing of organisations through technical and human resources.

Organisational socialisation is the process by which an organisational outsider gains the social knowledge and skills necessary to become a participating, effective and accepted member of an organisation.

Out-groups are social groups to which an individual believes he or she does not belong.

Perception originally comes from the Latin term 'perceptio', meaning comprehension, or literally, 'a taking in'.

Perceptual defence is discounting information in order to defend an existing perception.

Perceptual distortions are the errors that people make in their perception of others and events.

Perceptual filters are personal characteristics or perceptions that influence the way individuals take in and make sense of information, which can interfere with transmitting or receiving messages.

Perceptual set means a set of internal factors that influence what stimuli individuals select and pay attention to.

Personality is typically defined as the relatively stable set of psychological characteristics that can distinguish one individual from another and can provide generalised predictions about a person's behaviour.

Planned change is change that an organisation consciously thinks about and decides to engage in, which is designed to specifically change organisational outcomes.

Political behaviour is the conversion of power into action.

Positive action involves actions taken in order to achieve equality for group members who are economically and/or socially disadvantaged.

Positive affectivity is a dispositional tendency to experience pleasant moods such as enthusiasm and excitement.

Positive discrimination is preferential discriminatory treatment of members of a minority group over a majority group.

Power exists where person A can get person B to do something that B would not otherwise do.

Power tactics are the ways in which power bases are translated into actions.

Predictive validity is the extent to which a measurement tool accurately predicts future job behaviour or performance.

Prejudice can be defined as a negative attitude towards members of a specific group and can be either explicit or implicit.

Presenteeism refers to attending work while suffering with illness.

Proactive behaviour is a self-initiated behaviour that is focused on future results and aims to make change through the employee taking control.

Problem-solving teams are formed specifically to find a solution to an existing problem.

Process of perception means the process of how we attend to, organise, interpret and respond to stimuli.

Process theories focus on how people decide what actions to choose to engage in to meet their needs, and decide if these actions were successful.

Pro-social behaviours are those that benefit another party.

Psychological safety refers to the ability of someone to show their true self without fear of negative consequences to self-image, status or career.

'Pull' external forces are motivational forces which come from the environment that surrounds the person.

'Push' internal forces are motivational forces which come from the person.

Quantum or radical change is change that affects the entire organisation.

Reliability refers to the extent to which a measure is consistent or repeatable.

Resilience is the ability of a person to recover, re-bound, bounce back, adjust or even thrive in the face of adversity.

Resistance refers to action, overt or covert, exerted on behalf of maintaining the status quo.

Resources are anything perceived by an individual to help attain their goals.

Schema is a unique mental representation of the world around us and is based on information from our memories.

Scientific research is the systematic study of phenomena according to scientific principles.

Selective attention is the process through which we attend to certain stimuli and select out others.

Self-actualisation is a state of fulfilment in which a person is achieving at their highest level of capability.

Self-efficacy refers to an individual's judgement of their capacity to execute behaviours necessary to produce specific performance attainments.

Self-managed work teams consist of a small number of employees who have been given autonomy to plan and manage their team's day-to-day activities with relatively little supervision.

SMART goal setting means goals which are specific, measurable, achievable, realistic and time-bound.

Social identity theory describes a person's sense of who they are based on their group membership(s).

Social loafing is where a group member exerts less effort in the group than if they were working alone.

Socialisation is the process of learning how to think, feel and behave by conforming to and imitating influential others within social settings.

Stereotypes are generalised, pre-established expectations about the characteristics of a group of people.

Stereotyping is a preconceived belief that suggests that all members of a particular category share a set of characteristics.

Stress is a relationship with the environment that the person appraises as significant for his or her well-being and in which the demands tax or exceed available coping resources.

Stressors are events or conditions encountered by an individual that evoke strain.

Strong culture means one in which the company values are widely held and felt by all members of the organisation.

Strong situations are those in which the rules and expectations of the social context control the behaviour of people regardless of their personality.

Subcultures are those which hold the core assumptions of the dominant culture, as well as supplementary assumptions unique to members of that particular section of the organisation.

Subjective well-being refers to the extent to which individuals experience happiness, life satisfaction and positive affect.

Synergy is where the effect of combining efforts leads to more creative or effective outcomes than would have been achieved had each individual operated alone.

Systems thinking is an approach that considers the organisation as a structure made of different parts that affect and are affected by one another. Similarly, the organisation interacts with its larger environment.

Task groups are temporary groups designed to deal with specific issues and are dismantled once the task is completed.

Team refers to a group of people working together with a defined purpose in order to achieve a common goal.

Team roles are patterns of behaviour or sets of characteristics displayed in the way one team member interacts with another when serving to progress the performance of the team towards its aims.

Theory is a collection of assertions that specify how and why variables are related, as well as the circumstances in which they should and should not be related.

Town-hall meetings are meetings involving many, if not all, employees in an organisation, which are usually relatively informal in nature, wherein a leader/leaders convey(s) information to employees and asks for feedback, questions and discussion; the expression originates in politics.

Trait theories are theories that describe people in terms of enduring personality characteristics.

Transactional leadership is a leadership style that focuses on managing and supervising employees.

Transformational leadership is a leadership style that can inspire positive changes in those who follow.

Turnover intentions are an employee's self-reported intentions to leave their job.

Type theories are theories that place individuals into predetermined categories, thereby identifying them as a particular personality type.

Unplanned or emergent change is change that the organisation did not initiate or had no control over planning.

Upward communication flows from a lower level of an organisation to a higher level.

Valence is the extent to which an individual values a particular outcome.

Validity refers to the extent to which a measurement tool measures what it purports to measure.

Values refer to the degree of importance an individual ascribes to a particular belief they hold about an object.

Values and beliefs can be defined as basic convictions or ideals about desirable behaviour and outcomes.

Victimisation refers to negative consequences suffered by a person in reaction to her/his complaint about discrimination, or because of being a witness in a discrimination case.

Virtual teams are those where the team members are dispersed geographically and where the team communicates and collaborates together through the use of a variety of electronic systems.

Weak organisational culture means one in which the values of the company are not widely held by members of the organisation.

Work values are identified as the general and relatively stable goals that people try to reach through work.

BIBLIOGRAPHY

Accenture (2013) Our commitment to inclusion and diversity. Available at: https://www.accenture.com/ca-en/about/inclusion-diversity-index (accessed 20 May 2021).

Acquavita, S.P., Pittman, J., Gibbons, M. and Castellanos-Brown, K. (2009) Personal and organizational diversity factors' impact on social workers' job satisfaction: Results from a national internet-based survey. *Administration in Social Work*, 33, 151–166.

Adams, A., Freedland, M. and Prassl, J. (2015) *The Zero Hours Contract: Regulating Casual Work or Legitimising Precarity?* University of Oxford Legal Research Paper Series, no. 00/2015. Available at: https://ssrn.com/abstract=2507693

Adams, G.A. and Webster, J.R. (2013) Emotional regulation as a mediator between interpersonal mistreatment and distress. *European Journal of Work and Organizational Psychology*, 22(6), 697–710.

Adams, J.S. (1963) Towards an understanding of inequity. *Journal of Abnormal and Social Psychology*, 67, 422–436.

Adler, R.B, Rosenfeld, L.B. and Proctor, R.F. (2012) *Interplay: The Process of Interpersonal Communication*, 12th edn. New York: Oxford University Press.

Adriaenssens, J., De Gucht, V. and Maes, S. (2015) Determinants and prevalence of burnout in emergency nurses: A systematic review of 25 years of research. *International Journal of Nursing Studies*, 52(2), 649–661.

Ahola, K., Toppinen-Tanner, S., Huuhtanen, P., Koskinen, A. and Väänänen, A. (2009) Occupational burnout and chronic work disability: An eight-year cohort study on pensioning among Finnish forest industry workers. *Journal of Affective Disorders*, 115(1), 150–159.

Ajzen, I. (1991) The theory of planned behavior. *Organizational Behavior and Human Decision Processes*, 50(2), 179–211.

Alas, R. and Sharifi, S. (2002) Organizational learning and resistance to change in Estonian companies. *Human Resource Development International*, 5(3), 313–331.

Allen, N.J. and Meyer, J.P. (1990) Organizational socialization tactics: A longitudinal analysis of links to newcomers' commitment and role orientation. *Academy of Management Journal*, 33, 847–858.

Allen, N.J. and Meyer, J.P. (1990) The measurement and antecedents of affective, continuance and normative commitment to the organization. *Journal of Occupational Psychology*, 63(1), 1–18.

Allport, G.W. (1935) *Attitudes: A Handbook of Social Psychology*. Worcester, MA: Clark University Press.

Allport, G.W. (1954) *The Nature of Prejudice*. Reading, MA: Addison-Wesley.

Allport, G.W. and Odbert, H.S. (1936) Trait-names: A psycho-lexical study. *Psychological Monographs*, 47(1), i–171.

Amazon (2019) *Diversity and Inclusion at Amazon*. Available at: https://www.aboutamazon.com/workplace/diversity-inclusion/ (accessed 16 May 2021).

American Psychiatric Association (2013) *Diagnostic and Statistical Manual of Mental Disorders*, 5th edn. Washington, DC: American Psychiatric Association.

Andersson, L.M. and Pearson, C.M. (1999) Tit for tat? The spiraling effect of incivility in the workplace. *Academy of Management Review*, 24(3), 452–471.

Antonakis, J. and Dalgas, O. (2009) Predicting elections: Child's play! *Science*, 323(5918), 1183–1183.

Antonakis, J. and Eubanks, D.L. (2017) Looking leadership in the face. *Current Directions in Psychological Science*, 26(3), 270–275.

Anvari, F., Wenzel, M., Woodyatt, L. and Haslam, A. (2019) The social psychology of whistleblowing: An integrated model. *Organizational Psychology Review*, 9(1), 41–67.

Apple inc. (2019) *Different Together*. Available at: https://www.apple.com/diversity/ (accessed 10 October 2020).

Armenakis, A., Harris, S. and Mossholder, K. (1993) Creating readiness for organizational change. *Human Relations*, 46(6), 81–703.

Armstrong, C., Flood, P.C., Guthrie, J.P., Liu, W., MacCurtain, S. and Mkamwa, T. (2010) The impact of diversity and equality management on firm performance: Beyond high performance work systems. *Human Resource Management*, 49, 977–998.

Armstrong-Stassen, M. and Schlosser, F. (2011) Perceived organizational membership and the retention of older workers. *Journal of Organizational Behavior*, 32, 319–344.

Aronson, E. (2007) *The Social Animal*, 10th edn. New York and Oxford: Freeman.

Arvey, R.D., Harpaz, I. and Liao, H. (2004) Work centrality and post-award work behavior of lottery winners. *The Journal of Psychology*, 138(5), 404–420.

Asch, S.E. (1951) *Social Psychology*. New York: Prentice Hall.

Ashford, S.J. and Black, T.S. (1996) Proactivity during organizational entry: The role of desire for control. *Journal of Applied Psychology*, 81(2), 199–214.

Ashforth, B.E. and Saks, A.M. (1996) Socialization tactics: Longitudinal effects on newcomer adjustment. *Academy of Management Journal*, 39(1), 149–178.

Ashforth, B.E., Harrison, S.H. and Sluss, D.M. (2014) Becoming. The interaction of socialisation and identity in organizations over time. In A.J. Shipp and Y. Fried (eds), *Time and Work*, vol. 1. London and New York: Psychology Press, pp. 11–39.

Ashkanasy, N., Wilderom, C. and Peterson, M. (eds) (2000) *Handbook of Organizational Culture and Climate*. Thousand Oaks, CA: Sage.

Ashleigh, M.J. and Mansi, A. (2012) *The Psychology of People in Organisations*. Cambridge: Pearson.

Ashton, M.C. and Lee, K. (2007) Empirical, theoretical, and practical advantages of the HEXACO model of personality structure. *Personality and Social Psychology Review*, 11(2), 50–66.

Association of American Colleges and Universities (2013) *It Takes More Than a Major: Employer Priorities for College Learning and Student Success*. Washington, DC: Hart Research Associates. Available at: https://www.aacu.org/leap/presidentstrust/compact/2013SurveySummary (accessed 9 January 2020).

Atwater, L.E., Tringale, A.M., Sturm, R.E., Taylor, S.N. and Braddy, P.W. (2019) Looking ahead: How what we know about sexual harassment now informs us of the future. *Organizational Dynamics*, 48(4), 1–9.

Avolio, B.J. and Vogelgesang, G. (2011) Beginnings matter in genuine leadership development. In S.E. Murphy and R.J. Reichard (eds), *Early Development and Leadership: Building the Next Generation of Leaders*. New York: Routledge, pp. 179–204.

Bacharach, S. and Bamberger, P. (2007) 9/11 and New York City firefighters' post hoc unit support and control climates: A context theory of the consequences of involvement in traumatic work-related events. *Academy of Management Journal*, 50(4), 849–868.

Baker III, H.E. (1992) Employee socialization strategies and the presence of union representation. *Labor Studies Journal*, 17, 5–17.

Baker, H.E. and Feldman, D.C. (1990) Strategies of organizational socialization and their impact on newcomer adjustment. *Journal of Managerial Issues*, 2, 198–212.

Baker, J.P. and Berenbaum, H. (2007) Emotional approach and problem-focused coping: A comparison of potentially adaptive strategies. *Cognition and Emotion*, 21(1), 95–118.

Baker W.K. (2004) Antecedents and consequences of job satisfaction: Testing a comprehensive model using integrated methodology. *Journal of Applied Business Research*, 20(3), 31–43.

Bakker, A.B. and Demerouti, E. (2008) Towards a model of work engagement. *Career Development International*, 13(3), 209–223.

Bakker, A.B. and Derks, D. (2010) Positive occupational health psychology. In S. Leka and J. Houdmont (eds), *Occupational Health Psychology: A Key Text*. Oxford: Wiley-Blackwell, pp. 194–224.

Bakker, A.B. and Oerlemans, W.G.M. (2011) Subjective well-being in organizations. In K.S. Cameron and G.M. Spreitzer (eds), *The Oxford Handbook of Positive Organizational Scholarship*. New York: Oxford University Press, pp. 178–189.

Bakker, A., Demerouti, E. and Schaufeli, W. (2003) Dual processes at work in a call centre: An application of the job demands–resources model. *European Journal of Work and Organizational Psychology*, 12(4), 393–417.

Bandura, A. (1977) Self-efficacy: Toward a unifying theory of behavioral change. *Psychological Review*, 84(2), 191.

Bandura, A. (1986) *Social Foundations of Thought and Action: A Social-cognitive View*. Englewood Cliffs, NJ: Prentice Hall.

Barak, M.E.M. (2016) *Managing Diversity: Toward a Globally Inclusive Workplace*. London: Sage Publications.

Barnett, D. (2017) In the war between millennials and baby boomers we have forgotten about the work-hard, play-hard generation X. *The Independent*. Available at: https://www.independent.co.uk/life-style/health-and-families/millenials-generation-x-baby-boomers-a7570326.html

Baron, R.A. and Neuman, J.H. (1996) Workplace violence and workplace aggression: Evidence on their relative frequency and potential causes. *Aggressive Behaviour*, 22, 161–173.

Barrick, M.R., Mount, M.K. and Judge, T.A. (2001) Personality and performance at the beginning of the new millennium: What do we know and where do we go next? *International Journal of Selection and Assessment*, 9(1–2), 9–30.

Barrick, M.R., Patton, G.K. and Haugland, S.N. (2000) Accuracy of interviewer judgments of job applicant personality traits. *Personnel Psychology*, 53, 925–951.

Bartlett, C.A. and Beamish, P.W. (2018) *Transnational Management: Text and Cases in Cross-border Management*. Cambridge: Cambridge University Press.

Bass, B.M. (1985) *Leadership and Performance Beyond Expectations*. New York: Free Press.

Bass, B.M. (1990) *Bass & Stogdil's Handbook of Leadership*, 3rd edn. New York: Free Press.

Bass, B. (1999) Two decades of research and development in transformational leadership. *European Journal of Work and Organizational Psychology*, 8(1), 9–32.

Bass, B.M. (2008) *The Bass Handbook of Leadership: Theory, Research, and Managerial Applications*, 4th edn. New York: Free Press.

Bass, B. and Riggio, R. (2006) *Transformational Leadership*. Mahwah, NJ: Erlbaum.

Bass, B., Avolio, B., Jun, D. and Berson, Y. (2003) Predicting unit performance by assessing transformational and transactional leadership. *Journal of Applied Psychology*, 88(2), 207–218.

Batenburg, R., Walbeek, W. van, Maur, W. in der (2013) Belbin role diversity and team performance: Is there a relationship? *Journal of Management Development*, 32(8), 901–913.

Bauer, T.N. and Green, S.G. (1998) Testing the combined effects of newcomer information seeking and manager behavior on socialization. *Journal of Applied Psychology*, 83(1), 72–83.

Bauer, T.N., Bodner, T., Erdogan, B., Truxillo, D.M. and Tucker, J.S. (2007) Newcomer adjustment during organizational socialization: A meta-analytic review of antecedents, outcomes, and methods. *Journal of Applied Psychology*, 92, 707–721.

Bauer, T.N., Morrison, E.W. and Callister, R.R. (1998) Organizational socialization: A review and directions for future research. In G.R. Ferris (ed.), *Research in Personnel and Human Resource Management*, vol. 16. Greenwich, CT: JAI Press, pp. 149–214.

Beal, D.J., Cohen, R., Burke, M.J. and McLendon, C.L. (2003) Cohesion and performance in groups: A meta-analytic clarification of construct relation. *Journal of Applied Psychology*, 88, 989–1004.

Beattie, L. and Griffin, B. (2014) Day-level fluctuations in stress and engagement in response to workplace incivility: A diary study. *Work & Stress*, 28(2), 124–142.

Belbin, R.M. (1993) *Team Roles at Work*. Oxford: Butterworth-Heinemann.

Belle, N., Cantarelli, P. and Belardinelli, P. (2017) Cognitive biases in performance appraisal: Experimental evidence on anchoring and halo effects with public sector managers and employees. *Review of Public Personnel Administration*, 37(3), 275–294.

Bennis, W.G. (1959) Leadership theory and administrative behavior: The problem of authority. *Administrative Science Quarterly*, 259–301.

Bennis, W. (2007) The challenges of leadership in the modern world: Introduction to the special issue. *American Psychologist*, 62(1), 2.

Bennis, W. and Nanus, B. (1985) *Leaders: The Strategies for Taking Charge*. New York: Harper & Row.

Bennis, W. and Nanus, B. (2003) *Leaders: Strategies for Taking Charge*. New York: HarperCollins.

Bernstein, E.S., Turban, S. (2018) The impact of the 'open' workspace on human collaboration. *Philosophical Transactions of the Royal Society B: Biological Sciences*, 373(1753), 20170239.

Bertrand, M., Black, S.E., Jensen, S. and Lleras-Muney, A. (2018) Breaking the glass ceiling? The effect of board quotas on female labour market outcomes in Norway. *The Review of Economic Studies*, 86, 191–239.

Black, S. (2014) *It Starts with One: Changing Individuals Changes Organizations*, 3rd edn. Upper Saddle River, NJ: Pearson.

Blake, R.R. and Mouton, J.S. (1962) *The Managerial Grid*. Houston, TX: Gulf Publishing.

Blaschke, S., Schoeneborn, D. and Seidl, D. (2012) Organizations as networks of communication episodes: Turning the network perspective inside out. *Organization Studies*, 33(7), 879–906.

Blenko, M.W., Mankins M.C. and Rogers P. (2009) *Decide & Deliver: 5 Steps to Breakthrough Performance in your Organization*. Boston, MA: Harvard Business Review Press.

Bohlander, G. and Snell, S. (2009) *Managing Human Resource Management*. Mason, OH: Cengage Learning.

Bolden, R., Petrov, G. and Gosling, J. (2008) Tensions in higher education leadership: Towards a multilevel model of leadership practice. *Higher Education Quarterly*, 62(4), 358–376.

Bolger, N, and Zuckerman, A. (1995) A framework for studying personality in the stress process. *Journal of Personality and Social Psychology*, 69, 890–902.

Bondeson, U. (2017) *Prisoners in Prison Societies*. New York: Routledge.

Bono, J.E. and Judge, T.A. (2004) Personality and transformational and transactional leadership: A meta-analysis. *Journal of Applied Psychology*, 89(5), 901–910.

Bono, J.E., Glomb, T.M., Shen, W., Kim, E. and Koch, A.J. (2013) Building positive resources: Effects of positive events and positive reflection on work stress and health. *Academy of Management Journal*, 56(6), 1601–1627.

Boone, L.E. and Kurtz, D.L. (2010) *Contemporary Business*. Chichester: Wiley & Sons.

Bordia, P., Hobman, E., Joes, E., Gallois, C. and Callan, V. (2004) Uncertainty during organizational change: Types, consequences, and management strategies. *Journal of Business and Psychology*, 18(4), 507–532.

Bouckenooghe, D. (2010) Positioning change recipients' attitudes towards change in the organizational change literature. *Journal of Applied Behavioural Science*, 46(4), 500–531.

Bowditch, J.L. and Buono, A.F. (2005) *A Primer on Organizational Behaviour*, 6th edn. Hoboken, NJ: John Wiley and Sons.

Bowers, F. (2018) GPs criticise HSE over hospital waiting lists validation. Raidió Teilifís Éireann (RTE), 18 July. Available at: https://www.rte.ie/news/health/2018/0718/979524-health-waiting-lists/ (accessed 10 October 2019).

Boyce, A.S., Nieminen, L.R., Gillespie, M.A., Ryan, A.M. and Denison, D.R. (2015) Which comes first, organizational culture or performance? A longitudinal study of causal priority with automobile dealerships. *Journal of Organizational Behavior*, 36(3), 339–359.

Boydell, T., Burgoyne, J. and Pedler, M. (2004) Suggested development. *People Management*, 10(4), 32–34.

Brady, D. (2006) *#?@ the e-mail. Can we talk? *BusinessWeek*, 4 December, p. 109.

Brandstätter, H. (2011) Personality aspects of entrepreneurship: A look at five meta-analyses. *Personality and Individual Differences*, 51(3), 222–230.

Branson, J. (2014) *The Virgin Way: Everything I Know About Leadership*. New York: Penguin.

Bratton, J. (2020) *Work and Organisational Behaviour*, 4th edn. London: Red Globe Press.

Brief, A.P. and Weiss, H.M. (2002) Organizational behavior: Affect in the workplace. *Annual Review of Psychology*, 53(1), 279–307.

Briscoe, J.P., Henagan, S.C., Burton, J.P. and Murphy, W.M. (2012) Coping with an insecure employment environment: The differing roles of protean and boundaryless career orientations. *Journal of Vocational Behavior*, 80(2), 308–316.

Britt, T.W. (2003) Black Hawk Down at work. *Harvard Business Review*, 81(1), 16–17.

Britt, T.W., Shen, W., Sinclair, R.R., Grossman, M.R. and Klieger, D.M. (2016) How much do we really know about employee resilience? *Industrial and Organizational Psychology*, 9(2), 378–404.

Broucek, W.G. and Randell, G. (1996) An assessment of the construct validity of the Belbin self-perception inventory and Observer's assessment from the perspective of the Five-factor Model. *Journal of Occupational and Organizational Psychology* 69, 389–405.

Brown, K. (2018) To retain employees, focus on inclusion – not just diversity. *Harvard Business Review*, 4 December.

Brown, K.W. and Ryan, R.M. (2003) The benefits of being present: Mindfulness and its role in psychological well-being. *Journal of Personality and Social Psychology*, 84(4), 822–848.

Brown, M.E. and Treviño, L.K. (2006) Ethical leadership: A review and future directions. *The Leadership Quarterly*, 17(6), 595–616.

Brown, S.P. (1996) A meta-analysis and review of organizational research on job involvement. *Psychological Bulletin*, 120(2), 235–255.

Brunell, A.B., Gentry, W.A., Campbell, W.K., Hoffman, B.J., Kuhnert, K.W. and DeMarree, K.G. (2008) Leader emergence: The case of the narcissistic leader. *Personality and Social Psychology Bulletin*, 34(12), 1663–1676.

Brustein, J. (2013) How to cope with e-mail overload at work. *Bloomberg BusinessWeek*, 19 December. Available at: http://www.businessweek.com/articles/2013-12-19/asanas-justin-rosenstein-on-e-mail-overload (accessed 27 April 2014).

Bryman, A. (1992) *Charisma and Leadership in Organizations*. London: Sage.

Bucchi, M. (2019) The 'Greta Thunberg Effect': Some reflections on communication. *ESOF2020, Euroscience Open Forum*. Available at: https://www.esof.eu/en/news-reader/the-greta-thunberg-effect-some-reflections-on-communication-427.html (accessed 12 September 2019).

Buchanan, D. and Huczynski, A. (2020) *Organizational Behaviour: An Introductory Text*, 10th edn. Englewood Cliffs, NJ: Prentice Hall.

Business Insider (2011) Inside Apple's cult-like culture. Available at: http://www.businessinsider.com/10-ways-to-think-different-inside-apples-cult-like-culture-2011-3 (accessed 21 May 2021).

Byrne, M., Flood, B. and Shanahan, D. (2012) A qualitative exploration of oral communication apprehension. *Accounting Education: An International Journal*, 21(6), 565–581.

Cai, D.A. and Fink, E.L. (2009) Communicate successfully by seeking balance. In E.A. Locke (ed.), *Handbook of Principles of Organizational Behaviour: Indispensable Knowledge for Evidence-Based Management*. Chichester: Wiley.

Cameron, A.F. and Webster, J. (2005) Unintended consequences of emerging communication technologies: Instant messaging in the workplace. *Computers in Human Behavior*, 21(1), 85–103.

Cameron, K.S. and Quinn, R.E. (1999) *Diagnosing and Changing Organizational Culture Based on the Competing Values Framework*. Reading, MA: Addison-Wesley.

Campion, M.A., Medsker, G.J. and Higgs, A.C. (1993) Relations between work group characteristics and effectiveness: Implications for designing effective work groups. *Personnel Psychology*, 46, 823–847.

Carlström, E.D. and Ekman, I. (2012) Organisational culture and change: Implementing person-centred care. *Journal of Health Organization and Management*, 26(2), 175–191.

Carr, P.B., and Walton, G.M. (2014) Cues of working together fuel intrinsic motivation. *Journal of Experimental Social Psychology*, 53, 169–184.

Carron, A.V., Bray, S.R. and Eys, M.A. (2002) Team cohesion and team success in sport. *Journal of Sports Sciences*, 20(2), 119–127.

Carver, C.S. (1997) You want to measure coping but your protocol's too long: Consider the brief COPE. *International Journal of Behavioral Medicine*, 4(1), 92–100.

Carver, C.S. and Connor-Smith, J. (2010) Personality and coping. *Annual Review of Psychology*, 61, 679–704.

Carver, C.S., Scheier, M.F. and Weintraub, J.K. (1989) Assessing coping strategies – A theoretically based approach. *Journal of Personality and Social Psychology*, 56(2), 267–283.

Cascio, W.F. (2000) Managing a virtual workplace. *Academy of Management Executive*, 14(3), 81–90.

Cascio, W.F. (2006) *Managing Human Resources: Productivity, Quality of Life, Profits*. New York: McGraw-Hill/Irwin.

Casper, W.J., Wayne, J.H. and Manegold, J.G. (2013) Who will we recruit? Targeting deep- and surface-level diversity with human resource policy advertising. *Human Resource Management*, 52, 311–332.

Cattell, R.B. (1965) *The Scientific Analysis of Personality*. Baltimore, MD: Penguin Books.

Chamorro-Premuzic, T. (2017) Does diversity actually increase creativity? *Harvard Business Review*. Available at: https://hbr.org/2017/06/does-diversity-actually-increase-creativity

Channon, S.B., Davis, R.C., Goode, N.T. and May, S.A. (2017) What makes a 'good group'? Exploring the characteristics and performance of undergraduate student groups. *Advances in Health Sciences Education*, 22, 17–41.

Chappelow, J. (2019) *Service Sectors and Industries Analysis*. Investopedia. Available at: https://www.investopedia.com/terms/s/service-sector.asp (accessed 5 October 2019).

Charan, R., Drotter, S. and Noel, J. (2010) *The Leadership Pipeline: How to Build the Leadership Powered Company*. San Francisco, CA: John Wiley & Sons.

Chatman, J.A. and Spataro, S.E. (2005) Using self-categorization theory to understand relational demography-based variations in people's responsiveness to organizational culture. *Academy of Management Journal*, 48, 321–331.

Chen, Y., Ferris, D.L., Kwan, H.K., Yan, M., Zhou, M. and Hong, Y. (2012) Self-love's lost labor: A self-enhancement model of workplace incivility. *Academy of Management Journal*, 56(4), 1199–1219.

Cherry, K. (2020) *Muller-Lyer Illusion: History and Use in Psychology*. Available at: https://www.verywellmind.com/how-the-muller-lyer-illusion-works-4111110

Chiaburu, D.S., Van Dam, K. and Hutchins, H.M. (2010) Social support in the workplace and training transfer: A longitudinal analysis. *International Journal of Selection and Assessment*, 18(2), 187–200.

Child, J. (2005) *Organization: Contemporary Principles and Practices*. Oxford: Blackwell Publishing.

Cho, S., Kim, A. and Barak, M.E.M. (2017) Does diversity matter? Exploring workforce diversity, diversity management, and organizational performance in social enterprises. *Asian Social Work and Policy Review*, 11, 193–204.

CIPD (2020) Diversity and inclusion in the Workplace. In CIPD (ed.). London: CIPD.

Ciulla, J.B. (1995) Leadership ethics: Mapping the territory. *Business Ethics Quarterly*, 5–28.

Ciulla, J.B. (2005) The state of leadership ethics and the work that lies before us. *Business Ethics – Oxford – A European Review*, 14(4), 323.

Clark, R.E. (2003) Fostering the work motivation of individuals and teams. *Performance Improvement*, 42(3), 21–29.

Clark, R.E. and Estes, F. (2002) *Turning Research into Results: A Guide to Selecting the Right Performance Solutions*. Atlanta, GA: CEP Press.

Clark, R.P. (2019) What I learned about writing from reading Greta Thunberg's speech to the U.N. *Poynter*. Available at: https://www.poynter.org/reporting-editing/2019/what-i-learned-about-writing-from-reading-greta-thunbergs-speech-to-the-u-n/ (accessed 17 October 2019).

Clauss, E., Hoppe, A., O'Shea, D., Morales, M.G.G., Steidle, A. and Michel, A. (2018) Promoting personal resources and reducing exhaustion through positive work reflection among caregivers. *Journal of Occupational Health Psychology*, 23(1), 127–140.

Clegg, C. and Walsh, S. (2004) Change management: Time for change? *European Journal of Work and Organizational Psychology*, 13(2), 217–239.

Cohen, S.G. and Bailey, D.E. (1997) What makes teams work: Group effectiveness research from the shop floor to the executive suite. *Journal of Management*, 23(3), 239–290.

Cohn, S. (2019) *Race, Gender, and Discrimination at Work*. London and New York: Routledge.

Colbert, A.E., Bono, J.E. and Purvanova, R.K. (2016) Flourishing via workplace relationships: Moving beyond instrumental support. *Academy of Management Journal*, 59(4), 1199–1223.

Colligan, T.W. and Higgins, E.M. (2006) Workplace stress. *Journal of Workplace Behavioral Health*, 21(2), 89–97.

Colquitt, J.A., Conlon, D.E., Wesson, M.J., Porter, C.O. and Ng, K.Y. (2001) Justice at the millennium: A meta-analytic review of 25 years of organizational justice research. *Journal of Applied Psychology*, 86, 425.

Colquitt, J.A., Lepine, J.A. and Wesson, M.J. (2012) *Organizational Behavior: Improving Performance and Commitment in the Workplace*, 3rd edn. New York: McGraw-Hill Irwin.

Conger, J.A. and Kanungo, R.N. (1987) Toward a behavioral theory of charismatic leadership in organizational settings. *Academy of Management Review*, 12(4), 637–647.

Connell, R.W. (1972) Political socialization in the American family: The evidence re-examined. *Public Opinion Quarterly*, 36(3), 323–333.

Cordery, J.L., Mueller, W.S. and Smith, L.M. (1991) Attitudinal and behavioral effects of autonomous group working: A longitudinal field study. *Academy of Management Journal*, 34, 464–476.

Corritore, M., Goldberg, A. and Srivastava, S.B. (2020) Duality in diversity: How intrapersonal and interpersonal cultural heterogeneity relate to firm performance. *Administrative Science Quarterly*, 65(2), 359–394.

Cortina, L.M., Kabat-Farr, D., Leskinen, E.A., Huerta, M. and Magley, V.J. (2011) Selective incivility as modern discrimination in organizations: Evidence and impact. *Journal of Management*, 39(6), 1579–1605.

Costanza, D.P., Badger, J.M., Fraser, R.L., Severt, J.B. and Gade, P.A. (2012) Generational differences in work-related attitudes: A meta-analysis. *Journal of Business and Psychology*, 27(4), 375–394.

Cox, T. (1994) *Cultural Diversity in Organizations: Theory, Research and Practice*. San Francisco, CA: Berrett-Koehler Publishers.

Cox, T.H. and Blake, S. (1991) Managing cultural diversity: Implications for organizational competitiveness. *Academy of Management Perspectives*, 5, 45–56.

Crano, W.D., Cooper, J. and Forgas J.P. (2010) Attitudes and attitude change. An Introductory review. In J.P. Forgas, J. Cooper and W.D. Crano (eds), *The Psychology of Attitudes and Attitude Change*. Mahwah, NJ: Psychology Press.

Cropanzana, R., Bowen, D.E. and Gilliland, S.W. (2007) The management of organizational justice. *The Academy of Management Perspectives*, 34–48.

Cross, R., Rebele, R. and Grant, A. (2016) Collaborative overload. *Harvard Business Review*, January–February. Available at: https://hbr.org/2016/01/collaborative-overload

Crumley, B. (2010) The Game of Death: France's shocking TV experiment. *Time Magazine*. Available at: http://content.time.com/time/arts/article/0,8599,1972981,00.html

Cummings J.N., Butler, B. and Kraut R. (2000) The quality of online social relationships. *Communications of the ACM*, 45(2), 103–108.

Cunningham, I. (1986) Self-managed learning. In A. Mumford (ed.), *Handbook of Management Development*. Aldershot: Gower.

Dah, M.A., Jizi, M.I. and Kebbe, R. (2020) CEO gender and managerial entrenchment. *Research in International Business and Finance*, 54, 101237.

Dahl, R.A. (1957) The Concept of Power, *Behavioural Science*, 2(3), 201–215.

Dastin, J. (2018) Amazon scraps secret AI recruiting tool that showed bias against women. Available at: https://www.reuters.com/article/us-amazon-com-jobs-automation-insight/amazon-scraps-secret-ai-recruiting-tool-that-showed-bias-against-women-idUSKCN1MK08G? (accessed 18 January 2021).

Davies, B. (2011) *Leading the Strategically Focused School: Success and Sustainability*. London: Sage.

Day, D.V. (ed.) (2014) *Oxford Library of Psychology. The Oxford Handbook of Leadership and Organizations*. Oxford: Oxford University Press.

Day, D.V. and Harrison, M.M. (2007) A multilevel, identity-based approach to leadership development. *Human Resource Management Review*, 17(4), 360–373.

Day, D.V. and Lord, R.G. (1988) Executive leadership and organizational performance: Suggestions for a new theory and methodology. *Journal of Management*, 14(3), 453–464.

Day, D.V., Harrison, M.M. and Halpin, S.M. (2009) *An Integrative Approach to Leader Development*. New York: Routledge.

De Hauw, S. and De Vos, A. (2010) Millennials' career perspective and psychological contract expectations: Does the recession lead to lowered expectations? *Journal of Business and Psychology*, 25(2), 293–302.

De Mare, G. (1989) Communicating: The key to establishing good working relationships. *Price Waterhouse Review*, 33, 30–37.

De Neve, J.E., Mikhaylov, S., Dawes, C.T., Christakis, N.A. and Fowler, J.H. (2013) Born to lead? A twin design and genetic association study of leadership role occupancy. *The Leadership Quarterly*, 24(1), 45–60.

De Vos, A., Buyens, D. and Schalk, R. (2005) Making sense of a new employment relationship: Psychological contract-related information seeking and the role of work values and locus of control. *International Journal of Selection and Assessment*, 13(1), 41–52.

Deal T.E. and Kennedy, A.A. (1982) *Corporate Cultures: The Rites and Rituals of Corporate Life*. Harmondsworth: Penguin Books.

Delarue, A., Van Hootegem, G., Procter, S. and Burridge, M. (2008) Teamworking and organizational performance: A review of survey-based research. *International Journal of Management Reviews* 10(2), 127–148.

Delizonna, L. (2017) High-performance teams need psychological safety. Here's how to create it. *Harvard Business Review*, 24 August.

Deloitte (2017) Diversity and inclusion: The reality gap. *Wall Street Journal*, 10 November. Available at: https://www2.deloitte.com/us/en/insights/focus/human-capital-trends/2017/diversity-and-inclusion-at-the-workplace.html (accessed 17 May 2021).

Deloitte (2019) Government trends 2020: What are the most transformational trends in government today? *Report from Deloitte Center for Government Insights*. Available at: https://www2.deloitte.com/us/en/insights/industry/public-sector/government-trends/2020/government-nudge-thinking.htm (accessed 4 October 4 2019).

Deloitte Insights Report (2019) Organizational performance: It's a team sport. Available at: https://www2.deloitte.com/insights/us/en/focus/human-capital-trends/2019/team-based-organization.html

Dembe, A.E. (2001) The social consequences of occupational injuries and illnesses. *American Journal of Industrial Medicine*, 40(4), 403–417.

Demerouti, E. and Bakker, A.B. (2011) The job demands–resources model: Challenges for future research. *SA Journal of Industrial Psychology*, 37, 1–9.

Demerouti, E., Bakker, A B., Nachreiner, F. and Schaufeli, W.B. (2001) The job demands–resources model of burnout. *Journal of Applied Psychology*, 86(3), 499–512.

Denison, D.R. (1996) What is the difference between organizational culture and organizational climate? A native's point of view on a decade of paradigm wars. *Academy of Management Review*, 21(3), 619–654.

Denison, D.R. and Mishra, A.K. (1995) Toward a theory of organizational culture and effectiveness. *Organization Science*, 6(2), 204–223.

Dennis, A.R., Fuller, R.M. and Valacich, J.S. (2008) Media, tasks, and communication processes: A theory of media synchronicity. *MIS Quarterly*, 32(3), 575–600.

DeRosa, D.M., Smith, C.L. and Hantula, D.A. (2007) The medium matters: Mining the long-promised merit of group interaction in creative idea generation tasks in a meta-analysis of the electronic group brainstorming literature. *Computers in Human Behavior*, 23(3), 1549–1581.

DeRue, D.S. and Myers, C.G. (2014) Leadership development: A review and agenda for future research. In D.V. Day (ed.), *The Oxford Handbook of Leadership and Organizations*. Oxford Library of Psychology. Oxford: Oxford University Press, pp. 832–855.

Detert, J. and Burris, E. (2007) Leadership behavior and employee voice: Is the door really open? *Academy of Management Journal*, 50(4), 869–884.

Detert, J.R., Schroeder, R.G. and Mauriel, J.J. (2000) A framework for linking culture and improvement initiatives in organizations. *Academy of Management Review*, 25(4), 850–863.

Deutsch, M. and Collins, M.E. (1951) *Interracial Housing: A Psychological Evaluation of a Social Experiment*. Minneapolis, MN: University of Minnesota Press.

Development Dimensions International (2009) *Holding Women Back: Troubling Discoveries – And Best Practices for Helping Women Leaders Succeed*. Pittsburgh, PA: DDI Consulting.

Dhir, A.A. (2015) *Challenging Boardroom Homogeneity: Corporate Law, Governance, and Diversity*. Cambridge: Cambridge University Press.

Dianoux, C., Heitz-Spahn, S., Siadou-Martin, B., Thevenot, G. and Yildiz, H. (2019) Nudge: A relevant communication tool adapted for agile innovation. *Journal of Innovation Economics Management*, 1, 7–27.

Diener, E. (1984) Subjective well-being. *Psychological Bulletin*, 95(3), 542–575.

Diener, E. (2013) The remarkable changes in the science of subjective well-being. *Perspectives on Psychological Science*, 8(6), 663–666.

Diener, E., Oishi, S. and Lucas, R.E. (2003) Personality, culture, and subjective well-being: Emotional and cognitive evaluations of life. *Annual Review of Psychology*, 54, 403–425.

Dijk, R. and Dick, R. (2009) Navigating organizational change: Change leaders, employee resistance and work based identities. *Journal of Change Management*, 9(2), 143–163.

Dijkstra, M.T.M., Van Dierendonck, D., Evers, A. and De Dreu, C.K.W. (2004) Conflict and well-being at work: The moderating role of personality. *Journal of Managerial Psychology*, 20(2), 87–104.

Dipboye, R.L. and Colella, A. (2005) The dilemmas of workplace discrimination. In R. Dipboye and A. Colella (eds), *The Psychological and Organizational Bases Discrimination at Work*. Mahwah, NJ: Lawrence Erlbaum Associates, pp. 425–462.

Dixon, T. and O'Hara, M. (2013) *Communication Skills: Making Practice Based Learning Work*. Project No. 174/2. University of Ulster. Available at: http://cw.routledge.com/textbooks/9780415537902/data/learning/11_Communication%20Skills.pdf (accessed 11 December 2019).

Dobbin, F., Schrage, D. and Kalev, A. (2015) Rage against the iron cage: The varied effects of bureaucratic personnel reforms on diversity. *American Sociological Review*, 80, 1014–1044.

Dries, N. and De Gieter, S. (2014) Information asymmetry in high potential programs. *Personnel Review*, 43(1), 136–162.

Drucker, P.F. (2011) *Managing the Non-profit Organization*. London and New York: Routledge.

DuBrin, A.J. (2001) *Winning at Office Politics*. New York: Van Nostrand-Reinhold.

Dundon, T. and Rollinson, D. (2011) *Understanding Employment Relations*, 2nd edn. Maidenhead, Berkshire: McGraw-Hill.

Eagly, A.H. (2013) *Sex Differences in Social Behavior: A Social-role Interpretation*. Mahwah, NJ: Psychology Press.

Eagly, A.H., Nater, C., Miller, D.I., Kaufmann, M. and Sczesny, S. (2020) Gender stereotypes have changed: A cross-temporal meta-analysis of US public opinion polls from 1946 to 2018. *American Psychologist*, 75(3), 301–315.

Edmondson, A.C. and Lei, Z. (2014) Psychological safety: The history, renaissance, and future of an interpersonal construct. *Annual Review of Organizational Psychology and Organizational Behavior*, 1(1), 23–43.

Edwards, J. (2019) A false rumour on WhatsApp started a run on a London bank. *Business Insider*. Available at: https://www.businessinsider.com/whatsapp-rumour-started-run-on-metro-bank-2019-5?r=US&IR=Tsinessinsider.com (accessed 20 May 2021).

Egan, G. (1996) *Change Agent Skills: Managing Innovation and Change*. Englewood Cliffs, NJ: Prentice Hall.

Egan, T.M., Yang, B. and Bartlett, K.R. (2004) The effects of organizational learning culture and job satisfaction on motivation to transfer learning and turnover intention. *Human Resource Development Quarterly*, 15(3), 279–301.

Einarsen, S., Hoel, H., Zapf, D. and Cooper, C.L. (2011) The concept of bullying and harassment at work: The European tradition. In S. Einarsen, H. Hoel, D. Zapf

and C.L. Cooper (eds), *Bullying and Harassment in the Workplace: Developments in Theory, Research, and Practice*, 2nd edn. London: Taylor and Francis, pp. 3–40.

Ekvall, G. (1996) Organizational climate for creativity and innovation. *European Journal of Work and Organizational Psychology*, 5(1), 105–123.

Elias, S. (2008) Fifty years of influence in the workplace: The evolution of the French and Raven power taxonomy. *Journal of Management History*, 14(3), 267–283.

Ely, R.J. and Thomas, D.A. (1996) Making differences matter: A new paradigm for managing diversity. *Harvard Business Review*, 74, 79–90.

Ely, R.J., Ibarra, H. and Kolb, D.M. (2011) Taking gender into account: Theory and design for women's leadership development programs. *Academy of Management Learning & Education*, 10(3), 474–493.

Engel, D., Woolley, A.W., Jing, L.X., Chabris, C.F. and Malone, T.W. (2014) Reading the mind in the eyes or reading between the lines? Theory of mind predicts collective intelligence equally well online and face-to-face. *PLoS ONE*, 9(12), e115212.

Epitropaki, O., Kark, R., Mainemelis, C. and Lord, R.G. (2017) Leadership and followership identity processes: A multilevel review. *The Leadership Quarterly*, 28(1), 104–129.

Erez, M. and Earley, P.C. (1993) *Culture, Self-identity, and Work*. New York: Oxford University Press.

Evans, C.R. and Dion, K.L. (1991) Group cohesion and performance: A meta-analysis. *Small Group Research*, 22(2), 175–186.

Everuss, L., Carvalho, M., Casanova, J.L., Chaffee, D. and Lever-Tracy, C. (2017) Assessing the public willingness to contribute income to mitigate the effects of climate change: A comparison of Adelaide and Lisbon. *Journal of Sociology*, 53(2), 334–350.

Eysenck, H.J. (1947) *Dimensions of Personality: A Record of Research Carried Out in Collaboration with HT Himmelweit [and others]*. London: Kegan Paul, Trench, Trubner.

Eysenck, H.J. (1965) *Fact and Fiction in Psychology*. Harmondsworth: Penguin.

Eysenck, H.J. (1970) *The Structure of Human Personality*. London: Methuen.

Fay, D., Shipton, H., West, M.A. and Patterson, M. (2015) Teamwork and organizational innovation: The moderating role of the HRM context. *Creativity and Innovation Management*, 24(2), 261–277.

Feeney, B.C. and Collins, N.L. (2014) A new look at social support: A theoretical perspective on thriving through relationships. *Personality and Social Psychology Review*, 19(2), 113–147.

Feldman, D.C. (1976) A contingency theory of socialization. *Organization Dynamics*, 14, 5–23.

Feldman, D.C. (1976) Contingency theory of socialization. *Administrative Science Quarterly*, 21(3), 433–452.

Feldman, D.C. (1981) The multiple socialization of organization members. *Academy of Management Review*, 6(2), 309–318.

Feldman, D.C. (1984) The development and emergence of group norms. *Academy of Management Review*, 9, 47–53.

Feldman, D.C. (1997) Socialization in an international context. *International Journal of Selection and Assessment*, 5, 1–8.

Ferris, G.R., Liden, R.C., Munyon, T.P., Summers, J.K., Basik, K.J. and Buckley, M.R. (2009) Relationships at work: Toward a multidimensional conceptualization of dyadic work relationships. *Journal of Management*, 35(6), 1379–1403.

Festinger, L. (1957) *A Theory of Cognitive Dissonance*. Evanston, IL: Row Peterson.

Fiedler, F.E. (1971) Personality and situational determinants of leader behavior. Technical Report. Seattle: University of Washington, Department of Psychology.

Fiedler, F.E. and Chemers, M.M. (1974) *Leadership and Effective Management*. Glenview, IL: Scott, Foresman.

Filstad, C. (2011) Organizational commitment through organizational socialization tactics. *Journal of Workplace Learning*, 23(6), 376–390.

Fishbach, A. (2018) How to keep working when you're just not feeling it. *Harvard Business Review*, November/December.

Fisher, R. and Ury, W. (1981) *Getting to Yes: Negotiating Agreement Without Giving In*. New York: Penguin.

Fletcher, D. and Sarkar, M. (2013) Psychological resilience: A review and critique of definitions, concepts, and theory. *European Psychologist*, 18(1), 12–23.

Floyd, W.S. and Wooldridge, B. (1997) Middle management's strategic influence and organisational performance. *Journal of Management Studies*, 34, 465–485.

Floyd, W.S. and Wooldridge, B. (2000) *Building Strategy from the Middle: Reconceptualizing the Strategy Process*. Thousand Oaks, CA: Sage.

Folkman, S. and Lazarus, R.S. (1986) Stress processes and depressive symptomatology. *Journal of Abnormal Psychology*, 95(2), 107–113.

Forbes Insights (2017) *The Connected Culture: Unleashing the Power of Video in Everyday Collaboration*. Jersey City, NJ: Forbes Insights. Available at: https://i.forbesimg.com/forbesinsights/zoom/The_Connected_Culture.pdf (accessed 9 January 2020).

Forgas, J.P. (2007) When sad is better than happy: Negative affect can improve the quality and effectiveness of persuasive messages and social influence strategies. *Journal of Experimental Social Psychology*, 43(4), 513–528.

Forgas, J.P., Cooper, J. and Crano, W.D. (2010) Attitudes and attitude change: 'An introductory review'. In J.P. Forgas, J. Cooper and W.D. Crano (eds), *The Psychology of Attitudes and Attitude Change*. New York: Psychology Press, pp. 3–18.

Foss, N.J., Minbaeva, D., Pederseon, T. and Reinholt, M. (2009) The impact of autonomy, task identity, and feedback on employee motivation to share knowledge. *Human Resource Management*, 48(1), 871–893.

Fosslien, L. and Duffy, M.W. (2020) How to combat zoom fatigue. *Harvard Business Review*, 29.

Fox, A. (1966) Industrial Sociology and Industrial Relations. Research Paper No 3. Royal Commission on Trade Unions and Employers' Associations. London, HMSO.

Franzoi, S. (2009) *Social Psychology*, 5th edn. New York: McGraw-Hill.

French, J.R.P. and Raven, B. (1959) The bases of social power. In D. Cartwright (ed.), *Studies in Social Power*. Ann Arbor, MI: Institute for Social Research.

French, R., Rayner, C., Rees, G. and Rumbles, S. (2015) *Organizational Behaviour*, 3rd edn. Chichester: Wiley.

French, W. and Bell, C. (1978) *Organizational Development: Behavioural Science Interventions for Organization Improvement*, 2nd edn. Englewood Cliffs, NJ: Prentice Hall.

Frenkel-Brunswik, E. and Sanford, R.N. (1945) Some personality factors in anti-Semitism. *The Journal of Psychology*, 20(2), 271–291.

Frey, C. and Osborne, M. (2017) The future of employment: How susceptible are jobs to computerisation? *Technological Forecasting and Social Change*, 114, 254–280.

Fulmer, I.S., Gerhart, B. and Scott, K.S. (2003) Are the 100 Best better? An empirical investigation of the relationship between being a 'Great Place to Work' and firm performance. *Personnel Psychology*, 56, 965–993.

Fung, B. (2020) Twitter will let some employees work from home 'forever'. *CNN*. Available at: https://edition.cnn.com/2020/05/12/tech/twitter-work-from-home-forever/idex.html (accessed 9 May 2021).

Furnham, A., Steele, H. and Pendleton, D. (1993) A psychometric assessment of the Belbin Team-Role Self-Perception Inventory. *Journal of Occupational and Organizational Psychology*, 66(3), 245–257.

Future for Work Institute (2017) The dark side of strong organisational cultures. Available at: http://www.futureforwork.com/the-dark-side-of-strong-organisational-cultures/

Gagnon, S. and Cornelius, N. (2000) Re-examining workplace equality: The capabilities approach. *Human Resource Management Journal*, 10, 68–87.

Gallo, A. (2014) How to keep your team motivated. *Harvard Business Review*, December.

Gallup (2018) *Q12 Employee Engagement Center*. Available at: www.gallup.com/products/170969/q12-employee-engagement-center.aspx (accessed 20 April 2021).

Gambrel, P.A. and Cianci, R. (2003) Maslow's hierarchy of needs: Does it apply in a collectivist culture. *Journal of Applied Management and Entrepreneurship*, 8(2), 143–161.

Garcia-Dia, M.J., DiNapoli, J.M., Garcia-Ona, L., Jakubowski, R. and O'Flaherty, D. (2013) Concept analysis: Resilience. *Archives of Psychiatric Nursing*, 27(6), 264–270.

Gardner, W.L., Cogliser, C.C., Davis, K.M. and Dickens, M.P. (2011) Authentic leadership: A review of the literature and research agenda. *The Leadership Quarterly*, 22(6), 1120–1145.

Gibb, C.A. (1947) The principles and traits of leadership. *The Journal of Abnormal and Social Psychology*, 42(3), 267.

Giffords, E.D. (2009) An examination of organizational commitment and professional commitment and the relationship to work environment, demographic and organizational factors. *Journal of Social Work*, 9, 386–404.

Gill, C., Metz, I., Tekleab, A.G. and Williamson, I.O. (2018) The combined role of conscientiousness, social networks, and gender diversity in explaining individual performance in self-managed teams. *Journal of Business Research*, 106(C), 250–260.

Giumetti, G.W., Hatfield, A.L., Scisco, J.L., Schroeder, A.N., Muth, E.R. and Kowalski, R.M. (2013) What a rude e-mail! Examining the differential effects of incivility versus support on mood, energy, engagement, and performance in an online context. *Journal of Occupational Health Psychology*, 18(3), 297–309.

Glass, N. and Hume, T. (2013) The 'hallelujah moment' behind the invention of the Post-it note. CNN, 4 April. Available at: https://edition.cnn.com/2013/04/04/tech/post-it-note-history/ (accessed 17 January 2020).

Glick, P. and Fiske, S.T. (2001) Ambivalent stereotypes as legitimizing ideologies: Differentiating paternalistic and envious prejudice. In J. Jost and B. Major (eds), *The Psychology of Legitimacy*. Cambridge: Cambridge University Press, pp. 278–306.

Glisson, C. and James, L.R. (2002) The cross–level effects of culture and climate in human service teams. *Journal of Organizational Behavior: The International Journal of Industrial, Occupational and Organizational Psychology and Behavior*, 23(6), 767–794.

Goetzel, R.Z., Long, S.R., Ozminkowski, R.J., Hawkins, K., Wang, S. and Lynch, W. (2004) Health, absence, disability, and presenteeism cost estimates of certain physical and mental health conditions affecting US employers. *Journal of Occupational and Environmental Medicine*, 46(4), 398–412.

Gonzalez, J.A. and Denisi, A.S. (2009) Cross-level effects of demography and diversity climate on organizational attachment and firm effectiveness. *Journal of Organizational Behavior: The International Journal of Industrial, Occupational and Organizational Psychology and Behavior*, 30, 21–40.

Gonzalez-Morales, M.G. and Neves, P. (2015) When stressors make you work: Mechanisms linking challenge stressors to performance. *Work and Stress*, 29(3), 213–229.

Gonzalez-Roma, V., Schaufeli, W.B., Bakker, A.B. and Lloret, S. (2006) Burnout and work engagement: Independent factors or opposite poles? *Journal of Vocational Behavior*, 68(1), 165–174.

Gorgievski, M.J. and Hobfoll, S.E. (2008) Work can burn us out or fire us up: Conservation of resources in burnout and engagement. In J.R.B. Helbesleben (ed.), *Handbook of Stress and Burnout in Health Care*. New York: Nova Science Publishers, pp. 7–22.

Gosling, S.D., Rentfrow, P.J. and Swann Jr, W.B. (2003) A very brief measure of the Big-Five personality domains. *Journal of Research in Personality*, 37, 504–528.

Graen, G.B. and Uhl-Bien, M. (1995) Relationship-based approach to leadership: Development of leader–member exchange (LMX) theory of leadership over 25 years: Applying a multi-level multi-domain perspective. *The Leadership Quarterly*, 6(2), 219–247.

Graham, J. (2014) *Duke CFO Global Business Outlook Survey*. Available at: https://www.cfosurvey.org/press-release/few-companies-making-special-effort-to-attract-millenials-or-achieve-board-diversity-targets/

Grant, A. (2014) *Give and Take: Why Helping Others Drives Our Success*. New York: Penguin.

Greco, L.M. and Kraimer, M.L. (2019) Goal-setting in the career management process: An identity theory perspective. *Journal of Applied Psychology*, 105(1), 40–57.

Greenberg, J. (2011) *Behaviour in Organizations*, 10th edn. Harlow: Pearson Education.

Greenwald, A.G. (1968) Cognitive learning, cognitive response to persuasion, and attitude change. *Psychological Foundations of Attitudes*, 1, 147–170.

Gregory, B.T., Harris, S.G., Armenakis, A.A. and Shook, C.L. (2009) Organizational culture and effectiveness: A study of values, attitudes, and organizational outcomes. *Journal of Business Research*, 62(7), 673–679.

Grenny, J. and Maxfield, D. (2017) A study of 1,100 employees found that remote workers feel shunned and left out. *Harvard Business Review*. Available at: https://hbr. org/2017/11/a-study-of-1100-employees-found-that-remote-workers-feel-shunned-and-left-out

Grieg, A. (2013) All the lonely Facebook friends: Study shows social media makes us MORE lonely and unhappy and LESS sociable. Available at: http:// www.dailymail.co.uk/news/article-2419419/ All-lonely-Facebook-friends-Study-shows-social-media-makes-MORE-lonely-unhappy-LESS-sociable. html#ixzz33U3nWSHm (accessed 20 August 2019).

Griffin, M.A., Patterson, M.G. and West, M.A. (2001) Job satisfaction and teamwork: The role of supervisor support. *Journal of Organizational Behavior*, 22(5), 537–550.

Griffin, R.W. (2014) *Fundamentals of Management*. Mason, OH: South-Western Cengage Learning.

Gross, J.J. (1998) Antecedent- and response-focused emotion regulation: Divergent consequences for experience, expression, and physiology. *Journal of Personality and Social Psychology*, 74(1), 224–237.

Gross, J.J. (1999) Emotion regulation: Past, present, future. *Cognition & Emotion*, 13(5), 551–573.

Gross, J.J. and John, O.P. (2003) Individual differences in two emotion regulation processes: Implications for affect, relationships, and well-being. *Journal of Personality and Social Psychology*, 85(2), 348–362.

Gross, J.J. and Thompson, R.A. (2007) Emotion regulation: Conceptual foundations. In J.J. Gross (ed.), *Handbook of Emotion Regulation*. New York: Guilford Press, pp. 3–26.

Gruman, J.A. and Saks, A.M. (2011) Performance management and employee engagement. *Human Resource Management Review*, 21(2), 123–136.

Guest, D.E. (2004) The psychology of the employment relationship: An analysis based on the psychological contract. *Applied Psychology*, 53(4), 541–555.

Gurdjian, P., Halbeisen, T. and Lane, K. (2014) Why leadership-development programs fail. *McKinsey Quarterly*, 1(1), 121–126.

Hackman, J.R. and Oldham, G.R. (1976) Motivation through the design of work: Test of a theory. *Organizational Behavior and Human Performance*, 16, 256.

Halbesleben, J.R.B., Neveu, J.P., Paustian-Underdahl, S.C. and Westman, M. (2014) Getting to the 'COR': Understanding the role of resources in conservation of resources theory. *Journal of Management*, 40(5), 1334–1364.

Hall, D.T. (1996) Long live the career: A relational approach. In D.T. Hall (ed.), *The Career is Dead – Long Live the Career*. San Francisco, CA: Jossey-Bass, pp. 1–14.

Hallberg, U.E. and Schaufeli, W.B. (2006) 'Same Same' but different? Can work engagement be discriminated from job involvement and organizational commitment? *European Psychologist*, 11(2), 119.

Hamilton, B., Nickerson, J. and Owan, H. (2012) Diversity and productivity in production teams. In A. Bryson (ed.), *Advances in the Economic Analysis of Participatory and Labor-Managed Firms*. Bingley: Emerald Group Publishing, pp. 99–138.

Hanley, R. (2018) Rage against waiting lists validation. *Irish Medical Times*, 28 November. Available at: https://www.imt.ie/opinion/rage-waiting-lists-validation-28-11-2018/ (accessed 9 October 2019).

Hannah, S.T., Balthazard, P.A., Waldman, D.A., Jennings, P.L. and Thatcher, R.W. (2013) The psychological and neurological bases of leader self-complexity and effects on adaptive decision-making. *Journal of Applied Psychology*, 98, 393–411.

Harris, E. (2019) Why the world is watching young climate activists: Researchers break down why the movement and its message are gaining ground. *Nature, News in Focus*, 573, 471–472.

Harrison, D.A., Newman, D.A. and Roth, P.L. (2006) How important are job attitudes? Meta-analytic comparisons of integrative behavioral outcomes and time sequences. *Academy of Management Journal*, 49(2), 305–325.

Harrison, M.S. and Thomas, K.M. (2009) The hidden prejudice in selection: A research investigation on skin color bias. *Journal of Applied Social Psychology*, 39(1), 134–168.

Hart, E. (1996) Top teams. *Management Review*, February, 43–47.

Harter, J.K., Schmidt, F.L. and Hayes, T.L. (2002) Business-unit-level relationship between employee satisfaction, employee engagement, and business outcomes: A meta-analysis. *Journal of Applied Psychology*, 87(2), 268–279.

Hartnell, C.A., Ou, A.Y. and Kinicki, A. (2011) Organizational culture and organizational effectiveness: A meta-analytic investigation of the competing values framework's theoretical suppositions. *Journal of Applied Psychology*, 96(4), 677.

Harvard Business Review (2019) The Wrong Ways to Strengthen Culture. Available at: https://hbr. org/2019/07/the-wrong-ways-to-strengthen-culture (accessed 17 May 2021).

Hasin, D.S., Sarvet, A.L., Meyers, J.L., Saha, T.D., Ruan, W.J., Stohl, M. *et al.* (2018) Epidemiology of adult DSM-5 major depressive disorder and its specifiers in the United States. *JAMA Psychiatry*, 75(4), 336–346.

Hayes, J. (2002) *The Theory and Practice of Change Management*. New York: Palgrave.

Hayes, J. (2018) *The Theory and Practice of Change Management*, 5th edn. London: Red Globe Press.

Haynes, B. and Haines, A. (1998) Barriers and bridges to evidence based clinical practice. *British Medical Journal*, 317, 273–276.

He, J. and Kaplan, S. (2017) The gender equality challenge. *Gender and the Economy*, 5 October 2019.

Health Service Executive (2018) HSE Statement Re: Outpatient Waiting List Validation. Available at: https://www.hse.ie/eng/services/news/media/pressrel/hse-statement-re-outpatient-waiting-list-validation.html (accessed 9 October 2019).

Health Service Executive (2019a) About human resources. Available at: https://www.hse.ie/eng/about/who/hr/ (accessed 9 October 2019).

Health Service Executive (2019b) Who we are, what we do. Available at: https://www.hse.ie/eng/about/ (accessed 10 October 2019).

Heaphy, E.D., Byron, K., Ballinger, G.A., Gittell, J.H., Leana, C. and Sluss, D.M. (2018) Introduction to special topic forum: The Changing Nature of Work Relationships. *Academy of Management Review*, 43(4), 558–569.

Heath, R.G. and Isbell, M. (2015) Broadening organizational communication curricula: Collaboration as key to 21st-century organizing. *Management Communication Quarterly*, 29(2), 309–314.

Heider, F. (1958) *The Psychology of Interpersonal Relations*. Hoboken, NJ: John Wiley & Sons.

Heimler, R., Rosenberg, S. and Morote, E.S. (2012) Predicting career advancement with structural equation modelling. *Education & Training*, 54(2), 85–94.

Heine, S.J. and Buchtel, E.E. (2009) Personality: The universal and the culturally specific. *Annual Review of Psychology*, 60, 369–394.

Herold, D., Caldwell, S. and Liu, Y. (2008) The effects of transformational and change leadership on employees' commitment to change: A multilevel study. *Journal of Applied Psychology*, 93(2), 346–357.

Hersey, P. and Blanchard, K.H. (1969) Life cycle theory of leadership. *Training and Development Journal*, 23(2), 26–34.

Hersey, P. and Blanchard, K.H. (1972) The management of change. *Training and Development Journal*, 26(2), 20–24.

Hershcovis, M.S., Ogunfowora, B., Reich, T.C. and Christie, A.M. (2017) Targeted workplace incivility: The roles of belongingness, embarrassment, and power. *Journal of Organizational Behavior*, 38(7), 1057–1075.

Herzberg, F. (1966) *Work and the Nature of Man*. Cleveland, OH: World Publishing.

Hesketh, I. and Cooper, C.L. (2014) Leaveism at work. *Occupational Medicine*, 64(3), 146–147.

Hewlett, S.A., Rashid, R. and Sherbin, L. (2017) When employees think the boss is unfair, they're more likely to disengage and leave. *Harvard Business Review*, August.

Hicks-Clarke, D. and Iles, P. (2000) Climate for diversity and its effects on career and organisational attitudes and perceptions. *Personnel Review*, 29, 324–345.

Hirst, G., Walumbwa, F., Aryee, S., Butarbutar, I. and Chen, C.J.H. (2016) A Multi-level investigation of authentic leadership as an antecedent of helping behavior. *Journal of Business Ethics*, 139(3), 485–499.

Hitt, M.A., Black, S.J. and Porter, L.W. (2014) *Management* (International edn). Saddle River, NJ: Pearson.

Hitt, M.A., Miller, C.C. and Colella, A. (2009) *Organizational Behavior: A Strategic Approach*. Hoboken, NJ: John Wiley & Sons.

Hofstede, G. (1980) *Culture's Consequences: International Differences in Work Related Values*. Newbury Park, CA: Sage Publications.

Hofstede, G. (1991) *Cultures and Organizations*. London: McGraw-Hill.

Hofstede, G. (1994) Management scientists are human. *Management Science*, 40(1), 4–13.

Hofstede, G. (2011) Dimensionalizing cultures: The Hofstede Model in context. *Online Readings in Psychology and Culture*, 2(1), 1–26.

Hogan, J., Barrett, P. and Hogan, R. (2007) Personality measurement, faking, and employment selection. *Journal of Applied Psychology*, 92(5), 1270–1285.

Hogan, R. and Benson, M.J. (2009) Personality, leadership, and globalization: Linking personality to global organizational effectiveness. In Mobley, W.H., Wang, Y. and Li, M. (eds), *Advances in Global Leadership*. Advances in Global Leadership, 5. Bingley: Emerald Group Publishing, pp. 11–34.

Holland, J.L. (1997) *Making Vocational Choices*, 3rd edn. Lutz, FL: Psychological Assessment Resources.

Hope, V. and Hendry, J. (1995) Corporate cultural change – Is it relevant for the organisations of the 1990s? *Human Resource Management Journal*, 5, 61–73.

Hoppe, S., Loetscher, T., Morey, S.A. and Bulling, A. (2018) Eye movements during everyday behavior predict personality traits. *Frontiers in Human Neuroscience*, 12, 1–8.

House, R.J. (1977) A 1976 theory of charismatic leadership. In J.G. Hunt and L.L. Larson (eds), *Leadership: The Cutting Edge*. Carbondale, IL: Southern Illinois University Press.

House, R.J. and Aditya, R.N. (1997) The social scientific study of leadership: Quo vadis? *Journal of Management*, 23(3), 409–473.

House, R.J., Hanges, P.J., Javidan, M., Dorfman, P.W. and Gupta, V. (eds) (2004) *Culture, Leadership, and Organizations: The GLOBE Study of 62 Societies*. Thousand Oaks, CA: Sage Publications.

Hovland, C.I., Janis, I.L. and Kelley, H.H. (1953) *Communication and Persuasion: Psychological Studies of Obvious Change*. New Haven, CT: Yale University Press.

Howard, P.J. and Howard, J.M. (2001) *The Owner's Manual for Personality at Work: How the Big Five Personality Traits Affect your Performance, Communication, Teamwork, Leadership, and Sales*. Austin, TX: Bard Press.

Huczynski, A. and Buchanan, D. (2001) *Organizational Behaviour: An Introductory Text*. Harlow and London: Pearson Education.

Hughes, L.A. and Short, J.F. Jnr (2005) Disputes involving youth street gang members: Micro-social contexts. *Criminology*, 43(1), 43–76.

Hülsheger, U.R. (2015) Making sure that mindfulness is promoted in organizations in the right way and for the right goals. *Industrial and Organizational Psychology-Perspectives on Science and Practice*, 8(4), 674–679.

Hülsheger, U.R., Alberts, H., Feinholdt, A. and Lang, J.W.B. (2013) Benefits of mindfulness at work: The role of mindfulness in emotion regulation, emotional exhaustion, and job satisfaction. *Journal of Applied Psychology*, 98(2), 310–325.

Hülsheger, U.R., Lang, J.W.B., Depenbrock, F., Fehrmann, C., Zijlstra, F.R.H. and Alberts, H. (2014) The power of presence: The role of mindfulness at work for daily levels and change trajectories of psychological detachment and sleep quality. *Journal of Applied Psychology*, 99(6), 1113–1128.

Hunt, J.G. and Larson, L.L. (eds) (1977) *Leadership: The Cutting Edge*. Carbondale, IL: Southern Illinois University Press.

Hunt, V., Prince, S., Dixon-Fyle, S. and Yee, L. (2018) Delivering through diversity. McKinsey & Company. Available at: https://www.mckinsey.com/business-functions/organization/our-insights/delivering-through-diversity#> (accessed 17 May 2021).

Hyman, R. and Mason, B. (1995) *Managing Employee Involvement and Participation*. London: Sage.

Ihsan, Z. and Furnham, A. (2018) The new technologies in personality assessment: A review. *Consulting Psychology Journal: Practice and Research*, 70(2), 147.

Ilies, R., Aw, S.S.Y. and Pluut, H. (2015) Intraindividual models of employee well-being: What have we learned and where do we go from here? *European Journal of Work and Organizational Psychology*, 24(6), 827–838.

Ilies, R., Gerhardt, M.W. and Le, H. (2004) Individual differences in leadership emergence: Integrating meta-analytic findings and behavioral genetics estimates. *International Journal of Selection and Assessment*, 12(3), 207–219.

ILO (2015) *Women in business and management: Gaining momentum*. Global Report. Geneva: International Labour Office.

Isern, J. and Pung, C. (2007) Harnessing energy to drive organizational change. *The McKinsey Quarterly*, 1, 1–4.

Jack, R.E., Garrod, O.G., Yu, H., Caldara, R. and Schyns, P.G. (2012) Facial expressions of emotion are not culturally universal. *Proceedings of the National Academy of Sciences of the United States of America*, 109(19), 7241–7244.

Jackson, S.E. and Schuler, R.S. (1985) A meta-analysis and conceptual critique of research on role ambiguity and role conflict in work settings. *Organizational Behavior and Human Decision Processes*, 36(1), 16–78.

James, J.B., McKechnie, S. and Swanberg, J. (2011) Predicting employee engagement in an age-diverse retail workforce. *Journal of Organizational Behavior*, 32(2), 173–196.

James, L.A. and James, L.R. (1989) Integrating work environment perceptions: Explorations into the measurement of meaning. *Journal of Applied Psychology*, 74, 739–751.

Jamieson, J.P., Mendes, W.B. and Nock, M.K. (2013) Improving acute stress responses: The power of reappraisal. *Current Directions in Psychological Science*, 22(1), 51–56.

Janis, I.L. (1972) *Victims of Groupthink: A Psychological Study of Foreign-policy Decisions and Fiascos*. New York and Oxford: Houghton Mifflin.

Johns, G. (2010) Presenteeism in the workplace: A review and research agenda. *Journal of Organizational Behavior*, 31(4), 519–542.

Johnson, D.W. and Johnson, F. (2009) *Joining Together: Group Theory and Group Skills*, 10th edn. Boston, MA: Allyn & Bacon.

Johnson, M. and Senges, M. (2010) Learning to be a programmer in a complex organization: A case study on practice-based learning during the onboarding process at Google. *Journal of Workplace Learning*, 22(3), 181–194.

Jones, E., Watson, B., Gardner, J. and Gallois, C. (2004) Organization communication: Challenges for the new century. *Journal of Communication*, 54(4), 722–750.

Jones, R., Jimmieson, N. and Griffiths, A. (2005) The impact of organizational culture and reshaping capabilities on change implementation success: The mediating role of readiness for change. *Journal of Management Studies*, 42(2), 361–386.

Judge, T.A. and Bono, J.E. (2000) Five-factor model of personality and transformational leadership. *Journal of Applied Psychology*, 85, 751–765.

Judge, T.A. and Bono, J.E. (2001) Relationship of core self-evaluations traits – self-esteem, generalized self-efficacy, locus of control, and emotional stability – with job satisfaction and job performance: A meta-analysis. *Journal of Applied Psychology*, 86(1), 80–92.

Judge, T.A. and Cable, D.M. (2004) The effect of physical height on workplace success and income: Preliminary test of a theoretical model. *Journal of Applied Psychology*, 89(3), 428.

Judge, T. and Piccolo, R. (2004) Transformational and transactional leadership: A meta-analytic test of their relative validity. *Journal of Applied Psychology*, 89(5), 755–768.

Judge, T.A., Bono, J.E. and Thoresen, C.J. (2003) The core self-evaluation scale: Development of a measure. *Personnel Psychology*, 56, 303–331.

Judge, T.A., Heller, D. and Mount, M.K. (2002) Five-factor model of personality and job satisfaction: A meta-analysis. *Journal of Applied Psychology*, 87(3), 530–541.

Judge, T.A., Klinger, R., Simon, L.S. and Yang, I.W.F. (2008) The contributions of personality to organizational behavior and psychology: Findings, criticisms, and future research directions. *Social and Personality Psychology Compass*, 2(5), 1982–2000.

Judge, T.A., Lepine, J.A. and Rich, B.I. (2006) The narcissistic personality: Relationship with inflated self-ratings of leadership with task and contextual performance. *Journal of Applied Psychology*, 91(4), 762–776.

Judge, T.A., Piccolo, R.F. and Kosalka, T. (2009) The bright and dark sides of leader traits: A review and theoretical extension of the leader trait paradigm. *The Leadership Quarterly*, 20(6), 855–875.

Judge, T.A., Thoresen, C.J., Bono, J.E. and Patton, G.K. (2001) The job satisfaction–job performance relationship: A qualitative and quantitative review. *Psychological Bulletin*, 127(3), 376–407.

Kacmar, K.M., Collins, B.J., Harris, K.J. and Judge, T.A. (2009) Core self-evaluations and job performance: The role of the perceived work environment. *Journal of Applied Psychology*, 94(6), 1572.

Kahn, R.L. and Byosiere, P. (1992) Stress in organizations. In M.D. Dunnette and L.M. Hough (eds), *Handbook of Industrial and Organizational Psychology*. Palo Alto, CA: Consulting Psychologists Press, pp. 571–650.

Kahn, R.L., Wolfe, D.M., Quinn, R.P., Snoek, J.D. and Rosenthal, R.A. (1964) *Organizational Stress: Studies in Role Conflict and Ambiguity*. New York: John Wiley.

Kahn, W.A. (1990) Psychological conditions of personal engagement and disengagement at work. *Academy of Management Journal*, 33(4), 692–724.

Kakunja, M. (2017) Quality measurement in restaurant industry from the marketing perspective: A comparison of guests' and managers' quality perceptions. *Ekonomska Misao i Praksa*, 26(1), 41–61.

Kalkhoff, W. and Barnum, C. (2000) The effects of status-organizing and social identity processes on patterns of social influence. *Social Psychology Quarterly*, 95–115.

Kalogiannidis, S. (2020) Impact of effective business communication on employee performance. *European Journal of Business and Management Research*, 5(6), 1–6.

Kanter, R.M. (1977) *Men and Women on the Corporation*. New York: Basic Books.

Kanungo, R.N. (1982) Measurement of job and work involvement. *Journal of Applied Psychology*, 67(3), 341–349.

Kapoutsis, I., Papalexandris, A., Thanos, I.C. and Nikolopoulos, A.G. (2012) The role of political tactics on the organizational context–career success relationship. *The International Journal of Human Resource Management*, 23(9), 1908–1929.

Kapp, K.M. and O'Driscoll, T. (2009) *Learning in 3D: Adding a New Dimension to Enterprise Learning and Collaboration*. San Francisco, CA: John Wiley & Sons.

Karasek, R. (1990) Lower health risk with increased job control among white-collar workers. *Journal of Organizational Behavior*, 11(3), 171–185.

Karau, S.J. and Williams, K.D. (1993) Social loafing: A meta-analytic review and theoretical integration. *Journal of Personality and Social Psychology*, 65(4), 681–706.

Kase, R., Paauwe, J. and Zupan, N. (2009) HR practices, interpersonal relationships and intra-firm knowledge transfer in knowledge-intensive firms: A social network perspective. *Human Resource Management*, 48(4), 615–639.

Kast, F.E. and Rosenweig, J.E. (1972) General systems theory: Application for organizational and management. *Academy of Management Journal*, 15, 447–465.

Katzenbach, J.R. and Smith, D.K. (2005) The discipline of teams. *Harvard Business Review*, July.

Keegan, B. (1992) *An Evil Cradling*. London: Hutchinson.

Kelley, H.H. (1967) Attribution theory in social psychology. *Nebraska Symposium on Motivation*, 15, 192–238.

Khattab, J., Van Knippenberg, D., Pieterse, A.N. and Hernandez, M. (2020) A network utilization perspective on the leadership advancement of minorities. *Academy of Management Review*, 45(1), 109–129.

Kim, T., Hornung, S. and Rousseau, D. (2011) Change-supportive employee behavior: Antecedents and the moderating role of time. *Journal of Management*, 37(6), 1664–1693.

King, D.L. (2012) Social Media. *Library Technology Reports*, 48(6), 23–27.

Kinnunen, U., Mauno, S., Nätti, J. and Happonen, M. (1999) Perceived job insecurity: A longitudinal study among Finnish employees. *European Journal of Work and Organizational Psychology*, 8, 243–260.

Konrad, A.M. (2003) Special issue introduction: Defining the domain of workplace diversity scholarship. *Group & Organization Management*, 28, 4–17.

Korte, R. and Lim, S. (2012) Getting on board: Organizational socialization and the contribution of social capital. *Human Relations*, 66(3), 407–428.

Koschmann, M.A., Kuhn, T.R. and Pfarrer, M.D. (2012) A communicative framework of value in cross-sector partnerships. *Academy of Management Review*, 37, 332–354.

Kotter, J. (1980) An integrative model of organisational dynamics. In E. Lawler, D. Nadler and C. Cammann (eds), *Organizational Assessment*. New York: Wiley.

Kotter, J.P. (1988) *The Leadership Factor*. New York: The Free Press.

Kotter, J.P. (1995) Leading change: Why transformation efforts fail. *Harvard Business Review*, 73(2), 59–67.

Kotter, J. (1996) *Leading Change*. Boston, MA: Harvard Business School Press.

Kotter, J. (1998) Cultures and coalitions. In R. Gibson (ed.), *Rethinking the Future: Rethinking Business, Principles, Competition, Control and Complexity, Leadership, Markets and the World*. London: Nicholas Brealey, pp. 164–178.

Kotter, J. (2007) Leading change: Why transformation efforts fail. *Harvard Business Review*, 85(1), 96–103.

Kotter, J.P. (2008) *Corporate Culture and Performance*. New York: Simon and Schuster.

Kotter, J.P. and Heskett, J.L. (1992) *Corporate Culture and Performance*. New York: Free Press.

Kotter, J. and Schlesinger, L. (1979) Choosing strategies for change. *Harvard Business Review*, 57 (March–April), 106–114.

Kross, E., Verduyn, P., Demiralp, E., Park, J., Lee, D.S., Lin, N., Shablack, H., Jonides, J. and Ybarra, O. (2013) Facebook use predicts declines in subjective well-being in young adults. *PLoS One*, 8(8), e69841. Available at: http://www.ncbi.nlm.nih.gov/pmc/articles/PMC3743827/ (accessed 20 May 2019).

Kumar, P., Kaur, D. and Kalra, R. (2013) Role expectations, role perceptions and role performance of extension personnel. *American International Journal of Research in Humanities, Arts and Social Sciences*, 4, 6–13.

Lacerenza, C.N., Reyes, D.L., Marlow, S.L., Joseph, D.L. and Salas, E. (2017) Leadership training design, delivery, and implementation: A meta-analysis. *Journal of Applied Psychology*, 102(12), 1686–1718.

Lashinksy, A. (2013) *Inside Apple: How America's Most Admired – and Secretive – Company Really Works*. New York: Business Plus.

Latane, B., Williams, K. and Harkins, S. (1979) Many hands make light the work: The causes and consequences of social loafing. *Journal of Personality and Social Psychology*, 37, 822–832.

Lawrence, P.R. and Lorsch, J.W. (1967) Differentiation and Integration in Complex Organizations, *Administrative Science Quarterly*, 12(1), 1–4.

Lazarus, R.S. (1991) *Emotion and Adaptation*. Oxford: Oxford University Press.

Lazarus, R.S. (1993) From psychological stress to the emotions – A history of changing outlooks. *Annual Review of Psychology*, 44, 1–21.

Lazarus, R.S. (2000) Toward better research on stress and coping. *American Psychologist*, 55(6), 665–673.

Lazarus, R.S. and Folkman, S. (1986) Cognitive theories of stress and the issue of circularity. In M.H. Appley and R. Trumbull (eds), *Dynamics of Stress: Physiological, Psychological and Social Perspectives*. Boston, MA: Springer US, pp. 63–80.

Le, H., Oh, I.-S., Robbins, S.B., Ilies, R., Holland, E. and Westrick, P. (2011) Too much of a good thing: Curvilinear relationship between personality traits and job performance. *Journal of Applied Psychology*, 96(1), 113–133.

Lee, J. (2020) A neuropsychological exploration of zoom fatigue. *Psychiatric Times*. Available at: https://www.psychiatrictimes.com/view/psychological-exploration-zoom-fatigue

Lee, L., Frederick, S. and Ariely, D. (2006) Try it, you'll like it: The influence of expectation, consumption, and revelation on preferences for beer. *Journal of Psychological Science*, 17(12), 1054–1058.

Lehmann-Willenbrock, N., Lei, Z. and Kauffeld, S. (2012) Appreciating age diversity and German nurse well-being and commitment: Co-worker trust as the mediator. *Nursing & Health Sciences*, 14, 213–220.

Leslie, L.M., Mayer, D.M. and Kravitz, D.A. (2014) The stigma of affirmative action: A stereotyping-based theory and meta-analytic test of the consequences for performance. *Academy of Management Journal*, 57, 964–989.

Levesque, M.J. and Kenny, D.A. (1993) Accuracy of behavioral predictions at zero acquaintance: A social relations analysis. *Journal of Personality and Social Psychology*, 65, 1178–1187.

Lewin, K. (1948) *Resolving Social Conflicts*. New York: Harper & Row.

Lewin, K. (1951) *Field Theory in Social Science: Selected Theoretical Papers*, ed. D. Cartwright. New York: Harper & Row.

Lewis, L.K and Seibold, D.R. (2012) Reconceptualizing organizational change implementation as a communication problem: A review of literature and research agenda. In M.E Roloff (ed.) *Communication Yearbook* 21. New York: Routledge.

Likert, R. (1932) A technique for the measurement of attitudes. *Archives of Psychology*, 22, 1–55.

Lippitt, R. (1958) Dynamics of planned change. Available at: https://agris.fao.org/agris-search/search.do?recordID=US201300602467

Locke, E.A. (1968) Toward a theory of task performance and incentives. *Organizational Behavior and Human Performance*, 3, 157–189.

Locke, E.A. (1976) The nature and causes of job satisfaction. In M.D. Dunette (ed.), *Handbook of Industrial and Organizational Psychology*, vol. 1. Chicago, IL: Rand McNally, pp. 1297–1343.

Locke, E.A. and Latham, G.P. (1990) Work motivation: The high performance cycle. *Work Motivation*, 3–25.

Locke, E.A. and Latham, G.P. (2002) Building a practically useful theory of goal setting and task motivation. *American Psychologist*, 57(9), 705–717.

Loehlin, J.C. (1992) *Genes and Environment in Personality Development*. Newbury Park, CA: Sage.

Lok, P. and Crawford, J. (2004) The effect of organisational culture and leadership style on job satisfaction and organisational commitment: A cross-national comparison. *Journal of Management Development*, 23(4), 321–338.

Lord, R.G. and Hall, R.J. (2005) Identity, deep structure and the development of leadership skill. *The Leadership Quarterly*, 16(4), 591–615.

MacCann, C., Ziegler, M. and Roberts R.D. (2012) *Faking in Personality Assessment: Reflections and Recommendations*. Oxford: Oxford University Press.

MacDuffie, J.P. (1995) Human resource bundles and manufacturing performance. Organizational logic and flexible production systems in the world auto industry. *Industrial and Labor Relations Review*, 48(2), 197–221.

Madden, L., Mathias, B.D. and Madden, T.M. (2015) In good company: The impact of perceived organizational support and positive relationships at work on turnover intentions. *Management Research Review*, 38(3), 242–263.

Mamman, A., Kamoche, K. and Bakuwa, R. (2012) Diversity, organizational commitment and organizational citizenship behavior: An organizing framework. *Human Resource Management Review*, 22, 285–302.

Mann, S. (2013) Trust in virtual teams. *Leadership & Organization Development Journal*, 34(8), 805–806.

Marcus, B. (2015) The lack of diversity in tech is a cultural issue. *Forbes*. Available at: https://www.forbes.com/sites/bonniemarcus/2015/08/12/the-lack-of-diversity-in-tech-is-a-cultural-issue/?sh=3c53bdb579a2

Marianetti, O. and Passmore, J. (2010) Mindfulness at work: Paying attention to enhance well-being and performance. In P.A. Linley, S. Harrington and N. Garcea (eds), *Oxford Handbook of Positive Psychology and Work*. New York: Oxford University Press, pp. 189–200.

Maslach, C., Schaufeli, W.B. and Leiter, M.P. (2001) Job burnout. *Annual Review of Psychology*, 52(1), 397–422.

Maslow, A.H. (1943) A theory of human motivation. *Psychological Review*, 50(4), 370–396.

Masten, A.S. (2001) Ordinary magic: Resilience processes in development. *American Psychologist*, 56(3), 227–238.

Matsumoto, D. (1996) *Culture and Psychology*. Pacific Grove, CA: Brooks/Cole.

Matsumoto, D., Keltner, D., Shiota, M.N., O'Sullivan, M. and Frank, M. (2008) Facial expressions of emotion. In D. Matsumoto (ed.), *The Handbook of Emotions*. New York: Gilford Press, pp. 211–234.

Maznevski, M. (2007) IMD: Leading diverse teams Part 3. Available at: http://video.ft.com/62063401001/IMD-Leading-diverse-teams/Management (accessed 15 October 2019).

McCall, M.W. and Lombardo, M.M. (1983) *Off the Track: Why and How Successful Executives Get Derailed*. Technical Report, 21. Greensboro, NC: Center for Creative Leadership.

McCarthy, J., Heraty, N. and Bamberg, A. (2019) Lifespan perspectives on age-related stereotypes, prejudice, and discrimination at work (and beyond). In B.B. Baltes, C.W. Rudolph and H. Zacher (eds), *Work Across the Lifespan*. London: Academic Press, pp. 417–435.

McClelland, D.C. (1985) *Human Motivation*. Glenview, IL: Scott, Foresman.

McCord, P. (2014) How Netflix reinvented HR (cover story). *Harvard Business Review*, 92(1/2), 70–76.

McCrae, R.R. and Costa, P.T. Jr (1987) Validation of the five-factor model of personality across instruments and observers. *Journal of Personality and Social Psychology*, 52, 81–90.

McCrae, R.R., Terracciano, A. and Members of the Personality Profiles of Cultures Project (2005) Personality profiles of cultures: Aggregate personality traits. *Journal of Personality and Social Psychology*, 89(3), 407–425.

McDonald, S. (2011) What's in the 'old boys' network? Accessing social capital in gendered and racialized networks. *Social Networks*, 33, 317–330.

McDonald, S. and Day, J. (2010) Race, gender, and the invisible hand of social capital. *Sociology Compass*, 4, 532–543.

McKenna, E. (2012) *Business Psychology and Organizational Behaviour*, 5th edn. New York: Psychology Press.

McLean, J. (2011) Fayol – Standing the test of time. *Manager: British Journal of Administrative Management*, 74, 32–33.

McLuhan, M. (1964) *Understanding Media: The Extensions of Man*. New York: Signet Books.

McShane, S.L. (2006) *Canadian Organizational Behaviour*, 6th edn. Boston, MA: McGraw Hill.

Meaney, M. and Pung, C. (2008) McKinsey global results: Creating organizational transformations. *The McKinsey Quarterly*, August, pp. 1–7.

Meek, V.L. (1988) Organizational culture: Origins and weaknesses. *Organization Studies*, 9(4), 453–473.

Meissner, J.O. (2005) Relationship quality in the context of computer-mediated communication – A social constructionist approach (No. 05/01). *WWZ Discussion Paper*. Available at: https://www.researchgate.net/publication/46450925_Relationship_Quality_in_the_Context_of_Computer-Mediated_Communication_-_A_social_constructionist_approach (accessed 12 January 2020).

Meleady, R., Seger, C.R. and Vermue, M. (2017) Examining the role of positive and negative intergroup contact and anti-immigrant prejudice in Brexit. *British Journal of Social Psychology*, 56, 799–808.

Merton, R.K. (ed.) (1957) *Social Theory and Social Structure*. London: The Free Press.

Michel, A., Bosch, C. and Rexroth, M. (2014) Mindfulness as a cognitive–emotional segmentation strategy: An intervention promoting work–life balance. *Journal of Occupational and Organizational Psychology*, 87(4), 733–754.

Michie, S. and Williams, S. (2003) Reducing work related psychological ill health and sickness absence: A systematic literature review. *Occupational and Environmental Medicine*, 60(1), 3.

Microsoft (2019) *Diversity & Inclusion*. Available at: https://www.microsoft.com/en-us/diversity/default.aspx?icid=SSM_AS_Promo_Other_Diversity_CTA1 (accessed 17 May 2021).

Milgram, S. (1963) Behavioral study of obedience. *Journal of Abnormal and Social Psychology*, 67, 371–378.

Milgram, S. (1974) The perils of obedience. *Harper's*, 247, 62–77.

Milne, P. (2007) Motivation, incentives and organisational culture. *Journal of knowledge management*, 11, 28–38.

Mingers, J. (2011) Ethics and OR: Operationalising discourse ethics. *European Journal of Operational Research*, 210(1), 114–124.

Mintzberg, H. (1990) *Mintzberg on Management: Inside our Strange World of Organizations*. New York: Free Press; London: Macmillan.

Mishra, K., Boynton, L. and Mishra, A. (2014) Driving employee engagement: The expanded role of internal communications. *International Journal of Business Communication*, 51(2), 183–202.

Moore, K., McDonald, P. and Bartlett, J. (2018) Emerging trends affecting future employment opportunities for people with intellectual disability: The case of a large retail organisation. *Journal of Intellectual & Developmental Disability*, 43, 328–338.

Morgeson, F.P., Campion, M.A., Dipboye, R.L., Hollenbeck, J.R., Murphy, K. and Schmitt, N. (2007) Are we getting fooled again? Coming to terms with limitations in the use of personality tests for personnel selection. *Personnel Psychology*, 60(4), 1029–1049.

Morrison, E.W. (1993) Newcomer information seeking: Exploring types, modes, sources, and outcomes. *Academy of Management Journal*, 36(3), 557–589.

Mowday, R.T., Porter, L.W. and Steers, R. (1982) *Employee–Organizational Linkages: The Psychology of Commitment, Absenteeism, and Turnover*. New York: Academic Press.

Mowday, R.T., Steers, R.M. and Porter, L.W. (1979) The measurement of organizational commitment. *Journal of Vocational Behavior*, 14(2), 224–247.

Moyer, C.A. and Katz, K. (2007) Online patient–provider communication: How will it fit? *The Electronic Journal of Communication*, 17(3–4), 1–14.

Mullen, B., Johnson, C. and Salas, E. (1991) Productivity loss in brainstorming groups: A meta-analytic integration. *Basic and Applied Social Psychology*, 12(1), 3–23.

Mullins, L.J. (2007) *Management and Organisational Behaviour*. London: Pearson Education.

Mullins, L. and Christy, G. (2013) *Management and Organisational Behaviour*. London: Pearson Education.

Myers, I.B., Kirby, L.K. and Myers, K.D. (1993) *Introduction to Type: A Guide to Understanding your Results on the Myers-Briggs Type Indicator*. Palo Alto, CA: Consulting Psychologists Press.

Nadler, D. and Tushman, M. (1995) Types of organizational change: From incremental improvement to discontinuous transformation. In D. Nadler, R. Show and A. Walton (eds), *Discontinuous Change: Leading Organizational Transformation*. San Francisco, CA: Jossey-Bass, pp. 15–34.

National Treatment Purchase Fund (2019) Waiting list validation. Available at: https://www.ntpf.ie/home/Waiting_List_Validation.htm (accessed 10 October 2019).

Naylor, J. (2004) *Management*, 2nd edn. Harlow: Financial Times, Prentice Hall.

Neeley, T. and Leonardi, P. (2011) Effective managers say the same thing twice (or more). *Harvard Business Review*, May, 38–39.

Nelson, B. (2010) Creating high-performing teams: Characteristics of an effective team and team recognition tips. *Healthcare Registration*, 19(9), 10–13.

Ng, T.W. and Feldman, D.C. (2010) The relationships of age with job attitudes: A meta-analysis. *Personnel Psychology*, 63(3), 677–718.

Ng, T.W. and Feldman, D.C. (2012) Evaluating six common stereotypes about older workers with meta-analytical data. *Personnel Psychology*, 65, 821–858.

Ní Léime, Á., Duvvury, N. and Callan, A. (2015) *Delayed Retirement: Gender, Ageing and Work in Austerity*. Bristol: Policy Press.

Nicholson, N. (2003) How to motivate your problem people. *Harvard Business Review*, 81(1), 56–58.

Nicholson, N. and Johns, G. (1985) The absence culture and psychological contract – Who's in control of absence? *Academy of Management Review*, 10(3), 397–407.

Niedenthal, P.M., Krauth-Gruber, S. and Ric, F. (2006) *Psychology of Emotion: Interpersonal, Experiential, and Cognitive Approaches*. New York: Psychology Press.

Northcraft, G.B., Polzer, J.T., Neale, M.A. and Kramer, R.M. (1996) Diversity, social identity, and performance: Emergent social dynamics in cross-functional teams. In S.E. Jackson and M.N. Ruderman (eds), *Diversity in Work Teams: Research Paradigms for a Changing Workplace*. American Psychological Association. Available at: https://psycnet.apa.org/doi/10.1037/10189-003 (accessed 4 May 2021).

O'Brien, P. (2019) A false rumor on WhatsApp started a run on a London bank. Available at: https://www.businessinsider.com/whatsapp-rumour-started-run-on-metro-bank-2019-5?r=US&IR=T (accessed 10 October 2019).

O'Callaghan, J. (2014) The unsocial network? Facebook users who say they are 'lonely' are more likely to overshare personal information. Available at: http://www.dailymail.co.uk/sciencetech/article-2640390/The-unsocial-network-Facebook-users-say-lonely-likely-overshare-personal-information.html (accessed 19 October 2019).

Ogbonna, E. and Harris, L.C. (2015) Subcultural tensions in managing organisational culture: A study of an English Premier League football organisation. *Human Resource Management Journal*, 25(2), 217–232.

Ogbonna, E. and Wilkinson, B. (2003) The false promise of organizational culture change: A case study of middle managers in grocery retailing. *Journal of Management Studies*, 40(5), 1151–1178.

Oldham, G.R. and Cummings, A. (1996) Employee creativity: Personal and contextual factors at work. *Academy of Management Journal*, 39, 607–634.

O'Neill, K. (2019) Irish population rises by 64,500 bringing it to almost 5m. *The Irish Medical Examiner*, 28 August. Available at: https://www.irishexaminer.com/breakingnews/ireland/irish-population-rises-by-64500-bringing-it-to-almost-5m-946672.html (accessed 9 October 2019).

Ontario Securities Commission (2015) CSA Multilateral Staff Notice 58-307. Staff Review of Women on Boards and in Executive Officer Positions – Compliance with NI 58-101 Disclosure of Corporate Governance Practices. Available at: https://www.justice.gov.nt.ca/en/files/securities-regulatory-instruments/5/58-307/58-307.2015-09-28.01.en.pdf (accessed 17 May 2021).

Opstrup, N. and Villadsen, A.R. (2015) The right mix? Gender diversity in top management teams and financial performance. *Public Administration Review*, 75, 291–301.

O'Reilly, C. (1989) Corporations, culture, and commitment: Motivation and social control in organizations. *California Management Review*, 31(4), 9–25.

O'Reilly, C.A. and Pondy, L.R. (1979) Organizational communication. In Steve Kerr (ed.), *Organizational Behavior*. Columbia, OH: Grid.

O'Reilly III, C.A., Doerr, B. and Chatman, J.A. (2018) 'See you in court': How CEO narcissism increases firms' vulnerability to lawsuits. *The Leadership Quarterly*, 29(3), 365–378.

O'Reilly, L. (2018) Health Waiting Lists: Motion. Dáil Éireann debate, 20 June. Available at: https://www.

oireachtas.ie/en/debates/debate/dail/2018-06-20/32/ (accessed 10 October 2019).

Organ, D.W. (1997) Organizational citizenship behavior: It's construct clean-up time. *Human Performance*, 10(2), 85–97.

Orsburn, J.D., Moran, L., Musselwhite, E. and Zenger, J.H. (1990) *Self-Directed Work Teams: The New American Challenge*. Homewood, IL: Business One Irwin.

O'Shea, D., Monaghan, S. and Ritchie, T.D. (2014) Early career attitudes and satisfaction during recession. *Journal of Managerial Psychology*, 29(3), 226–245.

O'Shea, E. and Kennelly, B. (2008) *The Economics of Mental Healthcare in Ireland*. Galway: Mental Health Commission.

Ostroff, C., Kinicki, A.J. and Tamkins, M.M. (2003) Organizational culture and climate. In W.C. Borman, D.R. Ilgen, R.J. Klimoski and I. Weiner (eds), *Handbook of Psychology*, vol. 12. Hoboken, NJ: John Wiley & Sons.

O'Sullivan, M., Cross, C. and Lavelle, J. (2019) The forgotten workforce: Older female part-time workers' job characteristics. In A. Lopez-Cabrales and R. Valle-Cabrera (eds) *Human Resource Management at the Crossroads: Challenges and Future Directions*. Newcastle upon Tyne: Cambridge Scholars publishing.

Ozkan, A. and Ozdevecioğlu, M. (2013) The effects of occupational stress on burnout and life satisfaction: A study in accountants. *Quality & Quantity*, 47(5), 2785–2798.

Packard, V. (1962) *The Pyramid Climbers*. New York: McGraw-Hill.

Padilla, A., Hogan, R. and Kaiser, R.B. (2007) The toxic triangle: Destructive leaders, susceptible followers, and conducive environments. *The Leadership Quarterly*, 18(3), 176–194.

Park, S.-Y. and Bernstein, K.S. (2008) Depression and Korean American immigrants. *Archives of Psychiatric Nursing*, 22(1), 12–19.

Parker, L.D. and Ritson, P.A. (2005) Revisiting Fayol: Anticipating contemporary management. *British Journal of Management*, 16(3), 175–194.

Patra, N.K.D. (2017) *Digital Disruption and Electronic Resource Management in Libraries*. Oxford: Elsevier.

Peters, T. and Waterman, R. (1982) *In Search of Excellence – Lessons from America's Best-Run Companies*. London: HarperCollins Publishers.

Peters, T.J. and Waterman, R.H. (1984) *In Search of Excellence: Lessons from America's Best Run Companies*. New York: Harper & Row.

Pettigrew, T.F. and Meertens, R.W. (1995) Subtle and blatant prejudice in Western Europe. *European Journal of Social Psychology*, 25, 57–75.

Petty, R.E. and Cacioppo, J.T. (1986) The elaboration likelihood model of persuasion. *Advances in Experimental Social Psychology*, 19, 123–205.

Pfeffer, J. (1981) *Power in Organisations*. London: Harper Collins.

Piderit, S.K. (2000) Rethinking resistance and recognizing ambivalence: A multidimensional view of attitudes toward an organizational change. *Academy of Management Review*, 25(4), 783–794.

Pitts, D. (2009) Diversity management, job satisfaction, and performance: Evidence from US federal agencies. *Public Administration Review*, 69, 328–338.

Pitts, D.W. (2005) Diversity, representation, and performance: Evidence about race and ethnicity in public organizations. *Journal of Public Administration Research and Theory*, 15, 615–631.

Podsakoff, P.M. and Williams, L.J. (1986) The relationship between job performance and job satisfaction. In E.A. Locke (ed), *Generalizing from Laboratory to Field Settings*. Lexington, MA: Lexington Books.

Pogrebtsova, E., Craig, J., Chris, A., O'Shea, D. and Gonzalez-Morales, M.G. (2018) Exploring daily affective changes in university students with a mindful positive reappraisal intervention: A daily diary randomized controlled trial. *Stress and Health*, 34(1), 46–58.

Polley, D. and Ribbens, B. (1998) Sustaining self-managed teams: A process approach to team wellness. *Team Performance Management*, 4(1), 3–21.

Popovich, P. and Wanous, J.P. (1982) The realistic job preview as a persuasive communication. *Academy of Management Review*, 7(4), 570–578.

Porter, L.W., Lawler, E.E. III and Hackman, J.R. (1975) *Behavior in Organizations*. New York: McGraw-Hill.

Posthuma, R.A. and Campion, M.A. (2009) Age stereotypes in the workplace: Common stereotypes, moderators, and future research directions. *Journal of Management*, 35, 158–188.

Preti, E., Di Mattei, V., Perego, G., Ferrari, F., Mazzetti, M., Taranto, P., Di Pierro, R., Madeddu, F. and Calati, R. (2020) The psychological impact of epidemic and pandemic outbreaks on healthcare workers: Rapid review of evidence. *Current Psychiatry Reports*, 22(8), 1–22.

Probst, T.M., Jiang, L. and Benson, W. (2018) Job insecurity and anticipated job loss: A primer and exploration of possible interventions. In U.C. Klehe and E. Van Hooft (eds), *The Oxford Handbook of Job Search and Job Loss*. New York: Oxford University Press, pp. 31–56.

Procter & Gamble (2015) Diversity and inclusion annual report: Enabling a culture of innovation & productivity. Available at: https://legacymt.pg.com/pgcom-en-us/downloads/company/purpose_people/PG_Diversity_AR_2015.pdf (accessed 17 May 2021).

ença, T. (2010) Self-managed work teams: An enabling or coercive nature. *The International Journal of Human Resource Management*, 21(3), 337–354.

cell, J., Kinnie, N., Hutchinson, S., Rayton, B and Swart, J. (2003) *Understanding the People and Performance Link: Unlocking the Black Box*. London: CIPD

Qu, Y.E., Dasborough, M.T., Zhou, M. and Todorova, G. (2019) Should authentic leaders value power? A study of leaders' values and perceived value congruence. *Journal of Business Ethics*, 156(4), 1027–1044.

Quinn, R.E., Faerman, S.R., Thompson, M.P. and McGrath, M.R. (2003) *Becoming a Master Manager: A Competency Framework*, 3rd edn. New York: John Wiley.

Rauthmann, J.F., Seubert, C.T., Sachse, P. and Furtner, M.R. (2012) Eyes as windows to the soul: Gazing behavior is related to personality. *Journal of Research in Personality*, 46(2), 147–156.

Raven, B.H. (1993) The bases of power: Origins and recent developments. *Journal of Social Issues*, 49, 227–251.

Reich, B. and Adcock, C. (1976) *Values, Attitudes and Behaviour Change*. London: Methuen.

Reicher, S., Haslam, S.A. and Hopkins, N. (2005) Social identity and the dynamics of leadership: Leaders and followers as collaborative agents in the transformation of social reality. *The Leadership Quarterly*, 16(4), 547–568.

Rentsch, J.R. and McEwen, A.H. (2002) Comparing personality characteristics, values, and goals as antecedents of organizational attractiveness. *International Journal of Selection and Assessment*, 10(3), 225–234.

Reuters Institute (2019) *Digital News Report 2019*. Oxford: Reuters Institute for the Study of Journalism. Available at: https://reutersinstitute.politics.ox.ac.uk/sites/default/files/2019-06/DNR_2019_FINAL_0.pdf (accessed 9 January 2020).

Reynolds, A. and Lewis, D. (2018) The two traits of the best problem-solving teams. *Harvard Business Review*, 2 April.

Rice, D.J., Davidson, B.D., Dannenhoffer, J.F. and Gay, G.K. (2007) Improving the effectiveness of virtual teams by adapting team processes. *Computer Supported Cooperative Work (CSCW)*, 16(6), 567–594.

Rich, B.L., Lepine, J.A. and Crawford, E.R. (2010) Job engagement: Antecedents and effects on job performance. *Academy of Management Journal*, 53(3), 617–635.

Richard, O.C., Roh, H. and Pieper, J.R. (2013) The link between diversity and equality management practice bundles and racial diversity in the managerial ranks: Does firm size matter? *Human Resource Management*, 52, 215–242.

Richardson, G.E. (2002) The metatheory of resilience and resiliency. *Journal of Clinical Psychology*, 58(3), 307–321.

Riketta, M. (2008) The causal relation between job attitudes and performance: A meta-analysis of panel studies. *Journal of Applied Psychology*, 93(2), 472–481.

Robbins, S.P. and Judge, T.A. (2010) *Essentials of Organizational Behavior*, 10th edn. Saddle River, NJ: Pearson.

Robbins, S.P. and Judge, T.A. (2012) *Essentials of Organizational Behavior*, Global edn. Harlow: Pearson.

Robbins, S.P. and Judge, T.A. (2012) *Organizational Behavior*, 15th edn. Harlow: Pearson.

Roberge, M.-É. and Van Dick, R. (2010) Recognizing the benefits of diversity: When and how does diversity increase group performance? *Human Resource Management Review*, 20, 295–308.

Roberts, B.W., Walton, K.E. and Viechtbauer, W. (2006) Patterns of mean-level change in personality traits across the life course. A meta-analysis of longitudinal studies. *Psychological Bulletin*, 132, 1–25.

Robertson, I.T., Cooper, C.L., Sarkar, M. and Curran, T. (2015) Resilience training in the workplace from 2003 to 2014: A systematic review. *Journal of Occupational and Organizational Psychology*, 88(3), 533–562.

Robertson, L. and Kulik, C.T. (2007) Stereotype threat at work. *Academy of Management Perspectives*, 21(2), 24–40.

Roethlisberger, F.J. and Dickson, W.J., with Wright, H.A. (1939) *Management and the Worker*. Cambridge, MA: Harvard University Press.

Rogers, K. (2018) Do your employees feel respected? Show workers that they're valued, and your business will flourish. *Harvard Business Review*, July–August.

Rosenberg, S., Heimler, R. and Morote, E.S. (2012) Basic employability skills: A triangular design approach. *Education & Training*, 54(1), 7–20.

Ross, L. and Nisbett, R.E. (1991) *The Person and the Situation: Perspectives of Social Psychology*. Philadelphia, PA: Temple University Press.

Rouse, K.A.G. (2004) Beyond Maslow's hierarchy of needs what do people strive for? *Performance Improvement*, 43(10), 27–31.

Rousseau, D.M. (1995) *Psychological Contracts in Organizations: Understanding Written and Unwritten Agreements*. Thousand Oaks, CA: Sage.

Rousseau, D.M. (2006) Is there such a thing as 'evidence-based management'? *Academy of Management Review*, 31(2), 256–269.

Rousseau, D.M. (2011) Organizational climate and culture. In J.M. Stellman (ed.), *Encyclopedia of Occupational Health and Safety*. Geneva: International Labour Organization.

Rubin, E. (1915) Rubin's vase illusion. In E. Rubin, *Synsoplevede Figurer: Studier I psykologisk Analyse. Første Del* [*Visually Experienced Figures: Studies in Psychological Analysis. Part One*]. Copenhagen and Christiania: Gyldendalske Boghandel, Nordisk Forlag.

Rusaw, A.C. (2007) Changing public organizations: Four approaches. *International Journal of Public Administration*, 30(3), 347–361.

Russell, H., Maitre, B., Watson, D. and Fahey, E. (2018) *Job Stress and Working Conditions: Ireland in Comparative Perspective – An Analysis of the European Working Conditions Survey*. Dublin: Economic and Social Research Institute.

Russell, J.A. (2003) Core affect and the psychological construction of emotion. *Psychological Review*, 110(1), 145–172.

Russell, J.A. and Barrett, L.F. (1999) Core affect, prototypical emotional episodes, and other things called emotion: Dissecting the elephant. *Journal of Personality and Social Psychology*, 76(5), 805–819.

Rutter, M. (1987) Psychosocial resilience and protective mechanisms. *American Journal of Orthopsychiatry*, 57(3), 316–331.

Sacco, J.M. and Schmitt, N. (2005) A dynamic multilevel model of demographic diversity and misfit effects. *Journal of Applied Psychology*, 90, 203.

Sackett, S.J. (1998) Career counseling as an aid to self-actualization. *Journal of Career Development*, 24(3), 235–244.

Sackmann, S.A., Eggenhofer-Rehart, P.M. and Friesl, M. (2009) Sustainable change: Long-term efforts toward developing a learning organization. *Journal of Applied Behavioral Science*, 45, 521–549.

Sahdev, K. (2004) Revisiting the survivor syndrome: The role of leadership in implementing downsizing. *European Journal of Work and Organizational Psychology*, 13(2), 165–196.

Saks, A.M. (2008) The meaning and bleeding of employee engagement: How muddy is the water? *Industrial and Organizational Psychology*, 1(1), 40–43.

Salancik, G. and Pfeffer, J. (1978) A social information processing approach to job attitudes and task design. *Administrative Science Quarterly*, 23, 224–253.

Samson, A. (ed.) (2018) *The Behavioral Economics Guide 2018*. Available at: http://www.behavioraleconomics.com. (accessed 4 October 2019).

Sarros, J.C., Cooper, B.K. and Santora, J.C. (2008) Building a climate for innovation through transformational leadership and organizational culture. *Journal of Leadership & Organizational Studies*, 15(2), 145–158.

Saucier, G. (1994) Mini-markers: A brief version of Goldberg's unipolar Big-Five markers. *Journal of Personality Assessment*, 63(3), 506–516.

Schaufeli, W.B. and Bakker, A.B. (2004) Job demands, job resources, and their relationship with burnout and engagement: A multi-sample study. *Journal of Organizational Behavior*, 25(3), 293–315.

Schaufeli, W.B. and Taris, T.W. (2014) A critical review of the job demands–resources model: Implications for improving work and health. In G.F. Bauer and O. Hämmig (eds), *Bridging Occupational, Organizational and Public Health: A Transdisciplinary Approach*. Dordrecht: Springer Netherlands, pp. 43–68.

Schaufeli, W.B., Bakker, A.B., Hoogduin, K., Schaap, C. and Kladler, A. (2001) On the clinical validity of the Maslach Burnout Inventory and the Burnout Measure. *Psychology & Health*, 16(5), 565–582.

Schaufeli, W.B., Bakker, A.B. and Salanova, M. (2006) The measurement of work engagement with a short questionnaire – A cross-national study. *Educational and Psychological Measurement*, 66(4), 701–716.

Schaufeli, W.B., Salanova, M., González-Romá, V. and Bakker, A.B. (2002) The measurement of engagement and burnout: A two sample confirmatory factor analytic approach. *Journal of Happiness Studies*, 3(1), 71–92.

Schein, E.H. (1964) How to break in the college graduate. *Harvard Business Review*, 42, 68–76.

Schein, E.H. (1965) *Organizational Psychology*. Englewood Cliffs, NJ: Prentice Hall.

Schein, E.H. (1968) Organizational socialization and the profession of management. *Industrial Management Review*, 9, 1–16.

Schein, E.H. (1980) *Organizational Psychology*, 3rd edn. Englewood Cliffs, NJ: Prentice Hall.

Schein, E.H. (1984) Coming to a new awareness of organizational culture. *Sloan Management Review*, 25(2), 3–16.

Schein, E.H. (1985) *Organizational Culture and Leadership: A Dynamic View*. San Francisco, CA: Jossey-Bass.

Schein, E.H (1990) Organizational culture. *American Psychologist*, 45, 109–119.

Schein, E.H. (1996) Culture: The missing link in organization studies. *Administrative Science Quarterly*, 41(2), 229–240.

Schein, E.H. (2004) *Organizational Culture and Leadership*, 3rd edn. San Francisco, CA: Jossey-Bass.

Schneider, B. and Rentsch, J. (1988) Managing climates and cultures: A future perspective. In J. Hage (ed.) *Futures of Organizations*. Lexington, MA: Lexington Books, pp. 181–200.

olarios, D., Lockyer, C. and Johnson, H. (2003) Anticipatory socialisation: The effect of recruitment and selection experiences on career expectations. *Career Development International*, 8(4), 182–197.

honfeld, I.S. (2000) Short research paper: An updated look at depressive symptoms and job satisfaction in first-year women teachers. *Journal of Occupational and Organizational Psychology*, 73(3), 363–371.

Schooler, J. (2015) Bridging the objective/subjective divide – Towards a meta-perspective of science and experience. In T. Metzinger and J.M. Windt (eds), *Open MIND: 34(T)*. Frankfurt am Main: MIND Group. Available at: https://www.researchgate.net/publication/271842692_Bridging_the_ObjectiveSubjective_Divide_Towards_a_Meta-Perspective_of_Science_and_Experience (accessed 20 January 2021).

Schwartz, H. and Davis, D. (1981) Matching corporate culture and strategy. *Organizational Dynamics*, 10, 30–48.

Schyns, B. and Schilling, J. (2013) How bad are the effects of bad leaders? A meta-analysis of destructive leadership and its outcomes. *The Leadership Quarterly*, 24(1), 138–158.

Seibert, S.E. and Kraimer, M.L. (2001) The five-factor model of personality and career success. *Journal of Vocational Behavior*, 58(1), 1–21.

Seijts, G.H. and Latham, G.P. (2001) The effect of learning, outcome, and proximal goals on a moderately complex task. *Journal of Organizational Behavior*, 22, 291–307.

Seligman, M.E.P. (2011) Building resilience. *Harvard Business Review*, 89(4), 100–106.

Seligman, M.E.P., Steen, T.A., Park, N. and Peterson, C. (2005) Positive psychology progress – Empirical validation of interventions. *American Psychologist*, 60(5), 410–421.

Seo, M., Taylor, M., Hill, N., Zhang, X., Tesluk, P. and Lorinkova, N. (2012) The role of affect and leadership during organizational change. *Personnel Psychology*, 65(1), 121–165.

Seppala, E. (2016) To motivate employees, do 3 things well. *Harvard Business Review*, January.

Shannon, C.E. (1948) A mathematical theory of communication. *The Bell System Technical Journal*, 27, 379–423, 623–656.

Sharon Hill, N. and Bartil, M. (2018) Five ways to improve communication in virtual teams: New research reveals simple strategies that boost performance. *MIT Sloan Management Review*, 13 June. Available at: https://sloanreview.mit.edu/article/five-ways-to-improve-communication-in-virtual-teams/ (accessed 16 May 2021).

Sherman, L.W. (2002) Evidence-based policing: Social organization of information for social control. In E. Warring and D. Weisburd (eds), *Crime and Social Organization*. New Brunswick, NJ: Transaction, 217–248.

Sherman, U.P. and Morley, M.J. (2015) On the formation of the psychological contract: A schema theory perspective. *Group and Organization Management*, 40(2), 160–192.

Shi, X. and Wang, J. (2011) Interpreting Hofstede model and GLOBE model: Which way to go for cross-cultural research? *International Journal of Business and Management*, 6(5), 93.

Shin, J., Taylor, M.S. and Seo, M.G. (2012) Resources for change: The relationships of organizational inducements and psychological resilience to employees' attitudes and behaviors toward organizational change. *Academy of Management Journal*, 55(3), 727–748.

Shteynberg, G., Leslie, L.M., Knight, A.P. and Mayer, D.M. (2011) But affirmative action hurts us! Race-related beliefs shape perceptions of White disadvantage and policy unfairness. *Organizational Behavior and Human Decision Processes*, 115, 1–12.

Sidanius, J. and Pratto, F. (2003) Social dominance theory and the dynamics of inequality: A reply to Schmitt, Branscombe and Kappen, and Wilson and Liu. *The British Journal of Social Psychology*, 42, 207.

Siehl, C. and Martin, J. (1990) Organizational culture: A key to financial performance? In B. Schneider (ed.), *Organizational Climate and Culture*. San Francisco, CA: Jossey-Bass, pp. 241–281.

Simmons, B.L., Nelson, D.L. and Neal, L.J. (2001) A comparison of the positive and negative work attitudes of home health care and hospital nurses. *Health Care Management Review*, 26(3), 63–74.

Simon, H.A. (1965) *Administrative Behavior*, 2nd edn. New York: Free Press.

Siu, O.L., Cooper, C.L., Roll, L.C. and Lo, C. (2020) Occupational stress and its economic cost in Hong Kong: The role of positive emotions. *International Journal of Environmental Research and Public Health*, 17(22), 8601.

Skarbeck, D. (2012) Prison gangs, norms, and organizations. *Journal of Economic Behavior & Organization*, 82(1), 96–109.

Sliter, M., Sliter, K. and Jex, S. (2012) The employee as a punching bag: The effect of multiple sources of incivility on employee withdrawal behavior and sales performance. *Journal of Organizational Behavior*, 33(1), 121–139.

Smircich, L. (1983) Concepts of culture and organizational analysis. *Administrative Science Quarterly*, 28(3), 339–358.

Snell, S.A. (1992). Control theory in strategic human resource management: The mediating role of administrative information. *Academy of Management Journal*, 35(2): 292–327.

Sobek II, D.K., Liker, J.K. and Ward, A.C. (1998) Another look at how Toyota integrates product development. *Harvard Business Review*, 76(4), 36–47.

Society for Human Resource Management (2010) *Workplace Diversity Practices: How has Diversity and Inclusion Changed over Time?* Alexandria, VA: SHRM. Available at: http://www.thehrgroupinc.net/assets/galleries/Events/Diversity-Leadership-Conf-2010/PowerPoint-presentations/Workplace-Diversity-Practices-Change-Over-Time.pdf

Solinger, O.N., Van Olffen, W. and Roe, R.A. (2008) Beyond the three-component model of organizational commitment. *Journal of Applied Psychology*, 93(1), 70–83.

Somech, A. and Drach-Zahavy, A. (2001) Relative power and influence strategy: The effects of agent/target organizational power on superiors' choices of influence strategies. *Journal of Organizational Behavior*, 23(2), 167–179.

Song, Z. and Baicker, K. (2019) Effect of a workplace wellness program on employee health and economic outcomes: A randomized clinical trial. *JAMA* (15), 1491–1501.

Sonnentag, S. (2015) Dynamics of well-being. *Annual Review of Organizational Psychology and Organizational Behavior*, 2, 261–293.

Sørensen, J.B. (2002) The strength of corporate culture and the reliability of firm performance. *Administrative Science Quarterly*, 47(1), 7091.

Spain, S.M., Harms, P. and LeBreton, J.M. (2014) The dark side of personality at work. *Journal of Organizational Behavior*, 35(S1), S41–S60.

Spicer, A. (2017) Surveillance used to be a bad thing. Now, we happily let our employers spy on us. *The Guardian*, 4 August. Available at: https://theguardian.com/commentisfree/2017/aug/04/surveillance-employers-spy-implanted-chip (accessed 16 January 2021).

Spillane, J.P. and Diamond, J.B. (2007) *Distributed Leadership in Practice*. New York: Teachers College Press.

Spitzberg, B.H., Cupach, W.R., Hannawac, A.F. and Crowley, J.P. (2014) A preliminary test of a relational goal pursuit theory of obsessive relational intrusion and stalking. *Studies in Communication Sciences*, 14(1), 29–36.

Spitzer, D. (1995) *SuperMotivation*. New York: AMACOM Books.

Spoorthy, M.S., Pratapa, S.K. and Mahant, S. (2020) Mental health problems faced by healthcare workers due to the COVID-19 pandemic – A review. *Asian Journal of Psychiatry*, 51, 102119.

Sproull, L. and Kiesler, S. (1991) *Connections: New Ways Working in the Networked Organization*. Cambridge, MA: MIT Press.

Stahl, G.K., Maznevski, M.L., Voigt, A. and Jonsen, K. (2010) Unraveling the effects of cultural diversity in teams: A meta-analysis of research on multicultural work groups. *Journal of International Business Studies*, 41(4), 690–709.

Stajkovic, A.D. and Luthans, F. (1997) A meta-analysis of the effects of organizational behavior modification on task performance, 1975–95. *Academy of Management Journal*, 40(5), 1122–1149.

Stanford, N. (2010) *Organisation Culture: Getting it Right*. London: *The Economist* in association with Profile Books.

StatCounter GlobalStats (2019) Desktop vs Mobile vs Tablet Market Share Worldwide. Available at: https://gs.statcounter.com/platform-market-share/desktop-mobile-tablet (accessed 9 January 2020).

Steele, C.M. and Aronson, J. (1995) Stereotype threat and the intellectual test performance of African Americans. *Journal of Personality and Social Psychology*, 69(5), 797–811.

Steers, R.M., Bigley, G.A. and Porter, L.W. (2002) *Motivation and Leadership at Work*, 7th edn. New York: McGraw-Hill.

Stewart, G.L. and Carson, K.P. (1995) Personality dimensions and domains of service performance: A field investigation. *Journal of Business and Psychology*, 9, 365–378.

Stogdill, R.M. (1974) *Handbook of Leadership*. Chicago, IL: Free Press.

Stogdill, R.M. and Coons A.E. (1957) *Leader Behavior: Its Description and Measurement*. Columbus, OH: Ohio State University, Bureau of Business Research.

Sunstein, C.R. (2014) Nudging: A very short guide. *Journal of Consumer Policy*. 37(4), 583–588.

Super, D.E. and Šverko, B. (eds) (1995) *Life Roles, Values, and Careers*. San Francisco, CA: Jossey-Bass.

Surbhi, S. (2016) Difference between prejudice and discrimination. *Key Differences*. Available at: https://keydifferences.com/difference-between-prejudice-and-discrimination.html#ComparisonChart (accessed 17 May 2021).

Swanson, S.R., Kelley, S.W. and Dorsch, M.J. (1997) Inter-organizational ethical perceptions and buyer–seller relationships. *Journal of Business-to-Business Marketing*, 4, 3–31.

Swiercz, P.M. and Lydon, S.R. (2002) Entrepreneurial leadership in high-tech firms: A field study. *Leadership and Organization Development Journal*, 23(7), 380–389.

el, H. (1974) Social identity and intergroup behaviour. *Social Science Information*, 13, 65–93.

rmina, R.J. and Bauer, T.N. (2000) Organizational socialization in two cultures: Results from the United States and Hong Kong. *The International Journal of Organizational Analysis*, 8(3), 262–289.

haler, R.H. and Sunstein, C.R. (2008) *Nudge: Improving Decisions about Health, Wealth, and Happiness*. New Haven, CT: Yale University Press.

Thomas, H.D. and Anderson, N. (1998) Changes in newcomers' psychological contracts during organizational socialization: A study of recruits entering the British Army. *Journal of Organizational Behavior*, 19(s 1), 745–767.

Thompson, L. (2003) Improving the creativity of organizational work groups. *Academy of Management Executive*, 17, 96–109.

Thompson, N. (2013) *People Management*. London: Red Globe Press.

Thoresen, C.J., Kaplan, S.A., Barsky, A.P., Warren, C.R. and de Chermont, K. (2003) The affective underpinnings of job perceptions and attitudes: A meta-analytic review and integration. *Psychological Bulletin*, 129, 914–945.

Thrive Global (2019) How thoughtful communication can empower international teams. Available at: https://thriveglobal.com/stories/how-thoughtful-communication-can-empower-international-teams/

Thurstone, L.L. (1928) Attitudes can be measured. *American Journal of Sociology*, 33(4), 529–554.

Thurstone, L.L. (1931) The measurement of social attitudes. *The Journal of Abnormal and Social Psychology*, 26(3), 249–269.

Tjosvold, D., Andrews, I.R. and Struthers, J.T. (1992) Leadership influence: Goal interdependence and power. *Journal of Social Psychology*, 132(1), 39–50.

Toker, S., Heaney, C.A. and Ein-Gar, D. (2015) Why won't they participate? Barriers to participation in worksite health promotion programmes. *European Journal of Work and Organizational Psychology*, 24(6), 866–881.

Townsend, K., McDermott, A.M., Cafferkey, K. and Dundon, T. (2019) Theories used in employment relations and human resource management. In K. Townsend, K. Cafferkey, A.M. McDermott and T. Dundon (eds), *Introduction to Theories of Human Resources and Employment Relations*. Boston, MA: Elgar Publishing.

Trenholm, S. (2017) *Thinking through Communication: An Introduction to the Study of Human Communication*, 8th edn. London: Routledge.

Tuckman, B. (1965) Developmental sequence in small groups. *Psychological Bulletin*, 63(6), 384–399.

Tuckman, B.W. and Jensen, M.A. (1977) Stages in smallgroup development revisited. *Group and Organisation Studies*, 2, 419–427.

Turnipseed, L. (2002) Are good soldiers good? Exploring the link between organization citizenship behavior and personal ethics. *Journal of Business Research*, 55(1), 1–15.

Twenge, J.M., Campbell, S.M., Hoffman, B.J. and Lance, C.E. (2010) Generational differences in work values: Leisure and extrinsic values increasing, social and intrinsic values decreasing. *Journal of Management*, 36(5), 1117–1142.

Tymowski, J. (2016) The employment equality directive – European implementation assessment. European Parliamentary Research Service. Available at: https://epthinktank.eu/2016/02/10/the-employment-equality-directive-european-implementation-assessment/ (accessed 17 May 2021).

Tziner, A., Rabenu, E., Radomski, R. and Belkin, A. (2015) Work stress and turnover intentions among hospital physicians: The mediating role of burnout and work satisfaction. *Revista de Psicología del Trabajo y de las Organizaciones*, 31(3), 207–213.

Uhlaner, R. and West, A. (2011) McKinsey Global Survey results: Organizing for M&A. *The McKinsey Quarterly*, December, pp. 1–8.

United Nations (2019) *World Population Prospects 2019: Highlights*. United Nations, Department of Economic and Social Affairs, Population Division.

Urwin, P., Parry, E., Dodds, I., David, A. and Karuk, V. (2013) The business case for equality and diversity: A survey of the academic literature. London: Department for Business, Innovation and Skills.

US Bureau of Labor Statistics (2019) Economic and Employment Projections: 2019–2029 Summary. Available at: https://www.bls.gov/news.release/ecopro.nr0.htm (accessed 5 October 2019).

Van Hoye, G and Lievens, F. (2009) Tapping the grapevine: A closer look at word-of-mouth as a recruitment source. *Journal of Applied Psychology*, 94(2), 341–352.

Van Knippenberg, B. and Van Knippenberg, D. (2005) Leader self-sacrifice and leadership effectiveness: The moderating role of leader prototypicality. *Journal of Applied Psychology*, 90(1), 25–37.

Van Maanen, J. (1978) People processing: Strategies of organizational socialization. *Organizational Dynamics*, Summer 1978, pp. 19–36.

Van Maanen, J. and Schein, E.H. (1979) Towards a theory of organisational socialisation. In B.M. Staw (ed.), *Research in Organisational Behaviour*, vol. 1. Greenwich, CT: JAI Press, pp. 209–264.

Vigil, J.M. (2010) Political leanings vary with facial expression processing and psychosocial functioning. *Group Processes & Intergroup Relations*, 13, 547–558.

von Bertalanffy, L. (1968) *General System Theory: Essays on its Foundation and Development*, rev. edn. New York: George Braziller.

Vroom, V.H. (1964) *Work and Motivation*. New York: Wiley.

Wahba, M.A. and Bridwell, L.G. (1976) Maslow reconsidered: A review of research on the need hierarchy theory. *Organizational Behavior and Human Performance*, 15, 212–240.

Waizenegger, L., McKenna, B., Cai, W. and Bendz, T. (2020) An affordance perspective of team collaboration and enforced working from home during COVID-19. *European Journal of Information Systems*, 29(4), 429–442.

Wallace, J., Gunnigle, P., McMahon, G. and O'Sullivan, M. (2013) *Industrial Relations in Ireland*, 4th edn. Dublin: Gill & Macmillan.

Walther, J.B. (1996) Computer-mediated communication: Impersonal, interpersonal, and hyperpersonal interaction. *Human Communication Research* 23(1), 3–43.

Walzer, M. (1973) Political action: The problem of dirty hands. *Philosophy and Public Affairs*, 2(2), 160–180.

Wanous, J.P. (1990) Impression management at organizational entry. In R.A. Giacalone and P. Rosenfeld (eds), *Impression Management in the Organization*. Hillsdale, NJ: Lawrence Erlbaum.

Warm, J., Parasuraman, R. and Matthews, G. (2008) Vigilance requires hard mental work and is stressful. *Human Factors*, 50, 433–441.

Warr, P. (1990) The measurement of well-being and other aspects of mental-health. *Journal of Occupational Psychology*, 63(3), 193–210.

Warr, P., Bindl, U.K., Parker, S.K. and Inceoglu, I. (2014) Four-quadrant investigation of job-related affects and behaviours. *European Journal of Work and Organizational Psychology*, 23(3), 342–363.

Wassermann, M. and Hoppe, A. (2019) Perceived overqualification and psychological well-being among immigrants. *Journal of Personnel Psychology*, 18(1), 34–45.

Wasti, S.A. and Can, Ö. (2008) Affective and normative commitment to organization, supervisor, and coworkers: Do collectivist values matter? *Journal of Vocational Behavior*, 73(3), 404–413.

Watson, T. (2002) *Organising and Managing Work*. Harlow: Prentice Hall.

Waugh, C.E., Fredrickson, B.L. and Taylor, S.F. (2008) Adapting to life's slings and arrows: Individual differences in resilience when recovering from an anticipated threat. *Journal of Research in Personality*, 42(4), 1031–1046.

Weiner, B. (2009) A theory of organizational readiness for change. *Implementation Science*, 4(1), 67–75.

Werner, J.M. and DeSimone, R.L. (2006) *Human Resource Development*, 4th edn. Mason, OH: Thomson South-Western.

Wertheimer, M. (1923) Untersuchungen zur Lehre von der Gestalt II. *Psychologische Forschung*, 4, 301–350.

Wesson, M.G. and Gogus, C.I. (2005) Shaking hands with a computer: An examination of two methods of organizational newcomer orientation. *Journal of Applied Psychology*, 90(5), 1018–1026.

Wey Smola, K. and Sutton, C.D. (2002) Generational differences: Revisiting generational work values for the new millennium. *Journal of Organizational Behavior*, 23(4), 363–382.

Wheelan, S. (2009) Group size, group development, and group productivity. *Small Group Research*, 40, 247–262.

White, C.A., Uttl, B. and Holder, M.D. (2019) Meta-analyses of positive psychology interventions: The effects are much smaller than previously reported. *PLOS ONE*, 14(5), e0216588.

Wilkinson, A. (1998) Empowerment theory and practice. *Personnel Review*, 27(1), 40–56.

World Bank (2019) *ILO Labor force participation rate, female*. Available at: https://data.worldbank.org/indicator/SL.TLF.CACT.FE.ZS (accessed 5 October 2019).

Wright, L. (2018) New Survey explores the changing landscape of teamwork Available at: https://www.microsoft.com/en-us/microsoft-365/blog/2018/04/19/new-survey-explores-the-changing-landscape-of-teamwork/

Wright, P., Dunford, B. and Snell, S. (2001) Human resources and the resource based view of the firm. *Journal of Management*, 27(6), 701–721.

Wu, J. and LeBreton, J.M. (2011) Reconsidering the dispositional basis of counterproductive work behavior: The role of aberrant personality traits. *Personnel Psychology*, 64, 593–626.

Yang, S.-B. and Guy, M.E. (2006) GenXers versus boomers: Work motivators and management implications. *Public Performance & Management Review*, 29, 267–284.

Ye, L. (2017) The business case for hiring more women in sales. *The HubSpot Sales Blog*. Available at: https://blog.hubspot.com/sales/more-women-in-sales (accessed 1 February 2020).

Zaleznik, A. (1977) Managers and leaders: Are they different? *Harvard Business Review*, 55(3), 67–78.

Zanzi, A. and O'Neill, R.M. (2001) Sanctioned versus non-sanctioned political tactics. *Journal of Managerial Issues*, 13(2), 245–262.